MW01407365

GENESIS RETOLD

A RESTORED NAME, CRITICAL EDITION OF 1 ENOCH, JASHER, JUBILEES, AND THE TESTAMENTS OF THE TWELVE PATRIARCHS

Literal English Version

TRI

Textual Research Institute,
L.L.C
P.O. Box 384
Youngsville, NC 27596

Genesis Retold: *A Restored Name, Critical Edition of 1 Enoch, Jasher, Jubilees, and The Testaments of the Twelve Patriarchs ~ Literal English Version*

Textual Research Insititute, LLC
www.literalenglishversion.weebly.com
www.torahapologetics.weebly.com
levbible@outlook.com

Cover art & Design by J.A. Brown

Second printing, 2016

ISBN-13: 978-1512073355

Book of Enoch taken and edited from R.H. Charles' 1917 translation *The Book of Enoch*, which is in the public domain.

Book of Jasher taken and edited from J.H. Parry & Company's 1887 translation *The Book of Jasher*, which is in the public domain.

Book of Jubilees taken and edited from R.H. Charles' 1917 translation *The Book of Jubilees*, which is in the public domain.

The Testaments of the Twelve Patriarchs taken and edited from R.H. Charles' 1908 *The Testaments of the Twelve Patriarchs*, which in the public domain.

OTHER WORKS BY THE SAME AUTHOR

Treasured Books Volume 1: The Apocrypha ~ Literal English Version ©
ISBN-13: 978-0996171717

A Restored Name version of the standard Apocrypha. Also includes Psalms 151 – 155. All texts have been brought into modern American English and checked against newer manuscript discoveries. Hundreds of footnotes offer textual insights and critical notes. Includes a list of New Testament references to Apocryphal books.

Volume Preface

Introduction

This work does not stand alone; and it certainly would not be possible without the efforts of many scholars, researchers, translators, and archaeologists who have gone before me. As Sir Isaac Newton so eloquently explained it, "If I have seen further it is by standing on the shoulders of giants." I enjoy irony a bit, so given the material contained in this book regarding "giants" I believe this quote to be accurate and humorous all in one.

Surely it should be expected that with a work such as this, there is much to be said in introduction. However, rather than spend pages explaining each of the works contained in this publication, I will use only a brief space to explain the overall volume. Each individual book within this volume will have its own *Preface* to further explain it specifically.

For the most part, this book was written to meet a need. That is, in the growing community of individuals who believe that accuracy is important, that textual criticism is necessary, and that names, terms, phrases, idioms, and cultural context should never be ignored. Therefore, this book was created to be a member of the Literal English Version family, formerly titled the Shem Qadosh Version.

The four books chosen to be included in this present work were selected carefully. I resolved from the inception of this idea to include three books: 1 Enoch, Jasher, and Jubilees. However, the more I considered it, the more I felt it would add to the richness of the texts – and the insight of the reader – to include a slightly lesser-known work. From the onset I knew this volume would include extra-Biblical texts that cover the material of the Book of Genesis. So I decided to select material from other ancient texts that also cover this time period. Indeed, Jasher and Jubilees expand the time period covering Genesis as well as Exodus, but nonetheless they are fairly exhaustive accounts of the Genesis narrative.

So I chose The Testaments of the Twelve Patriarchs (T12P) for two reasons. The first simply being that this book contains material covered in the rest of this volume. The second being that some fragments of these texts (particularly the Testament of Naphtali) were also found at Qumran along with the other Dead Sea Scrolls. This should help to revive interest in this text to some extent.

What should be recognized in some of these texts (especially T12P) is that some sections are quite easily recognized as later additions. In most cases, they are sections added later into the Christian era to promote Christian doctrine and theology, such as the Virgin Birth (Testament of Joseph 19:8) or the dwelling of the Most High and His Son on earth (see Appendix E for Ethiopic version of 1 Enoch 105). Regardless of whether these texts should be considered canon or not, they provide good insight into the heart and mind of those who lived between the first two centuries BCE and CE. Such is the case with all of the books contained in this volume: they allow the reader to see how Biblical narratives were viewed and interpreted by those who lived much closer to the time, context, and culture of the events than we do today in modern times. And so it would seem that in numerous places, the very writers of the New Testament themselves drew on some of the information contained within the pages of Enoch, Jubilees, and T12P. (See Appendix F for more)

Table of Contents

The books are arranged in the following order:

1. Sefer Ḥanokh [Book of Enoch] .... Pages 1 – 62
2. Sefer Ha'Yashar [Book of Jasher] .... Pages 63 – 273
3. Sefer Yovelim [Book of Jubilees] .... Pages 274 – 352
4. Tsa'vavaot Ha'Shevatim [Test. of the 12 Patriarchs] .... Pages 353 – 357
   a) Tsava'ah Reuven [Testament of Reuben] .... Pages 358 – 360
   b) Tsava'ah Shimon [Testament of Simeon] .... Pages 361 – 363
   c) Tsava'ah Levi [Testament of Levi] .... Pages 364 – 371
   d) Tsava'ah Yehudah [Testament of Judah] .... Pages 372 – 378
   e) Tsava'ah Yissakhar [Testament of Issachar] .... Pages 379 – 381
   f) Tsava'ah Zevulun [Testament of Zebulun] .... Pages 382 – 384
   g) Tsava'ah Dan [Testament of Dan] .... Pages 385 – 387
   h) Tsava'ah Naphtali [Testament of Naphtali] .... Pages 388 – 391
   i) Tsava'ah Gad [Testament of Gad] .... Pages 392 – 394
   j) Tsava'ah Asher [Testament of Asher] .... Pages 395 – 396
   k) Tsava'ah Yoseph [Testament of Joseph] .... Pages 397 – 402
   l) Tsava'ah Benyamin [Testament of Benjamin] .... Pages 403 – 406
5. Appendix A: Explanatory Notes .... Pages 407 – 408
6. Appendix B: Names of the Messengers .... Pages 409 – 410
7. Appendix C: Alphabets .... Pages 411 – 412
8. Appendix D: Glossary of Terms .... Pages 413 – 415
9. Appendix E: Major Textual Variants .... Pages 416
10. Appendix F: Parallel New Testament Passages .... Pages 417 – 420

Names

What sets this version apart from others that are currently available is that this volume combines a critical approach with a careful restoration of names. While the most important Name is that of our Creator, all names are important, and all names *mean* something. Our Creator, the Almighty Eternal One, has a personal Name, though most Bibles and books today omit it. Rather than include His Name, the common practice for the translations of today is to replace the Name with a placeholder or filler. In most Bibles, His Name is replaced by the title "the LORD" or sometimes "GOD." However, in the Hebrew of the Tanakh ('Old Testament'), it does not call Him "the LORD" but rather, 𐤉𐤄𐤅𐤄. This four-letter name, yod-hey-vav-hey, has had its pronunciation debated and disputed for many centuries. The most common pronunciation now is Yahweh, though others include Yehovah, Yahuah, Yahveh, Yahuwah, and still more. The once-common rendering of 'Jehovah' has been all but abandoned, recognized as an impossibility given the limitations of the original languages. The reason being, that the letter J is not present in the Hebrew alphabet, and neither is the sound the letter J makes. Therefore it is not possible for the Name to be Jehovah, unless in the original German sense, where it is pronounced the same as Yehovah. For this publication, I have chosen not to take a particular dogmatic stance on pronunciation of the Name. Simply put, I believe it is most important to recognize that He does have a personal Name, and it is less important to argue the pronunciation. So rather than using the

English word Yahweh or Yahuah or Yehovah or whatever, I have simply written the Tetragrammaton: 𐤉𐤄𐤅𐤄.

While "Lord" and "God" are titles, His Name is personal. Therefore it is the practice of the current editor to "fix" the places where His Name was changed whenever possible. In many later Hebrew texts, it became common practice for scribes to use a double-yod as a placeholder for His Name, such as 𐤉𐤉. This is the case in the Book of Jasher. Rather than write the full, four-letter Name, 𐤉𐤄𐤅𐤄, the author (or later copyist) chose to use the double-yod instead. Another common placeholder is yod-vav-yod, 𐤉𐤅𐤉, which is seen in some of the Targumim (Aramaic Paraphrases of the Tanakh). Regardless of the mechanism chosen, however, the fact remains that these are merely placeholders for the Divine Name, 𐤉𐤄𐤅𐤄.

In Syriac Aramaic, as can be found in the Peshitta, another placeholder is used: ܡܪܝܐ (*Mar-ya*). This is used throughout the Peshitta Tanakh ('Old Testament') in place of 𐤉𐤄𐤅𐤄, and is used nowhere else. It is believed by some to be a contracted form of ܡܪܐ (*Moro*) which means "master" and ܝܐ (*Ya*), a shortened form of the Divine Name. Thus it could be rendered as "master Yah." However, the majority of Syriac scholarship states it does not denote the Name 'Yah' at all, and rather is simply the emphatic form of *Moro*: "The Master." Regardless of whether or not it is, indeed, a word meaning "Master Yah" however, it is clear that this is a word that is reserved only for the Most High.

The placeholder Mar-ya is also found in other Aramaic dialects, too, and not just the later Syriac. The Aramaic fragments of Enoch use this, מריא, the same way Syriac does.

In Greek, however, a placeholder is not used in most texts. Rather, it is exchanged for the generic Greek title Κυριος (*Kurios*), which means "lord" or "master." This is used in most copies of the Septuagint (LXX) for both a replacement of the Name, as well as an equivalent of the Hebrew 𐤀𐤃𐤍𐤉 (*Adonai*), which also means "master." This Greek word is used both in reference to the Almighty, as well as to men. Because of this, it can sometimes be difficult to discern when it stands in for the Name, and when it simply means "master." There are also some very small Greek fragments known from the Dead Sea Scrolls, such as 4Q120, a fragment of the book of Leviticus, which has the Tetragrammaton written as ΙΑΩ (IAŌ), which would properly be pronounced "Yah-Oh." However, it is very fragmentary, and little other evidence is known to show this type of placeholder in Greek. The Shelihim Writings ('New Testament') are extant completely in multiple languages, with the vast majority of early manuscript evidence being in Greek. However, none of these known manuscripts use a placeholder; they all continue the tradition of using *Kurios* instead.

In Ge'ez (Ethiopic), which is a Semitic language, we find the same treatment of the Name as we find with Syriac Aramaic. That is, a placeholder is used. We find the Ethiopic word እግዚአብሔር (*igzi'a'b'ḥeir*) in place where the Name would normally be present. This is a combined word of እግዚእ (*igzi'i*) meaning "master" and ብሔር (*b'ḥeir*) meaning "land" or "country." Thus, literally, it means, "Master of all the land." The significance of this title, however, is that it is used only in place of the Divine Name.

Since none of the texts that this volume is based on are the original autographs (and indeed, only Jasher is extant entirely in Hebrew), we do not find the Divine, four-letter Name in most of the source texts. Only in some of the Hebrew fragments from Qumran do we find the Tetragrammaton present. However, we do find the placeholders mentioned above; knowing, then, that these only appear in place of the Name, it is fair to assume that if there were Hebrew originals, the Name would be present. Therefore, we have sought to restore the Name wherever possible, replacing these placeholders with the Name written as יהוה.

Whenever books of Scripture are mentioned in footnotes for cross references, they are written in the following format: Book Title from the LEV [Common English Title] Chapter:Verse. Eg. Bereshiyt [Genesis] 1:1.

יברכך יהוה וישמרך יאר יהוה פניו אליך ויחנך ישא יהוה פניו אליך וישם לך שלום

May יהוה bless you and guard you. May יהוה make His face to shine upon, and show favor to you. May יהוה lift up His face upon you, and give you peace.

R. H. Charles' Preface: Enoch

[Editor's note: The following is the preface from R. H. Charles' 1912 edition of *The Book of Enoch or 1 Enoch*. My preface follows after. In his comments he mentions his second edition. His first edition was largely a revision of August Dillmann's translation. However, Charles then went on to collate many Ethiopic, Greek, and Latin manuscripts (MSS.) and then made his second edition from that.]

This is not so much a second edition as a new book. A brief comparison of the first edition and the present work will make this clear even to the cursory reader. Alike in the translation and in the commentary it forms a vast advance on its predecessor. I cannot claim to be satisfied with it even as it stands, and yet twenty additional years spent in Apocalyptic and Biblical studies have not, I would fain hope, been fruitless with regard to the present work.

The translation in the first edition was made from Dillmann's edition of the Ethiopic text, which was based on five MSS. With a view to this translation the present editor emended and revised Dillmann's text in accordance with nine hitherto uncollated Ethiopic MSS. in the British Museum, and the Greek and Latin fragments which had just come to light, but notwithstanding every care he felt his work in this respect to be of a wholly provisional character. From the date of the publication of the first edition in 1893 he steadily made preparation for an edition of the Ethiopic text and of the Greek and Latin fragments. This text, which is exhaustive of existing textual materials in these languages, was published by the University Press in 1906, and from this text the present translation is made.

A new and revolutionary feature in the translation is due to the editor's discovery of the poetical structure of a considerable portion of the work. I call it revolutionary; for such it proves to be in respect of the critical problems of the text. By its means the lost original of the text is not infrequently recovered, phrases and clauses recognized as obvious interpolations, and not a few lines restored to their original context, whose claims to a place in the text were hitherto ignored on the ground of the weakness of their textual attestation.

During the past eighteen years the criticism of the book has made undoubted headway, and that, I am glad to say, mainly in the direction defined in the first edition. The idea of a *Grundschrift*, which was accepted by most of the chief scholars in this field till its appearance, and to which I strove and not in vain to give the *coup de grace*, is now universally abandoned. The critical advance made in the present volume is not of a revolutionary character, but consists rather in a more detailed application of the principles of criticism pursued in the first edition.

In my first edition I said that a knowledge of 1 Enoch was indispensable to N.T. students. The further study of Apocalyptic and Biblical literature, Jewish and Christian, in the score of years that have since elapsed, has convinced me still more fully of this fact. And I might add here that to the O.T. student it is likewise indispensable, if we would understand many of the problems underlying O.T. prophecy. To the biblical scholar and to the student of Jewish and Christian theology 1 Enoch is the most important Jewish work written between 200 B.C. and 100 A.D. I cannot help expressing here my deep regret that Jewish scholars are still so backward in recognizing the value of this literature for their own history. Apocalyptic is the true child of Prophecy, and became its true representative to the Jews from the unhappy moment that the Law won an absolute autocracy in Judaism, and made the utterance of God-sent prophetic men impossible except through the medium of Pseudepigraphs, some of which, like Daniel, gained an entrance despite the Law into the O.T. Canon. It is true that eminent Jewish scholars in America and elsewhere have in part recognized the value of Apocalyptic literature but, as a whole, Orthodox Judaism still confesses and still champions the one-sided Judaism, which came into being after the Fall of Jerusalem in 70 A.D., a

Judaism lopped in the main of its spiritual and prophetic side and given over all but wholly to a legalistic conception of religion. It is not strange that since that disastrous period Judaism became to a great extent a barren faith, and lost its leadership in the spiritual things of the world.

I cannot close this Preface without recording my deep obligations to the officials of the University Press for the skill, care and expedition with which they have carried this work through; and likewise acknowledging the very helpful service rendered to me by a promising scholar, the Rev. A. L. Davies, in the correction of proofs, the verification of references, and at times the acquisition of fresh materials.

Editor's Preface: Enoch

Introduction

𐤎𐤐𐤓 𐤇𐤍𐤅𐤊 (*Sefer Ḥanokh*). Βιβλιο του Ενωχ (*Biblio tou Enoch*). መጽሐፈ ሄኖክ (*mats'hafa Henok*). Liber Enoch. Different titles across numerous languages, but regardless they all say the same thing: Book of Enoch.

The book of Enoch has long been a source of controversy. Its canonicity and authenticity have been debated many years. While it comes to us in various manuscripts, we still do not have it in its original. The foremost scholars of today are split in opinion of its original language. These two languages are Hebrew and Aramaic. R. H. Charles, who was perhaps the most eminent authority on the subject of the Ge'ez (Ethiopic) texts and the Book of Enoch in his day, stated in his translation that he believed the Book of Enoch to be much the same as the Biblical Book of Daniel: partly in Hebrew, and partly in Aramaic. While this may come as a shock to the layman, it is a well-established fact that the Biblical Book of Daniel has been wholly preserved in two languages, and not Hebrew alone. Fragments of 1 Enoch were found among the Dead Sea Scrolls that contain portions of the book in both languages, and thus it is still unknown which is the "original" language, if not both.

It is regarded as canonical by the Ethiopian Orthodox Tewahedo Church and Eritrean Orthodox Tewahedo Church, as well as Beta Israel; the latter also known by the term "Ethiopian Jews."

The Book of Enoch is split into various sections based on its content (shown in *The Divisions* section). It is because of these divisions (and the alternating writing style) that many scholars have come to the opinion that it was authored by one individual, and then later added to by another (or possibly multiple) author(s). Whether this is true or not is yet to be proven, as are many theories regarding the originality and authorship of the text. One thing should be clear, however, and that is the affect that this and other texts had on the ancient world. Indeed, between the Book of Enoch and the Book of Jubilees (the latter containing some quotations of the former) there have been many writings found to have spawned from them. There are, in circulation, two other primary texts that claim to be Enochian: 2 and 3 Enoch. While these texts bear this title, they are regarded by most authorities to be much the same as 3, 4, and 5 Maccabees: fraudulent. That is, they contain highly suspect and questionable material, as well as veering further and further from a Scriptural writing style.

The book claiming to be the Second Book of Enoch is found wholly extant in only the Slavonic language, though some Coptic fragments have been found in recent years. This book, claiming to be attributed to Enoch, details what happened to Enoch after he was "taken" according to Genesis 5:24. Part of this book details that Enoch ascended to become a priest, as well as stating that Melchizedek (a human) was born of a virgin, and the nephew of Noah. It states that Melchizedek was taken by the angel Gabriel to the Garden of Eden to be preserved from the coming flood. A similar story is also found within the Book of Jubilees, and thus 2 Enoch probably used Jubilees as a source. When giving a description of the birth of Melchizedek, its account is nearly identical to that of 1 Enoch 107's description of the birth of Noah, and thus probably used 1 Enoch as a source for this story.

3 Enoch is completely unrelated, and although is written in Hebrew, it is self-ascribed to "Rabbi Ishmael, the High Priest." The book reads strikingly similar to certain passages from the Talmud, and the language is most certainly post-Second Temple. This book follows certain other old Jewish writings, telling of an angel named "Metatron" who was the Scribe of God. According to 3 Enoch, Metatron is Enoch, who was transformed into an angel.

The Book of 1 Enoch, among others, is often presented as a "pseudepigraphal" work. That is, from the Greek: ψευδής, *pseudes*, "false" and ἐπιγραφή, *epigraphē*, "name" or "ascription"; "falsely ascribed." Simply defined, these are works that claim to be by a certain author, although they are not. I am, however, hesitant to state this book is pseudepigraphal, as the author is unknown, and therefore at least some portions of the book cannot be disproved as having been written by the Biblical Enoch. It is also worth noting that within this book itself are authors of different sections, such as Lamekh. Regardless of its author(s), however, the book contains much by way of information regarding the genesis of the Nephilim (giants), and the pre-flood world, as well as the courses of the sun, moon, and stars.

The Texts

For the Book of Enoch, we have numerous manuscripts (MSS) that are currently extant. Perhaps the most important work regarding this text was compiled by R.H. Charles in the early 1900s. Charles was able to create a critical edition of the text based on the MSS and fragments of three different languages: Ethiopic, Greek, and Latin. While the general consensus is that the book was originally Hebrew and/or Aramaic, the Greek Version was the first generation descendant. It was from this Greek Version that the Ethiopic and Latin Versions were translated. This, then, brings us to the primary faults in the text: the distance from the autograph. While the Ethiopic version was able to preserve the Greek (and, by extension, some of the Hebrew/Aramaic) very well, there are some pieces that are always "lost in translation." It is because of this that I esteem the work of Dr. Charles so highly, in that he compiled a critical edition of more than twenty different Ethiopic MSS. as well as the primary Greek MSS. and the Latin fragments. Since this collation, however, numerous other fragments have been discovered, including one of the most important discoveries of all regarding the Book of Enoch: the Aramaic and Hebrew fragments at Qumran.

While these Aramaic fragments differ little from the portions already known from Ethiopic and Greek, they do offer much by way of dating. They prove that, at the very least, parts of the Book of Enoch pre-date the Christian era, to no later than 100 B.C.E. While there have also been some very small Hebrew fragments, they offer no important variation or addition. Aside from the Aramaic fragments, there are now known to exist more than forty MSS. of the Ethiopic Version, and about sixteen of those contain all or almost all of the book. There are a dozen or so Aramaic fragments, containing numerous portions. There are four primary Greek MSS., containing approximately 40 chapters total. There were also some Greek fragments found at Qumran along with the Aramaic fragments. The Hebrew fragments are very small, and amount to roughly 30 verses total, including most of chapter 106. It should be noted that these are the extant manuscripts at the time of this publication. It has been stated by scholar John Strugnell, former Dead Sea Scrolls scholar and editor, that there is a whole copy of Enoch in Aramaic, compiled and written on one scroll that is being held in a private collection. However, aside from this statement, there is no known evidence that such a scroll exists, nor do we know which portions of the book were purported to be on it.

For this translation I have emended R. H. Charles' English translation published in 1917, as this work has since passed into the public domain. While Charles performed a marvelous work in his compilation, I have taken this even further by comparing some fragments and texts that were not available to him at the time. Sadly, he died in 1931, more than a decade prior to the major discoveries at the Qumran caves. For the most part, this is a revision of his translation. However it should be noted by the reader that I have gone to great lengths to incorporate not only the MSS. that were compiled and published by Charles, but also the fragments that are now known in Aramaic.

Written in Elizabethan English, Charles' version was a tedious read to most modern English-speakers. So among other alterations, the words "thee," "thou," and "ye" and so on have been changed to a more reader-friendly version of "you" and "your." Similarly, the words ending in "th" such as "hath" and "st" such as "dost" have also been rendered in a more modern way.

In many cases, where Charles chose a specific reading over a variant one, I considered the variant as well. Even if I did not change Charles' reading, I have noted many variants in the footnotes. This version presented here generally takes Greek precedence when the Aramaic is not available, as it is known to be closer to the original, though my purpose in all of this is to make it as Hebraic as possible, following along with the Shem Qadosh Version series of books.

One thing that should be recognized regarding the footnotes: Ge'ez (Ethiopic) is read left-to-right. While Hebrew, Aramaic, and most other Semitic languages are read right-to-left, Ge'ez is unique, in that it is read left-to-right, just as English, Latin, and Greek are read left-to-right. A table is included in Appendix C of the Ge'ez alphabet which should assist the reader in pronouncing the words noted in the footnotes.

The Names

Perhaps the most significant change in this version is that of the names of those involved in the book. Enoch is the anglicized form of the Hebrew name 𐤇𐤍𐤅𐤊 (*Ḥanokh*). Though since we can trace the origins of at least parts of the Book of Enoch back to Hebrew, it only makes sense to restore these names as well.

When dealing with the names of the Watchers, the angels who chose to take human wives, I was presented with an interesting dilemma. These names are recorded in both Greek and Ethiopic, as well as mostly in Aramaic, though many of these names do not appear in the 66 books of Scripture. This led me to work as diligently as I knew how to provide a restoration of these names, based on a reconstruction of Hebrew and/or Aramaic, to hopefully show the meaning of these names. Where the Aramaic presented a name, I took it over any other language. If the Aramaic was not available (that is, if a name is present in a section not preserved in Aramaic), I then attempted to reconstruct the name as best as possible. It should always be remembered that in most ancient cultures a name was not merely that which someone was called by, but rather it was a specific word or phrase. Adam is not merely a name, but rather means "mankind." All Hebrew (and similarly, Aramaic) names are words with specific meanings. I have provided a breakdown of the most likely grammatical roots for these specific names in Appendix B. Please remember, these are approximations based on my attempts to reconstruct the Hebrew/Aramaic originals based on the Greek and Ethiopic descendants, as well as some fragmentary Aramaic evidence. Perhaps the most difficult part of this is how different manuscripts will record the same name differently. For instance, in some verses (though not all) the name Sari'el was replaced by Uri'el, both of which are separate angels.

Titles for The Almighty remain translated from their Aramaic, Greek, and Ethiopic sources. The most common of these is the Ethiopic word አምላክ (*am'lak*), which stands in for the Greek word Θεος (*Theos*) (which itself stands in for the Aramaic 𐤀𐤋𐤄 [*Elah*]). This word is usually translated as "God" but, since I have sought for restoration of Hebraic terminology, I have transliterated it in the Hebrew form 𐤀𐤋𐤄𐤉𐤌 (*Elohim*), written in the text as "Elohim." The Name of the Almighty, and its use in this book, is explained in the *Volume Preface*.

The Divisions

The book of Enoch has classically been divided into five distinct sections. These fives sections are differentiated by subject matter, writing style, and in some cases, manuscript tradition. Many scholars believe each section to have a different author, being later redacted into what is now known as 1 Enoch. While some chapters do themselves claim to be by different authors, such as Lamekh in Enoch 60:8, the actual time these sections were written is still unknown. The divisions are:

1. The Book of the Watchers (1 – 36)
2. The Book of the Parables of Enoch (37 – 71) [Aka *The Similitudes of Enoch*]
3. The Astronomical Book (72 – 82) [Aka *The Book of the Heavenly Luminaries*]
4. The Book of Dream Visions (83 – 90)
5. The Epistle of Enoch (91 – 108)

Of these divisions, only the Book of the Parables of Enoch stands aside from the rest. This is because the general scholarly consensus is that these chapters were written well after the majority of the rest of the book. This division is the only one that has not had any manuscript evidence, however fragmentary, found among the Dead Sea Scrolls of Qumran. This, of course, does not definitively prove it is not original to the book; absence of evidence does not prove evidence of absence. Indeed, outside of the Ethiopic manuscripts, there are no witnesses known to exist (at the time of this publication) that support this division as authentic and original. In Greek only pieces of the Book of Watchers, a few scattered verses from chapters 77; 78; 85-87; 89; 98; and possibly 103 have been preserved. In Latin, there are even fewer, being 1:9 and 106:1-18. Thus we find that outside of Ethiopic, there is no manuscript support for the Book of the Parables of Enoch, and rather it is most likely to be a later addition. Dead Sea Scrolls scholar J. T. Milik estimated the Book of the Parables of Enoch was added sometime in the third century CE, giving the range of 260 CE to 270 CE; this, of course, places this section at least more than 300 years after the other divisions.

The individual section headings were added by the present editor, and do not exist in the original language texts. These were added in an attempt to aid the reader in locating a specific stories and section, since the book frequently changes topics and has many chapters.

Provenance

While it cannot be proven that the Biblical Enoch was, in fact, the author of all or part of this book, the opposite can also be asserted: that Enoch COULD be the author, at least of part of it. It is difficult to tell, however, how many sections could have been written so long ago. In the Aramaic fragments there are numerous words that are used that are related to much later Aramaic dialects, and other Semitic languages. This shows that the date range is significantly reduced closer to the turn of the millennium (from BCE to CE). Though as a matter of technicality, these Aramaic fragments could also be translations from another Semitic original, either Hebrew or perhaps an even older language. However it is also clear that even internally, the book does not claim Ḥanokh as its sole author: chapter 65 appears to be written from the perspective of Lamekh, while 67 seems to be from Noah's point of view.

Another point to note is in chapters 54 through 69, where the angel Azazel is mentioned. As pointed out in Appendix B, the name Azazel is known in the earlier sections of the book to actually a corruption of the name Asa'el. However, since there are no Aramaic or Hebrew fragments of these sections (54 – 69) we cannot tell for certain. Dead Sea Scrolls scholar J. T. Milik proposed that this section of the book, or really the entire Book of Parables, had a different author. Milik purports that the author of the Book of Parable confined the naming of angels to those with which he was familiar, and not having a Semitic copy of the rest of the book, mistook Shemiḥazah for an angel named Azazel.[a] Thus in the Book of Parables, when the judgment against the fallen angels is repeated, we find it being brought against "Azazel and his associates" rather than Shemiḥazah.

Conclusion

Overall, I believe this book to hold a great deal of information that is beneficial to the serious student of Scripture, especially those that study the Sheliḥim Writings ('New Testament'). There can be seen, in its text, numerous verses that appear strikingly similar to NT verses from the Gospels and even various epistles. Naturally, perhaps some of the most obvious similarities are found in the Apocalyptic visions, in the way they resemble the writings of Daniel and Revelation.

While it can be told rather definitively that the book is not, in its entirety, a work by the Biblical Enoch, we do know that it was highly regarded from the 2nd Century BCE onward. Indeed, at the very least it provides us with a look into the mind of a Jew living in and around Israel during that time.

It is the editor's personal recommendation that this books be read and studied with an open mind. As noted by Charles, the information gained by the study of these extra-Biblical books is by far indispensable.

---

[a] J. T. Milik, *The Books of Enoch*, Oxford University Press (**1976**), p. **252**.

Book I: Book of Watchers

Blessing of Ḥanokh

1 1 The blessing of Ḥanokh, with which he
blessed the elect and righteous, who will be
present in the day of affliction, when all the evil
and wicked are to be removed.

2 And Ḥanokh, a blessed and righteous man of
𐤉𐤄𐤅𐤄, whose eyes were open, said, "This is the
vision of the Set-Apart One in the heavens,
which the messengers showed me, and I heard
everything from the Watchers and the set-apart
ones, and I understood from them as I saw, but
not for this generation, but for a far-off one
which is to come.

3 "Concerning the elect I answered and said, 'The
Set-Apart and Great One, the Elohim of the
world, will come forth from His dwelling, 4 And
He will tread upon the earth, *even* on Mount
Sinai, and appear in the strength of His might
from the heavens. 5 And all shall be struck with
fear, and the Watchers shall quake, and great fear
and trembling shall seize them to the ends of the
earth. 6 And the high mountains shall be shaken,
and the high hills shall be made low, and shall
melt like wax before the flame. 7 And the earth
will be torn apart[a], and all that is on the earth will
perish, and there will be a judgment upon all
men. 8 But He will make peace with the
righteous, and will protect the elect; and
kindness will be upon them. And they will all
belong to Elohim, and they will prosper, and
they will all be blessed. And He will help them
all, and light will appear to them, and He will
make peace with them.

9 "And behold! He comes with ten thousand
times a thousand of His set-apart ones, to execute
judgment against all, and to destroy all the
wicked, and to convict all flesh of all the works
of everything which they have wickedly
committed; and of all the hard things which
wicked sinners have spoken against Him.'"[b]

Observation of the Seasons

2 1 Observe everything that takes place in the
heavens, how they do not change their orbits,
and the luminaries which are in the heavens, how
they all rise and set in order each in its season,
and do not transgress against their appointed
order. 2 Behold the earth, and observe the things
which take place on it, from first to last, how
steadfast they are, how none of the things on
earth change, but all [the works of Elohim][c]
appear to you. 3 Behold the summer and the
winter, how the whole earth is filled with water,
and the clouds cause the dew and rain to rest
upon it.

3 1 Observe and see how *in the winter* all the
trees seem as though they had withered and shed
all their leaves, except fourteen trees, which do
not lose their foliage but renew their foliage after
two to three years.

4 1 And again, observe the days of summer how
the sun is above her and ahead of her.[d] And you
seek shade and shelter because of the heat of the
sun, and the earth also burns with blazing heat,
and so you cannot walk on the earth, or on a rock
because of its heat.

5 1 Observe how the green trees are covered
with leaves and bear fruit. Now pay attention and
know with regard to all His works, and recognize
how He that lives forever has made them so.
2 And all His works go on from year to year
forever, and all prospers and obeys Him, and
does not change, but everything works according
to the way Elohim has ordained.

---

[a] **1**:7 The phrase "torn apart" is from the Ethiopic word ወትሠጠጥ (*wa't'sa'tat*). This reading is backed up by the Greek texts as well. However, some Ethiopic texts read ወትሠጠም (*wa't'sa'tam*) which means "submerged."

[b] **1:9** This verse is quoted in Yehudah [Jude] **1:14,15**.

[c] **2:2** Bracketed section indicates reading present in Ethiopic and Greek texts, but absent from Aramaic fragment.

[d] **4:1** The "her" mentioned here is usually taken to mean the earth, though some believe it refers to the moon.

3 And behold how the sea and the rivers in like manner accomplish and do not change their tasks from His commands.

4 But you: you have not been steadfast, nor done the commands of 𐤉𐤄𐤅𐤄, but you have turned away and spoken proud and hard words with your impure mouths against His greatness. Oh, you hardhearted, you shall find no peace.

5 Therefore you shall curse your days, and the years of your life shall perish, and the years of your destruction shall be multiplied in eternal cursing, and you shall find no kindness.

6 In those days you shall make your names an eternal curse to all the righteous, and by you shall all who curse, curse. And all the sinners and wicked shall curse by you, and for you the wicked there shall be a curse.

7 But for the elect there shall be light and joy and
peace, and they shall inherit the earth.[a] 8 And
then wisdom will be bestowed upon the elect,
and they will all live and never sin again, either
through wickedness or through pride. But the
wise will be humble. 9 And they will not
transgress again, nor will they sin all the days of
their life, nor will they die of *the* anger or wrath
of Elohim, but they shall complete the number of
the days of their life. 10 And their lives will be
increased in peace, and the years of their joy will
be multiplied in eternal gladness and peace, all
the days of their life.

The Fall of the Watchers

6 1 And it happened when the children of men
multiplied in those days that beautiful and fair
daughters were born to them.[b] 2 And the
Watchers, sons of heaven, saw and lusted after
them, and said to one another, "Come, let us
choose wives from among the children of men
and bring forth children for ourselves."[c]

3 And Shemiḥazah, who was their leader, said to them, "I fear you will not indeed agree to do this deed, and I alone will be guilty of a great sin."

4 And they all answered him and said, "Let us all swear an oath, and all bind ourselves by a curse not to abandon this plan but to do this thing."

5 Then they all swore together and bound
themselves by a curse upon it. 6 And they were,
in all, two hundred who descended in the days of
Yared on the summit of Mount Ḥermon[d], and
they called it Mount Ḥermon, because they had
sworn and bound themselves by a curse upon it.[e]
7 And these are the names of their leaders:
Shemiḥazah, their leader, Ar'taqoph, Ramt'el,
Kokhav'el, Tami'el, Ram'el, Dani'el, Ziqi'el,
Baraq'el, Asa'el, Ḥermoni, Matar'el, Anan'el,
Sataw'el, Shamshi'el, Sahari'el, Turi'el, Yomi'el,
and Yehaddi'el.[f] 8 These are their chiefs of tens.

7 1 And all the others together with them took
wives to themselves,[g] and each chose one for
himself, and they began to go in to them and to
defile themselves with them. And they taught
them charms and enchantments, and the cutting
of roots, and taught them *about* plants. 2 And *the*
women became pregnant, and they bore great
giants,[h] whose height was three thousand cubits;
3 who consumed all the labors of men. And when
men could no longer sustain them, 4 the giants
turned against them and devoured mankind.
5 And they began to sin against birds, and beasts,
and reptiles, and fish, and to devour one

---

[a] **5:7** Compare Mattithyahu [Matthew] **5**:**5**.

[b] **6:1** See also Bereshiyt [Genesis] **6**:**1**.

[c] **6:2** See also Bereshiyt [Genesis] **6**:**2**.

[d] **6:6** "Ḥermon" – Hebrew 𐤇𐤓𐤌𐤅𐤍 from the word 𐤇𐤓𐤌 (*ḥaram*): "accursed" or "devoted." Typically signifying in Scripture something "devoted" to an evil purpose. Cognate with the word *ḥerem* (same word, different vowels) which refers to objects "under the ban" such as in Devarim [Deuteronomy] **13**:**17** or Yehoshua [Joshua] **6**:**17**. This could also indicate a wordplay, as the word "oath" in verse **4** could, in a Hebrew or Aramaic original, have been 𐤇𐤓𐤌 (*ḥerem*).

[e] **6:6** See also Yehoshua [Joshua] **12**:**4**,**5**. The giants mentioned throughout Ḥanokh are usually called "Nephilim" in Scripture, but are also called "Rephaim."

[f] **6:7** Appendix B contains a list of etymological breakdowns for each of these names, showing their approximate meaning in Hebrew or Aramaic.

[g] **7:1** See Testament of Reuven **5**:**6**-**8**.

[h] **7:2** Some Greek texts add, "and the giants bore the Nephilim, and the Nephilim bore the Elioud." However, other Greek texts read "killed" instead of "bore."

another's flesh,[a] and drink the blood. 6 Then the earth laid accusation against the lawless ones.

8 1 And Asa'el taught men to make swords, and knives, and shields, and breastplates, and showed their successors the metals of the earth and the art of working them, and bracelets, and ornaments, and the use of cosmetics, and the beautifying of the eyelids, and all kinds of costly stones, and all coloring tinctures and alchemy[b].
2 And there were many wicked *ones*, and they committed whoring, and they were led astray, and became corrupt in all their ways.
3 Shemiḥazah taught enchantments, and root-cuttings; Ḥermoni *taught* the resolving of enchantments; Baraq'el *taught* astrology; Kokhav'el *taught* the constellations; Anan'el *taught* the knowledge of the clouds; Ar'taqoph *taught* the signs of the earth; Shamshi'el *taught* the signs of the sun; and Sahari'el *taught* the course of the moon, and the deception[c] of men.
4 And they cried *out*, and their cry went up to heaven.

9 1 And then Mikha'el, Sari'el[d], Rapha'el, and Gavri'el looked down from [the set-apart place of][e] heaven and saw much blood being shed on the earth, and all lawlessness being committed on the earth. 2 And the four, hearing this, went in and said to one another, "The earth, *which was* made without inhabitant, cries the voice of their crying up to the gates of heaven. 3 And now to you, the set-apart ones of heaven, the beings of men make their case, saying, 'Bring our cause before the Most High, [and our destruction before the majestic Glory, before the Master of masters in majesty.][f]'"

4 And [Rapha'el and Mikha'el, great Watchers and set-apart ones, went in and][g] said to their Master, "Master of masters, El of elohim, King of kings, and Elohim of the ages, the throne of Your glory is for every generation of the ages, and Your Name *is* set-apart, and glorious, and blessed to all the ages! 5 You have made all things, and You have power over all things: and all things are naked and open in Your sight, and You see all things, and nothing can hide itself from You.[h] 6 You see what Asa'el has done, who has taught all unrighteousness on earth and revealed the eternal secrets which were *preserved* in heaven, which men were striving to learn. 7 And Shemiḥazah, to whom You have given authority to bear rule over his associates.

8 "And they have gone to the daughters of men on the earth, and have slept with the women, and have defiled themselves, and revealed to them all kinds of sins. 9 And the women have borne giants, and the whole earth has thereby been filled with blood and unrighteousness. 10 And now, behold, the spirits of those who have died are crying and making their case to the gates of heaven, and their lamentations have ascended: and cannot cease because of the lawless deeds which are wrought on the earth. 11 And You know all things before they come to pass, and You see these things and You allow them, and You do not say to us what we are to do to them in regard to these."

---

[a] **7:5** A possible reference to the destruction of some of the "classes" of giants.
[b] **8:1** Some Ethiopic commentaries explain the use of alchemy not as changing non-precious metals into gold, but rather of changing one "kind" of creature into another, such as changing a man into a horse, or vice versa, or transferring an embryo from one womb to another. Most texts, however, omit the word "alchemy."
[c] **8:3** Some Ethiopic texts read "destruction" instead of "deception" here.
[d] **9:1** Ethiopic texts read "Uri'el" here, though the Aramaic reads "Sari'el."
[e] **9:1** Bracketed section indicates reading present in reconstructed Aramaic fragment, but absent from Greek and Ethiopic texts.
[f] **9:3** Bracketed section indicates reading present in reconstructed Aramaic fragment, but absent from Greek and Ethiopic texts.
[g] **9:4** Bracketed section indicates reading present in reconstructed Aramaic fragment, but absent from Greek and Ethiopic texts.
[h] **9:5** See Ivrim [Hebrews] **4:13**.

Judgment of the Watchers Pronounced

10 1 Then the Most High, the Set-Apart and Great One spoke, and sent Uri'el[a] to the son of Lamekh, and said to him:

2 "Go to Noaḥ, and tell him in My Name, 'Hide yourself!' and reveal to him the end that is approaching: that the whole earth will be destroyed, and a flood is about to come upon the whole earth, and will destroy all that is on it. 3 And now instruct him that he may escape and his seed may be preserved for all the generations of the world."

4 And again the Master said to Rapha'el, "Bind Asa'el hand and foot, and cast him into the darkness, and make an opening in the desert, which is in Dudael, and cast him in it. 5 And place rough and jagged rocks on him, and cover him with darkness, and let him stay there forever, and cover his face that he may not see light. 6 And on the day of the great judgment he will be cast into the fire. 7 And heal the earth which the messengers have corrupted, and proclaim the healing of the earth, that they may heal the plague, and that all the children of men may not perish through all the secret things that the Watchers have disclosed and have taught their sons. 8 And the whole earth has been corrupted through the works that were taught by Asa'el: ascribe all sin to him."

9 And to Gavri'el 𐤉𐤄𐤅𐤄 said, "Proceed against the illegitimate and the reprobates, and against the children of whoring, and destroy the children of whoring and the children of the Watchers from among men and cause them to go forth. Send them against one another that they may destroy each other in battle: for they shall not have length of days. 10 And no request that they or their fathers make of you will be granted to their fathers on their behalf; for they hope to live an eternal life, and that each one of them will live five hundred years."

11 And 𐤉𐤄𐤅𐤄 said to Mikha'el, "Go, make known to[b] Shemiḥazah and his associates who have united themselves with women so as to have defiled themselves with them in all their uncleanness. 12 And when their sons have slain one another, and they have seen the destruction of their beloved ones, bind them fast for seventy generations in the valleys of the earth, until the day of their judgment and of their consummation, until the judgment that is forever and ever is consummated.[c] 13 In those days they shall be led off to the abyss of fire; and to the torment and the prison in which they shall be confined forever. 14 And when they burn and die, those who collaborated with them will be bound together with them from now on, until the end of *all* generations. 15 And destroy all the beings of the reprobate and the children of the Watchers, because they have wronged mankind. 16 Destroy all wrong from the face of the earth and let every evil work come to an end: and let the plant of righteousness[d] and truth appear; and it shall prove a blessing: the works of righteousness and truth shall be planted in truth and joy for evermore. 17 And then shall all the righteous escape, and shall live until they bear thousands of children, and all the days of their youth and they shall complete their Sabbaths[e] in peace.

18 "And then shall the whole earth be tilled in righteousness, and shall all be planted with trees and be full of blessing. 19 And all desirable trees shall be planted on it, and they shall plant vines on it: and the vine which they plant on it shall yield wine in abundance, and as for all the seed which is sown on it, each measure *of it* shall bear a thousand, and each measure of olives shall yield ten presses of oil.

20 "And you, cleanse the earth from all oppression, and from all unrighteousness, and

---

[a] **10:1** Some Ethiopic texts read "Arsayalalur" instead of "Uriel" here.

[b] **10:11** Some Greek and Ethiopic texts read, "bind" instead of "make known to."

[c] **10:12** See also Kepha 𐤁 [2 Peter] **2:4**; Yehudah [Jude] **1:6**.

[d] **10:16** See Yovelim **1:16**.

[e] **10:17** The word rendered as "Sabbaths" here is ሰንበታት (*sanbatat*). Some texts use the singular form. In Greek, it is σαββατα (*sabbata*), which is also plural for "Sabbaths." In some Ethiopic commentaries, it is stated that the phrase "complete their Sabbaths" implies retirement at a ripe old age.

from all sin, and from all wickedness. And destroy all the uncleanness that is worked in the earth from off the earth. 21 And all the children of men will become righteous, and all nations will offer adoration and will praise Me, and all will bow before Me. 22 And the earth will be cleansed from all defilement, and from all sin, and from all punishment, and from all torment, and I will never send them upon it again, from generation to generation and forever."

11 1 "And in those days I will open the store chambers of blessing which are in the heaven, so as to send them down upon the earth over the work and labor of the children of men. 2 And truth and peace shall be associated together throughout all the days of the world and throughout all the generations of men."

Ḥanokh's Intercession for the Watchers

12 1 Before these things Ḥanokh was hidden, and no one of the children of men knew where he was hidden, and where he abode, and what had become of him. 2 And his activities had to do with the Watchers, and his days were with the set-apart ones.

3 And I, Ḥanokh was blessing the Master of Majesty, and the King of the ages, and behold, the Watchers called me 'Ḥanokh the scribe,' and *they* said to me:

4 "Ḥanokh, scribe of righteousness, go, declare to the Watchers of heaven who have left the high heaven,[a] the set-apart, eternal place, and have defiled themselves with women, and have done as the children of earth do, and have taken wives to themselves, 'You have worked great destruction on the earth. 5 And you will have no peace nor forgiveness of sin; and just as they delight themselves in their children, 6 they shall see the murder of their beloved ones, and they shall lament over the destruction of their children, and will make petition to eternity, but you will not attain kindness[b] and peace.'"

Ḥanokh's Intercession for Asa'el

13 1 And Ḥanokh went and said, "Asa'el, you shall have no peace. A severe sentence has gone forth against you, and he[c] will put you in bonds. 2 And you shall not have toleration nor request granted to you, because of the unrighteousness which you have taught, and because of all the works of wickedness and unrighteousness and sin which you have shown to men."

3 Then I went and spoke to them all together, and they were all afraid, and fear and trembling seized them. 4 And they implored me to draw up a petition for them that they might find forgiveness, and to read their petition in the presence of 𐤉𐤄𐤅𐤄 of heaven. 5 For from then on they could not speak *with Him* nor lift up their eyes to heaven for shame of their sins for which they had been condemned.

6 Then I wrote out their petition, and the prayer in regard to their beings and their deeds individually and in regard to their requests that they should have forgiveness and length of days. 7 And I went off and sat down at the waters of Dan, in the land of Dan, to the south of Ḥermon, at its western side. I read the book of their petition until I fell asleep.

Dream Vision

8 And behold a dream came to me, and visions fell down upon me, [and I lifted my eyelids to the windows of the palace of heaven,][d] and I saw visions of severe punishment, and a voice came bidding *me* to tell it to the sons of heaven, and reprimand them. 9 And when I awoke, I came to them, and they were all sitting gathered together, weeping in Havel-Mayya[e], which is between Levanon and Senir[f], with their faces covered.

---

[a] **12:4** See Yehudah [Jude] **6**.

[b] **12:6** Some texts omit "kindness" here.

[c] **13:1** The "he" mentioned here is Raphael, according to Ḥanokh **10:4**.

[d] **13:8** Bracketed section indicates reading present in reconstructed Aramaic fragment, but absent from Greek and Ethiopic texts.

[e] **13:9** Havel-Mayya – Aramaic for "waters of mourning."

[f] **13:9** In Greek, this is σενισηλ (*senisel*). In Ethiopic, it is ሰነሰር (*seneser*). However, these are most likely corruptions of the Hebrew word 𐤔𐤍𐤉𐤓 (*Shen'iyr*) which, according to Devarim [Deuteronomy] **3:9**, was the Amorite name for Mount Ḥermon. Note that there

10 And I recounted before them all the visions
which I had seen in sleep, and I began to speak
the words of righteousness, and to reprimand the
heavenly Watchers.

14 1 The book of the words of righteousness,
and of the reprimand of the eternal Watchers in
accordance with the command of the Set-Apart
Great One in that vision. 2 I saw in my sleep
what I will now say with a tongue of flesh and
with the breath of my mouth: which the Great
One has given to men to converse with, and
understand with the heart. 3 As He has created
and given to man the power of understanding the
word of wisdom, so has He created me also and
given me the power of reprimanding the
Watchers, the children of heaven.

4 "I wrote out your petition, and it appeared to
me in a vision, that your petition will not be
granted to you throughout all the days of
eternity, and that judgment has been finally
passed upon you. Yes, *your petition* will not be
granted to you. 5 And from now on you will not
ascend into heaven for all eternity; and the
decree has gone forth to bind you in the bonds of
the earth for all the days of the world.

6 "And before that you will see the destruction of
your beloved sons and you will have no pleasure
in them, but they will fall before you by the
sword. 7 And your petition on their behalf will
not be granted, nor yet on your own, even though
you weep and pray and speak all the words
contained in the writing which I have written.

8 "And this was the vision shown to me: Behold,
in the vision clouds invited me and a mist
summoned me, and the course of the stars and
the lightnings sped and hastened me, and the
winds in the vision caused me to fly and lifted
me upward, and bore me into heaven. 9 And I
went in until I drew near to a wall which is built
of crystals and surrounded by tongues of fire:
and it began to affright me. 10 And I went into
the tongues of fire and drew near to a large house
which was built of crystals: and the walls of the
house were like a tile floor *made* of crystals, and
its groundwork was of crystal. 11 Its ceiling was
like the path of the stars and the lightnings, and
between them were fiery kerubim, and their
heaven was water.[a] 12 A flaming fire surrounded
the walls, and its gates blazed with fire. 13 And I
entered into that house, and it was hot as fire and
cold as ice: there were no delights of life in
there: fear covered me, and trembling got hold
upon me. 14 And as I quaked and trembled, I fell
upon my face.

15 "And I beheld a vision, and behold: there was
a second house, greater than the former, and the
entire gate stood open before me, and it was built
of flames of fire. 16 And in every respect it so
excelled in splendor and magnificence to the
extent that I cannot describe to you its splendor
and its magnificence. 17 And its floor was of fire,
and above it were lightnings and the path of the
stars, and its ceiling also was flaming fire.
18 And I looked and saw in it a lofty throne: its
appearance was as crystal-glass, and its wheels
like the disc of the shining sun, and its sides
were kerubim. 19 And from underneath the
throne came streams of flaming fire so that I
could not look on. 20 And the Great Glory sat
thereon, and His garment was brighter than the
sun and was whiter than any snow. 21 None of
the messengers could enter and could behold His
face by reason of the magnificence and glory and
no flesh could behold Him.[b] 22 The flaming fire
was around Him, and a great fire stood before
Him, and none around could draw near Him. Ten
thousand times ten thousand *stood* before Him,
yet He needed no counselor. 23 And the most set-
apart ones who were near to Him did not leave
by night nor depart from Him. 24 And until then I
had been prostrate on my face, trembling: and
the Master called me with His own mouth, and

---

is only one letter difference between *Sheniyr* and *Shinar* (Heb. 𐤔𐤍𐤏𐤓), which was another name for Bavel (Babylon).

[a] **14:11** The Ethiopic text preserves the wordplay here. In Ethiopic, this phrase is ወሰማዮሙ ማይ, (*wa'samayomu may'*) which means "and their heaven" and "water" respectively. In Hebrew, these two words would be 𐤔𐤌𐤉𐤌 (*sha'mayim*) "heavens" and 𐤌𐤉𐤌 (*mayim*) "waters" respectively. In Aramaic, they are 𐤔𐤌𐤉𐤀 (*sha'maya*) "heaven" and 𐤌𐤉𐤀 (*maya*) "water." Thus whether the original were Hebrew or Aramaic, the wordplay remains as preserved properly in Ethiopic.

[b] **14:21** See Timotheos A [**1** Timothy] **6:16**.

said to me, 'Come here, Ḥanokh, and hear My
word.' **25** And one of the set-apart ones came to
me and waked me, and He made me rise up and
approach the door: and I bowed my face
downwards."

15 **1** And He answered and said to me, and I
heard His voice, "Fear not, Ḥanokh, righteous
man and scribe of righteousness: come here and
hear My voice.

2 "And go, say to the Watchers of heaven, who
have sent you to intercede for them: 'You should
intercede for men, and not men for you. **3** Why
have you left the high, set-apart, and eternal
heaven, and lain with women, and defiled
yourselves with the daughters of men and taken
to yourselves wives, and done like the children
of earth, and begotten giants as your sons? **4** And
though you were set-apart, spiritual, living the
eternal life, you have defiled yourselves with the
blood of women, and have begotten *children*
with the blood of flesh, and, as the children of
men, have lusted after flesh and blood as those
also do who die and perish.'

5 "Therefore have I given them wives also that
they might impregnate them, and beget children
by them, so that nothing might be lacking to
them on earth. **6** But you were formerly spiritual,
living the eternal life, and immortal for all
generations of the world. **7** And therefore I have
not appointed wives for you; for as for the
spiritual ones of the heaven, in heaven is their
dwelling. **8** And now the giants, who are
produced from the spirits and flesh, shall be
called 'evil spirits' upon the earth, and on the
earth shall be their dwelling. **9** Evil spirits have
proceeded from their bodies; because they are
born from men, and from the set-apart Watchers
is their beginning and primal origin; they shall be
evil spirits on earth, and evil spirits shall they be
called. [**10** As for the spirits of heaven, in heaven
shall be their dwelling, but as for the spirits of
the earth which were born upon the earth, on the
earth shall be their dwelling.][a]

11 "And the spirits of the giants afflict[b], oppress,
destroy, attack, do battle, and work destruction
on the earth, and cause trouble. They take no
food, but nevertheless hunger and thirst, and
cause offences. And these spirits shall rise up
against the children of men and against the
women, because they have proceeded from
them."

16 **1** "From the days of the slaughter and
destruction and death of the giants, from the
beings of whose flesh the spirits, having gone
forth, shall destroy without incurring judgment –
thus shall they destroy until the day of the
consummation, the great judgment in which the
age shall be consummated, over the Watchers
and the wicked; yes, *it* shall be wholly
consummated.

2 "And now as to the Watchers who have sent
you to intercede for them, who had previously
been in heaven, *say to them*: **3** 'You have been in
heaven, but all the mysteries had not yet been
revealed to you, and you knew worthless ones,
and these in the hardness of your hearts you have
made known to the women, and through these
mysteries women and men work much evil on
earth.' **4** Say to them therefore: 'You have no
peace.'"

Journey through Earth and Sheol

17 **1** And they took and brought me to a place in
which those who were there were like flaming
fire, and, whenever they willed, they appeared as
men. **2** And they brought me to the place of
darkness, and to a mountain the point of whose
summit reached to heaven. **3** And I saw the
places of the luminaries and the treasuries of the
stars and of the thunder and in the uttermost
depths, where were a fiery bow and arrows and
their quiver, and a fiery sword and all the

---

[a] **15:10** Some texts omit verse **10**.

[b] **15:11** Some Greek texts contain the word νεφελας (*nephalas*) which means "clouds" here. The Ethiopic also agrees with this reading, using ደመናት (*da'ma'na'ta*) which also means "clouds." Thus they read, "And the spirits of the giants are as clouds, and they oppress, destroy…" If this rendering is original, it is possibly a corruption of the Greek Ναφηλειμ (*Naphelim*) which is the Greek spelling of "Nephilim." Other Greek texts, however, use the word νεμομενα (*nemomena*) meaning "to lay waste" or "afflict."

lightnings. 4 And they took me to the living waters, and to the fire of the west, which receives every setting of the sun.

5 And I came to a river of fire in which the fire flows like water and discharges itself into the great sea towards the west. 6 I saw the great rivers and came to the great river and to the great darkness, and went to the place where no flesh walks. 7 I saw the mountains of the darkness of winter and the place whence all the waters of the deep flow. 8 I saw the mouths of all the rivers of the earth and the mouth of the deep.

18 1 I saw the treasuries of all the winds. I saw how He had furnished with them the whole creation and the firm foundations of the earth. 2 And I saw the corner-stone of the earth. I saw the four winds which bear the earth and the firmament of the heaven. 3 And I saw how the winds stretch out the vaults of heaven, and have their station between heaven and earth: these are the pillars of the heaven. 4 I saw the winds of heaven which turn and bring the roundness of the sun and all the stars to their setting. 5 I saw the winds on the earth carrying the clouds: I saw the paths of the messengers. I saw at the end of the earth the firmament of the heaven above. And I proceeded and saw a place which burns day and night, where there are seven mountains of magnificent stones, three towards the east, and three towards the south.

6 And as for those towards the east, one was of colored stone, and one of pearl, and one of jacinth, and those towards the south of red stone. 7 But the middle one reached to heaven like the throne of 𐤉𐤄𐤅𐤄, of alabaster, and the top of the throne was of sapphire. 8 And I saw a flaming fire. And beyond these mountains 9 is a region the end of the great earth: there the heavens[a] were completed. 10 And I saw a deep abyss, with columns of heavenly fire, and among them I saw columns of fire fall, which were beyond measure alike towards the height and towards the depth.

11 And beyond that abyss I saw a place which had no firmament of the heaven above, and no firmly founded earth beneath it: there was no water upon it, and no birds, but it was a waste and horrible place. 12 I saw there seven stars like great burning mountains, and to me, when I inquired regarding them, 13 the messenger said, "This place is the end of heaven and earth: this has become a prison for the stars and the host of heaven. 14 And the stars which roll over the fire are they which have transgressed the commandment of 𐤉𐤄𐤅𐤄 in the beginning of their rising, because they did not come forth at their appointed times. 15 And He was wroth with them, and bound them until the time when their guilt should be consummated, *even* for ten thousand years."

19 1 And Uri'el said to me, "Here the messengers who have joined themselves with women shall stand, and their spirits assuming many different forms are defiling mankind and shall lead them astray into sacrificing to demons as elohim,[b] *here shall they stand*, until the day of the great judgment in which they shall be judged until they are made an end of.

2 "And the women also, of the messengers who went astray, shall become sirens[c]." 3 And I, Ḥanokh, alone saw the vision, the ends of all things: and no man shall see as I have seen.

---

[a] **18:9** Some Ethiopic texts read ማያት (*maya't*) here, meaning "waters" (equivalent to the Hebrew 𐤌𐤉𐤌 [*mayim*]). Other texts, both Ethiopic and Greek, read ሰማያት (*sa'maya't*) meaning "heavens" as it is here (equivalent to the Hebrew 𐤔𐤌𐤉𐤌 (*sha'mayim*). It is possible that the rendering of *maya't* (waters) comes from a scribal error of leaving off the first letter ሰ (*sat*).

[b] **19:1** See Yovelim **1**:**11**; Korinthious A [**1** Corinthians] **10**:**20**.

[c] **19:2** The meaning "siren" comes from the Greek texts, which record this word as σειρηνας *(seirenas*), translating to "siren." This is used in place of the Hebrew 𐤉𐤏𐤍𐤄 (*ya'anah*), usually rendered as "ostrich" or "owl;" that is, a creature that screeches (see Mikhah [Micah] **1**:**8**). The Ethiopic word in some texts here is ሰላማውያን (*salama'w'yan*), which means "peaceful ones," an idiom for "friends." However, other Ethiopic texts use the word ሰላማዊያት (*salama'wiyat*). Although its meaning is debated, it is believed to more closely match the Greek version.

Names of the Set-Apart Messengers

20 1 And these are the names of the set-apart messengers who watch. 2 Uri'el, one of the set-apart messengers, who is over the world and over Tartarus. 3 Rapha'el, one of the set-apart messengers, who is over the spirits of men.
4 Rau'el, one of the set-apart messengers who takes vengeance on the world of the luminaries.
5 Mikha'el, one of the set-apart messengers, that is, he that is set over the best part of mankind and over chaos. 6 Sari'el, one of the set-apart messengers, who is set over the spirits, who sin in the spirit. 7 Gavri'el, one of the set-apart messengers, who is over Paradise and the serpents[a] and the kerubim. [8 Remi'el, one of the set-apart messengers, whom Elohim set over those who rise.][b]

Journey to Temporary and Final Place of Punishment for the Fallen Stars

21 1 And I proceeded to where nothing was done.[c] 2 [And I saw something terrible there:][d] I saw neither a heaven above nor a firmly founded earth, but a place chaotic and horrible. 3 And there I saw seven stars of the heaven bound together in it – like great mountains – and burning with fire.

4 Then I said, "What sin are they bound for, and why have they been cast in here?"

5 Then Uri'el, one of the set-apart messengers, who was with me, and was chief over them, said, "Ḥanokh, why do you ask, and why are you eager for the truth? 6 These are of the number of the stars of heaven, which have transgressed the command of 𐤉𐤄𐤅𐤄, and are bound here until ten thousand[e] years, the time entailed by their sins, are consummated."

7 And from there I went to another place, which was still more horrible than the former, and I saw a horrible thing: a great fire there which burned and blazed, and the place was cleft as far as the abyss, being full of great descending columns of fire. I could see neither its extent nor *its* magnitude, nor could I conjecture.[f]

8 Then I said, "How fearful is the place and how terrible to look upon!"

9 Then Uri'el answered me, one of the set-apart messengers who was with me, and said to me, "Ḥanokh, why do you have such fear and dread?" And I answered, "Because of this fearful place, and because of this sight of pain."

10 And he said to me, "This place is the prison of the messengers, and here they will be imprisoned forever."

22 1 And from there I went to another place, and he showed me in the west another great and high mountain and of hard rock.

2 And there were four hollow places in it, deep and wide and very smooth: three of them were dark and one bright; and there was a fountain of water in its midst. And I said, "How smooth are these hollow places, and deep and dark to view."

3 Then Rapha'el answered, one of the set-apart messengers who was with me, and said to me, "These hollow places have been created for this very purpose, that the spirits of the beings of the dead should assemble in them; yes that all the beings of the children of men should assemble here. 4 And these places have been made to receive them until the day of their judgment and until their appointed period; until the period appointed, until the great judgment *comes* upon them."

---

[a] **20:7** While the Ethiopic uses the word ወአክይስት (*wa'ak'iyst*) meaning "and serpents" here, the Greek actually uses δρακον (*drakon*) which, more specifically means "dragons." This is the Greek word used in place of the Hebrew 𐤕𐤍𐤉𐤍 (*tan'iyn*), usually translated as "sea monster" or "crocodile" or sometimes, due to Greek influence, "dragon." *Drakon* is also the word used in Hit'galut [Revelation] for "dragon."

[b] **20:8** Bracketed section indicates reading present in some Greek texts, but absent from Ethiopic. Some other Greek texts also add, "the names of the messengers."

[c] **21:1** Literally, "the place of void."

[d] **21:1** Bracketed section indicates reading present in some Greek and Ethiopic texts, but absent from others.

[e] **21:6** Some Ethiopic texts read, "ten million."

[f] **21:7-10** See Hit'galut [Revelation] **20:1-3**.

5 I saw the spirit of a dead man making accusation, and his voice went forth to heaven and made accusation, crying out unceasingly, and making accusations. 6 And I asked Rapha'el the Watcher and set-apart one who was with me, and I said to him, "This spirit which makes a case, whose is it, whose voice goes forth and makes a case to heaven?"

7 And he answered me saying, "This is the spirit which went forth from Havel, whom his brother Qayin killed; he makes accusation against him until his seed is destroyed from the face of the earth, and his seed is annihilated from among the seed of men."

8 Then I asked regarding all the hollow places, "Why is one separated from the other?"

9 And he answered me saying, "These three have been made that the spirits of the dead might be separated. And this division has been made for the spirits of the righteous, in which there is the bright spring of water.

10 "And this has been made for sinners when they die and are buried in the earth and judgment has not yet been executed upon them in their lifetime. 11 Here their spirits shall be set apart in this great pain, until the great day of judgment and scourgings and torments of the accursed forever, so that *there may be* retribution for their spirits. There He shall bind them forever.

12 "And this division has been made for the spirits of those who make their case, who make disclosures concerning their destruction, when they were slain in the days of the sinners.

13 "And this has been made for the spirits of men who shall not be righteous but sinners, who are wicked, and they shall be companions of the lawless: but their spirits shall not be punished in the day of judgment nor shall they be raised from there."

14 Then I blessed the Master of Glory and said, "Blessed are You, Master of righteousness, who rules over the world."

Fire of the Luminaries of Heaven

23 1 From there I was transported to another place to the west of the ends of the earth. 2 And I was shown a burning fire which ran without resting, and did not halt its running, day or night, at the same time remaining constant.

3 And I asked saying, "What is this which does not rest?" 4 Then Rau'el, one of the set-apart messengers who was with me, answered me, and said to me, "This course of fire which you have seen, this is the fire burning in the west, which is the luminaries of heaven." [a]

The Seven Mountains and the Tree of Life

24 1 And from there I went to another place of the earth, and he showed me a mountain range of fire which burned day and night. 2 And I went beyond it and saw seven magnificent mountains, all differing each from the other, and their stones were magnificent and beautiful, magnificent as a whole, of glorious appearance and fair exterior. *There were* three towards the east, one founded on the other, and three towards the south, one upon the other, and deep rough ravines, no one of which joined with any other. 3 And the seventh mountain was in the midst of these, and it surpassed them in height, resembling the seat of a throne; and fragrant trees encircled the throne. 4 And among them was a tree such as I had never yet smelled, neither was any among them nor were others like it: it had a fragrance beyond all fragrance, and its leaves and blooms and wood do not wither forever. And its fruit is beautiful, and its fruit resembles the dates of a palm.

5 Then I said, "How beautiful is this tree, and how fragrant, and its leaves are fair, and its blooms very delightful in appearance."

6 Then Mikha'el their leader, one of the set-apart and honored messengers who was with me, answered.

---

[a] **23:4** Charles translated this verse as, "This course of fire which you have seen is the fire burning in the west which persecutes all the luminaries of heaven." I have chosen an alternate reading, based on the sentence structure and some Ethiopic commentaries.

25 1 And he said to me, "Ḥanokh, why do you ask me regarding the fragrance of the tree, and why do you desire to learn the truth?"

2 Then I answered him saying, "I desire to know about everything, but especially about this tree."

3 And he answered saying, "This high mountain which you have seen, whose summit is like the throne of the Master, is His throne, where the Set-Apart Great One, the Master of Glory, the Eternal King, will sit, when He shall come down to visit the earth with goodness.[a] 4 And as for this fragrant tree no mortal is permitted to touch it until the great judgment, when He shall take vengeance on all and bring *everything* to its consummation forever. It shall then be given to the righteous and set-apart. 5 Its fruit shall be for food to the elect: it shall be transplanted to the set-apart place, to the Temple of the Master, the Eternal King. 6 Then shall they rejoice with joy and be glad, and they will enter into the set-apart place. And its fragrance shall be in their bones, and they will live a long life on earth, such as your fathers lived. And in their days shall no sorrow or plague or torment or calamity touch them." [b]

7 Then I blessed the Master of Glory, the Eternal King, who has prepared such things for the righteous, and has created them and promised to give to them.

Yerushalayim and its Surroundings

26 1 And I went from there to the center of the earth, and I saw a blessed place in which were trees with branches abiding and blooming from a dismembered tree. 2 And there I saw a set-apart mountain, and there was a stream underneath the mountain to the east, and it flowed towards the south. 3 And I saw towards the east another mountain higher than this, and between them was a deep and narrow ravine: a stream also ran in it underneath the mountain. 4 And to the west of it there was another mountain, lower than the former and of small elevation, and a ravine deep and dry between them. And another deep and dry ravine was at the extremities of the three mountains. 5 And all the ravines were deep and narrow, *formed* of hard rock, and trees were not planted upon them. 6 And I marveled at the mountains, and I marveled at the ravine; yes, I marveled very much.

Accursed Valley [Presumably Gehenna]

27 1 Then I said, "For what purpose does this blessed land, which is entirely filled with trees, have in its midst this accursed valley?"

2 Then Uri'el, one of the set-apart messengers who was with me, answered and said, "This accursed valley is for those who are accursed forever. Here all the accursed will be gathered together: *those* who utter with their lips against 𐤉𐤄𐤅𐤄 unseemly words; and speak hard things of His glory. They will be gathered together here, and this will be the place of their habitation. 3 In the last days, in the days of the true judgment in the presence of the righteous forever. Here the just will bless the Master of Glory, the Eternal King. 4 In the days of judgment of *the accursed*, they will bless Him for the kindness which He has given them."

5 Then I blessed the Master of Glory and gave Him the praise that suits His glory.

Journey East

28 1 And from there I went towards the east, into the midst of the mountain range of the desert, and I saw a wilderness and it was solitary, full of trees and plants. 2 And water gushed forth from above. 3 Rushing like a plentiful watercourse which flowed towards the northwest, it caused clouds and dew to ascend on every side.

29 1 And from there I went to another place in the wilderness, and approached to the east of this mountain range. 2 And there I saw wild trees excreting perfumes of frankincense and myrrh.

30 1 And beyond these, I went far to the east, and I saw another place, a valley *full* of water. 2 And in *the valley* were sweet-smelling reeds, like mastic. 3 And on the sides of those valleys I

---

[a] **25:3** See Yovelim **1:26**.

[b] **25:4-6** See Hit'galut [Revelation] **2**:7.

saw fragrant cinnamon. And beyond these I
proceeded to the east.

31 1 And I saw other mountains, and among
them were groves of trees, and nectar flowed
forth from them, which are called 'sarira'[a] and
'galbanum.'[b] 2 And beyond these mountains I
saw another mountain to the east of the ends of
the earth, where there were aloe trees, and the
whole forest was full of *trees*, being like sturdy
almond-trees. 3 And when one burned it[c], [a
pleasant odor came forth]; [when the bark was
ground][d] it smelled sweeter than any fragrant
odor.

32 1 To the northeast I saw seven mountains full
of choice nard and mastic and cinnamon and
pepper. 2 And from there I went over the
summits of all these mountains, far towards the
east of the earth, and passed above the Sea of
Reeds and went far from it, and passed over [the
darkness, far from it][e].

3 And I came to the Garden of Righteousness,
and from far off trees more numerous than these
trees, and *they were* great. *There were* two trees
there, very great, beautiful, and glorious, and
magnificent; and the tree of knowledge, whose
set-apart fruit they eat and know great wisdom.

4 That tree is like the fir in height, and its leaves
are like *those of* the Karob tree. And its fruit is
like the clusters of the vine, very beautiful: and
the fragrance of the tree penetrates far off.

5 Then I said, "How beautiful is the tree, and
how attractive is its appearance!"

6 Then Rapha'el the set-apart messenger who
was with me, answered me and said, "This is the
tree of wisdom, of which your father, old *in
years*, and your aged mother, who were before
you, have eaten, and they learned wisdom and
their eyes were opened, and they knew that they
were naked and they were driven out of the
garden."

33 1 And from there I went to the ends of the
earth and saw there great beasts, and each
differed from the other; and *I saw* birds also
differing in appearance and beauty and voice, the
one differing from the other. 2 And to the east of
those beasts I saw the ends of the earth upon
which the heaven rests, and the gates of the
heaven open. 3 And I saw how the stars of
heaven come forth, and I counted the gates out of
which they proceed, and wrote down all their
outlets, of each individual star by itself,
according to their number and their names, their
courses and their positions, and their times and
their months, as Uri'el the set-apart messenger
who was with me showed me. 4 He showed all
things to me and wrote them down for me. He
also wrote their names for me, and their laws and
their companies.

Journey North

34 1 And from there I went towards the north to
the ends of the earth, and there I saw a great and
glorious device at the ends of the whole earth.
2 And here I saw three gates of heaven open in
heaven: through each of them proceed north
winds. When they blow there is cold, hail, frost,
snow, dew, and rain. 3 And out of one gate they
blow for good; but when they blow through the
other two gates, it is with violence and affliction
on the earth, and they blow with violence.

---

[a] **31:1** Ethiopic word ሰሪራ (*sarira*) is left transliterated here. It is believed to actually be styrax, a genus of shrubs and small trees used both for its resin and for the sweet-smelling, aromatic incense that can be produced from it.

[b] **31:1** Ethiopic word ከልበኔን (*kal'banen*) is loosely transliterated from galbanum, referring to the resin and gum from the apiaceae (or umbelliferae) family of plants, which also includes celery, carrots and parsley.

[c] **31:3** Some texts read, "And when one picked the fruit of it..." here instead.

[d] **31:3** Bracketed section indicates reading present in reconstructed Aramaic fragment, but absent from Greek and Ethiopic texts.

[e] **32:2** Bracketed section indicates reading present in Aramaic fragment. Ethiopic text reads, "the messenger Zoti'el."

Journey West

35 1 And from there I went towards the west to the ends of the earth, and saw there three gates of heaven open such as I had seen in the east, the same number of gates, and the same number of outlets.

Journey South

36 1 And from there I went to the south to the ends of the earth, and saw there three open gates of heaven. And from there came the south wind, dew, rain, and wind. 2 And from there I went to the east to the ends of heaven, and saw here the three eastern gates of heaven open and small gates above them. 3 Through each of these small gates pass the stars of heaven and run their course to the west on the path which is shown to them.

4 And as often as I saw, I blessed always the Master of Glory, and I continued to bless the Master of Glory who has worked great and glorious wonders, to show the greatness of His work to the messengers and to spirits and to men, that they might praise His work and all His creation. That they might see the work of His might and praise the great work of His hands and bless Him forever.

Book II: Book of the Parables of Ḥanokh

37 1 The second vision which he saw, the vision of wisdom, which Ḥanokh the son of Yared, the son of Mahalalel, the son of Kenan, the son of Enosh, the son of Seth, the son of Adam, saw.

2 And this is the beginning of the words of wisdom which I lifted up my voice to speak and say to those who dwell on earth, "Hear, you men of old time, and see, you that come after, the words of the Set-Apart One which I will speak before the Master of Spirits. 3 It was better to declare *them only* to the men of old time, but we will not withhold the beginning of wisdom from those that come after. 4 Until the present day such wisdom has never been given by the Master of Spirits as I have received according to my insight, according to the good pleasure of the Master of Spirits, who has given me the lot of eternal life. 5 Now three parables were imparted to me, and I lifted up my voice and recounted them to those that dwell on the earth."

Prophecy of World Judgment

38 1 The First Parable. When the congregation of the righteous appears, and sinners are judged for their sins, and are driven from the face of the earth: 2 And when the Righteous One appears before the eyes of the righteous, whose elect works hang upon the Master of Spirits, and light will appear to the righteous and the elect who dwell on the earth, where then will the dwelling of the sinners be, and where *will* the resting-place of those who have denied the Master of Spirits *be*? It will have been better for them if they had not been born.[a]

3 When the secrets of the righteous are revealed and the sinners are judged, and the wicked are driven from the presence of the righteous and elect: 4 from that time, those that possess the earth will no longer be powerful and exalted. And they shall not be able to behold the face of the set-apart, for the Master of Spirits has caused His light to appear on the face of the set-apart, righteous, and elect.[b]

5 Then the kings and the mighty will die and be given into the hands of the righteous and set-apart. 6 And from then on, none *of them* will seek the kindness of the Master of Spirits for themselves, for their life is annihilated.

Home of the Righteous

39 1 And it will happen in those days, that elect and set-apart children will descend from the high heaven, and their seed will become one with the children of men. 2 And in those days Ḥanokh received the books of zeal and wrath, and the books of disquiet and disturbance. And kindness will not be given to them, says the Master of Spirits.

---

[a] **38:2** See Mattithyahu [Matthew] **26:24**; Yehudah [Jude] **4**.

[b] **38:4** See Korinthious B [2 Corinthians] **4:6**.

3 And in those days whirlwinds carried me off from the earth, and set me down at the end of the heavens.[a] **4** And there I saw another vision, the dwelling-places of the set-apart, and the resting-places of the righteous.[b]

5 Here my eyes saw their dwellings with His righteous messengers, and their resting-places with the set-apart ones. And they petitioned and interceded and prayed on behalf of the children of men, and righteousness flowed before them as water, and kindness like dew upon the earth. Thus it is among them forever and ever.

6 And in that place my eyes saw the Elect One of righteousness and of faith, and righteousness will prevail in His days, and the righteous and elect will be without number before Him forever and ever.

7 And I saw His dwelling-place under the wings of the Master of Spirits. And all the righteous and elect before Him will be as intense as the light of fire, and their mouths will be full of blessing, and their lips will praise the Name of the Master of Spirits, and righteousness will never fail before Him, and uprightness will never fail before Him.

8 And I desired to dwell there *under His wings*, and my spirit longed for that dwelling-place. And before now has been my portion, for so has it been established concerning me before the Master of Spirits.

9 In those days I praised and prayed to the Name of the Master of Spirits with blessings and praises, because He has strengthened me with blessings and praises, according to the good pleasure of the Master of Spirits. **10** For a long time my eyes regarded that place, and I blessed Him and praised Him, saying, "Blessed is He, and may He be blessed from the beginning and forevermore. **11** And before Him there is no ceasing. He knew before the world was created what would be forever and what would be from generation to generation. **12** Those who do not sleep bless You; they stand before Your glory and bless, praise, and exalt *You*, saying, "Set-Apart, Set-Apart, Set-Apart is the Master of Spirits. The spirits fill the earth.[c]"

13 And here my eyes saw all those who do not sleep: they stand before Him and bless and say, "Blessed be You, and blessed be the Name of 𐤉𐤄𐤅𐤄 forever and ever." [d]

14 And my face was changed; for I could no longer look.[e]

The Four Messengers

40 **1** And after that I saw thousands and thousands and ten thousand times ten thousand, I saw a multitude beyond number and reckoning, who stood before the Master of Spirits.[f] **2** And on the four sides of the Master of Spirits I saw four presences,[g] different from those that do not sleep, and I learned their names: for the messenger that went with me made their names known to me, and showed me all the hidden things.

3 And I heard the voices of those four presences as they uttered praises before the Master of Glory. **4** The first voice blesses the Master of Spirits forever and ever. **5** And the second voice I heard blessing the Elect One and the elect ones who hang upon the Master of Spirits. **6** And the third voice I heard prays and intercedes for those who dwell on the earth and petitions in the Name of the Master of Spirits. **7** And I heard the fourth voice fending off the Satans[h], and forbidding them to come before the Master of Spirits, to accuse them who dwell on the earth.

8 After that I asked the messenger of peace who went with me, who showed me everything that is hidden, "Who are these four presences which I

[a] **39:3** See Korinthious B [2 Corinthians] **12:2-4**.
[b] **39:4** See Yoḥanan [John] **14:2**.
[c] **39:12** Charles translated this last sentence as, "He fills the earth with spirits."
[d] **39:13** See Hit'galut [Revelation] **4:8**.
[e] **39:14** Literally, this reads, "for I hated to look."
[f] **40:1** See Hit'galut [Revelation] **5:11**.
[g] **40:2** See Hit'galut [Revelation] **4:6**.

[h] **40:7** Satans – Plural form of the name ሰይጣና (*say'tana*), borrowed from the Greek. This is merely a transliteration of the Hebrew 𐤔𐤈𐤍 (*Sah'tahn*), meaning "adversary." Thus, the phrase "fending off the Satans" could be read as, "fending off the adversaries." Note the function of the Satans is to accuse, the primary function of Satan (see Iyyov [Job] **1**; Yashar **22:46-55**; Yovelim **17:16**.).

have seen and whose words I have heard and written down?"

9 And he said to me, "This first is Mikha'el, the kind and patient. And the second, who is set over all the diseases and all the wounds of the children of men, is Rapha'el. And the third, who is set over all the powers, is Gavri'el. And the fourth, who is set over the repentance to hope of those who inherit eternal life, is named Phanu'el." And these are the four messengers of the Master of Spirits and the four voices I heard in those days.

The Master of Spirits & the Four Voices

41 1 And after that I saw all the secrets of the heavens, and how the kingdom is divided, and how the actions of men are weighed in the balance. 2 And there I saw the mansions of the elect and the mansions of the set-apart, and my eyes saw there all the sinners being driven from there; *those* who deny the Name of the Master of Spirits, and *they were* being dragged off. And they could not stay because of the punishment which proceeds from the Master of Spirits.

3 And there my eyes saw the secrets of the lightning and of the thunder, and the secrets of the winds, how they are divided to blow over the earth, and the secrets of the clouds and dew, and there I saw where they proceed from in that place and from where they saturate the dusty earth. 4 And there I saw closed chambers out of which the winds are divided, the chamber of the hail and winds, the chamber of the mist, and of the clouds, and the cloud thereof hovers over the earth from the beginning of the world.

5 And I saw the chambers of the sun and moon, where they proceed from and to which they come again, and their glorious return, and how one is superior to the other, and their stately orbit, and how they do not leave their orbit, and they add nothing to their orbit and they take nothing from it, and they keep faith with each other, in accordance with the oath by which they are bound together. 6 And first the sun goes forth and traverses his path according to the commandment of the Master of Spirits, and mighty is His Name forever and ever. 7 And after that I saw the hidden and the visible path of the moon, and she accomplishes the course of her path in that place by day and by night: the one holding a position opposite to the other before the Master of Spirits. And they give thanks and praise and do not rest; for to them their thanksgiving is rest.

8 For the sun changes often for a blessing or a curse, and the course of the path of the moon is light to the righteous and darkness to the sinners in the Name of the Master, who made a separation between the light and the darkness, and divided the spirits of men, and strengthened the spirits of the righteous, in the Name of His righteousness.

9 For no messenger hinders and no power is able to hinder; for He appoints a judge for them all and He judges them all before Him.[a]

Dwelling-Places of Wisdom and Unrighteousness

42 1 Wisdom found no place where she might dwell. Then a dwelling-place was assigned *to* her in the heavens. 2 Wisdom went forth to make her dwelling among the children of men, and found no dwelling-place. Wisdom returned to her place, and took her seat among the messengers. 3 And unrighteousness went forth from her chambers. *Those* whom she did not seek she found, and dwelled with them, as rain in a desert and dew on a thirsty land.

The Set-Apart Ones of the Earth

43 1 And I saw other lightnings and the stars of heaven, and I saw how He called them all by their names and they heard[b] Him. 2 And I saw how they are weighed in a righteous balance according to their proportions of light. *I saw* the width of their spaces and the day of their appearing, and how their revolution produces lightning. And *I saw* their revolution according

---

[a] **41**:**9** See Ma'asei [Acts] **17**:**31**.

[b] **43**:**1** Ethiopic word used here is ሰምዐ (*sam'a*) which is derived from the Hebrew word שמע (*sh'ma*) meaning "hear" with implied intent to obey. Thus it means not merely hearing, but also obeying.

to the number of the messengers, and *how* they keep faith with each other.

3 And I asked the messenger who went with me, who showed me what was hidden, "What are these?"

4 And he said to me, "The Master of Spirits has shown you their parable: these are the names of the set-apart who dwell on the earth and believe in [the Name of][a] the Master of Spirits forever and ever."

44 1 Also another phenomenon I saw in regard to the lightnings: how some of the stars arise and become lightnings and cannot dwell with them.

The Lot of Unbelievers

45 1 And this is the Second Parable concerning those who deny the name of the dwelling of the set-apart ones and the Master of Spirits.

2 And they will not ascend into heaven, and they will not be on the earth. Such shall be the lot of the sinners who have denied the Name of the Master of Spirits, who are thus preserved for the day of suffering and affliction.

3 On that day My Elect One will sit on the throne of glory and will try their works, and their places of rest will be without number. And their spirits will grow firm within them when they see My Elect Ones, and those who have called upon My glorious Name.[b]

New Heaven and New Earth

4 Then I will cause My elect ones to dwell among them. And I will transform the heaven and make it an eternal blessing and light.[c]

5 And I will transform the earth *also*, and make it a blessing, and I will cause My elect ones to dwell upon it. But the sinners and evil-doers shall not set foot on it. 6 For I have provided and satisfied My righteous ones with peace and have caused them to dwell before Me. But for the sinners there is judgment impending with Me, so that I shall destroy them from the face of the earth.

46 1 And there I saw One who had a head of days,[d] and His head was white like wool, and with Him was another, whose countenance had the appearance of a man, and his face was full of favor, like one of the set-apart messengers.

2 And I asked the messenger who went with me and showed me all the hidden things, concerning that Son of Man, who he was, and where he was from, *and* why he went with the Head of Days.

3 And he answered and said to me, "This is the Son of Man, who has righteousness, with whom dwells righteousness, and who reveals all the treasures of that which is hidden, because the Master of Spirits has chosen Him, and whose lot has the pre-eminence before the Master of Spirits in uprightness forever.[e]

4 "And this Son of Man whom you have seen shall raise up the kings and the mighty from their seats, and the strong from their thrones, and shall loosen the reins of the strong, and break the teeth of the sinners.[f] 5 And He shall put down the kings from their thrones and kingdoms because they do not extol and praise Him, nor humbly acknowledge from where the kingdom was bestowed upon them.

6 "And He shall put down the countenance of the strong, and shall fill them with shame. And darkness shall be their dwelling, and worms shall be their bed,[g] and they shall have no hope of rising from their beds, because they do not extol the Name of 𐤉𐤄𐤅𐤄 of Spirits.

7 "And these are those who judge the stars of heaven, and raise their hands against the Most High, and tread upon the earth and dwell upon it.

[a] **43:4** Bracketed section indicates reading present in some Ethiopic texts, though absent from others.
[b] **45:3** See Mattithyahu [Matthew] **25:31,32**.
[c] **45:4** See Hit'galut [Revelation] **7:15**.
[d] **46:1** Head of days – term referring to a time before time existed; preexistence.
[e] **44:3** See also Colossians [Kolossaeis] **2:2-3**.
[f] **46:4** See Tehillim [Psalms] **3:7**; Tehillim [Psalms] **58:6**.
[g] **46:6** See Yeshayahu [Isaiah] **66:24**; Markos [Mark] **9:48**.

And all their deeds manifest unrighteousness,
and their power rests upon their riches, and their
faith is in the elohim which they have made with
their hands, and they deny the Name of the
Master of Spirits. **8** And they persecute the
houses of His congregations, and the firm who
hang upon the Name of the Master of Spirits."

Prayer of the Righteous

47 **1** And in those days the prayer of the
righteous shall have ascended, and the blood of
the righteous from the earth before the Master of
Spirits. **2** In those days the set-apart ones who
dwell above in the heavens shall unite with one
voice and petition and pray and praise, and give
thanks and bless the Name of the Master of
Spirits on behalf of the blood of the righteous
which has been shed, and that the prayer of the
righteous may not be in vain before the Master of
Spirits, that judgment may be done to them, and
that they may not have to suffer forever.

3 In those days I saw the Head of Days when He
seated Himself upon the throne of His glory, and
the books of the living were opened before Him.
And all His host which is in heaven above and
His attendants stood before Him. **4** And the
hearts of the set-apart were filled with joy;
because the number of the righteous had been
offered, and the prayer of the righteous had been
heard, and the blood of the righteous had been
required before the Master of Spirits.

The Son of Man

48 **1** And in that place I saw the fountain of
righteousness which was inexhaustible, and
around it were many fountains of wisdom. And
all the thirsty drank from them, and were filled
with wisdom, and their dwellings were with the
righteous and holy and elect.[a]

2 And at that hour the Son of Man was named in
the presence of the Master Spirits, and His Name
before the Head of Days.[b] **3** Yes, before the sun
and the signs were created, before the stars of the
heaven were made, His Name was named before
the Master of Spirits. **4** He will be a staff to the
righteous on which to steady themselves and not
fall, and He will be the light of the Nations, and
the hope of those who are troubled of heart. **5** All
who dwell on earth shall fall down and worship
before Him, and will praise and bless and
celebrate the Master of Spirits with song.[c] **6** And
for this reason He has been chosen and hidden
before Him, before the creation of the world and
forevermore.

7 And He has revealed the wisdom of the Master
of Spirits to the righteous and set-apart ones;[d] for
He has preserved the lot of the righteous,
because they have hated and despised this world
of unrighteousness, and have hated all its works
and ways in the Name of the Master of Spirits.
For in His Name they are saved,[e] and according
to His good pleasure they have life.[f]

8 In these days the kings of the earth shall
become downcast in countenance, and the strong
who possess the land because of the works of
their hands. For on the day of their anguish and
affliction they shall not *be able to* save
themselves.

Judgment of the Kings of the Earth

9 "And I will give them over into the hands of
My elect. As straw in the fire so shall they burn
before the face of the set-apart. As lead in the
water they will sink before the face of the
righteous, and no trace of them will be found
anymore. **10** And on the day of their affliction
there shall be rest on the earth, and before them
they shall fall and not rise again: and there shall
be no one to take them with his hands and raise
them, for they have denied the Master of Spirits
and His Messiah[g]. The Name of the Master of
Spirits be blessed."[h]

---

[a] **48**:**1** See Hit'galut [Revelation] **21**:**6**.

[b] **48**:**2** See Mattithyahu [Matthew] **16**:**13**-**20**.

[c] **48**:**5** See Philippesious [Philippians] **2**:**10**.

[d] **48**:**1** Charles translated this sentence as, "And the wisdom of the Master of Spirits has revealed Him to the set-apart and righteous."

[e] **48**:**7** See Korinthious A [**1** Corinthians] **6**:**11**.

[f] **48**:7 See Yoḥanan 𐤀 [**1** John] **2**:**15**.

[g] **48**:**10** Ethiopic word መሲሕ (*ma'sich*) is derived from the Hebrew 𐤌𐤔𐤉𐤇 (*Mashiy'ach*) meaning "anointed one" or literally, "Messiah." In some translations it is rendered by its Greek form, "Christ." See also Yehudah [Jude] **4**.

[h] **48**:**10** See Tehillim [Psalms] **2**:**2**-**3**.

Wisdom and Power of the Elect One

49 1 For wisdom is poured out like water, and glory does not fail before Him forevermore.
2 For He is mighty in all the secrets of righteousness, and unrighteousness shall disappear as a shadow, and have no continuance, because the Elect One stands before the Master of Spirits, and His glory is forever and ever, and His might to all generations

3 And in Him dwells the spirit of wisdom, and the spirit which gives insight, and the spirit of understanding and of might, and the spirit of those who have fallen asleep in righteousness.
4 And He will judge the secret things, and no one will be able to utter a vain word before Him; for He is the Elect One before the Master of Spirits according to His good pleasure.[a]

Judgment of the Master of Spirits

50 1 And in those days a change shall take place for the set-apart and elect, and the light of days shall abide upon them, and glory and honor shall turn to the set-apart,[b] 2 on the day of affliction on which evil shall have been treasured up against the sinners. And the righteous shall be victorious in the Name of the Master of Spirits. And He will cause the others to witness *this* that they may repent and relinquish the works of their hands.

3 They shall have no honor through the Name of the Master of Spirits, yet through His Name they will be saved,[c] and the Master of Spirits will have compassion on them, for His compassion is great. 4 And He is righteous also in His judgment, and in the presence of His glory unrighteousness also shall not maintain itself. At His judgment the unrepentant shall perish before Him.

5 "And from now on I will have no kindness on them," says the Master of Spirits.

Resurrection of the Dead

51 1 "And in those days the earth will give back that which has been entrusted to her, and Sheol will also give back that which she has received, and destruction will give back that which it owes.[d]

2 "For in those days the Elect One shall arise, and He shall choose the righteous and set-apart from among them, for the day has drawn near that they should be saved. 3 And the Elect One will sit on My throne in those days, and His mouth will pour forth all the secrets of wisdom and counsel: for the Master of Spirits has given *them* to Him and has glorified Him.

4 "And in those days the mountains will leap like rams, and the hills also will skip like lambs satisfied with milk, and the faces of all the messengers in heaven will be lit up with joy.[e]
5 And the earth will rejoice, and the righteous will dwell upon it, and the elect will walk on it."

Mountains of Various Metals

52 1 And after those days in that place where I had seen all the visions of that which is hidden – for I had been carried off in a whirlwind and they had carried me towards the west – 2 There my eyes saw all the secret things of heaven that shall be, a mountain of iron, and a mountain of copper, and a mountain of silver, and a mountain of gold, and a mountain of soft metal, and a mountain of lead.

3 And I asked the messenger who went with me, saying, "What things are these which I have seen in secret?"

4 And he said to me, "All these things which you have seen shall serve the dominion of His Messiah, that He may be potent and mighty on the earth."

5 And that messenger of peace answered, saying to me, "Wait a little, and all the secret things which surround the Master of Spirits shall be revealed to you. 6 And these mountains which

[a] **49:4** See Ephesious [Ephesians] **1:9**.
[b] **50:1** See Korinthious A [**1** Corinthians] **15:51,52**.
[c] **50:3** See Ma'asei [Acts] **4:12**.
[d] **51:1** See Hit'galut [Revelation] **21:13**.
[e] **51:4** See Tehillim [Psalms] **114**.

your eyes have seen, the mountain of iron, and the mountain of copper, and the mountain of silver, and the mountain of gold, and the mountain of soft metal, and the mountain of lead, all these shall be in the presence of the Elect One as wax before the fire, and like the water which streams down from above upon those mountains, and they shall become powerless before His feet.

7 "And it shall come to pass in those days that none shall be saved either by gold or by silver, and none be able to escape. 8 And there shall be no iron for war, nor shall one clothe oneself with a breastplate. Copper shall be of no service, and tin shall be of no service and shall not be esteemed, and lead shall not be desired. 9 And all these things shall be denied and destroyed from the surface of the earth, when the Elect One shall appear before the face of the Master of Spirits."

Instruments of Destruction

53 1 There my eyes saw a deep valley with open mouths, and all who dwell on the earth and sea and islands shall bring to Him gifts and presents and tokens of homage, but that deep valley shall not become full. 2 And their hands commit lawless deeds, and the sinners devour all whom they lawlessly oppress, yet the sinners shall be destroyed before the face of the Master of Spirits, and they shall be banished from off the face of His earth, and they shall perish forever and ever.

3 For I saw all the messengers of punishment abiding *there* and preparing all the instruments of Satan. 4 And I asked the messenger of peace who went with me, "For whom are they preparing these instruments?"

5 And he said to me, "They prepare these for the kings and the mighty of this earth, that they may be destroyed by them. 6 And after this the Righteous and Elect One shall cause the house of His congregation to appear. From then on they shall be no more hindered in the Name of the Master of Spirits. 7 And these mountains shall not stand as the earth before His righteousness, but the hills shall be as a fountain of water, and the righteous shall have rest from the oppression of sinners."

54 1 And I looked and turned to another part of the earth, and saw there a deep valley with burning fire. 2 And they brought the kings and the mighty, and began to cast them into this deep valley. 3 And there my eyes saw how they made these their instruments, iron chains of immeasurable weight.

4 And I asked the messenger of peace who went with me, saying, "For whom are these chains being prepared?"

5 And he said to me, "These are being prepared for the hosts of Azazel, so that they may take them and cast them into the abyss of complete condemnation, and they shall cover their jaws with rough stones as the Master of Spirits commanded.[a] 6 And Mikha'el, and Gavri'el, and Rapha'el, and Phanu'el shall take hold of them on that great day, and cast them on that day into the burning furnace, that the Master of Spirits may take vengeance on them for their unrighteousness in becoming subject to Satan and leading astray those who dwell on the earth."[b]

Judgment through the Flood

7 "And in those days shall punishment come from the Master of Spirits, and He will open all the chambers of waters which are above the heavens, and of the fountains which are beneath the earth. 8 And all the waters shall be joined with the waters: that which is above the heavens is the male, and the water which is beneath the earth is the female.[c] 9 And they shall destroy all who dwell on the earth and those who dwell under the ends of the heaven. 10 And when they have recognized their unrighteousness which they have wrought on the earth, then by these shall they perish.

55 1 And after that the Head of Days relented

[a] **54:4-5** See Mattithyahu [Matthew] **25:41**.

[b] **54:6** See Hit'galut [Revelation] **13:14**.

[c] **54:8** Most Ethiopic commentaries interpret this as a comparison to reproduction: the male gives forth, the female receives, and life is produced.

and said, "In vain have I destroyed all who dwell on the earth."

2 And He swore by His great Name, "From here on I will not do so to all who dwell on the earth; and I will set a sign in the heaven. And this shall be a firm witness between Me and them forever, so long as heaven is above the earth. And this is in accordance with My command.[a]

Judgment of Azazel and His Associates

3 "When I have desired to take hold of them by the hand of the messengers on the day of affliction and pain because of this, I will cause My reprimand and My wrath to abide upon them," says the Master of Spirits. 4 "You mighty kings who dwell on the earth, you will see My Elect One, how He sits on the throne of glory and judges Azazel, and all his associates, and all his hosts in the Name of the Master of Spirits."

56 1 And I saw there the hosts of the messengers of punishment going, and they held scourges and chains of iron and copper. 2 And I asked the messenger of peace who went with me, saying, "To whom are these who hold the scourges going?"

3 And he said to me, "To their elect and beloved ones, that they may be cast into the chasm of the abyss of the valley. 4 And then that valley shall be filled with their elect and beloved, and the days of their lives shall be at an end, and the days of their leading astray shall not be reckoned from then on.

Struggles of the Elect with Their Enemies

5 "And in those days the messengers shall return and hurl themselves to the east upon the Parthians and Medes. They shall stir up the kings, so that a spirit of unrest shall come upon them, and they shall rouse them from their thrones, that they may break forth as lions from their lairs, and as hungry wolves among their flocks.

6 "And they shall go up and tread underfoot the land of His elect ones, and the land of His elect ones shall be before them a threshing-floor and a highway, 7 but the city of my righteous shall be a hindrance to their horses. And they shall begin to fight among themselves, and their right hand shall be strong against themselves, and a man shall not know his brother, nor a son his father or his mother, until there be no number of the corpses through their slaughter, and their punishment be not in vain.

8 "In those days Sheol shall open its jaws, and they shall be swallowed up in it and their destruction shall be at an end; Sheol shall devour the sinners in the presence of the elect."[b]

57 1 And it happened after this that I saw another host of wagons, and men riding on them, and coming on the winds from the east, and from the west to the south. 2 And the noise of their wagons was heard, and when this turmoil took place the set-apart ones from heaven remarked it, and the pillars of the earth were moved from their place, and that sound was heard from the one end of heaven to the other, in one day. 3 And they shall all fall down and worship the Master of Spirits. And this is the end of the second Parable.

Light of the Righteous and Elect

58 1 And I began to speak the third Parable concerning the righteous and elect.

2 Blessed are you, you righteous and elect, for your lot will be glorious. 3 And the righteous will be in the light of the sun. And the elect in the light of eternal life. The days of their life shall be unending, and the days of the set-apart without number. 4 And they shall seek the light and find righteousness with the Master of Spirits: there shall be peace to the righteous in the Name of the Eternal Master.

5 And after this it will be said to the set-apart in heaven that they should seek out the secrets of righteousness, the heritage of faith: for it has become bright as the sun upon earth, and the

[a] **55:2** Compare Bereshiyt [Genesis] **9:13**.

[b] **56:8** See Hit'galut [Revelation] **20:14-15**.

darkness is past.[a] 6 And there shall be a light that never ends, and they shall not come to a number of days, for the darkness shall first have been destroyed, and the light established before the Master of Spirits. And the light of uprightness established forever before the Master of Spirits.

Thunder and Lightnings

59 1 In those days my eyes saw the secrets of the lightnings, and of the lights, and their judgments; and they light up for a blessing or a curse as the Master of Spirits wills. 2 And there I saw the secrets of the thunder, and how when it resounds above in the heaven, its sound is heard, and He caused me to see the judgments executed on the earth, whether they be for well-being and blessing, or for a curse according to the word of the Master of Spirits. 3 And after that all the secrets of the lights and lightnings were shown to me, and they light up for blessing and for satisfying.

Quake in the Heavens

60 1 In the year five hundred, in the seventh month, on the fourteenth day of the month, in the life of Ḥanokh, in that Parable I saw how a mighty quaking made the heaven of heavens to quake, and the host of the Most High, and the messengers, a thousand thousands and ten thousand times ten thousand, were disquieted with a great disquiet. 2 And the Head of Days sat on the throne of His glory, and the messengers and the righteous stood around Him.

3 And a great trembling seized me, and fear took hold of me, and my loins gave way, and my reins were dissolved, and I fell upon my face. 4 And Mikha'el sent another messenger from among the set-apart ones and he raised me up, and when he had raised me up my spirit returned; for I had not been able to endure the look of this host, and the commotion and the quaking of the heaven.

5 And Mikha'el said to me, "Why are you disquieted with such a vision? Until this day the day of His kindness lasted; and He has been kind and patient towards those who dwell on the earth. 6 And when the day, and the power, and the punishment, and the judgment come, which the Master of Spirits has prepared for those who do not worships the righteous law, and for those who deny the righteous judgment, and for those who bring His Name to naught--that day is prepared, for the elect a covenant, but for sinners an inquisition.

[When the punishment of the Master of Spirits shall rest upon them, it shall rest in order that the punishment of the Master of Spirits may not come in vain, and it shall slay the children with their mothers and the children with their fathers. Afterwards the judgment shall take place according to His kindness and His patience.'][b]

Two Great Monsters

7 And on that day two monsters were[c] parted: a female monster named 'Livyathan[d],' to dwell in the abysses of the ocean over the fountains of the waters. 8 And the male named 'Behemoth[e],' who occupied with his breast a waste wilderness named 'Duidain[f],' on the east of the garden where the elect and righteous dwell, where my grandfather was taken up, the seventh from Adam, the first man whom the Master of Spirits created. 9 And I sought the other messenger that

---

[a] **58:5** See Yoḥanan 𐤀 [**1** John] **2:8**.

[b] **60:6** Some texts place bracketed section at the end of the chapter as verse **25**.

[c] **60:7** Some texts read, "will be."

[d] **60:7** Livyathan – Ethiopic word ሌዋታን (*lewa'tan*). This word is the Ethiopic equivalent of the Hebrew 𐤋𐤅𐤉𐤕𐤍 (*liv'ya'than*), which is most commonly translated as "Leviathan." See also Iyyov [Job] **3:8**; **41:1**; Tehillim [Psalms] **74:14**; **104:26**; Yeshayahu [Isaiah] **27:1**. Though widely debated, Livyathan was most likely a type of dinosaur or similar ancient water-dwelling creature.

[e] **60:8** Behemoth – Ethiopic word ብሔሞት (*B'hemot*). This word is the Ethiopic equivalent of the Hebrew 𐤁𐤄𐤌𐤅𐤕 (*B'hemoth*). See also Iyyov [Job] **40:15**. Though widely debated, Behemoth was most likely a type of dinosaur or similar pre-historic land-dwelling creature.

[f] **60:8** Duidain – Ethiopic word ዴንዳይን (*Den'dayn*). Charles attempted to restore the word "Dendain" to what he believed was more correct: Duidain. Noting that this area was east of Eden, it is possible that it is the same as the land of Nod mentioned in Bereshiyt [Genesis] **4:16**. Another theory is that it represents the land of Dedan mentioned in Yechezqel [Ezekiel] **27**.

he should show me the might of those monsters,
how they were parted on one day and cast, the
one into the abysses of the sea, and the other to
the dry land of the wilderness.

10 And he said to me, "You, son of man, in this
you seek to know what is hidden."

The Hidden Things of Nature

11 And the other messenger who went with me
and showed me what was hidden told me what is
first and last in the heaven in the height, and
beneath the earth in the depth, and at the ends of
the heaven, and on the foundation of the heaven.
12 And the chambers of the winds, and how the
winds are divided, and how they are weighed,
and *how* the gates of the winds are reckoned,
each according to the power of the wind, and the
power of the lights of the moon, and according to
the power that is fitting: and the divisions of the
stars according to their names, and how all the
divisions are divided. 13 And the thunders
according to the places where they fall, and all
the divisions that are made among the lightnings
that it may light up, and their host that they may
at once obey.

14 For the thunder has places of rest *which* are
assigned *to it* while it is waiting for its peal; and
the thunder and lightning are inseparable, and
although not one and undivided, they both go
together through the wind and do not separate.
15 For when the lightning lights up, the thunder
utters its voice, and the wind enforces a pause
during the peal, and divides equally between
them; for the treasury of their peals is like the
sand, and each one of them as it peals is held in
with a bridle, and turned back by the power of
the wind, and pushed forward according to the
many quarters of the earth. 16 And the wind of
the sea is male and strong, and according to the
might of his strength he draws it back with a
rein, and in like manner it is driven forward and
disperses amid all the mountains of the earth.

17 And the wind of the hoarfrost is his own
messenger, and the wind of the hail is a good
messenger. 18 And the wind of the snow has
forsaken his chambers on account of his strength.
There is a special wind therein, and that which
ascends from it is like smoke, and its name is
'frost.'

19 And the wind of the mist is not united with
them in their chambers, but it has a special
chamber; for its course is glorious both in light
and in darkness, and in winter and in summer,
and in its chamber is a messenger. 20 And the
wind of the dew has its dwelling at the ends of
the heaven, and is connected with the chambers
of the rain, and its course is in winter and
summer: and its clouds and the clouds of the
mist are connected, and the one gives to the
other.

21 And when the wind of the rain goes forth from
its chamber, the messengers come and open the
chamber and lead it out, and when it is diffused
over the whole earth it unites with the water on
the earth. And it is often united with the water on
the earth. 22 For the waters are for those who
dwell on the earth; for they are nourishment for
the earth from the Most High who is in heaven:
therefore there is a measure for the rain, and the
messengers take it in charge.

23 And these things I saw towards the Garden of
the Righteous. 24 And the messenger of peace
who was with me said to me, "These two
monsters, prepared conformably to the greatness
of 𐤉𐤄𐤅𐤄, shall feed."

Measures of the Righteous

61 1 And I saw in those days how long cords
were given to those messengers, and they took to
themselves wings and flew, and they went
towards the north.

2 And I asked the messenger, saying to him,
"Why have those *messengers* taken these cords
and gone off?" And he said to me, "They have
gone to measure."

3 And the messenger who went with me said to
me, "These shall bring the measures of the
righteous, and the ropes of the righteous to the
righteous, that they may stay themselves on the
Name of the Master of Spirits forever and ever.
4 The elect shall begin to dwell with the elect,
and those are the measures which shall be given
to faith and which shall strengthen righteousness.
5 And these measures shall reveal all the secrets

of the depths of the earth, and those who have
been destroyed by the desert, and those who have
been devoured by the beasts, and those who have
been devoured by the fish of the sea, that they
may return and steady themselves on the day of
the Elect One; for none shall be destroyed before
the Master of Spirits, and none can be destroyed.

Judgment and Praise of the Elect One

6 "And all who dwell above in the heaven
received a command and power and one voice
and one light like fire. 7 And that One *with* their
first words they blessed, and extolled and lauded
with wisdom, and they were wise in utterance
and in the spirit of life. 8 And the Master of
Spirits placed the Elect one on the throne of
glory. And He shall judge all the works of the
set-apart above in the heaven, and in the balance
shall their deeds be weighed. 9 And when He
shall lift up His countenance to judge their secret
ways according to the word of the Name of the
Master of Spirits, and their path according to the
way of the righteous judgment of the Master of
Spirits, then shall they all with one voice speak
and bless, and glorify and extol and sanctify the
Name of the Master of Spirits.

10 "And He will summon all the host of the
heavens, and all the set-apart ones above, and the
host of 𐤉𐤄𐤅𐤄, the Keruvim[a], Seraphim[b] and
Ophannim[c], and all the messengers of power,
and all the messengers of principalities, and the
Elect One, and the other powers on the earth *and*
over the water.[d]

11 "On that day one voice shall rise, and bless
and glorify and exalt in the spirit of faith, and in
the spirit of wisdom, and in the spirit of patience,
and in the spirit of kindness, and in the spirit of
judgment and of peace, and in the spirit of
goodness, and shall all say with one voice,
'Blessed is He, and may the Name of the Master
of Spirits be blessed forever and ever.'

12 "All who do not sleep above in heaven shall
bless Him. All the set-apart ones who are in
heaven shall bless Him, and all the elect who
dwell in the garden of life. And every spirit of
light who is able to bless, and glorify, and exalt,
and set apart Your blessed Name, and all flesh
shall glorify and bless Your Name beyond
measure forever and ever. 13 For great is the
kindness of the Master of Spirits, and He is
patient, and all His works and all that He has
created He has revealed to the righteous and
elect in the Name of the Master of Spirits."

Condemnation of the Mighty

62 1 And thus the Master commanded the kings
and the mighty and the exalted, and those who
dwell on the earth, and said, "Open your eyes
and lift up your horns if you are able to
recognize the Elect One."

2 And the Master of Spirits seated Him on the
throne of His glory, and the spirit of
righteousness was poured out upon Him, and the
word of His mouth slays all the sinners, and all
the unrighteous are destroyed from before His
face.

3 And all the kings and the mighty shall stand up
in that day, and the exalted and those who hold
the earth, and they shall see and recognize how
He sits on the throne of His glory, and
righteousness is judged before Him, and no lying
word is spoken before Him.

---

[a] **61:10** Keruvim – Ethiopic word ኪሩቤ (*kiru'be*), equivalent of the Hebrew word 𐤊𐤓𐤅𐤁𐤉𐤌 (*Keru'viym*). This is the plural form of 𐤊𐤓𐤁 (*kerub*). This is a class of messengers mentioned many times in Scripture. Its root and derivation is unknown, though it is possibly derived from an Assyrian word meaning "great, mighty."

[b] **31:10** Seraphim – Ethiopic word ሱራፌል (*suraph'el*), equivalent of the Hebrew word 𐤔𐤓𐤐𐤉𐤌 (*Seraph'iym*). This is the plural form of 𐤔𐤓𐤐 (*seraph*). This is a class of messengers mentioned a few times in Scripture. This is derived from the Hebrew word *saraph* (same spelling, different vowels) which means "burning, fiery." It is also the word for a certain time of serpent; see Bemidbar [Numbers] **21:6** for "fiery serpent."

[c] **61:10** Ophannim – Ethiopic word ኦፍኒን (*Oph'niyn'*). This class of messengers is not mentioned in Scripture. However, reconstructing a Hebrew word from this would render 𐤀𐤅𐤐𐤍𐤉𐤌 (*Ophan'iym*). This is the plural form of 𐤀𐤅𐤐𐤍 (*Oph'an*), which means "wheel." Compare Yechezqel [Ezekiel] **1:16**, where this word is rendered "wheel." According to Dead Sea Scroll **4Q405** and Jewish scholar Maimonides (Rambam), the Ophannim are, in fact, a class of messengers.

[d] **61:10** See Romaious [Romans] **8:38**.

4 Then pain shall come upon them as on a
woman in travail, when her child enters the
mouth of the womb, and she has pain in bringing
forth.[a]

5 And one portion of them will look on the other,
and they will be terrified, and their faces will be
downcast, and pain will seize them, when they
see the Son of Man sitting on the throne of His
glory.[b] 6 And the kings and the mighty and all
who possess the earth shall bless and glorify and
extol Him who rules over all, who was hidden.

7 For from the beginning the Son of Man was
hidden, and the Most High preserved Him in the
presence of His might, and revealed Him to the
elect.[c] 8 And the congregation of the elect and
set-apart shall be sown, and all the elect shall
stand before Him on that day.

9 And all the kings and the mighty and the
exalted and those who rule the earth shall fall
down before Him on their faces, and worship and
set their hope upon the Son of Man, and petition
Him and ask for kindness at His hands.[d]
10 Nevertheless the Master of Spirits will so
press them that they shall hastily go forth from
His presence, and their faces shall be filled with
shame, and the darkness grow deeper on their
faces. 11 And He will deliver them to the
messengers for punishment, to execute
vengeance on them because they have oppressed
His children and His elect.

12 And they will be a spectacle for the righteous
and for His elect: they shall rejoice over them,
because the wrath of the Master of Spirits rests
upon them, and His sword is drunk with their
blood. 13 And the righteous and elect will be
saved on that day, and from then on they will
never see the face of the sinners and unrighteous.
14 And the Master of Spirits will abide over
them, and shall they eat and lie down and rise up
with the Son of Man forever and ever.

Blessedness of the Righteous

15 And the righteous and elect shall have risen
from the earth, and ceased to have downcast
faces. And they will have been clothed with
garments of glory.[e] 16 And these will be the
garments of life from the Master of Spirits, and
your garments will not grow old, nor your glory
pass away before the Master of Spirits.[f]

The End of the Mighty

63 1 In those days the mighty and the kings who
possess the earth will implore *Him* to grant them
a little respite from His messengers of
punishment to whom they were delivered, that
they might fall down and worship before the
Master of Spirits, and confess their sins before
Him. 2 And they shall bless and glorify the
Master of Spirits, and say, "Blessed is the Master
of Spirits and the Master of kings, and the
Master of the mighty and the Master of the rich,
and the Master of glory and the Master of
wisdom.

3 "Your power is splendid in every secret thing
from generation to generation, and Your glory
forever and ever. All Your secrets are deep and
innumerable, and Your righteousness is beyond
reckoning. 4 We have now learned that we
should glorify and bless the Master of kings and
Him who is king over all kings."

5 And they shall say, "If only we had rest to
glorify and give thanks and confess our faith
before His glory! 6 And now we long for a little
rest but do not find it. We pursue it, but do not
obtain *it*. Light has vanished from before us, and
darkness is our dwelling-place forever and ever.
7 For we have not believed Him nor glorified the
Name of the Master of Spirits, nor glorified our
Master. But our hope was in the scepter of our
kingdom, and in our glory.

8 "And in the day of our suffering and affliction
He does not save us, and we find no respite for
confession that our Master is true in all His
works, and in His judgments and His justice, and

[a] **62:4** See Thessalonikeis A [**1** Thessalonians] **5:3**.
[b] **62:5** See Mattithyahu [Matthew] **19:28**.
[c] **62:7** Compare Kepha ✝ [**1** Peter] **1:5**; Romaious [Romans] **16:25-26**; Titus **1:1-3**.
[d] **62:9** Compare Philippesious [Philippians] **2:9-11**.
[e] **62:15** See Thessalonikeis A [**1** Thessalonians] **4:17**.
[f] **62:16** Compare Korinthious B [**2** Corinthians] **5:1-3**; Hit'galut [Revelation] **7:9-17**.

His judgments have no respect of persons. 9 And
we pass away from before His face on account of
our works, and all our sins are reckoned up in
righteousness."

10 Now they shall say to themselves, "Our beings
are full of unrighteous gain, but it does not
prevent us from descending from the midst
thereof into the burden of Sheol."

11 And after that their faces shall be filled with
darkness and shame before the Son of Man, and
they shall be driven from His presence, and the
sword shall abide before His face in their midst.

12 Thus spoke the Master of Spirits, "This is the
statute and judgment with respect to the mighty
and the kings and the exalted and those who
possess the earth before the Master of Spirits."

Fallen Messengers

64 1 And I saw other forms hidden in that place.
2 I heard the voice of the messenger saying,
"These are the messengers who descended to the
earth, and revealed what was hidden to the
children of men and seduced the children of men
into committing sin."

Prophecy of the Flood

65 1 And in those days Noaḥ saw the earth that
it had sunk down and its destruction was near.
2 And he arose from there and went to the ends
of the earth, and cried aloud to his grandfather
Ḥanokh. And Noaḥ said three times with an
embittered voice, "Hear me, hear me, hear me."

3 And I said to him, "Tell me what is being done
on the earth – for the earth is struggling and
shaken – lest perhaps I perish with it?"

4 And then there was a great commotion, on the
earth, and a voice was heard from heaven, and I
fell on my face. 5 And Ḥanokh my grandfather
came and stood by me, and said to me, "Why
have you cried to me with a bitter cry and
weeping? 6 A command has gone forth from the
presence of 𐤉𐤄𐤅𐤄 concerning those who dwell on
the earth, that their ruin is complete because they
have learned all the secrets of the messengers,
and all the violence of the Satans, and all their
powers – the most secret ones – and all the
power of those who practice sorcery, and the
power of witchcraft, and the power of those who
make molten images for the whole earth. 7 And
how silver is produced from the dust of the earth,
and how soft metal originates in the earth. 8 For
lead and tin are not produced from the earth like
the first: it is a fountain that produces them, and
a messenger stands in it, and that messenger
runs."

9 And after that my grandfather Ḥanokh took
hold of me by my hand and raised me up, and
said to me, "Go, for I have asked the Master of
Spirits as touching this commotion on the earth.
10 And He said to me, 'Because of their
unrighteousness their judgment has been
determined upon and shall not be withheld by
Me forever. Because of the sorceries which they
have searched out and learned, the earth and
those who dwell upon it shall be destroyed.'
11 And these have no place of repentance
forever, because they have shown them what was
hidden, and they are the condemned: but as for
you, my son, the Master of Spirits knows that
you are pure, and guiltless of this reproach
concerning the secrets.

12 "And He has destined your name to be among
the set-apart, and will preserve you among those
who dwell on the earth, and has destined your
righteous seed both for kingship and for great
honors, and from your seed shall proceed a
fountain of the righteous and set-apart *ones*
without number forever."

Messengers Over the Flood

66 1 And after that he showed me the
messengers of punishment who are prepared to
come and let loose all the powers of the waters
which are underground in order to bring
judgment and destruction on all who stay and
dwell on the earth. 2 And the Master of Spirits
gave command to the messengers who were
going forth, that they should not cause the waters
to rise but should hold them in check; for those
messengers were over the powers of the waters.
3 And I went away from the presence of Ḥanokh.

The Promise to Noaḥ

67 1 And in those days the word of 𐤉𐤄𐤅𐤄 came to me, and He said to me, "Noaḥ, your lot has come up before Me, a lot without blame, a lot of love and uprightness. 2 And now the messengers are making a wooden *ark*, and when they have completed it I will place My hand upon it and preserve it, and the seed of life will come forth from it, and a change will set in so that the earth will not remain without inhabitant. 3 And I will make your seed strong before Me forever and ever, and I will spread those who dwell with you abroad: they will not be unfruitful on the face of the earth, but will be blessed and multiply on the earth in the Name of the Master."

4 And He will imprison those messengers, who have shown unrighteousness, in that burning valley which my grandfather Ḥanokh had formerly shown to me in the west among the mountains of gold and silver and iron and soft metal and tin. 5 And I saw that valley in which there was a great disturbance and a stirring of the waters. 6 And when all this took place, from that fiery molten metal and from its stirring in that place, there was produced a smell of sulfur, and it mingled with those waters, and the valley of the messengers who had led *mankind* astray burned beneath the land. 7 And through its valleys proceed streams of fire, where these messengers who had led astray those who dwell upon the earth are punished.

Punishment of the Mighty

8 But in those days, those waters will serve for the kings and the mighty and the exalted, and those who dwell on the earth, for the healing of the body, for the punishment of the spirit. Now their spirit is full of lust, that they may be punished in their body, for they have denied the Master of Spirits and see their punishment daily, and yet do not believe in His Name. 9 And as the proportion of the burning of their bodies becomes severe, a corresponding change will take place in their spirit forever and ever; for none shall utter an idle word before the Master of Spirits. 10 For the judgment shall come upon them, because they believe in the lust of their body and deny the Master of Spirits. 11 And those same waters will also change in those days; for when those messengers are punished in these waters; the termperature of these water-springs shall change, and when the messengers ascend, this water of the springs shall become cold.

12 And I heard Mikha'el answering and saying, "This judgment with which the messengers are judged is a witness for the kings and the mighty who possess the earth."

13 Because these waters of judgment attend to the healing of the body of the kings and the lust of their body; therefore they will not see and will not believe that those waters will change and become a fire which burns forever.

Mikha'el and Rapha'el Discuss the Judgment

68 1 And after that my grandfather Ḥanokh gave me the teaching of all the secrets in the book in the Parables which had been given to him, and he put them together for me in the words of the book of the Parables. 2 And on that day Mikha'el answered Rapha'el and said, "The power of the spirit transports and makes me to tremble because of the severity of the judgment of the secrets, the judgment of the messengers: who can endure the severe judgment which has been executed, and before which they melt away?"

3 And Mikha'el answered again, and said to Rapha'el, "Who is he whose heart is not softened concerning it, and whose reins are not troubled by this word of judgment *that* has gone forth upon them because of those who have thus led them out?"

4 And it happened when he stood before the Master of Spirits, Mikha'el said to Rapha'el, "I will not take their part under the eye of the Master; for the Master of Spirits has been angry with them because they act as if they were the Master. 5 Therefore all that is hidden shall come upon them forever and ever; for neither messenger nor man shall have his portion *in it*, but alone they have received their judgment forever and ever."

Names of the Fallen Messengers

69 1 And after this judgment they shall be terrified, and *it shall* make them tremble because they have shown this to those who dwell on the earth.

2 And behold the names of those messengers: the first of them is Shemiḥazah, the second Ar'taqoph, and the third Ramt'el, the fourth Kokhav'el, the fifth Tami'el, the sixth Ram'el, the seventh Dani'el, the eighth Ziqi'el, the ninth Baraq'el, the tenth Asa'el, the eleventh Ḥermoni, the twelfth Matar'el, the thirteenth Anan'el, the fourteenth Sataw'el, the fifteenth Shamshi'el, and the sixteenth Sahari'el, the seventeenth Turi'el, the eighteenth Yom'el, the nineteenth Yehaddi'el, the twentieth Ruma'el, the twenty-first Azazel.[a]
3 And these are the chiefs of their messengers and their names, and their chief ones over hundreds and over fifties and over tens.

Misdeeds of the Fallen Messengers

4 The name of the first Yeqon: that is, the one who led astray all the set-apart messengers, and brought them down to the earth, and led them astray through the daughters of men. 5 And the second was named Asbe'el: he imparted to the set-apart messengers evil counsel, and led them astray so that they defiled their bodies with the daughters of men. 6 And the third was named Gadri'el: he showed the children of men all the blows of death, and he led Ḥavvah astray, and showed the weapons of death to the sons of men: the shield and the coat of mail, and the sword for battle, and all the weapons of death *she showed* to the children of men.[b] 7 And from his hand they have proceeded against those who dwell on the earth from that day and forevermore.

8 And the fourth was named Penemue: he taught the children of men the bitter and the sweet, and he taught them all the secrets of their wisdom.
9 And he instructed mankind in writing with ink and paper, and thereby many sinned from eternity to eternity and until this day. 10 For men were not created for such a purpose, to give confirmation to their good faith with pen and ink. 11 For men were created exactly like the messengers, to the intent that they should continue pure and righteous, and death, which destroys everything, could not have taken hold of them, but through this their knowledge they are perishing, and through this power it is consuming me.

12 And the fifth was named Kasdeya: this is he who showed the children of men all the wicked attacks of spirits and demons, and the attacks of the embryo in the womb, that it may pass away, and the attacks of the spirit the bites of the serpent, and the attacks which occur through the noontide heat, the son of the serpent named Taba'aet.

13 And this is the task of Kasbe'el, the chief of the oath which he showed to the set-apart ones when he dwelt high above in glory, and its name is Biqa. 14 This *messenger* asked Mikha'el to show him the hidden name, that he might enunciate it in the oath, so that those might quake before that name and oath who revealed all that was in secret to the children of men.
15 And this is the power of this oath, for it is powerful and strong, and he placed this oath Akae in the hand of Mikha'el. 16 And these are the secrets of this oath. And they are strong through his oath: and the heaven was suspended before the world was created, and forever.

17 And through it the earth was founded upon the water, and from the secret recesses of the mountains come beautiful waters, from the creation of the world and to eternity.

18 And through that oath the sea was created, and as its foundation He set for it the sand against the time of *its* anger, and it dare not pass beyond it from the creation of the world to eternity. 19 And through that oath the depths are made fast, and abide and stir not from their place from eternity to eternity.

20 And through that oath the sun and moon complete their course, and does not deviate from

[a] **69:2** I have rewritten the names of the messengers here to match chapter **6**. While most of these are written in the in their Ethiopic and Greek forms, some are different. To avoid confusion I have written them as they appear in chapter **6**. Two names are included here, however, that are not present in **6**. Those are Ruma'el and Azaz'el. It is possible that these were added later by mistake.

[b] **69:6** These events, namely the teaching of weapon-making, is attributed to Asa'el in chapter **8**. However, in that chapter there is no mention of who it was that led Ḥavvah astray.

their statute from eternity to eternity. **21** And through that oath the stars complete their course, and He calls them by their names, and they answer Him from eternity to eternity.

22 And in like manner the spirits of the water, and of the winds, and of all zephyrs, and *their* paths from all the quarters of the winds. **23** And the voices of the thunder and the light of the lightnings are preserved there. And the chambers of the hail and the chambers of the frost, and the chambers of the mist, and the chambers of the rain and the dew are preserved there.

24 And all these believe and give thanks before the Master of Spirits, and glorify *Him* with all their power, and their food is in every act of thanksgiving: they thank and glorify and extol the Name of the Master of Spirits forever and ever.

25 And this oath is mighty over them and through it they are preserved and their paths are preserved, and their course is not destroyed. **26** And there was great joy among them, and they blessed and glorified and extolled because the Name of the Son of Man had been revealed to them.

27 And He sat on the throne of His glory, and the sum of judgment was given to the Son of Man,[a] and He caused the sinners to pass away and be destroyed from off the face of the earth, and those who have led the world astray. **28** With chains shall they be bound, and in their assemblage-place of destruction shall they be imprisoned, and all their works vanish from the face of the earth.

29 And from then on there shall be nothing corruptible; for the Son of Man has appeared, and has seated Himself on the throne of His glory, and all evil shall pass away before His face, and the word of the Son of Man shall go forth and be strong before the Master of Spirits.

30 This is the Third Parable of Ḥanokh.

The Transportation of Ḥanokh

70 **1** And it happened after this that his name during his lifetime was raised high to the Son of Man and to the Master of Spirits from among those who dwell on the earth. **2** And he was raised high on the chariots of the wind and his name vanished among them. **3** And from that day I was no longer numbered among them. And He set me between the two winds, between the North and the West, where the messengers took the cords to measure for me the place for the elect and righteous. **4** And there I saw the first fathers and the righteous who dwell in that place from the beginning.

Vision of the House of Fire

71 **1** And it happened after this that my spirit was translated and it ascended into the heavens: and I saw the set-apart messengers. They were stepping on flames of fire, their garments and their raiment were white, and their faces shone like snow.

2 And I saw two streams of fire, and the light of that fire shone like hyacinth, and I fell on my face before the Master of Spirits.

3 And the messenger Mikha'el – one of the ruling messengers – seized me by my right hand, and lifted me up and led me into all the secrets, and he showed me all the secrets of righteousness. **4** And he showed me all the secrets of the ends of the heaven, and all the chambers of all the stars, and all the luminaries, where they proceed from before the face of the set-apart ones.

5 And he translated my spirit into the heaven of heavens, and I saw there as it were a structure built of crystals, and between those crystals tongues of living fire. **6** And my spirit saw the band which encompassed that house of fire, and on its four sides were streams full of living fire, and they encompassed that house. **7** And all around were Seraphim, Keruvim, and Ophannim. And these are they who do not sleep, and guard the throne of His glory.

---

[a] **69:27** See Yoḥanan [John] **5:22-27**.

8 And I saw messengers who could not be
counted, a thousand thousands, and ten thousand
times ten thousand, encircling that house. And
Mikha'el, and Rapha'el, and Gavri'el, and
Phanu'el, and the set-apart messengers who are
above the heavens, go in and out of that house.
9 And they came forth from that house, and
Mikha'el and Gavri'el, Rapha'el and Phanu'el,
and many set-apart messengers without number.
10 And with them the Head of Days, His head
white and pure as wool, and His garment was
indescribable. 11 And I fell on my face, and my
whole body became relaxed, and my spirit was
transformed; and I cried with a loud voice, with
the spirit of power, and blessed and glorified and
extolled. 12 And these blessings which went forth
out of my mouth were well pleasing before the
Head of Days.

13 And the Head of Days came with Mikha'el
and Gavri'el, Rapha'el and Phanu'el, thousands
and ten thousands of messengers without
number.

14 And he, *the messenger*, came to me and
greeted me with his voice, and said to me, "This
is the Son of Man who is born to righteousness;
and righteousness abides over Him, and the
righteousness of the Head of Days does not
forsake Him."

15 And he said to me, "He proclaims peace to
you in the name of the world to come; for from
now on peace has proceeded since the creation of
the world, and so it will be to you forever and
ever and ever. 16 And all will walk in His ways
since righteousness never forsakes Him. With
Him will be their dwelling-places, and with Him
their heritage, and they will not be separated
from Him forever and ever and ever. 17 And so
there will be length of days with the Son of Man,
and the righteous shall have peace and an upright
way in the Name of the Master of Spirits forever
and ever."

Book III: Astronomical Book

The Sun

72 1 The book of the courses of the luminaries
of the heaven, the relations of each, according to
their classes, their dominion and their seasons,
according to their names and places of origin,
and according to their months, which Uri'el, the
set-apart messenger who was with me, who is
their guide, showed me. And he showed me all
their calculations exactly as they are, and how it
is with regard to all the years of the world and to
eternity, until the new creation is accomplished
which endures until eternity.

2 And this is the first calculation of the
luminaries: the luminary the Sun has its rising in
the eastern gates of the heaven, and its setting in
the western gates of the heaven. 3 And I saw six
gates in which the sun rises, and six gates in
which the sun sets and the moon rises and sets in
these gates, and the leaders of the stars and those
whom they lead: six in the east and six in the
west, and all following each other in accurately
corresponding order: also many windows to the
right and left of these gates.[a]

4 And first there goes forth the great luminary,
named the Sun, and his roundness is like the
roundness of the heaven, and he is quite filled
with illuminating and heating fire. 5 The chariot
on which he ascends, the wind drives, and the
sun goes down from the heaven and returns
through the north in order to reach the east, and
is so guided that he comes to that gate and shines
in the face of the heaven. 6 In this way he rises in
the first month in the great gate, which is the
fourth; those six gates in the cast. 7 And in that
fourth gate from which the sun rises in the first
month are twelve window-openings, from which
proceed a flame when they are opened in their
season.

8 When the sun rises in the heaven, he comes
forth through that fourth gate thirty mornings in
succession, and sets accurately in the fourth gate
in the west of the heaven. 9 And during this

[a] **72:3** The twelve gates mentioned here, six to the east and six to the west, are believed by most scholar and commentators to be the twelve stations of the zodiac.

period the day becomes daily longer and the
night nightly shorter to the thirtieth morning.
10 On that day the day is longer than the night by
a ninth part, and the day amounts exactly to ten
parts and the night to eight parts.

11 And the sun rises from that fourth gate, and
sets in the fourth and returns to the fifth gate of
the east thirty mornings, and rises from it and
sets in the fifth gate. 12 And then the day
becomes longer by two parts and amounts to
eleven parts, and the night becomes shorter and
amounts to seven parts. 13 And it returns to the
east and enters into the sixth gate, and rises and
sets in the sixth gate thirty-one mornings on
account of its sign. 14 On that day the day
becomes longer than the night, and the day
becomes double the night, and the day becomes
twelve parts, and the night is shortened and
becomes six parts. 15 And the sun mounts up to
make the day shorter and the night longer, and
the sun returns to the east and enters into the
sixth gate, and rises from it and sets thirty
mornings.

16 And when thirty mornings are accomplished,
the day decreases by exactly one part, and
becomes eleven parts, and the night seven.
17 And the sun goes forth from that sixth gate in
the west, and goes to the east and rises in the
fifth gate for thirty mornings, and sets in the west
again in the fifth western gate. 18 On that day the
day decreases by two parts, and amounts to ten
parts and the night to eight parts. 19 And the sun
goes forth from that fifth gate and sets in the fifth
gate of the west, and rises in the fourth gate for
thirty-one mornings on account of its sign, and
sets in the west. 20 On that day the day is
equalized with the night, and becomes of equal
length, and the night amounts to nine parts and
the day to nine parts.

21 And the sun rises from that gate and sets in the
west, and returns to the east and rises thirty
mornings in the third gate and sets in the west in
the third gate. 22 And on that day the night
becomes longer than the day, and night becomes
longer than night, and day shorter than day until
the thirtieth morning, and the night amounts
exactly to ten parts and the day to eight parts.
23 And the sun rises from that third gate and sets
in the third gate in the west and returns to the
east, and for thirty mornings rises in the second
gate in the east, and in like manner sets in the
second gate in the west of the heaven. 24 And on
that day the night amounts to eleven parts and
the day to seven parts.

25 And the sun rises on that day from that second
gate and sets in the west in the second gate, and
returns to the east into the first gate for thirty-one
mornings, and sets in the first gate in the west of
the heaven. 26 And on that day the night becomes
longer and amounts to the double of the day: and
the night amounts exactly to twelve parts and the
day to six.

27 And the sun has traversed the divisions of his
orbit and turns again on those divisions of his
orbit, and enters that gate thirty mornings and
sets also in the west opposite to it. 28 And on that
night has the night decreased in length by a ninth
part, and the night has become eleven parts and
the day seven parts. 29 And the sun has returned
and entered into the second gate in the east, and
returns on those his divisions of his orbit for
thirty mornings, rising and setting.

30 And on that day the night decreases in length,
and the night amounts to ten parts and the day to
eight. 31 And on that day the sun rises from that
gate, and sets in the west, and returns to the east,
and rises in the third gate for thirty-one
mornings, and sets in the west of the heaven.
32 On that day the night decreases and amounts
to nine parts, and the day to nine parts, and the
night is equal to the day and the year is exactly,
as to its days, three hundred and sixty-four.
33 And the length of the day and of the night, and
the shortness of the day and of the night arise;
through the course of the sun they are separated.

34 So it comes that its course becomes daily
longer, and its course nightly shorter. 35 And this
is the calculation and the course of the sun, and
his return as often as he returns sixty times and
rises: the great luminary which is named the Sun,
forever and ever. 36 And that which rises is the
great luminary, and is so named according to its
appearance, as the Master commanded.

37 As he rises, so he sets and does not decrease,
and does not rest, but runs day and night, and his

light is seven times brighter than that of the moon; but regarding size they are both equal.[a]

The Moon

73 1 And after this calculation I saw another calculation dealing with the smaller luminary, which is named the Moon. 2 And her roundness is like the roundness of the heaven, and her chariot in which she rides is driven by the wind, and light is given to her in *definite* measure. 3 And her rising and setting change every month: and her days are like the days of the sun, and when her light is uniform,[b] it amounts to the seventh part of the light of the sun.

4 And thus she rises. And her first phase in the east comes forth on the thirtieth morning: and on that day she becomes visible, and constitutes for you the first phase of the moon on the thirtieth day together with the sun in the gate where the sun rises. 5 And the one half of her goes forth by a seventh part, and her whole roundness is empty, without light, with the exception of one-seventh part of it, *and* the fourteenth part of her light.

6 And when she receives one-seventh part of the half of her light, her light amounts to one-seventh part and the half. 7 And she sets with the sun, and when the sun rises the moon rises with him and receives the half of one part of light, and in that night in the beginning of her morning, in the commencement of the lunar day, the moon sets with the sun, and is invisible that night with the fourteen parts and the half of one of them. 8 And she rises on that day with exactly a seventh part, and comes forth and recedes from the rising of the sun, and in her remaining days she becomes bright in the *remaining* thirteen parts.

More Courses of the Moon

74 1 And I saw another course, a calculation for her, *and* how according to that calculation she performs her monthly revolution. 2 And all these Uri'el, the set-apart messenger who is the leader of them all, showed to me, and their positions, and I wrote down their positions as he showed them to me, and I wrote down their months as they were, and the appearance of their lights until fifteen days were accomplished. 3 In single seventh parts she accomplishes all her light in the east, and in single seventh parts accomplishes all her darkness in the west.

4 And in certain months she alters her settings, and in certain months she pursues her own peculiar course. 5 In two months the moon sets with the sun: in those two middle gates the third and the fourth. 6 She goes forth for seven days, and turns about and returns again through the gate where the sun rises, and accomplishes all her light: and she recedes from the sun, and in eight days enters the sixth gate from which the sun goes forth. 7 And when the sun goes forth from the fourth gate she goes forth seven days, until she goes forth from the fifth and turns back again in seven days into the fourth gate and accomplishes all her light: and she recedes and enters into the first gate in eight days. 8 And she returns again in seven days into the fourth gate from which the sun goes forth.

9 Thus I saw their position: how the moons rose and the sun set in those days. 10 And if five years are added together the sun has a surplus of thirty days, and all the days which accrue to it for one of those five years, when they are full, amount to three hundred and sixty-four days. 11 And the surplus of the sun and of the stars amounts to six days: in five years, six days every year come to thirty days: and the moon falls behind the sun and stars to the number of thirty days. 12 And the sun and the stars bring in all the years exactly, so that they do not advance or delay their position by a single day to eternity; but complete the years with perfect justice in three hundred and sixty-four days. 13 In three years there are one thousand and ninety-two days, and in five years *there are* one thousand eight hundred and twenty

[a] **72:37** Scientifically speaking, the sun is roughly **400** times larger than the moon, and roughly **400,000** times brighter than the moon. Compare Yeshayahu [Isaiah] **30:26**.

[b] **73:2** Uniform, meaning a full moon with no dark parts.

days, so that in eight years there are two
thousand nine hundred and twelve days.

14 For the moon alone the days amount in three
years to one thousand and sixty-two days, and in
five years she falls fifty days behind, to the sum
of sixty-two days. 15 And in five years there are
one thousand seven hundred and seventy days,
so that for the moon the days in eight years
amount to two thousand eight hundred and
thirty-two days. 16 For in eight years she falls
behind to the amount of eighty days, all the days
she falls behind in eight years are eighty. 17 And
the year is accurately completed in conformity
with their world-stations and the stations of the
sun, which rise from the gates through which it
the sun rises and sets thirty days.

Calendrical Comments

75 1 And the leaders of the heads of the
thousands, who are placed over the whole
creation and over all the stars, have also to do
with the four intercalary days, being inseparable
from their office, according to the reckoning of
the year, and these render service on the four
days which are not reckoned in the reckoning of
the year. 2 And owing to them men, go wrong in
them, for those luminaries truly render service on
the world-stations, one in the first gate, one in
the third gate of the heaven, one in the fourth
gate, and one in the sixth gate, and the exactness
of the year is accomplished through its separate
three hundred and sixty-four stations.

3 For the signs and the times and the years and
the days the messenger Uri'el showed to me,
whom 𐤉𐤄𐤅𐤄 of Glory has set forever over all the
luminaries of the heaven, in the heaven and in
the world, that they should rule on the face of the
heaven and be seen on the earth, and be leaders
for the day and the night: the sun, moon, and
stars, and all the ministering creatures which
make their revolution in all the chariots of the
heaven.

4 Similarly, Uri'el showed me twelve doors, open
in the roundness of the sun's chariot in the
heaven, through which the rays of the sun break
forth, and from them warmth is diffused over the
earth, when they are opened at their appointed
seasons. 5 And for the winds and the wind of the
dew when they are opened, standing open in the
heavens at the ends.

6 As for the twelve gates in the heaven, at the
ends of the earth, out of which go forth the sun,
moon, and stars, and all the works of heaven in
the east and in the west. 7 There are many
windows open to the left and right of them, and
one window at its *appointed* season produces
warmth, corresponding *as these do* to those
doors from which the stars come forth according
as He has commanded them, and in which they
set corresponding to their number.

8 And I saw chariots in the heaven, running in
the world, above those gates in which the stars
that never set revolve. 9 And one is larger than
all the rest, and it is that which makes its course
through the entire world.

The Twelve Winds and their Gates

76 1 And at the ends of the earth I saw twelve
gates open to all the quarters *of the heavens*,
from which the winds go forth and blow over the
earth. 2 Three of them are open on the face, *that
is, the east*, of the heavens, and three in the west,
and three on the right, *that is, the south,* of the
heaven, and three on the left, *that is, the north*.
3 And the three first are those of the east, and
three are of the north, and three after those on the
left of the south, and three of the west.

4 Through four of these come winds of blessing
and prosperity, and from those eight come
hurtful winds: when they are sent, they bring
destruction on all the earth and on the water upon
it, and on all who dwell thereon, and on
everything which is in the water and on the land.

5 And the first wind from those gates, called the
east wind, comes forth through the first gate
which is in the east, inclining towards the south:
from it come forth desolation, drought, heat, and
destruction. 6 And through the second gate in the
middle comes what is fitting, and from it there
come rain and fruitfulness and prosperity and
dew; and through the third gate which lies
toward the north come cold and drought. 7 And
after these come forth the south winds through
three gates: through the first gate of them
inclining to the east comes forth a hot wind.

8 And through the middle gate next to it there
come forth fragrant smells, and dew and rain,
and prosperity and health. 9 And through the
third gate lying to the west come forth dew and
rain, locusts and desolation.

10 And after these the north winds: from the
seventh gate in the east come dew and rain,
locusts and desolation. 11 And from the middle
gate come in a direct direction health and rain
and dew and prosperity; and through the third
gate in the west come cloud and hoarfrost, and
snow and rain, and dew and locusts.

12 And after these four are the west winds:
through the first gate adjoining the north come
forth dew and hoarfrost, and cold and snow and
frost. 13 And from the middle gate come forth
dew and rain, and prosperity and blessing; and
through the last gate which joins the south come
forth drought and desolation, and burning and
destruction. 14 And with this the twelve gates of
the four quarters of the heaven are completed,
and all their calculations and all their plagues
and all their benefactions have I shown to you,
my son Methushelaḥ.

Four Directions

77 1 And the first quarter is called the east,
because it is the first: and the second, the south,
because the Most High will descend there; yes,
there in quite a special sense will He who is
blessed forever descend. 2 And the west quarter
is named the diminished, because there all the
luminaries of the heaven wane and go down.
3 And the fourth quarter, named the north, is
divided into three parts: the first of them is for
the dwelling of men: and the second contains
seas of water, and the abysses and forests and
rivers, and darkness and clouds; and the third
part contains the Garden of Righteousness.

Seven Mountains & Rivers

4 I saw seven high mountains, higher than all the
mountains which are on the earth: and from there
comes forth hoar-frost, and days, seasons, and
years pass away. 5 I saw seven rivers on the earth
larger than all the rivers: one of them coming
from the west pours its waters into the Great Sea.
6 And these two come from the north to the sea
and pour their waters into the Sea of Reeds in the
east. 7 And the remaining four come forth on the
side of the north to their own sea, two of them to
the Sea of Reeds, and two into the Great Sea and
discharge themselves there and some say: into
the desert. 8 Seven great islands I saw in the sea
and in the mainland: two in the mainland and
five in the Great Sea.

Names of the Sun and Moon

78 1 And the names of the sun are the
following: the first Oryares[a], and the second
Tomas[b]. 2 And the moon has four names: the
first name is Asonya[c], the second Ebla[d], the third
Benase[e], and the fourth Erae[f]. 3 These are the
two great luminaries: their roundness is like the
roundness of the heaven, and the size of both
their roundness is alike. 4 In the roundness of the
sun there are seven portions of light which are
added to it more than to the moon, and in

---

[a] **78:1** Oryares – Ethiopic word ኦርያሬስ (*Or'ya'res*), an Ethiopic corruption of the Hebrew 𐤇𐤓𐤎 (*ḥer'es*) which is a synonym for "sun." Its literal meaning is "scrape" or "itch." However, it is used Scripturally as an idiom for the sun, probably on account of intense heat and sunburn.

[b] **78:1** Tomas – Ethiopic word ቶማስ (*to'mas*), an Ethiopic corruption of the Hebrew 𐤔𐤌𐤔 (*she'mesh*), the most commonly used Hebrew word for "sun."

[c] **78:2** Asonya – Ethiopic word አሶንያ (*a'so'n'ya*), most likely an Ethiopic corruption of the Hebrew 𐤀𐤉𐤔𐤅𐤍 (*iysh'on*), meaning "little man." It is used in Scripture as an idiomatic expression for the pupil of the eye, usually translated as "apple of the eye." See Devarim [Deuteronomy] **32:10**; Mishlei [Proverbs] **7:2** for "apple of the eye."

[d] **78:2** Ebla – Ethiopic word እብላ (*'ebla*), an Ethiopic corruption of the Hebrew 𐤋𐤁𐤍𐤄 (*l'banah*), meaning "white." It is used idiomatically in Scripture to mean "full moon." See Shir Ha'Shirim [Songs of Solomon] **6:10**; Yeshayahu [Isaiah] **24:23** for "moon."

[e] **78:2** Benase – Ethiopic word ብናሴ (*b'nase*), an Ethiopic corruption of the Hebrew 𐤁𐤊𐤎𐤄 (*b'kese*), meaning "covered." This describes a "covered" moon, meaning either a completely dark (conjunction) or a full moon. The exact meaning, be it conjunction or full, is debated.

[f] **78:2** Erae – Ethiopic word ኤራዕ (*era'*), an Ethiopic corruption of the Hebrew 𐤉𐤓𐤇 (*ya'reach*), meaning "moon."

definite measures it is transferred until the seventh portion of the sun is exhausted.

Phases & Levels of Lunar Illumination

5 And they set and enter the gates of the west, and make their revolution by the north, and come forth through the eastern gates on the face of the heaven. 6 And when the moon rises one-fourteenth part appears in the heaven. The light becomes full in her *and* on the fourteenth day she completes her light. 7 And fifteen parts of light are transferred to her until the fifteenth day *when* her light is completed, according to the sign of the year, and she becomes fifteen parts, and the moon grows by *individual* fourteenth parts. 8 And in her waning *she* decreases on the first day to fourteen parts of her light, on the second to thirteen parts of light, on the third to twelve, on the fourth to eleven, on the fifth to ten, on the sixth to nine, on the seventh to eight, on the eighth to seven, on the ninth to six, on the tenth to five, on the eleventh to four, on the twelfth to three, on the thirteenth to two, on the fourteenth to the half of a seventh, and all her remaining light disappears wholly on the fifteenth.

9 And in certain months the month has twenty-nine days and once twenty-eight. 10 And Uri'el showed me another calculation: when light is transferred to the moon, and on which side it is transferred to her by the sun.

11 During all the period in which the moon is growing in her light, she is transferring it to herself when opposite to the sun during fourteen days her light is completed in the heaven, and when she is illuminated throughout, her light is completed full in the heaven.

12 And on the first day she is called the 'new moon,' for on that day the light rises upon her. 13 She becomes full moon exactly on the day when the sun sets in the west, and from the east she rises at night, and the moon shines the whole night through until the sun rises over against her and the moon is seen over against the sun. 14 On the side from which the light of the moon comes forth, there again she wanes until all the light vanishes and all the days of the month are at an end, and her roundness is empty, void of light.

15 And three months she makes of thirty days, and at her time she makes three months of twenty-nine days each, in which she accomplishes her waning in the first period of time, and in the first gate for one hundred and seventy-seven days. 16 And in the time of her going out she appears for three months *of* thirty days each, and for three months she appears *of* twenty-nine each. 17 At night she appears like a man for twenty days each time, and by day she appears like the heaven, and there is nothing else in her save her light.

Completion of the Astronomical Calculations

79 1 "And now, my son, I have shown you everything, and the calculation of all the stars of the heaven is completed."

2 And he showed me all the calculations of these for every day, and for every season of bearing rule, and for every year, and for its going forth, and for the order prescribed to it every month and every week.

3 And the waning of the moon which takes place in the sixth gate: for in this sixth gate her light is completed, and after that there is the beginning of the waning. 4 And the waning which takes place in the first gate in its season, until one hundred and seventy-seven days are completed: reckoned according to weeks, twenty-five *weeks* and two days.

5 She falls behind the sun and the order of the stars exactly five days in the course of one period, and when this place which you see has been traversed. 6 Such is the picture and sketch of every luminary which Uri'el the ruling messenger, who is their leader, showed to me.

80 1 And in those days the messenger Uri'el answered and said to me, "Behold, I have shown you everything, Ḥanokh, and I have revealed everything to you that you should see this sun and this moon, and the leaders of the stars of the heaven and all those who turn them, their tasks and times and departures.

2 "And in the days of the sinners the years shall be shortened, and their seed shall be delayed on

their lands and fields, and all things on the earth
shall alter, and shall not appear in their time: and
the rain shall be kept back and the heaven shall
withhold *it*. **3** And in those times the fruits of the
earth shall be backward, and shall not grow in
their time, and the fruits of the trees shall be
withheld in their time. **4** And the moon shall alter
her order, and not appear at her time. **5** And in
those days the sun shall be seen and he shall
journey in the evening[a] on the extremity of the
great chariot in the west and shall shine more
brightly than accords with the order of light.

6 "And many chiefs of the stars shall transgress
the *prescribed* order. And these shall alter their
orbits and tasks, and not appear at the seasons
prescribed to them. **7** And the whole order of the
stars shall be concealed from the sinners, and the
thoughts of those on the earth shall err
concerning them, and they shall be altered from
all their ways. Yes, they shall err and take them
to be elohim. **8** And evil shall be multiplied upon
them, and punishment shall come upon them so
as to destroy all."

Ḥanokh's Commission

81 **1** And he said to me, "Observe, Ḥanokh,
these heavenly tablets, and read what is written
on them. And mark every individual fact."

2 And I observed the heavenly tablets, and read
everything which was written *on them*, and
understood everything, and read the book of all
the deeds of mankind, and of all the children of
flesh that shall be upon the earth to the furthest
generations. **3** And immediately I blessed the
Master, the King of glory forever, in that He has
made all the works of the world, and I glorified
the Master because of His patience, and blessed
Him because of the children of men.

4 And after that I said, "Blessed is the man who
dies in righteousness and goodness, concerning
whom there is no book of unrighteousness
written, and against whom no day of judgment
shall be found."

5 And those seven set-apart ones brought me and
placed me on the earth before the door of my
house, and said to me, "Declare everything to
your son Methushelaḥ, and show all your
children that no flesh is righteous in the sight of
the Master, for He is their Creator. **6** We will
leave you with your son for one year, until you
give your *last* commands, that you may teach
your children and record *it* for them, and witness
to all your children. And in the second year they
shall take you from their midst.

7 "Let your heart be strong, for the good shall
announce righteousness to the good. The
righteous shall rejoice with the righteous, and
shall congratulate one another. **8** But the sinners
shall die with the sinners, and the apostate go
down with the apostate. **9** And those who
practice righteousness shall die on account of the
deeds of men, and be taken away on account of
the doings of the wicked."

10 And in those days they ceased to speak to me,
and I came to my people, blessing the Master of
the world.

Additional Calendrical Teaching

82 **1** And now, my son Methushelaḥ, all these
things I am recounting to you and writing down
for you, and I have revealed to you everything,
and given you books concerning all these: so
preserve, my son Methushelaḥ, the books from
your father's hand, and *see* that you deliver them
to the generations of the world.

2 I have given wisdom to you and your children,
and your children that will be *born* to you, that
they may give it to their children for the
generations that are discerning. All the wise ones
shall give praise, and wisdom shall dwell upon
your consciousness. **3** And those who understand
it shall not sleep, but shall listen with the ear that
they may learn this wisdom, and it shall please
those that eat it more than good food.

4 Blessed are all the righteous, blessed are all
those who walk in the way of righteousness and
sin not as the sinners, in the reckoning of all their

---

[a] **80:5** Ethiopic texts actually read ዐበር (*'abar*), meaning "drought" or "famine." However, Charles believed this to be a corruption of the Hebrew 𐤏𐤓𐤁 (*erev*), meaning "evening." And so it has been rendered here, given the context.

days in which the sun traverses the heaven,
entering into and departing from the gates for
thirty days with the heads of thousands of the
order of the stars, together with the four which
are intercalated which divide the four portions of
the year, which lead them and enter with them
four days. 5 Owing to them, men shall be at fault
and not reckon them in the whole reckoning of
the year. Yes, men shall be at fault, and not
recognize them accurately. 6 For they belong to
the reckoning of the year and are truly recorded
in it forever, one in the first gate and one in the
third, and one in the fourth and one in the sixth,
and the year is completed in three hundred and
sixty-four days.

7 And this account is accurate and this recorded
reckoning is exact; for Uri'el has shown and
revealed to me the luminaries, and months and
festivals, and years and days, to whom 𐤉𐤄𐤅𐤄 of
the whole creation of the world has subjected the
host of heaven. 8 And he has power over night
and day in the heaven to cause the light to give
light to men--sun, moon, and stars, and all the
powers of the heaven which revolve in their
circular chariots. 9 And these are the orders of
the stars, which set in their places, and in their
seasons and festivals and months.

10 And these are the names of those who lead
them, who watch that they enter at their times, in
their orders, in their seasons, in their months, in
their periods of dominion, and in their positions.
11 Their four leaders who divide the four parts of
the year enter first; and after them the twelve
leaders of the orders who divide the months; and
for the three hundred and sixty *days* there are
heads over thousands who divide the days; and
for the four intercalary days there are the leaders
which separate the four parts of the year.

12 And these heads over thousands are
intercalated between leader and leader, each
behind a station, but their leaders make the
division. And these are the names of the leaders
who divide the four parts of the year which are
ordained: Milkiel, Helemmelekh, and Meleyal,
and Narel. 13 And the names of those who lead
them: Adnarel, and Yasusael, and Elome'el--
these three follow the leaders of the orders, and
there is one that follows the three leaders of the
orders which follow those leaders of stations that
divide the four parts of the year.

14 In the beginning of the year Melkeyal rises
first and rules, who is named Tam'aini and 'sun,'
and all the days of his dominion while he bears
rule are ninety-one days. 15 And these are the
signs of the days which are to be seen on earth in
the days of his dominion: sweat, and heat, and
calms; and all the trees bear fruit, and leaves are
produced on all the trees, and the harvest of
wheat, and the rose-flowers, and all the flowers
which come forth in the field, but the trees of the
winter season become withered. 16 And these are
the names of the leaders which are under them:
Berkael, Zelebsel, and another who is added a
head of a thousand, called Hiluyaseph: and the
days of the dominion of this *leader* are at an end.

17 The next leader after him is Helemmelekh,
whom one names 'the shining sun,' and all the
days of his light are ninety-one days. 18 And
these are the signs of *his* days on the earth:
glowing heat and dryness, and the trees ripen
their fruits and produce all their fruits ripe and
ready, and the sheep pair and become pregnant,
and all the fruits of the earth are gathered in, and
everything that is in the fields, and the
winepress: these things take place in the days of
his dominion. 19 These are the names, and the
orders, and the leaders of those heads of
thousands: Gedai'el, Ke'el, and He'el, and the
name of the head of a thousand which is added to
them, Asfa'el: and the days of his dominion are
at an end.

Book IV: Dream Visions

Vision of the Flood

83 1 And now, my son Methushelaḥ, I will
show you all my visions which I have seen, and
will recount them before you. 2 Two visions I
saw before I took a wife, and the one was quite
unlike the other: the first when I was learning to
write; the second before I took your mother *as
my wife*, *when* I saw a terrible vision. And I
prayed to the Master regarding them. 3 I was
lying down in the house of my grandfather
Mahalalel, *when* I saw in a vision how the
heaven collapsed and was borne off and fell to
the earth. 4 And when it fell to the earth I saw

how the earth was swallowed up in a great abyss,
and mountains were suspended on mountains,
and hills sank down on hills, and high trees were
torn from their stems, and hurled down and sunk
in the abyss. **5** And then a statement fell into my
mouth, and I lifted up *my voice* to cry aloud and
said, "The earth is destroyed!"

6 And my grandfather Mahalalel woke me as I
lay near him, and said to me, "Why do you cry
so, my son, and why do you make such
lamentation?"

7 And I recounted to him the whole vision which
I had seen, and he said to me, "You have seen a
terrible thing, my son, and your dream-vision is
of grave moment, *pertaining* to the secrets of all
the sin of the earth. It must sink into the abyss
and be destroyed with a great destruction. **8** And
now, my son, arise and make petition to the
Master of glory, since you affirm, that a remnant
may remain on the earth, and that He may not
destroy the whole earth. **9** My son, all this will
come upon the earth from heaven, and upon the
earth there will be great destruction."

10 After that I arose and prayed and implored and
sought, and wrote down my prayer for the
generations of the world, and I will show
everything to you, my son Methushelaḥ.

11 And when I had gone forth below and seen the
heaven, and the sun rising in the east, and the
moon setting in the west, and a few stars, and the
whole earth, and everything as He had known it
in the beginning, then I blessed the Master of
judgment and glorified Him because He had
made the sun to go forth from the windows of
the east, and he ascended and rose on the face of
the heaven, and set out and kept traversing the
path shown to him.

84 **1** And I lifted up my hands in righteousness
and blessed the Set-Apart and Great One, and
spoke with the breath of my mouth, and with the
tongue of flesh, which Elohim has made for the
children of the flesh of men, that they should
speak with it, and He gave them breath and a
tongue and a mouth that they should speak with
them this way:

2 "Blessed are You, O Master, King, Great and
Mighty in Your greatness, Master of the whole
creation of the heaven, King of kings and Elohim
of the whole world. And Your power and
kingship and greatness abide forever and ever,
and throughout all generations *of* Your
dominion; and all the heavens are Your throne
forever, and the whole earth *is* Your footstool
forever and ever. **3** For You have made, and You
rule all things, and nothing is too hard for You.
Wisdom does not depart from the place of Your
throne, nor does it turn away from Your
presence. And You know and see and hear
everything, and there is nothing hidden from
You, for You see everything."

4 "And now the messengers of Your heavens are
guilty of trespass, and Your wrath abides upon
the flesh of men until the great day of judgment.
5 And now, O Master and Elohim, and Great
King, I implore and ask You to fulfil my prayer,
to leave me a posterity on earth, and not destroy
all the flesh of man, and make the earth without
inhabitant, so that there should be an eternal
destruction.

6 "And now, Master, destroy the flesh from the
earth which has aroused Your wrath, but the
flesh of righteousness and uprightness establish
as a plant of the eternal seed, and do not hide
Your face from the prayer of Your servant, O
Master."

Vision of the Bulls

85 **1** "And after this I saw another dream, and I
will show the whole dream to you, my son."

2 And Ḥanokh lifted up *his voice* and spoke to
his son Methushelaḥ, "To you, my son, will I
speak. Hear my words, incline your ear to the
dream-vision of your father. **3** Before I took your
mother Edna[a] *as wife*, I saw in a vision on my

---

[a] **85:3** Ethiopic word እድና (*'edna*) is given as the name of Ḥanokh's wife. The exact meaning and etymological origin is unknown. If Hebrew, it is possibly related to אדן (*ed'en*) meaning "pedestal" or "foundation." This word is also related to the Hebrew אדון (*ad'own*) meaning "lord" or "master." However, if Aramaic in origin, it could be אדן (*'edna*) which means "ear" and, by implication, could be used to

bed, and behold a bull came forth from the earth,
and that bull was white; and after it came forth a
heifer, and along with this *latter* came forth two
bulls, one of them black and the other red. 4 And
that black bull gored the red one and pursued
him over the earth, and then I could no longer
see that red bull. 5 But that black bull grew and
that heifer went with him, and I saw that many
oxen proceeded from him which resembled and
followed him.

6 "And that cow, that first one, went from the
presence of that first bull in order to seek that red
one, but found him not, and lamented with a
great lamentation over him and sought him.
7 And I looked until that first bull came to her
and quieted her, and from that time onward she
cried no more. 8 And after that she bore another
white bull, and after him she bore many bulls
and black cows.

9 "And I saw in my sleep that white bull likewise
grow and become a great white bull, and from
Him proceeded many white bulls, and they
resembled him. And they began to beget many
white bulls, which resembled them, one
following the other, *even* many."

Vision of the Stars Among the Bulls

86 1 "And again I saw with my eyes as I slept,
and I saw the heaven above, and behold a star
fell from heaven,[a] and it arose and ate and
pastured among those oxen. 2 And after that I
saw the large and the black oxen, and behold
they all changed their stalls and pastures and
their cattle, and began to live with each other.
3 And again I saw in the vision, and looked
towards the heaven, and behold I saw many stars
descend and cast themselves down from heaven
to that first star, and they became bulls among
those cattle and pastured with them among them.
4 And I looked at them and saw, and behold they
all let out their privy members, like horses, and
began to mount upon the cows of the oxen, and
they all became pregnant and bore elephants,
camels, and donkeys. 5 And all the oxen feared
them and were afraid of them, and began to bite
with their teeth and to devour, and to gore with
their horns. 6 And they began, moreover, to
devour those oxen; and behold all the children of
the earth began to tremble and quake before
them and to flee from them."

Vision of the Four Heavenly Beings

87 1 "And again I saw how they began to gore
each other and to devour each other, and the
earth began to cry aloud. 2 And I raised my eyes
again to heaven, and I saw in the vision, and
behold there came forth from heaven beings who
were like white men: and four went forth from
that place and three with them. 3 And those three
that had come forth last grasped me by my hand
and took me up, away from the generations of
the earth, and raised me up to a lofty place, and
showed me a tower raised high above the earth,
and all the hills were lower. 4 And one said to
me, "Remain here until you see everything that
happens to those elephants, camels, and donkeys,
and the stars and the oxen, and all of them."

Vision of the Punishment of the Stars

88 1 "And I saw one of those four who had
come forth first, and he seized that first star
which had fallen from the heaven, and bound it
hand and foot and cast it into an abyss. That
abyss was narrow and deep, and horrible and
dark. 2 And one of them drew a sword, and gave
it to those elephants and camels and donkeys.
And then they began to strike each other, and the
whole earth quaked because of them. 3 And as I
was looking on in the vision, behold, one of
those four who had come forth stoned *them* from
heaven, and gathered and took all the many[b] stars
whose privy members were like those of horses,
and bound them all hand and foot, and cast them
in an abyss of the earth."

Vision of the Flood

89 1 "And one of those four went to that white
bull and instructed him in a secret, without him

describe a person that listens. Note this is not the same as 𐤏𐤃𐤍 (*E'den*) such as the Garden in Eden.

[a] **86**:**1** Compare Loukas [Luke] **10**:**18**; Hit'galut [Revelation] **9**:**1**.

[b] **88**:**3** Ethiopic texts contain various renderings here, including: "great," "stern," "powerful," and "mighty." However, the Aramaic reads "many."

being terrified: he was born a bull and became a
man, and built for himself a great vessel[a] and
dwelled on it; and three bulls[b] dwelled with him
in that vessel and they were shut in.

2 "And again I raised my eyes towards heaven
and saw a lofty roof, with seven water torrents
thereon, and those torrents flowed with much
water into an enclosure. **3** And I saw again, and
behold fountains were opened on the surface of
that great enclosure, and that water began to
swell and rise upon the surface, and I saw that
enclosure until all its surface was covered with
water.[c] **4** And the water, the darkness, and mist
increased upon it; and as I looked at the height of
that water, that water had risen above the height
of that enclosure, and was streaming over that
enclosure, and it stood upon the earth. **5** And all
the cattle of that enclosure were gathered
together until I saw how they sank and were
swallowed up and perished in that water.

6 "But that vessel floated on the water, while all
the oxen and elephants and camels and donkeys
sank to the bottom with all the animals, so that I
could no longer see them, and they were not able
to escape, *but* perished and sank into the depths.
7 And again I saw in the vision until those water
torrents were removed from that high roof, and
the chasms of the earth were levelled up and
other abysses were opened. **8** Then the water
began to run down into these, until the earth
became visible; but that vessel settled on the
earth, and the darkness retired and light
appeared. **9** But that white bull [which had
become a man][d] came out of that vessel, and the
three bulls with him, and one of those three was
white like that bull, and one of them was red as
blood, and one black: and that white bull
departed from them.

From the Flood to the Exodus

10 "And they began to bring forth beasts of the
field and birds, so that there arose different
kinds: lions, tigers, wolves, dogs, hyenas, wild
boars, foxes, squirrels, swine, falcons, vultures,
kites, eagles, and ravens; and among them was
born a white bull.[e] **11** And they began to bite one
another; but that white bull which was born
among them bore a wild donkey[f] and a white
bull[g] with it, and the wild donkeys multiplied.

12 "But that bull[h] which was born from him bore
a black wild boar[i] and a white sheep[j]; and the
former begat many boars, but that sheep begat
twelve sheep. **13** And when those twelve sheep
had grown, they gave up one[k] of them to the
donkeys, and those donkeys again gave up that
sheep to the wolves, and that sheep grew up
among the wolves. **14** And the Master brought
the eleven sheep to live with it and to pasture
with it among the wolves: and they multiplied
and became many flocks of sheep. **15** And the
wolves began to fear[l] them, and they oppressed
them until they destroyed their little ones, and
they cast their young into a river of much water:
but those sheep began to cry aloud on account of
their little ones, and to complain to their Master.

16 "And a sheep[m] which had been saved from the
wolves fled and escaped to the wild donkeys;
and I saw the sheep how they lamented and
cried, and petitioned their Master with all their
might, until the Master of the sheep descended at
the voice of the sheep from a lofty abode, and
came to them and pastured them. **17** And He
called that sheep which had escaped the wolves,

---

[a] **89:1** Some Ethiopic texts read መሥቀር (*mas'qar*) meaning "East" here. However, this is most likely a corruption of the Ethiopic መስቀረ (*mas'qara*), meaning "ship" or "vessel." The Aramaic fragment reads𐤏𐤓𐤁 𐤇𐤃𐤄 (*'arb chad'ah*) meaning "a boat."

[b] **89:1** Three bulls – presumably representing the three sons of Noaḥ: Shem, Ḥam, and Yepheth.

[c] **89:3** Aramaic fragment of 4QEn[e] reads 𐤔𐤁𐤏𐤄 𐤌𐤓𐤆𐤁𐤉𐤍 (*mar'zebiyn shab'ah*) meaning "seven spouts" rather than just "fountains."

[d] **89:9** Some scholars contest that the bracketed section is not original.

[e] **89:10** White bull – presumably Avraham.

[f] **89:11** Wild donkey – presumably Yishmael.

[g] **89:11** White bull – presumably Yitschaq.

[h] **89:12** Aramaic fragment of 4QEn[e] reads 𐤏𐤂𐤋𐤕 (*eg'el*) meaning "calf" and not "bull."

[i] **89:12** Black wild boar – presumably Esav/Edom.

[j] **89:12** White sheep – presumably Ya'aqov.

[k] **89:13** Presumably Yoseph.

[l] **89:15** Aramaic fragment of 4QEn[e] reads 𐤓𐤃𐤐𐤉𐤍 (*radep'iyn*) meaning "pursue" or "chase" and not "fear."

[m] **89:16** Sheep – presumably Moshe.

and spoke with it concerning the wolves that it should admonish them not to touch the sheep. 18 And the sheep went to the wolves according to the word of the Master, and another sheep[a] met it and went with it, and the two went and entered together into the assembly of those wolves, and spoke with them and admonished them not to touch the sheep from then onward.

19 "And then I saw the wolves, and how they oppressed the sheep exceedingly with all their power; and the sheep cried aloud. 20 And the Master came to the sheep and they began to strike those wolves: and the wolves began to make lamentation; but the sheep became quiet and immediately ceased to cry out. 21 And I saw the sheep until they departed from among the wolves; but the eyes of the wolves were blinded, and those wolves departed in pursuit of the sheep with all their power. 22 And the Master of the sheep went with them, as their leader, and all His sheep followed Him: and His face was dazzling and glorious and terrible to behold.

23 "But the wolves began to pursue those sheep until they reached a sea of water. 24 And that sea was divided, and the water stood on this side and on that before their face, and the Master led them and placed Himself between them and the wolves. 25 And as those wolves did not yet see the sheep, they proceeded into the midst of that sea, and the wolves followed the sheep, and those wolves ran after them into that sea. 26 And when they saw the Master of the sheep, they turned to flee before His face, but that sea gathered itself together, and became as it had been created, and the water swelled and rose until it covered those wolves. 27 And I saw until all the wolves who pursued those sheep perished and were drowned.

From the Exodus to the Promised Land

28 But the sheep escaped from that water and went forth into a wilderness, where there was no water and no grass; and they [began to open their eyes][b] and to see; and I saw the Master of the sheep pasturing them and giving them water and grass, and that sheep going and leading them.

29 "And that sheep ascended to the summit of that lofty rock, and the Master of the sheep gave *it* to them. 30 And after that I saw the Master of the sheep who stood before them, and His appearance was great and terrible and majestic, and all those sheep saw Him and were afraid before His face. 31 And they all feared and trembled because of Him, and they cried to that sheep with them which was among them, 'We are not able to stand before our Master or to behold Him.'

32 "And that sheep which led them again ascended to the summit of that rock, but the sheep began to be blinded and to wander from the way which he had showed them, but that sheep did not know it. 33 And the Master of the sheep was exceedingly wrathful against them, and that sheep discovered it, and went down from the summit of the rock, and came to the sheep, and found the greatest part of them blinded and fallen away. 34 And when they saw it they feared and trembled at its presence, and desired to return to their folds. 35 And that sheep took other sheep with it, and came to those sheep which had fallen away, and began to slay them. And the sheep feared its presence, and thus that sheep brought back those sheep that had fallen away, and they returned to their folds.

36 "And I saw in this vision until that sheep became a man and built a house[c] for the Master of the sheep, and placed all the sheep in that house. 37 And I saw until this sheep which had met that sheep which led them fell asleep. And I saw until all the great sheep perished and little ones arose in their place, and they came to a pasture, and approached a stream of water. 38 Then that sheep, their leader which had become a man, withdrew from them and fell asleep, and all the sheep sought it and cried over it with a great crying.

39 "And I saw until they left off crying for that sheep and crossed that stream of water, and there

[a] **89:18** Presumably Aharon.
[b] **89:28** Some Ethiopic texts read, "but they did not open their eyes." However, the Aramaic fragment reads 𐤅𐤏𐤉𐤍𐤉𐤄𐤅𐤍 𐤄𐤕𐤐𐤕𐤇𐤅 (*wa'eiyn'iy'hon ha't'pathaḥ*) meaning "and their eyes were opened."
[c] **89:36** House – presumably the Tabernacle.

arose the two sheep[a] as leaders in the place of those which had led them and fallen asleep.
40 And I saw until the sheep came to a good place, and a pleasant and glorious land, and I saw until those sheep were satisfied; and that house stood among them in the pleasant land.

From the Judges to the Building of the Temple

41 "And sometimes their eyes were opened, and sometimes blinded, until another sheep[b] arose and led them and brought them all back, and their eyes were opened.

42 "And the dogs and the foxes and the wild boars began to devour those sheep until the Master of the sheep raised up another sheep, a ram[c] from their midst, which led them. 43 And
that ram began to butt those dogs, foxes, and wild boars on either side until he had destroyed them all. 44 And that sheep whose eyes were
opened saw that ram, which was among the sheep, until it forsook its glory and began to butt those sheep, and trampled upon them, and behaved itself unseemly. 45 And the Master of
the sheep sent the lamb to another lamb[d] and raised it to being a ram and leader of the sheep instead of that ram which had forsaken its glory.

46 "And it went to it and spoke to it alone, and raised it to being a ram, and made it the prince and leader of the sheep; but during all these things those dogs oppressed the sheep.

47 "And the first ram pursued that second ram, and that second ram arose and fled before it; and I saw until those dogs pulled down the first ram.
48 And that second ram arose and led the little
sheep. 49 And those sheep grew and multiplied;
but all the dogs, and foxes, and wild boars feared and fled before it, and that ram butted and killed the wild beasts, and those wild beasts had no longer any power among the sheep and robbed them no more of ought. And that ram bore many sheep and fell asleep; and a little sheep[e] became ram in its stead, and became prince and leader of those sheep. 50 And that house became great and
broad, and it was built for those sheep. *And* a lofty and great tower was built on the house for the Master of the sheep, and that house was low, but the tower was elevated and lofty, and the Master of the sheep stood on that tower and they offered a full table before Him.

From the Split of Yisra'el & Yehudah to the Destruction of Yerushalayim

51 "And again I saw those sheep that they erred again and went many ways, and forsook that their house, and the Master of the sheep called some from among the sheep[f] and sent them to the sheep, but the sheep began to kill them. 52 And
one of them was saved[g] and was not slain, and it sped away and cried aloud over the sheep; and they sought to slay it, but the Master of the sheep saved it from the sheep, and brought it up to me, and caused it to dwell there. 53 And He sent
many other sheep to those sheep to witness to them and lament over them.

54 "And after that I saw that when they forsook the house of the Master and His tower, they fell away entirely, and their eyes were blinded; and I saw the Master of the sheep, how He wrought much slaughter among them in their herds until those sheep invited that slaughter and betrayed His place. 55 And He gave them over into the
hands of the lions and tigers, and wolves and hyenas, and into the hand of the foxes, and to all the wild beasts, and those wild beasts began to tear those sheep in pieces. 56 And I saw that He
forsook their house and their tower and gave them all into the hand of the lions, to tear and devour them, into the hand of all the wild beasts.

57 "And I began to cry aloud with all my power, and to appeal to the Master of the sheep, and to represent to Him in regard to the sheep that they were devoured by all the wild beasts. 58 But He
remained unmoved, though He saw it, and rejoiced that they were devoured and swallowed and robbed, and left them to be devoured in the hand of all the beasts. 59 And He called seventy
shepherds, and cast those sheep to them that they might pasture them, and He spoke to the

---

[a] **89:39** Two sheep – presumably Yehoshua and Kalev.
[b] **89:41** Presumably Shemuel.
[c] **89:42** Ram – presumably Sha'ul.
[d] **89:45** Lamb – presumably David.
[e] **89:49** Little sheep – presumably Shelomoh.
[f] **89:51** Presumably the prophets.
[g] **89:52** Presumably Eliyahu.

shepherds and their companions, 'Let each individual of you pasture the sheep from now on, and everything that I shall command you, that you shall do. **60** And I will deliver them over to you duly numbered, and tell you which of them are to be destroyed, and you destroy them.' And He gave them over to those sheep.

61 "And He called another and spoke to him, 'Observe and mark everything that the shepherds will do to those sheep; for they will destroy more of them than I have commanded them. **62** And every excess and the destruction which will be wrought through the shepherds, record how many they destroy according to My command, and how many according to their own whim. Record against every individual shepherd all the destruction he causes. **63** And read out before Me by number how many they destroy, and how many they deliver over for destruction, that I may have this as a witness against them, and know every deed of the shepherds, that I may comprehend and see what they do, whether or not they abide by My command which I have commanded them. **64** But they shall not know it, and you shall not declare it to them, nor admonish them, but only record against each individual all the destruction which the shepherds effect each in his time and lay it all before Me.'

65 "And I saw until those shepherds pastured in their season, and they began to slay and to destroy more than they were told, and they delivered those sheep into the hand of the lions. **66** And the lions and tigers ate and devoured the greater part of those sheep, and the wild boars ate along with them; and they burned that tower and demolished that house. **67** And I became exceedingly sorrowful over that tower because that house of the sheep was demolished, and afterwards I was unable to see if those sheep entered that house.

From the Destruction of Yerushalayim to the Return of the Exiles

68 "And the shepherds and their associates delivered over those sheep to all the wild beasts, to devour them, and each one of them received in his time a definite number: it was written by the other in a book how many each one of them destroyed of them. **69** And each one slew and destroyed many more than was prescribed; and I began to weep and lament on account of those sheep. **70** And thus in the vision I saw that one who wrote, how he wrote down every one that was destroyed by those shepherds, day by day, and carried up and laid down and showed the whole book to the Master of the sheep; everything that they had done, and all that each one of them had made away with, and all that they had given over to destruction. **71** And the book was read before the Master of the sheep, and He took the book from his hand and read it and sealed it and laid it down. **72** And immediately I saw how the shepherds pastured for twelve hours, and behold three of those sheep[a] turned back and came and entered and began to build up all that had fallen down of that house; and though the wild boars[b] tried to hinder them, they were not able.

From the Return of the Exiles to the Time of the Greeks

73 "And they began again to build as before, and they raised up that tower, and it was named the high tower; and they began again to place a table before the tower, but all the bread on it was polluted and not pure. **74** And as touching all this the eyes of those sheep were blinded so that they did not see, and *the eyes of* their shepherds likewise; and they delivered them in large numbers to their shepherds for destruction, and they trampled the sheep with their feet and devoured them. **75** And the Master of the sheep remained unmoved until all the sheep were dispersed over the field and mingled with *the beasts*, and *the shepherds* did not save them out of the hand of the beasts. **76** And this one who wrote the book carried it up, and showed it and read it before the Master of the sheep, and petitioned Him on their account, and asked Him on their account as he showed Him all the doings of the shepherds, and bore witness before Him

[a] **89:72** Presumably Zerubbavel, Yehoshua, and Nechemyah.

[b] **89:72** Wild boars – presumably Shomeronites.

against all the shepherds. And he took the actual book and laid it down beside Him and departed."

90 1 "And I saw until that in this manner thirty-five[a] shepherds undertook the pasturing *of the sheep*, and they individually completed their periods as did the first; and others received them into their hands, to pasture them for their period, each shepherd in his own period. 2 And after that I saw in my vision all the birds of heaven coming, the eagles, the vultures, the kites, the ravens; but the eagles led all the birds; and they began to devour those sheep, and to pick out their eyes and to devour their flesh. 3 And the sheep cried out because their flesh was being devoured by the birds, and as for me I looked and lamented in my sleep over that shepherd who pastured the sheep.

4 "And I saw until those sheep were devoured by the dogs and eagles and kites, and they left neither flesh nor skin nor sinew remaining on them until only their bones stood there. And their bones, too, fell to the earth, and the sheep became few. 5 And I saw until those twenty-three had undertaken the pasturing and completed in their several periods fifty-eight times.

From the Maccabean Revolt to the Establishment of the Messianic Kingdom

6 "But behold lambs were borne by those white sheep, and they began to open their eyes and to see, and to cry to the sheep. 7 Yes, they cried to them, but they did not listen to what they said to them, but were exceedingly deaf, and their eyes were very exceedingly blinded.

8 "And I saw in the vision how the ravens flew upon those lambs and took one of those lambs, and dashed the sheep in pieces and devoured them. 9 And I saw until horns grew upon those lambs, and the ravens cast down their horns; and I saw until a great horn sprouted from one of those sheep, and their eyes were opened. 10 And it looked at them and their eyes opened, and it cried to the sheep, and the rams saw it and all ran to it[b].

11 "And notwithstanding all this those eagles and vultures and ravens and kites still kept tearing the sheep and swooping down upon them and devouring them: still the sheep remained silent, but the rams lamented and cried out. 12 And those ravens fought and battled with it and sought to lay low its horn, but they had no power over it. 13 And I saw until the shepherds and eagles and those vultures and kites came, and they cried to the ravens that they should break the horn of that ram, and they battled and fought with it, and it battled with them and cried that its help might come.

14 "And I saw until that man, who wrote down the names of the shepherds and carried up into the presence of the Master of the sheep came and helped it and showed it everything: he had come down for the help of that ram. 15 And I saw until the Master of the sheep came to them in wrath, and all who saw Him fled, and they all fell into His shadow from before His face. 16 All the eagles and vultures and ravens and kites were gathered together, and all the sheep of the field came with them; yes, they all came together, and helped each other to break that horn of the ram.

17 "And I saw that man, who wrote the book according to the command of the Master, until he opened that book concerning the destruction which those twelve last shepherds had wrought, and showed that they had destroyed much more than their predecessors, before the Master of the sheep. 18 And I saw until the Master of the sheep came to them and took in His hand the staff of His wrath, and struck the earth, and the earth split apart, and all the beasts and all the birds of the heaven fell from among those sheep, and were swallowed up in the earth and it covered them.

19 "And I saw until a great sword was given to the sheep, and the sheep proceeded against all the beasts of the field to slay them, and all the beasts and the birds of the heaven fled before

---

[a] **90:1** Some Ethiopic texts read ፴ ወ ፯ meaning "thirty-seven." Charles' suggestion was to amend this to thirty-five, as other texts read. Also, verse **5** gives the numbers **23** and **58**, so the missing part of the equation must be **35** [**35** + **23** = **58**].

[b] **90:10** Presumably Alexander the Great.

their face. **20** And I saw until a throne was erected in the pleasant land, and the Master of the sheep sat Himself on it, and the other took the sealed books and opened those books before the Master of the sheep. **21** And the Master called those men the seven first white ones, and commanded that they should bring before Him, beginning with the first star which led the way, all the stars whose privy members were like those of horses, and they brought them all before Him.

22 "And He said to that man who wrote before Him, being one of those seven white ones, and said to him, 'Take those seventy[a] shepherds to whom I delivered the sheep, and who taking them on their own authority slew more than I commanded them.' **23** And behold they were all bound, I saw, and they all stood before Him. **24** And the judgment was held first over the stars, and they were judged and found guilty, and went to the place of condemnation, and they were cast into an abyss, full of fire and flaming, and full of pillars of fire.[b] **25** And those seventy shepherds were judged and found guilty, and they were cast into that fiery abyss.

26 "And I saw at that time how something like an abyss was opened in the midst of the earth, full of fire, and they brought those blinded sheep, and they were all judged and found guilty and cast into this fiery abyss, and they burned; now this abyss was to the right of that house. **27** And I saw those sheep burning and their bones burning. **28** And I stood up to see until they folded up that old house; and carried off all the pillars, and all the beams and ornaments of the house were at the same time folded up with it, and they carried it off and laid it in a place in the south of the land. **29** And I saw until the Master of the sheep brought a new house greater and loftier than that first, and set it up in the place of the first which had been folded up: all its pillars were new, and its ornaments were new and larger than those of the first, the old one which He had taken away, and all the sheep were within it.

30 "And I saw all the sheep which had been left, and all the beasts on the earth, and all the birds of the heaven, falling down and doing homage to those sheep and making petition to and obeying them in everything. **31** And after that, those three who were clothed in white[c] and had seized me by my hand who had taken me up before, and the hand of that ram also seizing hold of me, they took me up and set me down in the midst of those sheep before the judgment took place. **32** And those sheep were all white, and their wool was abundant and clean.

33 And all that had been destroyed and dispersed, and all the beasts of the field, and all the birds of the heaven, assembled in that house, and the Master of the sheep rejoiced with great joy because they were all good and had returned to His house. **34** And I saw until they laid down that sword, which had been given to the sheep, and they brought it back into the house, and it was sealed before the presence of the Master, and all the sheep were invited into that house, but it did not hold them. **35** And the eyes of them all were opened, and they saw the good, and there was not one among them that did not see. **36** And I saw that that house was large and broad and very full.

37 "And I saw that a white bull was born, with large horns and all the beasts of the field and all the birds of the air feared him and made petition to him all the time. **38** And I saw until all their generations were transformed, and they all became white bulls; and the first among them became a lamb, and that lamb became a great animal and had great black horns on its head; and the Master of the sheep rejoiced over it and over all the oxen.[d]

39 "And I slept in their midst: and I awoke and saw everything. **40** This is the vision which I saw while I slept, and I awoke and blessed the Master of righteousness and gave Him glory. **41** Then I wept with a great weeping and my tears did not stop until I could no longer endure it: when I saw, they flowed on account of what I had seen;

---

[a] **90:22** Some Ethiopic texts read ፯ meaning "seven" here.

[b] **90:24** Compare Yehudah [Jude] **6-7**; Hit'galut [Revelation] **12:4**; Kepha 𐤁 [2 Peter] **2:4-11**.

[c] **90:31** See Hit'galut [Revelation] **3:5**.

[d] **90:37-38** See Yoḥanan 𐤀 [1 John] **3:2**.

for everything shall come and be fulfilled, and all the deeds of men in their order were shown to me. 42 On that night I remembered the first dream, and because of it I wept and was troubled: because I had seen that vision."

Book V: Epistle of Ḥanokh

Ḥanokh's Exhortation for His Children

91 1 "And now, my son Methushelaḥ, call to me all your brothers and gather together to me all the sons of your mother. For the word calls me, and the spirit is poured out upon me, that I may show you everything that shall befall you forever."

2 And then Methushelaḥ went and summoned to him all his brothers and assembled his relatives. 3 And he spoke to all the children of righteousness and said, "Hear, you sons of Ḥanokh, all the words of your father, and listen to the voice of my mouth; for I exhort you and say to you, beloved: Love uprightness and walk in it. 4 And do not draw near to uprightness with a double heart, and do not associate with those of a double heart, but walk in righteousness, my sons. And it shall guide you on good paths, and righteousness shall be your companion.

5 "For I know that violence must increase on the earth, and a great chastisement be executed on the earth, and all unrighteousness come to an end: Yes, it shall be cut off from its roots, and its whole structure be destroyed. 6 And unrighteousness shall again be consummated on the earth, and all the deeds of unrighteousness and of violence and transgression shall prevail twice as much. 7 And when sin and unrighteousness and blasphemy and violence in all kinds of deeds increase, and apostasy and transgression and uncleanness increase, a great chastisement shall come from heaven upon all these, and the set-apart Master will come forth with wrath and chastisement to execute judgment on earth.

8 "In those days violence shall be cut off from its roots, and the roots of unrighteousness together with deceit, and they shall be destroyed from under heaven. 9 And all the idols of the heathen shall be abandoned, and the temples burned with fire, and they shall remove them from the whole earth, and *the heathen* shall be cast into the judgment of fire, and shall perish in wrath and in grievous judgment forever.

10 "And the righteous one shall arise from his sleep, and wisdom shall arise, and he shall be given to them. 11 And after that the roots of unrighteousness shall be cut off, and the sinners shall be destroyed by the sword, and they shall be cut off from the blasphemers in every place, and those who plan violence and those who commit blasphemy shall perish by the sword.

12 "Then after that, in the second eight week – the week of righteousness – a sword will be given to all the righteous, in to exact a righteous judgment on all the wicked, and they will be delivered into the hands of the righteous. 13 At its end, they will acquire riches in righteousness, and a royal Temple will be built for the Great King in glory forevermore.

14 "Then after that in the ninth week the righteous judgment will be revealed to the whole earth. All the deeds of the sinners will depart from the whole earth, and [they will be cast into the *eternal* pit][a], and all the people will look to the path of uprightness.

15 "Then after this matter, on the tenth week in the seventh part, there shall be the eternal judgment; and it shall be executed by the messengers of the eternal heaven – the great judgment which emanates from all of the messengers. 16 [And in the *end of the tenth week*][b] the first heaven will depart and pass away; a new heaven will appear, and all the powers of heaven will rise forever with sevenfold brightness.[c]

---

[a] **91:14** Bracketed section indicates reading present in Aramaic fragment. Ethiopic text reads, "written off for eternal destruction" here instead.

[b] **91:16** Bracketed section indicates reading present in Aramaic fragment but absent from Ethiopic texts.

[c] **91:16** See also Yeshayahu [Isaiah] **30:26**; Hit'galut [Revelation] **21:1**.

17 "Then after that there will be many weeks
without number forever; in which they will work
goodness and righteousness, and sin will not be
heard of anymore.

18 "And now I tell you, my sons, and show you
the paths of righteousness and the paths of
violence. Yes, I will show them to you again that
you may know what will come to pass. 19 And
now, listen to me, my sons, and walk in the paths
of righteousness, and do not walk in the paths of
violence; for all who walk in the paths of
unrighteousness shall perish forever."

92 1 The [a]book written by Ḥanokh – Ḥanokh
indeed wrote this complete doctrine of wisdom,
which is praised by all men and a judge of all the
earth, "for all my children who shall dwell on the
earth. And for the future generations who shall
observe uprightness and peace.

2 "Let your spirit not be troubled on account of
the times; for the Set-Apart and Great One has
appointed days for all things. 3 And the righteous
one shall arise from sleep, shall arise and walk in
the paths of righteousness, and all his path and
conversation shall be in eternal goodness and
favor. 4 He will show favor to the righteous and
give him eternal uprightness, and He will give
him power so that he will be *endowed* with
goodness and righteousness. And he will walk in
eternal light.[b]

5 "And sin shall perish in darkness forever, and
shall no more be seen from that day on, for all
generations forever."

Recounting of Weeks

93 1 And after that Ḥanokh both gave and began
to recount from the books. 2 And Ḥanokh said,
"Concerning the children of righteousness and
concerning the elect of the world, and
concerning the plant of uprightness, I will speak
these things: yes, I Ḥanokh will declare *them* to
you, my sons. According to that which appeared
to me in the heavenly vision, and which I have
known through the word of the set-apart
Watchers, and have learned from the heavenly
tablets."

3 And Ḥanokh began to recount from the books
and said, "I was born the seventh in the first
week, while judgment and righteousness still
endured. 4 And after me there shall arise in the
second week great wickedness, and deceit shall
have sprung up; and in it there shall be the first
end. And in it a man shall be saved; and after it
is ended unrighteousness shall grow up, and a
law shall be made for the sinners.[c]

5 "And after that in the third week at its close a
man shall be elected as the plant of righteous
judgment, and his posterity shall become the
plant of righteousness for evermore.

6 "And after that in the fourth week, at its close,
visions of the set-apart and righteous shall be
seen, and a law for all generations and an
enclosure shall be made for them.

7 "And after that in the fifth week, at its close,
the house of glory and dominion shall be built
forever.

8 "And after that in the sixth week all who live in
it shall be blinded, and all their hearts shall
wickedly forsake wisdom. And in it a man shall
ascend; and at its close the house of dominion
shall be burnt with fire, and the whole race of the
chosen root shall be dispersed.

9 "And after that in the seventh week shall an
apostate generation arise, and its deeds will be
numerous, and all its deeds will be done in
apostasy. 10 And at its end the elect will be
chosen, for witnesses to righteousness, from the
eternal plant of righteousness, to whom
sevenfold wisdom and knowledge[d] [concerning
all His flock][e] will be given.

11 "For who is there of all the children of men
that is able to hear the voice of the Set-Apart
One without being troubled? And who can think

[a] **92:1** Some Ethiopic texts state that this begins the "fifth" book.

[b] **92:4** See Yoḥanan ፊ [1 John] **1**:7.

[c] **93:4** See Timotheos A [1 Timothy] **1**:9.

[d] **93:10** Ethiopic text reads ትምህርት (*t'm'h'r't'*), meaning "instruction" here, rather than "wisdom and knowledge" as found in the Aramaic fragment.

[e] **93:10** Bracketed section not present in Aramaic text.

His thoughts? And who is there that can behold
all the works of heaven? **12** And how should
there be one who could behold the heaven, and
who is there that could understand the things of
heaven and see a being or a spirit and could tell
thereof, or ascend and see all their ends and think
them or do like them?

13 "And who is there of all men that could know
what is the breadth and the length of the earth,
and to whom has been shown the measure[a] of all
of them? **14** Or is there anyone who could discern
the length of the heaven and how great is its
height, and upon what it is founded, and how
great is the number of the stars, and where all the
luminaries rest?"

Ḥanokh's Advice to His Children & the Righteous

94 **1** "And now I say to you, my sons, love
righteousness and walk in it; for the paths of
righteousness are worthy of being embraced, but
the paths of unrighteousness will suddenly be
destroyed and vanish. **2** And to certain men of a
generation shall the paths of violence and of
death be revealed, and they shall hold themselves
afar from them, and shall not follow them. **3** And
now I say to you, the righteous: do not walk in
the paths of wickedness, nor in the paths of
death, and do not draw near to them, or else you
will be destroyed.

4 "But seek and choose for yourselves
righteousness and an elect life, and walk in the
paths of peace, and you shall live and prosper.
5 And hold fast my words in the thoughts of your
hearts, and do not allow them to be removed
from your hearts. For I know that sinners will
tempt men to evilly-entreat wisdom, so that no
place may be found for her, and no manner of
temptation may lessen.

Woes to the Unrighteous

6 "Woe to those who build unrighteousness and
oppression and lay deceit as a foundation, for
they shall be suddenly overthrown, and they
shall have no peace.

7 "Woe to those who build their houses with sin;
for shall they be overthrown from all their
foundations, and they shall fall by the sword.
And those who acquire gold and silver in
judgment suddenly shall perish.[b]

8 "Woe to you, you rich, for you have trusted in
your riches, and from your riches shall you
depart, because you have not remembered the
Most High in the days of your riches. **9** You have
committed blasphemy and unrighteousness, and
have become ready for the day of slaughter, and
the day of darkness and the day of the great
judgment.

10 "Thus I speak and declare to you: He who has
created you will overthrow you, and there will be
no compassion for your fall, and your Creator
will rejoice at your destruction. **11** And your
righteous ones will be a reproach to the sinners
and the wicked in those days."

Ḥanokh's Sorrow

95 **1** "Oh that my eyes were a cloud of waters
that I might weep over you, and pour down my
tears as a cloud of waters, so that I might rest
from my trouble of heart! **2** Who has permitted
you to practice reproaches and wickedness? And
so judgment shall overtake you, sinners.

3 "Do not fear the sinners, O you righteous; for
𐤉𐤄𐤅𐤄 will deliver them into your hands again,
that you may execute judgment upon them
according to your desires.

More Woes to the Unrighteous

4 "Woe to you who rant curses which cannot be
reversed. Because of your sins, healing shall be
far from you.

5 "Woe to you who repay your neighbor with
evil; for you shall be repaid according to your
works.[c]

---

[a] **93:13** Aramaic fragment reads 𐤑𐤅𐤓𐤕𐤀 (*tsur'tah*) meaning "image" or "shape" instead of "measure."

[b] **94:7** Compare Ya'aqov [James] **5:1-6**.

[c] **95:5** See also Mishlei [Proverbs] **24:12**; Mattithyahu [Matthew] **16:27**; Romaious [Romans] **2:6**.

6 "Woe to you, lying witnesses, and to those who weigh out injustice, for you shall suddenly perish.

7 "Woe to you, sinners, for you persecute the righteous. For you shall be delivered up and persecuted because of injustice, and its yoke shall be heavy upon you."

Hope for the Righteous

96 1 "Be hopeful, you righteous; for suddenly shall the sinners perish before you, and you shall have rule over them according to your desires.

2 "And in the day of the affliction of the sinners, your children shall mount and rise as eagles,[a] and your nest will be higher than the vultures and you shall ascend and enter the crevices of the earth, and the clefts of the rock forever as conies before the unrighteous, and the sirens shall sigh and weep because of you.

3 "So do not fear, you that have suffered; for healing shall be your portion, and a bright light shall enlighten you, and you shall hear the voice of rest from heaven.

4 "Woe to you, you sinners, for your riches make you appear like the righteous, but your hearts convict you of being sinners, and this fact shall be a witness against you for a memorial of your evil deeds.

More Woes to the Unrighteous

5 Woe to you who devour the finest of the wheat, and drink wine in large bowls, and tread underfoot the lowly with your might.

6 "Woe to you who drink water from every fountain, for suddenly you shall be consumed and wither away, because you have forsaken the fountain of life.

7 "Woe to you who work unrighteousness and deceit and blasphemy. It shall be a memorial against you for evil.

8 "Woe to you, you mighty, who with might oppress the righteous; for the day of your destruction is coming. In those days many and good days shall come to the righteous, *and this* in the day of your judgment."

The Judgment & Destruction of Sinners

97 1 "Believe, O you righteous, that the sinners will become ashamed and perish in the day of unrighteousness.

2 "Let it be known to you, sinners, that the Most High is mindful of your destruction, and the messengers of heaven rejoice over your
destruction. 3 What will you do, sinners, and where will you flee on that day of judgment, when you hear the voice of the prayer of the righteous?

4 "Yes, you shall be treated like them, against whom this word shall be a witness: 'You have
been companions of sinners.[b]' 5 And in those
days the prayer of the righteous shall reach to the Master, and for you the days of your judgment
shall come. 6 And all the words of your unrighteousness shall be read out before the Great Set-Apart One, and your faces shall be covered with shame, and He will reject every work which is grounded on unrighteousness.

More Woes to the Unrighteous

7 "Woe to you, you sinners, who live on the mid ocean and on the dry land, whose remembrance
is evil against you. 8 Woe to you who acquire silver and gold in unrighteousness and say, 'We have become rich with riches and have possessions; and have acquired everything we
have desired 9 And now let us do what we purposed; for we have gathered silver, and there are many workmen in our houses. And our granaries are full *to the* brim as with water.'[c]

10 "Yes and like water your lies shall flow away; for your riches shall not abide, but speedily ascend from you; for you have acquired it all in

---

[a] **96:2** Compare Shemoth [Exodus] **19:4**; Yeshayahu [Isaiah] **40:31**; Hit'galut [Revelation] **12:4**.
[b] **97:4** Compare Iyyov [Job] **34:8**; Korinthious A [1 Corinthians] **15:33**.
[c] **97:9** Compare Loukas [Luke] **12:16-21**.

unrighteousness, and you shall be given over to a great curse."

Overindulgence of the Rich

98 1 "And now I swear to you, to the wise and to the foolish, for you shall have various experiences on the earth. 2 For you men shall put on more adornments than a woman, and colored garments more than a virgin. In royalty and in grandeur and in power, and in silver and in gold and in purple, and in splendor and in food they shall be poured out as water.

3 "Therefore they shall be lacking doctrine and wisdom, and they shall perish thereby together with their possessions; and with all their glory and their splendor, and in shame and in slaughter and in great destitution, their beings shall be cast away. 4 I have sworn to you, you sinners, as a mountain has not become a slave, and a hill does not become the handmaid of a woman, even so sin has not been sent upon the earth; but man has created it himself, and all who commit it shall fall under a great curse.

5 "And barrenness has not been given to the woman, but on account of the deeds of her own hands she dies without children. 6 I have sworn to you, you sinners, by the Set-Apart Great One, that all your evil deeds are revealed in the heavens, and that none of your deeds of oppression are covered and hidden.

7 "And do not think in your spirit nor say in your heart that you do not know and that you do not see that every sin is recorded in heaven in the presence of the Most High daily. 8 From now on you know that all your oppression with which you oppress is written down every day until the day of your judgment.

More Woes to the Unrighteous

9 "Woe to you, you fools, for through your foolishness you shall perish; and *because* you transgress against the wise, so goodness shall not be your portion. 10 And now, know that you are prepared for the day of destruction; so do not hope to live, you sinners, but you shall depart and die; for you know no ransom; for you are prepared for the day of the great judgment, for the day of affliction and great shame for your spirits.

11 "Woe to you, you obstinate of heart, who work wickedness and eat blood.[a] Since when have you good things to eat and to drink and to be filled with? From all the good things which the Most High Master has placed in abundance on the earth; therefore you shall have no peace. 12 Woe to you who love the deeds of unrighteousness. Why do you hope for goodness to yourselves? Know that you shall be delivered into the hands of the righteous, and they shall cut off your necks and slay you, and have no kindness upon you. 13 Woe to you who rejoice in the affliction of the righteous; for no grave shall be dug for you. 14 Woe to you who bring the words of the righteous to nothing; for you shall have no hope of life. 15 Woe to you who write down lying and wicked words; for they write down their lies that men may hear them and act wickedly towards *their* neighbor.[b] 16 Therefore they shall have no peace but die a sudden death."

99 1 "Woe to you who work wickedness, and glory in lying and extol them; you shall perish, and shall not have a happy life. 2 Woe to them who pervert the words of uprightness, and transgress the eternal law[c], and transform themselves into what they were not: into sinners. They shall be trodden under foot upon the earth.

3 "In those days make ready, you righteous, to raise your prayers as a memorial, and place them as a witness before the messengers, that they may place the sin of the sinners for a memorial before the Most High.[d] 4 In those days the nations shall be stirred up, and the families of the nations shall arise on the day of destruction. 5 And in those days the *women* shall go forth and become pregnant, but *the sinners* shall cast out and tear out their infants, and cast them from

---

[a] **98:11** See also Bereshiyt [Genesis] **9:4**; Vayyiqra [Leviticus] **19:26**; Devarim [Deuteronomy] **12:23**; Ma'asei [Acts] **15:20-29**.

[b] **98:15** Compare Yirmeyahu [Jeremiah] **8:8**.

[c] **99:2** One Greek fragment reads διαθηκη (*diatheke*) meaning "covenant" instead of "law."

[d] **99:3** See Ma'asei [Acts] **10:4**.

their midst. Yes, they shall abandon their *other* children and their nurslings, and not return to them, and shall have no pity on their beloved ones.

6 "And again I swear to you, you sinners, that sin is prepared for a day of unceasing bloodshed.
7 And they who worship stones, and graven images of gold and silver and wood and stone and clay, and those who worship unclean spirits and demons, and all kinds of idols not according to knowledge, shall get no manner of help from them.[a]

8 "And they shall become wicked by reason of the foolishness of their hearts, and their eyes shall be blinded through the fear of their hearts
and through visions in their dreams. 9 They shall
become wicked and fearful through these; for they shall have worked all their work in a lie, and shall have worshiped a stone. Therefore in an instant they shall perish.

10 "But in those days blessed are all they who accept the words of wisdom, and understand them, and observe the paths of the Most High, and walk in the path of His righteousness, and do not *act* wickedly with the wicked; for they shall be saved.

11 "Woe to you who spread evil to your neighbors; for you shall be slain in Sheol.
12 Woe to you who make deceitful and false measures, and *to them* who cause bitterness on the earth, for they shall thereby be utterly
consumed. 13 Woe to you who build your houses
through the grievous toil of others, and all their building materials are the bricks and stones of sin; I tell you, you foolish men shall have no peace.

14 "Woe to them who reject the measure and eternal heritage of their fathers and whose beings follow after idols, for they shall have no rest.
15 Woe to them who work unrighteousness and assist oppression and slay their neighbors until
the day of the great judgment. 16 For He shall
cast down your glory, and bring affliction on your hearts, and shall arouse His fierce indignation, and destroy you all with the sword. And all the set-apart and righteous shall remember your sins."

Final Judgment

100 1 "And in those days the fathers shall be beaten in one place together with their sons and brothers one with another shall fall in death until
the streams flow with their blood. 2 For a man
shall not withhold his hand from slaying his sons and his sons' sons, and the sinner shall not withhold his hand from his honored brother[b], from dawn until sunset they shall slay one another.

3 "And the horse shall walk up to the breast in the blood of sinners, and the chariot shall be
submerged to its height.[c] 4 In those days the
messengers shall descend into the secret places and gather together into one place all those who brought down sin and the Most High will arise on that day of judgment to execute great judgment among sinners.

5 "And He will appoint guardians from among the set-apart messengers over all the righteous and set-apart to guard them as the apple of an eye, until He makes an end of all wickedness and all sin; and though the righteous sleep a long sleep, they have nothing to fear.

6 "And the children of the earth shall see the wise in security, and shall understand all the words of this book, and recognize that their riches shall not be able to save them in the overthrow of their sins.

7 "Woe to you, Sinners, on the day of strong anguish; you who afflict the righteous and burn them with fire. You shall be repaid according to
your works. 8 Woe to you, you obstinate of heart,
who watch in order to devise wickedness. Therefore fear shall come upon you, and there
shall be none to help you. 9 Woe to you, you
sinners, on account of the words of your mouth, and on account of the deeds of your hands which

---

[a] **99**:7 See Hit'galut [Revelation] **9**:**20**.
[b] **100**:2 Honored brother – Or, as it is in one Greek fragment, "man of worth."
[c] **100**:3 See Yeshayahu [Isaiah] **63**:**3**; Yechezqel [Ezekiel] **32**:**6**; Hit'galut [Revelation] **14**:**20**.

your wickedness has worked. You shall burn in
blazing flames burning worse than fire.

10 "And now, know that from the messengers He
will inquire as to your deeds in heaven, from the
sun and from the moon and from the stars in
reference to your sins because upon the earth you
execute judgment on the righteous. 11 And He
will summon every cloud and mist and dew and
rain to witness against you; for they shall all be
withheld because of you from descending upon
you, and they shall be mindful of your sins.
12 And now give presents to the rain so that it
will not be withheld from descending upon you,
nor yet the dew, when it has received gold and
silver from you that it may descend. 13 When the
hoar-frost and snow with their cold, and all the
snow-storms with all their plagues fall upon you,
in those days you shall not be able to stand
before them."

Fear of the Most High

101 1 "Observe the heavens, O you children of
heaven, and every work of the Most High, and
fear Him and work no evil in His presence. 2 If
He closes the windows of heaven, and withholds
the rain and the dew from descending on the
earth on your account, what will you do then?
3 And if He sends His anger upon you because of
your deeds, you cannot petition Him, for you
spoke proud and arrogant words against His
righteousness: therefore you shall have no peace.

4 Do you not see the sailors[a] of the ships, how
their ships are tossed to and fro by the waves,
and are shaken by the winds, and are in sore
trouble? 5 And therefore they fear because all
their good possessions go upon the sea with
them, and they have evil premonitions of heart
that the sea will swallow them and they will
perish in it.

6 "Is not the entire sea and all its waters, and all
its movements, the work of the Most High, and
has He not set limits to its doings, and confined
it throughout by the sand? 7 And at His reproof it
is afraid and dries up, and all its fish die and all
that is in it. But you sinners that are on the earth
do not fear Him. 8 Has He not made the heaven
and the earth, and all that is in them? Who has
given understanding and wisdom to everything
that moves on the earth and in the sea? 9 Do the
sailors of ships not fear the sea? Yet sinners do
not fear the Most High."

Terror of the Day of Judgment

102 1 "[In those days][b] when He has brought a
grievous fire upon you, to where will you flee,
and where will you find deliverance? And when
He launches forth His Word against you, will
you not be afraid and fear? 2 And all the
luminaries shall be afraid with great fear, and all
the earth shall be afraid and tremble and be
alarmed.

3 "And all the messengers shall execute their
commands and shall seek to hide themselves
from the presence of the Great Glory, and the
children of earth shall tremble and quake. And
you sinners shall be cursed forever, and you shall
have no peace.

Comfort for the Righteous who Suffer

4 "Fear not, O you beings of the righteous, and
be hopeful, you that have died in righteousness.
5 And do not grieve if your being has descended
into Sheol in grief, and that in your life your
body did not fare according to your goodness.
[But wait for the day of the judgment of sinners][c]
and for the day of cursing and chastisement.

6 "And yet when you die the sinners speak over
you, 'As we die, so the righteous also die, and
what benefit do they reap for their deeds?
7 Behold, even as we *die*, so do they die: in grief
and darkness, and what have they more than we?
From now on we are equal. 8 And what will they
receive and what will they see forever? Behold,

---

[a] **101:4** Ethiopic texts read ነገሥተ (*nagas'ta*) meaning "kings" here. *Nagas'* is the Ethiopic equivalent of the Hebrew / Aramaic מלך (*me'lekh*) which means "king." However, the word for sailor is מלח (*ma'laḥ*). In Greek it also reads "sailors" and thus it is possible that *ma'laḥ* is the original, and the Ethiopic translator mistakenly "restored" it to *nagas*, thinking the original to be *melek*.

[b] **102:1** Bracketed section not present in Greek fragment.

[c] **102:5** Bracketed section reads "the days that you lived were days of sinners" in the Greek fragment.

they too have died, and from now even forever they shall see no light.'

9 "I tell you, you sinners, you are content to eat and drink, and rob and sin, and strip men naked, and acquire wealth and see good days. 10 Have you seen the righteous; how their end falls out, that no manner of violence is found in them *even* until their death? 11 Nevertheless they perished and became as though they had not been, and their beings descended into Sheol in affliction.'"

The Ends of the Righteous and the Unrighteous

103 1 "Now, therefore, I swear to you, the righteous, by the glory of the Great and Honored and Mighty One in dominion, and by His greatness I swear to you:

2 "I know a mystery and have read the heavenly tablets, and have seen the set-apart books, and have found written in them and inscribed regarding them *this*:

3 "That all goodness and joy and glory are prepared for them, and written down for the spirits of those who have died in righteousness, and that manifold good shall be repaid to you for your labors, and that your lot is abundantly beyond the lot of the living. 4 And the spirits of you who have died in righteousness shall live and rejoice, and their spirits shall not perish, nor their memorial from before the face of the Great One, to all the generations of the world; so do not fear their reproach any longer.

5 "Woe to you, you sinners, when you have died, if you die in the wealth of your sins. And those who are like you say regarding you, 'Blessed are the sinners, for they have seen all their days.
6 And how they have died in prosperity and in wealth, and have not seen affliction or murder in their life. And they have died in honor, and judgment has not been executed on them during their life.'

7 "Know that their beings will be made to descend into Sheol and they shall be wretched in their great affliction. 8 And into darkness and chains and a burning flame – where there is grievous judgment – shall your spirits enter. And the great judgment shall be for all the generations of the world. Woe to you, for you shall have no peace.

9 "Do not say in regard to the righteous and good who are in life, 'In our troubled days we have toiled laboriously and experienced every trouble, and met with much evil and been consumed, and have become few and our spirit small. 10 And we have been destroyed and have not found any to help us even with a word. We have been tortured and destroyed, and not hoped to see life from day to day.

11 "'We hoped to be the head and have become the tail. We have toiled laboriously and had no satisfaction in our toil. We have become the food of the sinners and the unrighteous, and they have laid their yoke heavily upon us. 12 They have had dominion over us, *even those* that hated us and killed us; and to those that hated us we have bowed our necks but they have not pitied us.

13 "'We desired to get away from them that we might escape and be at rest, but found no place where we should flee to and be safe from them.
14 And have complained to the rulers in our affliction, and cried out against those who devoured us; but they did not attend to our cries and would not listen to our voice.

15 "'And they helped those who robbed us and devoured us and those who made us few; and they concealed their oppression, and they did not remove from us the yoke of those that devoured us and dispersed us and murdered us, and they concealed the fact of our being murdered, and did not remember that they had lifted up their hands against us.'"

104 1 "I swear to you, that in heaven the messengers remember you for good before the glory of the Great One, and your names are written before the glory of the Great One. 2 Be hopeful, for you were previously put to shame through illness and affliction. But now you shall shine as the lights of heaven, you shall shine and you shall be seen, and the gates of heaven shall be opened to you. 3 And in your cry, cry for judgment, and it shall appear to you; for all your affliction shall be visited on the rulers, and on all who helped those who plundered you. 4 Be hopeful, and do not cast away your hopes, for you shall have great joy as the messengers of heaven. **5** What shall you be obliged to do? You shall not have to hide on the day of the great judgment and you shall not be found as sinners, and the eternal judgment shall be far from you for all the generations of the world. **6** And now fear not, you righteous, when you see the sinners growing strong and prospering in their ways. Do not be companions with them, but keep far from their violence; for you shall become companions of the hosts of heaven.

7 "And although you sinners say, 'All our sins shall not be searched out and be written down,' nevertheless they shall write down all your sins every day. **8** And now I show to you that light and darkness, day and night, see all your sins. **9** Do not be wicked in your hearts, and do not lie, and do not alter the words of uprightness, nor charge with lying the words of the Set-Apart Great One, nor take account of your idols; for all your lying and all your wickedness do not go forth in righteousness but in great sin.

10 "And now I know this mystery, that sinners will alter and pervert the words of righteousness in many ways, and will speak wicked words, and lie, and practice great deceits, and write false books concerning their words.[a] **11** But when they write down truthfully all my words in their languages, and do not change or lessen anything from my words, but write them all down truthfully: all that I first witnessed concerning them. **12** Then, I know another mystery, that books will be given to the righteous and the wise to become a cause of joy and uprightness and much wisdom. **13** And the books will be given to them, and they will believe in them and rejoice over them, and then all the righteous who have learned from them all the paths of uprightness will be repaid."

Teaching Wisdom to the Children of the Earth

105 **1** In those days [𐤉𐤄𐤅𐤄 appointed *the righteous* over the children of the earth, to read *the books*, and to witness about them according to their wisdom, saying, "Show them *wisdom*, for you are to lead them, and you will receive your reward from all the children of earth. **2** And you will have reward. Be glad, O you children of righteousness."] [b]

Birth of Noaḥ

106 **1** And after some time [I, Ḥanokh, took a wife for my son Methushelaḥ, and she brought forth a son and called his name Lamekh, saying, 'Righteousness has indeed been brought low today.' And when he grew,][c] my son Methushelaḥ took a wife for his son Lamekh, and she became pregnant by him and bore a boy. **2** And *when he was born,* his body was as white as snow, and as red as[d] a rose, and the hair of his head and his long locks were white as wool, and his {demdema}[e] was beautiful. And when he opened his eyes, he lit up the whole house like the sun, and the whole house was very bright. **3** And then he arose in the hands of the midwife, opened his mouth, and spoke to the Master with righteousness.[f] **4** And his father Lamekh was afraid of him and fled, and came to his father Methushelaḥ. **5** And he said to him, "A strange son has been born to me, different than – and unlike – man, and resembling the sons of the messengers of heaven; and his nature is different and he is not like us, and his eyes are as the rays of the sun, and his face is glorious. **6** And it seems to me that he is not sprung from me but from the messengers, and I fear that in his days a wonder may be worked on the earth. **7** And now,

---

[a] **104:10** Compare Yirmeyahu [Jeremiah] **8:8**; Timotheos A [**1** Timothy] **4:1-2**.

[b] **105** The above section is how chapter **105** reads based on a reconstruction of the Aramaic fragment. The Ethiopic version varies greatly, most likely due to a later Christian interpolation. The Ethiopic reading is listed in Appendix E for the reader's benefit.

[c] **106:1** Bracketed section indicates reading present in Aramaic fragment, but absent from Ethiopic, Greek, and Latin texts.

[d] **106:2** Greek fragment reads, "redder than" and "whiter than" here.

[e] **106:2** Ethiopic word ድምድማ (*dem'dema*) has no exact English equivalent. It refers to long and curly hair that has been combed up straight; perhaps the closest equivalent would be the colloquial term "afro."

[f] **106:3** Greek fragment reads, "he blessed the Master."

my father, I am here to petition you and ask that you go to Ḥanokh, our father, and learn the truth from him, for his dwelling-place is among the messengers."

8 And when Methushelaḥ heard the words of his son, he came to me to the ends of the earth; for he had heard that I was there, and he cried aloud, and I heard his voice and I came to him. And I said to him, "Behold, here am I, my son. Why have you come to me?"

9 And he answered and said, "I have come to you because of a great anxiety, and have approached because of a disturbing vision. 10 And now, my father, hear me. A son has been born to my son Lamekh, the like of whom there is none, and his nature is not like man's nature, and the color of his body is whiter than snow and redder than the bloom of a rose, and the hair of his head is whiter than white wool, and his eyes are like the rays of the sun, and he opened his eyes and lit up the whole house. 11 And he arose in the hands of the midwife, and opened his mouth and blessed the Master of heaven. 12 And his father Lamekh became afraid and fled to me, and did not believe that he was sprung from him, but *thought* that he was *born* in the likeness of the messengers of heaven. And behold I have come to you that you may make the truth known to me."

13 And I, Ḥanokh, answered and said to him, "𐤉𐤄𐤅𐤄 will renew His Torah[a] on the earth, just as I saw, and made known to you that in the generation of my father Yared some of the messengers of heaven transgressed the word of the Master, the law of heaven. 14 And behold they commit sin and transgress the law, and have united themselves with women and commit sin with them, and have married some of them, and have begotten children by them. 15 And they shall produce giants on the earth; not according to the spirit, but according to the flesh, and there shall be a great punishment on the earth, and the earth shall be cleansed from all impurity. 16 Yes, a great destruction shall come over the whole earth, and there shall be a flood and a great destruction for one year. 17 And this son who has been born to you shall be left on the earth, and his three children shall be saved with him. When all mankind that are on the earth shall die, he and his sons shall be saved. 18 And now make known to your son Lamekh that he who has been born is in truth his son, and call his name Noaḥ; for he shall be left to you, and he and his sons shall be saved from the destruction, which shall come upon the earth on account of all the sin and all the unrighteousness, which shall be consummated on the earth in his days. 19 And after that there shall be still more unrighteousness than that which was first consummated on the earth; for I know the mysteries of the set-apart ones; for He, the Master, has showed me and informed me, and I have read *this* in the heavenly tablets."

Prophecy of Apostasy

107 1 "And I saw written on *the tablets* that generation upon generation will do evil, and evil will increase until a generation of righteousness arises, and transgression is destroyed and sin passes away from the earth, and all manner of good comes upon it. 2 And now, my son, go and make known to your son Lamekh that this son, which has been born, is in truth his son, and that *this* is no lie." 3 And when Methushelaḥ had heard the words of his father Ḥanokh – for he had shown to him everything in secret – he returned and showed *them* to *Lamekh*, and called the name of that son Noaḥ; for he will comfort the earth after all the destruction.

Exhortation to Keep the Torah

108 1 Another book which Ḥanokh wrote for his son Methushelaḥ and for those who will come after him, and keep the Torah in the last days. 2 You who have done good shall wait for those days until an end is made of those who work evil; and an end of the might of the transgressors. 3 And wait indeed until sin has passed away, for their names shall be blotted out of the book of life and out of the set-apart books, and their seed shall be destroyed forever, and their beings shall be slain, and they shall cry and make lamentation in a place that is a chaotic

[a] **106:13** Ethiopic and Latin texts read, "new things" instead of "His Torah" here.

wilderness, and in the fire shall they burn; for there is no earth there.

Vision of the Flame of Judgment

4 And I saw there something like an invisible cloud; for by reason of its depth I could not look over, and I saw a flame of fire blazing brightly, and things like shining mountains circling and sweeping to and fro. 5 And I asked one of the set-apart messengers who was with me and said to him, "What is this shining thing? For it is not a heaven but only the flame of a blazing fire, and the voice of weeping and crying and lamentation and strong pain."

6 And he said to me, "This place which you see: here are cast the spirits of sinners and blasphemers, and of those who work wickedness, and of those who pervert everything that the Master has spoken through the mouth of the prophets – *even* the things that shall be. 7 For some of them are written and inscribed above in the heaven, in order that the messengers may read them and know what will happen to the sinners, and the spirits of the humble, and of those who have afflicted their bodies, and been repaid by Elohim; and of those who have been put to shame by wicked men, 8 who love Elohim and did not love gold nor silver nor any of the good things which are in the world,[a] but gave over their bodies to torture. 9 Who, since they came into being, did not long after earthly food, but regarded everything as a passing breath, and lived accordingly, and the Master tried them much, and their spirits were found pure so that they should bless His Name. 10 And all the blessings destined for them I have recounted in the books. And he has assigned them their repayment, because they have been found to be such as loved heaven more than their life in the world, and though they were trodden under foot of wicked men, and experienced abuse and reviling from them and were put to shame, yet they blessed Me.

11 "And now I will summon the spirits of the good who belong to the generation of light, and I will transform those who were born in darkness, who in the flesh were not repaid with such honor as their faith deserved. 12 And I will bring forth in shining light those who have loved My Set-Apart Name, and I will seat each on the throne of his honor.[b] 13 And they shall be magnificent for times without number; for righteousness is the judgment of Elohim. For He will give faith to the faithful in the habitation of upright paths. 14 And they shall see those who were born in darkness led into darkness, while the righteous shall be magnificent. 15 And the sinners shall cry aloud and see them magnificent, and they indeed will go where days and seasons are prescribed for them."

---

[a] **108:8** See Yoḥanan ᚐ [1 John] **2:15**.

[b] **108:12** Compare Mattithyahu [Matthew] **19:28**; Hit'galut [Revelation] **3:21**.

Editor's Preface: Jasher

Introduction

The Book of Jasher has a long and rather involved history. Perhaps the first confusing point regarding this publication is that of its title. The word "Jasher" was thought, for some time, to have been a name. However, it is actually the Hebrew word ישר (*Yashar*) which means "upright." Thus the title of the book is actually "the Book of the Upright" or possibly "the Upright Record." In Hebrew, it is written as ספר הישר (*Sefer Ha'Yashar*). It can be deduced from this title that "Jasher" is, in fact, not a name at all. This is because Hebrew names are definite by nature, and never contain the ה- (*hey*) prefix, which represents the definite article "the." One would not say "the Dan went to the store" or "the Gavin bought a gallon of milk." Even in English we do not add the definite article "the" to proper nouns, except to stress singularity. That is, if one were to say for example, "you mean you saw THE Johnny Cash?"

Next it must be established which "version" is present in this text, and which is not. To those unaware, there are three different primary works that all bear the title of the "Sefer Ha'Yashar" and only one is thought to possibly be authentic.

The first of these three that I will mention was published in 1751, and has a title page that states, "The Book of Jasher: translated into English by Flaccus Albinus Alcuinus, of Britain, Abbot of Canterbury, who went on a pilgrimage into the Holy Land and Persia, where he discovered this volume in the city of Gazna." This work claims to be the book mentioned in the Scriptural books of Joshua and 2 Samuel. The provenance of the book was immediately questioned, as the English style was that of the 17th and 18th centuries, not that of the 8th century, in which Alcuin the abbot truly lived. During the 8th century only Old English (Anglo-Saxon) existed, and Latin was still the "ecclesiastical language" of the time. That is, any "religious" book of the Church was only written in Latin, or of the Jews written in Semitic (be it Hebrew or Aramaic), nothing else. A month after its publication the printer declared the book to be false, and was subsequently sentenced to prison.

There are, even to the date of this printing (2016) groups that consider this work to be inspired, namely the Rosicrucians. There was a revised version of this work released in 1829, and many of these reproductions exist even to this day. The text presented here is **NOT** this version.

Another book by the same title (or rather, its Hebrew title, *Sefer Ha'Yashar*) is a book written by Rabbi Jacob ben Meir (aka Rabbeinu Tam) in the 12th century. This book is a treatise which seeks to resolve Talmudic textual problems, without ever suggesting amending the text of the Talmud itself. Today there are multiple variations of this work known, as multiple copies have been reproduced from the extant fragments. Though this writing does not claim to be the Book of Jasher referenced in Scripture. The text presented here is **NOT** this version.

This version of the Book of Jasher is based on the 1887 publication by J. H. Parry and Company. This text is, itself, a revision of the 1840 English translation by Moses Samuel.

The original Hebrew has its own Preface (see section *Translation of the Hebrew Preface*) which claims to be from the 1st century CE. According to this writing – which appears to be from the original printer, either in 1552 or in 1625 – Jasher was well-known in his day, and had been preserved throughout Egypt (Mitsrayim). He claims that during the era of the Hasmoneans (the Maccabean era), king Ptolemy of Egypt demanded that his servants bring him all sorts of books so that he could study them and become wise. It states that the Jews (Yehudim) gave him the book of Jasher, but led him to believe it was the Torah. After a while Ptolemy learned the truth, and was greatly angered. So he gathered seventy elders of Yisrael and kept them all isolated from one another, and had them all write a copy of the Torah. Much to Ptolemy's delight, they all produced an identical copy of the Torah, which Ptolemy studied and loved. After his death, the Yisraelites then went into his treasuries and removed the Torah, since they believed it should never be given to a foreigner. However, they left Jasher in the treasury, so that it could be read by those of Mitsrayim.

Whether these claims are true or not can hardly be proved or disproved. However, even the Jewish-Roman historian Josephus writes about a book that described the sun standing still during the time of Joshua. He says this was one of the books "laid up in the Temple." (*Josephus, Antiquities of the Jews, Book V. 1.17*) Seeing he does not refer to this book in the same way as he does the books of the canonized Scriptures, it is quite possible that in this he refers to the Book of Jasher, though that cannot be ascertained for sure.

The Texts

For the source of the Book of Jasher, we sadly only have one text that is extant today. This is the Hebrew copy that was published in 1625. While we know the text was known at least as early as 1552, there is no known textual evidence aside from this.

For this translation I have chosen to emend the 1887 edition of J. H. Parry and Company's English text of Jasher, which was translated in 1840 by Moses Samuel. This work is in the public domain. Essentially, as with the other books in this publication, the English version was used as a "base" and has been emended and edited. For many readings this means going through the very slow process of completely re-translating the Hebrew text itself. I have found, through careful examination of the Hebrew text, that the 1840 translation is quite a faithful translation. However, I did discover that there were numerous times where Samuel mixed up the translation of the Hebrew 𐤀𐤋𐤄𐤉𐤌 (*Elohim*) and the placeholder for the Divine Name (𐤉𐤄𐤅𐤄), written in Hebrew as 𐤉𐤉 (see *Volume Preface* under section *The Names*). In most cases, Samuel rendered *Elohim* has "God" and the double yod (𐤉𐤉) as "the Lord." However, I found that in more than 20 instances, he rendered the double yod (𐤉𐤉) as "God" and in about a half-dozen instances rendered *Elohim* as "the Lord." In a small number of cases, one or both (God or Lord) were left out completely by Samuel, and in some places were added in when not present.

In other cases the way Samuel transliterated names of those in the book was restored to a more proper form to aid in pronunciation.

There are also certain sections that Samuel completely left out of the text. They are present in the Hebrew source, yet for some reason they did not make it into the English version.

These Hebrew sections have been added in as well. In a few isolated instances, it appears Samuel did not know the proper English *translation* for a certain word (such as in chapter 36, there were the terms "keephas" and "ducheemaths"), so he chose instead to transliterate it. For whatever reason, these terms have remained untranslated even in most modern emendations of Samuel's English translation. In these instances, such as the two listed above, I have translated these words into the English forms they take in most modern Scripture Versions (taking preference for the translation featured in the *Literal English Version of Scripture*).

One of the largest and strikingly obvious alterations made to the English text comes in the form of the language style. The original J. H. Parry publication was written in Elizabethan English, which was riddled with archaic terminology and dialogue. In order to make this a much more fluid translation I removed all of the "thees" and "thous" and "doests" and modernized the English. This should make it much easier to read to the vast majority of English-speakers.

There are numerous footnotes which help to further define certain Hebrew words, as well as to point to parallel passages in other books, particularly those in this publication. These are to assist the reader in gathering as much information about the text as possible, whether they can read Hebrew or not.

Divisions in the Text

The English version presented here follows the same chapter and verse arrangement as Samuel's English translation of 1840, since that has become the standard that most recognize. The Hebrew text of Jasher is not divided by verse numbers. Indeed, it is not even divided by chapter numbers. Rather, it is divided by *parashot*, or "portions." These portions appear in the Hebrew text and serve as dividers for the material covered in the following sections. These individual portion titles have been included in the English translation presented here as headers that are written ***bolded and italicized***. This allows the reader to see where the actual Hebrew text divides, rather than where Samuel arbitrarily chose to divide it into chapters.

As an example, the first *parashat* or "portion" that begins the book is written in the text as פרשת בראשית. This is *Parashat Bereshiyt*, or "portion in [the] beginning." It appears at the beginning of chapter 1 as ***פרשת בראשית – Parashat Bereshiyt***.

Authenticity

There are various reasons to question the authenticity of Jasher, though without a doubt there are also reasons to believe it is the authentic book referenced in Scripture. Among the supposed proofs of authenticity is the fact that it is referenced at least five times in the 66 book canon of Scripture. While only two of these are direct quotes, the other three are reasonable inferences. Consider the following passages:

> 13 The sun stood still, and the moon stayed, until the nation had avenged themselves of their enemies. Is this not written in the Book of the Upright? The sun stayed in the

> midst of the heavens, and did not hurry to go down about a whole day. – Joshua [Yehoshua] 10:13 (LEV)

Compare to that the following passage found in Jasher:

> 63 And when they were killing, the day was declining toward evening, and Yehoshua said in the sight of all the people, "Sun, you stand still upon Givon, and you, moon, in the valley of Ayalon, until the nation avenges itself upon its enemies."
>
> 64 And 𐤉𐤄𐤅𐤄 listened to the voice of Yehoshua, and the sun stood still in the midst of the heavens, and it stood still thirty-six moments, and the moon also stood still and did not hasten to go down a whole day. – Yashar 88:63-64

In the quotes above, it appears that Joshua is citing the Book of Jasher as source or reference to his own book. Now the next reference:

> 17 David lamented with this lamentation over Sha'ul and over Yehonathan his son; 18 and he commanded them to teach the children of Yehudah *to use* the bow: behold, it is written in the Book of the Upright. – 2 Samuel [Shemu'el] 1:17-18 (LEV)

Compared to:

> 9 Only teach your sons the bow and all weapons of war, in order that they may fight the battles of their brother who will rule over his enemies. – Yashar 56:9

Indeed, this appears to be two solid references from Jasher that found their way into the Tanakh. However, we could easily assume that if this book were a forgery, a Jewish scribe could have invented and simply placed those references into Jasher in an attempt to "prove" its authenticity. This, then brings us to the third reference. The third reference is not found in the Tanakh, but in the Sheliḥim Writings ('New Testament').

> 8 Even as Yanus and Yambrus opposed Moshe, so do these also oppose the truth; men corrupted in mind who, concerning the faith, are rejected.
> – 2 Timothy [Timotheos] 3:8 (LEV)

Now this does not make a reference to Jasher outright. However, which Scripture can we look up to see the story of two men, named Yanus [Jannes] and Yambrus [Jambres], opposing Moses? You can search every book in the Bible, and not once will you find these two men named. However, Jasher can answer this for us.

> 27 And when they had gone Pharaoh sent for Bil'am the magician and to Yanus and Yambrus his sons, and to all the magicians and conjurors and counsellors which belonged to the king, and they all came and sat before the king. – Yashar 79:27

The narrative here names the magicians of Pharaoh's court, the ones that performed a few signs (such as turning their staves into serpents), as the two sons of Bil'am [Balaam], Yochanai and Mambres. The narrative in Jasher continues by relating how these magicians opposed Moses and Aaron.

There is also another instance found twice in Jasher, that is possibly referenced in 1 Samuel. Here we read:

> 13 As the proverb of the ancients says, "Out of the wicked comes forth wickedness;" but my hand shall not be on you. – 1 Samuel [Shemu'el] 24:13 (LEV)

Compared to:

> 48 And everyone that heard of the acts of Mardon the son of Nimrod would say, concerning him, "Out of the wicked comes forth wickedness;" therefore it became a proverb in the whole earth, saying, "Out of the wicked comes forth wickedness," and it was current in the words of men from that time to this. – Yashar 7:48

Despite these "proofs" there are also a few issues within the text. There are some words used in the text that are written in Hebrew that did not exist at the time. These include a handful of place names that are used in chapter 10: Franza (France), Italia (Italy), Tuscanah (Tuscany), and Lumbardi (Lombard). Likewise, the territory of Afriqah (Africa) is also named. Clearly, over three thousand years ago the lands of France and Italy were not called by these names. So this must mean that Jasher was written at least around the 8th or 9th century CE at the earliest, right? Not quite. While it is clear that there were no such names lands in the time that the original book of Jasher was written (at the latest by the time of Joshua, since he mentions it), we cannot rule out the possibility of a copyist error. Indeed it is very possible that a later copier / redactor of the book filled in the modern place names, for whatever reason; such a process is somewhat common for Biblical literature, known as anachronism, and is found thoughout the Tanakh ('Old Testament'). Though it is also possible that this entire chapter is not original to the book, and was brought in as a later addition. Much in the same way that the *Book of the Parables of Enoch* may very well have been added hundreds or even thousands of years after the rest of the book was penned. We cannot rule out the very high likelihood that, if this is the real book of Jasher, it has probably been amended numerous times.

So we then must ask…if this book is a forgery of Jewish tradition, why then does it include information that is referenced by a book of Scripture which Jews reject (2 Timothy)? If the author of this book was attempting to make it look real, why would he use names that he knew were not found in the Hebrew Tanakh? Why not just copy the names of places straight from the Hebrew text of his day? Or at the very least use the names that were given to those places in Jewish tradition.

Conclusion

While the questions of authorship and authenticity remain unanswered, the Book of Jasher is, nonetheless, a fascinating read. Whether or not this book should be canonized is a matter of debate, but it is certainly interesting regardless. At worst, this book is a forgery, and provides nothing but an interesting story. In many of its passages it matches other writings of Jewish tradition, and thus perhaps can be afforded the same level of credibility as they. At best, this truly could be the actual Book of Jasher mentioned in the Scriptures, with perhaps a few inaccuracies and/or later additions.

Translation of the Hebrew Preface

This Book Is That Which Is Called The Upright Book

[Editor's note: all [bracketed] sections indicate words added for ease of reading]

It has at this time been determined by us that when the set-apart city Yerushalayim was destroyed by Titus, all the military heads went in to rob and plunder, and among the officers of Titus was one whose name was Sidrus, who went in to search, and found in Yerushalayim a house of great extent, and took away all the spoils which he found there. When he wished to leave to house, he looked at the wall and thought he saw treasures there, so he broke the wall down and the building and found a container full of various books of the Torah, the Prophets, and the Writings, as well as the books of the kings of Yisrael, and of the kings of other nations, as well as many other books of Yisrael, together with books of the Mishnah adopted and established; many rolls were also lying there. He found there all sorts of provisions and wine in abundance, and discovered an old man sitting there, who was reading the books.

When the officer saw this great sight he was exceedingly astonished. He said to the old man, "Why do you sit here alone in this place, without anyone else with you?" So the old man answered, "For many years I have been aware of this second destruction of Yerushalayim, so I built this house and made for myself a balcony, and I brought these books with me to read. I also brought many provisions, hoping to save my life with them."

And Elohim caused the old man to find favor in the eyes of the officer, who brought him forth with respect with all his books, and they went from city to city and from country to country until they reached Sevilia[a]. The officer found that this old man possessed much wisdom and understanding and was familiar with various kinds of science, upon discovering which he raised and honored him, was constantly in his house and was taught by him all sorts of wisdom, and they built for themselves a lofty and spacious house in the suburbs of Sevilia and placed all these books there.

This house is yet still in Sevilia to this day, and there they wrote all the events that would take place from now on among all the kings of the world until the coming of our Mashiach. And it came to pass that when Elohim carried us away with a mighty captivity by the hands of the kings of Edom, from city to city and country to country in bitter anxiety, this book, called "The Generations of Adam" together with other books came into our hands, for they came from that house in Sevilia, and they came afterward to our city Napuli[b], which city is under the influence of the king of Spain, (whose glory may be exalted.) And when we saw these books, that they were books of all wisdom, we resolved in our minds to print them like all the nooks that came to our hands. Now this book is the best and most valuable of all, and of this book twelve copies have reached us, and we searched in them and found them all

[a] Sevilia – Modern-day Seville, Spain.
[b] Napuli – Modern-day Naples, Italy.

of one copy, there was no difference: nothing added, and nothing removed; nor was there any alteration in letters, words, or events, for they were all alike as it were of one copy.

Since, therefore, we saw in this book great merit urging us to this decision, we are determined to print it – and it is found written that this book called the Book Yashar, because all its transactions are in that order as they had taken place in the world as regards priority and succession, for you will not find in this book any postponement of events that came before, or priority of those that came after, but everything is recorded in its place and time.

You will thus find that it relates the death of such a one at the particular time of the life of another and thus throughout. Owing to this it was called *Sefer Ha'Yashar*, but it is customary to call it the "Generations of Adam," the reason of which is that they call it by that with which it begins, but the chief name of it is the book "Yashar" owing to the reasons we have assigned. Now it is found that this book is translated into the *language* of the Greeks[a], entitled "*Lo libros de los diritos*."

It is also found written in the book of the Hasmoneans which has come down to us, that in the days of Ptolemy king of Mitsrayim, he ordered his servants to go and gather all of the books of laws, and all the books of chronicles which they could find in the world, so that he might become wise through them; and by examining them, become acquainted with the subjects and events of the world, and to compile from them a book in all matters of jurisdiction regarding the affairs of life, thereby to exercise pure justice. So they went and collected nine hundred and sixty-five books for him, and brought them to him. Then he commanded them to go again and seek to complete the number of a thousand books, and they did so. After this, some of the persecutors of Yisrael stood up before him and said, "O king, why do you trouble yourself this way? Send to the Yehudim in Yerushalayim that they bring to you the book of their Torah which was written for them from the mouth of יהוה, for they said, 'we cannot give the Torah of יהוה to a foreigner.'"

Now when this book came into the hands of Ptolemy he read it and it pleased him exceedingly, and he searched it in his wisdom, and he examined it and found in it what he desired, and he neglected all the other books which they had collected for him, and he blessed the one who had advised him to do this thing.

After some time the persecutors of Yisrael became aware of this, that the Yisraelites had not sent the book of the Torah to the king, and they came and said to him, "O king, the Yisraelites have treated you with contempt, for they did not send you the book of the Torah which we mentioned to you, but they sent you another book which they had in their hands. Therefore, send to them that they may send to you the book of the Torah, for you will obtain your desire much more from that book than from the book which they have sent to you." So when the king heard their words he became exceedingly wroth with the Yisraelites, and his

[a] This phrase in Hebrew is לו ליברוש די לוש דיריטוס, and is transliterated not from Greek but rather from Spanish, roughly meaning "the book of the rights." In Hebrew, the author uses the word היונים (*ha'Yavaniym*) where we read "the Greeks" in English. The definite article prefix *ha* (ה) and the masculine plural suffix *iym* (ים) are added to the word *Yavan*, the name of the ancestor of the Greeks (see Genesis **10**:**4** & Daniel **8**:**21**). Though there are numerous possible reasons the author chose to transliterate Spanish in Hebrew and call it Greek, the exact reason is unknown; however the author does inform the reader that he lives in Naples, and ancient Naples was known to be a hub for Hellenistic learning, containing numerous Greek settlements from the second millennia BCE. Thus it is possible that he refers to the people native to Naples as 'Greeks.'

anger burned within him until he sent again to them for them to send to him the book of the Torah. Fearing that they might still continue to scorn him, he acted cautiously with them and sent for seventy of their elders and placed them in seventy houses, that each should write the book of the Torah, so that no alteration might be found in them; and the set-apart spirit rested upon them, and they wrote seventy books for him, all of the same version, with no addition or diminution.[a] The king rejoiced greatly at this, and he honored the elders, together with all the Yehudim, and he sent offerings and gifts to Yerushalayim as it is written there [in the book of the Hasmoneans]. At his death, the Yisraelites acted cunningly with his son and took the book of the Torah from his treasures, but left this book there and did not take it away, in order that ever future king might know the wonders of 𐤉𐤄𐤅𐤄, blessed be His Name, and that He had chosen Yisrael from all nations, and there is no Elohim besides Him.

This book is therefore in Mitsrayim to this day, and from that time it became circulated throughout the earth, until it reached us in our captivity this day in the city of Napuli, which is in the domain of the king of Spain. Now you will find in the book that some of the kings of Edom, Kittim, and the kings of Africa who were in those days, are mentioned, although it might appear that such was not the aim or intent of this book; but the reason of this was to show every person obtaining this book the contrast between the wars of Yisrael and the wars of the nations, for the conquest of the kings of the nations one over the other was by accident, which is not so in the conquest of the kings of Yisrael over the nations, which is by a miracle from our blessed Master as long as the Yisraelites trusted in His exalted Name.

Now the uses of this book are many, all of which lead us to confidence in Elohim – whose Name be exalted – and to our adherence to Him and His ways.

The first use is the additional information it affords us on the subjects of the creation of man and the flood, recording also the years of the twenty generations and their misdeeds; also at what period they were born, and when they died; by which means our hearts might be inclined to adhere to 𐤉𐤄𐤅𐤄, when we see the mighty works which He performed in days of old.

The second use is in the additional account regarding the birth of Avraham and how it was that he cleaved to 𐤉𐤄𐤅𐤄, and the interactions that took place between him and Nimrod; and thus also of the account of the builders of the tower of Bavel[b], and how 𐤉𐤄𐤅𐤄 drove them to the four corners of the earth, and how they established the countries and lands called after their names to this day, by which we may draw near to our Creator.

---

[a] This is the legend of the creation of the Greek Septuagint (LXX). Though debated, it is commonly believed to have been created by **70** (or **72**) scholars and elders from all **12** tribes of Israel. Jewish Historian Philo considered the legend to be true, and wrote about it. The Pseudepigraphal book *The Letter of Aristeas* also tells of the legend, and there are even agreements found in the Talmud regarding the translation by the **70** elders. This shows that the author of this Preface believed this present book to be what was written by the **70** elders; however it is not clear if he intended his readers to believe that this book was real and the LXX was not what was written, or if he simply borrowed the story of Ptolemy and the **70** elders. Regardless, the two stories are nearly identical.

[b] In Hebrew, this reads 𐤃𐤅𐤓 𐤄𐤐𐤋𐤂𐤄 (*dur ha'pelegah*) meaning "generations divided." Compare Jasher **10**:**2** and Genesis **10**:**25**.

The third use is the explanation it gives us of how the patriarchs adhered to 𐤉𐤄𐤅𐤄, and of their interactions which convince us of their fear of Elohim.

The fourth use is in what it records of the affairs of Sodom and the iniquities of its people, and in what consisted their sins, as well as their punishment, by which means we may refrain from all evil doings.

The fifth use is in the account of the faith of Yitsḥaq and Ya'aqov in 𐤉𐤄𐤅𐤄, and the prayers and weeping of Sarah at the binding of Yitsḥaq, which is of great use in the inclining of our hearts to serving 𐤉𐤄𐤅𐤄.

The sixth use is in the information it affords us on the subject of the wars of the sons of Ya'aqov with the people of Shekem and the seven cities of the Amorites. This will rouse our hearts to faith in our Elohim; for how could ten men destroy seven cities, if their hearts had not been impressed with faith in 𐤉𐤄𐤅𐤄?

The seventh use is in the information it gives us of all the things that happened to Yoseph in Mitsrayim, with Potiphar and his wife and with the king of Mitsrayim, for this will also rouse our hearts to the fear of 𐤉𐤄𐤅𐤄, and to remove ourselves from all sin, so that it may be well with us in the latter end.

The eighth use is in the account it provides us of what happened to Moshe in Kush and in Midian, by which we may understand the wonders of 𐤉𐤄𐤅𐤄 which He performs for the righteous, and that we may adhere to Him by them.

The ninth use is in its recording of what happened to the Yisraelites in Mitsrayim, and when the commencement of their servitude took place, and how they served the Mitsrites in all manner of hard work, and to what purpose all this tended – how after this Elohim showed favor to them through their trusting in Him, and there is no doubt of this that he who reads the events of Mitsrayim from this book on the nights of Pesaḥ, will receive a great reward, as our Rabbis of blessed memory say, "He that is occupied in relating the flight from Mitsrayim is to be praised," in which this book is included, for this is the true narration which should be read after the Haggadah, for such person [reading this] may be assured that he will be greatly rewarded; we do so this day in our captivity in the countries of Spain, after having finished reading the Haggadah, we commence reading in this book of the whole affair of Mitsrayim, from the Yisraelites going down to Mitsrayim [even until] their flight, for in this books a person should read.

The eleventh[a] use is that some of the comments of our Rabbis and of other commentators who have explained the Torah, you will find illustrated in this book, such as the account of the messengers who met Ya'aqov[b] when he came from Mesopotamia after they had gone to Esaw, also the account of Gavri'el who taught Yoseph seventy languages, also the illustration it affords of him who struck the Midian in the fields of Moav,[c] and the like.

---

[a] The eleventh use – No mention is made of a "tenth use." This is most likely due to copyist error.

[b] See Yashar **31**.

[c] This is a rather puzzling statement found in Genesis **36**:**35**. Yashar **62** gives a deeper explanation.

The twelfth use is that every person lecturing in public may bring forward in his discourse, subject from this book, which the commentators have not explained, by which he may make an impression on the hearts of his audience.

The thirteenth use is that all merchants and travelers, who have an opportunity to study the Torah, may read this book and receive their reward, for the reward of the being as well as the delight of the body is in it, in the discovery of new matter not recorded in any other book, and by these means will man understand to know 𐤉𐤄𐤅𐤄, and cling to Him.

Now because we have seen the merit of this book, and the great usefulness of it, we have undertaken to print it without addition or diminution, and from this time we have commenced to print it in a book, that such books may be in the hands of the members of our covenant, the men of our captivity in order that it may be farther circulated throughout every generation and every city, family, and country, so that they may understand the wonders of 𐤉𐤄𐤅𐤄 which He performed for our ancestors, and His bounties toward them from the days of old, and that He chose us from all the nations. May they who devote their hearts to the fear of 𐤉𐤄𐤅𐤄 be rendered meritorious by studying in it while we confide in 𐤉𐤄𐤅𐤄, Elohim of elohim, and depend upon Him and seek salvation and help from Him, in this heavenly work, and may He cause us to prosper in the right path, and deliver us from errors, and acquit us from hidden errors, as His anointed said, "**Who can discern his errors? Acquit me of hidden [ones].**[a]" May Elohim teach us the good way and direct us in a prosperous path for the sake of His compassion and kindnesses, and may He favorably fulfill the desires of our hearts. Amein.

---

[a] See Psalm **19:12**.

The book of the generations of man, whom
Elohim created upon the earth on the day when
𐤉𐤄𐤅𐤄 Elohim created the heavens and the earth.

𐤐𐤓𐤔𐤕 𐤁𐤓𐤀𐤔𐤉𐤕 – *Parashat Bereshiyt*

1 1 And Elohim said, "Let Us make man in Our
image, after Our likeness;" and Elohim created
man in His own image. 2 And Elohim formed
man from the ground, and He blew into his
nostrils the breath of life, and man became a
living being, possessing speech.

3 And 𐤉𐤄𐤅𐤄 said, "It is not good for man to be
alone; I will make a helper for him."

4 And 𐤉𐤄𐤅𐤄 caused a deep sleep to fall upon the
man, and he slept, and He took away one of his
ribs, and He built flesh on it, and formed her and
brought her to the man, and Adam awoke from
his sleep, and behold a woman was standing
before him.

5 And he said, "This is a bone of my bones and
she shall be called 'Woman,' for she has been
taken from man." And Adam called her name
Ḥavvah, for she was the mother of all living.

6 And Elohim blessed them and called their
names 'Adam' and 'Ḥavvah' in the day that He
created them. And 𐤉𐤄𐤅𐤄 Elohim said, "Be
fruitful and multiply and fill the earth."

7 And 𐤉𐤄𐤅𐤄 Elohim took the man and his wife,
and He placed them in the garden of Eden to
serve it and to guard it. And He commanded
them and said to them, "From every tree of the
garden you may eat, but from the tree of the
knowledge of good and evil you shall not eat, for
in the day that you eat of it you shall surely die."

8 And when Elohim had blessed and commanded
them, He went from them, and the man and his
wife dwelled in the garden according to the
command which 𐤉𐤄𐤅𐤄 had commanded them.
9 And the serpent, which Elohim had created
with them in the earth, came to them to cause
them to transgress the command of Elohim
which He had commanded them. 10 And the
serpent enticed and persuaded the woman to eat
from the tree of knowledge, and the woman
listened to the voice of the serpent, and she
transgressed the word of 𐤉𐤄𐤅𐤄, and took from
the tree of the knowledge of good and evil, and
she ate, and she took from it and gave also to her
husband and he ate.

11 And the man and his wife transgressed the
command of Elohim which He commanded
them, and Elohim knew it, and His anger was
kindled against them and He cursed them.

12 And 𐤉𐤄𐤅𐤄 Elohim drove them that day from
the garden of Eden, to work the ground from
which they were taken. And they went and
dwelled at the east of the garden of Eden. And
Adam knew his wife Ḥavvah, and she bore two
sons and three daughters. 13 And she called the
name of the first born Qayin, saying, "I have
obtained a man *from* 𐤉𐤄𐤅𐤄," and the name of the
other she called Havel, for she said, "In vanity
we came into the earth, and in vanity we shall be
taken from it."

14 And the boys grew up and their father gave
them a possession in the land; and Qayin was a
worker of the ground, and Havel *was* a keeper of
sheep. 15 And it was at the expiration of a few
years, that they brought an approximating
offering to 𐤉𐤄𐤅𐤄, and Qayin brought from the
fruit of the ground, and Havel brought from the
firstlings of his flock from the fat of it, and
Elohim turned and inclined to Havel and his
offering, and a fire came down from 𐤉𐤄𐤅𐤄 from
the heavens and consumed it.

16 And 𐤉𐤄𐤅𐤄 did not turn to Qayin and his
offering, and He did not incline to it, for he had
brought from the inferior fruit of the ground
before 𐤉𐤄𐤅𐤄, and Qayin was jealous against his
brother Havel on account of this, and he sought
an excuse to slay him. 17 And in some time after,
Qayin and Havel his brother, went one day into
the field to do their work. And they were both in
the field, Qayin working and ploughing his
ground, and Havel feeding his flock. And the
flock passed that part which Qayin had ploughed
in the ground, and it sorely grieved Qayin on
account of this.

18 And Qayin approached his brother Havel in
anger, and he said to him, "What is there
between me and you, that you come to dwell and
bring your flock to feed in my land?"

19 And Havel answered his brother Qayin and
said to him, "What is there between me and you,
that you eat the flesh of my flock and clothe
yourself with their wool? 20 And now therefore,
put off the wool of my sheep with which you
have clothed yourself, and repay me for their
fruit and flesh which you have eaten. When you
have done this, I will then go from your land as
you have said."

21 And Qayin said to his brother Havel, "Surely
if I slay you today, who will require your blood
from me?"

22 And Havel answered Qayin, saying, "Surely
Elohim who has made us in the earth, He will
avenge my cause, and He will require my blood
from you, if you slay me. For 𐤉𐤄𐤅𐤄 is the judge
and mediator, and it is He who will repay man
according to his evil, and the wicked man
according to the wickedness that he may do upon
earth. 23 And now, if you slay me here, surely
Elohim knows your secret views, and will judge
you for the evil which you declared to do to me
today."

24 And when Qayin heard the words which
Havel his brother had spoken, behold the anger
of Qayin was kindled against his brother Havel
for declaring this thing. 25 And Qayin hurried
and rose up, and took the iron part of his
ploughing instrument, and he suddenly struck his
brother with it and he slew him. Qayin spilled
the blood of his brother Havel upon the earth,
and the blood of Havel streamed upon the earth
before the flock.

26 And after this Qayin was sorry for having
slain his brother, and he was sadly grieved, and
he wept over him and it aggravated him
exceedingly. 27 And Qayin rose up and dug a
hole in the field, and he put his brother's body in
it, and he turned the dust over it.

28 And 𐤉𐤄𐤅𐤄 knew what Qayin had done to his
brother, and 𐤉𐤄𐤅𐤄 appeared to Qayin and said to
him, "Where is Havel your brother that was with
you?"

29 And Qayin mislead, and said, "I do not know;
am I my brother's keeper?" And 𐤉𐤄𐤅𐤄 said to
him, "What have you done? The voice of your
brother's blood cries to me from the ground
where you have slain him. 30 For you have slain
your brother and have mislead before Me, and
imagined in your heart that I did not see you, nor
knew all your actions. 31 But you did this thing
and slew your brother for nothing, and because
he spoke rightly to you. And now, therefore, you
are cursed from the ground which opened its
mouth to receive your brother's blood from your
hand, and in which you buried him. 32 And it
shall be when you work it, it will no longer give
its strength to you as in the beginning, for the
ground shall produce thorns and thistles, and you
shall be moving and wandering in the earth until
the day of your death."

33 And at that time Qayin went out from the
presence of 𐤉𐤄𐤅𐤄, from the place where he was,
and he went moving and wandering in the land
toward the east of Eden, he and all belonging to
him.

34 And Qayin knew his wife in those days, and
she conceived and bore a son, and he called his
name Ḥanokh, saying, "In that time 𐤉𐤄𐤅𐤄 began
to give me rest and quiet in the earth."

35 And at that time Qayin also began to build a
city. And he built the city and he called the name
of the city Ḥanokh, according to the name of his
son; for in those days 𐤉𐤄𐤅𐤄 had given him rest
upon the earth, and he did not move about and
wander as in the beginning.

36 And Irad was born to Ḥanokh, and Irad
brought forth Mechuyael and Mechuyael brought
forth Methusael, and Methusael brought forth
Lamekh.

2
1 And it was in the hundred and thirtieth year
of the life of Adam upon the earth, that he again
knew Ḥavvah his wife, and she conceived and
bore a son in his likeness and in his image, and
she called his name Sheth, saying, "Because
Elohim has appointed me another seed in the
place of Havel, for Qayin killed him."

2 And Sheth lived one hundred and five years,
and he brought forth a son; and Sheth called the
name of his son Enosh, saying, "Because in that
time the sons of men began to multiply, and to

afflict their beings and hearts by transgressing and rebelling against Elohim."

3 And it was in the days of Enosh that the sons of men continued to rebel and transgress against Elohim, to increase the anger of 𐤉𐤄𐤅𐤄 against the sons of men. **4** And the sons of men went and they served other elohim, and they forgot 𐤉𐤄𐤅𐤄 who had created them in the earth. And in those days the sons of men made images of copper and iron, wood and stone, and they bowed down and served them. **5** And every man made his el and they bowed down to them, and the sons of men forsook 𐤉𐤄𐤅𐤄 all the days of Enosh and his children. And the anger of 𐤉𐤄𐤅𐤄 was kindled on account of their works and abominations which they did in the earth. **6** And 𐤉𐤄𐤅𐤄 caused the waters of the river Giḥon to overwhelm them, and He destroyed and consumed them, and He destroyed the third part of the earth, and despite this, the sons of men did not turn from their evil ways, and their hands were still extended to do evil in the sight of 𐤉𐤄𐤅𐤄.

7 And in those days there was neither sowing nor reaping in the earth; and there was no food for the sons of men and the famine was very great in those days. **8** And the seed which they sowed in those days in the ground became thorns, thistles and briers; for from the days of Adam was this declaration concerning the earth, of the curse of Elohim, which He cursed the earth, on account of the sin which Adam sinned before 𐤉𐤄𐤅𐤄.

9 And it was, when men continued to rebel and transgress against Elohim, and to corrupt their ways, that the earth also became corrupt.

10 And Enosh lived ninety years and he brought forth Qenan; **11** And Qenan grew up and he was forty years old, and he became wise and had knowledge and skill in all wisdom, and he reigned over all the sons of men, and he led the sons of men to wisdom and knowledge; for Qenan was a very wise man and had understanding in all wisdom, and with his wisdom he ruled over spirits and demons[a];

12 And Qenan knew by his wisdom that Elohim would destroy the sons of men for having sinned upon earth, and that 𐤉𐤄𐤅𐤄 would, in the latter days, bring upon them the waters of the flood. **13** And in those days Qenan wrote upon tablets of stone, what was to take place in time to come, and he put them in his treasures. **14** And Qenan reigned over the whole earth, and he turned some of the sons of men to the service of Elohim.

15 And when Qenan was seventy years old, he brought forth three sons and two daughters. **16** And these are the names of the children of Qenan; the name of the first born Mahalalel, the second Enan, and the third Mered, and their sisters were Adah and Tsillah; these are the five children of Qenan that were born to him.

17 And Lamekh, the son of Methushael, became related to Qenan by marriage, and he took his two daughters for his wives, and Adah conceived and bore a son to Lamekh, and she called his name Yaval. **18** And she again conceived and bore a son, and called his name Yuval; and Tsillah, her sister, was barren in those days and had no offspring. **19** For in those days the sons of men began to trespass against Elohim, and to transgress the commands which He had commanded to Adam, to be fruitful and multiply in the earth.

20 And some of the sons of men caused their wives to drink a draught that would render them barren, in order that they might retain their youthfulness and their beautiful appearance might not fade. **21** And when the sons of men caused some of their wives to drink, Tsillah drank with them. **22** And the child-bearing women appeared abominable in the sight of their husbands as widows, while their husbands lived, for they were only attached to the barren ones.

---

[a] **2:11** Demons – Hebrew word 𐤁𐤔𐤓𐤉𐤌 (*ba'sar'iym*). This could represent two words, which are not entirely distinguishable without vowel points. The Hebrew text of Yashar does not have these vowel points. Thus, it could be the plural of *Bas'ar* which means "good news" or "fresh tidings." By implication, this can mean messengers. Or, it could be the plural of *Ba'sar* (slightly different vowels) which means "flesh." In Bereshiyt [Genesis] **6:12** the word used for "flesh" is *ba'sar*, using this term to describe all fleshly creatures. This means the text actually reads either, "...spirits and flesh" or "...spirits and good news [messengers]."

23 And after many days and years, when Tsillah
became old, 𐤉𐤄𐤅𐤄 opened her womb. 24 And she
conceived and bore a son and she called his
name Tuval-Qayin[a], saying, "After I had
withered away have I obtained him from El
Shaddai."

25 And she conceived again and bore a daughter,
and she called her name Na'amah[b], for she said,
"After I had withered away have I obtained
pleasure and delight."

26 And Lamekh was old and advanced in years,
and his eyes were dim that he could not see, and
Tuval-Qayin, his son, was leading him and it was
one day that Lamekh went into the field and
Tuval-Qayin his son was with him, and while
they were walking in the field, Qayin the son of
Adam advanced towards them; for Lamekh was
very old and could not see well, and Tuval-Qayin
his son was very young. 27 And Tuval-Qayin
told his father to draw his bow, and with the
arrows he killed Qayin, who was still far off, and
he killed him, for he appeared to them to be an
animal. 28 And the arrows entered Qayin's body
although he was far from them, and he fell to the
ground and died.[c]

29 And 𐤉𐤄𐤅𐤄 avenged Qayin's evil according to
his wickedness, which he had done to his brother
Havel, according to the word of 𐤉𐤄𐤅𐤄 which He
had spoken.

30 And it happened when Qayin had died, that
Lamekh and Tuval-Qayin went to see the animal
which they had slain, and they saw, and behold
Qayin their grandfather was fallen dead upon the
earth. 31 And Lamekh was very much grieved at
having done this, and in striking his palms
together he struck his son and caused his death.
32 And the wives of Lamekh heard what Lamekh
had done, and they sought to kill him.

33 And the wives of Lamekh hated him from that
day, because he slew Qayin and Tuval-Qayin,
and the wives of Lamekh separated from him,
and would not listen to him in those days. 34 And
Lamekh came to his wives, and he pressed them
to listen to him about this matter.

35 And he said to his wives, "Adah and Tsillah,
hear my voice: O wives of Lamekh, attend to my
words, for now you have imagined and said that
I killed a man with my wounds, and a young lad
with my stripes for their having done no violence
to me, but surely know *this*: I am old and grey-
headed, and my eyes are heavy through age, and
I did this thing unknowingly."

36 And the wives of Lamekh listened to him in
this matter, and they returned to him with the
advice of their father Adam, but they bore no
children to him from that time, knowing that the
anger of Elohim was increasing in those days
against the sons of men, to destroy them with the
waters of the flood for their evil doings.

37 And Mahalalel the son of Qenan lived sixty-
five years and he brought forth Yared; and Yared
lived one hundred and sixty-two years and he
brought forth Ḥanokh.

3 1 And Ḥanokh lived sixty-five years and he
brought forth Methushelaḥ; and Ḥanokh walked
with Elohim after having begotten Methushelaḥ,
and he served 𐤉𐤄𐤅𐤄, and despised the evil ways
of men. 2 And the being of Ḥanokh clung to the
ways of 𐤉𐤄𐤅𐤄, in knowledge and in
understanding; and he wisely retired from the
sons of men, and secreted himself from them for
many days.

3 And it was at the expiration of many years,
while he was serving 𐤉𐤄𐤅𐤄, and praying before
Him in his house, that a messenger of 𐤉𐤄𐤅𐤄
called to him from the heavens, saying, "Ḥanokh,
Ḥanokh," and he said, "Here am I."

4 And he said, "Rise, go forth from your house
and from the place where you hide yourself, and
appear to the sons of men, in order that you may

---

[a] **2:24** Tuval-Qayin – Derived from the Hebrew words 𐤉𐤁𐤋 (*ya'val*) meaning "to bring forth" and 𐤒𐤉𐤍 (*qay'iyn*) meaning "spear." It is also possible that *Qayin* is derived from the root 𐤒𐤍𐤄 (*qa'nah*) meaning "to acquire" or "to buy." Thus Tuval-Qayin can mean "brought forth of Qayin" or "to bring forth the spear."

[b] **2:25** Na'amah – Derived from the Hebrew root word 𐤍𐤏𐤌 (*na'eim*) meaning "pleasant": "Pleasantness."

[c] **2:29** This account runs contradictory to Yovelim **4:31**.

teach them the way in which they should go, and the work which they must accomplish to emulate the ways of 𐤉𐤄𐤅𐤄."

5 And Ḥanokh rose up according to the word of 𐤉𐤄𐤅𐤄, and went forth from his house, from his place and from the chamber in which he was concealed; and he went to the sons of men and taught them the ways of 𐤉𐤄𐤅𐤄, and at that time he assembled the sons of men and taught them the instruction of 𐤉𐤄𐤅𐤄.

6 And he ordered it to be proclaimed in all places where the sons of men dwelled, saying, "Where is the man who wishes to know the ways of 𐤉𐤄𐤅𐤄 and good works? Let him come to Ḥanokh."

7 And all the sons of men then assembled to him,
for all who desired this thing went to Ḥanokh,
and Ḥanokh reigned over the sons of men
according to the word of 𐤉𐤄𐤅𐤄, and they came
and bowed to him and they heard his word.
8 And the Ruaḥ of Elohim was upon Ḥanokh,
and he taught all his men the wisdom of Elohim
and His ways, and the sons of men served 𐤉𐤄𐤅𐤄
all the days of Ḥanokh, and they came to hear his
wisdom.

9 And all the kings of the sons of men, both first
and last, together with their princes and judges,
came to Ḥanokh when they heard of his wisdom,
and they bowed down to him, and they also
requested that Ḥanokh reign over them, to which
he consented. 10 And they assembled in all, one
hundred and thirty kings and princes, and they
made Ḥanokh king over them and they were all
under his power and command. 11 And Ḥanokh
taught them wisdom, knowledge, and the ways
of 𐤉𐤄𐤅𐤄; and He made peace among them, and
peace was throughout the earth during the life of
Ḥanokh.

12 And Ḥanokh reigned over the sons of men two hundred and forty-three years, and he did justice and righteousness with all his people, and he led them in the ways of 𐤉𐤄𐤅𐤄.

13 And these are the generations of Ḥanokh:
Methushelaḥ, Elishua, and Elimelekh, three sons;
and their sisters were Melkah and Na'amah, and
Methushelaḥ lived one hundred and eighty-seven
years and he brought forth Lamekh. 14 And it
was in the fifty-sixth year of the life of Lamekh
when Adam died; he was nine hundred and thirty
years old at his death, and his two sons, with
Ḥanokh and Methushelaḥ his son, buried him
with great glory, as at the burial of kings, in the
cave which 𐤉𐤄𐤅𐤄 had told him.

15 And in that place all the sons of men made a
great mourning and weeping on account of
Adam; it has therefore become a custom among
the sons of men to this day. 16 And Adam died
because he ate of the tree of knowledge; he and
his children after him, as 𐤉𐤄𐤅𐤄 Elohim had
spoken.

17 And it was in the year of Adam's death which
was the two hundred and forty-third year of the
reign of Ḥanokh, in that time Ḥanokh decided to
separate himself from the sons of men and to
hide himself as at first in order to serve 𐤉𐤄𐤅𐤄.
18 And Ḥanokh did so, but did not entirely hide
himself from them, but kept away from the sons
of men three days and then went to them for one
day.

19 And during the three days that he was in his chamber, he prayed to, and praised 𐤉𐤄𐤅𐤄 his Elohim, and the day on which he went and appeared to his servants he taught them the ways of 𐤉𐤄𐤅𐤄, and all they asked him about Elohim he told them.

20 And he did in this manner for many years, and
he afterward concealed himself for six days, and
appeared to his people one day in seven; and
after that once in a month, and then once in a
year, until all the kings, princes and sons of men
sought for him, and desired again to see the face
of Ḥanokh, and to hear his word; but they could
not, as all the sons of men were greatly afraid of
Ḥanokh, and they feared to approach him
because they *saw* Elohim in his face, and upon
his countenance; therefore no man could look at
him, fearing he might be punished and die.
21 And all the kings and princes resolved to
assemble the sons of men, and to come to
Ḥanokh, thinking that they might all speak to
him at the time when he should come forth
among them, and they did so.

22 And the day came when Ḥanokh went forth and they all assembled and came to him, and Ḥanokh spoke to them the words of the fear of 𐤉𐤄𐤅𐤄, and he taught them wisdom and knowledge, and they bowed down before him and they said, "Let the king live! Let the king live!"

23 And some time after, when the kings and princes and the sons of men were speaking to Ḥanokh, and Ḥanokh was teaching them the ways of 𐤉𐤄𐤅𐤄, behold a messenger of 𐤉𐤄𐤅𐤄 called to Ḥanokh from the heavens, and desired to bring him up to the heavens to make him reign there over the sons of Elohim in the heavens, as he had reigned over the sons of men upon earth.

24 At that time Ḥanokh heard this, and he went
and assembled all the inhabitants of the earth,
and taught them wisdom and knowledge and
gave them chastisement, and he said to them, "I
have been required to ascend into the heavens, I
therefore do not know the day of my departure.
25 And now therefore I will teach you wisdom
and knowledge and will give you chastisement
before I leave you: how to act upon earth by
which you may live;" and he did so.

26 And he taught them wisdom and knowledge,
and gave them chastisement, and he reproved
them, and he placed before them statutes and
judgments to do on earth, and he made peace
among them, and he taught them eternal life, and
dwelled with them some time teaching them all
these things. 27 And at that time the sons of men
were with Ḥanokh, and Ḥanokh was speaking to
them, and they lifted up their eyes and the
likeness of a great horse descended from the
heavens, and the horse paced in the air[a];

28 And they told Ḥanokh what they had seen, and Ḥanokh said to them, "On my account does this horse descend upon earth; the time has come that I must go from you and I shall no more be seen by you."

29 And the horse descended at that time and stood before Ḥanokh, and all the sons of men that were with Ḥanokh saw him.

30 And Ḥanokh then again ordered a voice to be proclaimed, saying, "Where is the man who delights to know the ways of 𐤉𐤄𐤅𐤄 his Elohim? Let him come today to Ḥanokh before he is taken from us."

31 And all the sons of men assembled and came
to Ḥanokh that day; and all the kings of the earth
with their princes and counsellors remained with
him that day; and Ḥanokh taught the sons of men
wisdom and knowledge, and gave them
chastisement; and he charged them serve 𐤉𐤄𐤅𐤄
and walk in His ways all the days of their lives,
and he continued to make peace among them.
32 And it was after this that he rose up and rode
upon the horse; and he went forth and all the
sons of men went after him, about eight hundred
thousand men; and they went with him one day's
journey.

33 And the second day he said to them, "Return home to your tents, why will you go? Go, lest you die;" and some of them went from him, and those that remained went with him six days' journey; and Ḥanokh said to them every day, "Return to your tents, lest you die;" but they were not willing to return, and they went with him.

34 And on the sixth day some of the men remained and clung to him, and they said to him, "We will go with you to the place where you go; as 𐤉𐤄𐤅𐤄 lives, only death shall separate us."

35 And they urged so much to go with him that
he ceased speaking to them; and they went after
him and would not return. 36 And when the kings
returned they caused a census to be taken, in
order to know the number of remaining men that
went with Ḥanokh; and it was on the seventh day
that Ḥanokh ascended into the heavens in a
whirlwind, with horses and chariots of fire.

37 And on the eighth day all the kings that had been with Ḥanokh sent to bring back the number

[a] **3:27** In the air – Literally, this is "in spirit." This is the Hebrew word 𐤁𐤓𐤅𐤇 (*b'ru'aḥ*); *ruaḥ* means "spirit, breath, wind" and the *bet* (𐤁) prefix means "in."

of men that were with Ḥanokh, in that place from
which he ascended into the heavens.

38 And all those kings went to the place and they
found the earth there filled with snow, and upon
the snow were large stones of snow, and one said
to the other, "Come, let us break through the
snow and see, perhaps the men that remained
with Ḥanokh are dead, and are now under the
stones of snow," and they searched but could not
find him, for he had ascended into the heavens.

4 1 And all the days that Ḥanokh lived upon
earth, were three hundred and sixty-five years.

2 And when Ḥanokh had ascended into the
heavens, all the kings of the earth rose up and
took Methushelaḥ his son and anointed him, and
they caused him to reign over them in the place
of his father.

3 And Methushelaḥ acted uprightly in the eyes of
𐤉𐤄𐤅𐤄, as his father Ḥanokh had taught him, and
likewise during the whole of his life he taught
the sons of men wisdom, knowledge and the fear
of 𐤉𐤄𐤅𐤄, and he did not turn from the good way
either to the right or to the left. 4 But in the latter
days of Methushelaḥ, the sons of men turned
from 𐤉𐤄𐤅𐤄, they corrupted the earth, they robbed
and plundered each other, and they rebelled
against Elohim and they transgressed, and they
corrupted their ways, and would not listen to the
voice of Methushelaḥ, but rebelled against him.

5 And 𐤉𐤄𐤅𐤄 was exceedingly wroth against
them, and 𐤉𐤄𐤅𐤄 continued to destroy the seed in
those days, so that there was neither sowing nor
reaping in the earth. 6 For when they sowed the
ground in order that they might obtain food for
their support, behold, thorns and thistles were
produced which they did not sow. 7 And still the
sons of men did not turn from their evil ways,
and their hands were still extended to do evil in
the sight of 𐤉𐤄𐤅𐤄, and they provoked 𐤉𐤄𐤅𐤄 with
their evil ways, and 𐤉𐤄𐤅𐤄 was very angry, and
He was sorry that He had made man. 8 And He
thought to destroy and annihilate them, and He
did so.

9 In those days when Lamekh the son of
Methushelaḥ was one hundred and sixty-eight
years old, Sheth the son of Adam died. 10 And all
the days that Seth lived, were nine hundred and
twelve years, and he died. 11 And Lamekh was
one hundred and eighty-two years old when he
took as wife Ashmua, the daughter of Elishua the
son of Ḥanokh his uncle, and she conceived.
12 And at that time the sons of men sowed the
ground, and a little food was produced, yet the
sons of men did not turn from their evil ways,
and they trespassed and rebelled against the
ground.

13 And the wife of Lamekh conceived and bore
him a son at that time, at the revolution of the
year. 14 And Methushelaḥ called his name Noaḥ,
saying, "The ground was, in his days, at rest and
free from corruption," and Lamekh his father
called his name Menaḥem, saying, "This one will
give us rest from our work and from the pain of
our hands *arising* from the ground which 𐤉𐤄𐤅𐤄
has cursed."

15 And the child grew up and was weaned, and
he went in the ways of his father Methushelaḥ,
perfect and upright with 𐤉𐤄𐤅𐤄.

16 And all the sons of men departed from the
ways of 𐤉𐤄𐤅𐤄 in those days as they multiplied
upon the face of the earth with sons and
daughters, and they taught one another their evil
practices and they continued sinning against
𐤉𐤄𐤅𐤄. 17 And every man made himself an el, and
they robbed and plundered, every man his
neighbor as well as his relative, and they
corrupted the earth, and the earth was filled with
violence.

18 And their judges and rulers went to the
daughters of men and took their wives by force
from their husbands according to their choice,
and the sons of men in those days took from the
cattle of the earth, the beasts of the field and the
birds of the heavens, and taught the mixture of
animals of one kind with the other, in order to
provoke 𐤉𐤄𐤅𐤄; and Elohim saw the whole earth
and it was corrupt, for all flesh had corrupted its
ways upon earth, all men and all animals.

19 And 𐤉𐤄𐤅𐤄 said, "I will blot out man that I
created from the face of the earth, yes from man
to the birds of the heavens, together with cattle

and beasts that are in the field for I am sorry that
I made them."

20 And all men who walked in the ways of 𐤉𐤄𐤅𐤄,
died in those days, before 𐤉𐤄𐤅𐤄 brought the evil
upon man which He had declared, for this was
from 𐤉𐤄𐤅𐤄, that they should not see the evil
which 𐤉𐤄𐤅𐤄 spoke of concerning the sons of
men. 21 And Noaḥ found favor in the sight of
𐤉𐤄𐤅𐤄, and 𐤉𐤄𐤅𐤄 chose him and his children to
raise up seed from them upon the face of the
whole earth.

𐤐𐤓𐤔𐤕 𐤍𐤇 – Parashat Noaḥ

5 1 And it was in the eighty-fourth year of the
life of Noaḥ, that Enosh the son of Sheth died, he
was nine hundred and five years old at his death.
2 And in the one hundred and seventy-ninth year
of the life of Noaḥ, Qenan the son of Enosh died,
and all the days of Qenan were nine hundred and
ten years, and he died.

3 And in the two hundred and thirty-fourth year
of the life of Noaḥ, Mahalalel the son of Qenan
died, and the days of Mahalalel were eight
hundred and ninety-five years, and he died.
4 And Yared the son of Mahalalel died in those
days, in the three hundred and sixty-sixth year of
the life of Noaḥ; and all the days of Yared were
nine hundred and sixty-two years, and he died.
5 And all who followed 𐤉𐤄𐤅𐤄 died in those days,
before they saw the evil which was to be done on
the earth.

6 And after many days, in the four hundred and
eightieth year of the life of Noaḥ, when all those
men, who followed 𐤉𐤄𐤅𐤄 had died away from
among the sons of men, and only Methushelaḥ
was then left, 𐤉𐤄𐤅𐤄 said to Noaḥ and
Methushelaḥ, saying,

7 "Speak, and proclaim to the sons of men,
saying, 'Thus says 𐤉𐤄𐤅𐤄, return from your evil
ways and forsake your works, and 𐤉𐤄𐤅𐤄 will
relent of the evil that He declared to do to you,
so that it shall not come to pass. 8 For thus says
𐤉𐤄𐤅𐤄, "Behold I give you an appointed time of
one hundred and twenty years; if you will turn to
Me and forsake your evil ways, then will I also
turn away from the evil which I told you, and it
shall not exist," says 𐤉𐤄𐤅𐤄.'"

9 And Noaḥ and Methushelaḥ spoke all the
words of 𐤉𐤄𐤅𐤄 to all the sons of men, day after
day, constantly speaking to them. 10 But the sons
of men would not listen to them, nor incline their
ears to their words: they were stiff-necked.
11 And 𐤉𐤄𐤅𐤄 granted them an appointed time of
one hundred and twenty years, saying, "If they
will return, then 𐤉𐤄𐤅𐤄 will relent of the evil, so
as not to destroy the earth."

12 Noaḥ the son of Lamekh refrained from taking
a wife in those days, to beget children, for he
said, "Surely now 𐤉𐤄𐤅𐤄 will destroy the earth,
why then shall I beget children?"

13 And Noaḥ was a righteous man, he was
perfect in his generation, and 𐤉𐤄𐤅𐤄 chose him to
raise up seed from his seed upon the face of the
earth.

14 And 𐤉𐤄𐤅𐤄 said to Noaḥ, "Take to yourself a
wife, and beget children, for I have seen that you
are righteous before Me in this generation.
15 And you shall raise up seed, and your children
with you, in the midst of the earth." And Noaḥ
went and took a wife, and he chose Na'amah the
daughter of Ḥanokh, and she was five hundred
and eighty years old. 16 And Noaḥ was four
hundred and ninety-eight years old when he took
Na'amah as wife.

17 And Na'amah conceived and bore a son, and
he called his name Yepheth, saying, "Elohim has
enlarged me in the earth." And she conceived
again and bore a son, and he called his name
Shem, saying, "Elohim has made me a remnant,
to raise up seed in the midst of the earth."

18 And Noaḥ was five hundred and two years old
when Na'amah bore Shem, and the boys grew up
and went in the ways of 𐤉𐤄𐤅𐤄, in all that
Methushelaḥ and Noaḥ their father taught them.
19 And Lamekh the father of Noaḥ died in those
days; yet truly he did not go with all his heart in
the ways of his father, and he died in the five
hundred and ninety-fifth year of the life of Noaḥ.
20 And all the days of Lamekh were seven
hundred and seventy-seven years, and he died.

21 And all the sons of men who knew 𐤉𐤄𐤅𐤄 died
in that year before 𐤉𐤄𐤅𐤄 brought evil upon them;
for 𐤉𐤄𐤅𐤄 willed them to die, so as not to behold

the evil that 𐤉𐤄𐤅𐤄 would bring upon their
brothers and relatives, as He had so declared to
do.

22 In that time, 𐤉𐤄𐤅𐤄 said to Noaḥ and
Methushelaḥ, "Stand forth and proclaim to the
sons of men all the words that I spoke to you in
those days, that perhaps they may turn from their
evil ways, and I will then relent of the evil and
will not bring it."

23 And Noaḥ and Methushelaḥ stood forth, and
said in the ears of the sons of men, all that 𐤉𐤄𐤅𐤄
had spoken concerning them. 24 But the sons of
men would not listen, neither would they incline
their ears to all their declarations.

25 And it was after this that 𐤉𐤄𐤅𐤄 said to Noaḥ,
"The end of all flesh has come before Me, on
account of their evil deeds. Behold, I will destroy
the earth. 26 But you, take gopher wood, and go
to a certain place and make a large ark, and place
it in that spot. 27 And this is how you shall make
it; three hundred cubits long, fifty cubits wide
and thirty cubits high. 28 And you shall make a
door, open at its side, and to a cubit you shall
finish above, and cover it within and without
with pitch.

29 "And behold I will bring the flood of waters
upon the earth, and all flesh be destroyed, from
under the heavens all that is upon earth shall
perish. 30 And you and your household shall go
and gather two of all living things, male and
female, and shall bring them to the ark, to raise
up seed from them upon earth. 31 And gather all
food that is eaten by all the animals, that there
may be food for you and for them.

32 "And you shall choose for your sons three
young women, from the daughters of men, and
they shall be wives to your sons."

33 And Noaḥ rose up, and he made the ark, in the
place where 𐤉𐤄𐤅𐤄 had commanded him, and
Noaḥ did as 𐤉𐤄𐤅𐤄 had ordered him. 34 In his five
hundred and ninety-fifth year Noaḥ commenced
to make the ark, and he made the ark in five
years, as 𐤉𐤄𐤅𐤄 had commanded.

35 Then Noaḥ took the three daughters of
Elyaqim, son of Methushelaḥ, for wives for his
sons, as 𐤉𐤄𐤅𐤄 had commanded Noaḥ. 36 And it
was at that time Methushelaḥ the son of Ḥanokh
died, and he was nine hundred and sixty-nine
years old at his death.

6 1 At that time, after the death of Methushelaḥ,
𐤉𐤄𐤅𐤄 said to Noaḥ, "Go with your household
into the ark; behold I will gather to you all the
animals of the earth: the beasts of the field and
the birds of the heavens, and they shall all come
and surround the ark. 2 And you shall go and sit
by the doors of the ark, and all the beasts, the
animals, and the fowls, shall assemble and place
themselves before you, and such of them as shall
come and crouch before you, you shall take and
deliver into the hands of your sons, who shall
bring them to the ark, and all that will stand
before you shall leave."

3 And 𐤉𐤄𐤅𐤄 brought this about on the next day,
and animals, beasts and birds came in great
multitudes and surrounded the ark. 4 And Noaḥ
went and sat by the door of the ark, and of all
flesh that crouched before him, he brought into
the ark, and all that stood before him he left upon
earth.

5 And a lioness came, with her two cubs, male
and female, and the three crouched before Noaḥ,
and the two cubs rose up against the lioness and
struck her, and made her flee from her place, and
she went away, and they returned to their places,
and crouched upon the earth before Noaḥ. 6 And
the lioness ran away, and stood in the place of
the lions. 7 And Noaḥ saw this, and wondered
greatly, and he rose and took the two cubs, and
brought them into the ark.

8 And Noaḥ brought into the ark from all living
creatures that were upon earth, so that there was
none left but which Noaḥ brought into the ark.
9 Two and two came to Noaḥ into the ark, but
from the clean animals, and clean birds, he
brought seven couples, as Elohim had
commanded him. 10 And all the animals, and
beasts, and birds were still there, and they
surrounded the ark at every place, and the rain
did not descended until seven days later.

11 And on that day, the 𐤉𐤄𐤅𐤄 caused the whole
earth to shake, and the sun darkened, and the
foundations of the world raged, and the whole

earth was moved violently, and the lightning flashed, and the thunder roared, and all the fountains in the earth were broken up, such as was not known to the inhabitants before; and 𐤉𐤄𐤅𐤄 did this mighty act to cause the sons of men to fear 𐤉𐤄𐤅𐤄, that there might be no more evil in earth. **12** And still the sons of men would not return from their evil ways, and they increased the anger of 𐤉𐤄𐤅𐤄 at that time, and did not even direct their hearts to all of this.

13 And at the end of seven days, in the six hundredth year of the life of Noaḥ, the waters of the flood were upon the earth. **14** And all the fountains of the deep were broken up, and the windows of the heavens were opened, and the rain was upon the earth forty days and forty nights. **15** And Noaḥ and his household, and all the living creatures that were with him, came into the ark on account of the waters of the flood, and 𐤉𐤄𐤅𐤄 shut him in.

16 And all the sons of men that were left upon the earth became exhausted through evil on account of the rain, for the waters were coming more violently upon the earth, and the animals and beasts were still surrounding the ark. **17** And the sons of men assembled together, about seven hundred thousand men and women, and they came to Noaḥ to the ark.

18 And they called to Noaḥ, saying, "Open for us that we may come to you in the ark—why should we die?"

19 And Noaḥ, with a loud voice, answered them from the ark, saying, "Have you not all rebelled against 𐤉𐤄𐤅𐤄, and said that He does not exist? And therefore, 𐤉𐤄𐤅𐤄 brought this evil upon you, to destroy and cut you off from the face of the earth. **20** Is this not the thing that I spoke to you about, one hundred and twenty years ago, and you would not listen to the voice of 𐤉𐤄𐤅𐤄, and now do you desire to live upon earth?"

21 And they said to Noaḥ, "We are ready to return to 𐤉𐤄𐤅𐤄; only open for us that we may live and not die."

22 And Noaḥ answered them, saying, "Behold now that you see the trouble of your beings, you wish to return to 𐤉𐤄𐤅𐤄; why did you not return during these hundred and twenty years, which 𐤉𐤄𐤅𐤄 granted you as the appointed time? **23** But now you come and tell me this on account of the troubles of your beings, now also 𐤉𐤄𐤅𐤄 will not listen to you, neither will He give ear to you on today, so that you will not succeed in your desires."

24 And the sons of men approached in order to break into the ark, to come in on account of the rain, for they could not bear the rain upon them. **25** And 𐤉𐤄𐤅𐤄 sent all the beasts and animals that stood round the ark. And the beasts overpowered them and drove them from that place, and every man went his way and they again scattered themselves upon the face of the earth.

26 And the rain was still descending upon the earth, and it descended forty days and forty nights, and the waters prevailed greatly upon the earth; and all flesh that was upon the earth or in the waters died, whether men, animals, beasts, creeping things or birds of the heavens, and only Noaḥ and those that were with him in the ark remained. **27** And the waters prevailed and they greatly increased upon the earth, and they lifted up the ark and it was raised from the earth. **28** And the ark floated upon the face of the waters, and it was tossed upon the waters so that all the living creatures within were turned about like stew in a pot. **29** And great anxiety seized all the living creatures that were in the ark, and the ark was thought to be broken.

30 And all the living creatures that were in the ark were terrified, and the lions roared, and the oxen lowed, and the wolves howled, and every living creature in the ark spoke and lamented in its own language, so that their voices reached to a great distance, and Noaḥ and his sons cried and wept in their troubles; they feared that they had reached the gates of death.

31 And Noaḥ prayed to 𐤉𐤄𐤅𐤄, and cried to Him on account of this, and he said, "O 𐤉𐤄𐤅𐤄 save us now, for we have no strength to bear this evil that has encompassed us, for the waves of the waters have surrounded us, mischievous torrents have terrified us, the snares of death have come before us; answer us, O 𐤉𐤄𐤅𐤄, answer us, light up your countenance toward us and be gracious to us, redeem us and deliver us."

32 And יהוה listened to the voice of Noaḥ, and
יהוה remembered him. 33 And a wind passed
over the earth, and the waters were still and the
ark rested. 34 And the fountains of the deep and
the windows of the heavens were stopped, and
the rain from the heavens was restrained. 35 And
the waters decreased in those days, and the ark
rested upon the mountains of Ararat.

36 And Noaḥ then opened the windows of the
ark, and Noaḥ still called out to יהוה at that time
and he said, "O יהוה my Elohim, who formed
the earth and the heavens[a] and all that are in
them, bring our beings out from this
confinement, and from the prison in which You
have placed us, for I am very wearied with
sighing."

37 And יהוה listened to the voice of Noaḥ, and
said to him, "When you have completed a full
year, you shall go forth."

38 And at the revolution of the year, when a full
year was completed to Noaḥ's dwelling in the
ark, the waters were dried from off the earth, and
Noaḥ put off the cover of the ark. 39 At that time,
on the twenty-seventh day of the second month,
the earth was dry, but Noaḥ and his sons, and
those that were with him, did not go out from the
ark until יהוה told them.

40 And the day came that יהוה Elohim told them
to go out, and they all went out from the ark.

41 And they went and returned, everyone to his
way and to his place, and Noaḥ and his sons
dwelled in the land that יהוה had told them, and
they served יהוה all their days, and יהוה
blessed Noaḥ and his sons on their going out
from the ark.

42 And He said to them, "Be fruitful and fill all
the earth; become strong and increase abundantly
in the earth and multiply in it."

7

1 And these are the names of the sons of
Noaḥ: Yepheth, Ḥam and Shem; and children
were born to them after the flood, for they had
taken wives before the flood.

2 These are the sons of Yepheth; Gomer, Magog,
Madai, Yavan, Tuval, Meshekh, and Tiras, seven
sons. 3 And the sons of Gomer were Ashkinaz,
Rephath, and Tegarmah. 4 And the sons of
Magog were Eliḥaraph, and Luvav. 5 And the
sons of Madai were Achon, Zilo, Ḥuni, and
Lotai. 6 And the sons of Yavan were Elisha,
Tarshish, Kittim, and Dudenim. 7 And the sons
of Tuval were Ariphi, Kesed, and Ta'ari. 8 And
the sons of Meshekh were Ḥaron, Zadon, and
Shevashni.

9 And the sons of Tiras were Beniv, Gira, Kizon,
Luprion, and Gilaq; these are the sons of
Yepheth according to their families, and their
numbers in those days were about four hundred
and sixty men.

10 And these are the sons of Ḥam; Kush,
Mitsrayim, Phut, and Kana'an, four sons; and the
sons of Kush were Sheva, Ḥavilah, Sabtah,
Ra'ama and Sabteka, and the sons of Ra'ama
were Sheva and Dedan. 11 And the sons of
Mitsrayim were Lud, Anam, Lehav, Naphtuch,
Pathrus, Kaluch, and Kaphtor. 12 And the sons of
Phut were Gevul, Ḥadan, Benah, and Adan.
13 And the sons of Kana'an were Tsidon, Ḥeth,
Amori, Gergashi, Ḥivi, Arqi, Seni, Arodi,
Tsimod, and Ḥamath. 14 These are the sons of
Ham, according to their families, and their
numbers in those days were about seven hundred
and thirty men.

15 And these are the sons of Shem; Elam,
Ashuwr, Arpakshad, Lud, and Aram, five sons;
and the sons of Elam were Shushan, Machul and
Ḥarmon. 16 And the sons of Ashuwr were Miras
and Moqil; and the sons of Arpakshad were
Shelaḥ, Anar, and Ashkol. 17 And the sons of

---

[a] **6:36** The Hebrew text reads והימים (*v'ha'ya'mim*) meaning "and the days." However, this is most likely a copyist error, mistaken for והשמים (*v'ha'sha'ma'yim*) meaning "and the heavens." However, it could also be mistaken for והמים (*v'ha'ma'yim*) meaning "and the waters."

Lud were Pethor and Aziyon; and the sons of Aram were Uts, Ḥul, Gether and Mash.

18 These are the sons of Shem, according to their families; and their numbers in those days were about three hundred men.

19 These are the generations of Shem; Shem brought forth Arpakshad and Arpakshad brought forth Shelaḥ, and Shelaḥ brought forth Ever. And to Ever were born two sons, the name of the one was Peleg, for in his days the sons of men were divided, and in the latter days, the earth was divided. 20 And the name of the second was Yoqtan, meaning that in his day the lives of the sons of men were diminished and lessened.

21 These are the sons of Yoqtan; Almodad, Shelaf, Ḥatsarmoveth, Yeraḥ, Hadurom, Ozel, Diqlah, Oval, Abimael, Sheva, Ophir, Ḥavilah and Yovav; all these are the sons of Yoqtan.

22 And Peleg his brother brought forth Reu, and Reu brought forth, Serug, and Serug brought forth Naḥor and Naḥor brought forth Teraḥ, and Teraḥ was thirty-eight years old, and he brought forth Ḥaran and Naḥor.

23 And Kush the son of Ḥam, the son of Noaḥ, took a wife in those days in his old age, and she bore a son, and they called his name Nimrod, saying that at that time the sons of men again began to rebel and transgress against Elohim. And the child grew up, and his father loved him exceedingly, for he was the son of his old age.

24 And the garments of skin which Elohim made for Adam and his wife, when they went out of the garden, were given to Kush. 25 For after the death of Adam and his wife, the garments were given to Ḥanokh, the son of Yared, and when Ḥanokh was taken up toward Elohim, he gave them to Methushelaḥ, his son. 26 And at the death of Methushelaḥ, Noaḥ took them and brought them to the ark, and they were with him until he went out of the ark.

27 And in their going out, Ḥam stole those garments from Noaḥ his father, and he took them and hid them from his brothers. 28 And when Ḥam brought forth his firstborn, Kush, he gave him the garments in secret, and they were with Kush many days. 29 And Kush also concealed them from his sons and brothers, and when Kush had begotten Nimrod, he gave him those garments because of his love for him, and Nimrod grew up, and when he was twenty years old he put on those garments.

30 And Nimrod became strong when he put on the garments, and Elohim gave him might and strength, and he was a mighty hunter in the earth; yes, he was a mighty hunter in the field, and he hunted the animals and he built altars, and he offered upon them the animals before 𐤉𐤄𐤅𐤄. 31 And Nimrod strengthened himself, and he rose up from among his brethren, and he fought the battles of his brethren against all their enemies round about. 32 And 𐤉𐤄𐤅𐤄 delivered all the enemies of his brethren in his hands, and 𐤉𐤄𐤅𐤄 prospered him from time to time in his battles, and he reigned in earth.

33 Therefore it became current in those days, when a man accompanied those that he had trained up for battle, he would say to them, "Like Nimrod, who was a mighty hunter in the earth, and who succeeded in the battles that prevailed against his brethren, that he delivered them from the hands of their enemies, so may 𐤉𐤄𐤅𐤄 strengthen us and deliver us today."

34 And when Nimrod was forty years old, at that time there was a war between his brethren and the children of Yepheth, so that they were in the power of their enemies. 35 And Nimrod went forth at that time, and he assembled all the sons of Kush and their families, about four hundred and sixty men, and he hired also from some of his friends and acquaintances about eighty men, and be gave them their hire, and he went with them to battle, and when he was on the road, Nimrod strengthened the hearts of the people that went with him.

36 And he said to them, "Do not fear, neither be alarmed, for all our enemies will be delivered into our hands, and you may do with them as you please."

37 And all the men that went were about five hundred, and they fought against their enemies, and they destroyed them, and subdued them, and Nimrod placed officers over them in their respective places. 38 And he took some of their

children as collateral, and they were all servants to Nimrod and to his brethren, and Nimrod and all the people that were with him turned homeward. **39** And when Nimrod had joyfully returned from battle, after having conquered his enemies, all his brethren, together with those who knew him before, assembled to make him king over them, and they placed the kingdom's crown upon his head. **40** And he set over his subjects and people, princes, judges, and rulers, as is the custom of kings. **41** And he placed Teraḥ the son of Naḥor the prince of his host, and he dignified him and elevated him above all his princes. **42** And while he was reigning according to the desire of his being, after having conquered all his enemies around, he advised with his counselors to build a city for his palace, and they did so.

43 And they found a large valley opposite to the east *toward* the sun, and they built him a large and extensive city, and Nimrod called the name of the city that he built Shinar, for 𐤉𐤄𐤅𐤄 had vehemently shaken his enemies and destroyed them. **44** And Nimrod dwelled in Shinar, and he reigned securely, and he fought with his enemies and he subdued them, and he prospered in all his battles, and his kingdom became very great. **45** And all nations and tongues[a] heard of his fame, and they gathered themselves to him, and they bowed down to the earth, and they brought him offerings, and he became their master and king, and they all dwelled with him in the city at Shinar, and Nimrod reigned in the earth over all the sons of Noaḥ, and they were all under his hand and counsel.

46 And all the earth had the same language and the same words, but Nimrod did not go in the ways of 𐤉𐤄𐤅𐤄, and he was more wicked than all the men that were before him, from the days of the flood until those days. **47** And he made elohim of wood and stone, and he bowed down to them, and he rebelled against 𐤉𐤄𐤅𐤄, and taught all his servants and the people of the earth his wicked ways; and Mardon his son was more wicked than his father. **48** And everyone that heard of the acts of Mardon the son of Nimrod would say, concerning him, "Out of the wicked comes forth wickedness;" therefore it became a proverb in the whole earth, saying, "Out of the wicked comes forth wickedness," and it was current in the words of men from that time to this.[b]

49 And Teraḥ the son of Naḥor, prince of Nimrod's host, was very great in those days in the sight of the king and his subjects, and the king and princes loved him, and they elevated him highly. **50** And Teraḥ took a wife and her name was Amtheli the daughter of Kornevo; and the wife of Teraḥ conceived and bore him a son in those days. **51** Teraḥ was seventy years old when he brought forth him, and Teraḥ called the name of his son that was born to him Avram, for the king had raised him in those days, and dignified him above all his princes that were with him.

8

1 And it was in the night that Avram was born, that all the servants of Teraḥ, and all the wise men of Nimrod, and his magicians came and ate and drank in the house of Teraḥ, and they rejoiced with him on that night. **2** And when all the wise men and magicians went out from the house of Teraḥ, they lifted up their eyes toward the heavens that night to look at the stars, and they saw, and behold one very large star came from the east and ran in the heavens, and he swallowed up the four stars from the four sides of the heavens. **3** And all the wise men of the king and his magicians were astonished at the sight, and the wise men understood this matter, and they knew its importance.

4 And they said to each other, "This only heralds the child that has been born to Teraḥ this night, who will grow up and be fruitful, and multiply, and possess all the earth, he and his children forever, and he and his seed will slay great kings, and inherit their lands."

---

[a] **7:45** Tongues – Hebrew word 𐤋𐤔𐤅𐤍𐤅𐤕 (*liy'shon'owt*). This is the plural form of the word for tongue, the part of the body. However, verse **46** uses 𐤔𐤐𐤄 (*sa'pha*) meaning literally "lips."

[b] **7:48** See Shemu'el 𐤀 [1 Samuel] **24:13**.

5 And the wise men and magicians went home
that night, and in the morning all these wise men
and magicians rose up early, and assembled in an
appointed house.

6 And they spoke and said to each other, "Behold
the sight that we saw last night is hidden from
the king, it has not been made known to him.
7 And should this thing get known to the king in
the latter days, he will say to us, 'Why have you
concealed this matter from me?' And then we
shall all suffer death; therefore, now let us go
and tell the king the sight which we saw, and the
interpretation of it, and we shall then remain
clear."

8 And they did so, and they all went to the king
and bowed down to him to the ground, and they
said, "Let the king live, let the king live. 9 We
heard that a son was born to Teraḥ the son of
Naḥor, the prince of your host, and we came to
his house last night, and we ate and drank and
rejoiced with him that night. 10 And when your
servants went out from the house of Teraḥ, to go
to our respective homes to stay there for the
night, we lifted up our eyes to the heavens, and
we saw a great star coming from the east, and the
same star ran with great speed, and swallowed up
four great stars, from the four sides of the
heavens.

11 "And your servants were astonished at the
sight which we saw, and were greatly terrified,
and we made our judgment upon the sight, and
knew by our wisdom the proper interpretation of
it, that this thing applies to the child that is born
to Teraḥ, who will grow up and multiply greatly,
and become powerful, and kill all the kings of
the earth, and inherit all their lands, he and his
seed forever. 12 And now our master and king,
behold we have truly informed you of what we
have seen concerning this child. 13 If it seems
good to the king to give his father value for this
child, we will slay him before he shall grow up
and increase in the land, and his evil increase
against us, that we and our children perish
through his evil."

14 And the king heard their words and they
seemed good in his sight, and he sent and called
for Teraḥ, and Teraḥ came before the king.

15 And the king said to Teraḥ, "I have been told
that a son was born to you last night, and such
and such was observed in the heavens at his
birth. 16 And now therefore give me the child,
that we may slay him before his evil springs up
against us, and I will give you for his value, your
house full of silver and gold."

17 And Teraḥ answered the king and said to him:
"My master and king, I have heard your words,
and your servant shall do all that his king desires.
18 But my master and king, I will tell you what
happened to me last night, that I may see what
advice the king will give his servant, and then I
will answer the king upon what he has just
spoken;" and the king said, "Speak."

19 And Teraḥ said to the king, "Ayon, son of
Mored, came to me last night, saying, 20 'Give to
me the good and beautiful horse that the king
gave you, and I will give you silver and gold,
and straw and provender for its value;' and I said
to him, 'Wait until I see the king concerning your
words, and behold whatever the king says, that
will I do.' 21 And now my master and king,
behold I have made this thing known to you, and
the advice which my king will give to his
servant, that will I follow."

22 And the king heard the words of Teraḥ, and
his anger was kindled and he considered him in
the light of a fool.

23 And the king answered Teraḥ, and he said to
him, "Are you so foolish, ignorant, or deficient
in understanding, to do this thing, to give your
beautiful horse for silver and gold or even for
straw and provender? 24 Are you so short of
silver and gold, that you would do this thing,
because you cannot obtain straw and provender
to feed your horse? And what is silver and gold
to you, or straw and provender, that you should
give away that fine horse which I gave you, the
likes of which there is none to be had on the
whole earth?"

25 And the king left off speaking, and Teraḥ
answered the king, saying, "This is the way in
which the king has spoken to his servant; 26 I
entreat you, my master and king; what is this
which you said to me, saying, 'Give your son that
we may slay him, and I will give you silver and

gold for his value;' what shall I do with silver
and gold after the death of my son? Who shall be
my heir? Surely then at my death, the silver and
gold will return to my king who gave it."

27 And when the king heard the words of Teraḥ,
and the parable which he brought concerning the
king, it grieved him greatly and he was vexed at
this thing, and his anger burned within him.

28 And Teraḥ saw that the anger of the king was
kindled against him, and he answered the king,
saying, "All that I have is in the king's power;
whatever the king desires to do to his servant,
that let him do, yes, even my son, he is in the
king's power, without value in exchange, he and
his two brothers that are older than he."

29 And the king said to Teraḥ, "No, but I will
purchase your younger son for a price."

30 And Teraḥ answered the king, saying, "I
entreat you my master and king to let your
servant speak a word before you, and let the king
hear the word of his servant," and Teraḥ said,
"Let my king give me three days' time until I
consider this matter within myself, and consult
with my family concerning the words of my
king;" and he pressed the king greatly to agree to
this.

31 And the king listened to Teraḥ, and he did so
and he gave him three days' time, and Teraḥ
went out from the king's presence, and he came
home to his family and spoke to them all the
words of the king; and the people were greatly
afraid.

32 And it was in the third day that the king sent
to Teraḥ, saying, "Send me your son for a price
as I spoke to you; and if you do not do this, I will
send and slay all you have in your house, so that
you shall not even have one to urinate on a wall
remaining."

33 And Teraḥ hurried, (as the thing was urgent
from the king), and he took a child from one of
his servants, which his handmaid had born to
him that day, and Teraḥ brought the child to the
king and received value for him. **34** And 𐤉𐤄𐤅𐤄
was with Teraḥ in this thing, that Nimrod might
not cause Avram's death, and the king took the
child from Teraḥ and with all his might dashed
his head to the ground, for he thought it had been
Avram; and this was concealed from him from
that day, and it was forgotten by the king, as it
was the will of 𐤉𐤄𐤅𐤄 not to allow Avram's death.
35 And Teraḥ took Avram his son secretly,
together with his mother and nurse, and he
concealed them in a cave, and he brought them
their provisions monthly.

36 And 𐤉𐤄𐤅𐤄 was with Avram in the cave and he
grew up, and Avram was in the cave ten years,
and the king and his princes, magicians and wise
men, thought that the king had killed Avram.

9
1 And Haran, the son of Teraḥ, Avram's oldest
brother, took a wife in those days. **2** Haran was
thirty-nine years old when he took her; and the
wife of Haran conceived and bore a son, and he
called his name Lot.

3 And she conceived again and bore a daughter,
and she called her name Milkah; and she again
conceived and bore a daughter, and she called
her name Sarai. **4** Haran was forty-two years old
when he brought forth Sarai, which was in the
tenth year of the life of Avram; and in those days
Avram and his mother and nurse went out from
the cave, as the king and his subjects had
forgotten the affair of Avram.

5 And when Avram came out from the cave, he
went to Noaḥ and his son Shem, and he remained
with them to learn the correction of 𐤉𐤄𐤅𐤄 and
His ways, and no man knew where Avram was,
and Avram served Noaḥ and Shem his son for a
long time. **6** And Avram was in Noaḥ's house
thirty-nine years, and Avram knew 𐤉𐤄𐤅𐤄 from
three years old, and he went in the ways of 𐤉𐤄𐤅𐤄
until the day of his death, as Noaḥ and his son
Shem had taught him. And all the sons of the
earth in those days greatly transgressed against
𐤉𐤄𐤅𐤄, and they rebelled against Him and they
served other elohim, and they forgot 𐤉𐤄𐤅𐤄 who
had created them in the earth; and the inhabitants
of the earth made for themselves, at that time,
every man his *own* el; elohim of wood and stone
which could neither speak, hear, nor deliver, and
the sons of men served them and they became
their elohim.

7 And the king and all his servants, and Teraḥ
with all his household were then the first of those
that served elohim of wood and stone. 8 And
Teraḥ had twelve elohim of large size, made of
wood and stone, after the twelve new moons of
the year, and he served each one *in turn on its*
new moon, and every new moon Teraḥ would
bring his meat offering and drink offering to his
elohim; so Teraḥ did all the days.

9 And all that generation were wicked in the
sight of 𐤉𐤄𐤅𐤄, and they each made, every man,
his *own* el, but they forsook 𐤉𐤄𐤅𐤄 who had
created them. 10 And there was not found in
those days a man in the whole earth, who knew
𐤉𐤄𐤅𐤄 (for each man served his own el) except
Noaḥ and his household; and all those who were
under his counsel knew 𐤉𐤄𐤅𐤄 in those days.

11 And Avram the son of Teraḥ was waxing great
in those days in the house of Noaḥ, and no man
knew it, and 𐤉𐤄𐤅𐤄 was with him. 12 And 𐤉𐤄𐤅𐤄
gave Avram an understanding heart, and he
knew all the works of that generation were vain,
and that all their elohim were vain and were of
no avail. 13 And Avram saw the sun shining
upon the earth, and Avram said in his heart,
"Surely now this sun that shines upon the earth is
Elohim, and him will I serve."

14 And Avram served the sun in that day and he
prayed to it, and when evening came the sun set
according to its judgment, and Avram said in his
heart, "Surely this cannot be Elohim?"

15 And Avram still continued to speak in his
heart, "Who is He who made the heavens and the
earth? Who created *things* upon earth? Where is
He?"

16 And night darkened over him, and he lifted up
his eyes toward the west, north, south, and east,
and he saw that the sun had vanished from the
earth, and the day became dark.

17 And Avram saw the stars and moon before
him, and he said, "Surely this is the Elohim who
created the whole earth as well as man, and
behold these His servants are around Him:" and
Avram served the moon and prayed to it all that
night.

18 And in the morning when it was light and the
sun shone upon the earth according to its
judgment, Avram saw all the things that the
𐤉𐤄𐤅𐤄 Elohim had made in earth.

19 And Avram said in his heart, "Surely these are
not Elohim that made the earth and all mankind,
but these are the servants of Elohim," and Avram
remained in the house of Noaḥ and there knew
𐤉𐤄𐤅𐤄 and His ways' and he served 𐤉𐤄𐤅𐤄 all the
days of his life, and all that generation forgot
𐤉𐤄𐤅𐤄, and served other elohim of wood and
stone, and rebelled all their days.

20 And the king, Nimrod, reigned securely, and
all the earth was under his control, and all the
earth was of one language, and the same words.

21 And all the princes of Nimrod and his great
men took counsel together; Phut, Mitsrayim,
Kush and Kana'an with their families, and they
said to each other, "Come let us build ourselves a
city and in it a strong tower, and its top reaching
the heavens, and we will make ourselves famed,
so that we may reign upon the whole world, in
order that the evil of our enemies may cease
from us, that we may reign mightily over them,
and that we may not become scattered over the
earth on account of their wars.

22 And they all went before the king, and they
told the king these words, and the king agreed
with them in this affair, and he did so. 23 And all
the families assembled consisting of about six
hundred thousand men, and they went to seek an
extensive piece of ground to build the city and
the tower, and they sought in the whole earth and
they found none like one valley at the east of the
land of Shinar, about two days' walk, and they
journeyed there and they dwelled there. 24 And
they began to make bricks and burn fires to build
the city and the tower that they had imagined to
complete. 25 And the building of the tower was
to them a transgression and a sin, and they began
to build it, and while they were building against
𐤉𐤄𐤅𐤄 Elohim of the heavens, they imagined in
their hearts to war against Him and to ascend
into the heavens.

26 And all these people and all the families
divided themselves in three parts; the first said
"We will ascend into the heavens and fight

against Him;" the second said, "We will ascend
to the heavens and place our own elohim there
and serve them;" and the third part said, "We
will ascend to the heavens and kill Him with
bows and spears;" and Elohim knew all their
works and all their evil thoughts, and He saw the
city and the tower which they were building.

27 And when they were building they built
themselves a great city and a very high and
strong tower; and on account of its height the
mortar and bricks did not reach the builders in
their ascent to it, until those who went up had
completed a full year, and after that, they
reached to the builders and gave them the mortar
and the bricks; thus was it done daily. 28 And
behold these ascended and others descended the
whole day; and if a brick should fall from their
hands and get broken, they would all weep over
it, and if a man fell and died, none of them
would look at him. 29 And 𐤉𐤄𐤅𐤄 knew their
thoughts, and it happened when they were
building they cast the arrows toward the heavens,
and all the arrows fell upon them filled with
blood, and when they saw them they said to each
other, "Surely we have slain all those that are in
heaven."

30 For this was from 𐤉𐤄𐤅𐤄 in order to cause them
to err, and in order to destroy them from off the
face of the ground. 31 And they built the tower
and the city, and they did this thing daily until
many days and years were elapsed.

32 And Elohim said to the seventy messengers
who stood foremost before Him, to those who
were near to him, saying, "Come, let us descend
and confuse their language, that one man shall
not understand the language of his neighbor,"
and they did so to them.

33 And from that day following, they forgot each
man his neighbor's language, and they could not
understand to speak in one language, and when
the builder took from the hands of his neighbor
lime or stone which he did not order, the builder
would cast it away and throw it upon his
neighbor, that he would die. 34 And they did so
many days, and they killed many of them in this
manner.

35 And 𐤉𐤄𐤅𐤄 struck the three divisions that were
there, and He punished them according to their
works and designs; those who said, "We will
ascend to the heavens and serve our elohim,"
became like apes and elephants; and those who
said, "We will strike the heavens with arrows,"
𐤉𐤄𐤅𐤄 killed them, one man through the hand of
his neighbor; and the third division of those who
said, "We will ascend to the heavens and fight
against Him," 𐤉𐤄𐤅𐤄 scattered them throughout
the earth.

36 And those who were left among them, when
they knew and understood the evil which was
coming upon them, they forsook the building,
and they also became scattered upon the face of
the whole earth. 37 And they ceased building the
city and the tower; therefore he called that place
Bavel, for there 𐤉𐤄𐤅𐤄 confounded the language
of the whole earth; behold it was at the east of
the land of Shinar. 38 And as to the tower which
the sons of men built, the earth opened its mouth
and swallowed up one third part thereof, and a
fire also descended from the heavens and burned
another third, and the other third is left to this
day, and it is of that part which was aloft, and it
is a three days' walk around. 39 And many of the
sons of men died in that tower, a people without
number.

10 1 And Peleg the son of Ever died in those
days, in the forty-eighth year of the life of
Avraham son of Teraḥ, and all the days of Peleg
were two hundred and thirty-nine years.

2 And it happened when 𐤉𐤄𐤅𐤄 had scattered the
sons of men on account of their sin at the tower,
behold they spread forth into many divisions,
and all the sons of men were dispersed into the
four corners of the earth. 3 And all the families
became each according to its tongue, its land,
and its city. 4 And the sons of men built many
cities according to their families, in all the places
where they went, and throughout the earth where
𐤉𐤄𐤅𐤄 had scattered them. 5 And some of them
built cities in places from which they were
afterward abandoned, and they called these cities
after their own names, or the names of their
children, or after things that happened to them.
6 And the sons of Yepheth the son of Noaḥ went

and built themselves cities in the places where
they were scattered, and they called all their
cities after their names, and the sons of Yepheth
were divided upon the face of the earth into
many divisions and tongues. And these are the
names of their families according to all the cities
which they built in those days after the tower.

7 And these are the sons of Yepheth according to
their families: Gomer, Magog, Medai, Yavan,
Tuval, Meshekh, and Tiras; these are the sons of
Yepheth according to their generations.

8 And the sons of Gomer, according to their
cities, were the Fraqnum, who dwell in the land
of Frantsa, by the river Frantsa, by the river
Sinah.

9 And the sons of Rephath are the Bartonim, who
dwell in the land of Bartonia by the river Lidah,
which empties its waters in the great sea Giḥon,
that is, the ocean.

10 And the sons of Tugarma are ten families, and
these are their names: Buzar, Partsunakh, Balgar,
Eliqanum, Ragviv, Tarqi, Biz, Zebukh, Ongal
and Tilmats; all these spread and rested in the
north and built themselves cities. 11 And they
called their cities after their own names, those
are they who abide by the rivers Hithlah and
Italakh to this day.

12 But the families of Angoli, Balgar and
Partsunakh, they dwell by the great river Duvni;
and the names of their cities are also according to
their own names.

13 And the sons of Yavan are the Yavanim who
dwell in the land of Qandia, and the *sons of*
Medaiare are the Orzelos that dwell in the land
of Kurson. And the sons of Tuval are those that
dwell in the land of Tusqanah by the river
Pashiah.

14 And the sons of Meshekh are the Shibashni;
and the children of Tiras are Rushash, Kushni,
and Ongolis; all these went and built themselves
cities; those are the cities that are by the sea
Yavus, which empties itself in the river Toragan.

15 And the sons of Elishah are the Almanii, and
they also went and built themselves cities; those
are the cities situate between the mountains of
Iyyov and Shibathmo; and of them were the
people of Lumbardi who dwell opposite the
mountains of Iyyov and Shibathmo, and they
conquered the land of Italia and remained there
to this day.

16 And the sons of Kittim are the Romim who
dwell in the valley of Kanopia by the river
Tibereu.

17 And the sons of Dudonim are those who dwell
in the cities of the sea Giḥon, in the land of
Bordnah.

18 These are the families of the sons of Yepheth
according to their cities and tongues, when they
were scattered after the tower, and they called
their cities after their names and things that
happened to them; and these are the names of all
their cities according to their families, which
they built in those days after the tower.

19 And the sons of Ḥam the son of Noaḥ went
and built themselves cities in the places where
they were scattered, and they called all their
cities after their names and things that happened
to them. And these are the names of their
families according to all the cities which they
built in those days after the tower. And the sons
of Ḥam were Kush, Mitsrayim, Phut, and
Kana'an according to their generation and cities.
20 All these went and built themselves cities as
they found fit places for them, and they called
their cities after the names of their fathers Kush,
Mitsrayim, Phut, and Kana'an.

21 And the sons of Mitsrayim are the Ludim,
Anamim, Lehabim, Naphtuchim, Pathrusim,
Kasluchim, and Kaphtorim, seven families.
22 All these dwell by the river Siḥor, that is the
brook of Mitsrayim, and they built themselves
cities and called them after their own names.

23 And the sons of Pathros and the sons of
Kasloch intermarried together, and from them
went forth the Pelishtim, the Gerarim the
Azathim, the Githim, and the Eqronim, in all five
families; these also built themselves cities, and
they called their cities after the names of their
fathers to this day.

24 And the sons of Kana'an also built themselves
cities, and they called their cities after their
names, eleven cities and others without number.

25 And four men from the family of Ḥam went to
the land of the plain; these are the names of the
four men, Sodom, Gomorrah, Admah and
Tseboyim. 26 And these men built themselves
four cities in the land of the plain, and they
called the names of their cities after their own
names. 27 And they and their children and all
belonging to them dwelled in those cities, and
they were fruitful and multiplied greatly and
dwelled peaceably.

28 And Seir the son of Ḥur, son of Ḥivi, son of
Kana'an, went and found a valley opposite to
Mount Paran, and he built a city there, and he
and his seven sons and his household dwelled
there, and he called the city which he built Seir,
according to his name; that is the land of Seir to
this day. 29 These are the families of the children
of Ḥam, according to their tongues and cities,
when they were scattered to their countries after
the tower. 30 And some of the children of Shem
son of Noaḥ, father of all the children of Ever,
also went and built themselves cities in the
places where they were scattered, and they called
their cities after their names.

31 And the sons of Shem were Elam, Ashuwr,
Arpakshad, Lud and Aram, and they built
themselves cities and called the names of all
their cities after their names.

32 And Ashuwr son of Shem and his children and
household went forth at that time, a very large
body of them, and they went to a distant land
that they found, and they met with a very
extensive valley in the land that they went to,
and they built themselves four cities, and they
called them after their own names and things that
happened to them. 33 And these are the names of
the cities which the children of Ashuwr built:
Ninevah, Resen, Kalaḥ, and Rechoboth; and the
children of Ashuwr dwell there to this day.

34 And the sons of Aram also went and built
themselves a city, and they called the name of
the city Uts after their eldest brother, and they
dwell in it; that is the land of Uts to this day.

35 And in the second year after the tower a man
from the house of Ashuwr, whose name was
Bela, went from the land of Nineveh to sojourn
with his household wherever he could find a
place; and they came until opposite the cities of
the plain against Sodom, and they dwelled there.
36 And the man rose up and built a small city
there, and called its name Bela, after his name;
that is the land of Tsor to this day.

37 And these are the families of the children of
Shem according to their tongues and cities, after
they were scattered upon the earth after the
tower. 38 And every kingdom, city, and family of
the families of the children of Noaḥ built
themselves many cities after this. 39 And they
established governments in all their cities, in
order to be regulated by their orders. So all the
families of the children of Noaḥ did forever.

11

1 And Nimrod son of Kush was still in the
land of Shinar, and he reigned over it and
dwelled there, and he built cities in the land of
Shinar.

2 And these are the names of the four cities
which he built, and he called their names after
the things that happened to them in the building
of the tower.

3 And he called the first Bavel, saying, "Because
there 𐤉𐤄𐤅𐤄 confounded the language of the
whole earth;" and the name of the second he
called Erekh, because from there 𐤉𐤄𐤅𐤄 dispersed
them.

4 And the third he called Eked, saying there was
a great battle at that place; and the fourth he
called Kalnah, because his princes and mighty
men were consumed there, and they rebelled and
transgressed against him. 5 And when Nimrod
had built these cities in the land of Shinar, he
placed in them the remainder of his people, his
princes and his mighty men that were left in his
kingdom.

6 And Nimrod dwelled in Babel, and he there
renewed his reign over the rest of his subjects,
and he reigned securely, and the subjects and
princes of Nimrod called his name Amraphel,
saying that at the tower his princes and men fell
through his means.

7 And notwithstanding this, Nimrod did not
return to 𐤉𐤄𐤅𐤄, and he continued in wickedness
and teaching wickedness to the sons of men; and

Mardon, his son, was worse than his father, and
continued to add to the abominations of his
father. 8 And he caused the sons of men to sin,
therefore it is said, "Out of the wicked comes
forth wickedness."

9 At that time there was war between the families
of the children of Ḥam, as they were dwelling in
the cities which they had built.

10 And Kedorlaomer, king of Elam, went away
from the families of the children of Ḥam, and he
fought with them and he subdued them, and he
went to the five cities of the plain and he fought
against them and he subdued them, and they
were under his control. 11 And they served him
twelve years, and they gave him a yearly tax.

12 At that time Naḥor, son of Serug died, in the
forty-ninth year of the life of Avram son of
Teraḥ. 13 And in the fiftieth year of the life of
Avram son of Teraḥ, Avram came forth from the
house of Noaḥ, and went to his father's house.

14 And Avram knew 𐤉𐤄𐤅𐤄, and he went in His
ways and corrections, and 𐤉𐤄𐤅𐤄 his Elohim was
with him. 15 And Teraḥ his father was still
captain of the host of king Nimrod in those days,
and he still followed other elohim, of wood and
stone. 16 And Avram came to his father's house
and saw twelve elohim standing there in their
temples, and the anger of Avram was kindled
when he saw these images in his father's house.

17 And Avram said, "As 𐤉𐤄𐤅𐤄 lives, these
images shall not remain in my father's house! So
shall Elohim who created me do to me, if in three
days' time I do not break them all!"

18 And Avram went from them, and his anger
burned within him. And Avram hurried and went
from the chamber to his father's outer court, and
he found his father sitting in the court, and all his
servants with him, and Avram came and sat
before him.

19 And Avram asked his father, saying, "Father,
tell me, where is Elohim, who created the
heavens and the earth, and all the sons of men
upon earth, and who created you and I?" And
Teraḥ answered his son Avram and said,
"Behold, those who created us are all with us in
the house."

20 And Avram said to his father, "My master,
please show them to me." And Teraḥ brought
Avram into the chamber of the inner court, and
Avram saw, and behold the whole room was full
of elohim of wood and stone, twelve great
images and others less than they without number.

21 And Teraḥ said to his son, "Behold these are
they which made all that you see upon earth, and
which created you and I, and all mankind."

22 And Teraḥ bowed down to his elohim, and he
then went away from them, and Avram, his son,
went away with him. 23 And when Avram had
gone from them, he went to his mother and sat
before her, and he said to his mother, "Behold,
my father has shown me those who made the
heavens and the earth, and all the sons of men.
24 Now, therefore, hasten and fetch a kid from
the flock, and make of it savory meat, that I may
bring it to my father's elohim as an offering for
them to eat; perhaps I may become acceptable to
them."

25 And his mother did so, and she fetched a kid,
and made savory meat of it, and brought it to
Avram, and Avram took the savory meat from
his mother and brought it before his father's
elohim, and he drew near to them that they might
eat; and Teraḥ his father, did not know of it.
26 And Avram saw on the day when he was
sitting among them, that they had no voice, no
hearing, no motion, and not one of them could
stretch forth his hand to eat.

27 And Avram mocked them, and said, "Surely
the savory meat that I prepared has not pleased
them, or perhaps it was too little for them, and
for that reason they would not eat; therefore
tomorrow I will prepare fresh savory meat, better
and more plentiful than this, in order that I may
see the result."

28 And it was on the next day that Avram
directed his mother concerning the savory meat,
and his mother rose and fetched three fine kids
from the flock, and she made of them some
excellent savory meat, such as her son was fond
of, and she gave it to her son Avram; and Teraḥ
his father did not know of it.

29 And Avram took the savory meat from his
mother, and brought it before his father's elohim

into the chamber; and he came near to them that
they might eat, and he placed it before them, and
Avram sat before them all day, thinking perhaps
they might eat. **30** And Avram watched them, and
behold they had neither voice nor hearing, nor
did one of them stretch forth his hand to the meat
to eat.

31 And in the evening of that day in that house
Avram put on the Ruaḥ of Elohim.

32 And he called out and said, "Woe to my father
and this wicked generation, whose hearts are all
inclined to vanity, who serve these idols of wood
and stone which can neither eat, smell, hear nor
speak, who have mouths without words, eyes
without sight, ears without hearing, hands
without feeling, and legs which cannot move;
those that made them, and trust in them, are like
them."

33 And when Avram saw all these things his
anger was kindled against his father, and he
hurried and took an axe in his hand, and came to
the chamber of the elohim, and he broke all his
father's elohim. **34** And when he had finished
breaking the images, he placed the axe in the
hand of the great eloah which was there before
them, and he went out; and Teraḥ his father came
home, for he had heard at the door the sound of
the striking of the axe; so Teraḥ came into the
house to know what this was about.

35 And Teraḥ, having heard the noise of the axe
in the room of images, ran to the room to the
images, and he met Avram going out. **36** And
Teraḥ entered the room and found all the idols
fallen down and broken, and the axe in the hand
of the largest, which was not broken, and the
savory meat which Avram his son had made was
still before them. **37** And when Teraḥ saw this his
anger was greatly kindled, and he hurried and
went from the room to Avram.

38 And he found Avram his son still sitting in the
house; and he said to him, "What is this work
you have done to all my elohim?"

39 And Avram answered Teraḥ his father and he
said, "Not so my master, for I brought savory
meat before them, and when I came near to them
with the meat that they might eat, they all at once
stretched forth their hands to eat before the great
one had put forth his hand to eat. **40** And the
large one saw their works that they did before
him, and his anger was violently kindled against
them, and he went and took the axe that was in
the house and came to them and broke them all,
and behold the axe is yet in his hand as you see."

41 And Teraḥ's anger was kindled against his son
Avram, when he spoke this; and Teraḥ said to
Avram his son in his anger, "What is this false
word that you have told? You speak lies to me.
42 Is there a spirit, being, or power in these
elohim to do all that you have told me? Are they
not wood and stone, and have I not myself made
them, and how can you speak such lies, saying
that the great eloah that was with them struck
them? It was you who placed the axe in his
hands, and then said he struck them all."

43 And Avram answered his father and said to
him, "And how can you then serve these idols in
whom there is no power to do anything? Can
those idols in which you trust deliver you? Can
they hear your prayers when you call upon them?
Can they deliver you from the hands of your
enemies, or will they fight your battles for you
against your enemies, that you should serve
wood and stone which can neither speak nor
hear? **44** And now surely it is not good for you
nor for the sons of men that are connected with
you, to do these things; are you so simple, so
foolish or so short of understanding that you will
serve wood and stone, and do after this manner,
45 and forget 𐤄𐤅𐤄𐤉 Elohim who made the
heavens and the earth, and who created you in
the earth, and thereby bring a great evil upon
your beings in this matter by serving stone and
wood?

46 "Did not our fathers in days of old sin in this
matter, and 𐤄𐤅𐤄𐤉 Elohim of the universe brought
the waters of the flood upon them and destroyed
the whole earth? **47** And how can you continue to
do this and serve elohim of wood and stone, who
cannot hear, or speak, or deliver you from
oppression, thereby bringing down the anger of
the Elohim of the earth upon you? **48** Now
therefore my father refrain from this, and do not
bring evil upon your being and the beings of
your household."

49 And Avram hurried and sprang from before his father, and took the axe from his father's largest idol; and with it, Avram broke *the great idol* and ran away.

50 And Teraḥ, seeing all that Avram had done, hurried to go from his house, and he went to the king and he came before Nimrod and stood before him, and he bowed down to the king; and the king said, "What do you want?"

51 And he said, "I entreat you my master, to hear me: now, fifty years ago a child was born to me, and thus has he done to my elohim and thus has he spoken; and now therefore, my master and king, send for him that he may come before you, and judge him according to your judgment, that we may be delivered from his evil."

52 And the king sent three men of his servants, and they went and brought Avram before the king. And Nimrod and all his princes and servants were that day sitting before him, and Teraḥ sat also before them.

53 And the king said to Avram, "What is this that you have done to your father and to his elohim?" And Avram answered the king in the words that he spoke to his father, and he said, "The great eloah that was with them in the house did to them what you have heard."

54 And the king said to Avram, "Do they have power to speak and eat and do as you have said?" And Avram answered the king, saying, "And if there be no power in them why do you serve them, and cause the sons of men to err through your foolishness? 55 Do you imagine that they can deliver you or do anything small or great, that you should serve them? And why will you not serve the Elohim of the whole universe, who created you and in whose power it is to kill and keep alive? 56 Oh foolish, simple, and ignorant king, woe to you forever. 57 I thought you would teach your servants the upright way, but you have not done this; but *rather you* have filled the whole earth with your sins and the sins of your people who have followed your ways.

58 "Do you not know, or have you not heard, that this evil which you do, our ancestors sinned in *it the same*, in days of old, and the eternal Elohim brought the waters of the flood upon them and destroyed them all, and also destroyed the whole earth on their account? And will you and your people rise up now and do like this work, in order to bring down the anger of 𐤉𐤄𐤅𐤄 the Elohim of the whole universe, and to bring evil upon you and the whole earth? 59 Now therefore put away this evil deed which you do, and serve the Elohim of the universe, as your being is in His hands, and then it will be well with you.

60 "And if your wicked heart will not listen to my words to cause you to forsake your evil ways, and to serve the eternal Elohim, then you will die in shame in the latter days; you, your people, and all who are connected with you, hearing your words or walking in your evil ways."

61 And when Avram had ceased speaking before the king and princes, Avram lifted up his eyes to the heavens, and he said, "𐤉𐤄𐤅𐤄 sees all the wicked, and He will judge them."

12

1 And when the king heard the words of Avram he ordered him to be put into prison; and Avram was ten days in prison. 2 And at the end of those days the king ordered that all the kings, princes and governors of different provinces and the wise men should come before him, and they sat before him, and Avram was still in the house of confinement.

3 And the king said to the princes and wise men, "Have you heard what Avram, the son of Teraḥ, has done to his father? Thus has he done to him, and I ordered him to be brought before me, and thus has he spoken; his heart had no doubt, neither did he stir in my presence, and behold now he is confined in the prison. 4 And therefore, decide what judgment is due to this man who reviled the king; who spoke and did all the things that you heard."

5 And they all answered the king saying, "The man who reviles the king should be hanged upon a tree; but having done all the things that he said, and having despised our elohim, he must therefore be burned to death, for this is the judgment in this matter. 6 If it pleases the king to do this, let him order his servants to kindle a fire both night and day in your brick furnace, and then we will cast this man into it." And the king

did so; and he commanded his servants that they
should prepare a fire for three days and three
nights in the king's furnace, that is in Kasdim;
and the king ordered them to take Avram from
prison and bring him out to be burned. 7 And all
the king's servants, princes, mighty men,
governors, and judges, and all the lesser
inhabitants of the land, about nine hundred
thousand men, stood opposite the furnace to see
Avram. 8 And all the women and little ones
crowded upon the roofs and towers to see what
was happening with Avram, and they all stood
together at a distance; and there was not a man
left that did not come on that day to see.

9 And when Avram had come, the magicians of
the king and the wise men saw Avram, and they
cried out to the king, saying, "Our master the
king, surely this is the man whom we know to
have been the child at whose birth the great star
swallowed the four stars, which we declared to
the king fifty years ago. 10 And behold now his
father has also transgressed your commands, and
mocked you by bringing you another child,
which you killed."

11 And when the king heard their words, he was exceedingly wroth, and he ordered Teraḥ to be brought before him.

12 And the king said, "Have you heard what the magicians have spoken? Now tell me truly, how did you *do it*; and if you speak truth, you shall be spared."

13 And seeing that the king's anger was so much
kindled, Teraḥ said to the king, "My master and
king, you have heard the truth, and what the wise
men have spoken is right." And the king said,
"How could you do this thing, to transgress my
orders and to give me a child that you didst not
beget, and to take value for him?"

14 And Teraḥ answered the king, "Because my compassion was excited for my son, at that time, and I took a son of my handmaid, and I brought him to the king."

15 And the king said "Who advised you to this? Tell me, do not hide anything from me, and then you shall not die."

16 And Teraḥ was greatly terrified in the king's presence, and he said to the king, "It was Haran my eldest son who advised me to this; and Haran was in those days that Avram was born, thirty-two years old."

17 But Haran did not advise his father to anything, for Teraḥ said this to the king in order to deliver his being from the king, for he feared greatly; and the king said to Teraḥ, "Haran your son who advised you to this shall die through fire with Avram; for the sentence of death is upon him for having rebelled against the king's desire in doing this thing."

18 And Haran at that time felt inclined to follow the ways of Avram, but he kept it in his heart.

19 And Haran said in his heart, "Behold now the king has seized Avram on account of these things which Avram did, and it shall come to pass, that if Avram prevails over the king I will follow him, but if the king prevails, I will go after the king."

20 And when Teraḥ had spoken this to the king
concerning Haran his son, the king ordered
Haran to be seized with Avram. 21 And they
brought them both, Avram and Haran his
brother, to cast them into the fire; and all the
inhabitants of the land and the king's servants
and princes and all the women and little ones
were there, standing that day over them.

22 And the king's servants took Avram and his
brother, and they stripped them of all their
clothes excepting their lower garments which
were upon them. 23 And they bound their hands
and feet with linen cords, and the servants of the
king lifted them up and cast them both into the
furnace. 24 And 𐤉𐤄𐤅𐤄 loved Avram and He had
compassion on him, and 𐤉𐤄𐤅𐤄 came down and
delivered Avram from the fire and he was not
burned. 25 But all the cords with which they
bound him were burned, while Avram remained
and walked about in the fire.

26 And Haran died when they had cast him into the fire, and he was burned to ashes, for his heart was not complete with 𐤉𐤄𐤅𐤄; and those men who cast him into the fire, the flame of the fire spread over them, and they were burned, and twelve men of them died.

27 And Avram walked in the midst of the fire
three days and three nights, and all the servants
of the king saw him walking in the fire, and they
came and told the king, saying, "Behold we have
seen Avram walking about in the midst of the
fire, and even the lower garments which are upon
him are not burned, but the cord with which he
was bound is burned."

28 And when the king heard their words his heart
fainted and he would not believe them; so he
sent other faithful princes to see this matter, and
they went and saw it and told it to the king; and
the king rose to go and see it, and he saw Avram
walking to and fro in the midst of the fire, and he
saw Haran's body burned, and the king wondered
greatly.

29 And the king ordered Avram to be taken out
from the fire; and his servants approached to take
him out and they could not, for the fire was
round about and the flame ascending toward
them from the furnace. 30 And the king's servants
fled from it, and the king rebuked them, saying,
"Make haste and bring Avram out of the fire that
you shall not die."

31 And the servants of the king again approached
to bring Avram out, and the flames came upon
them and burned their faces so that eight of them
died. 32 And when the king saw that his servants
could not approach the fire lest they should be
burned, the king called to Avram, "O servant of
the Elohim who is in the heavens, go forth from
amidst the fire and come here before me;" and
Avram listened to the voice of the king, and he
went forth from the fire and came and stood
before the king.

33 And when Avram came out the king and all
his servants saw Avram coming before the king,
with his lower garments upon him, for they were
not burned, but the cord with which he was
bound was burned.

34 And the king said to Avram, "How is it that
you were not burned in the fire?"

35 And Avram said to the king, "The Elohim of
the heavens and the earth in whom I trust, and
who has all in His power, He delivered me from
the fire which you cast me into."

36 And Haran the brother of Avram was burned
to ashes, and they sought for his body, and they
found it consumed. 37 And Haran was eighty-two
years old when he died in the fire of Kasdim.
And the king, princes, and inhabitants of the
land, seeing that Avram was delivered from the
fire, they came and bowed down to Avram.

38 And Avram said to them, "Do not bow down
to me, but bow down to the Elohim of the world
who made you, and serve Him, and go in His
ways; for it is He who delivered me from this
fire, and it is He who created the beings and
spirits of all men, and formed man in his
mother's womb, and brought him forth into the
world; and it is He who will deliver those who
trust in Him from all pain."

39 And this thing seemed very wonderful in the
eyes of the king and princes, that Avram was
saved from the fire and that Haran was burned;
and the king gave Avram many presents and he
gave him his two head servants from the king's
house; the name of one was Ogi and the name of
the other was Eliezer. 40 And all the princes of
the king, and his servants gave Avram many
gifts of silver and gold and pearl, and the king
and his princes sent him away, and he went in
peace.

41 And Avram went forth from the king in peace,
and many of the king's servants followed him,
and about three hundred men joined him. 42 And
Avram returned on that day and went to his
father's house, he and the men that followed him,
and Avram served 𐤉𐤄𐤅𐤄 his Elohim all the days
of his life, and he walked in His ways and
followed His Torot. 43 And from that day
forward Avram inclined the hearts of the sons of
men to serve 𐤉𐤄𐤅𐤄. 44 And at that time Naḥor
and Avram took to themselves wives, the
daughters of their brother Haran. The name of
Naḥor's wife was Milkah and the name of
Avram's wife was Sarai. And Sarai, wife of
Avram, was barren; she had no offspring in those
days.

45 And at the expiration of two years from
Avram's going out of the fire, that is in the fifty-
second year of his life, behold king Nimrod sat
in Bavel upon the throne, and the king fell asleep
and dreamed that he was standing with his troops

and hosts in a valley opposite the king's furnace. 46 And he lifted up his eyes and saw a man in the likeness of Avram coming forth from the furnace, and that he came and stood before the king with his drawn sword, and then sprang to the king with his sword, when the king fled from the man, for he was afraid. And while he was running, the man threw an egg upon the king's head, and the egg became a great river. 47 And the king dreamed that all his troops sank in that river and died, and the king took flight with three men who were before him and he escaped. 48

And the king looked at these men and they were clothed in princely dresses as the garments of kings, and had the appearance and majesty of kings. 49 And while they were running, the river again turned to an egg before the king, and there came forth from the egg a young bird which came before the king, and flew at his head and plucked out the king's eye. 50 And the king was grieved at the sight, and he awoke out of his sleep and his spirit was agitated; and he felt a great terror.

51 And in the morning the king rose from his bed in fear, and he ordered all the wise men and magicians to come before him, when the king related his dream to them.

52 And a wise servant of the king, whose name was Anuqi, answered the king, saying, "This is nothing else but the evil of Avram and his seed which will spring up against my master and king in the latter days. 53 And behold the day will come when Avram and his seed and the children of his household will war with my king, and they will strike all the king's hosts and his troops. 54 And as to what you have said concerning three men which you saw like yourself, and which did escape, this means that only you will escape, with three kings from the kings of the earth who will be with you in battle. 55 And that which you saw of the river which turned to an egg as at first, and the young bird plucking out your eye, this means nothing else but the seed of Avram which will slay the king in latter days. 56 This is my king's dream, and this is its interpretation, and the dream is true, and the interpretation which your servant has given you is right.

57 "Now therefore my king, surely you know that it is now fifty-two years since your sages saw this at the birth of Avram, and if my king will allow Avram to live in the earth it will be to the injury of my master and king, for all the days that Avram lives neither you nor your kingdom will be established; for this was known formerly at his birth. And why will my king not slay him, that his evil may be kept from you in latter days?"

58 And Nimrod listened to the voice of Anuqi, and he sent some of his servants in secret to go and seize Avram, and bring him before the king to suffer death. 59 And Eliezer, Avram's servant whom the king had given him, was at that time in the presence of the king, and he heard what Anuqi had advised the king, and what the king had said to cause Avram's death.

60 And Eliezer said to Avram, "Hurry, rise up and save your being, that you not die through the hands of the king, for thus did he see in a dream concerning you, and thus did Anuqi interpret it, and thus also did Anuqi advise the king concerning you."

61 And Avram listened to the voice of Eliezer, and Avram hurried and ran for safety to the house of Noaḥ and his son Shem, and he concealed himself there and found a place of safety; and the king's servants came to Avram's house to seek him, but they could not find him, and they searched throughout the country and he was not to be found, and they went and searched in every direction and he was not to be found. 62 And when the king's servants could not find Avram they returned to the king, but the king's anger against Avram was stilled, as they did not find him, and the king drove this matter concerning Avram from his heart.

63 And Avram was concealed in Noaḥ's house for one month, until the king had forgotten this matter, but Avram was still afraid of the king; and Teraḥ came to see Avram his son secretly in the house of Noaḥ, and Teraḥ was very great in the eyes of the king.

64 And Avram said to his father, "Do you not know that the king thinks to kill me, and to annihilate my name from the earth by the advice

of his wicked counsellors? 65 Now who do you
have here and what do you have in this land?
Arise, let us go together to the land of Kana'an,
that we may be delivered from his hand, lest you
perish also through him in the latter days. 66 Do
you not know or have you not heard, that it is not
through love that Nimrod gives you all this
honor, but it is only for his benefit that he
bestows all this good upon you? 67 And if he
does to you greater good than this, surely these
are only vanities of the world, for wealth and
riches cannot avail in the day of wrath and anger.

68 "Now therefore listen to my voice, and let us
arise and go to the land of Kana'an, out of the
reach of injury from Nimrod; and serve 𐤉𐤄𐤅𐤄
who created you in the earth and it will be well
with you; and cast away all the vain things which
you pursue."

69 And Avram ceased to speak, when Noaḥ and
his son Shem answered Teraḥ, saying, "The
word which Avram has said to you is true."

70 And Teraḥ listened to the voice of his son
Avram, and Teraḥ did all that Avram said, for
this was from 𐤉𐤄𐤅𐤄, that the king should not
cause Avram's death.

13 1 And Teraḥ took his son Avram and his
grandson Lot, the son of Haran, and Sarai his
daughter-in-law, the wife of his son Avram, and
all the beings of his household and went with
them from Ur Kasdim to go to the land of
Kana'an. And when they came as far as the land
of Haran they remained there, for it was
exceedingly good land for pasture, and of
sufficient extent for those who accompanied
them. 2 And the people of the land of Haran saw
that Avram was good and upright with Elohim
and men, and that the 𐤉𐤄𐤅𐤄 his Elohim was with
him, and some of the people of the land of Haran
came and joined Avram, and he taught them the
correction of 𐤉𐤄𐤅𐤄 and His ways; and these men
remained with Avram in his house and they
adhered to him.

𐤐𐤓𐤔𐤕 𐤋𐤊 𐤋𐤊 – *Parashat Lekh-Lekha*

3 And Avram remained in the land three years,
and at the end of three years 𐤉𐤄𐤅𐤄 appeared to
Avram and said to him, "I am 𐤉𐤄𐤅𐤄 who brought
you out of Ur Kasdim, and delivered you from
the hands of all your enemies. 4 And now
therefore, if you will listen to My voice and keep
My commands, My statutes and My Torot, then
will I cause your enemies to fall before you, and
I will multiply your seed like the stars of the
heavens, and I will send My blessing upon all the
works of your hands, and you shall lack nothing.
5 Arise now, take your wife and all belonging to
you and go to the land of Kana'an and remain
there, and I will there be your Elohim, and I will
bless you." And Avram arose and took his wife
and all belonging to him, and he went to the land
of Kana'an as 𐤉𐤄𐤅𐤄 had told him; and Avram
was fifty-five years old when he went from
Haran.

6 And Avram came to the land of Kana'an and
dwelled in the midst of the city, and he pitched
his tent there among the children of Kana'an,
inhabitants of the land.

7 And 𐤉𐤄𐤅𐤄 appeared to Avram when he came to
the land of Kana'an, and said to him, "This is the
land which I give to you and to your seed after
you forever, and I will make your seed like the
stars of the heavens, and I will give all the lands
which you see to your seed for an inheritance."

8 And Avram built an altar in the place where
𐤉𐤄𐤅𐤄 had spoken to him, and Avram there called
upon the name of 𐤉𐤄𐤅𐤄.

9 At that time, at the end of three years of
Avram's dwelling in the land of Kana'an, in that
year Noaḥ died, which was the fifty-eighth year
of the life of Avram; and all the days that Noaḥ
lived were nine hundred and fifty years and he
died.

10 And Avram dwelled in the land of Kana'an;
he, his wife, and all belonging to him, and all
those that accompanied him, together with those
that joined him from the people of the land; but
Naḥor, Avram's brother, and Teraḥ his father,
and Lot the son of Haran and all belonging to
them dwelled in Haran.

11 In the fifth year of Avram's dwelling in the
land of Kana'an the people of Sodom and
Gomorrah and all the cities of the plain revolted
from the power of Kedorlaomer, king of Elam;

for all the kings of the cities of the plain had served Kedorlaomer for twelve years, and given him a yearly tax, but in those days in the thirteenth year, they rebelled against him. **12** And in the tenth year of Avram's dwelling in the land of Kana'an there was war between Nimrod king of Shinar and Kedorlaomer king of Elam, and Nimrod came to fight with Kedorlaomer and to subdue him. **13** For Kedorlaomer was at that time one of the princes of the hosts of Nimrod, and when all the people at the tower were dispersed and those that remained were also scattered upon the face of the earth, Kedorlaomer went to the land of Elam and reigned over it and rebelled against his master.

14 And in those days when Nimrod saw that the cities of the plain had rebelled, he came with pride and anger to war with Kedorlaomer, and Nimrod assembled all his princes and subjects, about seven hundred thousand men, and went against Kedorlaomer, and Kedorlaomer went out to meet him with five thousand men, and they prepared for battle in the valley of Bavel which is between Elam and Shinar. **15** And all those kings fought there, and Nimrod and his people were struck before the people of Kedorlaomer, and there fell from Nimrod's men about six hundred thousand, and Mardon the king's son fell among them. **16** And Nimrod fled and returned in shame and disgrace to his land, and he was under subjection to Kedorlaomer for a long time, and Kedorlaomer returned to his land and sent princes of his host to the kings that dwelled around him, to Ariokh king of Elasar, and to Tidal king of Goyim, and cut a covenant with them, and they were all obedient to his commands.

17 And it was in the fifteenth year of Avram's dwelling in the land of Kana'an, which is the seventieth year of the life of Avram, and 𐤉𐤄𐤅𐤄 appeared to Avram in that year and He said to him, "I am 𐤉𐤄𐤅𐤄 who brought you out of Ur Kasdim to give you this land for an inheritance. **18** Now therefore walk before Me and be perfect and guard My commands, for to you and to your seed I will give this land for an inheritance, from the river Mitsrayim to the great river Perath[a]. **19** And you shall go to your fathers in peace and in good age, and the fourth generation shall return here in this land and shall inherit it forever;" and Avram built an altar, and he called upon the name of 𐤉𐤄𐤅𐤄 who appeared to him, and he brought up ascension offerings upon the altar to 𐤉𐤄𐤅𐤄.

20 At that time Avram returned and went to Haran to see his father and mother, and his father's household, and Avram and his wife and all belonging to him returned to Haran, and Avram dwelled in Haran five years. **21** And many of the people of Haran, about seventy-two men, followed Avram and Avram taught them the correction of 𐤉𐤄𐤅𐤄 and His ways, and he taught them to know 𐤉𐤄𐤅𐤄.

22 In those days 𐤉𐤄𐤅𐤄 appeared to Avram in Haran, and He said to him, "Behold, I spoke to you twenty years ago saying, **23** 'Go forth from your land, from your birth-place and from your father's house, to the land which I have shown you to give it to you and to your children, for there in that land will I bless you, and make you a great nation, and make your name great, and in you shall the families of the earth be blessed.'

24 "Now therefore arise, go forth from this place, you, your wife, and all belonging to you, also everyone born in your house and all the beings you have made in Haran, and bring them out with you from here, and rise to return to the land of Kana'an."

25 And Avram arose and took his wife Sarai and all belonging to him and all that were born to him in his house and the beings which they had made in Haran, and they came out to go to the land of Kana'an. **26** And Avram went and returned to the land of Kana'an, according to the word of 𐤉𐤄𐤅𐤄. And Lot the son of his brother Haran went with him, and Avram was seventy-five years old when he went forth from Haran to return to the land of Kana'an. **27** And he came to the land of Kana'an according to the word of 𐤉𐤄𐤅𐤄 to Avram, and he pitched his tent and he

---

[a] **13:18** Perath – Most likely the Euphrates river, and probably the etymological origin of the name.

dwelled in the plain of Mamre, and with him was
Lot his brother's son, and all belonging to him.

28 And 𐤉𐤄𐤅𐤄 again appeared to Avram and said,
"To your seed will I give this land;" and he built
there an altar to 𐤉𐤄𐤅𐤄 who appeared to him,
which is still to this day in the plains of Mamre.

14

1 In those days there was in the land of
Shinar a wise man who had understanding in all
wisdom, and of a beautiful appearance, but he
was poor and indigent; his name was Riqayon
and he was hard set in his livelihood. 2 And he
resolved to go to Mitsrayim, to Oswiris[a] the son
of Anom king of Mitsrayim, to show the king his
wisdom; for perhaps he might find favor in his
sight, to raise him up and give him a livelihood;
and Riqayon did so.

3 And when Riqayon came to Mitsrayim he
asked the inhabitants of Mitsrayim concerning
the king, and the inhabitants of Mitsrayim told
him the custom of the king of Mitsrayim, for it
was then the custom of the king of Mitsrayim
that he went from his royal palace and was seen
abroad only one day in the year, and after that
the king would return to his palace to remain
there. 4 And on the day when the king went forth
he passed judgment in the land, and everyone
having a suit came before the king that day to
obtain his request.

5 And when Riqayon heard of the custom in
Mitsrayim and that he could not come into the
presence of the king, he grieved greatly and was
very sorrowful. 6 And in the evening Riqayon
went out and found a house in ruins, formerly a
bakers' house in Mitsrayim, and he stayed there
all night in bitterness of being and pinched with
hunger, and sleep was removed from his eyes.
7 And Riqayon considered in his heart what he
should do in the town until the king made his
appearance, and how he might maintain himself
there. 8 And he arose in the morning and walked
about, and met in his way those who sold
vegetables and various sorts of seed with which
they supplied the inhabitants. 9 And Riqayon
wished to do the same in order to get a livelihood
in the city, but he was unacquainted with the
custom of the people, and he was like a blind
man among them.

10 And he went and obtained vegetables to sell
them for his support, and the sons of Beliya'al
assembled about him and ridiculed him, and took
his vegetables from him and left him nothing.
11 And he arose up from there in bitterness of
being, and went sighing to the bakers' *house* in
which he had remained all the night before, and
he slept there the second night. 12 And on that
night again he reasoned within himself how he
could save himself from starvation, and he
devised a scheme how to act.

13 And he arose in the morning and acted wisely,
and went and hired thirty strong men of the sons
of Beliya'al, carrying their war instruments in
their hands, and he led them to the top of the
Mitsrite tomb, and he placed them there.

14 And he commanded them, saying, "Thus says
the king, 'Strengthen yourselves and be men of
valor, and let no man be buried here until two
hundred pieces of silver be given, and then he
may be buried;" and those men did according to
the order of Riqayon to the people of Mitsrayim
the whole of that year.

15 And in the time of eight new moons, Riqayon
and his men gathered great riches of silver and
gold, and Riqayon took a great quantity of horses
and other animals, and he hired more men, and
he gave them horses and they remained with
him. 16 And when the year came round, at the
time the king went forth into the town, all the
inhabitants of Mitsrayim assembled together to
speak to him concerning the work of Riqayon
and his men. 17 And the king went forth on the
appointed day, and all the Mitsrites came before
him and cried to him, saying,

18 "May the king live forever. What is this thing
you do in the town to your servants, not to allow
a dead body to be buried until so much silver and

---

[a] **14:2** Oswiris – Possibly the Hebrew transliteration of the Egyptian "Osiris." Osiris was worshiped in Mitsrayim as the el of the dead, as well as of resurrection. He is historically tied to Nimrod in mythology.

gold be given? Was there ever anything like this
done in the whole earth, from the days of former
kings, yes, even from the days of Adam, to this
day, that the dead should not be buried only for a
set price? 19 We know it to be the custom of
kings to take a yearly tax from the living, but
you not only do this, but from the dead you also
exact a yearly tax day by day. 20 Now, O king,
we can no more bear this, for the whole city is
ruined on this account; and do you not know it?"

21 And when the king heard all that they had
spoken he was very wroth, and his anger burned
within him at this affair, for he had known
nothing of it.

22 And the king said, "Who and where is he that
dares to do this wicked thing in my land without
my command? Surely you will tell me."

23 And they told him all the works of Riqayon
and his men, and the king's anger was aroused,
and he ordered Riqayon and his men to be
brought before him.

24 And Riqayon took about a thousand children,
sons and daughters, and clothed them in silk and
embroidery, and he set them upon horses and
sent them to the king by means of his men, and
he also took a great quantity of silver and gold
and precious stones, and a strong and beautiful
horse, as a present for the king, with which he
came before the king and bowed down to the
earth before him; and the king, his servants and
all the inhabitants of Mitsrayim wondered at the
work of Riqayon, and they saw his riches and the
present that he had brought to the king. 25 And it
greatly pleased the king and he wondered at it;
and when Riqayon sat before him the king asked
him concerning all his works, and Riqayon spoke
all his words wisely before the king, his servants
and all the inhabitants of Mitsrayim. 26 And
when the king heard the words of Riqayon and
his wisdom, Riqayon found grace in his sight,
and he met with grace and kindness from all the
servants of the king and from all the inhabitants
of Mitsrayim, on account of his wisdom and
good words, and from that time they loved him
exceedingly.

27 And the king answered and said to Riqayon,
"Your name shall no more be called Riqayon,
but Pharaoh shall be your name, since you
exacted a tax from the dead;" and he called his
name Pharaoh.

28 And the king and his subjects loved Riqayon
for his wisdom, and they consulted with all the
inhabitants of Mitsrayim to make him prefect
under the king. 29 And all the inhabitants of
Mitsrayim and its wise men did so, and it was
made a rule in Mitsrayim.

30 And they made Riqayon Pharaoh prefect
under Oswiris king of Mitsrayim, and Riqayon
Pharaoh governed over Mitsrayim, daily
administering justice to the whole city, but
Oswiris the king would judge the people of the
land one day in the year, when he went out to
make his appearance. 31 And Riqayon Pharaoh
cunningly usurped the government of Mitsrayim,
and he exacted a tax from all the inhabitants of
Mitsrayim.

32 And all the inhabitants of Mitsrayim greatly
loved Riqayon Pharaoh, and they made a statute
to call every king that should reign over them
and their seed in Mitsrayim, Pharaoh.
33 Therefore all the kings that reigned in
Mitsrayim from that time forward were called
Pharaoh to this day.

15 1 And in that year there was a heavy famine
throughout the land of Kana'an, and the
inhabitants of the land could not remain on
account of the famine for it was very heavy.
2 And Avram and all belonging to him rose and
went down to Mitsrayim on account of the
famine, and when they were at the brook
Mitsrayim they remained there some time to rest
from the fatigue of the road. 3 And Avram and
Sarai were walking at the border of the brook
Mitsrayim, and Avram beheld his wife Sarai that
she was exceedingly beautiful.

4 And Avram said to his wife Sarai, "Since
Elohim has created you with such a beautiful
countenance, I am afraid of the Mitsrites lest
they should kill me and take you away, for the
fear of Elohim is not in these places. 5 Surely
then you shall do this: say you are my sister to
all that may ask you, in order that it may be well

with me, and that we may live and not be put to
death."

6 And Avram commanded the same to all those
that came with him to Mitsrayim on account of
the famine; also his nephew Lot he commanded,
saying, "If the Mitsrites ask you concerning Sarai
say, 'she is the sister of Avram.'"

7 And yet with all these orders Avram did not put
confidence in them; he took Sarai and placed her
in an ark and concealed it among their vessels,
for Avram was very afraid about Sarai on
account of the evil of the Mitsrites. 8 And Avram
and all belonging to him rose up from the brook
Mitsrayim and came to Mitsrayim; and they had
scarcely entered the gates of the city when the
guards stood up to them saying, "Give tithe to
the king from what you have, and then you may
come into the town;" and Avram and those that
were with him did so.

9 And Avram with the people that were with him
came to Mitsrayim, and when they came they
brought the ark in which Sarai was concealed
and the Mitsrites saw the ark.

10 And the king's servants approached Avram,
saying, "What do you have here in this ark which
we have not seen? Now, open the ark and give
tithe to the king of all that it contains."

11 And Avram said, "This ark I will not open, but
all you demand upon it I will give." And
Pharaoh's officers answered Avram, saying, "It is
an ark of precious stones, give us the tithe of it."

12 Avram said, "All that you desire I will give,
but you must not open the ark."

13 And the king's officers pressed Avram, and
they reached the ark and opened it with force,
and they saw, and behold a beautiful woman was
in the ark. 14 And when the officers of the king
looked upon Sarai, they were struck with
admiration at her beauty, and all the princes and
servants of Pharaoh assembled to see Sarai, for
she was very beautiful. And the king's officers
ran and told Pharaoh all that they had seen, and
they praised Sarai to the king. And Pharaoh
ordered her to be brought, and the woman came
before the king.

15 And Pharaoh looked upon Sarai and she
pleased him exceedingly, and he was struck with
her beauty, and the king rejoiced greatly on her
account, and made presents to those who brought
him the news concerning her. 16 And the woman
was then brought to Pharaoh's house, and Avram
grieved on account of his wife, and he prayed to
𐤉𐤄𐤅𐤄 to deliver her from the hands of Pharaoh.

17 And Sarai also prayed at that time and said,
"O 𐤉𐤄𐤅𐤄 Elohim, You told my master Avram to
go from his land and from his father's house to
the land of Kana'an, and You promised to do
well with him if he would do Your commands;
now behold, we have done that which You
commanded us, and we left our land and our
families, and we went to a strange land and to a
people whom we have not known before. 18 And
we came to this land to avoid the famine, and
this evil accident has befallen me; now therefore,
O 𐤉𐤄𐤅𐤄 Elohim, deliver us and save us from the
hand of this oppressor, and do well with me for
the sake of Your kindness."

19 And 𐤉𐤄𐤅𐤄 listened to the voice of Sarai, and
𐤉𐤄𐤅𐤄 sent a messenger to deliver Sarai from the
power of Pharaoh. 20 And the king came and sat
before Sarai and behold a messenger of 𐤉𐤄𐤅𐤄
was standing over them, and he appeared to Sarai
and said to her, "Do not fear, for 𐤉𐤄𐤅𐤄 has heard
your prayer."

21 And the king approached Sarai and said to her,
"What is the man to you who brought you here?"
and she said, "He is my brother."

22 And the king said, "It is compulsory upon us
to make him great, to elevate him and to do to
him all the good which you command us;" and at
that time the king sent to Avram silver and gold
and precious stones in abundance, together with
cattle, men servants and maid servants; and the
king ordered Avram to be brought, and he sat in
the court of the king's house, and the king greatly
exalted Avram on that night. 23 And the king
approached to speak to Sarai, and when he
reached out his hand to touch her, the messenger
struck him heavily, and he was terrified and he
refrained from reaching to her. 24 And when the
king came near to Sarai, the messenger struck
him to the ground, and acted thus to him the
whole night, and the king was terrified. 25 And

the messenger on that night struck heavily all the servants of the king, and his whole household, on account of Sarai, and there was a great lamentation that night among the people of Pharaoh's house.

26 And Pharaoh, seeing the evil that happened to him, said, "Surely on account of this woman has this thing happened to me," and he removed himself some distance from her and spoke good words to her heart.

27 And the king said to Sarai, "Tell me, please, concerning the man with whom you cames here;" and Sarai said, "This man is my husband, and I said to you that he was my brother for I was afraid, lest you should put him to death through evil."

28 And the king kept away from Sarai, and the plagues of the messenger of 𐤉𐤄𐤅𐤄 ceased from him and his household; and Pharaoh knew that he was struck on account of Sarai, and the king was greatly astonished at this.

29 And in the morning the king called for Avram and said to him, "What is this you have done to me? Why did you say, 'She is my sister,' owing to which I took her to myself for a wife, and this heavy plague has therefore come upon me and my household? **30** Now therefore here is your wife, take her and go from our land lest we all die on her account." And Pharaoh took more cattle, manservants and maidservants, and silver and gold, to give to Avram, and he returned Sarai his wife to him.

31 And the king took a girl whom he brought forth by his concubines, and he gave her to Sarai for a handmaid.

32 And the king said to his daughter, "It is better for you my daughter to be a handmaid in this man's house than to be mighty woman in my house, after we have seen the evil that happened to us on account of this woman."

33 And Avram arose, and he and all belonging to him went away from Mitarayim; and Pharaoh ordered some of his men to accompany him and all that went with him. **34** And Avram returned to the land of Kana'an, to the place where he had made the altar, where he at first had pitched his tent. **35** And Lot the son of Haran, Avram's brother, had a heavy stock of cattle, flocks and herds and tents, for 𐤉𐤄𐤅𐤄 was bountiful to them on account of Avram.

36 And when Avram was dwelling in the land, the herdsmen of Lot quarreled with the herdsmen of Avram, for their property was too great for them to remain together in the land, and the land could not bear them on account of their cattle. **37** And when Avram's herdsmen went to feed their flock they would not go into the fields of the people of the land, but the cattle of Lot's herdsmen did otherwise, for they were allowed to feed in the fields of the people of the land. **38** And the people of the land saw this occurrence daily, and they came to Avram and quarreled with him on account of Lot's herdsmen.

39 And Avram said to Lot, "What is this you are doing to me, to make me odious to the inhabitants of the land, that you ordered your herdsman to feed your cattle in the fields of other people? Do you not know that I am a sojourner in this land among the children of Kana'an, and why do you do this to me?"

40 And Avram quarreled daily with Lot on account of this, but Lot would not listen to Avram, and he continued to do the same and the inhabitants of the land came and told Avram.

41 And Avram said to Lot, "How long will you be to me for a stumbling block with the inhabitants of the land? Now I entreat you, let there be no more quarrelling between us, for we are kinsmen. **42** But I ask you: separate from me, go and choose a place where you may dwell with your cattle and all belonging to you, but keep yourself at a distance from me, you and your household. **43** And do not be afraid to go from me, for if anyone injures you, let me know and I will avenge your cause from him; only remove from me."

44 And when Avram had spoken all these words to Lot, then Lot arose and lifted up his eyes toward the plain of the Yarden. **45** And he saw that the whole of this place was well watered, and good for man as well as affording pasture for the cattle. **46** And Lot went from Avram to that place, and there he pitched his tent, and he

dwelled in Sodom, and they were separated from
each other.

47 And Avram dwelled in the plain of Mamre,
which is in Ḥevron, and he pitched his tent there,
and Avram remained in that place many years.

16 1 At that time Kedorlaomer king of Elam
sent to all the neighboring kings, to Nimrod, king
of Shinar who was then under his power, and to
Tidal, king of Goyim, and to Ariokh, king of
Elasar, with whom he cut a covenant, saying,
"Come up to me and assist me, that we may
strike all the towns of Sodom and its inhabitants,
for they have rebelled against me these thirteen
years."

2 And these four kings went up with all their
camps, about eight hundred thousand men, and
they went as they were, and struck every man
they found in their road. 3 And the five kings of
Sodom and Gomorrah, Shinav king of Admah,
Shemever king of Tseboyim, Bera king of
Sodom, Bersha king of Gomorrah, and Bela king
of Tsor, went out to meet them, and they all
joined together in the valley of Siddim. 4 And
these nine kings made war in the valley of
Siddim; and the kings of Sodom and Gomorrah
were struck before the kings of Elam.

5 And the valley of Siddim was full of lime pits
and the kings of Elam pursued the kings of
Sodom, and the kings of Sodom with their camps
fled and fell into the lime pits, and all that
remained went to the mountain for safety, and
the five kings of Elam came after them and
pursued them to the gates of Sodom, and they
took all that there was in Sodom. 6 And they
plundered all the cities of Sodom and Gomorrah,
and they also took Lot, Avram's brother's son,
and his property, and they seized all the goods of
the cities of Sodom, and they went away; and
Og, Avram's servant, who was in the battle, saw
this, and told Avram all that the kings had done
to the cities of Sodom, and that Lot was taken
captive by them. 7 And Avram heard this, and he
rose up with about three hundred and eighteen
men that were with him, and he pursued these
kings that night, and struck them, and they all
fell before Avram and his men, and there was
none remaining but the four kings who fled, and
they went each his own road.

8 And Avram recovered all the property of
Sodom, and he also recovered Lot and his
property, their wives and little ones and all
belonging to them, so that Lot lacked nothing.

9 And when he returned from striking these
kings, he and his men passed the valley of
Siddim where the kings had made war together.
10 And Bera king of Sodom, and the rest of his
men that were with him, went out from the lime
pits into which they had fallen, to meet Avram
and his men. 11 And Adoni-tsedeq king of
Yerushalayim, who was Shem, went out with his
men to meet Avram and his people, with bread
and wine, and they remained together in the
valley of king. 12 And Adoni-tsedeq blessed
Avram, and Avram gave him a tenth from all
that he had brought from the spoil of his
enemies, for Adoni-tsedeq was a priest before
Elohim.

13 And all the kings of Sodom and Gomorrah
who were there, with their servants, approached
Avram and begged of him to return them their
servants whom he had made captive, and to take
for himself all the property.

14 And Avram answered the kings of Sodom,
saying, "As 𐤉𐤄𐤅𐤄 lives who created the heavens
and the earth, and who redeemed my being from
all affliction, and who delivered me today from
my enemies, and gave them into my hand, I will
not take anything belonging to you, that you may
not boast tomorrow, saying, 'Avram became rich
from our property that he saved.' 15 For 𐤉𐤄𐤅𐤄 my
Elohim in whom I trust said to me, 'You shall
lack nothing, for I will bless you in all the works
of your hands.' 16 And now therefore behold,
here is all that belongs to you, take it and go; as
𐤉𐤄𐤅𐤄 lives I will not take from you from a living
being down to a sandal strap or thread, excepting
the expense of the food of those who went out
with me to battle, as also the portions of the men
who went with me: Aner, Eshkol, and Mamre,
they and their men, as well as those also who had
remained to watch the baggage, they shall take
their portion of the spoil."

17 And the kings of Sodom gave Avram
according to all that he had said, and they
pressed him to take of whatever he chose, but he
would not. 18 And he sent away the kings of
Sodom and the remainder of their men, and he
gave them orders about Lot, and they went to
their respective places. 19 And Lot, his brother's
son, he also sent away with his property, and he
went with them, and Lot returned to his home, to
Sodom, and Avram and his people returned to
their home to the plains of Mamre, which is in
Ḥevron.

20 At that time 𐤉𐤄𐤅𐤄 again appeared to Avram in
Ḥevron, and He said to him, "Do not fear, your
reward is very great before Me, for I will not
leave you, until I have multiplied you, and
blessed you and made your seed like the stars in
the heavens, which cannot be measured nor
numbered. 21 And I will give to your seed all
these lands that you see with your eyes; to them
will I give them for an inheritance forever, only
be strong and do not fear, walk before Me and be
perfect."

22 And in the seventy-eighth year of the life of
Avram, in that year died Reu, the son of Peleg,
and all the days of Reu were two hundred and
thirty-nine years, and he died. 23 And Sarai, the
daughter of Haran, Avram's wife, was still barren
in those days; she did not bear to Avram either
son or daughter. 24 And when she saw that she
bore no children she took her handmaid Hagar,
whom Pharaoh had given her, and she gave her
to Avram her husband for a wife. 25 For Hagar
learned all the ways of Sarai as Sarai taught her:
she was not in any way deficient in following her
good ways.

26 And Sarai said to Avram, "Behold, here is my
handmaid Hagar, go to her that she may bring
forth upon my knees, that I may also obtain
children through her."

27 And at the end of ten years of Avram's
dwelling in the land of Kana'an, which is the
eighty-fifth year of Avram's life, Sarai gave
Hagar to him. 28 And Avram listened to the
voice of his wife Sarai, and he took her
handmaid Hagar and Avram came to her and she
conceived.

29 And when Hagar saw that she had conceived
she rejoiced greatly, and her mistress was
despised in her eyes, and she said within herself,
"This can only be that I am better before 𐤉𐤄𐤅𐤄
than Sarai my mistress, for all the days that my
mistress has been with my master, she did not
conceive, but I conceived by him in a short
time."

30 And when Sarai saw that Hagar had conceived
by Avram, Sarai was jealous of her handmaid,
and Sarai said within herself, "This is surely
nothing else but that she must be better than I
am."

31 And Sarai said to Avram, "My wrong be upon
you, for at the time when you prayed before
𐤉𐤄𐤅𐤄 for children, why did you not pray on my
account, that 𐤉𐤄𐤅𐤄 should give me seed from
you? 32 And when I speak to Hagar in your
presence, she despises my words, because she
has conceived, and you will say nothing to her;
may 𐤉𐤄𐤅𐤄 judge between me and you for what
you have done to me.

33 And Avram said to Sarai, "Behold your
handmaid is in your hand; do to her as it may
seem good in your eyes;" and Sarai afflicted her,
and Hagar fled from her to the wilderness.

34 And a messenger of 𐤉𐤄𐤅𐤄 found her in the
place where she had fled, by a well, and he said
to her, "Do not fear, for I will multiply your
seed, for you shall bear a son and you shall call
his name Yishma'el; now then return to Sarai
your mistress, and submit yourself under her
hands. 35 And Hagar called the place of that well
Beer-lahai-roi, it is between Qadesh and the
wilderness of Bered. 36 And Hagar at that time
returned to her master's house, and at the end of
days Hagar bore a son to Avram, and Avram
called his name Yishma'el; and Avram was
eighty-six years old when he brought forth him.

17 1 And in those days, in the ninety-first year
of the life of Avram, the sons of Kittim made
war with the sons of Tuval, for when 𐤉𐤄𐤅𐤄 had
scattered the sons of men upon the face of the
earth, the children of Kittim went and embodied
themselves in the plain of Kanopia, and they
built themselves cities there and dwelled by the

river Tibreu. 2 And the sons of Tuval dwelled in
Tuskanah, and their boundaries reached the river
Tibreu, and the sons of Tuval built a city in
Tuskanah, and they called the name Sabinah,
after the name of Sabinah son of Tuval their
father, and they dwelled there to this day.

3 And it was at that time the sons of Kittim made
war with the sons of Tuval, and the sons of
Tuval were struck before the sons of Kittim, and
the sons of Kittim caused three hundred and
seventy men to fall from the sons of Tuval.
4 And at that time the sons of Tuval swore to the
sons of Kittim, saying, "You shall not intermarry
among us, and no man shall give his daughter to
any of the sons of Kittim."

5 For all the daughters of Tuval were in those
days fair, for no women were then found in the
whole earth so fair as the daughters of Tuval.
6 And all who delighted in the beauty of women
went to the daughters of Tuval and took wives
from them, and the sons of men, kings and
princes, who greatly delighted in the beauty of
women, took wives in those days from the
daughters of Tuval. 7 And at the end of three
years after the sons of Tuval had sworn to the
sons of Kittim not to give them their daughters
for wives, about twenty men of the sons of
Kittim went to take some of the daughters of
Tuval, but they found none.

8 For the sons of Tuval kept their oaths not to
intermarry with them, and they would not break
their oaths. 9 And in the days of harvest the sons
of Tuval went into their fields to get in their
harvest, when the young men of Kittim
assembled and went to the city of Sabinah, and
each man took a young woman from the
daughters of Tuval, and they came to their cities.
10 And the sons of Tuval heard of it and they
went to make war with them, and they could not
prevail over them, for the mountain was
exceedingly high from them, and when they saw
they could not prevail over them they returned to
their land.

11 And at the revolution of the year the sons of
Tuval went and hired about ten thousand men
from those cities that were near them, and they
went to war with the sons of Kittim. 12 And the
sons of Tuval went to war with the sons of
Kittim, to destroy their land and to distress them,
and in this engagement the sons of Tuval
prevailed over the sons of Kittim, and the sons of
Kittim, seeing that they were greatly distressed,
lifted up the children which they had had by the
daughters of Tuval, upon the wall which had
been built, to be before the eyes of the sons of
Tuval.

13 And the sons of Kittim said to them, "Have
you come to make war with your own sons and
daughters, and have we not been considered your
flesh and bones from that time until now?"

14 And when the sons of Tuval heard this they
ceased to make war with the sons of Kittim, and
they went away. 15 And they returned to their
cities, and the sons of Kittim at that time
assembled and built two cities by the sea, and
they called one Purtu and the other Aritsah.
16 And Avram the son of Teraḥ was then ninety-
nine years old.

17 At that time 𐤉𐤄𐤅𐤄 appeared to him and He
said to him, "I will cut My covenant between Me
and you, and I will greatly multiply your seed,
and this is the covenant which I cut between Me
and you, that every male child be circumcised,
you and your seed after you. 18 At eight days old
shall he be circumcised, and this covenant shall
be in your flesh for an everlasting covenant.
19 And now therefore your name shall no more
be called Avram but Avraham, and your wife
shall no more be called Sarai but Sarah. 20 For I
will bless you both, and I will multiply your seed
after you that you shall become a great nation,
and kings shall come forth from you."

18 1 And Avraham rose and did all that Elohim
had ordered him, and he took the men of his
household and those bought with his money, and
he circumcised them as 𐤉𐤄𐤅𐤄 had commanded
him. 2 And there was not one left whom he did
not circumcise. And Avraham and his son
Yishma'el were circumcised in the flesh of their
foreskin; thirteen years old was Yishma'el when
he was circumcised in the flesh of his foreskin.

*𐤐𐤓𐤔𐤕 𐤅𐤉𐤓𐤀 – **Parashat Vayeira***

3 And in the third day Avraham went out of his
tent and sat at the tent doorway to warm himself
in the heat of the sun, during the pain of his
flesh.

4 And 𐤉𐤄𐤅𐤄 appeared to him in the plain of
Mamre, and sent three of His ministering
messengers to visit him; and he was sitting at the
door of the tent, and he lifted his eyes and saw,
and behold, three men were coming from a
distance, and he rose up and ran to meet them,
and he bowed down to them and brought them
into his house.

5 And he said to them, "If now I have found
favor in your sight, turn in and eat a morsel of
bread;" and he pressed them, and they turned in
and he gave them water and they washed their
feet, and he placed them under a tree at the door
of the tent.

6 And Avraham ran and took a calf, tender and
good, and he hurried to kill it, and gave it to his
servant Eliezer to dress.

7 And Avraham came to Sarah into the tent, and
he said to her, "Make ready quickly three
measures of fine meal, knead it and make cakes
to cover the pot containing the meat," and she
did so.

8 And Avraham hurried and brought before them
butter and milk, beef and lamb, and gave it
before them to eat before the flesh of the calf
was aged, and they did eat.

9 And when they had done eating one of them
said to him, "I will return to you according to the
time of life, and Sarah your wife shall have a
son."

10 And the men afterward departed and went
their ways, to the places to which they were sent.

11 In those days all the people of Sodom and
Gomorrah, and of the whole five cities, were
exceedingly evil and sinful against 𐤉𐤄𐤅𐤄 and
they provoked 𐤉𐤄𐤅𐤄 with their abominations,
and they grew in their abominations before
𐤉𐤄𐤅𐤄. And a cry arose in those days, and it was
great before 𐤉𐤄𐤅𐤄. 12 And they had in their land
a very extensive valley, about half a day's walk,
and in it there were fountains of water and a
great deal of herbage surrounding the water.
13 And all the people of Sodom and Gomorrah
went there four times in the year, with their
wives and children and all belonging to them,
and they rejoiced there with timbrels and dances.
14 And in the time of rejoicing they would all
rise and lay hold of their neighbor's wives, and
some, the virgin daughters of their neighbors,
and they abused them, and each man saw his
wife and daughter in the hands of his neighbor
and did not say a word. 15 And they did so from
morning to night, and they afterward returned
home each man to his house and each woman to
her tent; so they always did four times in the
year.

16 Also when a stranger came into their cities and
brought goods which he had purchased with
plans to sell them there, the people of these cities
would assemble, men, women, and children,
young and old, and go to the man and take his
goods by force, giving a little to each man until
there was an end to all the goods of the owner
which he had brought into the land. 17 And if the
owner of the goods quarreled with them, saying,
"What is this work which you have done to me?"
then they would approach to him one by one, and
each would show him the little which he took
and taunt him, saying, "I only took that little
which you gave me;" and when he heard this
from them all, he would arise and go from them
in sorrow and bitterness of being, when they
would all arise and go after him, and drive him
out of the city with great noise and tumult.

18 And there was a man from the country of
Elam who was leisurely going on the road,
seated upon his donkey, which carried a fine
mantle of diverse colors, and the mantle was
bound with a cord upon the donkey. 19 And the
man was on his journey passing through the
street of Sodom when the sun set in the evening,
and he remained there in order to stay during the
night, but no one would let him into his house.
And at that time there was in Sodom an evil and
worthless man; one skillful to do evil, and his
name was Hedad. 20 And he lifted up his eyes
and saw the traveler in the street of the city, and
he came to him and said, "Where have you come
from, and where are you going?"

21 And the man said to him, "I am traveling from Ḥevron to Elam where I belong, and as I passed the sun set and no one would allow me to enter his house, though I had bread and water and also straw and provender for my donkey, and am short of nothing."

22 And Hedad answered and said to him, "All that you need shall be supplied by me, but you shall not stay in the street all night."

23 And Hedad brought him to his house, and he
took off the mantle from the donkey with the
cord, and brought them to his house, and he gave
the donkey straw and provender while the
traveler ate and drank in Hedad's house, and he
stayed there that night. 24 And in the morning the
traveler rose up early to continue his journey,
when Hedad said to him, "Wait, comfort your
heart with a morsel of bread and then go," and
the man did so; and he remained with him, and
they both ate and drank together during the day,
when the man rose up to go.

25 And Hedad said to him, "Behold now the day is declining, you had better remain all night that your heart may be comforted;" and he pressed him so that he stayed there all night, and on the second day he rose up early to leave, when Hedad pressed him, saying, "Comfort your heart with a morsel of bread and then go," and he remained and ate with him also the second day, and then the man rose up to continue his journey.

26 And Hedad said to him, "Behold now the day is declining, remain with me to comfort your heart and in the morning rise up early and go your way."

27 And the man would not remain, but rose and saddled his donkey, and while he was saddling his donkey Hadad's wife said to her husband, "Behold this man has remained with us for two days eating and drinking and he has given us nothing, and now shall he go away from us without giving anything?" and Hedad said to her, "Be silent."

28 And the man saddled his donkey to go, and he asked Hedad to give him the cord and mantle to tie it upon the donkey.

29 And Hedad said to him, "What are you saying?" And he said to him, "That you, my master, should give me the cord and the mantle made with diverse colors which you concealed with you in your house to take care of it."

30 And Hedad answered the man, saying, "This is the interpretation of your dream: the cord which you saw, means that your life will be lengthened out like a cord, and having seen the mantle colored with all sorts of colors, means that you shall have a vineyard in which you will plant trees of all fruits."

31 And the traveler answered, saying, "Not so my
master, for I was awake when I gave you the
cord and also a mantle woven with diverse
colors, which you took off the donkey to put
them by for me;" and Hedad answered and said,
"Surely I have told you the interpretation of your
dream and it is a good dream, and this is the
interpretation of it. 32 Now the sons of men give
me four pieces of silver, which is my charge for
interpreting dreams, but I will only require three
pieces of silver from you."

33 And the man was provoked at the words of Hedad, and he cried bitterly, and he brought Hedad to Seraq judge of Sodom.

34 And the man laid his cause before Seraq the judge, when Hedad replied, saying, "It is not so, but thus the matter stands;" and the judge said to the traveler, "This man Hedad tells you truth, for he is famed in the cities for the accurate interpretation of dreams."

35 And the man cried at the word of the judge, and he said, "Not so my master, for it was in the day that I gave him the cord and mantle which was upon the donkey, in order to put them by in his house;" and they both disputed before the judge, the one saying, "Thus the matter was," and the other declaring otherwise.

36 And Hedad said to the man, "Give me four pieces of silver that I charge for my interpretations of dreams; I will not make any allowance; and give me the expense of the four meals that you ate in my house."

37 And the man said to Hedad, "Truly I will pay you for what I ate in your house, only give me

the cord and mantle which you concealed in your
house."

38 And Hedad replied before the judge and said
to the man, "Did I not tell you the interpretation
of your dream? The cord means that your days
shall be lengthened like a cord, and the mantle,
that you will have a vineyard in which you will
plant all kinds of fruit trees. 39 This is the proper
interpretation of your dream, now give me the
four pieces of silver that I require as a
compensation, for I will make you no
allowance."

40 And the man cried at the words of Hedad and
they both quarreled before the judge, and the
judge gave orders to his servants, who drove
them rashly from the house. 41 And they went
away quarreling from the judge, when the people
of Sodom heard them, and they gathered about
them and they exclaimed against the traveler,
and they drove him rashly from the city. 42 And
the man continued his journey upon his donkey
with bitterness of being, lamenting and weeping.
43 And while he was going along he wept at what
had happened to him in the corrupt city of
Sodom.

19 1 And the cities of Sodom had four judges to
four cities, and these were their names, Seraq in
the city of Sodom, Sharqad in Gomorrah,
Zavnakh in Admah, and Menon in Tseboyim.

2 And Eliezer Avraham's servant applied to them
different names, and he *changed* Seraq *to*
Shaqra, Sharqad *to* Shaqrura, Zevnakh *to*
Kezobin, and Menon to Matsoli-din.

3 And by desire of their four judges the people of
Sodom and Gomorrah had beds erected in the
streets of the cities, and if a man came to these
places they would lay hold of him and bring him
to one of their beds, and make him lie in them by
force. 4 And as he lay down, three men would
stand at his head and three at his feet, and
measure him by the length of the bed, and if the
man was less than the bed these six men would
stretch him at each end, and when he cried out to
them they would not answer him.

5 And if he was longer than the bed they would
draw together the two sides of the bed at each
end, until the man had reached the gates of death.

6 And if he continued to cry out to them, they
would answer him, saying, "Thus shall it be done
to a man that comes into our land."

7 And when men heard all these things that the
people of the cities of Sodom did, they refrained
from coming there. 8 And when a poor man
came to their land they would give him silver
and gold, and cause a proclamation in the whole
city not to give him a morsel of bread to eat, and
if the guest should remain there some days, and
die from hunger, not having been able to obtain a
morsel of bread, then at his death all the people
of the city would come and take their silver and
gold which they had given to him. 9 And those
that could recognize the silver or gold which
they had given him took it back, and at his death
they also stripped him of his garments, and they
would fight about them, and he that prevailed
over his neighbor took them. 10 They would after
that carry him and bury him under some of the
shrubs in the wildernesses; so they did all the
days to any one that came to them and died in
their land.

11 And in the course of time Sarah sent Eliezer to
Sodom, to see Lot and *see if he* fared in peace.

12 And Eliezer went to Sodom, and he met a man
of Sodom fighting with a foreigner, and the man
of Sodom stripped the poor man of all his clothes
and went away. 13 And this poor man cried to
Eliezer and pleaded his favor on account of what
the man of Sodom had done to him.

14 And he said to him, "Why do you act thus to
the poor man who came to your land?"

15 And the man of Sodom answered Eliezer,
saying, "Is this man your brother, or have the
people of Sodom made you a judge today, that
you speak about this man?"

16 And Eliezer strove with the man of Sodom on
account of the poor man, and when Eliezer
approached to recover the poor man's clothes
from the man of Sodom, he hurried and with a
stone struck Eliezer in the forehead.

17 And the blood flowed from Eliezer's forehead, and when the man saw the blood he caught hold of Eliezer, saying, "Give me my wage for having rid you of this evil blood that was in your forehead, for such is the statute and law in our land."

18 And Eliezer said to him, "You have wounded me and require me to pay you your hire;" and Eliezer would not listen to the words of the man of Sodom.

19 And the man laid hold of Eliezer and brought him to Shaqra the judge of Sodom for judgment.

20 And the man spoke to the judge, saying, "I entreat you my master, thus has this man done, for I struck him with a stone so that the blood flowed from his forehead, and he is unwilling to give me my wage."

21 And the judge said to Eliezer, "This man speaks truth to you, give him his wage, for this is the judgment in our land;" and Eliezer heard the words of the judge, and he lifted up a stone and struck the judge, and the stone struck on his forehead, and the blood flowed from the forehead of the judge, and Eliezer said, "If this then is the judgment in your land, then you give this man what I should have given him, for this has been your decision; you decreed it."

22 And Eliezer left the man of Sodom with the judge, and he went away.

23 And when the kings of Elam had made war with the kings of Sodom, the kings of Elam captured all the property of Sodom, and they took Lot captive, with his property, and when it was told to Avraham he went and made war with the kings of Elam, and he recovered from their hands all the property of Lot as well as the property of Sodom.

24 At that time the wife of Lot bore him a daughter, and he called her name Paltith, because Elohim had delivered him and his whole household from the kings of Elam; and Paltith daughter of Lot grew up, and one of the men of Sodom took her for a wife.

25 And a poor man came into the city to seek a
livelihood, and he remained in the city some
days, and all the people of Sodom caused a
proclamation of judgment not to give this man a
morsel of bread to eat, until he dropped dead
upon the earth, and they did so.
26 And Paltith
the daughter of Lot saw this man lying in the
streets starved with hunger, and no one would
give him anything to keep him alive, and he was
just upon the point of death.
27 And her being
was filled with pity on account of the man, and
she fed him secretly with bread for many days,
and the being of this man was revived.
28 For
when she went forth to fetch water she would put
the bread in the water pitcher, and when she
came to the place where the poor man was, she
took the bread from the pitcher and gave it him
to eat; so she did many days.

29 And all the people of Sodom and Gomorrah wondered how this man could bear starvation for so many days.

30 And they said to each other, "This can only be that he eats and drinks, for no man can bear starvation for so many days or live as this man has, without even his countenance changing;" and three people concealed themselves in a place where the poor man was located, to know who it was that brought him bread to eat.

31 And Paltith daughter of Lot went forth that day to fetch water, and she put bread into her pitcher of water, and she went to draw water by the poor man's place, and she took out the bread from the pitcher and gave it to the poor man and he ate it.

32 And the three men saw what Paltith did to the poor man, and they said to her, "It is you then who has been supporting him, and therefore has he not starved, nor changed in appearance nor died like the rest."

33 And the three men went out of the place in which they were concealed, and they seized Paltith and the bread which was in the poor man's hand.

34 And they took Paltith and brought her before their judges, and they said to them, "Thus did she do, and it is she who supplied the poor man with bread, therefore he did not die all this time; now therefore declare to us the punishment due to this woman for having disobeyed our judgment."

35 And the people of Sodom and Gomorrah
assembled and kindled a fire in the street of the
city, and they took the woman and cast her into
the fire and she was burned to ashes.

36 And in the city of Admah there was a woman
to whom they did the like. 37 For a traveler came
into the city of Admah to stay there all night,
with the intention of going home in the morning,
and he sat opposite the door of the house of the
young woman's father, to remain there, as the
sun had set when he had reached that place; and
the young woman saw him sitting by the door of
the house.

38 And he asked her for a drink of water and she
said to him, "Who are you?" and he said to her,
"I was today going on the road, and reached here
when the sun set, so I will stay here all night, and
in the morning I will arise early and continue my
journey."

39 And the young woman went into the house
and fetched the man bread and water to eat and
drink. 40 And this affair became known to the
people of Admah, and they assembled and
brought the young woman before the judges, that
they should judge her for this act.

41 And the judge said, "The judgment of death
must pass upon this woman because she
disobeyed our judgments, and this therefore is
the decision concerning her."

42 And the people of those cities assembled and
brought out the young woman, and anointed her
with honey from head to foot, as the judge had
decreed, and they placed her before a swarm of
bees which were then in their hives, and the bees
flew upon her and stung her that her whole body
was swelled. 43 And the young woman cried out
on account of the bees, but no one took notice of
her or pitied her, and her cries ascended to the
heavens.

44 And 𐤉𐤄𐤅𐤄 was provoked at this and at all the
works of the cities of Sodom, for they had
abundance of food, and had tranquility among
them, and still would not sustain the poor and the
needy, and in those days their evil doings and
sins became great before 𐤉𐤄𐤅𐤄.

45 And 𐤉𐤄𐤅𐤄 sent for two of the messengers that
had come to Avraham's house, to destroy Sodom
and its cities. 46 And the messengers rose up
from the door of Avraham's tent, after they had
eaten and drunk, and they reached Sodom in the
evening, and Lot was then sitting in the gate of
Sodom, and when he saw them he rose to meet
them, and he bowed down to the ground. 47 And
he pressed them greatly and brought them into
his house, and he gave them bread which they
ate, and they stayed all night in his house.

48 And the messengers said to Lot, "Arise, go
forth from this place, you and all belonging to
you, lest you be consumed in the iniquity of this
city, for 𐤉𐤄𐤅𐤄 will destroy this place."

49 And the messengers laid hold upon the hand
of Lot and upon the hand of his wife, and upon
the hands of his children, and all belonging to
him, and they brought him forth and set him
outside the cities.

50 And they said to Lot, "Escape for your life,"
and he fled and all belonging to him.

51 Then 𐤉𐤄𐤅𐤄 rained upon Sodom and upon
Gomorrah and upon all these cities brimstone
and fire from 𐤉𐤄𐤅𐤄 out of the heavens.

52 And He overthrew these cities, all the plain
and all the inhabitants of the cities, and that
which grew upon the ground; and Orit the wife
of Lot looked back to see the destruction of the
cities, for her compassion was moved on account
of her daughters who remained in Sodom, for
they did not go with her. 53 And when she looked
back she became a pillar of salt, and it is yet in
that place to this day. 54 And the oxen which
stood in that place daily licked up the salt to the
extremities of their feet, and in the morning it
would spring forth afresh, and they again licked
it up to this day.

55 And Lot and two of his daughters that
remained with him fled and escaped to the cave
of Adullam, and they remained there for some
time. 56 And Avraham rose up early in the
morning to see what had been done to the cities
of Sodom; and he looked and saw the smoke of
the cities going up like the smoke of a furnace.

57 And Lot and his two daughters remained in
the cave, and they made their father drink wine,
and they lay with him, for they said there was no
man upon earth that could raise up seed to them,
for they thought that the whole earth was
destroyed.

58 And they both lay with their father, and they
conceived and bore sons, and the firstborn called
the name of her son Moav, saying, "From my
father did I conceive him;" he is the father of the
Moavites to this day. 59 And the younger also
called her son Ben-Ammi; he is the father of the
children of Ammon to this day.

60 And after this Lot and his two daughters went
away from there, and he dwelled on the other
side of the Yarden with his two daughters and
their sons, and the sons of Lot grew up, and they
went and took themselves wives from the land of
Kana'an, and they brought forth children and
they were fruitful and multiplied.

20 1 And at that time Avraham journeyed from
the plain of Mamre, and he went to the land of
the Philistines, and he dwelled in Gerar; it was in
the twenty-fifth year of Avraham's being in the
land of Kana'an, and the hundredth year of the
life of Avraham, that he came to Gerar in the
land of the Philistines. 2 And when they entered
the land he said to Sarah his wife, "Say you are
my sister, to anyone that asks you, in order that
we may escape the evil of the inhabitants of the
land."

3 And as Avraham was dwelling in the land of
the Philistines, the servants of Avimelekh, king
of the Philistines, saw that Sarah was
exceedingly beautiful, and they asked Avraham
concerning her, and he said, "She is my sister."

4 And the servants of Avimelekh came and
praised Sarah to the king, saying, "A man from
the land of Kana'an is come to dwell in the land,
and he has a sister that is exceedingly beautiful."

5 And Avimelekh heard the words of his servants
who praised Sarah to him, and Avimelekh sent
his officers, and they brought Sarah to the king.
6 And Sarah came to the house of Avimelekh,
and the king saw that Sarah was beautiful, and
she pleased him exceedingly.

7 And he approached her and said to her, "What
is that man to you with whom you came to our
land?" and Sarah answered and said "He is my
brother, and we came from the land of Kana'an
to dwell wherever we could find a place."

8 And Avimelekh said to Sarah, "Behold my land
is before you; place your brother in any part of
this land that pleases you, and it will be our duty
to exalt and elevate him above all the people of
the land since he is your brother."

9 And Avimelekh sent for Avraham, and
Avraham came to Avimelekh.

10 And Avimelekh said to Avraham, "Behold I
have given orders that you shall be honored as
you desire on account of your sister Sarah."

11 And Avraham went forth from the king, and
the king's present followed him.

12 As at evening time, before men lie down to
rest, the king was sitting upon his throne, and a
deep sleep fell upon him, and he lay upon the
throne and slept till morning. 13 And he dreamed
that a messenger of 𐤉𐤄𐤅𐤄 came to him with a
drawn sword in his hand, and the messenger
stood over Avimelekh, and wished to slay him
with the sword. And the king was terrified in his
dream, and said to the messenger, "In what have
I sinned against you that you come to slay me
with your sword?"

14 And the messenger answered and said to
Avimelekh, "Behold, you die on account of the
woman whom you brought to your house last
night, for she is a married woman, the wife of
Avraham who came to your house; now
therefore return that man his wife, for she is his
wife; and if you do not return her, know that you
will surely die, you and all belonging to you."

15 And on that night there was a great outcry in
the land of the Philistines, and the inhabitants of
the land saw the figure of a man standing with a
drawn sword in his hand, and he struck the
inhabitants of the land with the sword; yes, he
continued to strike them. 16 And the messenger
of 𐤉𐤄𐤅𐤄 struck the whole land of the Philistines

on that night, and there was a great confusion on
that night and on the following morning. 17 And
every womb was closed, and all their issues, and
the hand of 𐤉𐤄𐤅𐤄 was upon them on account of
Sarah, wife of Avraham, whom Avimelekh had
taken.

18 And in the morning Avimelekh rose with
terror and confusion and with a great dread, and
he sent and had his servants called in, and he
related his dream to them, and the people were
greatly afraid.

19 And one man standing amongst the servants of
the king answered the king, saying, "O sovereign
king, restore this woman to her husband, for he
is her husband, for this also happened to the king
of Mitsrayim when this man came to Mitsrayim.
20 And he said concerning his wife, 'She is my
sister,' for such is his way when he comes to a
land in which he is a sojourner. 21 And Pharaoh
sent and took this woman for a wife and 𐤉𐤄𐤅𐤄
brought upon him grievous plagues until he
returned the woman to her husband. 22 Now
therefore, O sovereign king, know what
happened last night to the whole land, for there
was a very great confusion and great pain and
lamentation, and we know that it was on account
of the woman which you took. 23 Now, therefore,
restore this woman to her husband, lest it should
happen to us as it did to Pharaoh king of
Mitsrayim and his subjects, and that we may not
die;" and Avimelekh hurried and called and had
Sarah called for, and she came before him, and
he had Avraham called for, and he came before
him.

24 And Avimelekh said to them, "What is this
work you have been doing in saying you are
brother and sister, and I took this woman for a
wife?"

25 And Avraham said, "Because I thought I
should suffer death on account of my wife;" and
Avimelekh took flocks and herds, and
manservants and maidservants, and a thousand
pieces of silver, and he gave them to Avraham,
and he returned Sarah to him.

26 And Avimelekh said to Avraham, "Behold the
whole land is before you, dwell in it wherever
you choose."

27 And Avraham and Sarah, his wife, went forth
from the king's presence with honor and respect,
and they dwelled in the land, even in Gerar.
28 And all the inhabitants of the land of the
Philistines and the king's servants were still in
pain, through the plague which the messenger
had inflicted upon them the whole night on
account of Sarah.

29 And Avimelekh sent for Avraham, saying,
"Pray now for your servants to 𐤉𐤄𐤅𐤄 your
Elohim, that He may put away this death from
among us."

30 And Avraham prayed on account of
Avimelekh and his subjects, and 𐤉𐤄𐤅𐤄 heard the
prayer of Avraham, and He healed Avimelekh
and all his subjects.

21

1 And it was at that time at the end of a year
and four months of Avraham's dwelling in the
land of the Philistines in Gerar, that Elohim
visited Sarah, and 𐤉𐤄𐤅𐤄 remembered her, and
she conceived and bore a son to Avraham. 2 And
Avraham called the name of the son which was
born to him, which Sarah bore to him, Yitsḥaq.
3 And Avraham circumcised his son Yitsḥaq at
eight days old, as Elohim had commanded
Avraham to do to his seed after him. And
Avraham was one hundred, and Sarah ninety
years old, when Yitsḥaq was born to them.

4 And the child grew up and he was weaned, and
Avraham made a great banquet on the day that
Yitsḥaq was weaned. 5 And Shem and Ever and
all the great people of the land, and Avimelekh
king of the Philistines, and his servants, and
Phikol, the captain of his host, came to eat and
drink and rejoice at the banquet which Avraham
made upon the day of his son Yitsḥaq's being
weaned. 6 Also Teraḥ, the father of Avraham,
and Naḥor his brother, came from Haran, they
and all belonging to them, for they greatly
rejoiced on hearing that a son had been born to
Sarah. 7 And they came to Avraham, and they ate
and drank at the banquet which Avraham made
upon the day of Yitsḥaq's being weaned. 8 And
Teraḥ and Naḥor rejoiced with Avraham, and
they remained with him many days in the land of
the Philistines.

9 At that time Serug the son of Reu died, in the
first year of the birth of Yitsḥaq son of Avraham.
10 And all the days of Serug were two hundred
and thirty-nine years, and he died.

11 And Yishma'el the son of Avraham was grown
up in those days; he was fourteen years old when
Sarah bore Yitsḥaq to Avraham. 12 And Elohim
was with Yishma'el the son of Avraham, and he
grew up, and he learned to use the bow and
became an archer.

13 And when Yitsḥaq was five years old he was
sitting with Yishma'el at the door of the tent.
14 And Yishma'el came to Yitsḥaq and seated
himself opposite to him, and he took the bow and
drew it and put the arrow in it, and intended to
slay Yitsḥaq.

15 And Sarah saw the act which Yishma'el
desired to do to her son Yitsḥaq, and it grieved
her exceedingly on account of her son, and she
sent for Avraham, and said to him, "Cast out this
bondwoman and her son, for her son shall not be
heir with my son, for thus did he seek to do to
him today."

16 And Avraham listened to the voice of Sarah,
and he rose up early in the morning, and he took
twelve loaves and a skin of water which he gave
to Hagar, and sent her away with her son, and
Hagar went with her son to the wilderness, and
they dwelled in the wilderness of Paran with the
inhabitants of the wilderness, and Yishma'el was
an archer, and he dwelled in the wilderness a
long time. 17 And he and his mother afterward
went to the land of Mitsrayim, and they dwelled
there, and Hagar took a wife for her son from
Mitsrayim, and her name was Merivah.

18 And the wife of Yishma'el conceived and bore
four sons and two daughters, and Yishma'el and
his mother and his wife and children afterward
went and returned to the wilderness. 19 And they
made themselves tents in the wilderness, in
which they dwelled, and they continued to travel
and then to rest monthly and yearly. 20 And
Elohim gave Yishma'el flocks and herds and
tents on account of Avraham his father, and the
man increased in cattle. 21 And Yishma'el
dwelled in wildernesses and in tents, traveling
and resting for a long time, and he did not see the
face of his father.

22 And in some time after, Avraham said to
Sarah his wife, "I will go and see my son
Yishma'el, for I have a desire to see him, for I
have not seen him for a long time."

23 And Avraham rode upon one of his camels to
the wilderness to seek his son Yishma'el, for he
heard that he was dwelling in a tent in the
wilderness with all belonging to him. 24 And
Avraham went to the wilderness, and he reached
the tent of Yishma'el about noon, and he asked
after Yishma'el, and he found the wife of
Yishma'el sitting in the tent with her children,
and Yishma'el her husband and his mother were
not with them.

25 And Avraham asked the wife of Yishma'el,
saying, "Where has Yishma'el gone?" and she
said, "He has gone to the field to hunt," and
Avraham was still mounted upon the camel, for
he would not get off to the ground as he had
sworn to his wife Sarah that he would not get off
from the camel.

26 And Avraham said to Yishma'el's wife, "My
daughter, give me a little water that I may drink,
for I am weary and faint from the journey."

27 And Yishma'el's wife answered and said to
Avraham, "We have neither water nor bread,"
and she continued sitting in the tent and did not
notice Avraham, neither did she ask him who he
was.

28 But she was beating her children in the tent,
and she was cursing them, and she also cursed
her husband Yishma'el and reproached him, and
Avraham heard the words of Yishma'el's wife to
her children, and he was very angry and
displeased. 29 And Avraham called to the woman
to come out to him from the tent, and the woman
came and stood opposite to Avraham, for
Avraham was still mounted upon the camel.

30 And Avraham said to Yishma'el's wife, "When
your husband Yishma'el returns home say these
words to him, 31 'A very old man from the land
of the Philistines came here seeking you, and
thus was his appearance and figure; I did not ask
him who he was, and seeing you were not here

he spoke to me and said, "When Yishma'el your husband returns tell him thus did this man say," When you come home put away this nail of the tent which you have placed here, and place another nail in its stead.'"

32 And Avraham finished his instructions to the woman, and he turned and went off on the camel homeward. 33 And after that Yishma'el came from the chase he and his mother, and returned to the tent, and his wife spoke these words to him,

34 "A very old man from the land of the Philistines came here seeking you, and thus was his appearance and figure; I did not ask him who he was, and seeing you were not here he said to me, 'When your husband comes home tell him, thus says the old man, "Put away the nail of the tent which you have placed here and place another nail in its stead."'"

35 And Yishma'el heard the words of his wife, and he knew that it was his father, and that his wife did not honor him. 36 And Yishma'el understood his father's words that he had spoken to his wife, and Yishma'el listened to the voice of his father, and Yishma'el cast off that woman and she went away. 37 And Yishma'el afterward went to the land of Kana'an, and he took another wife and he brought her to his tent to the place where he then dwelled.

38 And at the end of three years Avraham said, "I will go again and see Yishma'el my son, for I have not seen him for a long time."

39 And he rode upon his camel and went to the wilderness, and he reached the tent of Yishma'el about noon.

40 And he asked after Yishma'el, and his wife came out of the tent and she said, "He is not here my master, for he has gone to hunt in the fields, and to feed the camels," and the woman said to Avraham, "Turn in my master into the tent, and eat a morsel of bread, for your being must be wearied and faint on account of the journey."

41 And Avraham said to her, "I will not stop for I am in haste to continue my journey, but give me a little water to drink, for I have thirst;" and the woman hurried and ran into the tent and she brought out water and bread to Avraham, which she placed before him and she urged him to eat, and he ate and drank and his heart was comforted and he blessed his son Yishma'el.

42 And he finished his meal and he blessed 𐤉𐤄𐤅𐤄, and he said to Yishma'el's wife, "When Yishma'el comes home say these words to him, 43 'A very old man from the land of the Philistines came here and asked about you, and you were not here; and I brought him out bread and water and he ate and drank and his heart was comforted. 44 And he spoke these words to me: "When Yishma'el your husband comes home, say to him, 'The nail of the tent which you have is very good, do not put it away from the tent.'"'"

45 And Avraham finished commanding the woman, and he rode off to his home to the land of the Philistines; and when Yishma'el came to his tent his wife went forth to meet him with joy and a cheerful heart.

46 And she said to him, "An old man came here from the land of the Philistines and thus was his appearance, and he asked about you and you were not here, so I brought out bread and water, and he ate and drank and his heart was comforted. 47 And he spoke these words to me, 'When Yishma'el your husband comes home say to him, "The nail of the tent which you have is very good, do not put it away from the tent."'"

48 And Yishma'el knew that it was his father, and that his wife had honored him, and 𐤉𐤄𐤅𐤄 blessed Yishma'el.

22

1 And Yishma'el then rose up and took his wife and his children and his cattle and all belonging to him, and he journeyed from there and he went to his father in the land of the Philistines. 2 And Avraham related to Yishma'el his son the transaction with the first wife that Yishma'el took, according to what she did. 3 And Yishma'el and his children dwelled with Avraham many days in that land, and Avraham dwelled in the land of the Philistines a long time.

4 And the days increased and reached twenty six years, and after that Avraham with his servants and all belonging to him went from the land of

the Philistines and removed to a great distance,
and they came near to Ḥevron, and they
remained there, and the servants of Avraham dug
wells of water, and Avraham and all belonging to
him dwelled by the water, and the servants of
Avimelekh king of the Philistines heard the
report that Avraham's servants had dug wells of
water in the borders of the land. 5 And they came
and quarreled with the servants of Avraham, and
they robbed them of the great well which they
had dug.

6 And Avimelekh king of the Philistines heard of this affair, and he with Phikol the captain of his host and twenty of his men came to Avraham, and Avimelekh spoke to Avraham concerning his servants, and Avraham rebuked Avimelekh concerning the well of which his servants had robbed him.

7 And Avimelekh said to Avraham, "As 𐤉𐤄𐤅𐤄 lives who created the whole earth, I did not hear of the act which my servants did to your servants until today."

8 And Avraham took seven ewe lambs and gave them to Avimelekh, saying, "Take these, I ask you, from my hands that it may be a witness for me that I dug this well."

9 And Avimelekh took the seven ewe lambs
which Avraham had given to him, for he had
also given him cattle and herds in abundance,
and Avimelekh swore to Avraham concerning
the well, therefore he called that well Beersheva,
for there they both swore concerning it. 10 And
they both cut a covenant in Beersheva, and
Avimelekh rose up with Phikol the captain of his
host and all his men, and they returned to the
land of the Philistines, and Avraham and all
belonging to him dwelled in Beersheva and he
was in that land a long time.

11 And Avraham planted a large grove in
Beersheva, and he made to it four gates facing
the four sides of the earth, and he planted a
vineyard in it, so that if a traveler came to
Avraham he entered any gate which was in his
road, and remained there and ate and drank and
satisfied himself and then departed. 12 For the
house of Avraham was always open to the sons
of men that passed and repassed, who came daily
to eat and drink in the house of Avraham. 13 And
any man who had hunger and came to Avraham's
house, Avraham would give him bread that he
might eat and drink and be satisfied, and any one
that came naked to his house he would clothe
with garments as he might choose, and give him
silver and gold and make known to him 𐤉𐤄𐤅𐤄
who had created him in the earth; this Avraham
did all his life.

14 And Avraham and his children and all
belonging to him dwelled in Beersheva, and he
pitched his tent as far as Ḥevron. 15 And
Avraham's brother Naḥor and his father and all
belonging to them dwelled in Haran, for they did
not come with Avraham to the land of Kana'an.

16 And children were born to Naḥor which Milkah the daughter of Haran, and sister to Sarah, Avraham's wife, bore to him.

17 And these are the names of those that were born to him: Uts, Buz, Qemuel, Kesed, Ḥazo, Pildash, Yidlaf, and Bethuel, being eight sons, these are the children of Milkah which she bore to Naḥor, Avraham's brother.

18 And Naḥor had a concubine and her name was Reumah, and she also bare to Naḥor, Tevaḥ, Gacham, Taḥash and Ma'akah, being four sons.

19 And the children that were born to Naḥor were twelve sons besides his daughters, and they also had children born to them in Haran.

20 And the children of Uts the first born of Naḥor were Aviḥeref, Gadin, Melus, and Devorah their sister.

21 And the sons of Buz were Berakel, Na'amath, Shevaḥ, and Madoni.

22 And the sons of Qemuel were Aram and Reḥov.

23 And the sons of Kesed were Anamelekh, Meishar, Benon, and Yifi; and the sons of Ḥazo were Pildash, Meki, and Opher.

24 And the sons of Pildash were Arud, Amoram, Merid, and Milokh.

25 And the sons of Yidlaf were Mushan, Kishan, and Mutsa.

26 And the children of Bethuel were Seḥar,
Lavan, and their sister Rivqah.

27 These are the families of the children of
Naḥor, that were born to them in Haran; and
Aram the son of Qemuel, and Reḥov his brother
went away from Haran, and they found a valley
in the land by the river Perath[a]. 28 And they built
a city there, and they called the name of the city
after the name of Pethor the son of Aram, that is
Aram-Naharayim to this day.

29 And the children of Kesed also went to dwell
where they could find a place, and they went and
they found a valley opposite to the land of
Shinar, and they dwelled there. 30 And they built
themselves a city there, and they called the name
at the city Kesed after the name of their father,
that is the land Kasdim to this day, and the
Kasdim dwelled in that land and they were
fruitful and multiplied exceedingly.

31 And Teraḥ, father of Naḥor and Avraham,
went and took another wife in his old age, and
her name was Pelilah, and she conceived and
bare him a son and he called his name Tsova.

32 And Teraḥ lived twenty-five years after he
brought forth Tsova. 33 And Teraḥ died in that
year, that is in the thirty-fifth year of the birth of
Yitsḥaq son of Avraham.

34 And the days of Teraḥ were two hundred and
five years, and he was buried in Haran.

35 And Tsova the son of Teraḥ lived thirty years
and he brought forth Aram, Aklon, and Meriq.

36 And Aram son of Tsova son of Teraḥ, had
three wives and he brought forth twelve sons and
three daughters; and 𐤉𐤄𐤅𐤄 gave to Aram the son
of Tsova, riches and possessions, and abundance
of cattle, and flocks and herds, and the man
increased greatly. 37 And Aram the son of Tsova
and his brother and all his household journeyed
from Haran, and they went to dwell where they
should find a place, for their property was too
great to remain in Haran; for they could not stop
in Haran together with their brethren the children
of Naḥor. 38 And Aram the son of Tsova went
with his brethren, and they found a valley at a
distance toward the eastern country and they
dwelled there. 39 And they also built a city there,
and they called its name Aram, after the name of
their eldest brother; that is Aram-Tsova to this
day.

40 And Yitsḥaq the son of Avraham was growing
in those days, and Avraham his father taught him
the way of 𐤉𐤄𐤅𐤄 to know 𐤉𐤄𐤅𐤄, and 𐤉𐤄𐤅𐤄 was
with him.

41 And when Yitsḥaq was thirty-seven years old,
Yishma'el his brother was going about with him
in the tent.

42 And Yishma'el boasted of himself to Yitsḥaq,
saying, "I was thirteen years old when 𐤉𐤄𐤅𐤄
spoke to my father to circumcise us, and I did
according to the word of 𐤉𐤄𐤅𐤄 which he spoke to
my father, and I gave my being to 𐤉𐤄𐤅𐤄, and I
did not transgress His word which He
commanded my father."

43 And Yitsḥaq answered Yishma'el, saying,
"Why do you boast to me about this, about a
little bit of your flesh which took from your
body, concerning which 𐤉𐤄𐤅𐤄 commanded you?
44 As 𐤉𐤄𐤅𐤄 lives, the Elohim of my father
Avraham, if 𐤉𐤄𐤅𐤄 should say to my father,
"Take now your son Yitsḥaq and offer him as a
ascension offering before me," I would not
refrain but I would joyfully do it."

45 And 𐤉𐤄𐤅𐤄 heard the word that Yitsḥaq spoke
to Yishma'el, and it seemed good in the sight of
𐤉𐤄𐤅𐤄, and He thought to try Avraham in this
matter.

46 And the day arrived when the sons of Elohim
came and placed themselves before 𐤉𐤄𐤅𐤄, and

[a] **22:27** Perath – Most likely the Euphrates river, and probably the etymological origin of the name.

the adversary[a] also came with the sons of Elohim
before 𐤉𐤄𐤅𐤄.[b]

47 And 𐤉𐤄𐤅𐤄 said to the adversary, "Where have
you come from?" and the adversary answered
𐤉𐤄𐤅𐤄 and said, "From going to and fro in the
earth, and from walking up and down in it."

48 And 𐤉𐤄𐤅𐤄 said to the adversary, "What is your
word to Me concerning all the children of the
earth?" and the adversary answered 𐤉𐤄𐤅𐤄 and
said, "I have seen all the children of the earth
who serve You and remember You when they
require anything from You. 49 And when You
give them the thing which they require from
You, they sit at their ease, and forsake You and
they remember You no more. 50 Have You seen
Avraham the son of Teraḥ, who at first had no
children, and he served You and built altars to
You wherever he went, and he offered ascension
offerings upon them, and he proclaimed Your
Name continually to all the children of the earth?
51 And now that his son Yitsḥaq is born to him,
he has forsaken You; he has made a great
banquet for all the inhabitants of the land, and he
has forgotten 𐤉𐤄𐤅𐤄. 52 For in all that he has done
he brought You no offering; neither ascension
offering nor peace offering, neither ox nor lamb
nor goat of all that he killed on the day that his
son was weaned. 53 Even from the time of his
son's birth until now, being thirty-seven years, he
built no altar before You, nor brought any
offering to You, for he saw that You gave him
what he requested before You, and he therefore
forsook You."

54 And 𐤉𐤄𐤅𐤄 said to the adversary, "Have you
set your heart on My servant Avraham? For there
is none like him upon earth, a perfect and an
upright man before Me, one that fears Elohim
and avoids evil; as I live, were I to say to him,
'Bring up Yitsḥaq your son before Me,' he would
not withhold him from Me, much more if I told
him to bring up a ascension offering before Me
from his flock or herds."

55 And the adversary answered 𐤉𐤄𐤅𐤄 and said,
"Speak now to Avraham then, as You have said,
and You will see whether or not he will
transgress and cast aside Your words today."

23 1 At that time the word of 𐤉𐤄𐤅𐤄 came to
Avraham, and He said to him, "Avraham," and
he said, "Here I am."

2 And He said to him, "Take now your son, your
only son whom you love, even Yitsḥaq, and go
to the land of Moriah, and offer him there for a
ascension offering upon one of the mountains
which shall be shown to you, for there will you
see a cloud and glory.

3 And Avraham said within in his heart, "How
shall I separate my son Yitsḥaq from Sarah his
mother, in order to bring him up for a ascension
offering before 𐤉𐤄𐤅𐤄?"

4 And Avraham came into the tent, and he sat
before Sarah his wife, and he spoke these words
to her, 5 "My son Yitsḥaq is grown and he has
not for some time studied the service of his
Elohim. Now tomorrow I will go and bring him
to Shem, and Ever his son, and there he will
learn the ways of 𐤉𐤄𐤅𐤄, for they will teach him
to know 𐤉𐤄𐤅𐤄 as well as to know that when he
prays continually before 𐤉𐤄𐤅𐤄, He will answer
him, therefore there he will know the way of
serving 𐤉𐤄𐤅𐤄 his Elohim."

6 And Sarah said, "You have spoken well; go my
master and do to him as you have said, but do
not take him far away from me, neither let him
remain there too long, for my being is bound
within his being."

---

[a] **22:46** Most translations render the name "Satan" here. However, the Hebrew word 𐤄𐤔𐤈𐤍 (*ha'satan*) is actually not a name. Rather, it is the definite article "the" (represented in Hebrew by the prefix 𐤄) and the word 𐤔𐤈𐤍 (*sa'tan*) which means "adversary."

[b] **22:46** Compare Iyyov [Job] chapters **1** & **2**.

7 And Avraham said to Sarah, "My daughter, let
us pray to 𐤉𐤄𐤅𐤄 our Elohim that He may do good
with us."

8 And Sarah took her son Yitsḥaq and he stayed
all that night with her, and she kissed and
embraced him, and gave him instructions until
morning.

9 And she said to him, "O my son, how can my
being separate itself from you?" And she still
kissed him and embraced him, and she gave
Avraham instructions concerning him.

10 And Sarah said to Avraham, "O my master, I
ask you: guard your son, and place your eyes
over him, for I have no other son nor daughter
but him." 11 O forsake him not. If he is hungry
give him bread, and if he is thirsty give him
water to drink; do not let him go on foot, neither
let him sit in the sun. 12 Neither let him go by
himself in the road, neither force him from
whatever he may desire, but do to him as he may
say to you."

13 And Sarah wept bitterly the whole night on
account of Yitsḥaq, and she gave him
instructions until morning. 14 And in the morning
Sarah selected a very fine and beautiful garment
from those garments which she had in the house,
that Avimelekh had given to her. 15 And she
dressed Yitsḥaq her son with them, and she put a
turban upon his head, and she enclosed a
precious stone in the top of the turban[a], and she
gave them provisions for the road, and they went
forth, and Yitsḥaq went with his father Avraham,
and some of their servants accompanied them to
see them off the road.

16 And Sarah went out with them, and she
accompanied them upon the road to see them off,
and they said to her, "Return to the tent."

17 And when Sarah heard the words of her son
Yitsḥaq she wept bitterly, and Avraham her
husband wept with her, and their son wept with
them a great weeping; also those who went with
them wept greatly.

18 And Sarah caught hold of her son Yitsḥaq, and
she held him in her arms, and she embraced him
and continued to weep with him, and Sarah said,
"Who knows if after today I shall ever see you
again?"

19 And they still wept together: Avraham, Sarah,
and Yitsḥaq, and all those that accompanied
them on the road wept with them, and Sarah
afterward turned away from her son, weeping
bitterly, and all her manservants and
maidservants returned with her to the tent.

20 And Avraham went with Yitsḥaq his son to
bring him up as an offering before 𐤉𐤄𐤅𐤄, as He
had commanded him.

21 And Avraham took two of his young men with
him: Yishma'el the son of Hagar, and Eliezer his
servant, and they went together with them, and
while they were walking in the road the young
men spoke these words to themselves;

22 And Yishma'el said to Eliezer, "Now my
father Avraham is going with Yitsḥaq to bring
him up for a ascension offering to 𐤉𐤄𐤅𐤄, as He
commanded him. 23 Now when he returns he
will give to me all that he possesses, to inherit
after him, for I am his firstborn."

24 And Eliezer answered Yishma'el and said,
"Surely Avraham did cast you away with your
mother, and swear that you should not inherit
anything of all he possesses, and to whom will
he give all that he has, with all his treasures, but
to me his servant, who has been faithful in his
house, who has served him night and day, and
has done all that he desired me? To me will he
leave at his death all that he possesses."

25 And while Avraham was proceeding with his
son Yitsḥaq along the road, the adversary came
and appeared to Avraham in the figure of a very

[a] **23:14** This could be a reference to a diadem. In ancient Near Eastern cultures, the symbol of royalty was not usually a crown, but rather a diadem. This was a precious stone hung on a headband and worn (usually) around a turban; the stone would then dangle onto the forehead. This was still worn into the **20th** century by some of the Ottoman Sultans.

aged man, humble and of contrite spirit, and he
approached Avraham and said to him, "Are you
simple or stupid, that you go to do this thing
today to your only son? 26 For Elohim gave you
a son in your latter days, in your old age. Will
you go and slaughter him today because he
committed no violence? And will you cause the
being of your only son to perish from the earth?
27 Do you not know and understand that this
thing cannot be from 𐤉𐤄𐤅𐤄? For 𐤉𐤄𐤅𐤄 cannot do
to man such evil upon earth to say to him, 'Go
slaughter your son.'"

28 And Avraham heard this and knew that it was
the word of the adversary who endeavored to
draw him aside from the way of 𐤉𐤄𐤅𐤄, but
Avraham would not listen to the voice of the
adversary, and Avraham rebuked him so that he
went away. 29 And the adversary returned and
came to Yitsḥaq; and he appeared to Yitsḥaq in
the figure of a young man good and well
favored.

30 And he approached Yitsḥaq and said to him,
"Do you not know and understand that your
simple old father is bringing you to the slaughter
today for nothing? 31 Now therefore, my son, do
not listen nor attend to him, for he is a simple old
man, and do not let your precious being and
beautiful appearance be lost from the earth."

32 And Yitsḥaq heard this, and said to Avraham,
"Have you heard, my father, that which this man
has spoken? Even thus has he spoken."

33 And Avraham answered his son Yitsḥaq and
said to him, "Guard against him and do not listen
to his words, nor attend to him, for he is the
adversary, endeavoring to draw us aside today
from the commands of Elohim.

34 And Avraham still rebuked the adversary, and
the adversary went from them, and seeing he
could not prevail over them he hid himself from
them, and he went and passed before them in the
road; and he transformed himself to a large
brook of water in the road, and Avraham and
Yitsḥaq and his two young men reached that
place, and they saw a brook large and powerful
as the mighty waters. 35 And they entered the
brook and passed through it, and the waters at
first reached their legs. 36 And they went deeper
in the brook and the waters reached up to their
necks, and they were all terrified on account of
the water; and whilst they were going over the
brook Avraham recognized that place, and he
knew that there was no water there before.

37 And Avraham said to his son Yitsḥaq, "I know
this place in which there was no brook nor water,
now therefore it is this the adversary who does
all this to us, to draw us aside today from the
commands of Elohim."

38 And Avraham rebuked him and said to him,
"𐤉𐤄𐤅𐤄 rebuke you, O adversary: be gone from us
for we go by the commands of Elohim."

39 And the adversary was terrified at the voice of
Avraham, and he went away from them, and the
place again became dry land as it was at first.
40 And Avraham went with Yitsḥaq toward the
place that Elohim had told him. 41 And on the
third day Avraham lifted up his eyes and saw the
place at a distance which Elohim had told him
about. 42 And a pillar of fire appeared to him that
reached from the earth to the heavens, and a
cloud of glory upon the mountain, and the glory
of 𐤉𐤄𐤅𐤄 was seen in the cloud.

43 And Avraham said to Yitsḥaq, "My son, do
you see in that mountain, which we perceive at a
distance, that which I see upon it?"

44 And Yitsḥaq answered and said to his father,
"I see, and behold, a pillar of fire and a cloud,
and the glory of 𐤉𐤄𐤅𐤄 is seen upon the cloud."

45 And Avraham knew that his son Yitsḥaq was
accepted before 𐤉𐤄𐤅𐤄 for a ascension offering.

46 And Avraham said to Eliezer and to Yishma'el
his son, "Do you also see that which we see upon
the mountain which is at a distance?"

47 And they answered and said, "We see nothing
more than like the other mountains of the earth."
And Avraham knew that they were not accepted
before 𐤉𐤄𐤅𐤄 to go with them, and Avraham said
to them, "Stay here with the donkey while
Yitsḥaq my son and I go to that mount and
worship there before 𐤉𐤄𐤅𐤄 and then return to
you."

48 And Eliezer and Yishma'el remained in that
place, as Avraham had commanded. 49 And

Avraham took wood for a ascension offering and
placed it upon his son Yitsḥaq, and he took the
fire and the knife, and they both went to that
place.

50 And when they were going along Yitsḥaq said
to his father, "Behold, I see here the fire and
wood, and where then is the lamb that is to be
the ascension offering before 𐤉𐤄𐤅𐤄?"

51 And Avraham answered his son Yitsḥaq,
saying, "𐤉𐤄𐤅𐤄 has chosen you, my son, to be a
perfect ascension offering instead of the lamb."

52 And Yitsḥaq said to his father, "I will do all
that 𐤉𐤄𐤅𐤄 spoke to you with joy and cheerfulness
of heart."

53 And Avraham again said to Yitsḥaq his son,
"Is there in your heart any thought or counsel
concerning this, which is not proper? Tell me my
son, I ask you, O my son do not hide it from
me."

54 And Yitsḥaq answered his father Avraham and
said to him, "O my father, as 𐤉𐤄𐤅𐤄 lives and as
your being lives, there is nothing in my heart to
cause me to deviate either to the right or to the
left from the word that He has spoken to you.
55 Neither limb nor muscle has moved or stirred
at this, nor is there in my heart any thought or
evil counsel concerning this. 56 But I am of
joyful and cheerful heart in this matter, and I say,
'Blessed is 𐤉𐤄𐤅𐤄 who has chosen me today to be
a ascension offering before Him."

57 And Avraham greatly rejoiced at the words of
Yitsḥaq, and they went on and came together to
that place that 𐤉𐤄𐤅𐤄 had spoken of. 58 And
Avraham approached to build the altar in that
place, and Avraham was weeping, and Yitsḥaq
took stones and mortar until they had finished
building the altar. 59 And Avraham took the
wood and placed it in order upon the altar which
he had built. 60 And he took his son Yitsḥaq and
bound him in order to place him upon the wood
which was upon the altar, to slay him for a
ascension offering before 𐤉𐤄𐤅𐤄.

61 And Yitsḥaq said to his father, "Bind me
securely and then place me upon the altar, lest I
should turn and move, and break loose from the
force of the knife upon my flesh and profane the
ascension offering;" and Avraham did so.

62 And Yitsḥaq still said to his father, "O my
father, when you have slain me and burned me
for an offering, take with you that which shall
remain of my ashes to bring to Sarah my mother,
and say to her, 'This is the sweet smelling savor
of Yitsḥaq;' but do not tell her this if she should
sit near a well or upon any high place, lest she
should cast her being after me and die."

63 And Avraham heard the words of Yitsḥaq, and
he lifted up his voice and wept when Yitsḥaq
spoke these words; and Avraham's tears gushed
down upon Yitsḥaq his son, and Yitsḥaq wept
bitterly, and he said to his father, "Hurry, O my
father, and do with me the will of 𐤉𐤄𐤅𐤄 our
Elohim as He has commanded you."

64 And the hearts of Avraham and Yitsḥaq
rejoiced at this thing which 𐤉𐤄𐤅𐤄 had
commanded them; but the eye wept bitterly
while the heart rejoiced. 65 And Avraham bound
his son Yitsḥaq, and placed him on the altar upon
the wood, and Yitsḥaq stretched forth his neck
upon the altar before his father, and Avraham
stretched forth his hand to take the knife to slay
his son as a ascension offering before 𐤉𐤄𐤅𐤄.

66 At that time the messengers of compassion
came before 𐤉𐤄𐤅𐤄 and spoke to Him concerning
Yitsḥaq, saying, 67 "O 𐤉𐤄𐤅𐤄, You art a kind and
compassionate King over all that You have
created in the heavens and in the earth, and You
support them all. Therefore, give ransom and
redemption instead of Your servant Yitsḥaq, and
be kind to and have compassion upon Avraham
and Yitsḥaq his son, who are today performing
Your commands. 68 Have You seen, O 𐤉𐤄𐤅𐤄,
how Yitsḥaq the son of Avraham Your servant is
bound down to the slaughter like an animal?
Now therefore, have compassion on them, O
𐤉𐤄𐤅𐤄."

69 At that time 𐤉𐤄𐤅𐤄 appeared to Avraham, and
called to him from the heavens, and said to him,
"Do not lay your hand upon the lad, neither do
anything to him, for now I know that you fear
Elohim in performing this act, and in not
withholding your son, your only son, from Me."

70 And Avraham lifted up his eyes and saw, and behold, a ram was caught in a thicket by his horns; that was the ram which 𐤉𐤄𐤅𐤄 Elohim had created in the earth in the day that He made the earth and the heavens. **71** For 𐤉𐤄𐤅𐤄 Elohim had prepared this ram from that day, to be a ascension offering instead of Yitsḥaq. **72** And this ram was advancing to Avraham when the adversary caught hold of him and entangled his horns in the thicket, that he might not advance to Avraham, in order that Avraham might slay his son. **73** And Avraham, seeing the ram advancing to him and the adversary withholding him, fetched him and brought him before the altar, and he loosened his son Yitsḥaq from his binding, and he put the ram in his stead, and Avraham killed the ram upon the altar, and brought it up as an offering in the place of his son Yitsḥaq.

74 And Avraham sprinkled some of the blood of the ram upon the altar, and he exclaimed and said, "This is in the place of my son, and may this be considered today as the blood of my son before 𐤉𐤄𐤅𐤄."

75 And all that Avraham did on this occasion by the altar, he would exclaim and say, "This is in the place of my son, and may it today be considered before 𐤉𐤄𐤅𐤄 in the place of my son;" and Avraham finished the whole of the service by the altar, and the service was accepted before 𐤉𐤄𐤅𐤄, and was accounted as if it had been Yitsḥaq; and 𐤉𐤄𐤅𐤄 blessed Avraham and his seed on that day.

76 And the adversary went to Sarah, and he appeared to her in the figure of a humble and meek old man, and Avraham was yet engaged in the ascension offering before 𐤉𐤄𐤅𐤄.

77 And he said to her, "Do you not know all the work that Avraham has made with your only son today? He took Yitsḥaq and built an altar, and killed him, and brought him up as a slaughtering upon the altar, and Yitsḥaq cried and wept before his father, but he did not look at him, neither did he have compassion over him."

78 And the adversary repeated these words, and he went away from her, and Sarah heard all the words of the adversary, and she imagined him to be an old man from among the sons of men who had been with her son, and had come and told her these things.

79 And Sarah lifted up her voice and wept and cried out bitterly on account of her son; and she threw herself upon the ground and she cast dust upon her head, and she said, "O my son, Yitsḥaq my son, O that I had today died instead of you!" And she continued to weep and said, "It grieves me for you.

80 "I have raised you and have brought you up; now my joy is turned into mourning over you, I that had a longing for you, and cried and prayed until I bore you at ninety years old; and now you have served today for the knife and the fire, to be made an offering. **81** But I console myself with you, my son, in that this is the word of 𐤉𐤄𐤅𐤄, for you performed the command of your Elohim; for who can transgress the word of our Elohim, in whose hands is the being of every living creature? **82** You are just, O 𐤉𐤄𐤅𐤄 our Elohim, for all Your works are good and righteous; for I also am rejoiced with Your word which You commanded, and while my eye weeps bitterly, my heart rejoices."

83 And Sarah laid her head upon the bosom of one of her handmaids, and she became as still as a stone. **84** She afterward rose up and went about making inquiries until she came to Ḥevron, and she inquired of all those whom she met walking in the road, and no one could tell her what had happened to her son. **85** And she came with her maidservants and manservants to Qiryath-arba, which is Ḥevron, and she asked concerning her son. And she remained there while she sent some of her servants to seek where Avraham had gone with Yitsḥaq; they went to seek him in the house of Shem and Ever, and they could not find him, and they sought throughout the land and he was not there.

86 And behold, the adversary came to Sarah in the shape of an old man, and he came and stood before her, and he said to her, "I spoke falsely to you, for Avraham did not kill his son and he is not dead;" and when she heard the word her joy was so exceedingly violent on account of her son, that her being went out through joy; she died and was gathered to her people.

87 And when Avraham had finished his service he returned with his son Yitsḥaq to his young men, and they rose up and went together to Beersheva, and they came home.

88 And Avraham sought for Sarah, and could not find her, and he made inquiries concerning her, and they said to him, "She went as far as Ḥevron to seek you both where you had gone, for thus was she informed."

89 And Avraham and Yitsḥaq went to her to Ḥevron, and when they found that she was dead they lifted up their voices and wept bitterly over her; and Yitsḥaq fell upon his mother's face and wept over her, and he said, "O my mother, my mother, how have you left me, and where have you gone? O how, how have you left me!"

90 And Avraham and Yitsḥaq wept greatly and all their servants wept with them on account of Sarah, and they mourned over her a great and heavy mourning.

פרשת חיי שרה – *Parashat Ḥaiyei Sarah*

24 1 And the life of Sarah was one hundred and twenty-seven years[a], and Sarah died. And Avraham rose up from before his dead to seek a burial place to bury his wife Sarah. And he went and spoke to the children of Ḥeth, the inhabitants of the land, saying,

2 "I am a guest and a sojourner with you in your land; give me a possession of a burial place in your land, that I may bury my dead from before me."

3 And the children of Ḥeth said to Avraham, "Behold the land is before you; in the choice of our tombs bury your dead, for no man shall withhold you from burying your dead."

4 And Avraham said to them, "If you are agreeable to this, go and ask Ephron, the son of Tsoḥar for me, requesting that he may give me the cave of Makhpelah, which is in the end of his field, and I will purchase it from him for whatever he desires for it."

5 And Ephron dwelled among the children of Ḥeth, and they went and called for him, and he came before Avraham, and Ephron said to Avraham, "Behold, all you require your servant will do;" and Avraham said, "No, but I will buy the cave and the field which you have for money, in order that it may be for a possession of a burial place forever."

6 And Ephron answered and said, "Behold the field and the cave are before you, give whatever you desire;" and Avraham said, "Only at full price will I buy it from your hand, and from the hands of those that go in at the gate of your city, and from the hand of your seed forever."

7 And Ephron and all his brethren heard this, and Avraham weighed to Ephron four hundred sheqels of silver in the hands of Ephron and in the hands of all his brethren; and Avraham wrote this transaction, and he wrote it and witnessed it with four witnesses.

8 And these are the names of the witnesses, Amigal son of Avishua the Ḥittite, Eliḥoreph son of Ashunah the Ḥivite, Adon son of Aḥira the Gerarite, Aqdil the son of Abudish the Tsidonite.

9 And Avraham took the book of the purchase, and placed it in his treasures, and these are the words that Avraham wrote in the book, namely:

10 "That the cave and the field Avraham bought from Ephron the Ḥittite, and from his seed, and from those that go out of his city, and from their seed forever, are to be a purchase to Avraham and to his seed and to those that go forth from his loins, for a possession of a burial place forever;" and he put a signet to it and witnessed it with witnesses.

11 And the field and the cave that was in it and
all that place were made sure to Avraham and to
his seed after him, from the children of Ḥeth;
behold it is before Mamre in Ḥevron, which is in
the land of Kana'an. 12 And after this Avraham
buried his wife Sarah there, and that place and all
its boundary became to Avraham and to his seed
for a possession of a burial place. 13 And
Avraham buried Sarah with splendor as observed
at the burial of kings, and she was buried in very

---

[a] **24:1** See Yovelim **19**:7; Bereshiyt [Genesis] **23**:**1**.

fine and beautiful garments. 14 And at her bed
was Shem, his sons Ever and Avimelekh,
together with Anar, Eshkol and Mamre, and all
the great *ones* of the land followed her bed.

15 And the days of Sarah were one hundred and
twenty-seven years and she died, and Avraham
made a great and heavy mourning, and he
performed the rites of mourning for seven days.
16 And all the inhabitants of the land comforted
Avraham and Yitsḥaq his son on account of
Sarah.

17 And when the days of their mourning passed
by Avraham sent away his son Yitsḥaq, and he
went to the house of Shem and Ever, to learn the
ways of 𐤉𐤄𐤅𐤄 and His corrections, and Avraham
remained there three years. 18 At that time
Avraham rose up with all his servants, and they
went and returned homeward to Beersheva, and
Avraham and all his servants remained in
Beersheva.

19 And at the revolution of the year Avimelekh
king of the Philistines died in that year; he was
one hundred and ninety-three years old at his
death; and Avraham went with his people to the
land of the Philistines, and they comforted the
whole household and all his servants, and he
then turned and went home. 20 And it was after
the death of Avimelekh that the people of Gerar
took Ben-melekh[a] his son, and he was only
twelve years old, and they made him sit in the
place of his father. 21 And they called his name
Avimelekh after the name of his father, for thus
was it their custom to do in Gerar, and
Avimelekh reigned instead of Avimelekh his
father, and he sat upon his throne.

22 And Lot the son of Haran also died in those
days, in the thirty-ninth year of the life of
Yitsḥaq, and all the days that Lot lived were one
hundred and forty-two years and he died.

23 And these are the children of Lot which were
born to him by his daughters: the name of the
firstborn was Moav, and the name of the second
was Ben-ammi.

24 And the two sons of Lot went and took
themselves wives from the land of Kana'an, and
they bore children to them, and the sons of Moav
were Er, Mayon, Tarsin, and Qanvil, four sons,
these are fathers to the children of Moav to this
day. And the sons of Ben-ammi were Gerim,
Ishon, Ravot, Tsilon, Eynon, and Mayom, six
sons. These are the fathers to the children of
Ammon to this day.

25 And all the families of the children of Lot
went to dwell wherever they should land, for
they were fruitful and increased abundantly.
26 And they went and built themselves cities in
the land where they dwelled, and they called the
names of the cities which they built after their
own names.

27 And Naḥor the son of Teraḥ, brother to
Avraham, died in those days in the fortieth year
of the life of Yitsḥaq, and all the days of Naḥor
were one hundred and seventy-two years and he
died and was buried in Haran.

28 And when Avraham heard that his brother was
dead he grieved sadly, and he mourned over his
brother many days. 29 And Avraham called for
Eliezer his head servant, to give him orders
concerning his house, and he came and stood
before him.

30 And Avraham said to him, "Behold I am old, I
do not know the day of my death; for I am
advanced in days. Now therefore rise up, go
forth and take a wife for my son from among my
family, and from the house of my father, from
Ḥaran. And now swear by 𐤉𐤄𐤅𐤄 Elohim of the
heavens, do not take a wife for my son from this
place and from this land, from the daughters of
the Kana'anites among whom we dwell. 31 But
go to my land and to my birthplace, and take
from there a wife for my son, and 𐤉𐤄𐤅𐤄 Elohim
of the heavens who took me from my father's
house and brought me to this place, and said to
me, 'To your seed will I give this land for an
inheritance forever,' He will send His messenger
before you and prosper your way, that you may

---

[a] **24:20** Ben-melekh – Hebrew 𐤁𐤉𐤍 (*beyn*) meaning "sons" and 𐤌𐤋𐤊 (*me'lekh*) meaning "king": "Son of the king."

obtain a wife for my son from my family and
from my father's house."

32 And the servant answered his master Avraham
and said, "Behold I go to your birthplace and to
your father's house, and take a wife for your son
from there; but if the woman is not willing to
follow me to this land, shall I take your son back
to the land of your birthplace?"

33 And Avraham said to him, "Guard that you do
not bring my son here again, for 𐤉𐤄𐤅𐤄 before
whom I have walked, He will send His
messenger before you and prosper your way."

34 And Eliezer did as Avraham ordered him, and
Eliezer swore to Avraham his master upon this
matter; and Eliezer rose up and took ten camels
of the camels of his master, and ten men from his
master's servants with him, and they rose up and
went to Haran, the city of Avraham and Naḥor,
in order to fetch a wife for Yitsḥaq the son of
Avraham; and while they were gone Avraham
sent to the house of Shem and Ever, and they
brought from there his son Yitsḥaq. 35 And
Yitsḥaq came home to his father's house to
Beersheva, while Eliezer and his men came to
Haran; and they stopped in the city by the
watering place, and he made his camels to kneel
down by the water and they remained there.

36 And Eliezer, Avraham's servant, prayed and
said, "O 𐤉𐤄𐤅𐤄 Elohim of Avraham my master;
send me, I ask You, good speed today and show
kindness to my master, that You shall appoint
today a wife for my master's son from his
family."

37 And 𐤉𐤄𐤅𐤄 listened to the voice of Eliezer, for
the sake of His servant Avraham; and he
happened to meet with the daughter of Bethuel,
the son of Milkah, the wife of Naḥor, brother to
Avraham. And Eliezer came to her house. 38 And
Eliezer related to them all his concerns, and that
he was Avraham's servant, and they greatly
rejoiced at him. 39 And they all blessed 𐤉𐤄𐤅𐤄
who brought this thing about, and they gave him
Rivqah, the daughter of Bethuel, for a wife for
Yitsḥaq. 40 And the young woman was of very
good appearance; she was a virgin, and no one
had known her. And Rivqah was ten[a] years old in
those days.

41 And Bethuel and Lavan and his children made
a banquet on that night, and Eliezer and his men
came and ate and drank and rejoiced there on
that night.

42 And Eliezer rose up in the morning, he and the
men that were with him, and he called to the
whole household of Bethuel, saying, "Send me
away that I may go to my master;" and they rose
up and sent away Rivqah and her nurse Devorah,
the daughter of Uts, and they gave her silver and
gold, manservants and maidservants, and they
blessed her. 43 And they sent Eliezer away with
his men; and the servants took Rivqah, and he
went and returned to his master to the land of
Kana'an.

44 And Yitsḥaq took Rivqah and she became his
wife, and he brought her into the tent. 45 And
Yitsḥaq was forty years old when he took
Rivqah, the daughter of his uncle Bethuel, for a
wife.

25 1 And it was at that time that Avraham again
took a wife in his old age, and her name was
Qeturah, from the land of Kana'an.

2 And she bore to him Zimran, Yoqshan, Medan,
Midian, Yishbaq and Shuaḥ, being six sons. And
the children of Zimran were Avihem, Molikh,
and Mariḥ.

3 And the sons of Yoqshan were Sheva and
Dedan, and the sons of Dedan[b] were Amida,

---

[a] **24:40** This recording of the number **10** is mostly likely a scribal error. Given that Ya'aqov and Esav were born when Yitschaq was **60** (see **26:16**), and that Ya'aqov was **99** when Rivqah died (**36:3**), and Rivqah was **133** when she died (**36:6**) we can calculate that she was **26** years younger than Yitschaq (his **60** years at their birth + Ya'aqov's **99** years means Yitschaq was **159** when Rivqah died, and she was **133**, being a difference of **26** years) thus making her **14** at marriage, not **10**. Given that the ages listed for Yitschaq and Ya'aqov are listed consistently, the age here for Rivqah must be the one that is wrong.

[b] **25:3** This should read "Medan" not "Dedan." Most likely a copyist error; Hebrew text reads 𐤃𐤃𐤍 (*de'dan*) instead of 𐤌𐤃𐤍 (*me'dan*).

Yoav, Gochi, Elisha, and Notha̱h. And the sons
of Midian were Ephah, Epher, Ḥanokh, Bidan[a],
and Dua'ah[b].

4 And the sons of Yishbaq were Makiri, Biydua,
and Tethor.

5 And the sons of Shua̱h were Bildad, Ḥamdad,
Mushan, and Mekan; all these are the families of
the sons of Keturah the Kana'anite woman which
she bore to Avraham the Hebrew.

6 And Avraham sent all these away, and he gave
them gifts, and they went away from his son
Yitsḥaq to dwell wherever they should find a
place. 7 And all these went to the mountains to
the east, and they built themselves six cities in
which they dwelled to this day. 8 But the
children of Sheva and Dedan, children of
Yoqshan, with their children, did not dwell with
their brethren in their cities, and they journeyed
and encamped in the countries and wildernesses
to this day.

9 And the children of Midian, son of Avraham,
went to the east of the land of Kush, and they
there found a large valley in the eastern country,
and they remained there and built a city, and they
dwelled in it; that is the land of Midian to this
day. 10 And Midian dwelled in the city which he
built, he and his five sons and all belonging to
him.

11 And these are the names of the sons of Midian
according to their names in their cities, Ephah,
Epher, Ḥanokh, Abida and Elda'ah.

12 And the sons of Ephah were Michah, Mishar,
Avi, and Atselua; and the sons of Epher were
Ephron, Tsur, Alirun, and Midon; and the sons
of Ḥanokh were Reuel, Reqem, Azi, Elioshuv,
and Ḥelad.

13 And the sons of Bira[c] were Ḥur, Melud,
Qeruil, Molchi; and the sons of Dua'ah[d] were
Yikir, and Reva, Malchum, and Gavol; these are
the names of the Midianites according to their
families; and afterward the families of Midian
spread throughout the land of Midian.

14 And these are the generations of Yishma'el the
son Avraham, whom Hagar, Sarah's handmaid,
bore to Avraham.

15 And Yishma'el took a wife from the land of
Mitsrayim, and her name was Rivah, the same is
Merivah. 16 And Rivah bore to Yishma'el
Nebayoth, Qedar, Adveel, Mivsam and their
sister Basemath.

17 And Yishma'el cast away his wife Rivah, and
she went from him and returned to Mitsrayim to
the house of her father, and she dwelled there,
for she had been very bad in the sight of
Yishma'el, and in the sight of his father
Avraham.

18 And Yishma'el afterward took a wife from the
land of Kana'an, and her name was Malkhuth,
and she bore to him Mishma, Dumah, Masa,
Ḥadad, Tima, Yetur, Naphish, and Qedmah.

19 These are the sons of Yishma'el, and these are
their names, being twelve princes according to
their nations; and the families of Yishma'el
afterward spread forth, and Yishma'el took his
children and all the property that he had gained,
together with the souls of his household and all
belonging to him, and they went to dwell where
they should find a place. 20 And they went and
dwelled near the wilderness of Paran, and their
dwelling was from Ḥavilah to Shur, that is
before Mitsrayim as you come toward
Ashuwrah. 21 And Yishma'el and his sons
dwelled in the land, and they had children born
to them, and they were fruitful and increased
abundantly.

22 And these are the names of the sons of
Nebayoth the firstborn of Yishma'el; Mied, Sied,

---

[a] **25:3** Bidan – Hebrew word recorded in Hebrew text as 𐤁𐤉𐤃𐤍 (*biy'dan*). Most likely a copyist error for the word 𐤀𐤁𐤉𐤃𐤏 (*avi'da*). Compare spelling in verse **11**. See also Bereshiyt [Genesis] **25:4**.

[b] **25:3** Dua'ah – Hebrew word recorded in Hebrew text as 𐤃𐤅𐤏𐤄 (*dua'ah*). Most likely a copyist error for the word 𐤀𐤋𐤃𐤏𐤄 (*el'da'ah*). Compare spelling in verse **11**. See also Bereshiyt [Genesis] **25:4**.

[c] **25:13** Bira – Hebrew word recorded in Hebrew text as 𐤁𐤉𐤓𐤏 (*biy'ra*). Most likely a copyist error for the word 𐤀𐤁𐤉𐤃𐤏 (*avi'da*). Compare spelling with verses **3** and **11**.

[d] **25:13** See footnote for **25:3** regarding the name Dua'ah.

Mayon; and the sons of Qedar were Alyon,
Qetsem, Ḥamad, and Eli.

23 And the sons of Adveel were Ḥamod and
Yavin; and the sons of Mibsam were Ovadyah,
Eved-melekh, and Yeush; these are the families
of the children of Rivah the wife of Yishma'el.

24 And the sons of Mishma the son of Yishma'el
were Shamua, Zekaryon, and Oved; and the sons
of Dumah were Qetsem, Eli, Machmad, and
Amed.

25 And the sons of Masa were Melon, Mulah,
and Evid-adon; and the sons of Ḥadad were
Na'atsar, Mintsar, and Eved-melekh; and the
sons of Tima were Seid, Sadon and Yakol.

26 And the sons of Yetur were Meriq, Yaish,
Alyo, and Pachith; and the sons of Naphish were
Eved-Tamed, Aviyasaph, and Mir; and the sons
of Qedma were Kaliph, Tachti, and Omir; these
were the children of Malkhuth the wife of
Yishma'el according to their families.

27 All these are the families of Yishma'el
according to their generations, and they dwelled
in those lands in which they had built themselves
cities to this day.

28 And Rivqah the daughter of Bethuel, the wife
of Avraham's son Yitsḥaq, was barren in those
days, she had no offspring. And Yitsḥaq dwelled
with his father in the land of Kana'an; and 𐤉𐤄𐤅𐤄
was with Yitsḥaq; and Arpakshad the son of
Shem the son of Noaḥ died in those days, in the
forty-eighth year of the life of Yitsḥaq, and all
the days that Arpakshad lived were four hundred
and thirty-eight years, and he died.

𐤐𐤓𐤔𐤕 𐤕𐤅𐤋𐤃𐤅𐤕 𐤉𐤑𐤇𐤒 – *Parashat Toldot Yitsḥaq*

26 1 And in the fifty-ninth year of the life of
Yitsḥaq the son of Avraham, Rivqah his wife
was still barren in those days.

2 And Rivqah said to Yitsḥaq, "Truly I have
heard, my master, that your mother Sarah was
barren in her days until my master Avraham,
your father, prayed for her and she conceived by
him. 3 Now therefore stand up, pray to Elohim
and He will hear your prayer and remember us
through His kindness."

4 And Yitsḥaq answered his wife Rivqah, saying,
"Avraham has already prayed for me to Elohim
to multiply his seed; now therefore this
barrenness must proceed to us from you."

5 And Rivqah said to him, "But arise now you
also and pray, that 𐤉𐤄𐤅𐤄 may hear your prayer
and grant me children," and Yitsḥaq listened to
the words of his wife, and Yitsḥaq and his wife
rose up and went to the land of Moriah to pray
there and to seek 𐤉𐤄𐤅𐤄. And when they had
reached that place Yitsḥaq stood up and prayed
to 𐤉𐤄𐤅𐤄 on account of his wife because she was
barren.

6 And Yitsḥaq said, "O 𐤉𐤄𐤅𐤄 Elohim of the
heavens and the earth, whose goodness and
mercies fill the earth, You who took my father
from his father's house and from his birthplace,
and brought him to this land, and said to him, 'To
your seed will I give the land,' and You promised
him and declared to him, 'I will multiply your
seed as the stars of the heavens and as the sand
of the sea,' now may Your words be verified
which You spoke to my father. 7 For You are
𐤉𐤄𐤅𐤄 our Elohim, our eyes are toward You to
give us seed of men, as You promised us, for
You are 𐤉𐤄𐤅𐤄 our Elohim and our eyes are
directed toward You only."

8 And 𐤉𐤄𐤅𐤄 heard the prayer of Yitsḥaq the son
of Avraham, and 𐤉𐤄𐤅𐤄 was entreated of him, and
Rivqah his wife conceived.

9 And in about seven months after the children
struggled together within her, and it pained her
greatly that she was wearied on account of them,
and she said to all the women who were then in
the land, "Did such a thing happen to you as it
has to me?" and they said to her, "No."

10 And she said to them, "Why am I alone in this
among all the women that were upon earth?" and
she went to the land of Moriah to seek 𐤉𐤄𐤅𐤄 on
account of this; and she went to Shem and Ever
his son to make inquiries of them in this matter,
and that they should seek 𐤉𐤄𐤅𐤄 in this thing
regarding her. 11 And she also asked Avraham to
seek and inquire of 𐤉𐤄𐤅𐤄 about all that had
happened to her.

12 And they all inquired of 𐤉𐤄𐤅𐤄 concerning this
matter, and they brought her word from 𐤉𐤄𐤅𐤄
and told her, "Two children are in our womb,
and two nations shall rise from them; and one
nation shall be stronger than the other, and the
greater shall serve the younger."

13 And when her days to deliver were completed,
she knelt down, and behold there were twins in
her womb, as 𐤉𐤄𐤅𐤄 had spoken to her.

14 And the first came out red all over like a hairy
garment, and all the people of the land called his
name Esaw, saying, "That this one was made
complete from the womb."

15 And after that came his brother, and his hand
took hold of Esaw's heel, therefore they called
his name Ya'aqov.

16 And Yitsḥaq, the son of Avraham, was sixty
years old when he brought forth them.

17 And the boys grew up to their fifteenth year,
and they came among the society of men. Esaw
was a designing and deceitful man, and an expert
hunter in the field, and Ya'aqov was a man
perfect and wise, dwelling in tents, feeding
flocks and learning the corrections of 𐤉𐤄𐤅𐤄 and
the commands of his father and mother. 18 And
Yitsḥaq and the children of his household
dwelled with his father Avraham in the land of
Kana'an, as Elohim had commanded them.

19 And Yishma'el the son of Avraham went with
his children and all belonging to them, and they
returned there to the land of Ḥavilah, and they
dwelled there.

20 And all the children of Avraham's concubines
went to dwell in the land of the east, for
Avraham had sent them away from his son, and
had given them gifts, and they went away.
21 And Avraham gave all that he had to his son
Yitsḥaq, and he also gave him all his treasures.

22 And he commanded him saying, "Do you not
know and understand 𐤉𐤄𐤅𐤄 is Elohim in the
heavens and in the earth, and there is no other
beside Him? 23 And it was He who took me from
my father's house, and from my birthplace, and
gave me all the delights upon earth; who
delivered me from the counsel of the wicked, for
I trusted in Him. 24 And He brought me to this
place, and He delivered me from Ur Kasdim; and
He said to me, 'To your seed will I give all these
lands, and they shall inherit them when they
guard My commands, My statutes, and My
judgments that I have commanded you, and
which I shall command them.' 25 Now therefore
my son, listen to my voice, and keep the
commands of 𐤉𐤄𐤅𐤄 your Elohim, which I
commanded you; do not turn from the correct
way either to the right or to the left, in order that
it may be well with you and your children after
you forever.

26 "And remember the wonderful works of 𐤉𐤄𐤅𐤄,
and His kindness that He has shown toward us,
in having delivered us from the hands of our
enemies. And 𐤉𐤄𐤅𐤄 our Elohim caused them to
fall into our hands; and now therefore guard all
that I have commanded you, and do not turn
away from the commands of your Elohim, and
serve none besides Him, in order that it may be
well with you and your seed after you. 27 And
teach your children and your seed the corrections
of 𐤉𐤄𐤅𐤄 and His commands, and teach them the
upright way in which they should go, in order
that it may be well with them forever."

28 And Yitsḥaq answered his father and said to
him, "That which my master has commanded,
that will I do, and I will not depart from the
commands of 𐤉𐤄𐤅𐤄 my Elohim. I will guard all
that He commanded me;" and Avraham blessed
his son Yitsḥaq, and also his children; and
Avraham taught Ya'aqov the corrections of 𐤉𐤄𐤅𐤄
and His ways.

29 And it was at that time that Avraham died, in
the fifteenth year of the life of Ya'aqov and
Esaw, the sons of Yitsḥaq, and all the days of
Avraham were one hundred and seventy-five
years, and he died and was gathered to his people
in good old age; old and satisfied with days, and
Yitsḥaq and Yishma'el his sons buried him.
30 And when the inhabitants of Kana'an heard
that Avraham was dead, they all came with their
kings and princes and all their men to bury
Avraham.

31 And all the inhabitants of the land of Haran,
and all the families of the house of Avraham, and
all the princes and great *ones*, and the sons of

Avraham by the concubines, all came when they
heard of Avraham's death, and they requited
Avraham's kindness, and comforted Yitsḥaq his
son, and they buried Avraham in the cave which
he bought from Ephron the Ḥittite and his
children, for the possession of a burial place.
32 And all the inhabitants of Kana'an, and all
those who had known Avraham, wept for
Avraham a whole year, and men and women
mourned over him.

33 And all the little children, and all the
inhabitants of the land wept on account of
Avraham, for Avraham had been good to them
all, and because he had been upright with Elohim
and men. **34** And not a man arose who feared
Elohim like Avraham, for he feared his Elohim
from his youth, and had served 𐤉𐤄𐤅𐤄, and had
gone in all His ways during his life, from his
childhood to the day of his death.

35 And 𐤉𐤄𐤅𐤄 was with him and delivered him
from the counsel of Nimrod and his people, and
when he made war with the four kings of Elam
he conquered them.

36 And he brought all the children of the earth to
the service of Elohim, and he taught them the
ways of 𐤉𐤄𐤅𐤄, and caused them to know 𐤉𐤄𐤅𐤄.
37 And he formed a grove and he planted a
vineyard in *the land*, and he always prepared in
his tent meat and drink to those that passed
through the land, that they might satisfy
themselves in his house. **38** And 𐤉𐤄𐤅𐤄 Elohim
delivered the whole earth on account of
Avraham.

39 And it was after the death of Avraham that
Elohim blessed his son Yitsḥaq and his children,
and 𐤉𐤄𐤅𐤄 was with Yitsḥaq as He had been with
his father Avraham, for Yitsḥaq guarded all the
commands of 𐤉𐤄𐤅𐤄 as Avraham his father had
commanded him; he did not turn to the right or
to the left from the correct path which his father
had commanded him.

27

1 And Esaw at that time, after the death of
Avraham, frequently went in the field to hunt.
2 And Nimrod king of Bavel, the same was
Amraphel, also frequently went with his mighty
men to hunt in the field, and to walk about with
his men in the cool of the day. **3** And Nimrod
was observing Esaw all the days, for a jealousy
was formed in the heart of Nimrod against Esaw
all the days.

4 And on a certain day Esaw went in the field to
hunt, and he found Nimrod walking in the
wilderness with his two men. **5** And all his
mighty men and his people were with him in the
wilderness, but they removed at a distance from
him, and they went from him in different
directions to hunt, and Esaw concealed himself
for Nimrod, and he lurked for him in the
wilderness. **6** And Nimrod and his men that were
with him did not know him, and Nimrod and his
men frequently walked about in the field at the
cool of the day, and to know where his men were
hunting in the field. **7** And Nimrod and two of his
men that were with him came to the place where
they were, when Esaw started suddenly from his
lurking place, and drew his sword, and hurried
and ran to Nimrod and cut off his head.

8 And Esaw fought a desperate fight with the two
men that were with Nimrod, and when they
called out to him, Esaw turned to them and
struck them to death with his sword. **9** And all
the mighty men of Nimrod, who had left him to
go to the wilderness, heard the cry at a distance,
and they knew the voices of those two men, and
they ran to know the cause of it, when they
found their king and the two men that were with
him lying dead in the wilderness. **10** And when
Esaw saw the mighty men of Nimrod coming at
a distance, he fled and escaped; and Esaw took
the valuable garments of Nimrod, which
Nimrod's father had left to Nimrod, and with
which Nimrod prevailed over the whole land,
and he ran and concealed them in his house.
11 And Esaw took those garments and ran into
the city on account of Nimrod's men, and he
came to his father's house wearied and exhausted
from fight, and he was ready to die through fear
when he approached his brother Ya'aqov and sat
before him.

12 And he said to his brother Ya'aqov, "Behold I
shall die today, and why then do I want the
birthright?" And Ya'aqov acted wisely with
Esaw in this matter, and Esaw sold his birthright
to Ya'aqov, for it was so brought about by 𐤉𐤄𐤅𐤄.

13 And Esaw's portion in the cave of the field of
Makhpelah, which Avraham had bought from
the children of Ḥeth for the possession of a
burial ground, Esaw also sold to Ya'aqov, and
Ya'aqov bought all this from his brother Esaw
for a set price. 14 And Ya'aqov wrote all of this
in a book, and he witnessed it with witnesses,
and he sealed it, and the book remained in the
hands of Ya'aqov.

15 And when Nimrod the son of Kush died, his
men lifted him up and brought him in confusion,
and buried him in his city, and all the days that
Nimrod lived were two hundred and fifteen years
and he died. 16 And the days that Nimrod reigned
upon the people of the land were one hundred
and eighty-five years; and Nimrod died by the
sword of Esaw in shame and contempt, and the
seed of Avraham caused his death as he had seen
in his dream. 17 And at the death of Nimrod his
kingdom became divided into many divisions,
and all those parts that Nimrod reigned over
were restored to the respective kings of the land,
who recovered them after the death of Nimrod,
and all the people of the house of Nimrod were
enslaved to all the other kings of the land for a
long time.

28

1 And in those days, after the death of
Avraham, in that year 𐤉𐤄𐤅𐤄 brought a heavy
famine in the land, and while the famine was
raging in the land of Kana'an, Yitsḥaq rose up to
go down to Mitsrayim on account of the famine,
as his father Avraham had done.

2 And 𐤉𐤄𐤅𐤄 appeared that night to Yitsḥaq and
He said to him, "Do not go down to Mitsrayim;
but rise and go to Gerar, to Avimelekh king of
the Philistines, and remain there until the famine
ceases."

3 And Yitsḥaq rose up and went to Gerar, as
𐤉𐤄𐤅𐤄 commanded him. And he remained there a
full year. 4 And when Yitsḥaq came to Gerar, the
people of the land saw that Rivqah his wife was
of a beautiful appearance, and the people of
Gerar asked Yitsḥaq concerning his wife, and he
said, "She is my sister," for he was afraid to say
she was his wife lest the people of the land slay
him on account of her. 5 And the princes of
Avimelekh went and praised the woman to the
king, but did not answer them, and neither did he
attend to their words. 6 But he heard them say
that Yitsḥaq declared her to be his sister, so the
king reserved this within himself.

7 And when Yitsḥaq had remained three months
in the land, Avimelekh looked out at the
window, and he saw, and behold Yitsḥaq was
laughing with Rivqah his wife, for Yitsḥaq
dwelled in the outer house belonging to the king,
so that the house of Yitsḥaq was opposite the
house of the king.

8 And the king said to Yitsḥaq, "What is this you
have done to us in saying of your wife, "She is
my sister"? How easily might one of the great
men of the people have lain with her, and then
you would have brought guilt upon us."

9 And Yitsḥaq said to Avimelekh, "Because I
was afraid lest I die on account of my wife,
therefore I said, 'She is my sister.'"

10 At that time Avimelekh gave orders to all his
princes and great men, and they took Yitsḥaq and
Rivqah his wife and brought them before the
king. 11 And the king commanded that they
should dress them in princely garments, and
make them ride through the streets of the city,
and proclaim before them throughout the land,
saying, "This is the man and this is his wife;
whoever touches this man or his wife shall surely
die." And Yitsḥaq returned with his wife to the
king's house, and 𐤉𐤄𐤅𐤄 was with Yitsḥaq and he
continued to become great and lacked nothing.

12 And 𐤉𐤄𐤅𐤄 caused Yitsḥaq to find favor in the
sight of Avimelekh, and in the sight of all his
subjects, and Avimelekh acted well with
Yitsḥaq, for Avimelekh remembered the oath
and the covenant that existed between his father
and Avraham.

13 And Avimelekh said to Yitsḥaq, "Behold the
whole earth is before you; dwell wherever it may
seem good in your eyes until you return to your
land;" and Avimelekh gave Yitsḥaq fields and
vineyards and the best part of the land of Gerar,
to sow and reap and eat the fruits of the ground
until the days of the famine should have passed
by.

14 And Yitsḥaq sowed in that land, and received
a hundred-fold in the same year, and 𐤉𐤄𐤅𐤄
blessed him. 15 And the man became great, and
he had possession of flocks and possession of
herds and great store of servants.

16 And when the days of the famine had passed
away 𐤉𐤄𐤅𐤄 appeared to Yitsḥaq and said to him,
"Rise up, go forth from this place and return to
your land, to the land of Kana'an;" and Yitsḥaq
rose up and returned to Ḥevron which is in the
land of Kana'an, he and all belonging to him as
𐤉𐤄𐤅𐤄 commanded him.

17 And after this Shelaḥ the son at Arpakshad
died in that year, which is the eighteenth year of
the lives of Ya'aqov and Esaw; and all the days
that Shelaḥ lived were four hundred and thirty-
three years and he died.

18 At that time Yitsḥaq sent his younger son
Ya'aqov to the house of Shem and Ever, and he
learned the instructions of 𐤉𐤄𐤅𐤄, and Ya'aqov
remained in the house of Shem and Ever for
thirty-two years, and Esaw his brother did not
go, for he was not willing to go, and he remained
in his father's house in the land of Kana'an.

19 And Esaw was continually hunting in the
fields to bring home what he could get, so did
Esaw all the days. 20 And Esaw was a cunning
and deceitful man, one who hunted after the
hearts of men and enticed them, and Esaw was a
valiant man in the field, and in the course of time
went as usual to hunt; and he came as far as the
field of Seir, the same is Edom. 21 And he
remained in the land of Seir hunting in the field a
year and four months.

22 And Esaw there saw in the land of Seir the
daughter of a man of Kana'an, and her name was
Yehudith, the daughter of Beeri, son of Epher,
from the families of Ḥeth the son of Kana'an.
23 And Esaw took her for a wife, and he came
into her; forty years old was Esaw when he took
her, and he brought her to Ḥevron, the land of his
father's dwelling place, and he dwelled there.

24 And it happened in those days, in the hundred
and tenth year of the life of Yitsḥaq, that is in the
fiftieth year of the life of Ya'aqov, in that year
Shem the son of Noaḥ died; Shem was six
hundred years old at his death.

25 And when Shem died Ya'aqov returned to his
father to Ḥevron which is in the land of Kana'an.
26 And in the fifty-sixth year of the life of
Ya'aqov, people came from Haran, and Rivqah
was told concerning her brother Lavan the son of
Bethuel.

27 For the wife of Lavan was barren in those
days, and bore no children, and also all his
handmaids bore none to him. 28 And afterward
𐤉𐤄𐤅𐤄 remembered Adinah the wife of Lavan,
and she conceived and bore twin daughters, and
Lavan called the names of his daughters: the
name of the elder Leah, and the name of the
younger Raḥel. 29 And those people came and
told these things to Rivqah, and Rivqah rejoiced
greatly that 𐤉𐤄𐤅𐤄 had visited her brother and that
he had gotten children.

29 1 And Yitsḥaq the son of Avraham became
old and advanced in days, and his eyes became
heavy through age; they were dim and could not
see.

2 At that time Yitsḥaq called to Esaw his son,
saying, "Please get your weapons – your quiver
and your bow – rise up and go forth into the field
and hunt game for me, and make me savory meat
and bring it to me, that I may eat in order that I
may bless you before my death, as I have now
become old and grey-headed."

3 And Esaw did so; and he took his weapon and
went forth into the field to hunt for game, as
usual, to bring to his father as he had ordered
him, so that he might bless him.

4 And Rivqah heard all the words that Yitsḥaq
had spoken to Esaw, and she hurried and called
her son Ya'aqov, saying, "Thus did your father
speak to your brother Esaw, and thus did I hear,
now therefore hurry and make that which I tell
you. 5 Rise up and go, I ask, to the flock and
fetch me two good kids of the goats, and I will
get the savory meat for your father, and you shall
bring the savory meat that he may eat before
your brother shall have come from the hunt, in
order that your father may bless you."

6 And Ya'aqov hurried and did as his mother had
commanded him, and he made the savory meat

and brought it before his father before Esaw had come from his hunt.

7 And Yitsḥaq said to Ya'aqov, "Who are you, my son?" And he said, "I am your first born Esaw, I have done as you ordered me; now therefore rise up I ask, and eat of my hunt, in order that your being may bless me as you spoke to me."

8 And Yitsḥaq rose up and he ate and he drank, and his heart was comforted, and he blessed Ya'aqov and Ya'aqov went away from his father; and as soon as Yitsḥaq had blessed Ya'aqov and he had gone away from him, behold Esaw came from his hunt from the field, and he also made savory meat and brought it to his father to eat, *so that he would* bless him.

9 And Yitsḥaq said to Esaw, "And who was he that has taken hunted game and brought it to me before you came, and whom I did bless?" And Esaw knew that his brother Ya'aqov had done this, and the anger of Esaw was kindled against his brother Ya'aqov that he had acted thus toward him.

10 And Esaw said, "Is he not rightly called Ya'aqov? For he has supplanted me twice. He took away my birthright and now he has taken away my blessing;" and Esaw wept greatly; and when Yitsḥaq heard the voice of his son Esaw weeping, Yitsḥaq said to Esaw, "What can I do, my son? Your brother came with subtlety and took away your blessing;" and Esaw hated his brother Ya'aqov on account of the blessing that his father had given him, and his anger was greatly roused against him.

11 And Ya'aqov was very much afraid of his brother Esaw, and he rose up and fled to the house of Ever the son of Shem, and he concealed himself there on account of his brother; and Ya'aqov was sixty-three years old when he went forth from the land of Kana'an from Ḥevron, and Ya'aqov was concealed in Ever's house fourteen years on account of his brother Esaw, and he there continued to learn the ways of 𐤉𐤄𐤅𐤄 and His commands.

12 And when Esaw saw that Ya'aqov had fled and escaped from his hand, and that Ya'aqov had cunningly obtained the blessing, then Esaw grieved exceedingly, and he was also angry at his father and mother; and he also rose up and took his wife and went away from his father and mother to the land of Seir, and he dwelled there; and Esaw saw there a woman from among the daughters of Ḥeth whose name was Basemath, the daughter of Elon the Ḥittite, and he took her for a wife in addition to his first wife, and Esaw called her name Adah, saying the blessing had in that time passed from him.

13 And Esaw dwelled in the land of Seir six months without seeing his father and mother, and afterward Esaw took his wives and rose up and returned to the land of Kana'an, and Esaw placed his two wives in his father's house in Ḥevron.

14 And the wives of Esaw angered and provoked
Yitsḥaq and Rivqah with their works, for they
did not walk in the ways of 𐤉𐤄𐤅𐤄, but served
their father's elohim of wood and stone as their
father had taught them, and they were more
wicked than their father. 15 And they went
according to the evil desires of their hearts, and
they slaughtered and burned incense to the
ba'alim[a], and Yitsḥaq and Rivqah became weary
of them.

16 And Rivqah said, "I am weary of my life because of the daughters of Ḥeth; if Ya'aqov take a wife of the daughters of Ḥeth such as these, which are of the daughters of the land, then what good is life to me?"

17 And in those days Adah the wife of Esaw conceived and bore him a son; and Esaw called the name of the son that was born to him Eliphaz, and Esaw was sixty-five years old when she bore him.

18 And Yishma'el the son of Avraham died in those days, in the sixty-forth year of the life of Ya'aqov, and all the days that Yishma'el lived

---

[a] **29:15** Ba'alim – Plural form of Hebrew word 𐤋𐤏𐤁 (*ba'al*) meaning "lord," "master," or "owner." Also the name of a Kana'anite deity.

were one hundred and thirty-seven years and he
died. 19 And when Yitsḥaq heard that Yishma'el
was dead he mourned for him, and Yitsḥaq
lamented over him many days.

20 And at the end of fourteen years of Ya'aqov's
residing in the house of Ever, Ya'aqov desired to
see his father and mother, and Ya'aqov came to
the house of his father and mother to Ḥevron,
and Esaw had in those days forgotten what
Ya'aqov had done to him in having taken the
blessing from him in those days. 21 And when
Esaw saw Ya'aqov coming to his father and
mother he remembered what Ya'aqov had done
to him, and he was greatly incensed against him
and he sought to kill him.

22 And Yitsḥaq the son of Avraham was old and
advanced in days, and Esaw said, "Now my
father's time is drawing near that he must die;
and when he dies I will kill my brother Ya'aqov."

23 And this was told to Rivqah, and she hurried
and sent and called for Ya'aqov her son, and she
said to him, "Arise, go and flee to Ḥaran to my
brother Lavan, and remain there for some time,
until your brother's anger is turned from you, and
then you shall come back."

24 And Yitsḥaq called to Ya'aqov and said to
him, "Do not take a wife from the daughters of
Kana'an, for thus did our father Avraham
command us according to the word of 𐤉𐤄𐤅𐤄
which He had commanded him, saying, 'To your
seed will I give this land; if your children keep
My covenant that I have cut with you, then will I
also perform to your children that which I have
said to you, and I will not forsake them.' 25 Now
therefore my son hear my voice, to all that I shall
command you, and refrain from taking a wife
from among the daughters of Kana'an; arise, go
to Ḥaran to the house of Bethuel your mother's
father, and take a wife from there from the
daughters of Lavan your mother's brother.

26 "Therefore guard lest you forget 𐤉𐤄𐤅𐤄 your
Elohim and all His ways in the lands where you
go, and should get connected with the people of
the land and pursue vanity and forsake 𐤉𐤄𐤅𐤄
your Elohim. 27 But when you come to the land,
serve 𐤉𐤄𐤅𐤄 there: do not turn to the right or to
the left from the way which I commanded you
and which you learned. 28 And may the El
Shaddai grant you favor in the sight of the
people of the earth, that you may take a wife
there according to your choice; one who is good
and upright in the ways of 𐤉𐤄𐤅𐤄. 29 And may
Elohim give you and your seed the blessing of
your father Avraham, and make you fruitful and
multiply you, and may you become a multitude
of people in the land where you go, and may
𐤉𐤄𐤅𐤄 cause you to return to this land, the land of
your father's dwelling, with children and with
great riches, with joy and with pleasure."

30 And Yitsḥaq finished commanding Ya'aqov
and blessing him, and he gave him many gifts,
together with silver and gold, and he sent him
away; and Ya'aqov listened to his father and
mother; he kissed them and arose and went to
Padan-aram; and Ya'aqov was seventy-seven
years old when he went out from the land of
Kana'an from Beersheva.

31 And when Ya'aqov went away to go to Ḥaran
Esaw called to his son Eliphaz, and secretly
spoke to him, saying, "Now hurry, take your
sword in your hand and pursue Ya'aqov and pass
before him in the road, and lurk for him, and kill
him with your sword in one of the mountains,
and take all that belongs to him and come back."

32 And Eliphaz the son of Esaw was an active
man and expert with the bow as his father had
taught him, and he was a noted hunter in the
field and a valiant man. 33 And Eliphaz did as his
father had commanded him, and Eliphaz was at
that time thirteen years old, and Eliphaz rose up
and went and took ten of his mother's brothers
with him and pursued Ya'aqov. 34 And he closely
followed Ya'aqov, and he lurked for him in the
border of the land of Kana'an opposite to the city
of Shekem.

35 And Ya'aqov saw Eliphaz and his men
pursuing him, and Ya'aqov stood still in the
place in which he was going, in order to know
what this was, for he did not know the thing; and
Eliphaz drew his sword and he went on
advancing, he and his men, toward Ya'aqov; and
Ya'aqov said to them, "What are you doing that
you have come here, and what does it mean that
you pursue with your swords?"

36 And Eliphaz came near to Ya'aqov and he
answered and said to him, "Thus did my father
command me, and now therefore I will not
deviate from the orders which my father gave
me;" and when Ya'aqov saw that Esaw had
spoken to Eliphaz to employ force, Ya'aqov then
approached and petitioned Eliphaz and his men,
saying to him, 37 "Behold all that I have and
which my father and mother gave to me, take it
and go from me, and do not kill me, and may this
thing be accounted to you a righteousness."

38 And 𐤉𐤄𐤅𐤄 caused Ya'aqov to find favor in the
sight of Eliphaz the son of Esaw, and his men,
and they listened to the voice of Ya'aqov, and
they did not put him to death, and Eliphaz and
his men took all belonging to Ya'aqov together
with the silver and gold that he had brought with
him from Beersheva; they left him nothing.
39 And Eliphaz and his men went away from him
and they returned to Esaw to Beersheva, and they
told him all that had occurred to them with
Ya'aqov, and they gave him all that they had
taken from Ya'aqov.

40 And Esaw was indignant at Eliphaz his son,
and at his men that were with him, because they
had not put Ya'aqov to death.

41 And they answered and said to Esaw,
"Because Ya'aqov petitioned us in this matter not
to kill him, our pity was excited toward him, and
we took all belonging to him and brought it to
you;" and Esaw took all the silver and gold
which Eliphaz had taken from Ya'aqov and he
put them in his house.

42 At that time when Esaw saw that Yitsḥaq had
blessed Ya'aqov, and had commanded him,
saying, "You shall not take a wife from among
the daughters of Kana'an," and that the daughters
of Kana'an were bad in the sight of Yitsḥaq and
Rivqah. 43 Then he went to the house of
Yishma'el his uncle, and in addition to his older
wives he took Machlath the daughter of
Yishma'el, the sister of Nevayoth, for a wife.

𐤐𐤓𐤔𐤕 𐤅𐤉𐤑𐤀 𐤉𐤏𐤒𐤁 – *Parashat Vayetse Ya'aqov*

30 1 And Ya'aqov went forth continuing his
road to Haran, and he came as far as mount
Moriah, and he stayed there all night near the
city of Luz; and 𐤉𐤄𐤅𐤄 appeared to Ya'aqov on
that night, and He said to him, "I am 𐤉𐤄𐤅𐤄
Elohim of Avraham and the Elohim of Yitsḥaq
your father; I will give the land on which you are
lying to you and your seed. 2 And behold, I am
with you and will keep you wherever you go,
and I will multiply your seed as the stars of the
heavens, and I will cause all your enemies to fall
before you; and when they make war with you
they shall not prevail over you, and I will bring
you to this land again with joy, with children,
and with great riches."

3 And Ya'aqov awoke from his sleep and he
rejoiced greatly at the vision which he had seen;
and he called the name of that place Beth-El.
4 And Ya'aqov rose up from that place quite
rejoiced, and when he walked his feet felt light to
him for joy, and he went from there to the land
of the children of the East, and he returned to
Ḥaran and he sat by the shepherd's well. 5 And
there he found some men going from Ḥaran to
feed their flocks, and Ya'aqov asked them, and
they said, "We are from Ḥaran."

6 And he said to them, "Do you know Lavan, the
son of Naḥor?" and they said, "We know him,
and behold his daughter Raḥel is coming along
to feed her father's flock."

7 While he was yet speaking with them, Raḥel
the daughter of Lavan came to feed her father's
sheep, for she was a shepherdess. 8 And when
Ya'aqov saw Raḥel, the daughter of Lavan, his
mother's brother, he ran and kissed her, and lifted
up his voice and wept. 9 And Ya'aqov told Raḥel
that he was the son of Rivqah, her father's sister,
and Raḥel ran and told her father, and Ya'aqov
continued to cry because he had nothing with
him to bring to the house of Lavan. 10 And when
Lavan heard that his sister's son Ya'aqov had
come, he ran and kissed him and embraced him
and brought him into the house and gave him
bread, and he ate. 11 And Ya'aqov related to
Lavan what his brother Esaw had done to him,
and what his son Eliphaz had done to him in the
road.

12 And Ya'aqov resided in Lavan's house for one
new moon, and Ya'aqov ate and drank in the
house of Lavan, and afterward Lavan said to

Ya'aqov, "Tell me what shall be your wages, for
how can you serve me for nothing?"

13 And Lavan had no sons, only daughters, and
his other wives and handmaids were still barren
in those days; and these are the names of Lavan's
daughters which his wife Adinah had borne to
him: the name of the elder was Leah and the
name of the younger was Raḥel; and Leah was
tender-eyed, but Raḥel was beautiful and well
favored, and Ya'aqov loved her.

14 And Ya'aqov said to Lavan, "I will serve you
seven years for Raḥel your younger daughter;"
and Lavan agreed to this and Ya'aqov served
Lavan seven years for his daughter Raḥel.

15 And in the second year of Ya'aqov's dwelling
in Ḥaran, that is in the seventy-ninth year of the
life of Ya'aqov, in that year Ever the son of
Shem died, he was four hundred and sixty-four
years old at his death. 16 And when Ya'aqov
heard that Ever was dead he grieved
exceedingly, and he lamented and mourned over
him many days.

17 And in the third year of Ya'aqov's dwelling in
Ḥaran, Basemath, the daughter of Yishma'el, the
wife of Esaw, bore him a son, and Esaw called
his name Reuel.

18 And in the fourth year of Ya'aqov's residence
in the house of Lavan, 𐤉𐤄𐤅𐤄 visited Lavan and
remembered him on account of Ya'aqov, and
sons were born to him, and his firstborn was
Beor, his second was Aliv, and the third was
Moresh.

19 And 𐤉𐤄𐤅𐤄 gave Lavan riches and honor, sons
and daughters, and the man increased greatly on
account of Ya'aqov. 20 And in those days
Ya'aqov served Lavan in all manner of work, in
the house and in the field, and the blessing of
𐤉𐤄𐤅𐤄 was in all that belonged to Lavan in the
house and in the field.

21 And in the fifth year Yehudith died, the
daughter of Beeri, the wife of Esaw, in the land
of Kana'an, and she had no sons but daughters
only. 22 And these are the names of her
daughters which she bore to Esaw: the name of
the elder was Martsith, and the name of the
younger was Puith. 23 And when Yehudith died,
Esaw rose up and went to Seir to hunt in the
field, as usual, and Esaw dwelled in the land of
Seir for a long time.

24 And in the sixth year Esaw took for a wife, in
addition to his other wives, Oholibamah, the
daughter of Tsivon the Ḥivite, and Esaw brought
her to the land of Kana'an. 25 And Oholibamah
conceived and bore three sons to Esaw: Yeush,
Ya'alam, and Qoraḥ.

26 And in those days, in the land of Kana'an,
there was a quarrel between the herdsmen of
Esaw and the herdsmen of the inhabitants of the
land of Kana'an, for Esaw's cattle and goods
were too abundant for him to remain in the land
of Kana'an, in his father's house, and the land of
Kana'an could not bear him on account of his
cattle. 27 And when Esaw saw that his quarreling
increased with the inhabitants of the land of
Kana'an, he rose up and took his wives and his
sons and his daughters, and all belonging to him,
and the cattle which he possessed, and all his
property that he had acquired in the land of
Kana'an, and he went away from the inhabitants
of the land to the land of Seir, and Esaw and all
belonging to him dwelled in the land of Seir.
28 But from time to time Esaw would go and see
his father and mother in the land of Kana'an, and
Esaw intermarried with the Ḥorites, and he gave
his daughters to the sons of Seir, the Ḥorite.

29 And he gave his elder daughter Martsith to
Anah, the son of Tsivon, his wife's brother, and
Puith he gave to Atsar, the son of Bilhan the
Ḥorite; and Esaw dwelled in the mountain, he
and his children, and they were fruitful and
multiplied.

31 1 And in the seventh year, Ya'aqov's service
which he served Lavan was completed, and
Ya'aqov said to Lavan, "Give me my wife, for
the days of my service are fulfilled; and Lavan
did so, and Lavan and Ya'aqov assembled all the
people of that place and they made a banquet.

2 And in the evening Lavan came to the house,
and afterward Ya'aqov came there with the
people of the banquet, and Lavan extinguished
all the lights that were there in the house.

3 And Ya'aqov said to Lavan, "Why do you do
this thing to us?" and Lavan answered, "Such is
our custom in this land."

4 And afterward Lavan took his daughter Leah,
and he brought her to Ya'aqov, and he came to
her and Ya'aqov did not know that she was Leah.
5 And Lavan gave his daughter Leah his maid
Zilpah for a handmaid. 6 And all the people at
the banquet knew what Lavan had done to
Ya'aqov, but they did not tell the thing to
Ya'aqov.

7 And all the neighbors came that night to
Ya'aqov's house, and they ate and drank and
rejoiced, and played before Leah upon timbrels,
and with dances, and they responded before
Ya'aqov, "Hiy'leah[a], Hiy'leah!"

8 And Ya'aqov heard their words but did not
understand their meaning, but he thought such
might be their custom in this land. 9 And the
neighbors spoke these words before Ya'aqov
during the night, and all the lights that were in
the house Lavan had that night extinguished.

10 And in the morning, when daylight appeared,
Ya'aqov turned to his wife and he saw, and
behold it was Leah that had been lying in his
bosom, and Ya'aqov said, "Behold now I know
what the neighbors said last night; "Hiy'leah,"
they said, and I did not know."

11 And Ya'aqov called Lavan, and said to him,
"What is this that you did to me? Surely I served
you for Raḥel, and why did you deceive me and
give me Leah?"

12 And Lavan answered Ya'aqov, saying, "It is
not done in our place to give the younger before
the elder. Now therefore, if you desire to take her
sister likewise, take her for the service which you
will serve me for another seven years."

13 And Ya'aqov did so, and he also took Raḥel
for a wife, and he served Lavan seven years
more, and Ya'aqov also came to Raḥel, and he
loved Raḥel more than Leah, and Lavan gave her
his maid Bilhah for a handmaid.

14 And when 𐤉𐤄𐤅𐤄 saw that Leah was hated, so
He opened her womb, and she conceived and
bore Ya'aqov four sons in those days. 15 And
these are their names: Reuven Shimon, Levi, and
Yehudah, and afterward she stopped bearing.

16 And at that time Raḥel was barren, and she
had no offspring, and Raḥel envied her sister
Leah, and when Raḥel saw that she bore no
children to Ya'aqov, she took her handmaid
Bilhah and gave her to Ya'aqov for a wife, and
she bore Ya'aqov two sons: Dan and Naphtali.

17 And when Leah saw that she had stopped
bearing, she also took her handmaid Zilpah, and
she gave her to Ya'aqov for a wife, and Ya'aqov
also came to Zilpah, and she also bore Ya'aqov
two sons: Gad and Asher. 18 And Leah again
conceived and bore Ya'aqov in those days two
sons and one daughter, and these are their names:
Yissakhar, Zevulun, and their sister Dinah.

19 And Raḥel was still barren in those days, and
Raḥel prayed to 𐤉𐤄𐤅𐤄 at that time, and she said,
"O 𐤉𐤄𐤅𐤄 Elohim, remember me and visit me, I
entreat You, for now my husband will cast me
off, for I have borne him no children. 20 Now O
𐤉𐤄𐤅𐤄 Elohim, hear my petition before You, and
see my affliction, and give me children like one
of the handmaids, that I may no more bear my
reproach."

21 And Elohim heard her, and Elohim
remembered her, and opened her womb, and
Raḥel conceived and bore a son, and she said,
"𐤉𐤄𐤅𐤄 has taken away my reproach, and she
called his name Yoseph, saying, "May 𐤉𐤄𐤅𐤄 add
to me another son;" and Ya'aqov was ninety-one
years old when she bore him.

22 At that time Ya'aqov's mother, Rivqah, sent
her nurse Devorah the daughter of Uts, and two
of Yitsḥaq's servants to Ya'aqov.

23 And they came to Ya'aqov to Ḥaran and they
said to him, "Rivqah has sent us to you that you
shall return to your father's house to the land of

---

[a] **31**:7 Hiy'leah – Combination of two Hebrew words, 𐤄𐤉𐤀 (*hi*) meaning "she" and 𐤋𐤀𐤄 (*leah*); literally it means "she [is] Leah!"

Kana'an;" and Ya'aqov listened to them in this
which his mother had spoken.

24 At that time, the other seven years which
Ya'aqov served Lavan for Raḥel were completed,
and it was at the end of fourteen years that he
had dwelled in Ḥaran that Ya'aqov said to Lavan,
"Give me my wives and send me away, that I
may go to my land, for behold my mother sent
for me from the land of Kana'an that I should
return to my father's house."

25 And Lavan said to him, "Not so I ask you; if I
have found favor in your sight do not leave me;
appoint me your wages and I will give them, and
remain with me."

26 And Ya'aqov said to him, "This is what you
shall give me for wages, that I shall today pass
through all your flock and take away from them
every lamb that is speckled and spotted and those
that are brown among the sheep, and among the
goats, and if you will do this thing for me I will
return and feed your flock and keep them as at
first."

27 And Lavan did so, and Lavan removed from
his flock all that Ya'aqov had said and gave them
to him. 28 And Ya'aqov placed all that he had
removed from Lavan's flock in the hands of his
sons, and Ya'aqov was feeding the remainder of
Lavan's flock. 29 And when the servants of
Yitsḥaq which he had sent to Ya'aqov saw that
Ya'aqov would not then return with them to the
land of Kana'an to his father, they then went
away from him, and they returned home to the
land of Kana'an. 30 And Devorah remained with
Ya'aqov in Ḥaran, and she did not return with the
servants of Yitsḥaq to the land of Kana'an, and
Devorah resided with Ya'aqov's wives and
children in Ḥaran.

31 And Ya'aqov served Lavan six years longer,
and when the sheep brought forth, Ya'aqov
removed from them such as were speckled and
spotted, as he had determined with Lavan, and
Ya'aqov did so at Lavan's for six years, and the
man increased abundantly and he had cattle and
maid servants and men servants, camels, and
asses. 32 And Ya'aqov had two hundred drove of
cattle, and his cattle were of large size and of
beautiful appearance and were very productive,
and all the families of the sons of men desired to
get some of the cattle of Ya'aqov, for they were
exceedingly prosperous. 33 And many of the sons
of men came to procure some of Ya'aqov's flock,
and Ya'aqov gave them a sheep for a manservant
or a maidservant or for a donkey or a camel, or
whatever Ya'aqov desired from them they gave
him. 34 And Ya'aqov obtained riches and honor
and possessions by means of these transactions
with the sons of men, and the children of Lavan
envied him of this honor.

35 And in the course of time he heard the words
of Lavan's sons, saying, "Ya'aqov has taken
away all that was our father's, and he has
acquired all this glory of that which was our
father's."

36 And Ya'aqov saw the countenance of Lavan
and his sons, and behold it was not *good* toward
him in those days as it had been before.

37 And 𐤉𐤄𐤅𐤄 appeared to Ya'aqov at the end of
the six years, and said to him, "Arise, go forth
out of this land, and return to the land of your
birthplace and I will be with you."

38 And Ya'aqov rose up at that time and he
mounted his children and wives and all
belonging to him upon camels, and he went forth
to go to the land of Kana'an to his father Yitsḥaq.
39 And Lavan did not know that Ya'aqov had
gone from him, for Lavan had been sheep-
shearing that day. 40 And Raḥel stole her father's
teraphim[a], and she took them and she concealed
them upon the camel upon which she sat, and she
went on.

41 And this is the manner of the teraphim; in
taking a man who is the first born and slaying
him and taking the hair off his head, and taking
salt and salting the head and anointing it in oil,
then taking a small tablet of copper or a tablet of
gold and writing the name upon it, and placing
the tablet under his tongue, and taking the head
with the tablet under the tongue and putting it in
the house, and lighting up lights before it and
bowing down to it. 42 And at the time when they

---

[a] **31:40** See Explanatory Note "Teraphim."

bow down to it, it speaks to them in all matters that they ask of it, through the power of the name which is written in it. 43 And some make them in the figures of men, of gold and silver, and go to them in times known to them, and the figures receive the influence of the stars, and tell them future things, and in this manner were the teraphim which Raḥel stole from her father.

44 And Raḥel stole these images which were her father's, in order that Lavan might not know through them where Ya'aqov had gone. 45 And Lavan came home and he asked concerning Ya'aqov and his household, and he was not to be found, and Lavan sought his teraphim to know where Ya'aqov had gone, and could not find them, and he went to some other teraphim, and he inquired of them and they told him that Ya'aqov had fled from him to his father's, to the land of Kana'an. 46 And Lavan then rose up and he took his brothers and all his servants, and he went forth and pursued Ya'aqov, and he overtook him in mount Gilad.

47 And Lavan said to Ya'aqov, "What is this you have done to me, to flee and deceive me, and lead my daughters and their children as captives taken by the sword? 48 And you did not allow me to kiss them and send them away with joy, and you stole my elohim and went away."

49 And Ya'aqov answered Lavan, saying, "Because I was afraid lest you would take your daughters by force from me; and now with whomever you find your elohim, he shall die."

50 And Lavan searched for the teraphim and he examined in all Ya'aqov's tents and furniture, but could not find them.

51 And Lavan said to Ya'aqov, "We will cut a covenant together and it shall be a witness between me and you; if you afflict my daughters, or take other wives besides my daughters, even Elohim shall be a witness between me and you in this matter."

52 And they took stones and made a heap, and Lavan said, "This heap is a witness between me and you," therefore he called the name of it Galeed.

53 And Ya'aqov and Lavan offered slaughtering upon the mount, and they ate there by the heap, and they stayed in the mount all night. And Lavan rose up early in the morning, and he wept with his daughters and he kissed them, and he returned to his place. 54 And he hurried and sent off his son Beor, who was seventeen years old, with Abiḥorof the son of Uts, the son of Naḥor, and with them were ten men. 55 And they hurried and went and passed on the road before Ya'aqov, and they came by another road to the land of Seir.

56 And they came to Esaw and said to him, "Thus says your brother and relative, your mother's brother Lavan, the son of Bethuel, saying, 57 'Have you heard what Ya'aqov your brother has done to me; who first came to me naked and bare, and I went to meet him, and brought him to my house with honor, and I made him great, and I gave him my two daughters for wives and also two of my maids. 58 And Elohim blessed him on my account, and he increased abundantly, and had sons, daughters and maid servants. 59 He has also an immense stock of flocks and herds, camels and donkeys, also silver and gold in abundance; and when he saw that his wealth increased, he left me while I went to shear my sheep, and he rose up and fled in secrecy.

60 "And he lifted his wives and children upon camels, and he led away all his cattle and property which he acquired in my land, and he lifted up his countenance to go to his father Yitsḥaq, to the land of Kana'an. 61 And he did not allow me to kiss my daughters and their children, and he led my daughters as captives taken by the sword, and he also stole my elohim and he fled. 62 And now I have left him in the mountain of the brook of Yabboq, him and all belonging to him; he lacks nothing. 63 If it be your wish to go to him, go then and there will you find him, and you can do to him as your being desires;" and Lavan's messengers came and told Esaw all these things.

64 And Esaw heard all the words of Lavan's messengers, and his anger was greatly kindled against Ya'aqov, and he remembered his hatred, and his anger burned within him. 65 And Esaw hurried and took his children and servants and

the beings of his household, sixty men, and he
went and assembled all the children of Seir the
Ḥorite and their people, three hundred and forty
men, and took all this number of four hundred
men with drawn swords, and he went to Ya'aqov,
to kill him.

66 And Esaw divided this number into several
parts, and he took the sixty men of his children
and servants and the beings of his household as
one head, and gave them in care of Eliphaz his
eldest son. 67 And the remaining heads he gave
to the care of the six sons of Seir the Ḥorite, and
he placed every man over his generations and
children. 68 And the whole of this camp went as
it was, and Esaw went among them toward
Ya'aqov, and he conducted them with speed.

69 And Lavan's messengers departed from Esaw
and went to the land of Kana'an, and they came
to the house of Rivqah the mother of Ya'aqov
and Esaw.

70 And they told her saying, "Behold, your son
Esaw has gone against his brother Ya'aqov with
four hundred men, for he heard that he was
coming, and he is gone to make war with him,
and to kill him and to take all that he has."

71 And Rivqah hurried and sent seventy-two men
from the servants of Yitsḥaq to meet Ya'aqov on
the road; for she said, "Perhaps Esaw may make
war in the road when he meets him."

72 And these messengers went on the road to
meet Ya'aqov, and they met him in the road of
the brook on the opposite side of the brook
Yabboq, and Ya'aqov said when he saw them,
"This camp is destined to me from Elohim," and
Ya'aqov called the name of that place
Machnayim.

73 And Ya'aqov knew all his father's people, and
he kissed them and embraced them and came
with them, and Ya'aqov asked them concerning
his father and mother, and they said, "They are
well."

74 And these messengers said to Ya'aqov,
"Rivqah your mother has sent us to you, saying,
'I have heard, my son, that your brother Esaw has
gone forth against you on the road with men
from the children of Seir the Ḥorite. 75 And
therefore, my son, listen to my voice and see
with your counsel what you will do, and when he
comes to you, petition him, and do not speak
rashly to him, and give him a present from what
you possess, and from what Elohim has favored
you with. 76 And when he asks you concerning
your affairs, conceal nothing from him. Perhaps
he may turn from his anger against you and you
will thereby save your being, you and all
belonging to you, for it is your duty to honor
him, for he is your elder brother.'"

77 And when Ya'aqov heard the words of his
mother which the messengers had spoken to him,
Ya'aqov lifted up his voice and wept bitterly, and
did as his mother commanded him.

פרשת וישלח יעקב – Parashat Vayishlaḥ Ya'aqov

32 1 And at that time Ya'aqov sent messengers
to his brother Esaw toward the land of Seir, and
he spoke to him words of petition.

2 And he commanded them, saying, "Thus you
shall say to my master, to Esaw, 'Thus says your
servant Ya'aqov, "Do not let my master imagine
that my father's blessing with which he blessed
me has proved beneficial to me. 3 For I have
been with Lavan these twenty years, and he
deceived me and changed my wages ten times, as
it has all been already told to my master. 4 And I
served him in his house very laboriously, and
Elohim afterward saw my affliction, my labor,
and the work of my hands, and He caused me to
find kindness and favor in His sight.

5 And afterward through the great favor and
kindness of Elohim, I acquired oxen and donkeys
and cattle, and menservants and maidservants.
6 And now I am coming to my land and my
home to my father and mother, who are in the
land of Kana'an; and I have sent to let my master
know all this in order to find favor in the sight of
my master, so that he may not imagine that I
have obtained wealth of myself, or that the
blessing with which my father blessed me has
benefited me."'"

7 And those messengers went to Esaw, and found
him on the borders of the land of Edom going
toward Ya'aqov, and four hundred men of the

children of Seir the Ḥorite were standing with
drawn swords. 8 And the messengers of Ya'aqov
told Esaw all the words that Ya'aqov had spoken
to them concerning Esaw.

9 And Esaw answered them with pride and
contempt, and said to them, "Surely I have heard
and truly it has been told to me what Ya'aqov has
done to Lavan, who exalted him in his house and
gave him his daughters for wives, and he brought
forth sons and daughters, and abundantly
increased in wealth and riches in Lavan's house
through his means. 10 And when he saw that his
wealth was abundant and his riches great he fled
with all belonging to him, from Lavan's house,
and he led Lavan's daughters away from the face
of their father, as captives taken by the sword
without telling him of it. 11 And not only to
Lavan has Ya'aqov done this, but also to me has
he done so and has twice supplanted me; and
shall I be silent? 12 Now therefore I have today
come with my camps to meet him, and I will do
to him according to the desire of my heart."

13 And the messengers returned and came to
Ya'aqov and said to him, "We came to your
brother, to Esaw, and we told him all your
words, and thus has he answered us, and behold
he comes to meet you with four hundred men.
14 Now then know and see what you shall do,
and pray before Elohim to deliver you from
him."

15 And when he heard the words of his brother
which he had spoken to the messengers of
Ya'aqov, Ya'aqov was greatly afraid and he was
distressed.

16 And Ya'aqov prayed to 𐤉𐤄𐤅𐤄 his Elohim, and
he said, "O 𐤉𐤄𐤅𐤄 Elohim of my fathers,
Avraham and Yitsḥaq, You spoke to me when I
went away from my father's house, saying, 17 'I
am 𐤉𐤄𐤅𐤄 Elohim of your father Avraham and the
Elohim of Yitsḥaq; I give this land to you and
your seed after you, and I will make your seed as
the stars of the heavens, and you shall spread
forth to the four winds of the heavens, and in you
and in your seed shall all the families of the earth
be blessed.'

18 "And You established Your words, and gave
me riches and children and cattle; as the utmost
desires of my heart You have given to Your
servant; You gave me all that I asked from You,
so that I lacked nothing. 19 And You afterward
said to me, 'Return to your parents and to your
birth place and I will still do well with you.'

20 "And now that I have come, and You
delivered me from Lavan, I shall fall in the hands
of Esaw who will slay me, yes, together with the
mothers of my children. 21 Now therefore, O
𐤉𐤄𐤅𐤄 Elohim, deliver me, I ask You, from the
hands of my brother Esaw, for I am greatly
afraid of him. 22 And if there is no righteousness
in me, do it for the sake of Avraham and my
father Yitsḥaq. 23 For I know that through
kindness and favor have I acquired this wealth;
now therefore I entreat You to deliver me today
with Your clouds of kindness, and answer me."

24 And Ya'aqov ceased praying to 𐤉𐤄𐤅𐤄, and he
divided the people that were with him with the
flocks and cattle into two camps, and he gave the
half to the care of Dammeseq, the son of Eliezer,
Avraham's servant, for a camp, with his children,
and the other half he gave to the care of his
brother Elianus the son of Eliezer, to be for a
camp with his children.

25 And he commanded them, saying, "Keep
yourselves at a distance with your camps, and do
not come too near each other. And if Esaw come
to one camp and slay it, the other camp at a
distance from it will escape him."

26 And Ya'aqov stayed there that night, and
during the whole night he gave his servants
instructions concerning the forces and his
children. 27 And 𐤉𐤄𐤅𐤄 heard the prayer of
Ya'aqov on that day, and 𐤉𐤄𐤅𐤄 delivered
Ya'aqov from the hands of his brother Esaw.

28 And 𐤉𐤄𐤅𐤄 sent three messengers of the
exalted messengers, and they went before Esaw
and came to him. 29 And these messengers
appeared to Esaw and his people as two thousand
men, riding upon horses furnished with all sorts
of war instruments, and they appeared in the
sight of Esaw and all his men to be divided into
four camps, with four chiefs to them. 30 And one
camp went on and they found Esaw coming with
four hundred men toward his brother Ya'aqov,
and this camp ran toward Esaw and his people

and terrified them, and Esaw fell off the horse in alarm, and all his men separated from him in that place, for they were greatly afraid.

31 And the whole of the camp shouted after them when they fled from Esaw, and all the warlike men answered, saying, **32** "Surely we are the servants of Ya'aqov, who is the servant of Elohim, and who then can stand against us?" And Esaw said to them, "O then, my master and brother Ya'aqov is your master, whom I have not seen for these twenty years, and now that I have today come to see him, do you treat me in this manner?"

33 And the messengers answered him saying, "As 𐤉𐤄𐤅𐤄 lives, if Ya'aqov of whom you speak was not your brother, we would not let one remain from you and your people; but only on account of Ya'aqov we will do nothing to them."

34 And this camp passed from Esaw and his men and it went away, and Esaw and his men had gone from them about a league when the second camp came toward him with all sorts of weapons, and they also did to Esaw and his men as the first camp had done to them.

35 And when they had left it to go on, behold the third camp came toward him and they were all terrified, and Esaw fell off the horse, and the whole camp cried out, and said, "Surely we are the servants of Ya'aqov, who is the servant of Elohim, and who can stand against us?"

36 And Esaw again answered them saying, "O then, Ya'aqov my master and your master is my brother, and for twenty years I have not seen his face and hearing today that he was coming, I went today to meet him, and do you treat me in this manner?"

37 And they answered him, and said to him, "As 𐤉𐤄𐤅𐤄 lives, if Ya'aqov were not your brother as you said, we would not have left a remnant of you and your men; but on account of Ya'aqov of whom you speak being your brother, we will not meddle with you or your men."

38 And the third camp also passed from them, and he still continued his road with his men toward Ya'aqov, when the fourth camp came toward him, and they also did to him and his men as the others had done. **39** And when Esaw beheld the evil which the four messengers had done to him and to his men, he became greatly afraid of his brother Ya'aqov, and he went to meet him in peace. **40** And Esaw concealed his hatred against Ya'aqov, because he was afraid of his life on account of his brother Ya'aqov, and because he imagined that the four camps that he had lighted upon were Ya'aqov's servants.

41 And Ya'aqov stayed that night with his servants in their camps, and he resolved with his servants to give Esaw a present from all that he had with him, and from all his property; and Ya'aqov rose up in the morning, he and his men, and they chose from among the cattle a present for Esaw. **42** And this is the amount of the present which Ya'aqov chose from his flock to give to his brother Esaw: and he selected two hundred and forty heads from the flocks, and he selected from the camels and donkeys thirty each, and of the herds he chose fifty cows. **43** And he put them all in ten droves, and he placed each sort by itself, and he delivered them into the hands of ten of his servants, each drove by itself.

44 And he commanded them, and said to them, "Keep yourselves at a distance from each other, and put a space between the droves, and when Esaw and those who are with him shall meet you and ask you, saying, 'Whose are you, and where do you go, and to whom does all this before you belong,' you shall say to them, 'We are the servants of Ya'aqov, and we come to meet Esaw in peace, and behold Ya'aqov cometh behind us. **45** And that which is before us is a present sent from Ya'aqov to his brother Esaw.'

46 And if they shall say to you, 'Why does he delay behind you, from coming to meet his brother and to see his face?' then you shall say to them, 'Surely he comes joyfully behind us to meet his brother, for he said, "I will appease him with the present that goes to him, and after this I will see his face, perhaps he will accept of me."'"

47 So the whole present passed on in the hands of his servants, and went before him on that day, and he lodged that night with his camps by the border of the brook of Yabboq, and he rose up in the midst of the night, and he took his wives and

his maid servants, and all belonging to him, and
that night he passed them over the river Yabboq.
48 And when he passed all belonging to him over
the brook, Ya'aqov was left by himself, and a
man met him, and he wrestled with him that
night until the breaking of the day, and the
hollow of Ya'aqov's thigh was out of joint
through wrestling with him. 49 And at the break
of day the man left Ya'aqov there, and he blessed
him and went away, and Ya'aqov passed the
brook at the break of day, and he halted upon his
thigh. 50 And the sun rose upon him when he had
passed the brook, and he came up to the place of
his cattle and children.

51 And they went on until midday, and while
they were going the present was passing on
before them. 52 And Ya'aqov lifted up his eyes
and looked, and behold Esaw was at a distance,
coming along with many men, about four
hundred, and Ya'aqov was greatly afraid of his
brother. 53 And Ya'aqov hurried and divided his
children to his wives and his handmaids, and his
daughter Dinah he put in an ark, and delivered
her into the hands of his servants.

54 And he passed before his children and wives
to meet his brother, and he bowed down to the
ground, yes he bowed down seven times until he
approached his brother, and Elohim caused
Ya'aqov to find kindness and favor in the sight of
Esaw and his men, for Elohim had heard the
prayer of Ya'aqov. 55 And the fear of Ya'aqov
and his terror fell upon his brother Esaw, for
Esaw was greatly afraid of Ya'aqov for what the
messengers of Elohim had done to Esaw, and
Esaw's anger against Ya'aqov was turned into
kindness.

56 And when Esaw saw Ya'aqov running toward
him, he also ran toward him and he embraced
him, and he fell upon his neck, and he kissed
him, and they wept. 57 And Elohim put fear and
kindness toward Ya'aqov in the hearts of the men
that came with Esaw, and they also kissed
Ya'aqov and embraced him.

58 And also Eliphaz, the son of Esaw, with his
four brothers, sons of Esaw, wept with Ya'aqov,
and they kissed him and embraced him, for the
fear of Ya'aqov had fallen upon them all. 59 And
Esaw lifted up his eyes and saw the women with
their offspring, the children of Ya'aqov, walking
behind Ya'aqov and bowing along the road to
Esaw.

60 And Esaw said to Ya'aqov, "Who are these
with you, my brother? Are they your children or
your servants?" and Ya'aqov answered Esaw and
said, "They are my children which Elohim has
graciously given to your servant."

61 And while Ya'aqov was speaking to Esaw and
his men, Esaw saw the whole camp, and he said
to Ya'aqov, "Where did you get the whole of the
camp that I met last night?" and Ya'aqov said,
"To find favor in the sight of my master, it is that
which Elohim graciously gave to your servant."

62 And the present came before Esaw, and
Ya'aqov pressed Esaw, saying, "Please take the
present that I have brought to my master," and
Esaw said, "What would be the purpose? Keep
that which you have to yourself."

63 And Ya'aqov said, "It is incumbent upon me
to give all this, since I have seen your face, that
you still live in peace."

64 And Esaw refused to take the present, and
Ya'aqov said to him, "I entreat you, my master, if
now I have found favor in your sight, then
receive my present at my hand, for I have seen
your face, as though I had seen the face of
Elohim, because you were pleased with me."

65 And Esaw took the present, and Ya'aqov also
gave to Esaw silver and gold and bdellium, for
he pressed him so much that he took them.
66 And Esaw divided the cattle that were in the
camp, and he gave the half to the men who had
come with him, for they had come on hire, and
the other half he delivered to the hands of his
children. 67 And the silver and gold and bdellium
he gave in the hands of Eliphaz his eldest son,
and Esaw said to Ya'aqov, "Let us remain with
you, and we will go slowly along with you until
you come to my place with me, that we may
dwell there together."

68 And Ya'aqov answered his brother and said, "I
would do as my master says to me, but my
master knows that the children are tender, and
the flocks and herds with their young who are
with me go very slowly, for if they went swiftly

they would all die, for you know their burdens
and their fatigue. 69 Therefore let my master pass
on before his servant, and I will go on slowly for
the sake of the children and the flock, until I
come to my master's place to Seir."

70 And Esaw said to Ya'aqov, "I will place with
you some of the people that are with me to take
care of you in the road, and to bear your fatigue
and burden," and he said, "What for, my master,
if I may find favor in your sight? 71 Behold I will
come to you to Seir to dwell there together as
you have spoken; go then with your people for I
will follow you."

72 And Ya'aqov said this to Esaw in order to
remove Esaw and his men from him, so that
Ya'aqov might afterward go to his father's house
to the land of Kana'an. 73 And Esaw listened to
the voice of Ya'aqov, and Esaw returned with the
four hundred men that were with him on their
road to Seir, and Ya'aqov and all belonging to
him went that day as far as the extremity of the
land of Kana'an in its borders, and he remained
there some time.

33 1 And in some time after Ya'aqov went away
from the borders of the land, and he came to the
land of Shalem, that is the city of Shekhem,
which is in the land of Kana'an, and he rested in
front of the city. 2 And he bought a parcel of the
field which was there, from the children of
Ḥamor the people of the land, for five sheqels.
3 And Ya'aqov built himself a house there, and
he pitched his tent there, and he made
tabernacles for his cattle, therefore he called the
name of that place Sukkot. 4 And Ya'aqov
remained in Sukkot a year and six months.

5 At that time some of the women of the
inhabitants of the land went to the city of
Shekhem to dance and rejoice with the daughters
of the people of the city. And when they went
forth, then Raḥel and Leah the wives of Ya'aqov
with their families also went to see the rejoicing
of the daughters of the city.

6 And Dinah the daughter of Ya'aqov also went
along with them and saw the daughters of the
city, and they remained there before these
daughters while all the people of the city were
standing by them to see their rejoicings, and all
the great people of the city were there. 7 And
Shekhem the son of Ḥamor, the captain of the
land was also standing there to see them.

8 And Shekhem saw Dinah the daughter of
Ya'aqov sitting with her mother before the
daughters of the city, and the girl pleased him
greatly, and he asked his friends and his people
there, saying, "Whose daughter is that sitting
among the women, whom I do not know in this
city?"

9 And they said to him, "Surely this is the
daughter of Ya'aqov the son of Avraham the
Hebrew, who has dwelled in this city for some
time; and when it was reported that the daughters
of the land were going forth to rejoice she went
with her mother and maidservants to sit among
them as you see."

10 And Shekhem saw Dinah the daughter of
Ya'aqov, and when he looked at her his being
became fixed upon Dinah. 11 And he sent and
had her taken by force, and Dinah came to the
house of Shekhem and he seized her forcibly and
lay with her and humbled her, and he loved her
exceedingly and placed her in his house.

12 And they came and told the thing to Ya'aqov,
and when Ya'aqov heard that Shekhem had
defiled his daughter Dinah, Ya'aqov sent twelve
of his servants to fetch Dinah from the house of
Shekhem, and they went and came to the house
of Shekhem to take away Dinah from there.
13 And when they came Shekhem went out to
them with his men and drove them from his
house, and he would not allow them to come
before Dinah, but Shekhem was sitting with
Dinah kissing and embracing her before their
eyes.

14 And the servants of Ya'aqov came back and
told him, saying, "When we came, he and his
men drove us away, and thus did Shekhem do to
Dinah before our eyes."

15 And Ya'aqov knew moreover that Shekhem
had defiled his daughter, but he said nothing, and
his sons were feeding his cattle in the field, and
Ya'aqov remained silent until their return. 16 And

before his sons came home Ya'aqov sent two girls from his servants' daughters to take care of Dinah in the house of Shekhem, and to remain with her, and Shekhem sent three of his friends to his father Ḥamor the son of Ḥiddeqem, the son of Pered, saying, "Get me this girl for a wife."

17 And Ḥamor the son of Ḥiddeqem the Ḥivite came to the house of Shekhem his son, and he sat before him, and Ḥamor said to his son Shekhem, "Is there then no woman among the daughters of your people that you would take a Hebrew woman, who is not of your people?"

18 And Shekhem said to him, "Only her you must get for me, for she is delightful in my sight;" and Ḥamor did according to the word of his son, for he greatly loved him. 19 And Ḥamor went forth to Ya'aqov to speak with him concerning this matter, and when he had gone from the house of his son Shekhem, before he came to Ya'aqov to speak to him, behold the sons of Ya'aqov had come from the field, as soon as they heard the thing that Shekhem the son of Ḥamor had done. 20 And the men were very much grieved concerning their sister, and they all came home fired with anger, before the time of gathering in their cattle.

21 And they came and sat before their father and they spoke to him kindled with wrath, saying, "Surely death is due to this man and to his household, because 𐤉𐤄𐤅𐤄 Elohim of the whole earth commanded Noaḥ and his children that man shall never rob, nor commit adultery; now behold, Shekhem has both ravaged and whored with our sister, and not one of all the people of the city spoke a word to him. 22 Surely you know and understand that the judgment of death is due to Shekhem, and to his father, and to the whole city on account of the thing which he has done."

23 And while they were speaking before their father in this matter, behold Ḥamor the father of Shekhem came to speak to Ya'aqov the words of his son concerning Dinah, and he sat before Ya'aqov and before his sons.

24 And Ḥamor spoke to them, saying, "The being of my son Shekhem longs for your daughter; I ask that you give her to him for a wife and intermarry with us; give us your daughters and we will give you our daughters, and you shall dwell with us in our land and we will be as one people in the land. 25 For our land is very extensive; so dwell and trade in it and get possessions in it, and do in it as you desire, and no one shall prevent you by saying a word to you."

26 And Ḥamor ceased speaking to Ya'aqov and his sons, and behold Shekhem his son had come after him, and he sat before them.

27 And Shekhem spoke before Ya'aqov and his sons, saying, "May I find favor in your sight that you will give me your daughter, and whatever you say to me that will I do for her. 28 Ask me for abundance of bride-price and gift, and I will give it, and whatever you shall say to me, that I will do; and whoever rebels against your orders, he shall die; only give me the girl for a wife."

29 And Shimon and Levi answered Ḥamor and Shekhem his son deceitfully, saying, "All you have spoken to us we will do for you. 30 And behold our sister is in your house, but keep away from her until we send to our father Yitsḥaq concerning this matter, for we can do nothing without his consent. 31 For he knows the ways of our father Avraham, and whatever he says to us we will tell you; we will conceal nothing from you."

32 And Shimon and Levi spoke this to Shekhem and his father in order to gain advice, and to seek counsel what was to be done to Shekhem and to his city in this matter. 33 And when Shekhem and his father heard the words of Shimon and Levi, it seemed good in their sight, and Shekhem and his father came forth to go home.

34 And when they had gone, the sons of Ya'aqov spoke to their father, saying, "Behold, we know that death is due to these wicked ones and to their city, because they transgressed that which our Elohim commanded Noaḥ and his children and his seed after them. 35 And also because Shekhem did this thing to our sister Dinah in defiling her, for such vileness shall never be done among us. 36 Now therefore know and see what you will do, and seek counsel and advice what is to be done to them, in order to kill all the inhabitants of this city."

37 And Shimon said to them, "Here is proper
advice for you: tell them to circumcise every
male among them as we are circumcised, and if
they do not wish to do this, we shall take our
daughter from them and go away. 38 And if they
consent to do this and will do it, then when they
are sunk down with pain, we will attack them
with our swords, as upon one who is quiet and
peaceable, and we will slay every male among
them."

39 And Shimon's advice pleased them, and
Shimon and Levi resolved to do to them as it was
proposed.

40 And on the next morning Shekhem and Ḥamor
his father came again to Ya'aqov and his sons, to
speak concerning Dinah, and to hear what
answer the sons of Ya'aqov would give to their
words.

41 And the sons of Ya'aqov spoke deceitfully to
them, saying, "We told our father Yitsḥaq all
your words, and your words pleased him. 42 But
he spoke to us, saying thus did Avraham his
father command him from Elohim, Master of the
whole earth, that any man who is not of his
descendants that should wish to take one of his
daughters, shall cause every male belonging to
him to be circumcised, as we are circumcised,
and then we may give him our daughter for a
wife. 43 Now we have made known to you all our
ways that our father spoke to us, for we cannot
do this of which you spoke to us, to give our
daughter to an uncircumcised man, for it is a
disgrace to us.

44 "But this is how we will consent to you, to
give you our daughter, and we will also take to
ourselves your daughters, and will dwell among
you and be one people as you have spoken, if
you will listen to us, and consent to be like us, to
circumcise every male belonging to you, as we
are circumcised. 45 And if you will not listen to
us, to have every male circumcised as we are
circumcised, as we have commanded, then we
will come to you, and take our daughter from
you and go away."

46 And Shekhem and his father Ḥamor heard the
words of the sons of Ya'aqov, and the thing
pleased them exceedingly, and Shekhem and his
father Ḥamor hurried to do the wishes of the
sons of Ya'aqov, for Shekhem was very fond of
Dinah, and his being was wrapped up in her.

47 And Shekhem and his father Ḥamor hurried to
the gate of the city, and they assembled all the
men of their city and spoke to them the words of
the sons of Ya'aqov, saying, 48 "We came to
these men, the sons of Ya'aqov, and we spoke to
them concerning their daughter, and these men
will consent to do according to our wishes, and
behold our land is of great extent for them, and
they will dwell in it, and trade in it, and we shall
be one people; we will take their daughters, and
our daughters we will give to them for wives.
49 But only on this condition will these men
consent to do this thing: that every male among
us be circumcised as they are circumcised, as
their Elohim commanded them, and when we
shall have done according to their instructions to
be circumcised, then will they dwell among us,
together with their cattle and possessions, and we
shall be as one people with them."

50 And when all the men of the city heard the
words of Shekhem and his father Ḥamor, then all
the men of their city agreed to this proposal, and
they obeyed to be circumcised, for Shekhem and
his father Ḥamor were greatly esteemed by them,
being the captains of the land. 51 And on the next
day, Shekhem and Ḥamor his father rose up early
in the morning, and they assembled all the men
of their city into the middle of the city, and they
called for the sons of Ya'aqov, who circumcised
every male belonging to them on that day and the
next.

52 And they circumcised Shekhem and Ḥamor
his father, and the five brothers of Shekhem, and
then everyone rose up and went home, for this
thing was from 𐤉𐤄𐤅𐤄 against the city of
Shekhem, and from 𐤉𐤄𐤅𐤄 was Shimon's counsel
in this matter, in order that 𐤉𐤄𐤅𐤄 might deliver
the city of Shekhem into the hands of Ya'aqov's
two sons.

34 1 And the number of all the males that were
circumcised, were six hundred and forty-five
men, and two hundred and forty-six children.

2 But Ḥiddeqem, son of Pered, the father of
Ḥamor, and his six brothers, would not listen to
Shekhem and his father Ḥamor, and they would
not be circumcised, for the proposal of the sons
of Ya'aqov was loathsome in their sight, and
their anger was greatly roused at this, that the
people of the city had not listened to them.

3 And in the evening of the second day, they
found eight small children who had not been
circumcised, for their mothers had concealed
them from Shekhem and his father Ḥamor, and
from the men of the city. 4 And Shekhem and his
father Ḥamor sent to have them brought before
them to be circumcised, when Ḥiddeqem and his
six brothers sprang at them with their swords,
and sought to kill them. 5 And they sought to kill
Shekhem and his father Ḥamor also, and they
sought to kill Dinah with them on account of this
matter.

6 And they said to them, "What is this thing that
you have done? Are there no women among the
daughters of your brethren the Kana'anites, that
you wish to take to yourselves daughters of the
Hebrews, whom you did not know before; and
will do this act which your fathers never
commanded you? 7 Do you think that you will
succeed through this act which you have done?
And what will you answer in this affair to your
brethren the Kana'anites, who will come
tomorrow and ask you concerning this thing?
8 And if your act shall not appear just and good
in their sight, what will you do for your lives,
and me for our lives, since you have not listened
to our voices? 9 And if the inhabitants of the land
and all your brethren the children of Ḥam, shall
hear of your act, saying, 10 'On account of a
Hebrew woman did Shekhem and Ḥamor his
father, and all the inhabitants of their city, do that
with which they had been unacquainted and
which their ancestors never commanded them,'
to where then will you flee or where will you
conceal your shame, all your days before your
brethren, the inhabitants of the land of Kana'an?

11 "Now therefore we cannot bear up against this
thing which you have done, neither can we be
burdened with this yoke upon us, which our
ancestors did not command us. 12 Behold
tomorrow we will go and assemble all our
brethren, the Kana'anite brethren who dwell in
the land, and we will all come and kill you and
all those who trust in you, and there shall not be
a remnant left from you or them."

13 And when Ḥamor and his son Shekhem and
all the people of the city heard the words of
Ḥiddeqem and his brothers, they were terribly
afraid of their lives at their words, and they
repented of what they had done.

14 And Shekhem and his father Ḥamor answered
their father Ḥiddeqem and his brethren, and they
said to them, "All the words which you spoke to
us are true. 15 Now do not say, nor imagine in
your hearts that on account of the love of the
Hebrews we did this thing that our ancestors did
not command us. 16 But because we saw that it
was not their intention and desire to agree to our
desires concerning their daughter since we took
her, except on this condition, so we listened to
their voices and did this act which you saw, in
order to obtain our desire from them. 17 And
when we shall have obtained our request from
them, we will then return to them and do to them
that which you say to us.

18 "We entreat you, then, to wait and stay until
our flesh shall is healed and we become strong
again, and we will then go together against them,
and do to them that which is in your hearts and
in ours.

19 And Dinah the daughter of Ya'aqov heard all
these words which Ḥiddeqem and his brothers
had spoken, and what Ḥamor and his son
Shekhem and the people of their city had
answered them.

20 And she hurried and sent one of the girls that
her father had sent to take care of her in the
house of Shekhem, to Ya'aqov her father and to
her brethren, saying, 21 "Thus did Ḥiddeqem and
his brothers advise concerning you, and thus did
Ḥamor and Shekhem and the people of the city
answer them."

22 And when Ya'aqov heard these words he was
filled with wrath, and he was indignant at them,
and his anger was kindled against them.

23 And Shimon and Levi swore and said, "As
𐤉𐤄𐤅𐤄 lives, the Elohim of the whole earth, by

this time tomorrow, there shall not be a remnant
left in the whole city."

24 And twenty young men had concealed
themselves who were not circumcised, and these
young men fought against Shimon and Levi, and
Shimon and Levi killed eighteen of them, and
two fled from them and escaped to some lime
pits that were in the city, and Shimon and Levi
sought for them, but could not find them. 25 And
Shimon and Levi continued to go about in the
city, and they killed all the people of the city at
the edge of the sword, and they left none
remaining. 26 And there was a great disquiet in
the midst of the city, and the cry of the people of
the city ascended to the heavens, and all the
women and children cried aloud. 27 And Shimon
and Levi slew all the city; they did not leave a
male remaining in the whole city.

28 And they slew Ḥamor and Shekhem his son
with the edge of the sword, and they brought
away Dinah from the house of Shekhem and they
went from there. 29 And the sons of Ya'aqov
went and returned, and came upon the slain, and
spoiled all their property which was in the city
and the field. 30 And while they were taking the
spoil, three hundred men stood up and threw dust
at them and struck them with stones; then
Shimon turned to them and he slew them all with
the edge of the sword, and Shimon turned before
Levi, and came into the city. 31 And they took
away their sheep and their oxen and their cattle,
and also the remainder of the women and little
ones, and they led all these away, and they
opened a gate and went out and came to their
father Ya'aqov bravely.

32 And when Ya'aqov saw all that they had done
to the city, and saw the spoil that they took from
them, Ya'aqov was very angry at them, and
Ya'aqov said to them, "What is this that you have
done to me? Behold I obtained rest among the
Kana'anite inhabitants of the land, and none of
them bothered me. 33 And now you have made
me odious to the inhabitants of the land, among
the Kana'anites and the Perizzites. I am but of a
small number, and they will all assemble against
me and kill me when they hear of your work
with their brethren, and I and my household will
be destroyed."

34 And Shimon and Levi and all their brothers
with them answered their father Ya'aqov and
said to him, "Behold we live in the land; shall
Shekhem do this to our sister? Why are you
silent at all that Shekhem has done? And shall he
treat our sister as a whore in the streets?"

35 And the number of women whom Shimon and
Levi took captives from the city of Shekhem,
whom they did not kill, was eighty-five who had
not known a man. 36 And among them was a
young woman of beautiful appearance and well
favored, whose name was Bunah, and Shimon
took her for a wife. And the number of the males
which they took captives and did not kill, was
forty-seven men, and the rest they killed. 37 And
all the young men and women that Shimon and
Levi had taken captives from the city of
Shekhem, were servants to the sons of Ya'aqov
and to their children after them, until the day of
the sons of Ya'aqov going forth from the land of
Mitsrayim.

38 And when Shimon and Levi had gone forth
from the city, the two young men that were left,
who had concealed themselves in the city, and
did not die among the people of the city, rose up,
and these young men went into the city and
walked about in it, and found the city desolate
without man, and only women weeping, and
these young men cried out and said, "Behold,
this is the evil which the sons of Ya'aqov the
Hebrew did to this city in destroying one of the
Kana'anite cities today, and were not afraid of
their lives of all the land of Kana'an."

39 And these men left the city and went to the
city of Tapuaḥ, and they came there and told the
inhabitants of Tapuaḥ all that happened to them,
and all that the sons of Ya'aqov had done to the
city of Shekhem. 40 And the information reached
Yashuv king of Tapuaḥ, and he sent men to the
city of Shekhem to see those young men, for the
king did not believe them in this account, saying,
"How could two men destroy such a large town
as Shekhem?"

41 And the messengers of Yashuv came back and
told him, saying, "We came to the city, and it is
destroyed, there is not a man there; only weeping
women; neither is any flock or cattle there, for

all that was in the city the sons of Ya'aqov took
away."

42 And Yashuv wondered at this, saying, "How
could two men do this thing, to destroy so large a
city, and not one man able to stand against them?
43 For the like has not been from the days of
Nimrod; and not even from the most remote
time, has something like this taken place;" and
Yashuv, king of Tapuaḥ, said to his people, "Be
courageous and we will go and fight against
these Hebrews, and do to them as they did to the
city, and we will avenge the cause of the people
of the city."

44 And Yashuv, king of Tapuaḥ, consulted with
his counsellors about this matter, and his
advisers said to him, "You will not prevail over
the Hebrews alone, for they must be powerful to
do this to the whole city. 45 If two of them laid
waste the whole city, and no one stood against
them, surely if you went against them, they
would all rise against us and destroy us likewise.
46 But if you send to all the kings that surround
us, and let them come together, then we will go
with them and fight against the sons of Ya'aqov;
then you will prevail against them."

47 And Yashuv heard the words of his
counsellors, and their words pleased him and his
people, and he did so; and Yashuv king of
Tapuaḥ sent to all the kings of the Amorites that
surrounded Shekhem and Tapuaḥ, saying, 48 "Go
up with me and assist me, and we will strike
Ya'aqov the Hebrew and all his sons, and destroy
them from the earth, for thus did he do to the city
of Shekhem; and do you not know of it?"

49 And all the kings of the Amorites heard the
evil that the sons of Ya'aqov had done to the city
of Shekhem, and they were greatly astonished at
them. 50 And the seven kings of the Amorites
assembled with all their armies, about ten
thousand men with drawn swords, and they came
to fight against the sons of Ya'aqov; and Ya'aqov
heard that the kings of the Amorites had
assembled to fight against his sons, and Ya'aqov
was greatly afraid, and it distressed him.

51 And Ya'aqov exclaimed against Shimon and
Levi, saying, "What is this act that you did? Why
have you injured me, to bring against me all the
children of Kana'an to destroy me and my
household? For I was at rest, even I and my
household, and you have done this thing to me,
and provoked the inhabitants of the land against
me by your proceedings."

52 And Yehudah answered his father, saying,
"Was it for nothing that my brothers Shimon and
Levi killed all the inhabitants of Shekhem?
Surely it was because Shekhem had defiled our
sister, and transgressed the command of our
Elohim to Noaḥ and his children, for Shekhem
took our sister away by force, and whored with
her. 53 And Shekhem did all this evil and not one
of the inhabitants of his city interfered with him,
to say, 'Why do you do this?' surely for this my
brothers went and struck the city, and 𐤉𐤄𐤅𐤄
delivered it into their hands, because its
inhabitants had transgressed the commands of
our Elohim. Is it then for nothing that they have
done all this? 54 And now why are you afraid or
distressed, and why are you displeased at my
brothers, and why is your anger kindled against
them?

55 "Surely our Elohim who delivered the city of
Shekhem and its people into their hand, he will
also deliver into our hands all the Kana'anite
kings who are coming against us, and we will do
to them as my brothers did to Shekhem. 56 Now
be at peace about them and cast away your fears,
and trust in 𐤉𐤄𐤅𐤄 our Elohim, and pray to Him to
assist us and deliver us, and deliver our enemies
into our hands."

57 And Yehudah called to one of his father's
servants and said, "Go now and see where those
kings, who are coming against us, are situated
with their armies."

58 And the servant went and looked far off, and
went up opposite Mount Sion[a], and saw all the
camps of the kings standing in the fields, and he
returned to Yehudah and said, "Behold the kings
are situated in the field with all their camps, a

[a] **34:58** Mount Sion – Not to be confused with Mount Tsion (Zion). Per Devarim [Deuteronomy] **4:48**, this is also Mount Ḥermon.

people exceedingly numerous, like the sand upon
the sea shore.

59 And Yehudah said to Shimon and Levi, and to
all his brothers, "Strengthen yourselves and be
sons of valor, for 𐤉𐤄𐤅𐤄 our Elohim is with us; do
not fear them. 60 Stand forth each man, fortified
with his weapons of war, his bow and his sword,
and we will go and fight against these
uncircumcised men; 𐤉𐤄𐤅𐤄 is our Elohim, He will
save us."

61 And they rose up, and each put on his
weapons of war, great and small, eleven sons of
Ya'aqov, and all the servants of Ya'aqov with
them. 62 And all the servants of Yitsḥaq who
were with Yitsḥaq in Ḥevron, all came to them
equipped with all sorts of war instruments, and
the sons of Ya'aqov and their servants, being one
hundred and twelve men, went towards these
kings, and Ya'aqov also went with them.

63 And the sons of Ya'aqov sent to their father
Yitsḥaq the son of Avraham to Ḥevron, the same
is Qiryath-arba, saying, 64 "Pray for us, we ask,
to 𐤉𐤄𐤅𐤄 our Elohim, to protect us from the hands
of the Kana'anites who are coming against us,
and to deliver them into our hands."

65 And Yitsḥaq the son of Avraham prayed to
𐤉𐤄𐤅𐤄 for his sons, and he said, "O 𐤉𐤄𐤅𐤄 Elohim,
You promised my father, saying, 'I will multiply
your seed as the stars of the heavens,' and You
also promised me. And *now* establish Your
word, now that the kings of Kana'an are coming
together, to make war with my sons because they
committed no violence. 66 Now therefore, O
𐤉𐤄𐤅𐤄 Elohim, Elohim of the whole earth, I ask
that You pervert the counsel of these kings that
they may not fight against my sons. 67 And
impress the hearts of these kings and their people
with the terror of my sons and bring down their
pride, and that they may turn away from my
sons. 68 And with Your strong hand and
outstretched arm deliver my sons and their
servants from them, for power and might are in
Your hands to do all this."

69 And the sons of Ya'aqov and their servants
went toward these kings, and they trusted in
𐤉𐤄𐤅𐤄 their Elohim. And while they were going,
Ya'aqov their father also prayed to 𐤉𐤄𐤅𐤄 and
said, "O 𐤉𐤄𐤅𐤄 Elohim, powerful and exalted
Elohim, who has reigned from days of old, from
then *even* until now and forever; 70 You are He
who stirs up wars and causes them to cease; in
Your hand are power and might to exalt and to
bring down; O may my prayer be acceptable
before You that You may turn to me with Your
favor, to impress the hearts of these kings and
their people with the terror of my sons, and
terrify them and their camps, and with Your
great kindness deliver all those that trust in You,
for it is You who can bring people under us and
reduce nations under our power.

35 1 And all the kings of the Amorites came and
took their stand in the field to consult with their
counsellors what was to be done with the sons of
Ya'aqov, for they were still afraid of them,
saying, "Behold, two of them killed the whole of
the city of Shekhem."

2 And 𐤉𐤄𐤅𐤄 heard the prayers of Yitsḥaq and
Ya'aqov, and He filled the hearts of all these
kings' advisers with great fear and terror that
they unanimously exclaimed, 3 "Are you *so*
simple today, or is there no understanding in
you, that you will fight with the Hebrews? And
why will you take a delight in your own
destruction today? 4 Behold two of them came to
the city of Shekhem without fear or terror, and
they killed all the inhabitants of the city, that no
man stood up against them, and how will you be
able to fight with them all? 5 Surely you know
that their Elohim is exceedingly fond of them,
and has done mighty things for them, such as
have not been done from days of old, and among
all the elohim of *the* nations there is none that
can do like His mighty deeds.

6 "Surely He delivered their father Avraham, the
Hebrew, from the hand of Nimrod, and from the
hand of all his people who had many times
sought to kill him. 7 He delivered him also from
the fire in which king Nimrod had cast him, and
his Elohim delivered him from it. 8 And who else
can do the like? Surely it was Avraham who
killed the five kings of Elam, when they had
touched his brother's son who in those days
dwelled in Sodom. 9 And took his servant that
was faithful in his house and a few of his men,

and they pursued the kings of Elam in one night
and killed them, and restored to his brother's son
all his property which they had taken from him.
10 And surely you know the Elohim of these
Hebrews is much delighted with them, and they
are also delighted with Him, for they know that
He delivered them from all their enemies.

11 "And behold through his love toward his
Elohim, Avraham took his only and precious son
and intended to bring him up as a ascension
offering to his Elohim, and had it not been for
Elohim who prevented him from doing this, he
would then have done it for his love to his
Elohim. **12** And Elohim saw all his works, and
swore to him, and promised him that He would
deliver his sons and all his seed from every
trouble that would happen to them, because he
had done this thing, and through his love to his
Elohim stifled his compassion for his child.

13 "And have you not heard what their Elohim
did to Pharaoh king of Mitsrayim, and to
Avimelekh king of Gerar, through taking
Avraham's wife, who said of her, 'She is my
sister,' lest they might kill him on account of her,
and think of taking her for a wife? And Elohim
did to them and their people all that you heard of.

14 And behold, we ourselves saw with our eyes
that Esaw, the brother of Ya'aqov, came to him
with four hundred men, with the intention of
killing him, for he called to mind that he had
taken away from him his father's blessing.
15 And he went to meet him when he came from
Aram, to kill the mother with the children, and
who delivered him from his hands but his
Elohim in whom he trusted? He delivered him
from the hand of his brother and also from the
hands of his enemies, and surely He will protect
them again. **16** Who does not know that it was
their Elohim who inspired them with strength to
do to the town of Shekhem the evil which you
heard of? **17** Could it then be with their own
strength that two men could destroy such a large
city as Shekhem had it not been for their Elohim
in whom they trusted? He said and did to them
all this to kill the inhabitants of the city in their
city.

18 "And can you then prevail over them who
have come forth together from your city to fight
with the whole of them, even if a thousand times
as many more should come to your assistance?
19 Surely you know and understand that you do
not come to fight with them, but you come to
war with their Elohim who chose them, and you
have therefore all come today to be destroyed.
20 Now therefore refrain from this evil which
you are endeavoring to bring upon yourselves,
and it will be better for you not to go to battle
with them, although they are but few in number,
because their Elohim is with them."

21 And when the kings of the Amorites heard all
the words of their advisers, their hearts were
filled with terror, and they were afraid of the
sons of Ya'aqov and would not fight against
them. **22** And they inclined their ears to the
words of their advisers, and they listened to all
their words, and the words of the counsellors
greatly pleased the kings, and they did so. **23** And
the kings turned and refrained from the sons of
Ya'aqov, for they did not dare approach them to
make war with them, for they were greatly afraid
of them, and their hearts melted within them
from their fear of them. **24** For this proceeded
from 𐤉𐤄𐤅𐤄 to them, for He heard the prayers of
His servants Yitsḥaq and Ya'aqov, for they
trusted in Him; and all these kings returned with
their camps on that day, each to his own city, and
they did not at that time fight with the sons of
Ya'aqov. **25** And the sons of Ya'aqov kept their
station that day until evening opposite mount
Sion, and seeing that these kings did not come to
fight against them, the sons of Ya'aqov returned
home.

36 **1** At that time 𐤉𐤄𐤅𐤄 appeared to Ya'aqov
saying, Arise, go to Beth-El and remain there,
and make an altar there to 𐤉𐤄𐤅𐤄 who appeared to
you, who delivered you and your sons from
affliction."

2 And Ya'aqov rose up with his sons and all
belonging to him, and they went and came to
Beth-El according to the word of 𐤉𐤄𐤅𐤄. **3** And
Ya'aqov was ninety-nine years old when he went
up to Beth-El, and Ya'aqov and his sons and all
the people that were with him, remained in Beth-
El in Luz, and he built an altar there to 𐤉𐤄𐤅𐤄

who appeared to him, and Ya'aqov and his sons remained in Beth-El six months.

4 At that time Devorah the daughter of Uts, the nurse of Rivqah died, who had been with Ya'aqov; and Ya'aqov buried her beneath Beth-El under an oak that was there. 5 And Rivqah the daughter of Bethuel, the mother of Ya'aqov, also died at that time in Ḥevron, the same is Qiryath-arba, and she was buried in the cave of Makhpelah which Avraham had bought from the children of Ḥeth.

6 And the life of Rivqah was one hundred and thirty-three years, and she died; and when Ya'aqov heard that his mother Rivqah was dead he wept bitterly for his mother, and made a great mourning for her, and for Devorah her nurse beneath the oak, and he called the name of that place Allon-bakhuth.

7 And Lavan the Aramean died in those days, for Elohim killed him because he transgressed the covenant that existed between him and Ya'aqov.

8 And Ya'aqov was a hundred years old when 𐤉𐤄𐤅𐤄 appeared to him, and blessed him and called his name Yisra'el, and Raḥel the wife of Ya'aqov conceived in those days.

9 And at that time Ya'aqov and all belonging to him journeyed from Beth-El to go to his father's house, to Ḥevron. 10 And while they were going on the road, and there was yet but a little way to come to Ephrath, Raḥel bore a son and she had hard labor and she died.

11 And Ya'aqov buried her in the way to Ephrath, which is Beth-lechem, and he set a pillar upon her grave, which is there to this day; and the days of Raḥel were forty-five years and she died.
12 And Ya'aqov called the name of his son that was born to him, which Raḥel bore to him, Benyamin, for he was born to him in the land on the right hand.[a]

13 And it was after the death of Raḥel, that Ya'aqov pitched his tent in the tent of her handmaid Bilhah. 14 And Reuven was jealous for his mother Leah on account of this, and he was filled with anger, and he rose up in his anger and went and entered the tent of Bilhah and he tore his father's bed. 15 At that time the portion of birthright, together with the kingdom and priesthood, was removed from the sons of Reuven, for he had profaned his father's bed, and the birthright was given to Yoseph, the kingdom to Yehudah, and the priesthood to Levi, because Reuven had defiled his father's bed.

16 And these are the generations of Ya'aqov who were born to him in Padan-aram: there were twelve sons of Ya'aqov.

17 The sons of Leah were Reuven the firstborn, and Shimon, Levi, Yehudah, Yissakhar, Zevulun, and their sister Dinah; and the sons of Raḥel were Yoseph and Benyamin.

18 The sons of Zilpah, Leah's handmaid, were Gad and Asher, and the sons of Bilhah, Raḥel's handmaid, were Dan and Naphtali; these are the sons of Ya'aqov which were born to him in Padan-aram.

19 And Ya'aqov and his sons and all belonging to him journeyed and came to Mamre, which is Qiryath-arba, that is in Ḥevron, where Avraham and Yitsḥaq sojourned, and Ya'aqov with his sons and all belonging to him, dwelled with his father in Ḥevron.

20 And his brother Esaw and his sons, and all belonging to him went to the land of Seir and dwelled there, and had possessions in the land of Seir, and the children of Esaw were fruitful and multiplied exceedingly in the land of Seir.
21 And these are the generations of Esaw that were born to him in the land of Kana'an: there were five sons of Esaw.

22 And Adah bore to Esaw his firstborn Eliphaz, and she also bore to him Reuel, and Oholibamah bore to him Yeush, Ya'alam and Qoraḥ.

23 These are the sons of Esaw who were born to him in the land of Kana'an; and the sons of Eliphaz the son of Esaw were Teman, Omar, Tsepho, Gatam, Qenaz and Amaleq, and the sons

[a] **36:12** Benyamin – Hebrew word 𐤁𐤍𐤉𐤌𐤉𐤍 (*ben'ya'miyn*) means "son of [the] right hand."

of Reuel were Nachath, Zeraḥ, Shamah and Mizzah.

24 And the sons of Yeush were Timnah, Alvah, Yetheth; and the sons of Ya'alam were Alah, Phinon and Qenaz.

25 And the sons of Qoraḥ were Teman, Mivtsar, Magdiel and Eram; these are the families of the sons of Esaw according to their regions in the land of Seir.

26 And these are the names of the sons of Seir the Ḥorite, inhabitants of the land of Seir: Lotan, Shoval, Tsivon, Anah, Dishon, Etser and Dishan, being seven sons.

27 And the children of Lotan were Ḥori, Heman and their sister Timna, that is Timna who came to Ya'aqov and his sons, and they would not give ear to her, and she went and became a concubine to Eliphaz the son of Esaw, and she bore to him Amaleq.

28 And the sons of Shoval were Alvan,
Manaḥath, Eyval, Shepho, and Onam, and the
sons of Tsivon were Ayah and Anah, this was
that Anah who found the hot spring in the
wilderness when he fed the donkeys of Tsivon
his father. 29 And while he was feeding his
father's donkeys he led them to the wilderness at
different times to feed them. 30 And there was a
day that he brought them to one of the deserts on
the sea shore, opposite the wilderness of the
people, and while he was feeding them, behold a
very heavy storm came from the other side of the
sea and rested upon the donkeys that were
feeding there, and they all stood still. 31 And
afterward about one hundred and twenty great
and terrible animals came out from the
wilderness at the other side of the sea, and they
all came to the place where the donkeys were,
and they placed themselves there.

32 And those animals, from their middle downward, were in the shape of the children of men, and from their middle upward, some had the likeness of bears, and some the likeness of apes, with tails behind them from between their shoulders reaching down to the earth, like the tails of the hoopoe, and these animals came and mounted and rode upon these donkeys, and led them away, and they went away to this day.

33 And one of these animals approached Anah and struck him with his tail, and then fled from that place.

34 And when he saw this work he was
exceedingly afraid of his life, and he fled and
escaped to the city. 35 And he related to his sons
and brothers all that had happened to him, and
many men went to seek the donkeys but could
not find them, and Anah and his brothers went
no more to that place from that day following,
for they were greatly afraid of their lives.

36 And the children of Anah the son of Seir, were Dishon and his sister Oholibamah, and the children of Dishon were Ḥemdan, Eshvan, Yithran and Ḥeran, and the children of Etser were Bilhan, Za'avan and Aqan, and the children of Dishan were Uts and Aran.

37 These are the families of the children of Seir the Ḥorite, according to their regions in the land of Seir.

38 And Esaw and his children dwelled in the land of Seir the Ḥorite, the inhabitant of the land, and they had possessions in it and were fruitful and multiplied exceedingly, and Ya'aqov and his children and all belonging to them, dwelled with their father Yitsḥaq in the land of Kana'an, as 𐤉𐤄𐤅𐤄 had commanded Avraham their father.

37

1 And in the one hundred and fifth year of
the life of Ya'aqov, that is the ninth year of
Ya'aqov's dwelling with his children in the land
of Kana'an, he came from Padan-aram. 2 And in
those days Ya'aqov journeyed with his children
from Ḥevron, and they went and returned to the
city of Shekhem, they and all belonging to them,
and they dwelled there, for the children of
Ya'aqov obtained good and fat pasture land for
their cattle in the city of Shekhem; the city of
Shekhem was then rebuilt, and there were about
three hundred men and women in it. 3 And
Ya'aqov and his children and all belonging to
him dwelled in the part of the field which
Ya'aqov had bought from Ḥamor the father of
Shekhem, when he came from Padan-aram
before Shimon and Levi had struck the city.

4 And all those kings of the Kana'anites and
Amorites that surrounded the city of Shekhem,
heard that the sons of Ya'aqov had again come to
Shekhem and dwelled there.

5 And they said, "Shall the sons of Ya'aqov the
Hebrew again come to the city and dwell in it,
after that they have struck its inhabitants and
driven them out? Shall they now return and also
drive out those who are dwelling in the city or
kill them?"

6 And all the kings of Kana'an again assembled,
and they came together to make war with
Ya'aqov and his sons. 7 And Yashuv king of
Tapuaḥ sent also to all his neighboring kings, to
Elon king of Ga'ash, and to Ihuri king of Shiloh,
and to Parathon king of Ḥatsor, and to Susi king
of Sarton, and to Lavan king of Bethḥoron, and
to Shabir king of Machanehem, saying, 8 "Come
up to me and assist me, and let us kill Ya'aqov
the Hebrew and his sons, and all belonging to
him, for they are again come to Shekhem to
possess it and to kill its inhabitants as before."

9 And all these kings assembled together and
came with all their camps, a people exceedingly
plentiful like the sand upon the seashore, and
they were all opposite to Tapuaḥ. 10 And Yashuv
king of Tapuaḥ went forth to them with all his
army, and he encamped with them opposite to
Tapuaḥ outside the city, and all these kings
divided into seven divisions, being seven camps
against the sons of Ya'aqov.

11 And they sent a declaration to Ya'aqov and his
son, saying, "Come forth, all of you, to us that
we may have an meeting together in the plain,
and revenge the cause of the men of Shekhem
whom you killed in their city, and you will now
again return to the city of Shekhem and dwell in
it, and kill its inhabitants as before."

12 And the sons of Ya'aqov heard this and their
anger was kindled exceedingly at the words of
the kings of Kana'an, and ten of the sons of
Ya'aqov hastened and rose up, and each of them
put on his weapons of war; and there were one
hundred and two of their servants with them
equipped in battle array. 13 And all these men,
the sons of Ya'aqov with their servants, went
toward these kings, and Ya'aqov their father was
with them, and they all stood upon the heap of
Shekhem.

14 And Ya'aqov prayed to 𐤉𐤄𐤅𐤄 for his sons, and
he spread forth his hands to 𐤉𐤄𐤅𐤄, and he said,
"O Elohim, You are El Shaddai, You are our
Father, You formed us, and we are the works of
Your hands; I ask You, deliver my sons through
Your favor from the hand of their enemies, who
are today coming to fight with them and save
them from their hand, for in Your hand is power
and might, to save the few from the many.
15 And give to my sons, Your servants, strength
of heart and might to fight with their enemies, to
subdue them, and make their enemies fall before
them, and do not let my sons and their servants
die through the hands of the children of Kana'an.
16 But if it seems good in Your eyes to take away
the beings of my sons and their servants, take
them in Your great mercy through the hands of
Your ministers, that they may not perish today
by the hands of the kings of the Amorites."

17 And when Ya'aqov ceased praying to 𐤉𐤄𐤅𐤄
the earth shook from its place, and the sun
darkened, and all these kings were terrified and a
great consternation seized them. 18 And 𐤉𐤄𐤅𐤄
listened to the prayer of Ya'aqov, and 𐤉𐤄𐤅𐤄
impressed the hearts of all the kings and their
hosts with the terror and awe of the sons of
Ya'aqov.

19 For 𐤉𐤄𐤅𐤄 caused them to hear the voice of
chariots, and the voice of mighty horses from the
sons of Ya'aqov, and the voice of a great army
accompanying them. 20 And these kings were
seized with great terror at the sons of Ya'aqov,
and while they were standing in their quarters,
behold the sons of Ya'aqov advanced upon them,
with one hundred and twelve men, with a great
and tremendous shouting. 21 And when the kings
saw the sons of Ya'aqov advancing toward them,
they were still more panic struck, and they were
inclined to retreat from before the sons of
Ya'aqov as at first, and not to fight with them.

22 But they did not retreat, saying, "It would be a
disgrace to us to retreat from before the Hebrews
twice."

23 And the sons of Ya'aqov came near and
advanced against all these kings and their armies,

and they saw, and behold it was a very mighty
people, numerous as the sand of the sea.

24 And the sons of Ya'aqov called to 𐤉𐤄𐤅𐤄 and
said, "Help us O 𐤉𐤄𐤅𐤄, help us and answer us,
for we trust in You, and do not let us die by the
hands of these uncircumcised men, who today
have come against us."

25 And the sons of Ya'aqov put on their weapons
of war, and they took in their hands each man his
shield and his javelin, and they approached to
battle. 26 And Yehudah, the son of Ya'aqov, ran
first before his brethren, and ten of his servants
with him, and he went toward these kings.
27 And Yashuv, king of Tapuaḥ, also came forth
first with his army before Yehudah, and
Yehudah saw Yashuv and his army coming
toward him, and Yehudah's wrath was kindled,
and his anger burned within him, and he
approached to battle in which Yehudah ventured
his life.

28 And Yashuv and all his army were advancing
toward Yehudah, and he was riding upon a very
strong and powerful horse, and Yashuv was a
very valiant man, and covered with iron and
copper from head to foot. 29 And while he was
on the horse, he shot arrows with both hands
from before and behind, as was his manner in all
his battles; and he never missed the place to
which he aimed his arrows.

30 And when Yashuv came to fight with
Yehudah, and was shooting many arrows at
Yehudah, 𐤉𐤄𐤅𐤄 bound the hand of Yashuv, and
all the arrows that he shot rebounded upon his
own men. 31 And despite this, Yashuv kept
advancing toward Yehudah, to challenge him
with the arrows, but the distance between them
was about thirty cubits, and when Yehudah saw
Yashuv shooting his arrows against him, he ran
to him in his wrath *and* might. 32 And Yehudah
took up a large stone from the ground, and its
weight was sixty sheqels, and Yehudah ran
toward Yashuv, and with the stone struck him on
his shield, that Yashuv was stunned by the blow,
and fell off his horse to the ground. 33 And the
shield broke out of the hand of Yashuv, and
through the force of the blow sprang to the
distance of about fifteen cubits, and the shield
fell before the second camp.

34 And the kings that came with Yashuv saw at a
distance the strength of Yehudah, the son of
Ya'aqov, and what he had done to Yashuv, and
they were terribly afraid of Yehudah.

35 And they assembled near Yashuv's camp,
seeing his confusion, and Yehudah drew his
sword and killed forty-two men of the camp of
Yashuv, and the whole of Yashuv's camp fled
before Yehudah, and no man stood against him,
and they left Yashuv and fled from him, and
Yashuv was still fallen upon the earth. 36 And
Yashuv seeing that all the men of his camp had
fled from him, hurried and rose up with terror
against Yehudah, and stood upon his legs
opposite Yehudah.

37 And Yashuv had fought with Yehudah,
placing shield against shield, and Yashuv's men
all fled, for they were greatly afraid of Yehudah.
38 And Yashuv took his spear in his hand to
strike Yehudah on his head, but Yehudah had
quickly placed his shield to his head against
Yashuv's spear, so that the shield of Yehudah
received the blow from Yashuv's spear, and the
shield was split in half.

39 And when Yehudah saw that his shield was
split, he quickly drew his sword and struck
Yashuv at his ankles, and cut off his feet so that
Yashuv fell upon the ground, and the spear fell
from his hand. 40 And Yehudah quickly picked
up Yashuv's spear, with which he severed his
head and cast it next to his feet.

41 And when the sons of Ya'aqov saw what
Yehudah had done to Yashuv, they all ran into
the ranks of the other kings, and the sons of
Ya'aqov fought with the army of Yashuv, and the
armies of all the kings that were there. 42 And the
sons of Ya'aqov caused fifteen thousand of their
men to fall, and they struck them as if striking at
gourds, and the rest fled for their lives.

43 And Yehudah was still standing by the body
of Yashuv, and stripped Yashuv of his coat of
mail. 44 And Yehudah also took off the iron and
copper that was on Yashuv, and behold nine men
of the captains of Yashuv came along to fight
against Yehudah. 45 And Yehudah hurried and
took up a stone from the ground, and with it
struck one of them on the head, and his skull was

split, and the body also fell from the horse to the
earth. 46 And the eight captains that remained,
seeing the strength of Yehudah, were greatly
afraid and they fled, and Yehudah with his ten
men pursued them, and they overtook them and
killed them.

47 And the sons of Ya'aqov were still striking the
armies of the kings, and they killed many of
them, but those kings daringly kept their stand
with their captains, and did not retreat from their
places, and they exclaimed against those of their
armies that fled from before the sons of Ya'aqov,
but none would listen to them, for they were
afraid of their lives lest they should die. 48 And
all the sons of Ya'aqov, after having struck the
armies of the kings, returned and came before
Yehudah, and Yehudah was still killing the eight
captains of Yashuv, and stripping off their
garments.

49 And Levi saw Elon, king of Ga'ash, advancing
toward him, with his fourteen captains to strike
him, but Levi did not know it for certain. 50 And
Elon with his captains approached nearer, and
Levi looked back and saw that battle was coming
from behind, and Levi ran with twelve of his
servants, and they went and killed Elon and his
captains with the edge of the sword.

38 1 And Ihuri king of Shiloh came up to assist
Elon, and he approached Ya'aqov, when Ya'aqov
drew his bow that was in his hand and with an
arrow struck Ihuri which caused his death.

2 And when Ihuri king of Shiloh was dead, the
four remaining kings fled from their station with
the rest of the captains, and they endeavored to
retreat, saying, "We have no more strength with
the Hebrews after they killed the three kings and
their captains who were more powerful than we
are."

3 And when the sons of Ya'aqov saw that the
remaining kings had removed from their station,
they pursued them, and Ya'aqov also came from
the heap of Shekhem from the place where he
was standing, and they went after the kings and
they approached them with their servants. 4 And
the kings and the captains with the rest of their
armies, seeing that the sons of Ya'aqov
approached them, were afraid of their lives and
fled till they reached the city of Ḥatsor. 5 And the
sons of Ya'aqov pursued them to the gate of the
city of Ḥatsor, and they struck a great attack
against the kings and their armies, about four
thousand men, and while they were striking the
army of the kings, Ya'aqov was occupied with
his bow confining himself to killing the kings,
and he killed them all. 6 And he killed Parathon
king of Ḥatsor at the gate of the city of Ḥatsor,
and he afterward killed Susi king of Sarton, and
Lavan king of Bethḥoron, and Shavir king of
Machanehem, and he killed them all with arrows,
an arrow to each of them, and they died.

7 And the sons of Ya'aqov, seeing that all the
kings were dead and that they were broken up
and retreating, continued to carry on the battle
with the armies of the kings opposite the gate of
Ḥatsor, and they still killed about four hundred
of their men. 8 And three men of the servants of
Ya'aqov fell in that battle, and when Yehudah
saw that three of his servants had died, it grieved
him greatly, and his anger burned within him
against the Amorites. 9 And all the men that
remained of the armies of the kings were greatly
afraid of their lives, and they ran and broke the
gate of the walls of the city of Ḥatsor, and they
all entered the city for safety. 10 And they
concealed themselves in the midst of the city of
Ḥatsor, for the city of Ḥatsor was very large and
extensive, and when all these armies had entered
the city, the sons of Ya'aqov ran after them to the
city.

11 And four mighty men, experienced in battle,
went forth from the city and stood against the
entrance of the city, with drawn swords and
spears in their hands, and they placed themselves
opposite the sons of Ya'aqov, and would not
allow them to enter the city.

12 And Naphtali ran and came between them and
with his sword killed two of them, and cut off
their heads at one stroke. 13 And he turned to the
other two, and behold they had fled, and he
pursued them, overtook them, struck them, and
killed them.

14 And the sons of Ya'aqov came to the city and
saw, and behold there was another wall to the
city, and they sought for the gate of the wall and

could not find it, and Yehudah sprang up on top
of the wall, and Shimon and Levi followed him,
and they all three descended from the wall into
the city. 15 And Shimon and Levi killed all the
men who ran for safety into the city. And also
the inhabitants of the city with their wives and
little ones, they killed with the edge of the
sword, and the cries of the city ascended up to
the heavens.

16 And Dan and Naphtali sprang upon the wall to
see what caused the noise of lamentation, for the
sons of Ya'aqov felt anxious about their brothers,
and they heard the inhabitants of the city
speaking with weeping and petitions, saying,
"Take all that we possess in the city and go
away, only do not put us to death."

17 And when Yehudah, Shimon, and Levi had
ceased striking the inhabitants of the city, they
ascended the wall and called to Dan and
Naphtali, who were on the wall, and to the rest of
their brothers, and Shimon and Levi informed
them of the entrance into the city, and all the
sons of Ya'aqov came to fetch the spoil. 18 And
the sons of Ya'aqov took the spoil of the city of
Ḥatsor, the flocks and herds, and the property,
and they took all that could be captured, and
went away that day from the city.

19 And on the next day the sons of Ya'aqov went
to Sarton, for they heard that the men of Sarton
who had remained in the city were assembling to
fight with them for having killed their king, and
Sarton was a very high and fortified city, and it
had a deep rampart surrounding the city. 20 And
the pillar of the rampart was about fifty cubits
and its breadth forty cubits, and there was no
place for a man to enter the city on account of
the rampart, and the sons of Ya'aqov saw the
rampart of the city, and they sought an entrance
in it but could not find it. 21 For the entrance to
the city was at the rear, and every man that
wished to come into the city came by that road
and went around the whole city, and he
afterwards entered the city.

22 And the sons of Ya'aqov seeing they could not
find the way into the city, their anger was
kindled greatly, and the inhabitants of the city
seeing that the sons of Ya'aqov were coming to
them were greatly afraid of them, for they had
heard of their strength and what they had done to
Ḥatsor. 23 And the inhabitants of the city of
Sarton could not go out toward the sons of
Ya'aqov after having assembled in the city to
fight against them, lest they might thereby get
into the city, but when they saw that they were
coming toward them, they were greatly afraid of
them, for they had heard of their strength and
what they had done to Ḥatsor.

24 So the inhabitants of Sarton quickly took away
the bridge of the road of the city, from its place,
before the sons of Ya'aqov came, and they
brought it into the city. 25 And the sons of
Ya'aqov came and sought the way into the city,
and could not find it and the inhabitants of the
city went up to the top of the wall, and saw, and
behold the sons of Ya'aqov were seeking an
entrance into the city. 26 And the inhabitants of
the city reproached the sons of Ya'aqov from the
top of the wall, and they cursed them, and the
sons of Ya'aqov heard the reproaches, and they
were greatly incensed, and their anger burned
within them. 27 And the sons of Ya'aqov were
provoked at them, and they all rose and sprang
over the rampart with the force of their strength,
and through their might passed the forty cubits'
breadth of the rampart.

28 And when they had passed the rampart they
stood under the wall of the city, and they found
all the gates of the city enclosed with iron doors.
29 And the sons of Ya'aqov came near to break
open the doors of the gates of the city, and the
inhabitants did not let them, for from the top of
the wall they were casting stones and arrows
upon them. 30 And the number of the people that
were upon the wall was about four hundred men,
and when the sons of Ya'aqov saw that the men
of the city would not let them open the gates of
the city, they sprang and ascended the top of the
wall, and Yehudah went up first to the east part
of the city. 31 And Gad and Asher went up after
him to the west corner of the city, and Shimon

and Levi to the north, and Dan and Reuven to the south.[a]

32 And the men who were on the top of the wall, the inhabitants of the city, seeing that the sons of Ya'aqov were coming up to them, they all fled from the wall, descended into the city, and concealed themselves in the midst of the city.

33 And Yissakhar and Naphtali remained under
the wall, and approached and broke the gates of
the city, and kindled a fire at the gates of the city,
that the iron melted, and all the sons of Ya'aqov
came into the city, they and all their men, and
they fought with the inhabitants of the city of
Sarton, and struck them with the edge of the
sword, and no man stood up before them. 34 And
about two hundred men fled from the city, and
they all went and hid themselves in a certain
tower in the city, and Yehudah pursued them to
the tower and he broke down the tower, which
fell upon the men, and they all died.

35 And the sons of Ya'aqov went up the road of the roof of that tower, and they saw, and behold there was another strong and high tower at a distance in the city, and the top of it reached to the heavens, and the sons of Ya'aqov hastened and descended, and went with all their men to that tower, and found it filled with about three hundred men, women and little ones.

36 And the sons of Ya'aqov struck a great attack
among those men in the tower and they ran away
and fled from them. 37 And Shimon and Levi
pursued them, when twelve mighty and valiant
men came out to them from the place where they
had concealed themselves. 38 And those twelve
men fought a strong battle against Shimon and
Levi, and Shimon and Levi could not prevail
over them, and those valiant men broke the
shields of Shimon and Levi, and one of them
struck at Levi's head with his sword, when Levi
quickly placed his hand to his head, for he was
afraid of the sword, and the sword struck Levi's
hand, and it was close to cutting off Levi's hand.
39 And Levi seized the sword of the valiant man
in his hand, and took it forcibly from the man,
and with it he struck at the head of the powerful
man, and he severed his head.

40 And *the* eleven men *that were left* approached
to fight with Levi, for they saw that one of them
was killed, and the sons of Ya'aqov fought, but
the sons of Ya'aqov could not prevail over them,
for those men were very powerful. 41 And the
sons of Ya'aqov seeing that they could not
prevail over them, Shimon gave a loud and
tremendous cry, and the eleven powerful men
were stunned at the voice of Shimon's cry.

42 And Yehudah knew the voice of Shimon's
shouting from a distance, and Naphtali and
Yehudah ran with their shields to Shimon and
Levi, and found them fighting with those
powerful men, unable to prevail over them as
their shields were broken. 43 And Naphtali saw
that the shields of Shimon and Levi were broken,
and he took two shields from his servants and
brought them to Shimon and Levi. 44 And
Shimon, Levi, and Yehudah all three fought
against the eleven mighty men on that day until
the time of sunset, but they could not prevail
over them. 45 And this was told to Ya'aqov, and
he was sorely grieved, and he prayed to 𐤉𐤄𐤅𐤄,
and he and Naphtali his son went against these
mighty men.

46 And Ya'aqov approached and drew his bow,
and came near to the mighty men, and killed
three of their men with the bow, and the
remaining eight turned back, and behold, the war
waged against them in the front and rear, and
they were greatly afraid for their lives, and could
not stand before the sons of Ya'aqov, and they
fled from before them. 47 And in their flight they
met Dan and Asher coming toward them, and
they suddenly fell upon them, and fought with
them, and killed two of them, and Yehudah and
his brothers pursued them, and struck the
remainder of them, and killed them.

48 And all the sons of Ya'aqov returned and walked about the city, searching if they could find any men, and they found about twenty young men in a cave in the city, and Gad and Asher killed them all, and Dan and Naphtali

[a] **38**:**31** Compare Testament of Yehudah **5**:**2** and accompanying footnote.

lighted upon the rest of the men who had fled
and escaped from the second tower, and they
killed them all. **49** And the sons of Ya'aqov
struck all the inhabitants of the city of Sarton,
but the women and little ones they left in the city
and did not kill them.

50 And all the inhabitants of the city of Sarton
were powerful men, one of them would pursue a
thousand, and two of them would not flee from
ten thousand of the rest of men. **51** And the sons
of Ya'aqov killed all the inhabitants of the city of
Sarton with the edge of the sword, that no man
stood up against them, and they left the women
in the city. **52** And the sons of Ya'aqov took all
the spoil of the city, and captured what they
desired, and they took flocks and herds and
property from the city, and the sons of Ya'aqov
did to Sarton and its inhabitants as they had done
to Ḥatsor and its inhabitants, and they turned and
went away.

39 **1** And when the sons of Ya'aqov went from
the city of Sarton, they had gone about two
hundred cubits when they met the inhabitants of
Tapuaḥ coming toward them, for they went out
to fight with them, because they had killed the
king of Tapuaḥ and all his men. **2** So all that
remained in the city of Tapuaḥ came out to fight
with the sons of Ya'aqov, and they thought to
retake from them the plunder and the spoil which
they had captured from Ḥatsor and Sarton. **3** And
the rest of the men of Tapuaḥ fought with the
sons of Ya'aqov in that place, and the sons of
Ya'aqov struck them, and they fled before them,
and they pursued them to the city of Arvelan,
and they all fell before the sons of Ya'aqov.

4 And the sons of Ya'aqov returned and came to
Tapuaḥ, to take away the spoil of Tapuaḥ, and
when they came to Tapuaḥ they heard that the
people of Arvelan had gone out to meet them to
save the spoil of their brethren, and the sons of
Ya'aqov left ten of their men in Tapuaḥ to
plunder the city, and they went out toward the
people of Arvelan. **5** And the men of Arvelan
went out with their wives to fight with the sons
of Ya'aqov, for their wives were experienced in
battle, and they went out, about four hundred
men and women. **6** And all the sons of Ya'aqov
shouted with a loud voice, and they all ran
toward the inhabitants of Arvelan, and with a
great and tremendous voice.

7 And the inhabitants of Arvelan heard the noise
of the shouting of the sons of Ya'aqov, and their
roaring like the noise of lions and like the
roaring of the sea and its waves. **8** And fear and
terror possessed their hearts on account of the
sons of Ya'aqov, and they were terribly afraid of
them, and they retreated and fled before them
into the city, and the sons of Ya'aqov pursued
them to the gate of the city, and they came upon
them in the city. **9** And the sons of Ya'aqov
fought with them in the city, and all their women
were engaged in slinging *stones* against the sons
of Ya'aqov, and the battle was very severe
among them all that day until evening.

10 And the sons of Ya'aqov could not prevail
over them, and the sons of Ya'aqov had almost
perished in that battle, and the sons of Ya'aqov
cried to 𐤉𐤄𐤅𐤄 and greatly gained strength toward
evening, and the sons of Ya'aqov struck all the
inhabitants of Arvelan by the edge of the sword,
men, women and little ones.

11 And also the remainder of the people who had
fled from Sarton, the sons of Ya'aqov struck
them in Arvelan, and the sons of Ya'aqov did to
Arvelan and Tapuaḥ as they had done to Ḥatsor
and Sarton, and when the women saw that all the
men were dead, they went up onto the roofs of
the city and struck the sons of Ya'aqov by
showering down stones like rain. **12** And the sons
of Ya'aqov hurried and came into the city and
seized all the women and struck them with the
edge of the sword, and the sons of Ya'aqov
captured all the spoil and plunder, flocks and
herds and cattle.

13 And the sons of Ya'aqov did to Machanehem
as they had done to Tapuaḥ, to Ḥatsor, and to
Shiloh, and they turned from there and went
away.

14 And on the fifth day the sons of Ya'aqov heard
that the people of Ga'ash had gathered against
them to battle, because they had killed their king
and their captains, for there had been fourteen
captains in the city of Ga'ash, and the sons of
Ya'aqov had killed them all in the first battle.

15 And the sons of Ya'aqov put on their weapons
of war that day, and they marched to battle
against the inhabitants of Ga'ash, and in Ga'ash
there was a strong and mighty people of the
people of the Amorites, and Ga'ash was the
strongest and most fortified city of all the cities
of the Amorites, and it had three walls. 16 And
the sons of Ya'aqov came to Ga'ash and they
found the gates of the city locked, and about five
hundred men standing at the top of the outermost
wall, and a people numerous as the sand upon
the seashore were in ambush for the sons of
Ya'aqov from outside the rear of the city.

17 And the sons of Ya'aqov approached to open
the gates of the city, and while they were
drawing near, behold those who were in ambush
at the rear of the city came forth from their
places and surrounded the sons of Ya'aqov.
18 And the sons of Ya'aqov were enclosed
between the people of Ga'ash, and the battle was
both to their front and rear; and all the men that
were upon the wall were casting arrows and
stones from the wall *down* upon them.

19 And Yehudah, seeing that the men of Ga'ash
were getting too heavy for them, gave a most
piercing and tremendous cry and all the men of
Ga'ash were terrified at the voice of Yehudah's
cry, and men fell from the wall at his powerful
cry, and all those that were outside and inside the
city were greatly afraid for their lives.

20 And the sons of Ya'aqov still came near to
break the doors of the city, when the men of
Ga'ash threw stones and arrows upon them from
the top of the wall, and made them flee from the
gate. 21 And the sons of Ya'aqov returned against
the men of Ga'ash who were with them from
without the city, and they struck them terribly, as
striking against gourds, and they could not stand
against the sons of Ya'aqov, for fright and terror
had seized them at the cry of Yehudah.

22 And the sons of Ya'aqov killed all those men
who were outside the city, and the sons of
Ya'aqov still drew near to make an entrance into
the city, and to fight under the city walls, but
they could not for all the inhabitants of Ga'ash
who remained in the city had surrounded the
walls of Ga'ash in every direction, so that the
sons of Ya'aqov were unable to approach the city
to fight with them. 23 And as the sons of Ya'aqov
came near to one corner to fight under the wall,
the inhabitants of Ga'ash threw arrows and
stones upon them like showers of rain, and they
fled from under the wall.

24 And the people of Ga'ash who were upon the
wall, seeing that the sons of Ya'aqov could not
prevail over them from under the wall,
reproached the sons of Ya'aqov in these words,
saying, 25 "What is the matter with you in the
battle that you cannot prevail? Can you then do
to the mighty city of Ga'ash and its inhabitants as
you did to the cities of the Amorites that were
not so powerful? Surely to those weak ones
among us you did those things, and killed them
in the entrance of the city, for they had no
strength when they were terrified at the sound of
your shouting. 26 And will you now then be able
to fight in this place? Surely here you will all
die, and we will avenge the cause of those cities
that you have laid waste."

27 And the inhabitants of Ga'ash greatly
reproached the sons of Ya'aqov and reviled them
and their Elohim, and continued to cast arrows
and stones upon them from the wall. 28 And
Yehudah and his brothers heard the words of the
inhabitants of Ga'ash and their anger was greatly
roused, and Yehudah was jealous of his Elohim
in this matter, and he called out and said, "O
𐤉𐤄𐤅𐤄, save us; save us, O 𐤉𐤄𐤅𐤄; send help to us
and our brothers."

29 And he ran at a distance with all his might,
with his drawn sword in his hand, and he sprang
from the earth into *the* heavens, and by his
strength mounted the wall, and his sword fell
from his hand. 30 And Yehudah shouted on the
wall, and all the men that were upon the wall
were terrified, and some of them fell from the
wall into the city and died, and those who were
still on the wall, when they saw Yehudah's
strength, they were greatly afraid and fled for
their lives into the city for safety.

31 And some were emboldened to fight with
Yehudah upon the wall, and they came near to
kill him when they saw there was no sword in
Yehudah's hand. And they thought of casting
him from the wall to his brothers, and twenty
men of the city came up to assist them, and they

surrounded Yehudah and they all shouted over
him, and approached him with drawn swords,
and they terrified Yehudah, and Yehudah cried
out to his brothers from the wall.

32 And Ya'aqov and his sons drew the bow from
under the wall, and struck three of the men that
were upon the top of the wall, and Yehudah
continued to cry and he exclaimed, "O 𐤉𐤄𐤅𐤄 help
us, O 𐤉𐤄𐤅𐤄 deliver us," and he cried out with a
loud voice upon the wall, and the cry was heard
at a great distance. **33** And after this cry he
shouted again, and all the men who surrounded
Yehudah on the top of the wall were terrified,
and they each threw his sword from his hand at
the sound of Yehudah's shouting and his tremor,
and fled. **34** And Yehudah took the swords which
had fallen from their hands, and Yehudah fought
with them and killed twenty of their men upon
the wall. **35** And about eighty men and women
still ascended the wall from the city and they all
surrounded Yehudah, and 𐤉𐤄𐤅𐤄 impressed the
fear of Yehudah in their hearts, that they were
unable to approach him.

36 And Ya'aqov and all who were with him drew
the bow from under the wall, and they killed ten
men upon the wall, and they fell below the wall,
before Ya'aqov and his sons. **37** And the people
upon the wall seeing that twenty of their men
had fallen, they still ran toward Yehudah with
drawn swords, but they could not approach him
for they were greatly terrified at Yehudah's
strength.

38 And one of their mighty men whose name was
Arud approached to strike Yehudah upon the
head with his sword, when Yehudah quickly put
his shield to his head, and the sword hit the
shield, and it was split in two. **39** And this mighty
man, after he had struck Yehudah, ran for his life
at the fear of Yehudah, and his feet slipped upon
the wall and he fell among the sons of Ya'aqov
who were below the wall, and the sons of
Ya'aqov struck him and killed him.

40 And Yehudah's head pained him from the
blow of the powerful man, and Yehudah had
nearly died from it. **41** And Yehudah cried out
upon the wall owing to the pain produced by the
blow, when Dan heard him, and his anger burned
within him, and he also rose up and went at a
distance and ran and sprang from the earth and
mounted the wall with his wrath *and* might.
42 And when Dan came upon the wall near
Yehudah all the men who had stood against
Yehudah on the wall fled, and they went up to
the second wall, and they threw arrows and
stones upon Dan and Yehudah from the second
wall, and endeavored to drive them from the
wall. **43** And the arrows and stones struck Dan
and Yehudah, and they were nearly killed on the
wall, and wherever Dan and Yehudah fled from
the wall, they were attacked with arrows and
stones from the second wall.

44 And Ya'aqov and his sons were still at the
entrance of the city below the first wall, and they
were not able to draw their bow against the
inhabitants of the city, as they could not see
them, since they were on the second wall. **45** And
Dan and Yehudah, when they could no longer
bear the stones and arrows that fell upon them
from the second wall, both sprang upon the
second wall near the people of the city, and when
the people of the city who were on the second
wall saw that Dan and Yehudah had come to
them upon the second wall, they all cried out and
descended below between the walls.

46 And Ya'aqov and his sons heard the noise of
the shouting from the people of the city, and they
were still at the entrance of the city, and they
were anxious about Dan and Yehudah who were
not seen by them, they being upon the second
wall. **47** And Naphtali went up in his wrath *and*
might and sprang upon the first wall to see what
caused the noise of shouting which they had
heard in the city, and Yissakhar and Zevulun
drew near to break the doors of the city, and they
opened the gates of the city and came into the
city. **48** And Naphtali leapt from the first wall to
the second, and came to assist his brothers, and
the inhabitants of Ga'ash who were upon the
wall, seeing that Naphtali was the third who had
come up to assist his brothers, they all fled and
descended into the city, and Ya'aqov and all his
sons and all their young men came into the city
to them.

49 And Yehudah and Dan and Naphtali
descended from the wall into the city and
pursued the inhabitants of the city, and Shimon
and Levi were outside the city and did not know

that the gate was opened, and they went up from there to the wall and came down to their brothers into the city. **50** And the inhabitants of the city had all descended into the city, and the sons of Ya'aqov came to them in different directions, and the battle waged against them from the front and the rear, and the sons of Ya'aqov struck them terribly, and killed about twenty thousand of them, men and women, not one of them could stand up against the sons of Ya'aqov. **51** And the blood flowed plentifully in the city, and it was like a brook of water, and the blood flowed like a brook to the outer part of the city, and reached the desert of Bethḥoron.

52 And the people of Bethḥoron saw at a distance the blood flowing from the city of Ga'ash, and about seventy men from among them ran to see the blood, and they came to the place where the blood was. **53** And they followed the track of the blood and came to the wall of the city of Ga'ash, and they saw the blood issue from the city, and they heard the voice of crying from the inhabitants of Ga'ash, for it ascended to the heavens, and the blood was continuing to flow abundantly like a brook of water.

54 And all the sons of Ya'aqov were striking the inhabitants of Ga'ash, and were killing them until evening; about twenty thousand men and women. And the people of Ḥor said, "Surely this is the work of the Hebrews, for they are still carrying on war in all the cities of the Amorites."

55 And those people hurried and ran to Bethḥoron, and each took his weapons of war, and they cried out to all the inhabitants of Bethḥoron, who also put on their weapons of war to go and fight with the sons of Ya'aqov. **56** And when the sons of Ya'aqov had finished striking the inhabitants of Ga'ash, they walked about the city to strip all the dead, and coming in the innermost part of the city and farther on they met three exceedingly mighty men, and there was no sword in their hand.

57 And the sons of Ya'aqov came up to the place where they were, and the mighty men ran away, and one of them had taken Zevulun, whom he saw was a young lad and of short stature, and with his might threw him to the ground. **58** And Ya'aqov ran to him with his sword and Ya'aqov struck him below his loins with the sword, and cut him in two, and the body fell upon Zevulun. **59** And the second one approached and seized Ya'aqov to throw him to the ground, and Ya'aqov turned to him and shouted to him, while Shimon and Levi ran and struck him on the hips with the sword and threw him to the ground. **60** And the mighty man rose up from the ground with wrath *and* might, and Yehudah came to him before he had gained his footing, and struck him upon the head with the sword, and his head was split and he died.

61 And the third mighty man, seeing that his companions were killed, ran from before the sons of Ya'aqov, and the sons of Ya'aqov pursued him in the city; and while the mighty man was fleeing he found one of the swords of the inhabitants of the city, and he picked it up and turned to the sons of Ya'aqov and fought them with that sword. **62** And the mighty man ran to Yehudah to strike him upon the head with the sword, and there was no shield in Yehudah's hand; and while he was aiming to strike him, Naphtali quickly took his shield and put it to Yehudah's head, and the sword of the mighty man hit the shield of Naphtali and Yehudah escaped the sword. **63** And Shimon and Levi ran upon the mighty man with their swords and struck at him forcibly with their swords, and the two swords entered the body of the mighty man and divided it in two, length-wise.

64 And the sons of Ya'aqov struck the three mighty men at that time, together with all the inhabitants of Ga'ash, and the day was about to decline.

65 And the sons of Ya'aqov walked about Ga'ash and took all the spoil of the city, even the little ones and women they did not allow to live, and the sons of Ya'aqov did to Ga'ash as they had done to Sarton and Shiloh.

40 **1** And the sons of Ya'aqov led away all the spoil of Ga'ash, and went out of the city by night.

2 They were going out marching toward the height[a] of Bethḥoron, and the inhabitants of Bethḥoron were going to the height to meet them, and on that night the sons of Ya'aqov fought with the inhabitants of Bethḥoron, in the height of Bethḥoron. 3 And all the inhabitants of Bethḥoron were mighty men, one of them would not flee from before a thousand men, and they fought on that night on the height, and their shouts were heard on that night from afar, and the earth quaked at their shouting.

4 And all the sons of Ya'aqov were afraid of those men, as they were not accustomed to fight in the dark, and they were greatly confounded, and the sons of Ya'aqov cried to 𐤉𐤄𐤅𐤄, saying, "Save us O 𐤉𐤄𐤅𐤄, deliver us that we may not die by the hands of these uncircumcised men."

5 And 𐤉𐤄𐤅𐤄 listened to the voice of the sons of Ya'aqov, and 𐤉𐤄𐤅𐤄 caused great terror and confusion to seize the people of Bethḥoron, and they fought among themselves: one with the other in the darkness of night, and struck each other in great numbers. 6 And the sons of Ya'aqov, knowing that 𐤉𐤄𐤅𐤄 had brought a spirit of perverseness among those men, and that they fought each man with his neighbor, went forth from among the bands of the people of Bethḥoron and went as far as the descent of the height of Bethḥoron, and farther, and they stayed there securely with their young men on that night.

7 And the people of Bethḥoron fought all night, one man with his brother, and the other with his neighbor, and they cried out in every direction upon the height, and their cry was heard at a distance, and the whole earth shook at their voice, for they were powerful above all the people of the earth. 8 And all the inhabitants of the cities of the Kana'anites, the Ḥittites, the Amorites, the Ḥivites and all the kings of Kana'an, and also those who were on the other side of the Yarden, heard the noise of the shouting on that night.

9 And they said, "Surely these are the battles of the Hebrews who are fighting against the seven cities, who came near to them; and who can stand against those Hebrews?"

10 And all the inhabitants of the cities of the Kana'anites, and all those who were on the other side of the Yarden, were greatly afraid of the sons of Ya'aqov, for they said, "Behold the same will be done to us as was done to those cities, for who can stand against their mighty strength?"

11 And the cries of the Ḥorites were very great on that night, and continued to increase; and they struck each other until morning, and numbers of them were killed. 12 And the morning appeared, and all the sons of Ya'aqov rose up at daybreak and went up to the height, and they struck those who remained of the Ḥorites in a terrible manner, and they were all killed in the height.

13 And the sixth day came, and all the inhabitants of Kana'an saw at a distance all the people of Bethḥoron lying dead in the height of Bethḥoron, and strewn about as the carcasses of lambs and goats. 14 And the sons of Ya'aqov led all the spoil which they had captured from Ga'ash and went to Bethḥoron, and they found the city full of people like the sand of the sea, and they fought with them, and the sons of Ya'aqov struck them there until evening time. 15 And the sons of Ya'aqov did to Bethḥoron as they had done to Ga'ash and Tapuaḥ, and as they had done to Ḥatsor, to Sarton and to Shiloh.

16 And the sons of Ya'aqov took with them the spoil of Bethḥoron and all the spoil of the cities, and on that day they went home to Shekhem. 17 And the sons of Ya'aqov came home to the city of Shekhem, and they remained outside the city, and they then rested there from the war, and stayed there all night. 18 And all their servants together with all the spoil that they had taken from the cities, they left outside the city, and

---

[a] **40:2** Samuel's translation reads "castle." The Hebrew word rendered as "height" here is 𐤌𐤏𐤋𐤄 (*ma'alah*), derived from the word 𐤏𐤋𐤄 (*alah*) meaning "to ascend" or "to raise up." Thus here it refers to a height or "high ground" of the city.

they did not enter the city, for they said, "Perhaps there may be yet more fighting against us, and they may come to besiege us in Shekhem."

19 And Ya'aqov and his sons and their servants remained on that night and the next day in the portion of the field which Ya'aqov had purchased from Ḥamor for five sheqels, and all that they had captured was with them. 20 And all the plunder which the sons of Ya'aqov had captured, was in the portion of the field, *as* immense as the sand upon the sea shore.

21 And the inhabitants of the land observed them from afar, and all the inhabitants of the land were afraid of the sons of Ya'aqov who had done this thing, for no king from the days of old had ever done the like. 22 And the seven kings of the Kana'anites resolved to make peace with the sons of Ya'aqov, for they were greatly afraid of their lives, on account of the sons of Ya'aqov.

23 And on that day, being the seventh day, Yaphia king of Ḥevron sent secretly to the king of Ai, and to the king of Givon, and to the king of Shalem, and to the king of Adulam, and to the king of Lakish, and to the king of Ḥatsor, and to all the Kana'anite kings who were in subjection to them, saying, 24 "Go up with me, and come to me that we may go to the sons of Ya'aqov, and I will make peace with them, and form a treaty with them, lest all your lands be destroyed by the swords of the sons of Ya'aqov, as they did to Shekhem and the cities around it, as you have heard and seen. 25 And when you come to me, do not come with many men, but let every king bring his three head captains, and every captain bring three of his officers. 26 And come all of you to Ḥevron, and we will go together to the sons of Ya'aqov, and petition them that they shall form a treaty of peace with us."

27 And all those kings did as the king of Ḥevron had sent to them, for they were all under his counsel and command, and all the kings of Kana'an assembled to go to the sons of Ya'aqov, to make peace with them; and the sons of Ya'aqov returned and went to the portion of the field that was in Shekhem, for they did not trust the kings of the land. 28 And the sons of Ya'aqov returned and remained in the portion of the field ten days, and no one came to make war with them. 29 And when the sons of Ya'aqov saw that there was no appearance of war, they all assembled and went to the city of Shekhem, and the sons of Ya'aqov remained in Shekhem.

30 And at the end of forty days, all the kings of the Amorites assembled from all their places and came to Ḥevron, to Yaphia, king of Ḥevron.

31 And the number of kings that came to Ḥevron, to make peace with the sons of Ya'aqov, was twenty-one kings, and the number of captains that came with them was sixty-nine, and their men were one hundred and eighty-nine, and all these kings and their men rested by Mount Ḥevron. 32 And the king of Ḥevron went out with his three captains and nine men, and these kings resolved to go to the sons of Ya'aqov to make peace.

33 And they said to the king of Ḥevron, "Go before us with your men, and speak for us to the sons of Ya'aqov, and we will come after you and confirm your words," and the king of Ḥevron did so.

34 And the sons of Ya'aqov heard that all the kings of Kana'an had gathered together and rested in Ḥevron, and the sons of Ya'aqov sent four of their servants as spies, saying, "Go and spy these kings, and search and examine their men whether they are few or many, and if they are but few in number, number them all and come back."

35 And the servants of Ya'aqov went secretly to these kings, and did as the sons of Ya'aqov had commanded them, and on that day they came back to the sons of Ya'aqov, and said to them, "We came to those kings, and they are but few in number, and we numbered them all, and behold, they were two hundred and eighty-eight, kings and men."

36 And the sons of Ya'aqov said, "They are but few in number, therefore we will not all go out to them;" and in the morning the sons of Ya'aqov rose up and chose sixty two of their men, and ten of the sons of Ya'aqov went with them; and they put on their weapons of war, for they said, "They are coming to make war with us," for they did

not know that they were coming to make peace with them.

37 And the sons of Ya'aqov went with their servants to the gate of Shekhem, toward those kings, and their father Ya'aqov was with them.
38 And when they had come forth, behold, the king of Ḥevron and his three captains and nine men with him were coming along the road against the sons of Ya'aqov, and the sons of Ya'aqov lifted up their eyes, and saw at a distance Yaphia, king of Ḥevron, with his captains, coming toward them, and the sons of Ya'aqov took their stand at the place of the gate
of Shekhem, and did not proceed. 39 And the
king of Ḥevron continued to advance, he and his captains, until he came near to the sons of Ya'aqov, and he and his captains bowed down to them to the ground, and the king of Ḥevron sat with his captains before Ya'aqov and his sons.

40 And the sons of Ya'aqov said to him, "What happened to you, king of Ḥevron? Why have you come to us today? What do you require from us?" And the king of Ḥevron said to Ya'aqov, "I entreat you my master, all the kings of the Kana'anites have today come to make peace with you."

41 And the sons of Ya'aqov heard the words of the king of Ḥevron, and they would not consent to his proposals, for the sons of Ya'aqov put no faith in him, for they imagined that the king of Ḥevron had spoken deceitfully to them.

42 And the king of Ḥevron knew from the words of the sons of Ya'aqov, that they did not believe his words, and the king of Ḥevron approached nearer to Ya'aqov, and said to him, "I entreat you, my master, to be assured that all these kings have come to you on peaceable terms, for they have not come with all their men, neither did they bring their weapons of war with them, for they have come to seek peace from my master and his sons."

43 And the sons of Ya'aqov answered the king of Ḥevron, saying, "Send to all these kings, and if you speak truth to us, let them each come individually before us, and if they come to us unarmed, we shall then know that they seek peace from us."

44 And Yaphia, king of Ḥevron, sent one of his men to the kings, and they all came before the sons of Ya'aqov, and bowed down to them to the ground, and these kings sat before Ya'aqov and
his sons, and they spoke to them, saying, 45 "We
have heard all that you did to the kings of the Amorites with your sword and exceedingly mighty arm, so that no man could stand up before you, and we were afraid of you for the sake of our lives, lest it should happen to us as it
did to them. 46 So we have come to you to form a
treaty of peace between us, and now therefore cut a covenant of peace and truth with us, that you will not meddle with us, inasmuch as we have not meddled with you."

47 And the sons of Ya'aqov knew that they had really come to seek peace from them, and the sons of Ya'aqov listened to them, and cut a
covenant with them. 48 And the sons of Ya'aqov
swore to them that they would not meddle with them, and all the kings of the Kana'anites swore also to them, and the sons of Ya'aqov made them
tributary from that day forward. 49 And after this
all the captains of these kings came with their men before Ya'aqov, with presents in their hands for Ya'aqov and his sons, and they bowed down to him to the ground.

50 And these kings then urged the sons of Ya'aqov and begged of them to return all the spoil they had captured from the seven cities of the Amorites, and the sons of Ya'aqov did so, and they returned all that they had captured, the women, the little ones, the cattle and all the spoil which they had taken, and they sent them off,
and they went away each to his city. 51 And all
these kings again bowed down to the sons of Ya'aqov, and they sent or brought them many gifts in those days, and the sons of Ya'aqov sent off these kings and their men, and they went peaceably away from them to their cities, and the sons of Ya'aqov also returned to their home, to
Shekhem. 52 And there was peace from that day
forward between the sons of Ya'aqov and the kings of the Kana'anites, until the children of Yisra'el came to inherit the land of Kana'an.

41 1 And at the turn of the year the sons of Ya'aqov journeyed from Shekhem, and they

came to Ḥevron, to their father Yitsḥaq, and they
dwelled there, but their flocks and herds they fed
daily in Shekhem, for there was good and fat
pasture there in those days, and Ya'aqov and his
sons and all their household dwelled in the valley
of Ḥevron.

2 And it was in those days, in that year, being the
hundred and sixth year of the life of Ya'aqov, in
the tenth year of Ya'aqov's coming from Padan-
aram, that Leah the wife of Ya'aqov died; she
was fifty-one years old when she died in Ḥevron.
3 And Ya'aqov and his sons buried her in the
cave of the field of Makhpelah, which is in
Ḥevron, which Avraham had bought from the
children of Ḥeth, for the possession of a burial
place. 4 And the sons of Ya'aqov dwelled with
their father in the valley of Ḥevron, and all the
inhabitants of the land knew their strength and
their fame went throughout the land.

5 And Yoseph the son of Ya'aqov, and his
brother Benyamin, the sons of Raḥel, the wife of
Ya'aqov, were yet young in those days, and did
not go out with their brethren during their battles
in all the cities of the Amorites. 6 And when
Yoseph saw the strength of his brethren, and
their greatness, he praised them and extolled
them, but he ranked himself greater than them,
and extolled himself above them; and Ya'aqov
his father also loved him more than any of his
sons, for he was a son of his old age, and through
his love toward him, he made him a varicolored
tunic.

7 And when Yoseph saw that his father loved
him more than his brethren, he continued to exalt
himself above his brethren, and he brought to his
father evil reports concerning them. 8 And the
other sons of Ya'aqov seeing the whole of
Yoseph's conduct toward them, and that their
father loved him more than any of them, hated
him and could not speak peaceably to him all the
days.

9 And Yoseph was seventeen years old, and he
was still magnifying himself above his brethren,
and thought of raising himself above them. 10 At
that time he dreamed a dream, and he came to his
brothers and told them his dream, and he said to
them, "I dreamed a dream, and behold we were
all binding sheaves in the field, and my sheaf
rose and placed itself upon the ground and your
sheaves surrounded it and bowed down to it."

11 And his brethren answered him and said to
him, "What does this dream mean that you
dreamt? Do you imagine in your heart to reign or
rule over us?"

12 And he still came, and told the thing to his
father Ya'aqov, and Ya'aqov kissed Yoseph
when he heard these words from his mouth, and
Ya'aqov blessed Yoseph. 13 And when the sons
of Ya'aqov saw that their father had blessed
Yoseph and had kissed him, and that he loved
him exceedingly, they became jealous of him
and hated him the more.

14 And after this Yoseph dreamed another dream
and related the dream to his father in the
presence of his brethren, and Yoseph said to his
father and brothers, "Behold I have again
dreamed a dream, and behold the sun and the
moon and the eleven stars bowed down to me."

15 And his father heard the words of Yoseph and
his dream, and seeing that his brethren hated
Yoseph on account of this matter, Ya'aqov
therefore rebuked Yoseph before his brothers on
account of this thing, saying, "What does this
dream mean that you dreamt, and this
magnifying yourself before your brothers who
are older than you? 16 Do you imagine in your
heart that I and your mother and your eleven
brothers will come and bow down to you, that
you speak these things?"

17 And his brothers were jealous of him on
account of his words and dreams, and they
continued to hate him, but Ya'aqov reserved the
dreams in his heart. 18 And the sons of Ya'aqov
went one day to feed their father's flock in
Shekhem, for they were still herdsmen in those
days; and while the sons of Ya'aqov were that
day feeding in Shekhem they delayed, and the
time of gathering in the cattle was passed, and
they had not arrived.

19 And Ya'aqov saw that his sons were delayed
in Shekhem, and Ya'aqov said within himself,
"Perhaps the people of Shekhem have risen up to
fight against them, therefore they have delayed
coming today."

20 And Ya'aqov called Yoseph his son and commanded him, saying, "Behold your brothers are feeding in Shekhem today, and behold they have not yet come back; go now therefore and see where they are, and bring me word back concerning the welfare of your brothers and the welfare of the flock."

21 And Ya'aqov sent his son Yoseph to the valley
of Ḥevron, and Yoseph came for his brothers to
Shekhem, and could not find them, and Yoseph
went about the field which was near Shekhem, to
see where his brothers had turned, and he missed
his road in the wilderness, and knew not which
way he should go. 22 And a messenger of 𐤉𐤄𐤅𐤄
found him wandering in the road toward the
field, and Yoseph said to the messenger of 𐤉𐤄𐤅𐤄,
"I am looking for my brothers; have you not
heard where they are feeding?" and the
messenger of 𐤉𐤄𐤅𐤄 said to Yoseph, "I saw your
brothers feeding here, and I heard them say they
would go to feed in Dothan."

23 And Yoseph listened to the voice of the
messenger of 𐤉𐤄𐤅𐤄, and he went to his brethren
in Dothan and he found them in Dothan feeding
the flock. 24 And Yoseph advanced to his
brethren, and before he had drawn near to them,
they had decided to kill him.

25 And Shimon said to his brothers, "Behold the man of dreams is coming to us today, and now therefore come and let us kill him and cast him into one of the pits that are in the wilderness, and when his father seeks him from us, we will say an evil beast has devoured him."

26 And Reuven heard the words of his brethren concerning Yoseph, and he said to them, "You should not do this thing, for how can we look up to our father Ya'aqov? Cast him into this pit to die there, but do not stretch forth a hand upon him to spill his blood;" and Reuven said this in order to deliver him from their hand, to bring him back to his father.

27 And when Yoseph came to his brethren he sat
before them, and they rose upon him and seized
him and knocked him to the earth, and stripped
him of is varicolored tunic which he had on.
28 And they took him and cast him into a pit, and
in the pit there was no water, but naḥashim and
scorpions. And Yoseph was afraid of the
naḥashim and scorpions that were in the pit. And
Yoseph cried out with a loud voice, and 𐤉𐤄𐤅𐤄
hid the naḥashim and scorpions in the sides of
the pit, and they did no evil to Yoseph.

29 And Yoseph called out from the pit to his brothers, and said to them, "What have I done to you, and in what have I sinned? Why do you not fear 𐤉𐤄𐤅𐤄 concerning me? Am I not of your bones and flesh, and is not Ya'aqov your father, my father *also*? Why do you do this thing to me today, and how will you be able to look up to our father Ya'aqov?"

30 And he continued to cry out and call to his
brothers from the pit, and he said, "O Yehudah,
Reuven, Shimon, and Levi, my brothers, lift me
up from the place of darkness in which you have
placed me, and look before 𐤉𐤄𐤅𐤄, and before
Ya'aqov my father. And if I have sinned against
you, are you not the sons of Avraham, Yitsḥaq,
and Ya'aqov? If they saw an orphan they had
compassion over him, or one that was hungry,
they gave him bread to eat, or one that was
thirsty, they gave him water to drink, or one that
was naked, they covered him with garments!
31 And how then will you withhold your pity
from your brother, for I am of your flesh and
bones, and if I have sinned against you, surely
you will do this on account of my father!"

32 And Yoseph spoke these words from the pit, and his brothers did not hear him, nor incline their ears to the words of Yoseph, and Yoseph was crying and weeping in the pit.

33 And Yoseph said, "O that my father knew, today, the act which my brothers have done to me, and the words which they have spoken to me today."

34 And all his brothers heard his cries and weeping in the pit, and his brothers went and removed themselves from the pit, so that they might not hear the cries of Yoseph and his weeping in the pit.

42 1 And they went and sat on the opposite side, about the distance of a bow-shot, and they sat there to eat bread, and while they were eating

they held counsel together what was to be done
with him, whether to kill him or to bring him
back to his father. 2 They were holding the
counsel, when they lifted up their eyes, and saw,
and behold there was a company of
Yishma'elites coming at a distance by the road of
Gilad, going down to Mitsrayim.

3 And Yehudah said to them, "What would we
gain if we killed our brother? Perhaps Elohim
will require him from us. This, then, is the
counsel proposed concerning him, which you
shall do to him. See this company of
Yishma'elites going down to Mitsrayim? 4 Now
therefore, come let us dispose of him to them, so
that our hand be will not upon him, and they will
lead him along with them, and he will be lost
among the people of the land, and we will not
put him to death with our own hands." And the
proposal pleased his brothers and they did
according to the word of Yehudah.

5 And while they were discussing the matter, and
before the company of Yishma'elites had come
up to them, seven trading men of Midian passed
by them, and as they passed they were thirsty,
and they lifted up their eyes and saw the pit
where Yoseph was, and they looked, and behold
every kind of bird was upon him. 6 And these
Midianites ran to the pit to drink water, for they
thought that it contained water, and on coming
before the pit they heard the voice of Yoseph
crying and weeping in the pit, and they looked
down into the pit, and they saw and behold there
was a youth of good appearance and well
favored.

7 And they called to him and said, "Who are you
and who brought you here, and who placed you
in this pit, in the wilderness?" And they all
helped to raise Yoseph up, and they drew him
out, and brought him up from the pit, and took
him and went away on their journey and passed
by his brothers.

8 And *the brothers* said to them, "Why do you do
this, to take our servant from us and to go away?
Surely we placed this youth in the pit because he
rebelled against us, and you come and bring him
up and lead him away; now then give us back
our servant."

9 And the Midianites answered and said to the
sons of Ya'aqov, "Is this your servant, or does
this man attend you? Perhaps you are all his
servants, for he is more good and well favored
than any of you, and why do you all speak
falsely to us? 10 Now therefore we will not listen
to your words, nor attend to you, for we found
the youth in the pit in the wilderness, and we
took him; we will therefore go on."

11 And all the sons of Ya'aqov approached them
and rose up to them and said to them, "Give us
back our servant. Why should you all die by the
edge of the sword?" And the Midianites cried out
against them, and they drew their swords, and
approached to fight with the sons of Ya'aqov.

12 And behold Shimon rose up from his seat
against them, and sprang upon the ground and
drew his sword and approached the Midianites
and he gave a terrible shout before them, so that
his shouting was heard at a distance, and the
earth shook at Shimon's shouting. 13 And the
Midianites were terrified on account of Shimon
and the noise of his shouting, and they fell upon
their faces, and were excessively alarmed.

14 And Shimon said to them, "Truly, I am
Shimon, the son of Ya'aqov the Hebrew, who
have, with only my brother, destroyed the city of
Shekhem and the cities of the Amorites; so shall
Elohim moreover do to me, that if all your
brethren the people of Midian, and also the kings
of Kana'an, were to come with you, they could
not fight against me. 15 Now therefore give us
back the youth whom you have taken, lest I give
your flesh to the birds of the heavens and the
beasts of the earth."

16 And the Midianites were more afraid of
Shimon, and they approached the sons of
Ya'aqov with terror and fright, and with pathetic
words, saying, 17 "Surely you have said that the
young man is your servant, and that he rebelled
against you, and therefore you placed him in the
pit; what then will you do with a servant who
rebels against his master? Now therefore sell him
to us, and we will give you all that you require
for him;" and 𐤉𐤄𐤅𐤄 was pleased to do this so that
the sons of Ya'aqov would not kill their brother.

18 And the Midianites saw that Yoseph was of a
good appearance and well-favored; they desired
him in their hearts and were urgent to purchase
him from his brethren. 19 And the sons of
Ya'aqov listened to the Midianites and they sold
their brother Yoseph to them for twenty pieces of
silver, and Reuven their brother was not with
them, and the Midianites took Yoseph and
continued their journey to Gilad.

20 They were going along the road, and the
Midianites repented of what they had done, in
having purchased the young man, and one said to
the other, "What is this thing that we have done,
in taking this youth from the Hebrews, who is of
good appearance and well favored? 21 Perhaps
this youth is stolen from the land of the Hebrews,
and why then have we done this thing? If
someone looks for him and he is found in our
hands we shall die because of him. 22 Now
surely hardy and powerful men have sold him to
us, the strength of one of whom you saw today;
perhaps they stole him from his land with their
might and with their powerful arm, and have
therefore sold him to us for the small value
which we gave to them."

23 And while they were discussing together, they
looked, and behold the company of Yishma'elites
which was coming at first, and which the sons of
Ya'aqov saw, was advancing toward the
Midianites, and the Midianites said to each other,
"Come let us sell this youth to the company of
Yishma'elites who are coming toward us, and we
will take for him the little that we gave for him,
and we will be delivered from his evil."

24 And they did so, and they reached the
Yishma'elites, and the Midianites sold Yoseph to
the Yishma'elites for twenty pieces of silver
which they had given to his brothers for him.
25 And the Midianites went on their road to
Gilad, and the Yishma'elites took Yoseph and
they let him ride upon one of the camels, and
they were leading him to Mitsrayim. 26 And
Yoseph heard that the Yishma'elites were
proceeding to Mitsrayim, and Yoseph lamented
and wept at this thing that he was to be so far
removed from the land of Kana'an, from his
father. And he wept bitterly while he was riding
on the camel, and one of their men observed him,
and made him go down from the camel and walk
on foot, and despite this Yoseph continued to cry
and weep, and he said, "O my father, my father."

27 And one of the Yishma'elites rose up and
struck Yoseph on the cheek, and still he
continued to weep. And Yoseph was fatigued in
the road, and was unable to proceed on account
of the bitterness of his being, and they all struck
him and afflicted him in the road, and they
terrified him in order that he might stop weeping.

28 And 𐤉𐤄𐤅𐤄 saw the sorrow of Yoseph and his
toil, and 𐤉𐤄𐤅𐤄 brought down upon those men
darkness and confusion, and the hand of
everyone that struck him became withered.

29 And they said to each other, "What is this
thing that Elohim has done to us in the road?"
and they did not know that this happened to them
on account of Yoseph. And the men proceeded
on the road, and they passed along the road of
Ephrath where Raḥel was buried. 30 And Yoseph
reached his mother's grave, and Yoseph hurried
and ran to his mother's grave, and fell upon the
grave and wept.

31 And Yoseph cried aloud upon his mother's
grave, and he said, "O my mother, my mother, O
you who gave birth to me, wake up; rise and see
your son, how he has been sold for a slave, and
no one pities him. 32 Rise and see your son, weep
with me on account of my troubles, and see the
heart of my brothers. 33 Arouse my mother,
arouse, awake from your sleep for me, and direct
your battles against my brothers. O how have
they stripped me of my tunic, and sold me
already twice for a slave, and separated me from
my father, and there is no one to pity me.
34 Arouse and lay your cause against them before
Elohim, and see whom Elohim will declare right
in the judgment, and whom He will condemn.
35 Rise, O my mother, rise, awake from your
sleep and see my father how his being is with me
today, and comfort him and ease his heart."

36 And Yoseph continued to speak these words,
and Yoseph cried aloud and wept bitterly upon
his mother's grave; and he ceased speaking, and
from bitterness of heart he became still as a stone
upon the grave. 37 And Yoseph heard a voice
speaking to him from beneath the ground, which

answered him with bitterness of heart, and with a voice of weeping and praying in these words:

38 "My son, my son Yoseph, I have heard the
voice of your weeping and the voice of your
lamentation; I have seen your tears; I know your
troubles, my son, and it grieves me for your sake,
and abundant grief is added to my grief. 39 Now
therefore my son, Yoseph my son, hope in 𐤉𐤄𐤅𐤄,
and wait for him and do not fear, for 𐤉𐤄𐤅𐤄 is
with you. He will deliver you from all trouble.
40 Rise my son, go down to Mitsrayim with your
masters, and do not fear, for 𐤉𐤄𐤅𐤄 is with you,
my son." And she continued to speak these
words to Yoseph, and she was still.

41 And Yoseph heard this, and he wondered greatly at this, and he continued to weep; and after this one of the Yishma'elites observed him crying and weeping upon the grave, and his anger was kindled against him, and he drove him from there, and he struck him and cursed him.

42 And Yoseph said to the men, "May I find favor in your sight to take me back to my father's house, and he will give you abundance of riches."

43 And they answered him, saying, "Are you not a slave? Where *then* is your father? And if you had a father, you would not have been sold twice for a slave for so little value;" and their anger was still roused against him, and they continued to strike him and to beat him, and Yoseph wept bitterly.

44 And 𐤉𐤄𐤅𐤄 saw Yoseph's affliction, and 𐤉𐤄𐤅𐤄 again struck these men, and beat them, and 𐤉𐤄𐤅𐤄 caused darkness to envelope them upon the earth, and the lightning flashed and the thunder roared, and the earth shook at the voice of the thunder and of the mighty wind, and the men were terrified and did not know where they should go.

45 And the beasts and camels stood still, and they led them, but they would not go, they struck them, and they crouched upon the ground; and the men said to each other, "What is this that Elohim has done to us? What are our transgressions, and what are our sins that this thing has happened to us?"

46 And one of them answered and said to them, "Perhaps on account of the sin of afflicting this slave has this thing happened today to us; now therefore beg him strongly to forgive us, and then we shall know on whose account this evil happened to us, and if Elohim shall have compassion over us, then we shall know that all this comes to us on account of the sin of afflicting this slave."

47 And the men did so, and they petitioned Yoseph and pressed him to forgive them; and they said, "We have sinned against 𐤉𐤄𐤅𐤄 and against you. Now therefore promise to request of your Elohim that He shall put away this death from among us, for we have sinned against Him."

48 And Yoseph did according to their words, and 𐤉𐤄𐤅𐤄 listened to Yoseph, and 𐤉𐤄𐤅𐤄 put away the plague which He had inflicted on those men on account of Yoseph, and the beasts rose up from the ground and they conducted them, and they went on, and the raging storm settled and the earth became tranquil, and the men proceeded on their journey to go down to Mitsrayim, and the men knew that this evil happened to them on account of Yoseph.

49 And they said to each other, "Behold we know that it was on account of his affliction that this evil happened to us; now therefore why shall we bring this death upon our beings? Let us hold counsel what to do to this slave."

50 And one answered and said, "Surely he told us to bring him back to his father; now therefore come, let us take him back and we will go to the place that he will tell us, and take from his family the price that we gave for him and we will then go away."

51 And one answered again and said, "Behold this counsel is very good, but we cannot do so for the way is very far from us, and we cannot go out of our road."

52 And one more answered and said to them, "This is the counsel that we should do: we will not swerve from it; behold we are going to Mitsrayim today, and when we have come to Mitsrayim, we will sell him there at a high price, and we will be delivered from his evil."

53 And this thing pleased the men and they did so, and they continued their journey to Mitsrayim with Yoseph.

43 1 And when the sons of Ya'aqov had sold their brother Yoseph to the Midianites, their hearts were struck on account of him, and they repented of their acts, and they sought for him to bring him back, but could not find him.

2 And Reuven returned to the pit in which Yoseph had been put, in order to lift him out, and restore him to his father, and Reuven stood by the pit, and he did not hear a word. And he called out, "Yoseph! Yoseph!" and no one answered or uttered a word.

3 And Reuven said, "Yoseph has died through fright, or some naḥash has caused his death;" and Reuven descended into the pit, and he searched for Yoseph and could not find him in the pit, and he came out again.

4 And Reuven tore his garments and he said, "The child is not there, and how shall I reconcile my father about him if he be dead?" and he went to his brethren and found them grieving on account of Yoseph, and counseling together how to reconcile their father about him, and Reuven said to his brethren, "I came to the pit and behold Yoseph was not there, what then shall we say to our father, for my father will only seek the lad from me."

5 And his brothers answered him saying, "Thus and thus we did, and our hearts afterward struck us on account of this act, and we now sit to plot how we shall reconcile our father to it."

6 And Reuven said to them, "What is this you have done to bring down the grey hairs of our father in sorrow to Sheol? The thing that you have done is not good."

7 And Reuven sat with them, and they all rose up and swore to each other not to tell a word to Ya'aqov, and they all said, "The man who tells this to our father or his household, or who will report this to any of the children of the land, we will all rise up against him and kill him with the sword."

8 And the sons of Ya'aqov feared each other in this matter, from the youngest to the oldest, and no one spoke a word, and they concealed the
thing in their hearts. 9 And they afterward sat
down to determine and invent something to say to their father Ya'aqov concerning all these things.

10 And Yissakhar[a] said to them, "Here is advice for you, if it seems good in your eyes to do this thing: take the coat which belonged to Yoseph and tear it, and kill a kid of the goats and dip it in
its blood. 11 And *then* send it to our father and
when he sees it he will say an evil beast has devoured him. Therefore tear his coat and behold his blood will be upon his coat, and by doing this we shall be free of our father's grumblings."

12 And Yissakhar's advice pleased them, and they listened to him and they did according to the word of Yissakhar which he had counselled
them. 13 And they hurried and took Yoseph's
coat and tore it, and they killed a kid of the goats and dipped the coat in the blood of the kid, and then trampled it in the dust, and they sent the coat to their father Ya'aqov by the hand of Naphtali, and they commanded him to say these words:

14 "We had gathered in the cattle and had come as far as the road to Shekhem and farther, when we found this coat on the road in the wilderness dipped in blood and in dust; now therefore know if it is your son's coat or not."

15 And Naphtali went and he came to his father and he gave him the coat, and he spoke to him all the words which his brother had commanded
him. 16 And Ya'aqov saw Yoseph's coat and he
knew it and he fell upon his face to the ground, and became as still as a stone, and he afterward rose up and cried out with a loud and weeping voice and he said, "It is the coat of my son Yoseph!"

17 And Ya'aqov hurried and sent one of his servants to his sons, who went to them and found

[a] **43:10** See Testament of Zevulun **4:8** and accompanying footnote.

them coming along the road with the flock.
18 And the sons of Ya'aqov came to their father
about evening, and behold their garments were
torn and dust was upon their heads, and they
found their father crying out and weeping with a
loud voice.

19 And Ya'aqov said to his sons, "Tell me truly
what evil have you suddenly brought upon me
today?" and they answered their father Ya'aqov,
saying, "We were coming along after the flock
had been gathered in today, and we came as far
as the city of Shekhem by the road in the
wilderness, and we found this coat filled with
blood upon the ground, and we knew it and we
sent to you if you knew it."

20 And Ya'aqov heard the words of his sons and
he cried out with a loud voice, and he said, "It is
the coat of my son, an evil beast has devoured
him; Yoseph is torn to pieces, for I sent him
today to see whether it was well with you and
well with the flocks and to bring me word again
from you, and he went as I commanded him, and
this has happened to him today while I thought
my son was with you."

21 And the sons of Ya'aqov answered and said,
"He did not come to us, neither have we seen
him from the time of our going out from you
until now."

22 And when Ya'aqov heard their words he again
cried out aloud, and he rose up and tore his
garments, and he put sackcloth on his loins, and
he wept bitterly and he mourned and lifted up his
voice in weeping and exclaimed and said these
words,

23 "Yoseph my son, O my son Yoseph, I sent you
after the welfare of your brothers today, and
behold you have been torn to pieces; through my
hand has this happened to my son. 24 It grieves
me for you Yoseph my son, it grieves me for
you; how sweet you were to me during life, and
now how exceedingly bitter is your death to me.
25 O that I had died in instead of you, Yoseph my
son, for it grieves me sadly for you my son, O
my son, my son. Yoseph my son, where are you,
and where have you been drawn? Arouse, arouse
from your place, and come and see my grief for
you, O my son Yoseph. 26 Come now and
number the tears pouring from my eyes down my
face, and bring them up before 𐤉𐤄𐤅𐤄, that His
anger may turn from me.

27 "O Yoseph my son, how did you fall, by the
hand of one by whom no one had fallen from the
beginning of the world to this day; for you have
been put to death by the striking of an enemy,
inflicted with cruelty, but surely I know that this
has happened to you on account of the multitude
of my sins. 28 Arouse now and see how bitter is
my trouble for you my son, although I did not
raise you, nor fashion you, nor give you breath
and being, but it was Elohim who formed you
and built your bones and covered them with
flesh, and breathed in your nostrils the breath of
life, and then He gave you to me. 29 Now truly
Elohim who gave you to me, He has taken you
from me, and such has happened to you."

30 And Ya'aqov continued to speak these *kinds of*
words concerning Yoseph, and he wept bitterly;
he fell to the ground and became still. 31 And all
the sons of Ya'aqov seeing their father's trouble,
they repented of what they had done, and they
also wept bitterly.

32 And Yehudah rose up and lifted his father's
head from the ground, and placed it upon his lap,
and he wiped his father's tears from his face, and
Yehudah wept an exceedingly great weeping,
while his father's head was reclining upon his
lap, still as a stone. 33 And the sons of Ya'aqov
saw their father's trouble, and they lifted up their
voices and continued to weep, and Ya'aqov was
still lying upon the ground still as a stone. 34 And
all his sons and his servants and his servant's
children rose up and stood around him to
comfort him, and he refused to be comforted.

35 And the whole household of Ya'aqov rose up
and mourned a great mourning on account of
Yoseph and their father's trouble, and the news
reached Yitsḥaq, the son of Avraham, the father
of Ya'aqov, and he wept bitterly on account of
Yoseph, he and all his household, and he went
from the place where he dwelled in Ḥevron, and
his men with him, and he comforted Ya'aqov his
son, and he refused to be comforted.

36 And after this, Ya'aqov rose up from the
ground, and his tears were running down his

face, and he said to his sons, "Rise up and take
your swords and your bows, and go forth into the
field, and seek whether you can find my son's
body and bring it to me that I may bury it.
37 Seek also, I ask you, among the beasts and
hunt them, and that which shall come the first
before you seize and bring it to me; perhaps
𐤉𐤄𐤅𐤄 will pity my affliction today, and prepare
before you that which tore my son in pieces.
Bring it to me, and I will avenge the cause of my
son."

38 And his sons did as their father had
commanded them, and they rose up early in the
morning, and each took his sword and his bow in
his hand, and they went forth into the field to
hunt the beasts.

39 And Ya'aqov was still crying aloud and
weeping and walking to and fro in the house, and
striking his hands together, saying, "Yoseph my
son, Yoseph my son."

40 And the sons of Ya'aqov went into the
wilderness to seize the beasts, and behold a wolf
came toward them, and they seized it, and
brought it to their father, and they said to him,
"This is the first we have found, and we have
brought him to you as you commanded us, and
we could not find your son's body."

41 And Ya'aqov took the beast from the hands of
his sons, and he cried out with a loud and
weeping voice, holding the beast in his hand, and
he spoke with a bitter heart to the beast, "Why
did you devour my son Yoseph, and why did you
not fear the Elohim of the earth, or of my trouble
for my son Yoseph? 42 And you devoured my
son for nothing, because he committed no
violence, and thus you rendered me liable on his
account; therefore Elohim will require him that is
persecuted."

43 And 𐤉𐤄𐤅𐤄 opened the mouth of the beast in
order to comfort Ya'aqov with its words, and it
answered Ya'aqov and spoke these words to him,

44 "As Elohim lives who created us in the earth,
and as your being lives, my master, I did not see
your son, neither did I tear him to pieces, but
from a distant land I also came to seek my son
who went from me today, and I do not know if
he is living or dead. 45 And I came into the field
to seek my son today, and your sons found me,
and seized me and increased my grief, and have
brought me before you today, and I have now
spoken all my words to you. 46 And now
therefore, O son of man, I am in your hands; do
to me today as it may seem good in your eyes,
but by the life of Elohim who created me, I did
not see your son, nor did I tear him to pieces,
neither has the flesh of man entered my mouth
all the days of my life."

47 And when Ya'aqov heard the words of the
beast he was greatly astonished, and sent the
beast forth from his hand, and she went her way.
48 And Ya'aqov was still crying aloud and
weeping for Yoseph day after day, and he
mourned for his son many days.

44

1 And the sons of Yishma'el who had bought
Yoseph from the Midianites, who had bought
him from his brothers, went to Mitsrayim with
Yoseph, and they came upon the borders of
Mitsrayim, and when they came near Mitsrayim,
they met four men of the sons of Medan[a] the son
of Avraham, who had gone forth from the land
of Mitsrayim on their journey.

2 And the Yishma'elites said to them, "Do you
desire to purchase this slave from us?" and they
said, "Deliver him over to us," and they
delivered Yoseph over to them, and they saw
him, that he was a very good youth and they
purchased him for twenty sheqels.

3 And the Yishma'elites continued their journey
to Mitsrayim and the Medanites also returned
that day to Mitsrayim, and the Medanites said to
each other, "Behold we have heard that Potiphar,
an officer of Pharaoh, captain of the guard, seeks
a good servant who shall stand before him to
attend him, and to make him overseer over his
house and all belonging to him. 4 Now therefore
come let us sell *this youth* to him for whatever

---

[a] **44:1** Sons of Medan – Not to be confused with the sons of Midian. As shown in Yashar **25:2** (see also Bereshiyt [Genesis] **25:2**) Avraham had other sons by Qeturah, including both Medan and Midian.

price we desire, if he be able to give to us that
which we shall require for him."

5 And these Medanites went and came to the
house of Potiphar, and said to him, "We have
heard that you seek a good servant to attend you;
behold we have a servant that will please you, if
you can give us that which we desire, and we
will sell him to you."

6 And Potiphar said, "Bring him before me, and I
will see him, and if he please me I will give you
that which you require for him."

7 And the Medanites went and brought Yoseph
and placed him before Potiphar, and he saw him,
and he pleased *Potiphar* exceedingly, and
Potiphar said to them, "Tell me what you require
for this youth."

8 And they said, "Four hundred pieces of silver *is
the price* we desire for him," and Potiphar said,
"I will give it you if you bring me the record of
his sale to you, and tell me his history, for
perhaps he may be stolen, for this youth is
neither a slave, nor the son of a slave, but I
observe in him the appearance of a good and
handsome man."

9 And the Medanites went and brought to him the
Yishma'elites who had sold him to them, and
they told him, saying, "He is a slave and we sold
him to them."

10 And Potiphar heard the words of the
Yishma'elites and he gave the silver to the
Medanites, and the Medanites took the silver and
went on their journey, and the Yishma'elites also
returned home.

11 And Potiphar took Yoseph and brought him to
his house that he might serve him, and Yoseph
found favor in the eyes of Potiphar; and *Potiphar*
placed confidence in him, and made him
overseer over his house, and all that belonged to
him he delivered over into his hand. 12 And
𐤉𐤄𐤅𐤄 was with Yoseph and he became a
prosperous man, and 𐤉𐤄𐤅𐤄 blessed the house of
Potiphar for the sake of Yoseph. 13 And Potiphar
left all that he had in the hand of Yoseph, and
Yoseph was he that caused things to come in and
go out, and everything was regulated by his
desire in the house of Potiphar.

14 And Yoseph was eighteen years old, a youth
with beautiful eyes and of good appearance, and
there was no one like him in the whole land of
Mitsrayim.

15 At that time while he was in his master's
house, going in and out of the house and
attending to 𐤉𐤄𐤅𐤄, Zelikhah[a], his master's wife,
lifted up her eyes toward Yoseph and she looked
at him, and behold he was a good and well
favored youth. 16 And she coveted his beauty in
her heart, and her being was fixed upon Yoseph,
and she enticed him day after day, and Zelikhah
tried to persuade Yoseph daily, but Yoseph did
not lift up his eyes to behold his master's wife.

17 And Zelikhah said to him, "How good is your
appearance and form; truly I have looked at all
the slaves, and have not seen so beautiful a slave
as you are;" and Yoseph said to her, "Surely He
who created me in my mother's womb created all
mankind."

18 And she said to him, "How beautiful are your
eyes, with which you have dazzled all the
inhabitants of Mitsrayim, men and women;" and
he said to her, "How beautiful they are while we
are alive, but if you were to see them in the
grave, surely you would move away from them."

19 And she said to him, "How beautiful and
pleasing are all your words. Now then, please
take the harp which is in the house, and play
with your hands and let us hear your words."

20 And he said to her, "How beautiful and
pleasing are my words when I speak the praise of
my Elohim and His glory;" and she said to him,
"How very beautiful is the hair of your head;
behold the golden comb which is in the house,
please take it and curl the hair of your head."

21 And he said to her, "How long will you speak
these words? Stop saying these words to me, and
rise and see to your business affairs."

---

[a] **44:15** Zelikhah – Name of unknown meaning, most likely a Mitsrite word.

22 And she said to him, "There is no one in my house, and there is nothing to attend to but to your words and to your desire;" yet despite all this, she could not bring Yoseph to her, neither did he place his eye upon her, but directed his eyes below to the ground.

23 And Zelikhah desired Yoseph in her heart, that he should lie with her. At the time that Yoseph was sitting in the house doing his work, Zelikhah came and sat before him, and she enticed him daily with her discourse to lie with her, or even to look at her, but Yoseph would not listen to her.

24 And she said to him, "If you will not do according to my words, I will punish you with the judgment of death, and put an iron yoke upon you."

25 And Yoseph said to her, "Surely Elohim who created man loosens the fetters of prisoners, and it is He who will deliver me from your prison and from your judgment."

26 And when she could not prevail over him, to persuade him, and her being was still fixed upon him, her desire threw her into a grievous sickness.

27 And all the women of Mitsrayim came to visit her, and they said to her, "Why are you so lowly and lean? You lack nothing; surely your husband is a great and esteemed prince in the eyes of the king, should you lack anything of what your heart desires?"

28 And Zelikhah answered them, saying, "Today
it shall be made known to you, where this
disorder comes from which you see *in* me," and
she commanded her maid servants to prepare
food for all the women, and she made a banquet
for them, and all the women ate in the house of
Zelikhah. 29 And she gave them knives to peel
the citrons[a] *in order* to eat them, and she
commanded that they should dress Yoseph in
costly garments, and that he should appear
before them, and Yoseph came before their eyes
and all the women looked on Yoseph, and could
not take their eyes from off him, and they all cut
their hands with the knives that they had in their
hands, and all the citrons that were in their hands
were filled with blood. 30 And they did not know
what they had done but they continued to look at
the beauty of Yoseph, and did not turn their
eyelids from him.

31 And Zelikhah saw what they had done, and she said to them, "What is this work that you have done? See, I gave you citrons to eat and you have all cut your hands."

32 And all the women saw their hands, and behold they were full of blood, and their blood flowed down upon their garments, and they said to her, "this slave in your house has overcome us, and we could not turn our eyelids from him on account of his beauty."

33 And she said to them, "Surely this happened to you in the moment that you looked at him, and you could not contain yourselves from him; how then can I refrain when he is constantly in my house, and I see him day after day going in and out of my house? How then can I keep from declining or even from dying on account of this?"

34 And they said to her, "The words are true, for who can see this beautiful form in the house and refrain from him. Is he not your slave and attendant in your house? Why do you not tell him that which is in your heart, and allow your being to die through this matter?"

35 And she said to them, "I am daily endeavoring to persuade him, and he will not consent to my desires, and I promised him everything that is good, and yet I could meet with no return from him; I am therefore in a lowly state as you see."

36 And Zelikhah became very sick on account of her desire toward Yoseph, and she was heavily lovesick on account of him, and all the people of the house of Zelikhah and her husband knew nothing of this matter, that Zelikhah was sick on account of her love for Yoseph.

37 And all the people of her house asked her, saying, "Why are you sick and lowly, and *yet*

---

[a] **44:29** Citron – Specifically the Etrog (Heb. אתרוג).

lack nothing?" and she said to them, "I do not know what thing is daily increasing upon me."

38 And all the women and her friends came daily to see her, and they spoke with her, and she said to them, "This can only be through the love of Yoseph;" and they said to her, "Entice him and seize him secretly, perhaps he may listen to you, and put this death off from you."

39 And Zelikhah became worse from her love for Yoseph, and she continued to decline, until she hardly had enough strength to stand.

40 And on a certain day Yoseph was doing his master's work in the house, and Zelikhah came secretly and fell suddenly upon him, and Yoseph rose up against her, and he was more powerful than she, and he brought her down to the ground.
41 And Zelikhah wept on account of the desire of her heart toward him, and she petitioned him with weeping, and her tears flowed down her face, and she spoke to him in a voice of petition and in bitterness of being, saying,

42 "Have you ever heard, seen, or known of so beautiful a woman as I am, or better than myself – who speaks to you daily – *and* fall into a decline through love for you, give all this honor upon you, and still you will not listen to my
voice? 43 And if it be through fear of your master lest he punish you, as the king lives no harm shall come to you from your master through this thing. Now, therefore please listen to me, and consent for the sake of the honor which I have given to you, and put off this death from me; and why should I die for your sake?" And she stopped speaking.

44 And Yoseph answered her, saying, "Refrain from me, and leave this matter to my master; behold my master does not know what there is with me in the house, for all that belongs to him he has delivered into my hand; how shall I do
these things in my master's house? 45 For he has greatly honored me in his house, and he has also made me overseer over his house, and he has exalted me, and there is no one greater in this house than I am, and my master has not kept anything from me, except for you, who are his wife; how then can you speak these words to me, and how can I do this great evil and sin to
Elohim and to your husband? 46 Now therefore refrain from me, and do not speak these words anymore, for I will not listen to your words." But Zelikhah would not listen to Yoseph when he spoke these words to her, but she daily enticed him to listen to her.

47 And it was after this that the brook of Mitsrayim was filled above all its sides, and all the inhabitants of Mitsrayim went forth with song; and also the king and princes went forth to the shore with dancing, for it was a great rejoicing in Mitsrayim, and a celebration at the time of the inundation of the sea Siḥor, and they went there to rejoice all the day.

48 And when the Mitsrites went out to the river to rejoice, as was their custom, all the people of the house of Potiphar went with them, but Zelikhah would not go with them, for she said, "I am unwilling," and she remained alone in the house, for Yoseph found her that day, and no other person was with her in the house.

49 And she rose up and ascended to her temple in the house, and put on royal garments, and she placed upon her head precious stones of onyx, inlaid with silver and gold; and she beautified her face and skin with all sorts of women's cosmetics, and she perfumed the temple and the house with cassia and frankincense, and she spread myrrh and aloes, and she afterward sat in the entrance of the temple, in the passage of the house, through which Yoseph passed to do his work. And behold Yoseph came from the field, and entered the house to do his master's work.
50 And he came to the place through which he had to pass, and he saw all the work of Zelikhah, and he turned back.

51 And Zelikhah saw Yoseph turning back from her, and she called out to him, saying "What ails you, Yoseph? Come to your work, and behold I will make room for you until you pass to your seat."

52 And Yoseph returned and came to the house, and passed from there to the place of his seat, and he sat down to do his master's work as usual and behold Zelikhah came to him and stood before him in royal garments, and the scent from her clothes was spread to a distance.

53 And she hastened and caught hold of Yoseph and his garments, and she said to him, "As the king lives if you will not do as I say you shall die today," and she hurried and stretched forth her other hand and drew a sword from beneath her garments, and she placed it upon Yoseph's neck, and she said, "Rise and do as I say, and if not then you will die today."

54 And Yoseph was afraid of her for her doing this thing, and he rose up to flee from her, and she seized the front of his garments, and in the terror of his flight the garment which Zelikhah seized was torn, and Yoseph left the garment in the hand of Zelikhah, and he fled and got out, for he was in fear. 55 And when Zelikhah saw that Yoseph's garment was torn, and that he had left it in her hand, and had fled, she was afraid of her life, lest the report should spread concerning her, and she rose up and acted with cunning, and put off the garments in which she was dressed, and she put on her other garments. 56 And she took Yoseph's garment, and she laid it beside her, and she went and seated herself in the place where she had sat in her sickness, before the people of her house had gone out to the river, and she called a young lad who was then in the house, and she ordered him to call the people of the house to her.

57 And when she saw them she said to them with a loud voice and lamentation, "See what a Hebrew your master has brought to me in the house, for he came to lie with me today. 58 For when you had gone out he came to the house, and seeing that there was no person in the house, he came to me, and caught hold of me, with intent to lie with me. 59 And I seized his garments and tore them and called out against him with a loud voice, and when I had lifted up my voice he was afraid of his life and left his garment before me, and fled."

60 And the people of her house spoke nothing, but their wrath was kindled against Yoseph, and they went to his master and told him the words of his wile.

61 And Potiphar came home enraged, and his wife cried out to him, saying, "What is this thing that you have done to me in bringing a Hebrew servant into my house? For he came to me today to play with me; thus did he do to me today."

62 And Potiphar heard the words of his wife, and he ordered Yoseph to be punished with severe stripes, and they did so to him.

63 And while they were striking him, Yoseph called out with a loud voice, and he lifted up his eyes to the heavens, and he said, "O 𐤉𐤄𐤅𐤄 Elohim, You know that I am innocent of all these things; why should I die today through falsehood, by the hand of these uncircumcised *and* wicked men, whom You know?"

64 And whilst Potiphar's men were beating Yoseph, he continued to cry out and weep, and there was a child there eleven months old, and 𐤉𐤄𐤅𐤄 opened the mouth of the child, and he spoke these words before Potiphar's men, who were striking Yoseph, saying,

65 "What do you want of this man, and why do you do this evil to him? My mother spoke falsely and uttered lies; thus was the what actually transpired."

66 And the child told them accurately all that happened, and he declared to them all the words of Zelikhah to Yoseph day after day. 67 And all the men heard the words of the child and they wondered greatly at the child's words, and the child ceased to speak and became still. 68 And Potiphar was very much ashamed at the words of his son, and he commanded his men not to beat Yoseph anymore, and the men ceased beating Yoseph.

69 And Potiphar took Yoseph and ordered him to be brought to judgment before the priests, who were judges belonging to the king, in order to judge him concerning this affair.

70 And Potiphar and Yoseph came before the priests who were the king's judges, and he said to them, "Judge, please, what judgment is due to a servant, for thus has he done."

71 And the priests said to Yoseph, "Why did you do this thing to your master?" and Yoseph answered them, saying, "Not so my masters, thus was the matter;" and Potiphar said to Yoseph, "Surely I entrusted in all that belonged to me into

your hands, and I withheld nothing from you but
my wife; how could you do this evil?"

72 And Yoseph answered saying, "Not so my
master, as 𐤉𐤄𐤅𐤄 lives, and as your being lives,
my master, the word which you heard from your
wife is false, for thus was the affair today. 73 A
year has elapsed to me since I have been in your
house;[a] have you seen any iniquity in me, or
anything which might cause you to demand my
life?"

74 And the priests said to Potiphar, "Send, please, and let them bring before us Yoseph's torn garment, and let us see the tear in it, and if it shall be that the tear is in front of the garment, then his face must have been opposite to her and she must have caught hold of him, to come to her, and your wife has done all that she has spoken with deceit."

75 And they brought Yoseph's garment before the priests who were judges, and they saw and behold the tear was in front of Yoseph*'s garment*, and all the judging priests knew that she had pressed him, and they said, "The judgment of death is not due to this slave for he has done nothing, but his judgment is, that he be placed in the prison house on account of the report, which has gone forth through him against you wife."

76 And Potiphar heard their words, and he placed him in the prison house, the place where the king's prisoners are confined, and Yoseph was in the house of confinement twelve years.

77 And despite this, his master's wife did not turn from him, and she did not cease from speaking to him day after day to listen to her. And at the end of three months Zelikhah continued going to Yoseph to the house of confinement day by day, and she enticed him to listen to her, and Zelikhah said to Yoseph, "How long will you remain in this house? Listen now to my voice, and I will bring you out of this house."

78 And Yoseph answered her, saying, "It is better for me to remain in this house than to listen to your words, to sin against Elohim;" and she said to him, "If you will not do as I desire, I will pluck out your eyes, add fetters to your feet, and deliver you into the hands of them whom you have not known before."

79 And Yoseph answered her and said, "Behold the Elohim of the whole earth is able to deliver me from all that you can do to me, for He opens the eyes of the blind, and loosens those that are bound,[b] and preserves all sojourners who are unacquainted with the land."

80 And when Zelikhah was unable to persuade Yoseph to listen to her, she stopped going to entice him; and Yoseph was still confined in the house of confinement. And Ya'aqov the father of Yoseph, and all his brothers who were in the land of Kana'an still mourned and wept in those days on account of Yoseph, for Ya'aqov refused to be comforted for his son Yoseph, and Ya'aqov cried aloud, and wept and mourned all those days.

45 1 And it was at that time in that year, which
is the year of Yoseph's going down to Mitsrayim
after his brothers had sold him, that Reuven the
son of Ya'aqov went to Timnah and took
Eliuram, the daughter of Azi the Kana'anite for a
wife for himself, and he came to her. 2 And
Eliuram the wife of Reuven conceived and bare
him Ḥanokh, Palu, Ḥetsron and Karmi, four
sons; and Shimon his brother took his sister
Dinah for a wife, and she bore to him Memuel,
Yamin, Ohad, Yakin and Tsoḥar, five sons.

3 And he afterward came to Bunah the Kana'anite woman, the same is Bunah whom Shimon took captive from the city of Shekhem, and Bunah was before Dinah and attended to her; and Shimon came to her, and she bore to him Sha'ul.

4 And Yehudah went at that time to Adulam, and he came to a man of Adulam, and his name was Ḥirah, and Yehudah saw there the daughter of a man from Kana'an, and her name was Aliyath, the daughter of Shua; and he took her, and came

[a] **44**:**73** See footnote at Yovelim **39**:**8**.

[b] **44**:**79** See also Yeshayahu [Isaiah] **61**:**1**; Loukas [Luke] **4**:**18**.

to her, and Aliyath bore to Yehudah, Er, Onan and Shelah; three sons.

5 And Levi and Yissakhar went to the land of the east, and they took to themselves for wives the daughters of Yovav the son of Yoktan, the son of Ever; and Yovav the son of Yoktan had two daughters; the name of the elder was Adinah, and the name of the younger was Aridah. 6 And Levi took Adinah, and Yissakhar took Aridah, and they came to the land of Kana'an, to their father's house, and Adinah bore to Levi, Gershon, Qohath, and Merari; three sons.

7 And Aridah bore to Yissakhar Tola, Puvvah, Yov, and Shimron, four sons; and Dan went to the land of Moav and took for a wife Aphlaleth, the daughter of Ḥamudan the Moavite, and he brought her to the land of Kana'an. 8 And Aphlaleth was barren, she had no offspring, and Elohim afterward remembered Aphlaleth the wife of Dan, and she conceived and bore a son, and she called his name Ḥushim.

9 And Gad and Naphtali went to Ḥaran and took from there the daughters of Amuram the son of Uts, the son of Naḥor, for wives. 10 And these are the names of the daughters of Amuram; the name of the elder was Merimah, and the name of the younger Utsit; and Naphtali took Merimah, and Gad took Utsit; and brought them to the land of Kana'an, to their father's house. 11 And Merimah bore to Naphtali Yaḥtseel, Guni, Yetser and Shillem, four sons; and Utsit bore to Gad Tsiphion, Ḥaggi, Shuni, Etsbon, Eri, Arodi and Areli, seven sons.

12 And Asher went forth and took Adon the daughter of Aphlal, the son of Ḥadad, the son of Yishma'el, for a wife, and he brought her to the land of Kana'an. 13 And Adon the wife of Asher died in those days: she had no offspring; and it was after the death of Adon that Asher went to the other side of the river and took for a wife Hadurah the daughter of Avimael, the son of Ever, the son of Shem. 14 And the young woman was of a comely appearance, and a woman of sense, and she had been the wife of Malki'el the son of Elam, the son of Shem. 15 And Hadurah bore a daughter to Malki'el, and he called her name Seraḥ, and Malki'el died after this, and Hadurah went and remained in her father's house. 16 And after the death of the wife of Asher, he went and took Hadurah for a wife, and brought her to the land of Kana'an, and he also brought Seraḥ her daughter with them, and she was three years old, and the girl was brought up in Ya'aqov's house.17 And the girl was of a fine appearance, and she went in the set-apart ways of the children of Ya'aqov; she lacked nothing, and 𐤄𐤅𐤄𐤉 gave her wisdom and understanding.

18 And Hadurah the wife of Asher conceived and bore to him Yimnah, Yishvah, Ishvi and Beriah; four sons.

19 And Zevulun went to Midian, and took for a wife Merishah the daughter of Molad, the son of Avida, the son of Midian, and brought her to the land of Kana'an. 20 And Merushah bore to Zevulun Sered, Elon and Yaḥleel; three sons.

21 And Ya'aqov sent to Aram, the son of Tsova, the son of Teraḥ, and he took for his son Benyamin Meḥalya the daughter of Aram, and she came to the land of Kana'an to the house of Ya'aqov; and Benyamin was ten years old when he took Meḥalya the daughter of Aram for a wife. 22 And Meḥalya conceived and bore to Benyamin Bela, Beḥer, Ashbel, Gera and Na'aman, five sons; and Benyamin went afterward and took for a wife Aribath, the daughter of Zimran, the son of Avraham, in addition to his first wife, and he was eighteen years old; and Aribath bore to Benyamin Eḥi, Rosh, Muppim, Ḥuppim, and Ard; five sons.

23 And in those days Yehudah went to the house of Shem and took Tamar the daughter of Elam, the son of Shem, for a wife for his first born Er.[a] 24 And Er came to his wife Tamar, and she became his wife, and when he came to her he outwardly destroyed his seed, and his work was evil in the eyes of 𐤄𐤅𐤄𐤉, and 𐤄𐤅𐤄𐤉 killed him. 25 And it was after the death of Er, Yehudah's firstborn, that Yehudah said to Onan, "Go in to your brother's wife, and perform your duty as a brother-in-law to her, and raise up seed for your brother."

---

[a] **45:23** See footnote at Yovelim **41:1**.

26 And Onan took Tamar for a wife and he came
to her, and Onan also did the thing that his
brother did, and his work was evil in the eyes of
𐤉𐤄𐤅𐤄, and He killed him also. 27 And when
Onan died,
Yehudah said to Tamar, "Remain in your father's
house until my son Shelah is grown up," and
Yehudah did not delight in Tamar anymore, to
give her to Shelah, for he said, "Perhaps he will
also die like his brothers."

28 And Tamar rose up and went and remained in
her father's house, and Tamar was in her father's
house for some time.

29 And at the revolution of the year, Aliyath the
wife of Yehudah died; and Yehudah was
comforted for his wife, and after the death of
Aliyath, Yehudah went up with his friend Ḥirah
to Timnah to shear their sheep. 30 And Tamar
heard that Yehudah had gone up to Timnah to
shear the sheep, and that Shelah was grown up,
and Yehudah did not delight in her. 31 And
Tamar rose up and put off the garments of her
widowhood, and she put on a veil, and she
entirely covered herself, and she went and sat in
the public square, which is on the road to
Timnah. 32 And Yehudah passed and saw her
and took her and he came to her, and she
conceived by him, and at the time of giving
birth, behold, there were twins in her womb, and
he called the name of the first Perets, and the
name of the second Zeraḥ. [a]

46 1 In those days Yoseph the son of Ya'aqov
was still confined in the prison house in the land
of Mitsrayim. 2 At that time the attendants of
Pharaoh were standing before him, the chief of
the cupbearers and the chief of the bakers which
belonged to the king of Mitsrayim.

3 And the cupbearer took wine and placed it
before the king to drink, and the baker placed
bread before the king to eat, and the king drank
of the wine and ate of the bread, he and his
servants and ministers that ate at the king's table.
4 And while they were eating and drinking, the
cupbearer and the baker remained there, and
Pharaoh's ministers found many flies in the wine,
which the cupbearer had brought, and stones of
lye[b] were found in the baker's bread. 5 And the
captain of the guard placed Yoseph as an
attendant on Pharaoh's officers, and Pharaoh's
officers were in confinement one year.

6 And at the end of the year, they both dreamed
dreams in one night, in the place of confinement
where they were, and in the morning Yoseph
came to them to attend to them as usual, and he
saw them, and saw that their faces were evil and
sad.

7 And Yoseph asked them, "Why are your faces
evil and sad today?" and they said to him, "We
dreamed a dream, and there is no one to interpret
it;" and Yoseph said to them, "Please, tell me
your dream, and Elohim shall give you an
answer of peace as you desire."

8 And the cupbearer related his dream to Yoseph,
and he said, "I saw in my dream, and behold a
large vine was before me, and upon that vine I
saw three branches, and the vine quickly
blossomed and reached a great height, and its
clusters were ripened and became grapes. 9 And I
took the grapes and pressed them in a cup, and
placed it in Pharaoh's hand and he drank;" and
Yoseph said to him, "The three branches that
were upon the vine are three days. 10 In three
days, the king will order you to be brought out
and he will restore you to your office, and you
shall give the king his wine to drink as at first
when you were his cupbearer. But let me find
favor in your eyes, that you remember me to
Pharaoh when it is well with you, and do
kindness to me, and have me brought forth from
this prison, for I was stolen away from the land
of Kana'an and was sold for a slave in this place.

---

[a] **45** See footnotes c – d at Yovelim **34**:**20** (pg. **329**) and footnotes a – i (pg. **330**).

[b] **46**:**4** Lye – Hebrew word 𐤍𐤕𐤓 (*ne'ther*) describes something bubbly or effervescent. It is derived from *na'thar* (same word, different vowels) which means "to jump" and thus describes the behavior of effervescent materials. This is the etymological origin of the word nitre (which is how Moses Samuel translated the word), as well as the origin of the word "nitrate." Strictly defined, it refers to the *state* an object is in (ie. a bubbly state) rather than a specific object itself. In this context, it most likely refers to pieces of lye soap.

11 "And also that which you were told
concerning my master's wife is false, for they
placed me in this pit for nothing;" and the
cupbearer answered Yoseph, saying, "If the king
deals well with me as at first, as you interpreted
to me, I will do all that you desirest, and get you
brought out of this pit."

12 And the baker, seeing that Yoseph had
accurately interpreted the cupbearer's dream, also
approached, and related the whole of his dream
to Yoseph.

13 And he said to him, "In my dream I saw and
behold three white baskets upon my head, and I
looked, and behold there were in the all kinds of
baked food for Pharaoh in the top basket, and
behold the birds were eating them from off my
head."

14 And Yoseph said to him, "The three baskets
which you saw are three days; in three days
Pharaoh will take off your head, and hang you on
a tree, and the birds will eat your flesh from off
you, as you saw in your dream."

15 In those days the queen was about to be
delivered, and upon that day she bore a son to the
king of Mitsrayim, and they proclaimed that the
king had gotten his firstborn son and all the
people of Mitsrayim together with the officers
and servants of Pharaoh rejoiced greatly. 16 And
upon the third day of his birth Pharaoh made a
banquet for his officers and servants, for the
hosts of the land of Tsoar and of the land of
Mitsrayim. 17 And all the people of Mitsrayim
and the servants of Pharaoh came to eat and
drink with the king at the banquet of his son, and
to rejoice at the king's rejoicing.

18 And all the officers of the king and his
servants were rejoicing at that time for eight days
at the banquet, and they made merry with all
sorts of musical instruments, with timbrels and
with dances in the king's house for eight days.
19 And the cupbearer whose dream Yoseph had
interpreted forgot Yoseph, and he did not
mention him to the king as he had promised, for
this thing was from 𐤉𐤄𐤅𐤄 in order to punish
Yoseph because he had trusted in man. 20 And
Yoseph remained in the prison house for two
years after this, until he had completed twelve
years.

47 1 And Yitsḥaq the son of Avraham was still
living in those days in the land of Kana'an; he
was very aged, one hundred and eighty years old,
and Esaw his son, the brother of Ya'aqov, was in
the land of Edom, and he and his sons had
possessions in it among the children of Seir.
2 And Esaw heard that his father's time was
drawing near to die, and he and his sons and
household came to the land of Kana'an, to his
father's house, and Ya'aqov and his sons went
forth from the place where they dwelled in
Ḥevron, and they all came to their father
Yitsḥaq, and they found Esaw and his sons in the
tent.

3 And Ya'aqov and his sons sat before his father
Yitsḥaq, and Ya'aqov was still mourning for his
son Yoseph.

4 And Yitsḥaq said to Ya'aqov, "Bring me your
sons and I will bless them;" and Ya'aqov brought
his eleven sons before his father Yitsḥaq.

5 And Yitsḥaq placed his hands upon all the sons
of Ya'aqov, and he took hold of them and
embraced them, and kissed them one by one, and
Yitsḥaq blessed them on that day, and he said to
them, "May the Elohim of your fathers bless you
and multiply your seed like the stars of the
heavens in number."

6 And Yitsḥaq also blessed the sons of Esaw,
saying, "May God cause you to be a dread and a
terror to all that will behold you, and to all your
enemies."

7 And Yitsḥaq called Ya'aqov and his sons, and
they all came and sat before Yitsḥaq, and
Yitsḥaq said to Ya'aqov, "𐤉𐤄𐤅𐤄 Elohim of the
whole earth said to me, 'To your seed will I give
this land for an inheritance if your children keep
My statutes and My ways, then I will perform
the oath which I swore to your father Avraham.
8 Now therefore my son, teach your children and
your children's children to fear 𐤉𐤄𐤅𐤄, and to go
in the better way which will please 𐤉𐤄𐤅𐤄 your
Elohim, for if you keep the ways of 𐤉𐤄𐤅𐤄 and
His statutes 𐤉𐤄𐤅𐤄 will also keep His covenant

with Avraham, and will do well with you and your seed all the days."

9 And when Yitsḥaq had finished commanding Ya'aqov and his children, he expired and died, and was gathered to his people. **10** And Ya'aqov and Esaw fell upon the face of their father Yitsḥaq, and they wept, and Yitsḥaq was one hundred and eighty years old when he died in the land of Kana'an, in Ḥevron, and his sons carried him to the cave of Makhpelah, which Avraham had bought from the children of Ḥeth for a possession of a burial place. **11** And all the kings of the land of Kana'an went with Ya'aqov and Esaw to bury Yitsḥaq, and all the kings of Kana'an showed Yitsḥaq great honor at his death.

12 And the sons of Ya'aqov and the sons of Esaw went barefooted round about, walking and lamenting until they reached Qiryath-arba. **13** And Ya'aqov and Esaw buried their father Yitsḥaq in the cave of Makhpelah, which is in Qiryath-arba in Ḥevron, and they buried him with very great honor, as at the funeral of kings. **14** And Ya'aqov and his sons, and Esaw and his sons, and all the kings of Kana'an made a great and heavy mourning, and they buried him and mourned for him many days.

15 And at the death of Yitsḥaq, he left his cattle and his possessions and all belonging to him to his sons; and Esaw said to Ya'aqov, "Behold, please, all that our father has left we will divide it in two parts, and I will have the choice," and Ya'aqov said, "We will do so."

16 And Ya'aqov took all that Yitsḥaq had left in the land of Kana'an, the cattle and the property, and he placed them in two parts before Esaw and his sons, and he said to Esaw, "Behold all this is before you, choose for yourself the half which you will take."

17 And Ya'aqov said to Esaw, "Please, hear now what I will speak to you, saying, '𐤉𐤄𐤅𐤄 Elohim of the heavens and the earth spoke to our fathers Avraham and Yitsḥaq, saying, "To your seed will I give this land for an inheritance forever."' **18** Now therefore all that our father has left is before you, and behold all the land is before you; choose from them what you desire. **19** If you desire the whole land take it for you and your children forever, and I will take these riches. And if you desire the riches then take them for yourself, and I will take this land for me and for my children to inherit it forever."

20 And Nebayoth, the son of Yishma'el, was then in the land with his children, and Esaw went on that day and consulted with him, saying, **21** "Thus has Ya'aqov spoken to me, and thus has he answered me; now give your advice and we will hear."

22 And Nebayoth said, "What is this that Ya'aqov hath spoken to you? Behold all the children of Kana'an are dwelling securely in their land, and Ya'aqov says he will inherit it with his seed all the days. **23** Go now therefore and take all your father's riches and leave Ya'aqov your brother in the land, as he has spoken."

24 And Esaw rose up and returned to Ya'aqov, and did all that Nebayoth the son of Yishma'el had advised; and Esaw took all the riches that Yitsḥaq had left, the beings, the beasts, the cattle and the property, and all the riches; he gave nothing to his brother Ya'aqov; and Ya'aqov took all the land of Kana'an, from the brook of Mitsrayim to the river Perath; and he took it for an everlasting possession, and for his children and for his seed after him forever. **25** Ya'aqov also took from his brother Esaw the cave of Makhpelah, which is in Ḥevron, which Avraham had bought from Ephron for a possession of a burial place for him and his seed forever. **26** And Ya'aqov wrote all these things in the book of purchase, and he signed it, and he witnessed it all with four faithful witnesses.

27 And these are the words which Ya'aqov wrote in the book, saying: "The land of Kana'an and all the cities of the Ḥittites, the Ḥivites, the Yevusites, the Amorites, the Perizzites, and the Girgashites, all the seven nations from the river of Mitsrayim to the river Perath."

28 And the city of Ḥevron Qiryath-arba, and the cave which is in it, the whole did Ya'aqov buy from his brother Esaw for value, for a possession and for an inheritance for his seed after him forever. **29** And Ya'aqov took the book of purchase and the signature, the command and the statutes and the revealed book, and he placed them in an earthen vessel in order that they should remain for a long time, and he delivered them into the hands of his children.

30 Esaw took all that his father had left him after his death from his brother Ya'aqov, and he took all the property, from man and beast, camel and donkey, ox and lamb, silver and gold, stones and bdellium, and all the riches which had belonged to Yitsḥaq the son of Avraham; there was nothing left which Esaw did not take to himself, from all that Yitsḥaq had left after his death. 31 And Esaw took all this, and he and his children went home to the land of Seir the Ḥorite, away from his brother Ya'aqov and his children. 32 And Esaw had possessions among the children of Seir, and Esaw did not return to the land of Kana'an from that day forward. 33 And the whole land of Kana'an became an inheritance to the children of Yisra'el for an everlasting inheritance, and Esaw with all his children inherited the mountain of Seir.

*𐤐𐤓𐤔𐤕 𐤌𐤒𐤑 – **Parashat Miqqets***

48 1 In those days, after the death of Yitsḥaq, 𐤉𐤄𐤅𐤄 commanded and caused a famine upon the whole earth.

2 At that time Pharaoh king of Mitsrayim was sitting on his throne in the land of Mitsrayim, and lay in his bed and dreamed dreams, and Pharaoh saw in his dream that he was standing by the side of the river of Mitsrayim. 3 And while he was standing he saw seven fat-fleshed and well favored cows came up out of the river. 4 And seven other cows, thin and evil in appearance, came up after them, and the seven *that were* evil in appearance swallowed up the well favored ones, and still their appearance was as evil as at first. 5 And he awoke, and he slept again and he dreamed a second time, and he saw and behold seven ears came up on one stalk, full and good, and seven thin ears blasted with the east wind sprang up after them, and the thin ears swallowed up the full ones, and Pharaoh awoke out of his dream. 6 And in the morning the king remembered his dreams, and his spirit was sadly troubled on account of his dreams, and the king hurried and sent and called for all the magicians of Mitsrayim, and the wise men, and they came and stood before Pharaoh.

7 And the king said to them, "I have dreamed dreams, and there is none to interpret them;" and they said to the king, "Relate your dreams to your servants and let us hear them."

8 And the king related his dreams to them, and they all answered and said with one voice to the king, "May the king live forever; and this is the interpretation of your dreams. 9 The seven good cows which you saw are seven daughters that will be born to you in the latter days, and the seven cows which you saw come up after them, and swallowed them up, are for a sign that the daughters which will be born to you will all die in the life-time of the king.

10 "And that which you saw in the second dream of seven full good ears coming up on one stalk, this is their interpretation: that you will build to yourself in the latter days seven cities throughout the land of Mitsrayim; and that which you saw of the seven blasted ears springing up after them and swallowing them up while you beheld them with your eyes, is for a sign that the cities which you will build will all be destroyed in the latter days, in the life-time of the king."

11 And when they spoke these words the king did not incline his ear to their words, neither did he fix his heart upon them, for the king knew in his wisdom that they did not give a proper interpretation of the dreams; and when they had finished speaking before the king, the king answered them, saying, "What is this thing that you have spoken to me? Surely you have uttered falsehood and spoken lies; therefore now give the proper interpretation of my dreams, that you may not die."

12 And the king commanded after this, and he sent and called again for other wise men, and they came and stood before the king, and the king related his dreams to them, and they all answered him according to the first interpretation, and the king's anger was kindled and he was very wroth, and the king said to them, "Surely you speak lies and utter falsehood in what you have said."

13 And the king commanded that a proclamation should be issued throughout the land of Mitsrayim, saying, "It is resolved by the king and

his great men, that any wise man who knows and
understands the interpretation of dreams, and
will not come this day before the king, shall die.
14 And the man who declares to the king the
proper interpretation of his dreams, shall be
given all that he will require from the king." And
all the wise men of the land of Mitsrayim came
before the king, together with all the magicians
and sorcerers that were in Mitsrayim and in
Goshen, in Rameses, in Tachpanches, in Tsoar,
and in all the places on the borders of Mitsrayim,
and they all stood before the king.

15 And all the nobles and the princes, and the
attendants belonging to the king, came together
from all the cities of Mitsrayim, and they all sat
before the king, and the king related his dreams
before the wise men, and the princes, and all that
sat before the king were astonished at the vision.

16 And all the wise men who were before the
king were greatly divided in their interpretation
of his dreams; some of them interpreted them to
the king, saying, "The seven good cows are
seven kings, who will be raised over Mitsrayim
from the king's issue. 17 And the seven evil cows
are seven princes, who will stand up against
them in the latter days and destroy them; and the
seven ears are the seven great princes belonging
to Mitsrayim, who will fall in the hands of the
seven less powerful princes of their enemies, in
the wars of our master the king."

18 And some of them interpreted to the king in
this manner, saying, "The seven good cows are
the strong cities of Mitsrayim, and the seven evil
cows are the seven nations of the land of
Kana'an, who will come against the seven cities
of Mitsrayim in the latter days and destroy them.
19 And that which you saw in the second dream,
of seven good and evil ears, is a sign that the
government of Mitsrayim will again return to
your seed as at first. 20 And in his reign the
people of the cities of Mitsrayim will turn
against the seven cities of Kana'an who are
stronger than they are, and will destroy them,
and the government of Mitsrayim will return to
your seed."

21 And some of them said to the king, "This is
the interpretation of your dreams; the seven good
cows are seven queens, whom you will take for
wives in the latter days, and the seven evil cows
mean that those women will all die in the
lifetime of the king. 22 And the seven good and
evil ears which you saw in the second dream are
fourteen children, and it will be in the latter days
that they will stand up and fight among
themselves, and seven of them will strike the
seven that are more powerful."

23 And some of them said these words to the
king, saying, "The seven good cows mean that
seven children will be born to you, and they will
kill seven of your children's children in the latter
days; and the seven good ears which you saw in
the second dream, are those princes against
whom seven other less powerful princes will
fight and destroy them in the latter days, and
avenge your children's cause, and the
government will again return to your seed."

24 And the king heard all the words of the wise
men of Mitsrayim and their interpretation of his
dreams, and none of them pleased the king.

25 And the king knew in his wisdom that they did
not altogether speak correctly in all these words,
for this was from 𐤉𐤄𐤅𐤄 to frustrate the words of
the wise men of Mitsrayim, in order that Yoseph
might go forth from the house of confinement,
and in order that he should become great in
Mitsrayim. 26 And the king saw that none among
all the wise men and magicians of Mitsrayim
spoke correctly to him, and the king's wrath was
kindled, and his anger burned within him. 27 And
the king commanded that all the wise men and
magicians should go out from before him, and
they all went out from before the king with
shame and disgrace. 28 And the king commanded
that a proclamation be sent throughout
Mitsrayim to kill all the magicians that were in
Mitsrayim, and not one of them should be
allowed to live. 29 And the captains of the guards
belonging to the king rose up, and each man
drew his sword, and they began to strike the
magicians of Mitsrayim, and the wise men.

30 And after this Merod, chief cupbearer to the
king, came and bowed down before the king and
sat before him.

31 And the cupbearer said to the king, "May the
king live forever, and his government be exalted

in the land. 32 You were angry with your servant in those days, now two years past, and placed me in the prison, and I was for some time in the ward, I and the chief of the bakers. 33 And there was a Hebrew servant with us, belonging to the captain of the guard; his name was Yoseph, for his master had been angry with him and placed him in the house of confinement, and he attended us there. 34 And in some time later when we were in the prison, we dreamed dreams in one night, I and the chief of the bakers; we dreamed, each man according to the interpretation of his dream. 35 And we came in the morning and told them to that servant, and he interpreted to us our dreams, and he interpreted to each man correctly according to his dream. 36 And it happened as he interpreted to us, so was the event; none of his words fell to the ground.

37 "And now therefore my master and king, do not kill the people of Mitsrayim for nothing; behold that slave is still confined in the house by the captain of the guard his master, in the house of confinement. 38 If it pleases the king, let him send for him that he may come before you and he will make known the correct interpretation of the dream which you dreamed to you."

39 And the king heard the words of the chief cupbearer, and the king ordered that the wise men of Mitsrayim should not be killed.

40 And the king ordered his servants to bring Yoseph before him, and the king said to them, "Go to him and do not terrify him, lest he be confused and will not know to speak properly."

41 And the servants of the king went to Yoseph, and they quickly brought him out of the pit, and the king's servants shaved him, and he changed his prison garment and he came before the king. 42 And the king was sitting upon his royal throne in a royal robe, with a golden ephod, and the fine gold which was upon it sparkled, and the carbuncle and the ruby and the emerald, together with all the precious stones that were upon the king's head, dazzled the eye, and Yoseph wondered greatly at the king. 43 And the throne upon which the king sat was covered with gold and silver, and with onyx stones, and it had seventy steps.

44 And it was their custom throughout the land of Mitsrayim, that every man who came to speak to the king, if he was a prince or one that was worthy in the sight of the king, he ascended to the king's throne as far as the thirty-first step, and the king would descend to the thirty-sixth step, and speak with him. 45 If he was one of the common people, he ascended to the third step, and the king would descend to the fourth and speak to him, and their custom was, moreover, that any man who understood to speak in all the seventy tongues, he ascended the seventy steps, and went up and spoke until he reached the king. 46 And any man who could not complete the seventy, he ascended as many steps as the tongues which he knew to speak in. 47 And it was customary in those days in Mitsrayim that no one should reign over them, but who understood to speak in the seventy tongues.

48 And when Yoseph came before the king he bowed down to the ground before the king, and he ascended to the third step, and the king sat upon the fourth step and spoke with Yoseph.

49 And the king said to Yoseph, "I dreamed a dream, and there is no interpreter to interpret it properly, and I commanded this day that all the magicians and the wise men of Mitsrayim should come before me, and I related my dreams to them, and no one has properly interpreted them to me. 50 And after this I heard about you today, that you are a wise man, and can correctly interpret every dream that you hear."

51 And Yoseph answered Pharaoh, saying, "Let Pharaoh relate his dreams that he dreamed; surely the interpretations belong to Elohim;" and Pharaoh related his dreams to Yoseph, the dream of the cows, and the dream of the ears, and the king left off speaking.

52 And Yoseph was then clothed with the Ruaḥ of Elohim before the king, and he knew all the things that would happen to the king from that day forward, and he knew the proper interpretation of the king's dream, and he spoke before the king.

53 And Yoseph found favor in the eyes of the king, and the king inclined his ears and his heart, and he heard all the words of Yoseph. And

Yoseph said to the king, "Do not imagine that
they are two dreams, for it is only one dream: for
that which Elohim has chosen to do throughout
the land, He has shown to the king in his dream.
And this is the proper interpretation of your
dream: 54 the seven good cows and ears are
seven years, and the seven evil cows and ears are
also seven years; it is one dream. 55 Behold the
seven years that are coming there will be a great
abundance throughout the land, and after that the
seven years of famine will follow them, a very
heavy famine; and all the abundance will be
forgotten from the land, and the famine will
consume the inhabitants of the land. 56 The king
dreamed one dream, and the dream was therefore
repeated to Pharaoh because the thing is
established by Elohim, and Elohim will make it
happen soon.

57 "Now therefore I will give you counsel and
deliver your being and the beings of the
inhabitants of the land from the evil of the
famine. *I counsel* that you seek throughout your
kingdom for a man very discreet and wise, who
knows all the affairs of government, and appoint
him to overseer over the land of Mitsrayim.
58 And let the man whom you place over
Mitsrayim appoint officers under him, that they
gather in all the food of the good years that are
coming, and let them lay up grain and deposit it
in your appointed storehouses. 59 And let them
keep that food for the seven years of famine, that
it may be found for you and your people and
your whole land, so that you and your land will
not be cut off by the famine. 60 Let all the
inhabitants of the land be also ordered that they
gather in, every man the produce of his field, of
all sorts of food, during the seven good years,
and that they place it in their storehouses, that it
may be found for them in the days of the famine
and that they may live on it. 61 This is the proper
interpretation of your dream, and this is the
counsel I give you to save your being, and the
beings of all your people."

62 And the king answered and said to Yoseph,
"Who says and who knows that your words are
correct?" And he said to the king, "This shall be
a sign for you concerning all my words, that they
are true and that my advice is good for you:
63 behold your wife sits upon the stool of
delivery today, and she will bare a son to you,
and you will rejoice with him; when your son
has gone forth from his mother's womb, your
firstborn son that was born two years ago shall
die, and you will be comforted in the child that
will be born to you today."

64 And Yoseph finished speaking these words to
the king, and he bowed down to the king and he
went out, and when Yoseph had gone out from
the king's presence, those signs which Yoseph
had spoken to the king happened on that day.
65 And the queen bore a son on that day, and the
king heard the glad tidings about his son, and he
rejoiced, and when the messenger had gone forth
from the king's presence, the king's servants
found the firstborn son of the king fallen dead
upon the ground.

66 And there was great lamentation and noise in
the king's house, and the king heard it, and he
said, "What is the noise and lamentation that I
have heard in the house?" and they told the king
that his firstborn son had died; then the king
knew that all Yoseph's words that he had spoken
were correct, and the king was consoled for his
son by the child that was born to him on that day
as Yoseph had spoken.

49 1 After these things the king sent and
assembled all his officers and servants, and all
the princes and nobles belonging to the king, and
they all came before the king.

2 And the king said to them, "Behold you have
seen and heard all the words of this Hebrew man,
and all the signs which he declared would come
to pass, and none of his words have fallen to the
ground. 3 You know that he has given a proper
interpretation of the dream, and it will surely
come to pass; now therefore take counsel, and
know what you will do and how the land will be
delivered from the famine. 4 Seek now and see
whether someone, in whose heart there is
wisdom and knowledge, can be found, and I will
appoint him over the land. 5 For you have heard
what the Hebrew man has advised concerning
this to save the land from the famine, and I know
that the land will not be delivered from the
famine except by the advice of the Hebrew man,
the one that advised me."

6 And they all answered the king and said, "The
counsel which the Hebrew has given concerning
this is good; now therefore, our master and king,
behold the whole land is in your hand, do what
seems good in your eyes. 7 Whomever you
choose, and whomever you, in your wisdom,
know to be wise and capable of delivering the
land with his wisdom, the king shall appoint him
to be under him over the land."

8 And the king said to all the officers, "I have
thought that since Elohim has made known to the
Hebrew man all that he has spoken, there is none
so discreet and wise in the whole land as he is; if
it seem good in your eyes I will place him over
the land, for he will save the land with his
wisdom."

9 And all the officers answered the king and said,
"But surely it is written in the decrees of
Mitsrayim, and it should not be violated, that no
man shall reign over Mitsrayim, nor be the
second to the king, except one who has
knowledge in all the languages of the sons of
men. 10 Now therefore our master and king,
behold this Hebrew man can only speak the
Hebrew language, and how then can he be over
us the second under government, a man who
does not even know our language? 11 Now
please, send for him, and let him come before
you, and prove him in all things, and do as you
see fit."

12 And the king said, "It shall be done tomorrow,
and the thing that you have spoken is good;" and
all the officers came on that day before the king.

13 And on that night 𐤉𐤄𐤅𐤄 sent one of His
attending messengers, and he came into the land
of Mitsrayim to Yoseph, and the messenger of
𐤉𐤄𐤅𐤄 stood over Yoseph, and behold Yoseph
was lying in the bed at night in his master's
house in the pit, for his master had put him back
into the pit on account of his wife. 14 And the
messenger roused him from his sleep, and
Yoseph rose up and stood upon his legs, and
behold the messenger of 𐤉𐤄𐤅𐤄 was standing
opposite to him; and the messenger of 𐤉𐤄𐤅𐤄
spoke with Yoseph, and he taught him all the
tongues of man in that night, and he called his
name Yehoseph[a].

15 And the messenger of 𐤉𐤄𐤅𐤄 went from him,
and Yoseph returned and lie upon his bed, and
Yoseph was astonished at the vision which he
saw.

16 And it happened in the morning that the king
sent for all his officers and servants, and they all
came and sat before the king, and the king
ordered Yoseph to be brought, and the king's
servants went and brought Yoseph before
Pharaoh. 17 And the king came forth and
ascended the steps of the throne, and Yoseph
spoke to the king in all tongues, and Yoseph
went up to him and spoke to the king until he
arrived before the king in the seventieth step, and
he sat before the king. 18 And the king greatly
rejoiced on account of Yoseph, and all the king's
officers rejoiced greatly with the king when they
heard all the words of Yoseph. 19 And the word
seemed good in the eyes of the king and the
officers, to appoint Yoseph to be second to the
king over the whole land of Mitsrayim, and the
king spoke to Yoseph, saying,

20 "Now you gave me counsel to appoint a wise
man over the land of Mitsrayim, so that with his
wisdom he would save the land from the famine;
now therefore, since Elohim has made all this
known to you, and all the words which you have
spoken, there is no man in all the land as discreet
and as wise as you. 21 And your name shall no
longer be called Yoseph, but Zaphnath Pa'aneach
shall be your name; you shall be second to me,
and all the affairs of my government shall be
according to your word, and at your word my
people shall go out and come in. 22 And all my
servants and officers shall receive their monthly
salary from under your hand, and all the people
of the land shall bow down to you. Only in my
throne will I be greater than you."

---

[a] **49:14** Yoseph's name is spelled 𐤉𐤅𐤎𐤐, though here is it spelled 𐤉𐤄𐤅𐤎𐤐, with an added *hey* (𐤄). This is similar to some names in the Tanakh being written with an extra *hey*, such as Yonathan → Yehonathan. Though the reason is debated, it is most commonly believed to show that honor was added to the name due to the *hey* infix.

23 And the king took off his ring from his hand
and put it upon the hand of Yoseph, and the king
dressed Yoseph in a royal garment, and he put a
golden crown upon his head, and he put a golden
chain around his neck. 24 And the king
commanded his servants, and they made him ride
in the second chariot belonging to the king, that
went opposite to the king's chariot, and he
caused him to ride on a great and strong horse
from the king's horses, and to be conducted
through the streets of the land of Mitsrayim.
25 And the king commanded that all those that
played upon timbrels, harps and other musical
instruments should go forth with Yoseph; one
thousand timbrels, one thousand dancers, and
one thousand harpists went after him. 26 And five
thousand men, with drawn swords glittering in
their hands, and they went marching and playing
before Yoseph, and twenty thousand of the great
men of the king with sashes of skin covered with
gold, marched at the right hand of Yoseph, and
twenty thousand at his left, and all the women
and girls went up on the roofs or stood in the
streets playing and rejoicing at Yoseph, and
gazed at the appearance of Yoseph and at his
beauty.

27 And the king's people went before him and
behind him, perfuming the road with
frankincense and with cassia, and with all sorts
of fine perfume, and scattered myrrh and aloes
along the road, and twenty men proclaimed these
words before him throughout the land in a loud
voice: 28 "Do you see this man whom the king
has chosen to be his second? All the affairs of
government shall be regulated by him, and
anyone that transgresses his orders, or that does
not bow down to the ground before him, shall
die, for he rebels against the king and his
second."

29 And when the heralds had ceased proclaiming,
all the people of Mitsrayim bowed down to the
ground before Yoseph and said, "May the king
live, also may his second live;" and all the
inhabitants of Mitsrayim bowed down along the
road, and when the heralds approached them,
they bowed down, and they rejoiced with all
sorts of timbrels, dancing, and harps before
Yoseph.

30 And while upon his horse, Yoseph lifted up
his eyes to the heavens, and called out and said,
"He raises the poor man from the dust, He lifts
up the needy from the dunghill. O 𐤉𐤄𐤅𐤄 Tsevaot,
happy is the man who trusts in You.[a]"

31 And Yoseph passed throughout the land of
Mitsrayim with Pharaoh's servants and officers,
and they showed him the whole land of
Mitsrayim and all the king's treasures. 32 And
Yoseph returned and came on that day before
Pharaoh, and the king gave to Yoseph a
possession in the land of Mitsrayim, a possession
of fields and vineyards, and the king gave to
Yoseph three thousand talents of silver and one
thousand talents of gold, and onyx stones and
bdellium and many gifts. 33 And on the next day
the king commanded all the people of Mitsrayim
to bring to Yoseph offerings and gifts, and that
he that violated the command of the king should
die; and they made a high place[b] in the street of
the city, and they spread out garments there, and
whoever brought anything to Yoseph put it on
the high place. 34 And all the people of
Mitsrayim cast something onto the high place,
one man a golden earring[c], and the other pieces
of money and round rings[d], and different vessels
of gold and silver work, and onyx stones and
bdellium were cast upon the high place; every
one gave something of what he possessed.
35 And Yoseph took all these and placed them in
his treasuries, and all the officers and nobles
belonging to the king exalted Yoseph, and they

---

[a] **49:30** See also Tehillim [Psalms] **84:12**; Mishlei [Proverbs] **16:20**.

[b] **49:33** High place – Hebrew 𐤁𐤌𐤄 (*ba'mah*); Litterally "a stage." Also root of the word bimah as is used in synagogues.

[c] **49:34** Earring – Hebrew word 𐤍𐤆𐤌 (*ne'zem*) does mean earring, though not specifically. It can also mean nose-ring or another type of ring worn in a piercing.

[d] **49:34** Round rings – Hebrew words 𐤈𐤁𐤏𐤅𐤕 𐤅𐤏𐤂𐤋𐤉𐤌 (*ta'ba'owt v'agol'im*) means literally "and round rings." The word for rings (𐤈𐤁𐤏𐤅𐤕) means a ring as worn on the hand, including a signet ring. This is distinguished from *nezem*, which refers to a ring as worn in a piercing.

gave him many gifts, seeing that the king had
chosen him to be his second.

36 And the king sent to Potiphera, the son of
Aḥiram priest of On, and he took his young
daughter Asenath and gave her to Yoseph for a
wife. 37 And the girl was very beautiful, a virgin,
one whom man had not known, and Yoseph took
her for a wife; and the king said to Yoseph, "I am
Pharaoh, and besides you no one shall dare to lift
up his hand or his foot to regulate my people
throughout the land of Mitsrayim."

38 And Yoseph was thirty years old when he
stood before Pharaoh, and Yoseph went out from
before the king, and he became the king's second
in Mitsrayim. 39 And the king gave Yoseph a
hundred servants to attend him in his house, and
Yoseph also sent and purchased many servants
and they remained in the house of Yoseph.
40 Yoseph then built for himself a very
magnificent house like the houses of kings,
before the court of the king's palace, and he
made in the house a large temple, very elegant in
appearance and convenient for his residence;
three years was Yoseph in erecting his house.
41 And Yoseph made himself a very elegant
throne of abundance of gold and silver, and he
covered it with onyx stones and bdellium, and he
made on it the likeness of the whole land of
Mitsrayim, and the likeness of the river of
Mitsrayim that waters the whole land of
Mitsrayim; and Yoseph sat securely on his
throne in his house and 𐤉𐤄𐤅𐤄 increased Yoseph's
wisdom. 42 And all the inhabitants of Mitsrayim
and Pharaoh's servants and his princes loved
Yoseph exceedingly, for this thing was from
𐤉𐤄𐤅𐤄 to Yoseph.

43 And Yoseph had an army that made war,
going out in hosts and troops to the number of
forty thousand six hundred men, capable of
bearing arms to assist the king and Yoseph
against the enemy, besides the king's officers and
his servants and inhabitants of Mitsrayim
without number. 44 And Yoseph gave to his
mighty men, and to all his host, shields and
javelins, and caps and coats of mail and stones
for slinging.

50 1 At that time the children of Tarshish came
against the sons of Yishma'el, and made war
with them, and the children of Tarshish spoiled
the Yishma'elites for a long time. 2 And the
children of Yishma'el were small in number in
those days, and they could not prevail over the
children of Tarshish, and they were sorely
oppressed. 3 And the old men of the
Yishma'elites sent a book to the king of
Mitsrayim, saying, "Please send officers and
hosts to your servants to help us to fight against
the children of Tarshish, for we have been
consuming away for a long time."

4 And Pharaoh sent Yoseph with the mighty men
and host which were with him, and also his
mighty men from the king's house. 5 And they
went to the land of Ḥavilah to the children of
Yishma'el, to assist them against the children of
Tarshish, and the children of Yishma'el fought
with the children of Tarshish, and Yoseph struck
the Tarshishites and he subdued all their land,
and the children of Yishma'el dwell in it to this
day. 6 And when the land of Tarshish was
subdued, all the Tarshishites ran away, and came
on the border of their brethren the children of
Yavan, and Yoseph with all his mighty men and
host returned to Mitsrayim, not one man of them
missing.

7 And at the revolution of the year, in the second
year of Yoseph's reigning over Mitsrayim, 𐤉𐤄𐤅𐤄
gave great plenty throughout the land for seven
years as Yoseph had spoken, for 𐤉𐤄𐤅𐤄 blessed
all the produce of the earth in those days for
seven years, and they ate and were greatly
satisfied. 8 And Yoseph at that time had officers
under him, and they collected all the food of the
good years, and stored up grain year by year, and
they placed it in the treasuries of Yoseph. 9 And
at any time when they gathered the food Yoseph
commanded that they should bring the ears, and
also bring with it some of the soil of the field,
that it should not spoil.

10 And Yoseph did this year by year, and he
stored up grain like the sand of the sea for
abundance, for his storehouses were immense
and could not be numbered for abundance.
11 And also all the inhabitants of Mitsrayim
gathered all sorts of food in their stores in great
abundance during the seven good years, but they
did not do it as Yoseph did. 12 And all the food

which Yoseph and the Mitsrites had gathered during the seven years of plenty was secured for the land in storehouses for the seven years of famine, for the support of the whole land. **13** And the inhabitants of Mitsrayim filled each man his storehouse and his concealed place with grain, to be for support during the famine. **14** And Yoseph placed all the food that he had gathered in all the cities of Mitsrayim, and he closed all the stores and placed sentinels over them.

15 And Yoseph's wife Asenath the daughter of Potiphera bore two sons to him: Menasheh and Ephrayim, and Yoseph was thirty-four years old when he brought them forth. **16** And the lads grew up and they went in his ways and in his instructions, they did not deviate from the way which their father taught them, either to the right or left. **17** And 𐤉𐤄𐤅𐤄 was with the lads, and they grew up and had understanding and skill in all wisdom and in all the affairs of government, and all the king's officers and his great men of the inhabitants of Mitsrayim exalted the lads, and they were brought up among the king's children.

18 And the seven years of plenty that were throughout the land were at an end, and the seven years of famine came after them as Yoseph had spoken, and the famine was throughout the land. **19** And all the people of Mitsrayim saw that the famine had commenced in the land of Mitsrayim, and all the people of Mitsrayim opened their storehouses of grain for the famine prevailed over them. **20** And they found all the food that was in their stores, full of vermin and not fit to eat, and the famine prevailed throughout the land, and all the inhabitants of Mitsrayim came and cried before Pharaoh, for the famine was heavy upon them.

21 And they said to Pharaoh, "Give food to your servants; why should we die through hunger before your eyes, even we and our little ones?"

22 And Pharaoh answered them, saying, "Why do you cry to me? Did Yoseph not command that the grain should be laid up during the seven years of plenty for the years of famine? Why did you not listen to his voice?"

23 And the people of Mitsrayim answered the king, saying, "As your being lives, our master, your servants have done all that Yoseph ordered, for your servants also gathered in all the produce of their fields during the seven years of plenty and laid it in the storehouses *even* to this day. **24** And when the famine prevailed over your servants, we opened our storehouses, and behold all our produce was filled with vermin and was not fit for food."

25 And when the king heard all that had happened to the inhabitants of Mitsrayim, the king was greatly afraid on account of the famine, and he was terrified; and the king answered the people of Mitsrayim, saying, "Since all this has happened to you, go to Yoseph, do whatever he says to you, do not transgress his commands."

26 And all the people of Mitsrayim went forth and came to Yoseph, and said to him, "Give us food; why should we die before you through hunger? For we gathered in our produce during the seven years as you commanded, and we put it in storehouses, and thus has it happened to us."

27 And when Yoseph heard all the words of the people of Mitsrayim and what had happened to them, Yoseph opened all his storehouses of the produce and he sold it to the people of Mitsrayim.

28 And the famine prevailed throughout the land, and the famine was in all countries, but in the land of Mitsrayim there was produce for sale. **29** And all the inhabitants of Mitsrayim came to Yoseph to buy grain, for the famine prevailed over them, and all their grain was spoiled, and Yoseph sold it daily to all the people of Mitsrayim.

30 And all the inhabitants of the land of Kana'an and the Philistines, and those beyond the Yarden, and the children of the east and all the cities of the lands far and near heard that there was grain in Mitsrayim, and they all came to Mitsrayim to buy grain, for the famine prevailed over them. **31** And Yoseph opened the storehouses of grain and placed officers over them, and they stood and sold daily to all that came. **32** And Yoseph knew that his brothers would also come to Mitsrayim to buy grain, for the famine prevailed throughout the earth. And Yoseph commanded all his people that they should cause it to be proclaimed throughout the land of Mitsrayim, saying,

33 "It is the pleasure of the king, of his second and of their great men, that any person who wishes to buy grain in Mitsrayim shall not send his servants to Mitsrayim to purchase, but his sons; and also any Mitsrite or Kana'anite, who shall come from any of the storehouses from buying grain in Mitsrayim, and shall go and sell it throughout the land, he shall die, for no one shall buy but for the support of his household.
34 And any man leading two or three beasts shall die, for a man shall only lead his own beast."

35 And Yoseph placed sentinels at the gates of Mitsrayim, and commanded them, saying, "Any person who may come to buy grain, do not allow him to enter until his name, and the name of his father, and the name of his father's father be written down, and whatever is written by day, send their names to me in the evening that I may know their names."

36 And Yoseph placed officers throughout the
land of Mitsrayim, and he commanded them to
do all these things. 37 And Yoseph did all these
things, and made these statutes, so that he might
know when his brothers would come to
Mitsrayim to buy grain; and Yoseph's people
caused it to be proclaimed daily in Mitsrayim
according to these words and statutes which
Yoseph had commanded. 38 And all the
inhabitants of the east and west country, and of
all the earth, heard of the statutes and regulations
which Yoseph had enacted in Mitsrayim, and the
inhabitants of the extreme parts of the earth came
and they bought grain in Mitsrayim day after
day, and then went away.

39 And all the officers of Mitsrayim did as Yoseph had commanded, and all that came to Mitsrayim to buy grain, the gate keepers would write their names, and their fathers' names, and daily bring them in the evening before Yoseph.

51

1 And Ya'aqov heard that there was grain in Mitsrayim, and he called to his sons to go to Mitsrayim to buy grain, for the famine also prevailed over them; and he called to his sons, saying,

2 "Behold I hear that there is grain in Mitsrayim, and all the people of the earth go there to purchase *it*. Now therefore, why will you show yourselves satisfied before the whole earth? Go down to Mitsrayim and buy us a little grain among those that come there, that we may not die."

3 And the sons of Ya'aqov listened to the voice of their father, and they rose up to go down to Mitsrayim in order to buy grain among the rest that came there.

4 And Ya'aqov their father commanded them, saying, "When you come into the city do not enter together in one gate, on account of the inhabitants of the land."

5 And the sons of Ya'aqov went forth and they went to Mitsrayim, and the sons of Ya'aqov did all as their father had commanded them, and Ya'aqov did not send Benyamin, for he said, "Lest an accident happen to him on the road like his brother;" and ten of Ya'aqov's sons went forth.

6 And while the sons of Ya'aqov were going on the road, they repented of what they had done to Yoseph, and they spoke to each other, saying, "We know that our brother Yoseph went down to Mitsrayim, and now we will seek him where we go, and if we find him we will take him from his master for a ransom, and if not, by force, and we will die for him."

7 And the sons of Ya'aqov agreed to this thing and strengthened themselves on account of Yoseph, to deliver him from the hand of his master; and the sons of Ya'aqov went to Mitsrayim. And when they came near to Mitsrayim they separated from each other, and they came through ten gates of Mitsrayim, and the gate keepers wrote their names on that day, and brought them to Yoseph in the evening.
8 And Yoseph read the names from the hand of the gate-keepers of the city, and he found that his brothers had entered at the ten gates of the city, and Yoseph commanded at that time that it should be proclaimed throughout the land of Mitsrayim, saying,

9 "Go forth, all storehouse guards: close all the
grain storehouses and let only one remain open,
that those who come may purchase from it."

10 And all the officers of Yoseph did so at that
time, and they closed all the storehouses and left
only one open.

11 And Yoseph gave the written names of his
brothers to him that was set over the open
storehouse, and he said to him, "Whoever comes
to you to buy grain, ask his name, and when men
of these names come before you, seize them and
send them," and they did so.

12 And when the sons of Ya'aqov came into the
city, they joined together in the city to seek
Yoseph before they bought themselves grain.
13 And they went to the walls of the whores, and
they sought Yoseph in the walls of the whores
for three days, for they thought that Yoseph
would come in the walls of the whores, for
Yoseph was very handsome and well favored,
and the sons of Ya'aqov sought Yoseph for three
days, and they could not find him. 14 And the
man who was set over the open storehouse
sought those names which Yoseph had given
him, and he did not find them.

15 And he sent to Yoseph, saying, "These three
days have passed, and those men whose names
you gave me have not come;" and Yoseph sent
servants to seek the men in all Mitsrayim, and to
bring them before Yoseph. 16 And Yoseph's
servants went and came into Mitsrayim and
could not find them, and went to Goshen and
they were not there, and then went to the city of
Rameses and could not find them.

17 And Yoseph continued to send sixteen
servants to seek his brothers, and they went and
spread themselves in the four corners of the city,
and four of the servants went into the house of
the whores, and they found the ten men there
seeking their brother.

18 And those four men took them and brought
them before him, and they bowed down to him to
the ground, and Yoseph was sitting upon his
throne in his temple, clothed with royal
garments, and there was a large crown of gold on
his head, and all the mighty men were sitting
around him. 19 And the sons of Ya'aqov saw
Yoseph, and his figure and handsomeness and
dignity of countenance seemed wonderful in
their eyes, and they again bowed down to him to
the ground. 20 And Yoseph saw his brothers, and
he knew them, but they did not know him, for
Yoseph was very great in their eyes, therefore
they did not know him.

21 And Yoseph spoke to them, saying, "Where
have you come from?" and they all answered and
said, "Your servants have come from the land of
Kana'an to buy grain, for the famine prevails
throughout the earth, and your servants heard
that there was grain in Mitsrayim, so they have
come among the others to buy grain for their
support."

22 And Yoseph answered them, saying, "If you
have come to purchase as you say, why did you
come through ten gates of the city? It can only be
that you have come to spy out the land."

23 And they all together answered Yoseph, and
said, "Not so my master, we are right; your
servants are not spies, but we have come to buy
grain, for your servants are all brothers, the sons
of one man in the land of Kana'an, and our father
commanded us, saying, 'When you come to the
city do not enter together at one gate on account
of the inhabitants of the land.'"

24 And Yoseph again answered them and said,
"That is the thing which I spoke to you, you have
come to spy out the land, therefore you all came
through ten gates of the city; you have come to
see the nakedness of the land. 25 Surely everyone
that comes to buy grain goes his way, and you
are already three days in the land; and what did
you do in the walls of *the* whores in which you
have been for these three days? Surely spies do
these sorts of things."

26 And they said to Yoseph, "Far be it from our
master to speak such; we are twelve brothers, the
sons of our father Ya'aqov, in the land of
Kana'an, the son of Yitsḥaq, the son of Avraham,
the Hebrew. And behold the youngest is with our
father this day in the land of Kana'an, and one is
not, for he was lost from us, and we thought
perhaps he might be in this land, so we are
seeking him throughout the land, and have come
even to the houses of whores to seek him there."

27 And Yoseph said to them, "And have you then sought him throughout the earth, that there only remained Mitsrayim for you to seek him in? And what would your brother be doing in the houses of the whores, if he were in Mitsrayim? Have you not said, that you are from the sons of Yitsḥaq, the son of Avraham? What shall the sons of Ya'aqov do then in the houses of whores?"

28 And they said to him, "Because we heard that Yishma'elites stole him from us, and we were told that they sold him in Mitsrayim, and your servant, our brother, is very handsome and well favored, so we thought he would surely be in the houses of *the* whores, therefore your servants went there to seek him and give ransom for him."

29 And Yoseph still answered them, saying, "Surely you speak falsely and utter lies, to say of yourselves that you are the sons of Abraham! As Pharaoh lives you are spies; that is why you have come to the houses of *the* whores that you should not be known."

30 And Yoseph said to them, "And now if you find him, and his master requires a great price, will you give it for him?" and they said, "It shall be given."

31 And he said to them, "And if his master will not consent to part with him for a great price, what will you do to him on account *of your brother*?" and they answered him, saying, "If he will not give him to us we will slay him, and take our brother and go away."

32 And Yoseph said to them, "That is the thing
which I have spoken to you; you are spies, for
you have come to kill the inhabitants of the land;
for we heard that two of your brothers struck all
the inhabitants of Shekhem, in the land of
Kana'an, on account of your sister, and you now
come to do the same in Mitsrayim on account of
your brother. 33 Only hereby shall I know that
you are true men; if you will send home one
from among you to fetch your youngest brother
from your father, and to bring him here to me,
and by doing this thing I will know that you are
right."

34 And Yoseph called to seventy of his mighty men, and he said to them, "Take these men and bring them into the ward."

35 And the mighty men took the ten men, they laid hold of them and put them into the ward, and they were in the ward three days.

36 And on the third day Yoseph had them brought out of the ward, and he said to them, "Do this for yourselves if you be true men, so that you may live: one of your brothers shall be confined in the ward while you go and take home the grain for your household to the land of Kana'an, and fetch your youngest brother, and bring him here to me, that I may know that you are true men when you do this thing."

37 And Yoseph went out from them and came
into the chamber, and wept a great weeping, for
his pity was excited for them, and he washed his
face, and returned to them again, and he took
Shimon from them and ordered him to be bound,
but Shimon was not willing to be *bound*, for he
was a very powerful man and they could not
bind him. 38 And Yoseph called to his mighty
men and seventy valiant men came before him
with drawn swords in their hands, and the sons
of Ya'aqov were terrified at them.

39 And Yoseph said to them, "Seize this man and
confine him in prison until his brothers come to
him," and Yoseph's valiant men hurried and they
all laid hold of Shimon to bind him, and Shimon
gave a loud and terrible shriek and the cry was
heard at a distance. 40 And all the valiant men of
Yoseph were terrified at the sound of the shriek,
that they fell upon their faces, and they were
greatly afraid and fled. 41 And all the men that
were with Yoseph fled, for they were greatly
afraid of their lives, and only Yoseph and
Menasheh his son remained there, and Menasheh
the son of Yoseph saw the strength of Shimon,
and he was exceedingly angry. 42 And Menasheh
the son of Yoseph rose up to Shimon, and
Menasheh struck Shimon a heavy blow with his
fist against the back of his neck, and Shimon's
rage was calmed. 43 And Menasheh laid hold of
Shimon and he seized him violently and he
bound him and brought him into the house of
confinement, and all the sons of Ya'aqov were
astonished at the act of the youth.

44 And Shimon said to his brothers, "None of you may say that this is the striking of a Mitsrite, but it is the striking of the house of my father."

45 And after this Yoseph ordered him to be called who was set over the storehouse, to fill their sacks with grain as much as they could carry, and to restore every man's money into his sack, and to give them provision for the road, and thus he did to them.

46 And Yoseph commanded them, saying, "Be on guard lest you transgress my orders to bring your brother as I have told you, and it shall be when you bring your brother here to me, then will I know that you are true men, and you shall buy and sell in the land, and I will restore your brother to you, and you shall return in peace to your father."

47 And they all answered and said, "As our master speaks so will we do," and they bowed down to him to the ground.

48 And every man lifted his grain upon his donkey, and they went out to go to the land of Kana'an to their father; and they came to the inn and Levi spread his sack to give provender to his donkey, when he saw and behold his money in full weight was still in his sack.

49 And the man was greatly afraid, and he said to his brothers, "My money is restored, and see, it is even in my sack," and the men were greatly afraid, and they said, "What is this that Elohim has done to us?"

50 And they all said, "And where is kindness of 𐤉𐤄𐤅𐤄 with our fathers, with Avraham, Yitsḥaq, and Ya'aqov, that 𐤉𐤄𐤅𐤄 has delivered us today into the hands of the king of Mitsrayim to plot against us?"

51 And Yehudah said to them, "Surely we are guilty sinners before 𐤉𐤄𐤅𐤄 our Elohim in having sold our brother, our own flesh; why do you say, 'Where is the kindness of 𐤉𐤄𐤅𐤄 with our fathers?'"

52 And Reuven said to them, "Did I not say to you, 'do not sin against the lad,' and you would not listen to me? Now Elohim requires him from us, and how dare you say, 'Where is the kindness of 𐤉𐤄𐤅𐤄 with our fathers,' while you have sinned against 𐤉𐤄𐤅𐤄?"

53 And they stayed overnight in that place, and
they rose up early in the morning and loaded
their donkeys with their grain, and they led them
and went on and came to their father's house in
the land of Kana'an. 54 And Ya'aqov and his
household went out to meet his sons, and
Ya'aqov saw and behold their brother Shimon
was not with them, and Ya'aqov said to his sons,
"Where is your brother Shimon, whom I do not
see?" and his sons told him all that had happened
to them in Mitsrayim.

52 1 And they entered their house, and every man opened his sack and they saw and behold every man's bundle of money was there, at which they and their father were greatly terrified.

2 And Ya'aqov said to them, "What is this that
you have done to me? I sent your brother Yoseph
to inquire after your welfare and you said to me,
'A wild beast devoured him.' 3 And Shimon went
with you to buy food and you say, 'the king of
Mitsrayim has confined him in prison,' and you
wish to take Benyamin to cause his death also,
and bring my grey hairs down with sorrow to the
grave on account of Benyamin and his brother
Yoseph. 4 Now therefore my son shall not go
down with you, for his brother is dead and he is
left alone, and mischief might happen to him by
the way in which you go, as it happened to his
brother."

5 And Reuven said to his father, "You can kill my two sons if I do not bring your son *back* and place him before you;" and Ya'aqov said to his sons, "Stay here and do not go down to Mitsrayim, for my son shall not go down with you to Mitsrayim, nor die like his brother."

6 And Yehudah said to them, "Refrain from him until the grain is finished, and he will then say, 'Take your brother,' when he finds his own life and the life of his household in danger from the famine."

7 And in those days the famine was heavy throughout the land, and all the people of the earth went and came to Mitsrayim to buy food,

for the famine prevailed greatly among them, and the sons of Ya'aqov remained in Kana'an a year and two months until their grain was finished.

8 And it happened after their grain was finished, the whole household of Ya'aqov was pinched with hunger, and all the infants of the sons of Ya'aqov came together and they approached Ya'aqov, and they all surrounded him, and they said to him, "Give us bread; why should we all perish through hunger in your presence?"

9 Ya'aqov heard the words of his sons' children, and he wept a great weeping, and his pity was roused for them, and Ya'aqov called to his sons and they all came and sat before him.

10 And Ya'aqov said to them, "Have you not seen how your children have been weeping over me this day, saying, 'Give us bread,' and there is none? Now therefore return and buy for us a little food."

11 And Yehudah answered and said to his father, "If you send our brother with us we will go down and buy grain for you, but if you will not send him then we will not go down; for surely the king of Mitsrayim specifically commanded us, saying, 'You shall not see my face unless your brother be with you,' for the king of Mitsrayim is a strong and mighty king, and behold if we shall go to him without our brother we shall all be put to death. 12 Do you not know and have you not heard that this king is very powerful and wise, and there is no one like him in all the earth? Behold we have seen all the kings of the earth and we have not seen one like that king, the king of Mitsrayim; surely among all the kings of the earth there is none greater than Avimelekh king of the Philistines, yet the king of Mitsrayim is greater and mightier than he, and Avimelekh can only be compared to one of his officers.

13 "Father, you have not seen his palace and his throne, and all his servants standing before him. You have not seen that king upon his throne in his splendor and royal appearance, dressed in his royal robes with a large golden crown upon his head. You have not seen the honor and glory which Elohim has given to him, for there is no one like him in all the earth. 14 Father, you have not seen the wisdom, the understanding, and the knowledge which Elohim has put in his heart, nor heard his sweet voice when he spoke to us.

15 "We do not know, father, who made him acquainted with our names and all that happened to us, yet he asked also after you, saying, 'Is your father still living, and is it well with him?' 16 You have not seen the affairs of the government of Mitsrayim regulated by him, without inquiring of Pharaoh his master; you have not seen the awe and fear which he impressed upon all the Mitsrites. 17 And also when we went from him, we threatened to do to Mitsrayim like to the rest of the cities of the Amorites, and we were exceedingly wroth against all his words which he spoke concerning us as spies, and now when we shall again come before him his terror will fall upon us all, and not one of us will be able to speak to him either a little or a great thing.

18 "Now therefore father, please send the lad with us, and we will go down and buy food for our support, and not die through hunger." And Ya'aqov said, "Why have you dealt so ill with me to tell the king you had a brother? What is this thing that you have done to me?"

19 And Yehudah said to Ya'aqov his father, "Give the lad into my care and we will rise up and go down to Mitsrayim and buy grain, and then return, and it shall be when we return if the lad is not with us, then let me bear your blame forever. 20 Have you seen all our infants weeping over you through hunger and there is no power in your hand to satisfy them? Now let your pity be roused for them and send our brother with us and we will go. 21 For how will the kindness of 𐤉𐤄𐤅𐤄 to our ancestors be manifested to you when you say that the king of Mitsrayim will take away your son? As 𐤉𐤄𐤅𐤄 lives, I will not leave him until I bring him and place him before you; but pray to 𐤉𐤄𐤅𐤄 for us, that He may deal kindly with us, to cause us to be received favorably and kindly before the king of Mitsrayim and his men, for if we had not delayed we could have returned twice with your son."

22 And Ya'aqov said to his sons, "I trust in 𐤉𐤄𐤅𐤄 Elohim that He will deliver you and give you favor in the sight of the king of Mitsrayim, and in the sight of all his men. 23 Now therefore rise

up and go to the man, and take for him in your
hands a present from what can be obtained in the
land and bring it before him, and may the El
Shaddai give you mercy before him that he may
send Benyamin and Shimon your brothers with
you."

24 And all the men rose up, and they took their
brother Benyamin, and they took in their hands a
large present of the best of the land, and they
also took a double portion of silver.

25 And Ya'aqov strictly commanded his sons
concerning Benyamin, saying, "Guard him in the
way in which you are going, and do not separate
yourselves from him in the road, neither in
Mitsrayim."

26 And Ya'aqov rose up from his sons and spread
forth his hands and he prayed to 𐤉𐤄𐤅𐤄 on
account of his sons, saying, "𐤉𐤄𐤅𐤄 Elohim of the
heavens and the earth: remember Your covenant
with our father Avraham, remember it with my
father Yitsḥaq, and deal kindly with my sons and
do not deliver them into the hands of the king of
Mitsrayim; please do it, O Elohim, for the sake
of Your kindnesses and redeem all my children
and rescue them from power of the Mitsrite, and
send them their two brothers."

27 And all the wives of the sons of Ya'aqov and
their children lifted up their eyes to the heavens
and they all wept before 𐤉𐤄𐤅𐤄, and cried to Him
to deliver their fathers from the hand of the king
of Mitsrayim. 28 And Ya'aqov wrote a record to
the king of Mitsrayim and placed it into the hand
of Yehudah and into the hands of his sons for the
king of Mitsrayim, saying,

29 "From your servant Ya'aqov, son of Yitsḥaq,
son of Avraham the Hebrew, the prince of
Elohim: to the powerful and wise king, the
revealer of secrets, king of Mitsrayim. 30 Be it
known to my master the king of Mitsrayim, the
famine was heavily upon us in the land of
Kana'an, and I sent my sons to you to buy us a
little food from you for our support. 31 For my
sons surrounded me and I, being very old, cannot
see with my eyes, for my eyes have become very
heavy through age, as well as with daily weeping
for my son, Yoseph, who was lost from before
me; and I commanded my sons that they should
not enter the gates of the city when they came to
Mitsrayim, on account of the inhabitants of the
land.

32 "And I also commanded them to go about
Mitsrayim to seek for my son Yoseph, perhaps
they might find him there, and they did so, and
you considered them as spies of the land.
33 Have we not heard concerning you that you
interpreted Pharaoh's dream and spoke truly to
him? How then do you not know in your wisdom
whether my sons are spies or not? 34 Now
therefore, my master and king, behold I have
sent my son before you, as you spoke to my
sons; I ask you to put your eyes upon him until
he is returned to me in peace with his brothers.
35 For do you not know, or have you not heard
that which our Elohim did to Pharaoh when he
took my *grand*mother Sarah, and what He did to
Avimelekh king of the Philistines on account of
her, and also what our father Avraham did to the
nine kings of Elam, how he struck them all with
a few men that were with him?

36 "And also what my two sons Shimon and Levi
did to the eight cities of the Amorites, how they
destroyed them on account of their sister Dinah?
37 And also on account of their brother
Benyamin they consoled themselves for the loss
of his brother Yoseph; what will they then do for
him when they see the hand of any people
prevailing over them, for his sake? 38 Do you not
know, O king of Mitsrayim, that the power of
Elohim is with us, and that Elohim always hears
our prayers and does not ever forsake us?

39 "And when my sons told me of your dealings
with them, I did not call to 𐤉𐤄𐤅𐤄 on account of
you, for then you would have perished with your
men before my son Benyamin came before you,
but I thought that as Shimon my son was in your
house, perhaps you might deal kindly with him,
therefore I did not do this thing to you. 40 Now
therefore behold Benyamin my son comes to you
with my sons: guard him and put your eyes upon
him, and then will Elohim place His eyes over
you and throughout your kingdom. 41 Now I
have told you all that is in my heart, and behold
my sons are coming to you with their brother:
examine the face of the whole earth for their sake
and send them back in peace with their brothers."

42 And Ya'aqov gave the record to his sons into the care of Yehudah to give it to the king of Mitsrayim.

53 1 And the sons of Ya'aqov rose up and took
Benyamin and the whole of the presents, and
they went and came to Mitsrayim and they stood
before Yoseph. 2 And Yoseph saw his brother
Benyamin with them and he saluted them, and
these men came to Yoseph's house. 3 And
Yoseph commanded the keeper of his house to
give to his brothers *something* to eat, and he did
so to them.

4 And at noon time Yoseph sent for the men to come before him with Benyamin, and the men told the keeper of Yoseph's house concerning the silver that was returned in their sacks, and he said to them, "It will be well with you, fear not," and he brought their brother Shimon to them.

5 And Shimon said to his brothers, "The master of the Mitsrites has acted very kindly to me; he did not keep me bound, as you saw with your eyes, for when you went out from the city he let me free and dealt kindly with me in his house."

6 And Yehudah took Benyamin by the hand, and they came before Yoseph, and they bowed down to him to the ground.

7 And the men gave the present to Yoseph and they all sat before him, and Yoseph said to them, "Is it well with you, is it well with your children, is it well with your aged father?" And they said, "It is well," and Yehudah took the record which Ya'aqov had sent and gave it into the hand of Yoseph.

8 And Yoseph read the letter and knew his father's writing, and he wished to weep and he went into an inner room and he wept a great weeping; and he went out.

9 And he lifted up his eyes and beheld his brother Benyamin, and he said, "Is this your brother of whom you spoke?" And Benyamin approached Yoseph, and Yoseph placed his hand upon his head and he said to him, "May Elohim be kind to you my son."

10 And when Yoseph saw his brother, the son of his mother, he again wished to weep, and he entered the chamber, and he wept there, and he washed his face, and went out and refrained from weeping, and he said, "Prepare food."

11 And Yoseph had a cup from which he drank, and it was of silver beautifully inlaid with onyx stones and bdellium, and Yoseph struck the cup in the sight of his brethren while they were sitting to eat with him.

12 And Yoseph said to the men, "I know by this cup that Reuven the firstborn, Shimon and Levi and Yehudah, Yissakhar and Zevulun are children from one mother; seat yourselves to eat according to your births."

13 And he also placed the others according to their births, and he said, "I know that this your youngest brother has no brother, and I, like him, have no brother, he shall therefore sit down to eat with me."

14 And Benyamin went up before Yoseph and sat upon the throne, and the men saw the acts of Yoseph, and they were astonished at them; and the men ate and drank at that time with Yoseph, and he then gave presents to them, and Yoseph gave one gift to Benyamin, and Menasheh and Ephrayim saw the acts of their father, and they also gave presents to him, and Asenath gave him one present, and they totaled five presents in the hand of Benyamin.

15 And Yoseph brought out wine for them to drink, and they would not drink, and they said, "From the day on which Yoseph was lost we have not drunk wine, nor eaten any delicacies."

16 And Yoseph swore to them, and he pressed them hard, and they drank plentifully with him on that day, and Yoseph afterward turned to his brother Benyamin to speak with him, and Benyamin was still sitting upon the throne before Yoseph.

17 And Yoseph said to him, "Have you begotten any children?" and he said, "Your servant has ten sons, and these are their names: Bela, Beḥer, Ashbel, Gera, Na'aman, Eḥi, Rosh, Muppim, Ḥuppim, and Ard, and I called their names after my brother whom I have not seen."

18 And he ordered them to bring before him his map of the stars, whereby Yoseph knew all the times, and Yoseph said to Benyamin, "I have heard that the Hebrews have all wisdom; do you know anything of this?"

19 And Benyamin said, "Your servant knows all the wisdom which my father taught me," and Yoseph said to Benyamin, "Now, look at this instrument and discern where your brother Yoseph is in Mitsrayim, whom you said went down to Mitsrayim."

20 And Benyamin beheld that instrument with the map of the stars of heaven, and he was wise and looked in it to know where his brother was, and Benyamin divided the whole land of Mitsrayim into four divisions, and he found that he who was sitting upon the throne before him was his brother Yoseph, and Benyamin wondered greatly, and when Yoseph saw that his brother Benyamin was greatly astonished, he said to Benyamin, "What have you seen, and why are you astonished?"

21 And Benyamin said to Yoseph, "I can see by
this that Yoseph my brother sits here with me
upon the throne," and Yoseph said to him, "I am
Yoseph your brother; do not reveal this thing to
your brothers; behold I will send you with them
when they go away, and I will command them to
be brought back again into the city, and I will
take you away from them. 22 And if they risk
their lives and fight for you, then I will know
that they have repented for what they did to me,
and I will make myself known to them. But if
they forsake you when I take you, then you will
remain with me, and I will wrangle with them,
and they shall go away, and I will not become
known to them."

23 At that time Yoseph commanded his officer to
fill their sacks with food, and to put each man's
money into his sack, and to put the cup in the
sack of Benyamin, and to give them provision
for the road, and they did so to them. 24 And on
the next day the men rose up early in the
morning, and they loaded their donkeys with
their grain, and they went forth with Benyamin,
and they went to the land of Kana'an with their
brother Benyamin.

25 They had not gone far from Mitsrayim when Yoseph commanded him that was set over his house, saying, "Rise, pursue these men before they get too far from Mitsrayim, and say to them, 'Why have you stolen my master's cup?'"

26 And Yoseph's officer rose up and he reached them, and he spoke to them all the words of Yoseph; and when they heard this thing they became exceedingly wroth, and they said, "He with whom your master's cup is found shall die, and we will also become slaves."

27 And they hurried and each man brought down his sack from his donkey, and they looked in their bags and the cup was found in Benyamin's bag, and they all tore their garments and they returned to the city, and they struck Benyamin in the road, continually striking him until he came into the city, and they stood before Yoseph.

28 And Yehudah's anger was kindled, and he said, "This man has only brought me back to destroy Mitsrayim this day."

29 And the men came to Yoseph's house, and they found Yoseph sitting upon his throne, and all the mighty men standing at his right and left.

30 And Yoseph said to them, "What is this act that you have done, that you took away my silver cup and went away? I know that you took my cup in order to use it to know which part of the land your brother is in."

31 And Yehudah said, "What shall we say to our master, *and* what shall we speak, and how shall we declare ourselves right? Elohim has found the iniquity of all your servants today, so He has done this to us today."

32 And Yoseph rose up and caught hold of Benyamin and took him from his brethren with violence, and he came to the house and locked the door before them, and Yoseph commanded him that was set over his house that he should say to them, "Thus says the king, 'Go in peace to your father; behold I have taken the man in whose hand my cup was found.'"

𐤐𐤓𐤔𐤕 𐤅𐤉𐤂𐤔 – *Parahsat Vayigash*

54 1 And when Yehudah saw the dealings of

Yoseph with them, Yehudah approached him
and broke open the door, and came with his
brethren before Yoseph.

2 And Yehudah said to Yoseph, "Do not let it
seem grievous in the eyes of my master; may
your servant please speak a word before you?"
and Yoseph said to him, "Speak."

3 And Yehudah spoke before Yoseph, with his
brothers standing before them; and Yehudah said
to Yoseph, "Surely when we first came to our
master to buy food, you thought we were spies of
the land. And we *have* brought Benyamin before
you, and you still make sport of us today. 4 Now
therefore let the king hear my words, and please
send out our brother that he may go along with
us to our father, lest your being perish today with
all the beings of the inhabitants of Mitsrayim.
5 Do you not know what two of my brothers,
Shimon and Levi, did to the city of Shekhem,
and to seven cities of the Amorites, on account
of our sister Dinah, and also what they would do
for the sake of their brother Benyamin?

6 "And I, with my strength, who am greater and
mightier than both of them, will come to you and
your land today if you are unwilling to send our
brother *with us*. 7 Have you not heard what our
Elohim who chose us did to Pharaoh on account
of Sarah our mother, whom he took away from
our father, how He struck him and his household
with plagues so heavy, that even to this day the
Mitsrites still relate this wonder to each other?
So will our Elohim do to you on account of
Benyamin whom you have taken today from his
father; and on account of the evils which you
heap over us today in your land; for our Elohim
will remember His covenant with our father
Avraham and bring evil upon you, because you
have grieved the being of our father today.
8 Now therefore, hear the words that I have
spoken to you today, and send *out* our brother
that he may go away *with us*, lest you and the
people of your land die by the sword: for you
cannot all prevail over me."

9 And Yoseph answered Yehudah, saying, "Why
have you opened wide your mouth and why do
you boast over us, saying that you are strong? As
Pharaoh lives, if I command all my valiant men
to fight with you, surely you and your brothers
would sink in the mud."

10 And Yehudah said to Yoseph, "Surely it suits
you and your people to fear me; as 𐤉𐤄𐤅𐤄 lives if
I once draw my sword I shall not sheathe it again
until I have killed all Mitsrayim today. I will
begin with you and finish with Pharaoh your
master."

11 And Yoseph answered and said to him,
"Surely you are not the only one possessing
strength; I am stronger and mightier than you;
surely if you draw your sword I will put it to
your neck and the necks of all your brothers."

12 And Yehudah said to him, "Surely if I open
my mouth against you today I would swallow
you up that you be destroyed from off the earth
and perish from your kingdom today." And
Yoseph said, "Surely if you open your mouth, I
have power and might to close your mouth with
a stone until you are not be able to utter a word;
see how many stones are before us? Truly I can
take a stone, and force it into your mouth and
break your jaws."

13 And Yehudah said, "Elohim is witness
between us, that we have not desired to fight
with you here; only give us our brother and we
will go from you." And Yoseph answered and
said, "As Pharaoh lives, if all the kings of
Kana'an came together with you, you *still* would
not take him from my hand. 14 Now therefore go
your way to your father, and your brother shall
be my slave, for he has robbed the king's house."
And Yehudah said, "What is it to you or to the
name of the king? Surely the king sends forth
from his house, throughout the land, silver and
gold either in gifts or expenses, and you still
speak about your cup which you placed in our
brother's bag, and say that he has stolen it from
you? 15 Elohim forbid that our brother Benyamin
or any of the seed of Avraham should do this
thing, to steal from you, or from anyone else,
whether king, prince, or any man. 16 Now
therefore cease this accusation lest the whole
earth hear your words, saying, 'For a little silver
the king of Mitsrayim wrangled with the men,
and he accused them and took their brother for a
slave.'"

17 And Yoseph answered and said, "Take this cup and go from me and leave your brother for a slave, for it is the judgment of a thief to be a slave."

18 And Yehudah said, "Why are you not ashamed of your words, to leave our brother and to take your cup? Surely if you gave us your cup, or a thousand times as much, we would not leave our brother for the silver which is found in the hand of any man, for we are willing to die for him."

19 And Yoseph answered, "And why did you forsake your brother and sell him for twenty pieces of silver to this day? Why then will you not do the same to this your brother?"

20 And Yehudah said, "𐤉𐤄𐤅𐤄 is witness between me and you that we do not desire to fight; now therefore give us our brother and we will go from you without quarreling."

21 And Yoseph answered and said, "If all the kings of the land should assemble they will not be able to take your brother from my hand;" and Yehudah said, "What shall we say to our father, when he sees that our brother does not come with us, and will grieve over him?"

22 And Yoseph answered and said, "This is the thing which you shall tell your father, saying, 'The rope has gone after the bucket.'"

23 And Yehudah said, "Surely you are a king, and why do you say these things, giving a false judgment? Woe to the king who is like you."

24 And Yoseph answered and said, "There is no false judgment in the word that I spoke on account of your brother Yoseph, for you all sold him to the Midianites for twenty pieces of silver, and you all denied it to your father and said to him, 'An evil beast has devoured him, Yoseph has been torn to pieces.'"

25 And Yehudah said, "Behold the fire of Shekhem burns in my heart, now I will burn all your land with fire;" and Yoseph answered and said, "Surely your wife, who killed your sons, extinguished the fire of Shekhem."

26 And Yehudah said, "As 𐤉𐤄𐤅𐤄 lives, if I pluck out a single hair from my flesh, I will fill all Mitsrayim with its blood."

27 And Yoseph answered and said, "Such is your custom to do as you did to your brother whom you sold, and you dipped his coat in blood and brought it to your father in order that he might say an evil beast devoured him and here is his blood."

28 And when Yehudah heard this thing he was
exceedingly wroth and his anger burned within
him, and there was before him in that place a
stone, the weight of which was about four
hundred sheqels[a], and Yehudah's anger was
kindled and he took the stone in one hand and
cast it to the heavens and caught it with his left
hand. 29 And afterward he placed it under his
legs, and he sat upon it with all his strength and
the stone was turned into dust from the force of
Yehudah.

30 And Yoseph saw the act of Yehudah and he was very much afraid, but he commanded Menasheh his son *to do so*, and he also did with another stone what Yehudah *had done*, and Yehudah said to his brothers, "Let none of you say, 'this man is an Mitsrite,' but by his doing this thing he is of our father's family."

31 And Yoseph said, "You are not the only one given strength, for we are also powerful men, and why will you boast over us all?" and Yehudah said to Yoseph, "Please send our brother and do not ruin your land today."

32 And Yoseph answered and said to them, "Go and tell your father, 'an evil beast has devoured him' as you said concerning your brother Yoseph."

33 And Yehudah spoke to his brother Naphtali, and he said to him, "Hurry, go now and number all the streets of Mitsrayim and come and tell me;" and Shimon said to him, "Do not let this thing trouble you; now I will go to the mount and

---

[a] **54:28** Four hundred sheqels is equal to approximately **10** US lbs (**4.5** kg).

take up one large stone from the mount and level
it at everyone in Mitsrayim, and kill all that are
in it."

34 And Yoseph heard all these words that his
brothers spoke before him, and they did not
know that Yoseph understood them, for they
imagined that he did not know Hebrew.

35 And Yoseph was greatly afraid at the words of
his brethren lest they should destroy Mitsrayim,
and he commanded his son Menasheh, saying,
"Go now hurry and gather to me all the
inhabitants of Mitsrayim, and all the valiant men
together, and let them come to me now on
horseback and on foot and with all sorts of
musical instruments," and Menasheh went and
did so.

36 And Naphtali went as Yehudah had
commanded him, for Naphtali was light-footed
as one of the swift deer, and he would go upon
the ears of grain and they would not break under
him. **37** And he went and numbered all the streets
of Mitsrayim, and found them to be twelve, and
he came quickly and told Yehudah, and Yehudah
said to his brethren, "Hurry, every man, and put
his sword on upon his loins and we will come
over Mitsrayim, and strike them all, and do not
let a remnant remain."

38 And Yehudah said, "Behold, I will destroy
three of the streets with my strength, and you
shall each destroy one street;" and when
Yehudah was speaking this thing, behold the
inhabitants of Mitsrayim and all the mighty men
came toward them with all sorts of musical
instruments and with loud shouting. **39** And their
number was five hundred horsemen and ten
thousand infantry, and four hundred men who
could fight without sword or spear, only with
their hands and strength. **40** And all the mighty
men came with great storming and shouting, and
they all surrounded the sons of Ya'aqov and
terrified them, and the ground quaked at the
sound of their shouting. **41** And when the sons of
Ya'aqov saw these troops they were greatly
afraid of their lives, and Yoseph did so in order
to terrify the sons of Ya'aqov to become calm.

42 And Yehudah, seeing some of his brothers
terrified, said to them, "Why are you afraid while
the favor of Elohim is with us?" and when
Yehudah saw all the people of Mitsrayim
surrounding them at the command of Yoseph to
terrify them, only Yoseph commanded them,
saying, "Do not touch any of them."

43 Then Yehudah hurried and drew his sword,
and uttered a loud and bitter scream, and he
struck *the ground* with his sword, and he sprang
upon the ground and he still continued to shout
against all the people.

44 And when he did this thing 𐤉𐤄𐤅𐤄 caused the
terror of Yehudah and his brethren to fall upon
the valiant men and all the people that
surrounded them. **45** And they all fled at the
sound of the shouting, and they were terrified
and fell one upon the other, and many of them
died as they fell, and they all fled from before
Yehudah and his brethren and from before
Yoseph. **46** And while they were fleeing,
Yehudah and his brothers pursued them to the
house of Pharaoh, and they all escaped, and
Yehudah again sat before Yoseph and roared at
him like a lion, and gave a great and tremendous
shriek at him. **47** And the shriek was heard at a
distance, and all the inhabitants of Sukoth heard
it, and all Mitsrayim quaked at the sound of the
shriek, and *some of* the walls of Mitsrayim and
of the land of Goshen fell in from the shaking of
the earth, and Pharaoh also fell from his throne
to the ground, and also all the children of the
pregnant women of Mitsrayim and Goshen fell
from the womb when they heard the noise of the
shaking, for they were terribly afraid.[a]

48 And Pharaoh sent word, saying, "What is this
thing that has happened in the land of Mitsrayim
today?" and they came and told him all the
things from beginning to end, and Pharaoh was
alarmed and he wondered and was greatly afraid.

---

[a] **54:47** "Children of the pregnant women…fell from the womb…" - Hebrew text is slightly ambiguous here. Samuel's translation read "pregnant women…miscarried." However, the word usually used for "miscarry" is 𐤔𐤊𐤋 (*sha'khol*), and is not present here. Rather, it uses 𐤍𐤐𐤋 (*na'fal*) meaning "to fall" and 𐤌𐤏𐤉 (*me'ai*) meaning "inward parts" or "belly." This may mean miscarriage, though it could be interpreted also as premature birth. Compare verse **50**, which says the women "have dropped their children."

49 And his fear increased when he heard all these
things, and he sent to Yoseph, saying, "You have
brought the Hebrews to me to destroy all
Mitsrayim; what will you do with that thieving
slave? Send him away and let him go with his
brothers, and let us not perish through their evil,
even we, you and all Mitsrayim. 50 And if you do
not desire to do this thing, cast off all my
valuable things, and go with them to their land, if
you delight in it, for they will destroy my whole
country and kill all my people today; even all the
women of Mitsrayim have dropped their children
through their screams; see what they have done
merely by their shouting and speaking! If they
fight with the sword, they will destroy the land;
now therefore choose that which you desire,
whether me or the Hebrews, whether Mitsrayim
or the land of the Hebrews."

51 And they came and told Yoseph all the words
of Pharaoh that he had said concerning him, and
Yoseph was greatly afraid at the words of
Pharaoh and Yehudah and his brothers were still
standing before Yoseph indignant and enraged,
and all the sons of Ya'aqov roared at Yoseph,
like the roaring of the sea and its waves. 52 And
Yoseph was greatly afraid of his brothers and on
account of Pharaoh, and Yoseph sought a way to
make himself known to his brothers, lest they
destroy all Mitsrayim. 53 And Yoseph
commanded his son Menasheh, and Menasheh
went and approached Yehudah, and placed his
hand on his shoulder, and the anger of Yehudah
was calmed.

54 And Yehudah said to his brothers, "Let none
of you say that this is the act of a Mitsrite youth
for this is the work of my father's house."

55 And Yoseph, seeing and knowing that
Yehudah's anger was calmed, approached to
speak to Yehudah in a soft tongue.

56 And Yoseph said to Yehudah, "Surely you
speak truth and have verified your assertions
concerning your strength today; may your
Elohim who delights in you increase your
welfare; but tell me truly why from among all
your brothers do you wrangle with me on
account of the lad, as none of them have spoken
one word to me concerning him."

57 And Yehudah answered Yoseph, saying,
"Surely you must know that I was collateral for
the lad to his father, saying if I did not bring him
back to him I should bear his blame forever.
58 Therefore have I approached you from among
all my brothers, for I saw that you were
unwilling to allow him to go from you; now
therefore may I find favor in your eyes that you
would send him to go with us, and behold I will
remain as a substitute for him, to serve you in
whatever you desire; for wherever you send me I
will go to serve you with great energy. 59 Send
me now to a mighty king who has rebelled
against you, and you will know what I will do to
him and to his land; although he may have
horsemen and infantry or an exceedingly mighty
people, I will kill them all and bring the king's
head before you. 60 Do you not know or have
you not heard that our father Avraham with his
servant Eliezer struck all the kings of Elam with
their hosts in one night, and no one was left
remaining? And ever since that day our father's
strength was given to us for an inheritance: for
us and our seed forever."

61 And Yoseph answered and said, "You speak
truth, and falsehood is not in your mouth, for it
was also told to us that the Hebrews have power
and that 𐤉𐤄𐤅𐤄 their Elohim delighted greatly in
them; and who then can stand before them?
62 However, on this condition will I send your
brother, if you will bring before me his brother
the son of his mother, of whom you said that he
had gone from you down to Mitsrayim; and it
shall come to pass when you bring to me his
brother I will take him in his stead, because not
one of you was collateral for him to your father,
and when he comes to me, I will then send with
you his brother for whom you have been
collateral."

63 And Yehudah's anger was kindled against
Yoseph when he spoke this thing, and his eyes
dropped blood with anger, and he said to his
brothers, "Oh how this man seeks his own
destruction and that of all Mitsrayim today!"

64 And Shimon answered Yoseph, saying, "Did
we not tell you at first that we did not know the
particular place where he went, and whether he
be dead or alive? And did we not tell these things
to my master?"

65 And Yoseph, observing the countenance of Yehudah, discerned that his anger began to kindle when he spoke to him, saying, "Bring me your other brother instead of this brother."

66 And Yoseph said to his brothers, "Surely you said that your brother was either dead or lost; now if I should call him today and he should come before you, would you give him to me instead of his brother?"

67 And Yoseph began to speak and call out, "Yoseph, Yoseph, come before me today, and appear to your brothers and sit before them."

68 And when Yoseph spoke this thing before them, they looked each a different way to see where Yoseph would come from.

69 And Yoseph observed all their acts, and said to them, "Why do you look here and there? I am Yoseph whom you sold to Mitsrayim, now therefore do not let it grieve you that you sold me, for Elohim sent me before you to be support through the famine."

70 And his brothers were terrified at him when
they heard the words of Yoseph, and Yehudah
was exceedingly terrified at him. 71 And when
Benyamin heard the words of Yoseph he
appeared before them in the inner part of the
house, and Benyamin ran to Yoseph his brother,
and embraced him and fell upon his neck, and
they wept. 72 And when Yoseph's brothers saw
that Benyamin had fallen upon his brother's neck
and wept with him, they also fell upon Yoseph
and embraced him, and they wept a great
weeping with Yoseph. 73 And the voice was
heard in the house of Yoseph that they were
Yoseph's brothers, and it pleased Pharaoh
exceedingly, for he was afraid of them lest they
should destroy Mitsrayim.

74 And Pharaoh sent his servants to Yoseph to commend him concerning his brothers who had come to him, and all the captains of the armies and troops that were in Mitsrayim came to rejoice with Yoseph, and all Mitsrayim rejoiced greatly about Yoseph's brethren.

75 And Pharaoh sent his servants to Yoseph, saying, "Tell your brothers to fetch all that belongs to them and let them come to me, and I will place them in the best part of the land of Mitsrayim," and they did so.

76 And Yoseph commanded him that was set
over his house to bring out gifts and garments to
his brothers, and he brought out to them many
garments being royal robes and many gifts, and
Yoseph divided them among his brothers. 77 And
he gave to each of his brothers a change of
garments of gold and silver, and three hundred
pieces of silver, and Yoseph commanded them
all to be dressed in these garments, and to be
brought before Pharaoh. 78 And Pharaoh seeing
that all Yoseph's brothers were valiant men, and
of beautiful appearance, he greatly rejoiced.
79 And they afterward went out from the
presence of Pharaoh to go to the land of Kana'an,
to their father, and their brother Benyamin was
with them.

80 And Yoseph rose up and gave them eleven
chariots from Pharaoh, and Yoseph gave them
his chariot, upon which he rode on the day of his
being crowned in Mitsrayim, to fetch his father
to Mitsrayim; and Yoseph sent garments to all
his brothers' children, according to their
numbers, and a hundred pieces of silver to each
of them, and he also sent garments to the wives
of his brothers from the garments of the king's
wives. 81 And he gave to each of his brothers ten
men to go with them to the land of Kana'an to
serve them, to serve their children and all
belonging to them in coming to Mitsrayim.
82 And Yoseph sent by the hand of his brother
Benyamin ten changes of garments for his ten
sons, a portion above the rest of the children of
the sons of Ya'aqov.

83 And he sent to each *one of them* fifty pieces of
silver, and ten chariots from Pharaoh, and he sent
to his father ten donkeys laden with all the
luxuries of Mitsrayim, and ten female donkeys
laden with grain and bread and nourishment for
his father, and to all that were with him as
provisions for the road. 84 And he sent to his
sister Dinah garments of silver and gold, and
frankincense and myrrh, and aloes and women's
ornaments in great plenty, and he sent the same
from the wives of Pharaoh to the wives of
Benyamin.

85 And he gave to all his brothers, and also to
their wives, all sorts of onyx stones and
bdellium, and from all the valuable things among
the great people of Mitsrayim, nothing of all the
costly things was left but what Yoseph sent to
his father's household. **86** And he sent his
brothers away, and they went, and he sent his
brother Benyamin with them. **87** And Yoseph
went out with them to accompany them on the
road to the borders of Mitsrayim, and he
commanded them concerning his father and his
household, to come to Mitsrayim.

88 And he said to them, "Do not quarrel on the road, for this thing was from 𐤉𐤄𐤅𐤄 to keep a great people from starvation, for there will still be five more years of famine in the land."

89 And he commanded them, saying, "When you come to the land of Kana'an, do not come suddenly before my father in this affair, but act in your wisdom."

90 And Yoseph ceased to command them, and he turned and went back to Mitsrayim, and the sons of Ya'aqov went to the land of Kana'an with joy and cheerfulness to their father Ya'aqov.

91 And they came to the borders of the land, and they said to each other, "What shall we do in this matter before our father? For if we come suddenly to him and tell him the matter, he will be greatly alarmed at our words and will not believe us."

92 And they went along until they came near to their houses, and they found Seraḥ, the daughter of Asher, going forth to meet them, and the girl was very good and subtle, and knew how to play the harp.

93 And they called to her and she came before them, and she kissed them, and they took her and gave her a harp, saying, "Go now before our father, and sit before him, and strike upon the harp, and speak these words."

94 And they commanded her to go to their house, and she took the harp and hurried before them, and she came and sat near Ya'aqov.

95 And she played well and sang, and uttered in the sweetness of her words, "Yoseph my uncle is living, and he rules throughout the land of Mitsrayim, and is not dead."

96 And she continued to repeat and utter these
words, and Ya'aqov heard her words and they
were agreeable to him. **97** He listened while she
repeated them two and then three times, and joy
entered the heart of Ya'aqov at the sweetness of
her words, and the Ruaḥ of Elohim was upon
him, and he knew all her words to be true.

98 And Ya'aqov blessed Seraḥ when she spoke these words before him, and he said to her, "My daughter, may death never prevail over you, for you have revived my spirit; only continue to speak before me as you have been speaking, for you have gladdened me with all your words."

99 And she continued to sing these words, and Ya'aqov listened and it pleased him, and he rejoiced, and the Ruaḥ of Elohim was upon him.

100 While he was still speaking with her, behold
his sons came to him with horses and chariots
and royal garments and servants running before
them. **101** And Ya'aqov rose up to meet them, and
saw his sons dressed in royal garments and he
saw all the treasures that Yoseph had sent to
them.

102 And they said to him, "Be informed that our brother Yoseph is living, and it is he who rules throughout the land of Mitsrayim, and it is he who spoke to us as we told you."

103 And Ya'aqov heard all the words of his sons,
and his heart raced at their words, for he could
not believe them until he saw all that Yoseph had
given them and what he had sent him, and all the
signs which Yoseph had spoken to them. **104** And
they opened out before him, and showed him all
that Yoseph had sent, and they gave to each what
Yoseph had sent him, and he knew that they had
spoken the truth, and he rejoiced exceedingly an
account of his son.

105 And Ya'aqov said, "It is enough for me that my son Yoseph is alive; I will go and see him before I die."

106 And his sons told him all that had happened to them, and Ya'aqov said, "I will go down to Mitsrayim to see my son and his offspring."

107 And Ya'aqov rose up and put on the garments
which Yoseph had sent him, and after he had
washed, and shaved his hair, he put upon his
head the turban which Yoseph had sent him.
108 And all the people of Ya'aqov's house and
their wives put on the garments which Yoseph
had sent them, and they greatly rejoiced at
Yoseph that he was alive and that he was ruling
in Mitsrayim. 109 And all the inhabitants of
Kana'an heard of this thing, and they came and
rejoiced much with Ya'aqov that he was alive.

110 And Ya'aqov made a banquet for them for
three days, and all the kings of Kana'an and great
ones of the land ate and drank and rejoiced in the
house of Ya'aqov.

55 1 And it happened after this that Ya'aqov
said, "I will go and see my son in Mitsrayim and
will then come back to the land of Kana'an of
which Elohim had spoken to Avraham, for I
cannot leave the land of my birth-place."

2 Behold the word of 𐤉𐤄𐤅𐤄 came to him, saying,
"Go down to Mitsrayim with all your household
and remain there; and do not fear going down to
Mitsrayim for I will make you a great nation
there."

3 And Ya'aqov said in his heart, "I will go and
see my son whether the fear of his Elohim is yet
in his heart in the midst of all the inhabitants of
Mitsrayim."

4 And 𐤉𐤄𐤅𐤄 said to Ya'aqov, "Do not fear for
Yoseph, for he retains his integrity to serve Me,
as will seem good in your eyes," and Ya'aqov
rejoiced exceedingly concerning his son.

5 At that time Ya'aqov commanded his sons and
household to go to Mitsrayim according to the
word of 𐤉𐤄𐤅𐤄 to him, and Ya'aqov rose up with
his sons and all his household, and he went out
from the land of Kana'an from Beersheva, with
joy and gladness of heart, and they went to the
land of Mitsrayim. 6 And it happened when they
came near Mitsrayim, Ya'aqov sent Yehudah
before him to Yoseph that he might show him a
situation in Mitsrayim, and Yehudah did
according to the word of his father, and he
hurried and ran and came to Yoseph, and they
assigned for them a place in the land of Goshen
for all his household, and Yehudah returned and
came along the road to his father.

7 And Yoseph harnessed the chariot, and he
assembled all his mighty men and his servants
and all the officers of Mitsrayim in order to go
and meet his father Ya'aqov, and Yoseph's
mandate was proclaimed in Mitsrayim, saying,
"All that do not go to meet Ya'aqov shall die."

8 And on the next day Yoseph went forth with all
Mitsrayim a great and mighty host, all dressed in
garments of fine linen and purple and with
instruments of silver and gold and with their
instruments of war with them. 9 And they all
went to meet Ya'aqov with all sorts of musical
instruments, with drums and timbrels, strewing
myrrh and aloes all along the road, and they all
went after this fashion, and the earth shook at
their shouting. 10 And all the women of
Mitsrayim went upon the roofs of Mitsrayim and
upon the walls to meet Ya'aqov, and Pharaoh's
regal crown was on the head of Yoseph, for
Pharaoh had sent it to him to put on at the time
of his going to meet his father.

11 And when Yoseph came within fifty cubits of
his father, he alighted from the chariot and he
walked toward his father, and when all the
officers of Mitsrayim and the princes saw that
Yoseph had gone on foot toward his father, they
also alighted and walked on foot toward
Ya'aqov. 12 And when Ya'aqov approached the
camp of Yoseph, Ya'aqov observed the camp
that was coming toward him with Yoseph, and it
gratified him and Ya'aqov was astonished at it.

13 And Ya'aqov said to Yehudah, "Who is that
man whom I see in the camp of Mitsrayim
dressed in royal robes with a very red garment on
and a royal crown on his head, who has alighted
from his chariot and is coming toward us?" And
Yehudah answered his father, saying, "He is
your son Yoseph the king;" and Ya'aqov rejoiced
in seeing the glory of his son.

14 And Yoseph came near to his father and he
bowed to his father, and all the men of the camp
bowed to the ground with him before Ya'aqov.
15 And behold Ya'aqov ran and hurried to his son
Yoseph and fell upon his neck and kissed him,

and they wept, and Yoseph also embraced his father and kissed him, and they wept and all the people of Mitsrayim wept with them.

16 And Ya'aqov said to Yoseph, "Now I will die cheerfully after I have seen your face, that you are alive and with glory."

17 And the sons of Ya'aqov and their wives and their children and their servants, and all the household of Ya'aqov wept exceedingly with Yoseph, and they kissed him and wept greatly
with him. 18 And Yoseph and all his people afterward returned home to Mitsrayim, and Ya'aqov and his sons and all the children of his household came with Yoseph to Mitsrayim, and Yoseph placed them in the best part of Mitsrayim, in the land of Goshen.

19 And Yoseph said to his father and to his brothers, "I will go up and tell Pharaoh, 'My brothers and my father's household and all belonging to them have come to me, and behold they are in the land of Goshen.'"

20 And Yoseph did so and took from his brothers Reuven, Yissakhar, Zevulun, and his brother Benyamin and he placed them before Pharaoh.

21 And Yoseph spoke to Pharaoh, saying, "My brothers and my father's household and all belonging to them, together with their flocks and cattle have come to me from the land of Kana'an, to sojourn in Mitsrayim; for the famine was heavy upon them."

22 And Pharaoh said to Yoseph, "Place your father and brothers in the best part of the land; do not withhold anything good from them, and cause them to eat of the fat of the land."

23 And Yoseph answered, saying, "Behold I have stationed them in the land of Goshen, for they are shepherds; therefore let them remain in Goshen to feed their flocks apart from the Mitsrites."

24 And Pharaoh said to Yoseph, "Do with your brothers all that they say to you;" and the sons of Ya'aqov bowed down to Pharaoh, and they went forth from him in peace, and Yoseph afterward brought his father before Pharaoh.

25 And Ya'aqov came and bowed down to Pharaoh, and Ya'aqov blessed Pharaoh, and he then went out; and Ya'aqov and all his sons, and all his household dwelled in the land of Goshen.

26 In the second year, that is in the hundred and thirtieth year of the life of Ya'aqov, Yoseph maintained his father and his brethren, and all his father's household, with bread according to their little ones, all the days of the famine; they lacked
nothing. 27 And Yoseph gave them the best part of the whole land; they had the best of Mitsrayim all the days of Yoseph; and Yoseph also gave them and all of his father's household, clothes and garments year by year; and the sons of Ya'aqov remained securely in Mitsrayim all the
days of their brother. 28 And Ya'aqov always ate at Yoseph's table, Ya'aqov and his sons did not leave Yoseph's table day or night, besides what Ya'aqov's children consumed in their houses.

29 And all Mitsrayim ate bread during the days of the famine from the house of Yoseph, for all the Mitsrites sold all belonging to them on account
of the famine. 30 And Yoseph purchased all the lands and fields of Mitsrayim for bread on the account of Pharaoh, and Yoseph supplied all Mitsrayim with bread all the days of the famine, and Yoseph collected all the silver and gold that came to him for the grain which they bought throughout the land, and he accumulated much gold and silver, besides an immense quantity of onyx stones, bdellium and valuable garments which they brought to Yoseph from every part of the land when their money was spent.

31 And Yoseph took all the silver and gold that came into his hand, about seventy two talents of gold and silver, and also onyx stones and bdellium in great abundance, and Yoseph went and concealed them in four parts: and he concealed one part in the wilderness near the Sea of Reeds, and one part by the river Perath, and the third and fourth part he concealed in the wilderness opposite to the wilderness of Persia
and Media. 32 And he took part of the gold and silver that was left, and gave it to all his brothers and to all his father's household, and to all the women of his father's household, and the rest he brought to the house of Pharaoh, about twenty talents of gold and silver.

33 And Yoseph gave all the gold and silver that
was left to Pharaoh, and Pharaoh placed it in the
treasury, and the days of the famine ceased after
that in the land, and they sowed and reaped in the
whole land, and they obtained their usual
quantity year by year; they lacked nothing.
34 And Yoseph dwelled securely in Mitsrayim,
and the whole land was under his control. And
his father and all his brothers dwelled in the land
of Goshen and took possession of it.

35 And Yoseph was very aged, advanced in days,
and his two sons, Ephrayim and Menasheh
remained constantly in the house of Ya'aqov,
together with the children of the sons of Ya'aqov
their brothers, to learn the ways of 𐤉𐤄𐤅𐤄 and His
Torah. 36 And Ya'aqov and his sons dwelled in
the land of Mitsrayim in the land of Goshen, and
they took possession in it, and they were fruitful
and multiplied in it.

*𐤐𐤓𐤔𐤕 𐤅𐤉𐤇𐤉 – **Parashat Vayeḥi***

56 1 And Ya'aqov lived in the land of Mitsrayim
seventeen years, and the days of Ya'aqov, and
the years of his life were a hundred and forty
seven years. 2 At that time Ya'aqov was attacked
with the illness of which he died and he sent and
called for his son Yoseph from Mitsrayim, and
Yoseph his son came from Mitsrayim and
Yoseph came to his father.

3 And Ya'aqov said to Yoseph and to his sons,
"Behold I die, and the Elohim of your ancestors
will visit you, and bring you back to the land
which 𐤉𐤄𐤅𐤄 swore to give to you and your
children after you; now therefore when I am
dead, bury me in the cave which is in Makhpelah
in Ḥevron in the land of Kana'an, near my
fathers."

4 And Ya'aqov made his sons swear to bury him
in Makhpelah, in Ḥevron, and his sons swore to
him concerning this thing.

5 And he commanded them, saying, "Serve 𐤉𐤄𐤅𐤄
your Elohim, for He who delivered your fathers
will also deliver you from all trouble."

6 And Ya'aqov said, "Call all your children to
me," and all the children of Ya'aqov's sons came
and sat before him, and Ya'aqov blessed them,
and he said to them, "𐤉𐤄𐤅𐤄 Elohim of your
fathers shall grant you a thousand times as much
and bless you, and may He give you the blessing
of your father Avraham;" and all the children of
Ya'aqov's sons went forth on that day after he
had blessed them.

7 And on the next day Ya'aqov again called for
his sons, and they all assembled and came to him
and sat before him, and Ya'aqov blessed his sons
on that day before his death; each man he blessed
according to his blessing; behold it is written in
the book of the Torah of 𐤉𐤄𐤅𐤄 pertaining to
Yisra'el.

8 And Ya'aqov said to Yehudah, "I know my son
that you are a mighty man for your brothers;
reign over them, and your sons shall reign over
their sons forever. 9 Only **teach your sons the
bow** and all the weapons of war, in order that
they may fight the battles of their brother who
will rule over his enemies.[a]"

10 And Ya'aqov again commanded his sons on
that day, saying, "Behold I shall be gathered to
my people today; carry me up from Mitsrayim,
and bury me in the cave of Makhpelah as I have
commanded you. 11 Nevertheless please guard,
that none of your sons carry me, only yourselves,
and this is the manner you shall do to me, when
you carry my body to go with it to the land of
Kana'an to bury me: 12 Yehudah, Yissakhar and
Zevulun shall carry my bier at the eastern side;
Reuven, Shimon and Gad at the south,
Ephrayim, Menasheh and Benyamin at the west,
Dan, Asher and Naphtali at the north.[b] 13 Do not
let Levi carry with you, for he and his sons will
carry the ark of the covenant of 𐤉𐤄𐤅𐤄 with the
Yisra'elites in the camp; neither let Yoseph my
son carry, for as a king so let his glory be;
however, Ephrayim and Menasheh shall be in
their stead. 14 Thus shall you do to me when you
carry me away; do not neglect any thing of all
that I command you; and it shall come to pass
when you do this for me, that 𐤉𐤄𐤅𐤄 will

---

[a] **56:9** See also Shemu'el 𐤁 [2 Samuel] **1:18**.

[b] **56:12** See Bemidbar [Numbers] **2:1-31**.

remember you favorably and your children after
you forever. **15** And you my sons, honor each his
brother and his relative, and command your
children and your children's children after you to
serve 𐤉𐤄𐤅𐤄 Elohim of your fathers all the days.
16 In order that you may prolong your days in the
land, you and your children and your children's
children forever, when you do what is good and
upright in the sight of 𐤉𐤄𐤅𐤄 your Elohim, to go
in all His ways.

17 "And you, Yoseph my son, please forgive the
prongs of your brothers and all their misdeeds in
the injury that they heaped upon you, for Elohim
intended it for your and your children's benefit.
18 And my son, do not leave your brothers to the
inhabitants of Mitsrayim, neither hurt their
feelings, for behold I entrust them to the hand of
Elohim and in your hand to guard them from the
Mitsrites;" and the sons of Ya'aqov answered
their father saying, "O, our father, all that you
have commanded us, so will we do; may Elohim
only be with us."

19 And Ya'aqov said to his sons, "So may Elohim
be with you when you keep all His ways; do not
turn from His ways either to the right or the left
in performing what is good and upright in His
eyes. **20** For I know that many grievous troubles
will happen you in the latter days in the land;
yes, to your children and children's children,
only serve 𐤉𐤄𐤅𐤄 and He will save you from all
trouble. **21** And it shall come to pass when you
shall go after Elohim to serve Him and will teach
your children after you, and your children's
children, to know 𐤉𐤄𐤅𐤄, then will 𐤉𐤄𐤅𐤄 raise up
to you and your children a servant from among
your children, and 𐤉𐤄𐤅𐤄 will deliver you through
his hand from all affliction, and bring you out of
Mitsrayim and bring you back to the land of your
fathers to inherit it securely."

22 And Ya'aqov ceased commanding his sons,
and he drew his feet into the bed, he died and
was gathered to his people.

23 And Yoseph fell upon his father and he cried
out and wept over him and he kissed him, and he
called out in a bitter voice, and he said, "O my
father, my father."

24 And his son's wives and all his household
came and fell upon Ya'aqov, and they wept over
him, and cried in a very loud voice concerning
Ya'aqov. **25** And all the sons of Ya'aqov rose up
together, and they tore their garments, and they
all put sackcloth upon their loins, and they fell
on their faces, and they cast dust upon their
heads toward the heavens.

26 And the thing was told to Asenath Yoseph's
wife, and she rose up and put on sackcloth and
she, with all the Mitsrite women with her, came
and mourned and wept for Ya'aqov. **27** And also
all the people of Mitsrayim who knew Ya'aqov
came all on that day when they heard this thing,
and all Mitsrayim wept for many days. **28** And
also from the land of Kana'an did the women
come to Mitsrayim when they heard that Ya'aqov
was dead, and they wept for him in Mitsrayim
for seventy days.

29 And it happened after this that Yoseph
commanded his servants the doctors to embalm
his father with myrrh and frankincense and all
manner of incense and perfume, and the
physicians embalmed Ya'aqov as Yoseph had
commanded them. **30** And all the people of
Mitsrayim and the elders and all the inhabitants
of the land of Goshen wept and mourned over
Ya'aqov, and all his sons and the children of his
household lamented and mourned over their
father Ya'aqov many days.

31 And after the days of his weeping had passed
away, at the end of seventy days, Yoseph said to
Pharaoh, "I will go up and bury my father in the
land of Kana'an as he made me swear, and then I
will return."

32 And Pharaoh sent Yoseph, saying, "Go up and
bury your father as he said, and as he made you
swear;" and Yoseph rose up with all his brothers
to go to the land of Kana'an to bury their father
Ya'aqov as he had commanded them.

33 And Pharaoh commanded that it should be
proclaimed throughout Mitsrayim, saying,
"Whoever does not go up with Yoseph and his
brothers to the land of Kana'an to bury Ya'aqov,
shall die."

34 And all Mitsrayim heard of Pharaoh's
proclamation, and they all rose up together, and

all the servants of Pharaoh, and the elders of his
house, and all the elders of the land of Mitsrayim
went up with Yoseph, and all the officers and
princes of Pharaoh went up as the servants of
Yoseph, and they went to bury Ya'aqov in the
land of Kana'an. 35 And the sons of Ya'aqov
carried the bier upon which he lay; according to
all that their father commanded them, so did his
sons to him.

36 And the bier was of pure gold, and it was
inlaid round about with onyx stones and
bdellium; and the covering of the bier was gold
woven work, joined with threads, and over them
were hooks of onyx stones and bdellium. 37 And
Yoseph placed a large golden crown on his
father Ya'aqov's head, and he put a golden
scepter in his hand, and they surrounded the bier
as was the custom of kings during their lives.
38 And all the troops of Mitsrayim went before
him in this array, at first all the mighty men of
Pharaoh, and the mighty men of Yoseph, and
after them the rest of the inhabitants of
Mitsrayim, and they all carried swords and were
equipped with coats of mail, and the trappings of
war were upon them. 39 And all the weepers and
mourners went at a distance opposite to the bier,
going and weeping and lamenting, and the rest of
the people went after the bier.

40 And Yoseph and his household went together
near the bier barefooted and weeping, and the
rest of Yoseph's servants went around him; each
man had his ornaments upon him, and they were
all armed with their weapons of war. 41 And fifty
of Ya'aqov's servants went in front of the bier,
and they strewed along the road myrrh and aloes,
and all manner of perfume, and all the sons of
Ya'aqov that carried the bier walked upon the
perfumery, and the servants of Ya'aqov went
before them strewing the perfume along the road.

42 And Yoseph went up with a heavy camp, and
they did after this manner every day until they
reached the land of Kana'an, and they came to
the threshing floor of Atad, which was on the
other side of the Yarden, and they mourned an
exceedingly great and heavy mourning in that
place.

43 And all the kings of Kana'an heard of this
thing and they all went forth, each man from his
house, thirty-one kings of Kana'an, and they all
came with their men to mourn and weep over
Ya'aqov. 44 And all these kings saw Ya'aqov's
bier, and behold Yoseph's crown was on it, and
they also put their crowns upon the bier, and
encircled it with crowns.

45 And all these kings made in that place a great
and heavy mourning with the sons of Ya'aqov
and Mitsrayim over Ya'aqov, for all the kings of
Kana'an knew the valor of Ya'aqov and his sons.

46 And the report reached Esaw, saying,
"Ya'aqov died in Mitsrayim, and his sons and all
Mitsrayim are conveying him to the land of
Kana'an to bury him."

47 And Esaw heard this thing, and he was
dwelling in mount Seir, and he rose up with his
sons and all his people and all his household, a
people exceedingly great, and they came to
mourn and weep over Ya'aqov. 48 And it
happened, when Esaw came, he mourned for his
brother Ya'aqov, and all Mitsrayim and all
Kana'an again rose up and mourned a great
mourning with Esaw over Ya'aqov in that place
49 And Yoseph and his brothers brought their
father Ya'aqov from that place, and they went to
Ḥevron to bury Ya'aqov in the cave by his
fathers.

50 And they came to Qiryath-arba, to the cave,
and as they came Esaw stood with his sons
against Yoseph and his brethren as a hindrance
in the cave, saying, "Ya'aqov shall not be buried
here, for *the cave* belongs to us and to our
father."

51 And Yoseph and his brethren heard the words
of Esaw's sons, and they were exceedingly
wroth, and Yoseph approached Esaw, saying,
"What is this thing which they have spoken?
Surely my father Ya'aqov bought it from you for
great riches after the death of Yitsḥaq, now
twenty-five years ago, and also he bought all the
land of Kana'an from you and from your sons,
and your seed after you. 52 And Ya'aqov bought
it for his sons and his seed after him for an
inheritance forever; and why do you speak these
things today?"

53 And Esaw answered, saying, "You speak
falsely and utter lies, for I did not sell anything

belonging to me in all this land, as you say; neither did my brother Ya'aqov buy anything belonging to me in this land."

54 And Esaw spoke these things in order to deceive Yoseph with his words, for Esaw knew that Yoseph was not present in those days when Esaw sold all belonging to him in the land of Kana'an to Ya'aqov.

55 And Yoseph said to Esaw, "Surely my father wrote these things with you in the record of purchase, and witnessed the record with witnesses, and behold it is with us in Mitsrayim."

56 And Esaw answered him, saying, "Bring the record, whatever you find in the record, so will we do."

57 And Yoseph called to Naphtali his brother, and he said, "Hurry, go quickly, do not stay: please run to Mitsrayim and bring all the records; the record of the purchase, the sealed record and the open record, and also all the first records in which all the transactions of the birth-right are written: fetch them.
58 And you will bring them to us here, that we may know from them all the words of Esaw and his sons which they spoke today."

59 And Naphtali listened to the voice of Yoseph and he hurried and ran down to Mitsrayim, and Naphtali was lighter on foot than any of the deer that were in the wilderness, for he would go upon ears of grain without crushing them.
60 And when Esaw saw that Naphtali had gone to fetch the records, he and his sons increased their resistance against the cave, and Esaw and all his people rose up against Yoseph and his brothers to battle.

61 And all the sons of Ya'aqov and the people of Mitsrayim fought with Esaw and his men, and the sons of Esaw and his people were struck before the sons of Ya'aqov, and the sons of Ya'aqov killed forty of Esaw's people.

62 And Ḥushim the son of Dan, the son of Ya'aqov, was with Ya'aqov's sons at that time, but he was about a hundred cubits distant from the place of battle, for he remained with the children of Ya'aqov's sons by Ya'aqov's bier to guard it.
63 And though Ḥushim was mute and deaf, still he understood the voice of disquiet among the men.

64 And he asked, saying, "Why do you not bury the dead, and what is this great disquiet?" and they answered him the words of Esaw and his sons; and he ran to Esaw in the midst of the battle, and he killed Esaw with the sword, and he cut off his head, and it sprang to a distance, and Esaw fell among the people of the battle.[a]
65 And when Ḥushim did this thing the sons of Ya'aqov prevailed over the sons of Esaw, and the sons of Ya'aqov buried their father Ya'aqov by force in the cave, and the sons of Esaw saw it.

66 And Ya'aqov was buried in Ḥevron, in the cave of Makhpelah which Avraham had bought from the sons of Ḥeth for the possession of a burial place, and he was buried in very costly garments.
67 And no king had such honor paid to him as Yoseph paid to his father at his death, for he buried him with great honor like the burial of kings.
68 And Yoseph and his brothers made a mourning of seven days for their father.

57 1 And it was after this that the sons of Esaw waged war with the sons of Ya'aqov, and the sons of Esaw fought with the sons of Ya'aqov in Ḥevron, and Esaw was still lying dead, and not buried.

2 And the battle was heavy between them, and the sons of Esaw were struck before the sons of Ya'aqov, and the sons of Ya'aqov killed eighty men of the sons of Esaw, and not one died of the people of the sons of Ya'aqov; and the hand of Yoseph prevailed over all the people of the sons of Esaw, and he took Tsepho, the son of Eliphaz, the son of Esaw, and fifty of his men captive, and he bound them with chains of iron, and gave them into the hand of his servants to bring them to Mitsrayim.
3 And it happened when the sons of Ya'aqov had taken Tsepho and his people

[a] **56**:**64** Compare conflicting account in Yovelim **38**:**2**. See accompanying footnote. See also Testament of Yehudah **9**.

captive, all those that remained were greatly afraid for their lives from the house of Esaw, lest they should also be taken captive, and they all fled with Eliphaz the son of Esaw and his people, with Esaw's body, and they went on their road to Mount Seir. 4 And they came to Mount Seir and they buried Esaw in Seir, but they had not brought his head with them to Seir, for it was buried in that place where the battle had been in Ḥevron.

5 And it happened when the sons of Esaw had fled from before the sons of Ya'aqov, the sons of Ya'aqov pursued them to the borders of Seir, but they did not kill a single man from among them when they pursued them, for Esaw's body which they carried with them excited their confusion, so they fled and the sons of Ya'aqov turned back from them and came up to the place where their brothers were in Ḥevron, and they remained there on that day, and on the next day until they rested from the battle. 6 And it happened on the third day they assembled all the sons of Seir the Ḥorite, and they assembled all the children of the east, a multitude of people like the sand of the sea, and they went and came down to Mitsrayim to fight with Yoseph and his brothers, in order to free their brothers.

7 And Yoseph and all the sons of Ya'aqov heard that the sons of Esaw and the children of the east had come upon them to battle in order to free their brothers. 8 And Yoseph and his brothers and the strong men of Mitsrayim went forth and fought in the city of Rameses, and Yoseph and his brethren dealt out a tremendous blow against the sons of Esaw and the children of the east. 9 And they killed six hundred thousand men of them, and they killed all the mighty men of the children of Seir the Ḥorite *that were* among them; there were only a few of them left. And they also killed a great many of the children of the east, and of the children of Esaw; and Eliphaz the son of Esaw, and the children of the east all fled before Yoseph and his brothers.

10 And Yoseph and his brothers pursued them until they came to Sukkoth, and they killed thirty men of them in Sukkoth, and the rest escaped and they fled each to his city. 11 And Yoseph and his brothers and the mighty men of Mitsrayim turned back from them with joy and cheerfulness of heart, for they had struck all their enemies.

12 And Tsepho the son of Eliphaz and his men were still slaves in Mitsrayim to the sons of Ya'aqov, and their pains increased. 13 And when the sons of Esaw and the sons of Seir returned to their land, the sons of Seir saw that they had all fallen into the hands of the sons of Ya'aqov, and the people of Mitsrayim, on account of the battle of the sons of Esaw.

14 And the sons of Seir said to the sons of Esaw, "You have seen, therefore you know that this camp was on your account, and neither mighty man nor novice remains. 15 Now therefore go forth from our land, go from us to the land of Kana'an to the land of the dwelling of your fathers; why should your children inherit the effects of our children in latter days?"

16 And the children of Esaw would not listen to the children of Seir, and the children of Seir considered to make war with them. 17 And the children of Esaw sent secretly to Angias king of Afriqah, the same is Dinhabah, saying, 18 "Send us some of your men and let them come to us, and we will fight together against the children of Seir the Ḥorite, for they have resolved to fight with us to drive us away from the land."

19 And Angias king of Dinhabah did so, for in those days he was friendly to the children of Esaw, and Angias sent five hundred valiant infantry to the children of Esaw, and eight hundred horsemen. 20 And the children of Seir sent to the children of the east and to the children of Midian, saying, "You have seen what the children of Esaw have done to us, upon whose account we are almost all destroyed, in their battle with the sons of Ya'aqov. 21 Now therefore come to us and assist us, and we will fight them together, and we will drive them from the land and be avenged of the cause of our brethren who died for their sakes in their battle with their brethren the sons of Ya'aqov."

22 And all the children of the east listened to the children of Seir, and they came to them about eight hundred men with drawn swords, and the children of Esaw fought with the children of Seir at that time in the wilderness of Paran. 23 And

the children of Seir prevailed over the sons of
Esaw then; and the children of Seir killed on that
day of the children of Esaw in that battle about
two hundred men of the people of Angias king of
Dinhabah. 24 And on the second day the children
of Esaw came again to fight a second time with
the children of Seir, and the battle was sore upon
the children of Esaw this second time, and it
troubled them greatly on account of the children
of Seir. 25 And when the children of Esaw saw
that the children of Seir were more powerful than
they were, some men of the children of Esaw
turned and assisted the children of Seir their
enemies. 26 And there fell of the people of the
children of Esaw in the second battle fifty-eight
men of the people at Angias king of Dinhabah.
27 And on the third day the children of Esaw
heard that some of their brethren had turned from
them to fight against them in the second battle;
and the children of Esaw mourned when they
heard this thing.

28 And they said, "What shall we do to our
brethren who turned from us to assist the
children of Seir our enemies?" and the children
of Esaw again sent to Angias king of Dinhabah,
saying, 29 "Send us other men again that we may
fight with the children of Seir, for they have
already twice been heavier than we were."

30 And Angias again sent to the children of Esaw
about six hundred valiant men, and they came to
assist the children of Esaw.

31 And for ten days the children of Esaw again
waged war with the children of Seir in the
wilderness of Paran, and the battle was very
severe upon the children of Seir, and the children
of Esaw prevailed over the children of Seir this
time, and the children of Seir were struck before
the children of Esaw, and the children of Esaw
killed about two thousand men from them.
32 And all the mighty men of the children of Seir
died in this battle, and there only remained their
young ones that were left in their cities.

33 And all Midian and the children of the east
took flight from the battle, and they left the
children of Seir and fled when they saw that the
battle was severe upon them, and the children of
Esaw pursued all the children of the east until
they reached their land. 34 And the children of
Esaw killed about two hundred and fifty men of
them; and from the people of the children of
Esaw about thirty men fell in that battle, but this
evil came upon them through their brethren
turning from them to assist the children of Seir
the Ḥorite, and the children of Esaw again heard
of the evil doings of their brethren, and they
again mourned on account of this thing.

35 And it happened after the battle, the children
of Esaw turned back and came home to Seir, and
the children of Esaw killed those who had
remained in the land of the children of Seir; they
also killed their wives and little ones, they did
not leave a being alive except fifty young boys
and girls whom they allowed to live, and the
children of Esaw did not put them to death, and
the boys became their slaves, and the girls they
took for wives. 36 And the children of Esaw
dwelled in Seir in the place of the children of
Seir, and they inherited their land and took
possession of it. 37 And the children of Esaw
took all belonging in the land to the children of
Seir, also their flocks, their bulls and their goods,
and the children of Esaw took all belonging to
the children of Seir, and the children of Esaw
dwelled in Seir in the place of the children of
Seir to this day, and the children of Esaw divided
the land into divisions to the five sons of Esaw,
according to their families.

38 And it happened in those days, that the
children of Esaw resolved to crown a king over
them in the land of which they became
possessed. And they said to each other, "Not so,
for he shall reign over us in our land, and we
shall be under his counsel and he shall fight our
battles, against our enemies, and they did so."

39 And all the children of Esaw swore, saying
that none of their brethren should ever reign over
them, but a strange man who is not of their
brethren, for the beings of all the children of
Esaw were embittered every man against his son,
brother and friend, on account of the evil they
sustained from their brethren when they fought
with the children of Seir. 40 Therefore the sons of
Esaw swore, saying from that day forward they
would not choose a king from their brethren, but
one from a strange land to this day.

41 And there was a man there from the people of Angias king of Dinhabah; his name was Bela the son of Beor, who was a very valiant man, beautiful and handsome and wise in all wisdom, and a man of sense and counsel; and there was none of the people of Angias like him. 42 And all the children of Esaw took him and anointed him and they crowned him for a king, and they bowed down to him, and they said to him, "May the king live, may the king live."

43 And they spread out the sheet, and they brought him each man earrings of gold and silver or rings or bracelets, and they made him very rich in silver and in gold, in onyx stones and bdellium, and they made him a royal throne, and they placed a regal crown upon his head, and they built a palace for him and he dwelled in it, and he became king over all the children of Esaw. 44 And the people of Angias took their hire for their battle from the children of Esaw, and they went and returned at that time to their master in Dinhabah. 45 And Bela reigned over the children of Esaw thirty years, and the children of Esaw dwelled in the land instead of the children of Seir, and they dwelled securely in their stead *even* to this day.

58 1 And it happened in the thirty-second year of the Yisra'elites going down to Mitsrayim, that is in the seventy-first year of the life of Yoseph, in that year Pharaoh king of Mitsrayim died, and Magron his son reigned in his stead.

2 And Pharaoh commanded Yoseph before his death to be a father to his son, Magron, and that Magron should be under the care of Yoseph and under his counsel. 3 And all Mitsrayim consented to this thing that Yoseph should be king over them, for all the Mitsrites loved Yoseph before, only Magron the son of Pharaoh sat upon his father's throne, and he became king in those days in his father's stead. 4 Magron was forty-one years old when he began to reign, and he reigned forty years in Mitsrayim, and all Mitsrayim called his name Pharaoh after the name of his father, as it was their custom to do in Mitsrayim to every king that reigned over them. 5 And it happened when Pharaoh reigned in his father's stead, he placed the rules of Mitsrayim and all the affairs of government in the hand of Yoseph, as his father had commanded him. 6 And Yoseph became king over Mitsrayim, for he oversaw over all Mitsrayim, and all Mitsrayim was under his care and under his counsel, for all Mitsrayim inclined to Yoseph after the death of Pharaoh, and they loved him exceedingly to reign over them.

7 But there were some people among them who did not like him, saying, "No foreigner shall reign over us;" still the whole government of Mitsrayim declined in those days upon Yoseph, after the death of Pharaoh, *since* he was the regulator, doing as he liked throughout the land without any one interfering. 8 And all Mitsrayim was under the care of Yoseph, and Yoseph made war with all his surrounding enemies, and he subdued them; also all the land and all the Philistines, to the borders of Kana'an, Yoseph subdued; and they were all under his power and they gave a yearly tax to Yoseph. 9 And Pharaoh king of Mitsrayim sat upon his throne in his father's stead, but he was under the control and counsel of Yoseph, as he was at first under the control of his father. 10 Neither did he reign only in the land of Mitsrayim, under the counsel of Yoseph, but Yoseph reigned over the whole country at that time, from Mitsrayim *even* to the great river Perath. 11 And Yoseph was successful in all his ways, and 𐤉𐤄𐤅𐤄 was with him, and 𐤉𐤄𐤅𐤄 gave Yoseph additional wisdom, and honor, and glory, and love toward him in the hearts of the Mitsrites and throughout the land, and Yoseph reigned over the whole country forty years.

12 And all the countries of the Philistines and Kana'an and Tsidon, and on the other side of *the* Yarden, brought presents to Yoseph all his days, and the whole country was in the hand of Yoseph, and they brought him a yearly tribute as it was regulated, for Yoseph had fought against all his surrounding enemies and subdued them, and the whole country was in the hand of Yoseph, and Yoseph sat securely upon his throne in Mitsrayim. 13 And also all his brethren the sons of Ya'aqov dwelled securely in the land, all the days of Yoseph, and they were fruitful and multiplied exceedingly in the land, and they

served 𐤉𐤄𐤅𐤄 all their days, as their father
Ya'aqov had commanded them.

14 And it happened at the end of many days and
years, when the children of Esaw were dwelling
quietly in their land with Bela their king, that the
children of Esaw were fruitful and multiplied in
the land, and they resolved to go and fight with
the sons of Ya'aqov and all Mitsrayim, and to
deliver their brother Tsepho, the son of Eliphaz,
and his men, for they were still slaves to Yoseph
in those days. 15 And the children of Esaw sent
to all the children of the east, and they made
peace with them, and all the children of the east
came to them to go with the children of Esaw to
Mitsrayim to battle. 16 And the people of Angias,
king of Dinhabah also came to them, and they
also sent to the children of Yishma'el and they
also came to them. 17 And all this people
assembled and came to Seir to assist the children
of Esaw in their battle, and this camp was very
large and heavy with people, numerous as the
sand of the sea, about eight hundred thousand
men, infantry and horsemen, and all these troops
went down to Mitsrayim to fight with the sons of
Ya'aqov, and they encamped by Rameses.

18 And Yoseph went forth with his brothers *and*
with the mighty men of Mitsrayim, about six
hundred men, and they fought with them in the
land of Rameses; and the sons of Ya'aqov fought
with the children of Esaw again at that time, in
the fiftieth year of the sons of Ya'aqov going
down to Mitsrayim, that is the thirtieth year of
the reign of Bela over the children of Esaw in
Seir. 19 And 𐤉𐤄𐤅𐤄 gave all the mighty men of
Esaw and the children of the east into the hand of
Yoseph and his brothers, and the people of the
children of Esaw and the children of the east
were struck before Yoseph.

20 And of the people of Esaw and the children of
the east that were killed, there fell before the
sons of Ya'aqov about two hundred thousand
men, and their king Bela the son of Beor fell
with them in the battle, and when the children of
Esaw saw that their king had fallen in battle and
was dead, their hands became weak in the
combat.

21 And Yoseph and his brothers and all
Mitsrayim were still striking the people of the
house of Esaw, and all Esaw's people were afraid
of the sons of Ya'aqov and fled from before
them. 22 And Yoseph and his brothers and all
Mitsrayim pursued them a day's journey, and
they killed from them about three hundred more
men, continuing to strike them in the road; and
they afterward turned back from them. 23 And
when Yoseph and all his brothers returned to
Mitsrayim, not one man was missing from them;
but of the Mitsrites twelve men fell. 24 And when
Yoseph returned to Mitsrayim he ordered Tsepho
and his men to be additionally bound, and they
bound them in irons and they increased their
grief.

25 And all the people of the children of Esaw,
and the children of the east, returned in shame
each to his city, for all the mighty men that were
with them had fallen in battle. 26 And when the
children of Esaw saw that their king had died in
battle they hastened and took a man from the
people of the children of the east; his name was
Yovav the son of Tseraḥ, from the land of
Botsrah, and they caused him to reign over them
instead of Bela their king. 27 And Yovav sat on
the throne of Bela as king in his stead, and
Yovav reigned in Edom over all the children of
Esaw ten years, and the children of Esaw did not
go out to fight with the sons of Ya'aqov from that
day forward; for the sons of Esaw knew the valor
of the sons of Ya'aqov, and they were greatly
afraid of them. 28 But from that day forward the
children of Esaw hated the sons of Ya'aqov, and
the hatred and enmity were very strong between
them all the days, even to this day.

29 And it happened after this, at the end of ten
years, Yovav, the son of Tseraḥ, king of Edom,
died, and the children of Esaw took a man whose
name was Ḥusham, from the land of Teman, and
they made him king over them instead of Yovav,
and Ḥusham reigned in Edom over all the
children of Esaw for twenty years.

30 And Yoseph, king of Mitsrayim, and his
brothers, and all the children of Yisra'el dwelled
securely in Mitsrayim in those days, together
with all the children of Yoseph and his brothers,
having no hindrance or evil accident; and the
land of Mitsrayim was, at that time, at rest from
war in the days of Yoseph and his brothers.

פרשת שמות – *Parashat Shemoth*
ספר שמות – *Sefer Shemoth*

59 1 And these are the names of the sons of Yisra'el who dwelled in Mitsrayim, who had come with Ya'aqov, all the sons of Ya'aqov came to Mitsrayim, every man with his household.

2 The children of Leah were Reuven, Shimon, Levi, Yehudah, Yissakhar and Zevulun, and their sister Dinah.

3 And the sons of Raḥel were Yoseph and Benyamin.

4 And the sons of Zilpah, the handmaid of Leah, were Gad and Asher.

5 And the sons of Bilhah, the handmaid of Raḥel, were Dan and Naphtali.

6 And these were their offspring that were born to them in the land of Kana'an, before they came to Mitsrayim with their father Ya'aqov.

7 The sons of Reuven were Ḥanokh, Pallu, Ḥetsron, and Karmi.

8 And the sons of Shimon were Yemuel, Yamin, Ohad, Yakin, Tsoḥar, and Sa'ul, the son of a Kana'anite woman.

9 And the children of Levi were Gershon, Qohath and Merari, and their sister Yokeved, who was born to them in their going down to Mitsrayim.

10 And the sons of Yehudah were Er, Onan, Shelah, Perets, and Zeraḥ.

11 And Er and Onan died in the land of Kana'an; and the sons of Perets were Ḥetsron and Ḥamul.

12 And the sons of Yissakhar were Tola, Puvvah, Yashu, and Shimron.

13 And the sons of Zevulun were Sered, Elon, and Yaḥleel, and the son of Dan was Ḥushim.

14 And the sons of Naphtali were Yaḥtseel, Guni, Yetser and Shillem.

15 And the sons of Gad were Tsiphion, Ḥaggi, Shuni, Etsbon, Eri, Arodi and Areli.

16 And the children of Asher were Yimnah, Yishvah, Ishvi, Beriah and their sister Seraḥ; and the sons of Beriah were Ḥeber and Malki'el.

17 And the sons of Benyamin were Bela, Beḥer, Ashbel, Gera, Na'aman, Eḥi, Rosh, Muppim, Ḥuppim and Ard.

18 And the sons of Yoseph, that were born to him in Mitsrayim, were Menasheh and Ephrayim.

19 And all the beings that went forth from the
loins of Ya'aqov, were seventy beings; these are
they who came with Ya'aqov their father to
Mitsrayim to dwell there: and Yoseph and all his
brothers dwelled securely in Mitsrayim, and they
ate of the best of Mitsrayim all the days of the
life of Yoseph. 20 And Yoseph lived in the land
of Mitsrayim ninety-three years, and Yoseph
reigned over all Mitsrayim eighty years. 21 And
when the days of Yoseph drew near for him to
die, he sent and called for his brothers and all his
father's household, and they all came together
and sat before him.

22 And Yoseph said to his brothers and to all of
his father's household, "Behold I die, and Elohim
will surely visit you and bring you up from this
land to the land which He swore to your fathers
to give them. 23 And it shall be when Elohim
visits you to bring you up from here to the land
of your fathers, then bring up my bones with you
from here."

24 And Yoseph made the sons of Yisra'el to swear for their seed after them, saying, "Elohim will surely visit you and you shall bring up my bones with you from here."

25 And it happened after this that Yoseph died in
that year, the seventy-first year of the Yisra'elites
going down to Mitsrayim. 26 And Yoseph was
one hundred and ten years old when he died in
the land of Mitsrayim, and all his brothers and all
his servants rose up and they embalmed Yoseph,
as was their custom, and his brothers and all
Mitsrayim mourned for him seventy days.
27 And they put Yoseph in a coffin filled with
spices and all sorts of perfume, and they buried
him by the side of the river, that is Siḥor, and his
sons and all his brothers, and the whole of his
father's household mourned for him for one
week. 28 And it happened after the death of

Yoseph, all the Mitsrites began in those days to
rule over the children of Yisra'el, and Pharaoh,
king of Mitsrayim, who reigned in his father's
stead, took all the statutes of Mitsrayim and
conducted the whole government of Mitsrayim
under his counsel, and he reigned securely over
his people.

60 1 And when the year came round, being the
seventy-second year from the Yisra'elites going
down to Mitsrayim, after the death of Yoseph,
Tsepho, the son of Eliphaz, the son of Esaw, fled
from Mitsrayim, he and his men, and they went
away. 2 And he came to Afriqah, which is
Dinhabah, to Angias king of Afriqah, and Angias
received them with great honor, and he made
Tsepho the captain of his host. 3 And Tsepho
found favor in the eyes of Angias and in the eyes
of his people, and Tsepho was captain of the host
to Angias king of Afriqah for many days.

4 And Tsepho enticed Angias king of Afriqah to
collect all his army to go and fight with the
Mitsrites, and with the sons of Ya'aqov, and to
avenge of them the cause of his brethren. 5 But
Angias would not listen to Tsepho to do this
thing, for Angias knew the strength of the sons
of Ya'aqov, and what they had done to his army
in their warfare with the children of Esaw. 6 And
Tsepho was in those days very great in the eyes
of Angias and in the eyes of all his people, and
he continually enticed them to make war against
Mitsrayim, but they would not.

7 And it happened in those days there was in the
land of Kittim a man in the city of Putsimna,
whose name was Utsu, and he was worshiped *as*
an eloah by the children of Kittim, and the man
died and had no son, only one daughter whose
name was Yania. 8 And the girl was exceedingly
beautiful, comely, and intelligent, there was none
seen like her for beauty and wisdom throughout
the land. 9 And the people of Angias king of
Afriqah saw her and they came and praised her
to him, and Angias sent to the children of Kittim,
and he requested to take her to himself as wife,
and the people of Kittim consented to give her to
him as wife.

10 And when the messengers of Angias were
going forth from the land of Kittim to take their
journey, behold the messengers of Turgos king
of Bivintu came to Kittim, for Turgos king of
Bivintu also sent his messengers to request
Yania for him, to take her to himself as wife, for
all his men had also praised her to him, therefore
he sent all his servants to her.

11 And the servants of Turgos came to Kittim,
and they asked for Yania, to be taken to Turgos
their king as wife.

12 And the people of Kittim said to them, "We
cannot give her, because Angias king of Afriqah
desired her to take her as wife before you came,
and that we should give her to him, and now
therefore we cannot do this thing to deprive
Angias of the girl in order to give her to Turgos.
13 For we are greatly afraid of Angias lest he
come in battle against us and destroy us, and
Turgos your master will not be able to deliver us
from his hand."

14 And when the messengers of Turgos heard all
the words of the children of Kittim, they turned
back to their master and told him all the words of
the children of Kittim.

15 And the children of Kittim sent a memorial to
Angias, saying, "Behold Turgos has sent for
Yania to take her as wife, and thus have we
answered him; and we heard that he has
collected his whole army to go to war against
you, and he intends to pass by the road of
Sardunia to fight against your brother Lukus, and
after that he will come to fight against you."

16 And Angias heard the words of the children of
Kittim which they sent to him in the book, and
his anger was kindled and he rose up and
assembled his whole army and came through the
islands of the sea, the road to Sardunia, to his
brother Lukus king of Sardunia.

17 And Givlos, the son of Lukus, heard that his
uncle Angias was coming, and he went out to
meet him with a heavy army, and he kissed him
and embraced him, and Givlos said to Angias,
"When you ask my father about his welfare, and
I go with you to fight with Turgos, ask him to
make me captain of his host,' and Angias did so,
and he came to his brother and his brother came
to meet him, and he asked him about his welfare.
18 And Angias asked his brother Lukus about his

welfare, and to make his son Givlos captain of
his host, and Lukus did so, and Angias and his
brother Lukus rose up and they went toward
Turgos to battle, and there was with them a great
army and a heavy people.

19 And he came in ships, and they came into the
province of Ashtorash, and behold Turgos came
toward them, for he went forth to Sardunia, and
intended to destroy it and afterward to pass on
from there to Angias to fight with him. 20 And
Angias and Lukus his brother met Turgos in the
valley of Kanopia, and the battle was strong and
mighty between them in that place. 21 And the
battle was severe upon Lukus king of Sardunia,
and all his army fell, and Givlos his son fell also
in that battle.

22 And his uncle Angias commanded his servants
and they made a golden coffin for Givlos and
they put him in it, and Angias again waged battle
toward Turgos, and Angias was stronger than he,
and he killed him, and he struck all his people
with the edge of the sword, and Angias avenged
the cause of Givlos his brother's son and the
cause of the army of his brother Lukus. 23 And
when Turgos died, the hands of those that
survived the battle became weak, and they fled
from before Angias and Lukus his brother.
24 And Angias and his brother Lukus pursued
them to the highway, which is between Alphanu
and Romah, and they killed the whole army of
Turgos with the edge of the sword.

25 And Lukus king of Sardunia commanded his
servants that they should make a coffin of
copper, and that they should place the body of
his son Givlos in it, and they buried him in that
place.

26 And they built a high tower on it, there upon
the highway, and they called its name after the
name of Givlos *even* to this day, and they also
buried Turgos king of Bivintu there in that place
with Givlos. 27 And behold upon the highway
between Alphanu and Romah the grave of
Givlos is on one side and the grave of Turgos on
the other, and a pathway between them to this
day.

28 And when Givlos was buried, Lukus his father
returned with his army to his land Sardunia, and
Angias his brother king of Afriqah went with his
people to the city of Bivintu, that is the city of
Turgos. 29 And the inhabitants of Bivintu heard
of his fame and they were greatly afraid of him,
and they went forth to meet him with weeping
and petition, and the inhabitants of Bivintu asked
Angias to not kill them, and to not destroy their
city; and he did so, for Bivintu was, in those
days, reckoned as one of the cities of the children
of Kittim; therefore he did not destroy the city.
30 But from that day forward the troops of the
king of Afriqah would go to Kittim to spoil and
plunder it, and whenever they went, Tsepho the
captain of the host of Angias would go with
them.

31 And it was after this that Angias turned with
his army and they came to the city of Putsimna,
and Angias took Yania the daughter of Utsu
from there as wife and brought her to his city to
Afriqah.

61

1 And it happened at that time Pharaoh king
of Mitsrayim commanded all his people to make
for him a strong palace in Mitsrayim. 2 And he
also commanded the sons of Ya'aqov to assist the
Mitsrites in the building, and the Mitsrites made
a beautiful and elegant palace for a royal
habitation, and he dwelled in it and he renewed
his government and he reigned securely.

3 And Zevulun the son of Ya'aqov died in that
year, that is the seventy-second year of the going
down of the Yisra'elites to Mitsrayim, and
Zevulun died a hundred and fourteen years old,
and was put into a coffin and given into the
hands of his children.

4 And in the seventy-fifth year his brother
Shimon died; he was a hundred and twenty years
old at his death, and he was also put into a coffin
and given into the hands of his children.

5 And Tsepho the son of Eliphaz the son of
Esaw, captain of the host to Angias king of
Dinhabah, was still enticing Angias daily to
prepare for battle to fight with the sons of
Ya'aqov in Mitsrayim, and Angias was unwilling
to do this thing, for his servants had related to
him all the might of the sons of Ya'aqov, what
they had done to them in their battle with the

children of Esaw. 6 And Tsepho was enticing
Angias daily in those days to fight with the sons
of Ya'aqov. 7 And after some time Angias
listened to the words of Tsepho and consented to
him to fight with the sons of Ya'aqov in
Mitsrayim, and Angias got all his people in
order, a people as numerous as the sand which is
upon the sea shore, and he formed his resolution
to go to Mitsrayim to battle.

8 And among the servants of Angias was a youth
fifteen years old, Bil'am the son of Beor was his
name and the youth was very wise and
understood the art of divination.

9 And Angias said to Bil'am, "Divine for us,
please, with divination, that we may know who
will prevail in this battle to which we are now
proceeding."

10 And Bil'am ordered that they should bring him
wax, and he made it into the likeness of chariots
and horsemen representing the army of Angias
and the army of Mitsrayim, and he put them in
the cunningly prepared waters that he had for
that purpose, and he took boughs of myrtle trees
in his hand, and he exercised his cunning, and he
joined them over the water, and there appeared to
him in the water images resembling the hosts of
Angias falling before the images resembling the
Mitsrites and the sons of Ya'aqov. 11 And Bil'am
told this thing to Angias, and Angias despaired
and did not arm himself to go down to Mitsrayim
to battle, and he remained in his city. 12 And
when Tsepho the son of Eliphaz saw that Angias
despaired, and did not go forth to battle with the
Mitsrites, Tsepho fled from Angias from
Afriqah, and he went and came to Kittim.

13 And all the people of Kittim received him with
great honor, and they hired him to fight their
battles all the days, and Tsepho became
exceedingly rich in those days, and the troops of
the king of Afriqah still spread themselves out in
those days, and the children of Kittim assembled
and went to Mount Kupatitsia on account of the
troops of Angias king of Afriqah, who were
advancing upon them. 14 And it happened one
day that Tsepho lost a young heifer, and he went
to seek it, and he heard it lowing round about the
mountain. 15 And Tsepho went and he saw and
behold, there was a large cave at the bottom of
the mountain, and there was a great stone there at
the entrance of the cave, and Tsepho split the
stone and he came into the cave and he looked
and behold, a large animal was devouring the ox;
from the middle upward it resembled a man, and
from the middle downward it resembled an
animal, and Tsepho rose up against the animal
and killed it with his swords.

16 And the inhabitants of Kittim heard of this
thing, and they rejoiced exceedingly, and they
said, "What shall we do to this man who has
killed this animal that devoured our cattle?"

17 And they all assembled to set apart one day in
the year to him, and they called the name of it
Tsepho after his name, and they brought him
drink offerings year after year on that day, and
they brought him gifts.

18 At that time Yania the daughter of Utsu wife
of king Angias became ill, and her illness was
heavily felt by Angias and his officers, and
Angias said to his wise men, "What shall I do to
Yania and how shall I heal her from her illness?"
And his wise men said to him, "Because the air
of our country is not like the air of the land of
Kittim, and our water is not like their water, this
has made her ill. 19 For through the change of air
and water she became ill, and also because in her
country she drank only the water which came
from Purmah, which her ancestors had brought
up with bridges."

20 And Angaas commanded his servants, and
they brought him the waters of Purmah
belonging to Kittim in vessels, and they weighed
those waters with all the waters of the land of
Afriqah, and they found those waters lighter than
the waters of Afriqah.

21 And Angias saw this thing, and he
commanded all his officers to assemble the
hewers of stone in thousands and tens of
thousands, and they hewed stone without
number, and the builders came and they built an
exceedingly strong bridge, and they conveyed
the spring of water from the land of Kittim to
Afriqah, and those waters were for Yania the
queen and for all her concerns, to drink from and
to bake, wash, and bathe with, and also to water
all seed from which food can be obtained, and all

fruit of the ground. 22 And the king commanded
that they should bring of the soil of Kittim in
large ships, and they also brought stones to build
with, and the builders built palaces for Yania the
queen, and the queen became healed of her
illness.

23 And at the revolution of the year the troops of
Afriqah continued coming to the land of Kittim
to plunder as usual, and Tsepho son of Eliphaz
heard their report, and he gave orders concerning
them and he fought with them, and they fled
before him, and he delivered the land of Kittim
from them. 24 And the children of Kittim saw the
valor of Tsepho, and the children of Kittim
resolved and they made Tsepho king over them,
and he became king over them, and while he
reigned they went to subdue the children of
Tuval, and all the surrounding islands. 25 And
their king Tsepho went at their head and they
made war with Tuval and the islands, and they
subdued them, and when they returned from the
battle they renewed his government for him, and
they built a very large palace for him for his
royal habitation and throne, and they made a
large throne for him, and Tsepho reigned over
the whole land of Kittim and over the land of
Italia fifty years.

62 1 In that year, being the seventy-ninth year of
the Yisra'elites going down to Mitsrayim,
Reuven the son of Ya'aqov died in the land of
Mitsrayim; Reuven was a hundred and twenty-
five years old when he died, and they put him
into a coffin, and he was given into the hands of
his children.[a]

2 And in the eightieth year his brother Dan died;
he was a hundred and twenty years at his death,
and he was also put into a coffin and given into
the hands of his children.

3 And in that year Ḥusham king of Edom died,
and after him reigned Hadad the son of Bedad,
for thirty-five years; and in the eighty-first year
Yissakhar the son of Ya'aqov died in Mitsrayim,
and Yissakhar was a hundred and twenty-two
years old at his death, and he was put into a
coffin in Mitsrayim, and given into the hands of
his children.

4 And in the eighty-second year Asher his
brother died. He was a hundred and twenty-three
years old at his death, and he was placed in a
coffin in Mitsrayim, and given into the hands of
his children.

5 And in the eighty-third year Gad died. He was
a hundred and twenty-five years old at his death,
and he was put into a coffin in Mitsrayim, and
given into the hands of his children.

6 And it happened in the eighty-fourth year, that
is the fiftieth year of the reign of Hadad, son of
Bedad, king of Edom, that Hadad assembled all
the children of Esaw, and he got his whole army
in readiness, about four hundred thousand men,
and he directed his way to the land of Moav, and
he went to fight with Moav and to make them
tributary to him.

7 And the children of Moav heard this thing, and
they were very much afraid, and they sent to the
children of Midian to assist them in fighting with
Hadad, son of Bedad, king of Edom. 8 And
Hadad came to the land of Moav, and Moav and
the children of Midian went out to meet him, and
they placed themselves in battle array against
him in the field of Moav. 9 And Hadad fought
with Moav, and there fell of the children of
Moav and the children of Midian many slain
ones, about two hundred thousand men. 10 And
the battle was very severe upon Moav, and when
the children of Moav saw that the battle was sore
upon them, they weakened their hands and
turned their backs, and left the children of
Midian to carry on the battle.

11 And the children of Midian did not know the
intentions of Moav, but they strengthened
themselves in battle and fought with Hadad and
all his host, and all Midian fell before him.
12 And Hadad struck all Midian with a heavy
strike, and he killed them with the edge of the
sword, he left none remaining of those who came
to assist Moav. 13 And when all the children of
Midian had perished in battle, and the children at
Moav had escaped, Hadad made all Moav at that

[a] **62**:**1** See also Testament of Reuven **1**:**1** and
accompanying footnote.

time tributary to him, and they came under his
hand, and they gave a yearly tax as it was
ordered, and Hadad turned and went back to his
land.

14 And at the revolution of the year, when the
rest of the people of Midian that were in the land
heard that all their brethren had fallen in battle
with Hadad for the sake of Moav, because the
children of Moav had turned their backs in battle
and left Midian to fight, then five of the captains
of Midian resolved with the rest of their brethren
who remained in their land, to fight with Moav
to avenge the cause of their brethren.

15 And the children of Midian sent to all their
brethren the children of the east, and all their
brethren, all the children of Qeturah came to
assist Midian to fight with Moav. 16 And the
children of Moav heard this thing, and they were
greatly afraid that all the children of the east had
assembled together against them for battle, and
they the children of Moav sent a memorial to the
land of Edom to Hadad the son of Bedad, saying,

17 "Come to us and assist us and we will strike
Midian, for they all assembled together and have
come against us with all their brethren the
children of the east to battle, to avenge the cause
of Midian that fell in battle."

18 And Hadad, son of Bedad, king of Edom,
went forth with his whole army and went to the
land of Moav to fight with Midian, and Midian
and the children of the east fought with Moav in
the field of Moav, and the battle was very fierce
between them. 19 And Hadad struck all the
children of Midian and the children of the east
with the edge of the sword, and Hadad delivered
Moav at that time from the hand of Midian, and
those that remained of Midian and of the
children of the east fled before Hadad and his
army, and Hadad pursued them to their land, and
struck them with a very heavy slaughter, and the
slain fell in the road.

20 And Hadad delivered Moav from the hand of
Midian, for all the children of Midian had fallen
by the edge of the sword, and Hadad turned and
went back to his land. 21 And from that day
forth, the children of Midian hated the children
of Moav, because they had fallen in battle for
their sake, and there was a great and mighty
enmity between them all the days.

22 And all that were found of Midian in the road
of the land of Moav perished by the sword of
Moav, and all that were found of Moav in the
road of the land of Midian, perished by the
sword of Midian; thus Midian did to Moav and
Moav to Midian for many days.

23 And it happened at that time that Yehudah the
son of Ya'aqov died in Mitsrayim, in the eighty-
sixth year of Ya'aqov's going down to
Mitsrayim, and Yehudah was a hundred and
twenty-nine years old at his death, and they
embalmed him and put him into a coffin, and he
was given into the hands of his children. And in
the eighty-seventh year his brother Benyamin
died, and he was a hundred and seventeen years
old at his death, and they embalmed him and put
him into a coffin, and he was given into the
hands of his children.

24 And in the eighty-ninth year Naphtali died, he
was a hundred and thirty-two years old, and he
was put into a coffin and given into the hands of
his children.

25 And it happened in the ninety-first year of the
Yisra'elites going down to Mitsrayim, that is in
the thirtieth year of the reign of Tsepho the son
of Eliphaz, the son of Esaw, over the children of
Kittim, the children of Afriqah came upon the
children of Kittim to plunder them as usual, but
they had not come upon them for these thirteen
years. 26 And they came to them in that year, and
Tsepho the son of Eliphaz went out to them with
some of his men and struck them desperately,
and the troops of Afriqah fled from before
Tsepho and the slain fell before him, and Tsepho
and his men pursued them, going on and striking
them until they were near Afriqah. 27 And
Angias king of Afriqah heard the thing which
Tsepho had done, and it vexed him exceedingly,
and Angias was afraid of Tsepho all the days.

63 1 And in the ninety-third year Levi the son of
Ya'aqov died in Mitsrayim, and Levi was a
hundred and thirty-seven years old when he died,
and they put him into a coffin and he was given
into the hands of his children. 2 And it happened

after the death of Levi, when all Mitsrayim saw
that the sons of Ya'aqov the brothers of Yoseph
were dead, all the Mitsrites began to afflict the
children of Ya'aqov, and to embitter their lives
from that day *even* to the day of their going forth
from Mitsrayim, and they took all the vineyards
and fields from their hands which Yoseph had
given them, and all the elegant houses in which
the people of Yisra'el lived, and all the fat of
Mitsrayim, the Mitsrites took all from the sons of
Ya'aqov in those days. **3** And the hand of all
Mitsrayim became more grievous in those days
against the children of Yisra'el, and the Mitsrites
injured the Yisra'elites until the children of
Yisra'el were wearied of their lives on account of
the Mitsrites.

4 And it happened in those days, in the hundred
and second year of Yisra'el's going down to
Mitsrayim, that Pharaoh king of Mitsrayim died,
and Melol his son reigned in his stead, and all
the mighty men of Mitsrayim and all that
generation which knew Yoseph and his brethren
died in those days. **5** And another generation rose
up in their stead, which had not known the
children of Ya'aqov and all the good which they
had done to them, and all their might in
Mitsrayim. **6** Therefore all Mitsrayim began from
that day forth to embitter the lives of the children
of Ya'aqov, and to afflict them with all manner
of hard labor, because they had not known their
ancestors who had delivered them in the days of
the famine.

7 And this was also from 𐤉𐤄𐤅𐤄 for the children
of Yisra'el, to benefit them in their latter days, in
order that all the children of Yisra'el might know
𐤉𐤄𐤅𐤄 their Elohim. **8** And in order to know the
signs and mighty wonders which 𐤉𐤄𐤅𐤄 would do
in Mitsrayim on account of His people Yisra'el,
in order that the children of Yisra'el might fear
𐤉𐤄𐤅𐤄 the Elohim of their ancestors, and walk in
all His ways, they and their seed after them all
the days.

9 Melol was twenty years old when he began to
reign, and he reigned ninety-four years, and all
Mitsrayim called his name Pharaoh after the
name of his father, as it was their custom to do to
every king who reigned over them in Mitsrayim.
10 At that time all the troops of Angias king of
Afriqah went forth to spread along the land of
Kittim as usual for plunder. **11** And Tsepho the
son of Eliphaz the son of Esaw heard their
report, and he went forth to meet them with his
army, and he fought them there in the road.
12 And Tsepho struck the troops of the king of
Afriqah with the edge of the sword, and left none
remaining of them, and not even one returned to
his master in Afriqah.

13 And Angias heard of this which Tsepho the
son of Eliphaz had done to all his troops, that he
had destroyed them, and Angias assembled all
his troops, all the men of the land of Afriqah, a
people numerous like the sand by the sea shore.

14 And Angias sent to Lukus his brother, saying,
"Come to me with all your men and help me to
strike Tsepho and all the children of Kittim who
have destroyed my men," and Lukus came with
his whole army, a very great force, to assist
Angias his brother to fight with Tsepho and the
children of Kittim.

15 And Tsepho and the children of Kittim heard
this thing, and they were greatly afraid and a
great terror fell upon their hearts. **16** And Tsepho
also sent a letter to the land of Edom to Hadad
the son of Bedad king of Edom and to all the
children of Esaw, saying,

17 "I have heard that Angias king of Afriqah is
coming to us with his brother for battle against
us, and we are greatly afraid of him, for his army
is very great, particularly as he comes against us
with his brother and his army likewise. **18** Now
therefore come up with me and help me, and we
will fight together against Angias and his brother
Lukus, and you will save us out of their hands.
But if not, know that we shall all die."

19 And the children of Esaw sent a letter to the
children of Kittim and to Tsepho their king,
saying, "We cannot fight against Angias and his
people for a covenant of peace has been between
us these many years, from the days of Bela the
first king, and from the days of Yoseph the son
of Ya'aqov king of Mitsrayim, with whom we
fought on the other side of Yarden when he
buried his father."

20 And when Tsepho heard the words of his
brethren the children of Esaw he withdrew from
them, and Tsepho was greatly afraid of Angias.

21 And Angias and Lukus his brother arrayed all
their forces, about eight hundred thousand men,
against the children of Kittim.

22 And all the children of Kittim said to Tsepho,
"Pray for us to the Elohim of your fathers;
perhaps He may deliver us from the hand of
Angias and his army, for we have heard that He
is a great Elohim and that He delivers all who
trust in Him."

23 And Tsepho heard their words, and Tsepho
sought 𐤉𐤄𐤅𐤄 and he said,

24 "O 𐤉𐤄𐤅𐤄 Elohim of Avraham and Yitsḥaq my
fathers: today I know that You are a true Elohim,
and all the elohim of the nations are vain and
useless. 25 Remember now Your covenant with
Avraham our father, which our fathers related to
us, and act favorably with me today for the sake
of Avraham and Yitsḥaq our fathers, and save
me and the children of Kittim from the hand of
the king of Afriqah who comes against us for
battle."

26 And 𐤉𐤄𐤅𐤄 listened to the voice of Tsepho, and
He had regard for him on account of Avraham
and Yitsḥaq, and 𐤉𐤄𐤅𐤄 delivered Tsepho and the
children of Kittim from the hand of Angias and
his people. 27 And Tsepho fought Angias king of
Afriqah and all his people on that day, and 𐤉𐤄𐤅𐤄
gave all the people of Angias into the hands of
the children of Kittim. 28 And the battle was
severe upon Angias, and Tsepho struck all the
men of Angias and Lukus his brother, with the
edge of the sword, and about four hundred
thousand men fell from them to the evening of
that day.

29 And when Angias saw that all his men
perished, he sent a letter to all the inhabitants of
Afriqah to come to him, to assist him in the
battle, and he wrote in the letter, saying, "All
who are found in Afriqah let them come to me
from ten years old and upward; let them all come
to me, and behold he who does not come shall
die, and all that he has, with his whole
household, the king will take."

30 And all the rest of the inhabitants of Afriqah
were terrified at the words of Angias, and there
went out of the city about three hundred
thousand men and boys, from ten years upward,
and they came to Angias. 31 And at the end of
ten days Angias renewed the battle against
Tsepho and the children of Kittim, and the battle
was very great and strong between them. 32 And
from the army of Angias and Lukus, Tsepho sent
many of the wounded to his hand, about two
thousand men; and Sosiphtar the captain of the
host of Angias fell in that battle

33 And when Sosiphtar had fallen, the Afriqahn
troops turned their backs to flee, and they fled,
and Angias and Lukus his brother were with
them. 34 And Tsepho and the children of Kittim
pursued them, and they struck them heavily on
the road, about two hundred men, and they
pursued Azdruval the son of Angias who had
fled with his father, and they struck twenty of his
men in the road, and Azdruval escaped from the
children of Kittim, and they did not kill him.
35 And Angias and Lukus his brother fled with
the rest of their men, and they escaped and came
into Afriqah with terror and confusion, and
Angias feared all the days lest Tsepho the son of
Eliphaz should go to war with him.

64 1 And Bil'am the son of Beor was at that time
with Angias in the battle, and when he saw that
Tsepho prevailed over Angias, he fled from there
and came to Kittim. 2 And Tsepho and the
children of Kittim received him with great honor,
for Tsepho knew Bil'am's wisdom, and Tsepho
gave Bil'am many gifts and he remained with
him. 3 And when Tsepho had returned from the
war, he commanded all the children of Kittim to
be numbered who had gone into battle with him,
and behold not one was missed. 4 And Tsepho
rejoiced at this thing, and he renewed his
kingdom, and he made a banquet to all his
subjects.

5 But Tsepho did not remember 𐤉𐤄𐤅𐤄 and did
not consider that 𐤉𐤄𐤅𐤄 had helped him in battle,
and that He had delivered him and his people
from the hand of the king of Afriqah; but *he* still
walked in the ways of the children of Kittim and
the wicked children of Esaw, to serve other
elohim which his brethren the children of Esaw
had taught him; it is therefore said, "Out of the
wicked comes forth wickedness."

6 And Tsepho reigned over all the children of
Kittim securely, but did not know 𐤉𐤄𐤅𐤄 who had
delivered him and all his people from the hand of
the king of Afriqah; and the troops of Afriqah
did not come to Kittim anymore to plunder as
usual, for they knew of the power of Tsepho who
had struck them all at the edge of the sword. So
Angias was afraid of Tsepho the son of Eliphaz,
and of the children of Kittim all the days.

7 At that time when Tsepho had returned from
the war, and when Tsepho had seen how he
prevailed over all the people of Afriqah and had
struck them in battle at the edge of the sword,
then Tsepho advised with the children of Kittim,
to go to Mitsrayim to fight with the sons of
Ya'aqov and with Pharaoh king of Mitsrayim.
8 For Tsepho heard that the mighty men of
Mitsrayim were dead and that Yoseph and his
brothers, the sons of Ya'aqov, were dead *as well*,
and that all their children the children of Yisra'el
remained in Mitsrayim. 9 And Tsepho considered
to go to fight against them and all Mitsrayim, to
avenge the cause of his brethren the children of
Esaw, whom Yoseph, with his brothers and all
Mitsrayim, had struck in the land of Kana'an,
when they went up to bury Ya'aqov in Ḥevron.
10 And Tsepho sent messengers to Hadad, son of
Bedad, king of Edom, and to all his brethren the
children of Esaw, saying,

11 "Did you not say that you would not fight
against the king of Afriqah for he is a member of
your covenant? Behold, I fought with him and
struck him and all his people. 12 Now therefore I
have decided to fight against Mitsrayim and the
children of Ya'aqov who are there, and I will be
revenged of them for what Yoseph, his brothers,
and his ancestors did to us in the land of Kana'an
when they went up to bury their father in
Ḥevron. 13 Now then if you are willing to come
to me to assist me in fighting against them and
Mitsrayim, then shall we avenge the cause of our
brethren."

14 And the children of Esaw listened to the words
of Tsepho, and the children of Esaw gathered
themselves together, a very great people, and
they went to assist Tsepho and the children of
Kittim in battle. 15 And Tsepho sent to all the
children of the east and to all the children of
Yishma'el with words like these, and they
gathered themselves and came to the assistance
of Tsepho and the children of Kittim in the war
upon Mitsrayim. 16 And all these kings, the king
of Edom and the children of the east, and all the
children of Yishma'el, and Tsepho the king of
Kittim went forth and arrayed all their hosts in
Ḥevron. 17 And the camp was very heavy,
extending in length a distance of three days'
journey, a people numerous as the sand on the
seashore which cannot be counted.

18 And all these kings and their hosts went down
and came against all Mitsrayim in battle, and
encamped together in the valley of Pathros.
19 And all Mitsrayim heard their report, and they
also gathered themselves together, all the people
of the land of Mitsrayim, and of all the cities
belonging to Mitsrayim, about three hundred
thousand men. 20 And the men of Mitsrayim sent
also to the children of Yisra'el who were in those
days in the land of Goshen, to come to them in
order to go and fight with these kings. 21 And the
men of Yisra'el assembled and were about one
hundred and fifty men, and they went into battle
to assist the Mitsrites. 22 And the men of Yisra'el
and of Mitsrayim went forth, about three
hundred thousand men and one hundred and fifty
men, and they went toward these kings to battle,
and they placed themselves outside the land of
Goshen opposite Pathros.

23 And the Mitsrites did not believe in Yisra'el to
go with them in their camps together for battle,
for all the Mitsrites said, "Perhaps the children of
Yisra'el will deliver us into the hand of the
children of Esaw and Yishma'el, for they are
their brethren."

24 And all the Mitsrites said to the children of
Yisra'el, "Remain here together in your stand and
we will go and fight against the children of Esaw
and Yishma'el; and if these kings should prevail
over us, then come you altogether upon them and
assist us," and the children of Yisra'el did so

25 And Tsepho the son of Eliphaz the son of
Esaw king of Kittim, and Hadad the son of
Bedad king of Edom, and all their camps, and all
the children of the east, and children of
Yishma'el, a people numerous as sand, encamped
together in the valley of Pathros opposite
Tachpanches. 26 And Bil'am the son of Beor the

Aramean was there in the camp of Tsepho, for he
came with the children of Kittim to the battle,
and Bil'am was a man highly honored in the eyes
of Tsepho and his men.

27 And Tsepho said to Bil'am, "Perform
divination for us that we may know who will
prevail in the battle, we or the Mitsrites."

28 And Bil'am rose up and performed the art of
divination. He was skillful in the knowledge of
it, but he was confused and the work was
destroyed in his hand. 29 And he tried it again but
it did not succeed, and Bil'am despaired *because*
of it and left it and did not complete it, for this
was from 𐤉𐤄𐤅𐤄, in order to cause Tsepho and his
people to fall into the hand of the children of
Yisra'el, who had trusted in 𐤉𐤄𐤅𐤄, the Elohim of
their ancestors, in their war. 30 And Tsepho and
Hadad put their forces in battle array, and all the
Mitsrites went alone against them, about three
hundred thousand men, and not one man of
Yisra'el was with them.

31 And all the Mitsrites fought with these kings
opposite Pathros and Tachpanches, and the battle
was severe against the Mitsrites. 32 And the
kings were stronger than the Mitsrites in that
battle, and about one hundred and eighty men of
Mitsrayim fell on that day, and about thirty men
of the forces of the kings, and all the men of
Mitsrayim fled from before the kings, so the
children of Esaw and Yishma'el pursued the
Mitsrites, continuing to strike them *even* to the
place where the camp of the children of Yisra'el
was.

33 And all the Mitsrites cried to the children of
Yisra'el, saying, "Hurry to us and assist us and
save us from the hand of Esaw, Yishma'el and
the children of Kittim."

34 And the hundred and fifty men of the children
of Yisra'el ran from their station to the camps of
these kings, and the children of Yisra'el cried
𐤉𐤄𐤅𐤄 their Elohim to deliver them. 35 And 𐤉𐤄𐤅𐤄
listened to Yisra'el, and 𐤉𐤄𐤅𐤄 gave all the men of
the kings into their hand, and the children of
Yisra'el fought against these kings, and the
children of Yisra'el struck about four thousand of
the kings' men. 36 And 𐤉𐤄𐤅𐤄 threw a great
confusion in the camp of the kings, so that the
fear of the children of Yisra'el fell upon them.
37 And all the hosts of the kings fled from before
the children of Yisra'el and the children of
Yisra'el pursued them continuing to strike them
even to the borders of the land of Kush. 38 And
the children of Yisra'el killed two thousand men
of them in the road, and not one of the children
of Yisra'el fell. 39 And when the Mitsrites saw
that the children of Yisra'el had fought with such
few men with the kings, and that the battle was
so very severe against them, 40 all the Mitsrites
were greatly afraid of their lives on account of
the strong battle, and all Mitsrayim fled, every
man hiding himself from the arrayed forces, and
they hid themselves in the road, and they left the
Yisra'elites to fight. 41 And the children of
Yisra'el inflicted a terrible blow upon the kings'
men, and they returned from them after they had
driven them to the border of the land of Kush.
42 And all Yisra'el knew the thing which the men
of Mitsrayim had done to them, that they had
fled from them in battle, and had left them to
fight alone.

43 So the children of Yisra'el also acted with
cunning, and as the children of Yisra'el returned
from battle, they found some of the Mitsrites in
the road and struck them there. 44 And while
they killed them, they said these words to them:

45 "Why did you go from us and leave us, being
a few people, to fight against these kings who
had a great people to strike us, that you might
deliver your own beings?"

46 And of some which the Yisra'elites met on the
road, they the children of Yisra'el spoke to each
other, saying, "Strike, strike, for he is a
Yishma'elite," or "an Edomite," or "from the
children of Kittim," and they stood over him and
killed him, and they knew that he was a Mitsrite.

47 And the children of Yisra'el did these things
cunningly against the Mitsrites, because they had
deserted them in battle and had fled from them.
48 And the children of Yisra'el killed about two
hundred men of the men of Mitsrayim in the
road in this manner. 49 And all the men of
Mitsrayim saw the evil which the children of
Yisra'el had done to them, so all Mitsrayim
feared greatly the children of Yisra'el, for they
had seen their great power, and that not one man

of them had fallen. 50 So all the children of
Yisra'el returned with joy on their road to
Goshen, and the rest of Mitsrayim returned each
man to his place.

65 1 And it happened after these things, that all
the counsellors of Pharaoh, king of Mitsrayim,
and all the elders of Mitsrayim assembled and
came before the king and bowed down to the
ground, and they sat before him. 2 And the
counsellors and elders of Mitsrayim spoke to the
king, saying,

3 "Behold the people of the children of Yisra'el
are greater and mightier than we are, and you
know all the evil which they did to us in the road
when we returned from battle. 4 And you have
seen their strong power, for this power is in them
from their fathers; for but a few men stood up
against a people numerous as the sand, and
struck them with the edge of the sword, and not
one of them has fallen, so that if they had been
numerous they would then have utterly destroyed
them. 5 Now therefore give us counsel what to
do with them, until we gradually destroy them
from among us, lest they become too numerous
for us in the land. 6 For if the children of Yisra'el
should increase in the land, they will become an
obstacle to us, and if any war should happen to
take place, they with their great strength will join
our enemy against us, and fight against us,
destroy us from the land and go away from it."

7 So the king answered the elders of Mitsrayim
and said to them, "This is the plan advised
against Yisra'el, from which we will not depart:
8 Behold in the land are Pithom and Rameses,
cities unfortified against battle. It is incumbent
upon you and us to build them, and to fortify
them. 9 Now therefore go you also and act
cunningly toward them, and proclaim a voice in
Mitsrayim and in Goshen at the command of the
king, saying,

10 'All men of Mitsrayim, Goshen, Pathros and
all their inhabitants! The king has commanded us
to build Pithom and Rameses, and to fortify them
for battle; who among you of all Mitsrayim, of
the children of Yisra'el and of all the inhabitants
of the cities, are willing to build with us, shall
each have his wages given to him daily at the
king's order;' so go first and act cunningly, and
gather yourselves and come to Pithom and
Rameses to build. 11 And while you are building,
cause a proclamation of this kind to be made
throughout Mitsrayim every day at the command
of the king. 12 And when some of the children of
Yisra'el shall come to build with you, you shall
give them their wages daily for a few days.
13 And after they have built with you for their
daily hire, drag yourselves away from them daily
one by one in secret, and then you shall rise up
and become their task-masters and officers, and
you shall leave them afterward to build without
wages, and should they refuse, then force them
with all your might to build. 14 And if you do
this it will be well with us to strengthen our land
against the children of Yisra'el, for on account of
the fatigue of the building and the work, the
children of Yisra'el will decrease, because you
will deprive them of their wives day by day."

15 And all the elders of Mitsrayim heard the
counsel of the king, and the counsel seemed
good in their eyes and in the eyes of the servants
of Pharaoh, and in the eyes of all Mitsrayim, and
they did according to the word of the king.
16 And all the servants went away from the king,
and they caused a proclamation to be made in all
Mitsrayim, in Tachpanches and in Goshen, and
in all the cities which surrounded Mitsrayim,
saying,

17 "You have seen what the children of Esaw and
Yishma'el did to us. *How they* came to war
against us and wished to destroy us. 18 Now
therefore the king commanded us to fortify the
land, to build the cities Pithom and Rameses, and
to fortify them for battle, if they should again
come against us. 19 Whosoever of you from all
Mitsrayim and from the children of Yisra'el will
come to build with us, he shall have his daily
wages given by the king, as his command is to
us."

20 And when Mitsrayim and all the children of
Yisra'el heard all that the servants of Pharaoh
had spoken, there came from the Mitsrites, and
the children of Yisra'el, to build with the servants
of Pharaoh, Pithom and Rameses, but the
children of Levi did not go with Yisra'el their
brethren. 21 And all the servants of Pharaoh and
his princes came at first with deceit to build with

all Yisra'el as daily hired laborers, and they gave to Yisra'el their daily hire at the beginning. **22** And the servants of Pharaoh built with all Yisra'el, and were employed in that work with Yisra'el for a new moon. **23** And at the end of the new moon, all the servants of Pharaoh began to withdraw secretly from the people of Yisra'el daily.

24 And Yisra'el went on with the work at that time, but they *still* received their daily hire, because some of the men of Mitsrayim were still carrying on the work with Yisra'el at that time; therefore the Mitsrites gave Yisra'el their hire in those days, in order that they, the Mitsrites their fellow-workmen, might also take the pay for their labor. **25** And at the end of days and four new moons all the Mitsrites had withdrawn from the children of Yisra'el, so that the children of Yisra'el were left alone engaged in the work.[a] **26** And after all the Mitsrites had withdrawn from the children of Yisra'el they returned and became oppressors and officers over them, and some of them stood over the children of Yisra'el as taskmasters, to receive from them all that they gave them for the pay of their labor. **27** And the Mitsrites did in this manner to the children of Yisra'el day by day, in order to afflict in their work. **28** And all the children of Yisra'el were alone engaged in the labor, and the Mitsrites refrained from giving any pay to the children of Yisra'el from that time forward.

29 And when some of the men of Yisra'el refused to work on account of the wages not being given to them, then the exactors and the servants of Pharaoh oppressed them and struck them with heavy blows, and made them return by force, to labor with their brethren; thus all the Mitsrites did to the children of Yisra'el all the days. **30** And all the children of Yisra'el were greatly afraid of the Mitsrites in this matter, and all the children of Yisra'el returned and worked alone without pay. **31** And the children of Yisra'el built Pithom and Rameses, and all the children of Yisra'el did the work, some making bricks, and some building, and the children of Yisra'el built and fortified all the land of Mitsrayim and its walls, and the children of Yisra'el were engaged in work for many years and days, until the time came when יהוה remembered them and brought them out of Mitsrayim.

32 But the children of Levi were not employed in the work with their brethren of Yisra'el, from the beginning *of their labor* to the day of their going forth from Mitsrayim. **33** For all the children of Levi knew that the Mitsrites had spoken all these words with deceit to the Yisra'elites; therefore the children of Levi refrained from approaching to the work with their brethren. **34** And the Mitsrites did not direct their attention to make the children of Levi work afterward, since they had not been with their brethren at the beginning, therefore the Mitsrites left them alone.

35 And the hands of the men of Mitsrayim were directed with continued severity against the children of Yisra'el in that work, and the Mitsrites made the children of Yisra'el work with rigor. **36** And the Mitsrites embittered the lives of the children of Yisra'el with hard work, in mortar and bricks, and also in all manner of work in the field. **37** And the children of Yisra'el called Melol[b] the king of Mitsrayim "Meror[c], king of Mitsrayim," because in his days the Mitsrites had embittered their lives with all manner of work. **38** And all the work wherein the Mitsrites made the children of Yisra'el labor, they exacted rigorously, in order to afflict the children of Yisra'el. But the more they afflicted them, the more they increased and grew, and the Mitsrites were grieved because of the children of Yisra'el.

---

[a] **65:25** The phrase "…the end of days and four new moons" is generally understood to mean "a year and four months." However, the Hebrew word for year, שנה (*sha'nah*) is not present here; rather the word is ימים (*ya'mim*) which is the plural of "day." Thus it could also be understood as meaning "four months worth of days."

[b] **65:37** Melol – The name of Pharaoh at the time. It is not entirely clear if this was his name in Hebrew or in Mitsrite (Egyptian). In Hebrew it is מלול (*me'lol*) which is most likely derived from the root מלל (*ma'lal*) which means "to say, utter, speak."

[c] **65:37** Meror – While the origin and exact definition of Pharaoh's name is debatable, the name which the children of Yisra'el gave him is clear in meaning. מרור (*me'ror*) is derived from the root מרר (*ma'rar*) which means "to be bitter."

66 1 At that time Hadad the son of Bedad king
of Edom died, and Samlah from Mesreqah, from
the country of the children of the east, reigned in
his place. 2 In the thirteenth year of the reign of
Pharaoh king of Mitsrayim, which was the
hundred and twenty-fifth year of the Yisra'elites
going down into Mitsrayim, Samlah had reigned
over Edom eighteen years. 3 And when he
reigned, he drew forth his hosts to go and fight
against Tsepho the son of Eliphaz and the
children of Kittim, because they had made war
against Angias king of Afriqah, and they
destroyed his whole army.

4 But he did not engage with him, for the
children of Esaw prevented him, saying he was
their brother. So Samlah listened to the voice of
the children of Esaw, and turned back with all
his forces to the land of Edom, and did not
proceed to fight against Tsepho the son of
Eliphaz.

5 And Pharaoh king of Mitsrayim heard this
thing, saying, "Samlah king of Edom has
resolved to fight the children of Kittim, and
afterward he will come to fight against
Mitsrayim."

6 And when the Mitsrites heard this word, they
increased the labor upon the children of Yisra'el,
lest the Yisra'elites should do to them as they did
to them in their war with the children of Esaw in
the days of Hadad.

7 So the Mitsrites said to the children of Yisra'el,
"Hurry and do your work, and finish your task,
and strengthen the land, lest the children of Esaw
your brethren should come to fight against us,
for on account of you they will come out against
us."

8 And the children of Yisra'el did the work of the
men of Mitsrayim day by day, and the Mitsrites
afflicted the children of Yisra'el in order to
reduce them in the land. 9 But as the Mitsrites
increased the labor upon the children of Yisra'el,
so did the children of Yisra'el increase and
multiply, and all Mitsrayim was filled with the
children of Yisra'el. 10 And in the hundred and
twenty-fifth year of Yisra'el's going down into
Mitsrayim, all the Mitsrites saw that their
counsel did not succeed against Yisra'el, but that
they increased and grew, and the land of
Mitsrayim and the land of Goshen were filled
with the children of Yisra'el. 11 So all the elders
of Mitsrayim and its wise men came before the
king and bowed down to him and sat before him.

12 And all the elders of Mitsrayim and the wise
men said to the king, "May the king live forever;
you counseled us against the children of Yisra'el,
and we did to them according to the word of the
king. 13 But in proportion to the increase of the
labor so do they increase and grow in the land,
and behold the whole country is filled with them.
14 Now therefore our master and king, the eyes
of all Mitsrayim are on you to give them advice
with your wisdom, by which they may prevail
over Yisra'el to destroy them, or to reduce them
from the land;" and the king answered them
saying, "Give counsel in this matter that we may
know what to do to them."

15 And a eunuch, one of the king's counsellors,
whose name was Iyyov, from Aram-Naharayim,
in the land of Uts, answered the king, saying,
16 "If it please the king, let him hear the counsel
of his servant;" and the king said to him,
"Speak."

17 And Iyyov spoke before the king, the princes,
and before all the elders of Mitsrayim, saying,
18 "Behold the counsel of the king which he
advised formerly respecting the labor of the
children of Yisra'el is very good, and you must
not remove from them that labor forever. 19 But
this is the advice counselled by which you may
reduce them, if it seems good to the king to
afflict them. 20 Behold, we have feared war for a
long time, and we said, 'When Yisra'el becomes
fruitful in the land, they will drive us from the
land if a war should take place.' 21 If it please the
king, let a word from the king go forth, and let it
be written in the decrees of Mitsrayim which
shall not be revoked, that every male child born
to the Yisra'elites, his blood shall be spilled upon
the ground. 22 And by your doing this, when all
the male children of Yisra'el shall have died, the
evil of their wars will cease. Let the king do this,
and send for all the Hebrew midwives and order
them in this matter to execute it;" so the thing
pleased the king and the princes, and the king did
according to the word of Iyyov.

23 And the king sent for the Hebrew midwives to
be called, one of which was named Shiphrah,
and the name of the other Puah. 24 And the
midwives came before the king, and stood in his
presence.

25 And the king said to them, "When you are
helping the Hebrew women to give birth and see
them upon the birthstool, if it is a son, then you
shall put him to death; but if it is a daughter, then
she shall live. 26 But if you will not do this thing,
then will I burn you up and all your houses with
fire."

27 But the midwives feared Elohim and did not
listen to the king of Mitsrayim nor to his words,
and when the Hebrew women brought forth to
the midwife son or daughter, then the midwife
did all that was necessary to the child and let him
live; thus did the midwives all the days.

28 And this word was told to the king, and he
sent and called for the midwives and he said to
them, "Why have you done this thing and have
saved the sons alive?"

29 And the midwives answered and spoke
together before the king, saying, 30 "The Hebrew
women are not as the Mitsrite women, for all the
daughters of Yisra'el are vigorous, and before the
midwife comes to them they have brought forth,
and as for us your handmaids, for many days no
Hebrew woman has brought forth upon us, for
all the Hebrew women are their own midwives,
because they are vigorous."

31 And Pharaoh heard their words and believed
them in this matter, and the midwives went away
from the king, and Elohim dealt kindly with
them, and the people multiplied and grew
exceedingly.

67 1 There was a man in the land of Mitsrayim
of the seed of Levi, whose name was Amram, the
son of Qohath, the son of Levi, the son of
Yisra'el. 2 And this man went and took a wife,
namely Yokheved the daughter of Levi his
father's sister, and she was one hundred and
twenty-six years old, and he came to her. 3 And
the woman conceived and brought forth a
daughter, and she called her name Miryam[a],
because in those days the Mitsrites had
embittered the lives of the children of Yisra'el.
4 And she conceived again and brought forth a
son and she called his name Aharon[b], for in the
days of her conception, Pharaoh began to spill
the blood of the male children of Yisra'el.

5 In those days Tsepho the son of Eliphaz, son of
Esaw, king of Kittim died, and Yaneas reigned in
his stead. 6 And the time that Tsepho reigned
over the children of Kittim was fifty years, and
he died and was buried in the city of Navna in
the land of Kittim. 7 And Yaneas, one of the
mighty men of the children of Kittim, reigned
after him and he reigned fifty years.

8 And it was after the death of the king of Kittim
that Bil'am the son of Beor fled from the land of
Kittim, and he went and came to Mitsrayim to
Pharaoh king of Mitsrayim. 9 And Pharaoh
received him with great honor, for he had heard
of his wisdom, and he gave him presents and
made him a counsellor, and magnified him.
10 And Bil'am dwelled in Mitsrayim, in honor
with all the nobles of the king, and the nobles
exalted him, because they all desired to learn his
wisdom.

11 And in the hundred and thirtieth year of
Yisra'el's going down to Mitsrayim, Pharaoh
dreamed that he was sitting upon his kingly
throne, and lifted up his eyes and saw an old man
standing before him, and there were scales in the
hands of the old man, such scales as are used by
merchants. 12 And the old man took the scales
and hung them before Pharaoh. 13 And the old

[a] **67:3** Miryam – Hebrew word (𐤌𐤓𐤉𐤌) usually understood to mean "rebellious." The word is believed to derive from 𐤌𐤓𐤄 (*ma'rah*) meaning "to be rebellious." It also shares etymological roots with the word 𐤌𐤓𐤓 (*ma'rar*) and its short form 𐤌𐤓 (*mar*) which mean "bitter." Thus there is a wordplay here between the name, Miryam, and the lives of the people being made bitter.

[b] **67:4** Aharon – Hebrew word (𐤀𐤄𐤓𐤍) of uncertain meaning. It is possibly related to the word 𐤄𐤓𐤂 (*ha'rag*) meaning "to slay" or "to kill." Thus maintaining the theme that during his days the children were killed by Pharaoh.

man took all the elders of Mitsrayim and all its nobles and great men, and he tied them together and put them in one scale. 14 And he took a milk-kid and put it into the other scale, and the kid prevailed over all. 15 And Pharaoh was astonished at this dreadful vision, why the kid should preponderate over all, and Pharaoh awoke and behold it was a dream.

16 And Pharaoh rose up early in the morning and called all his servants and related to them the dream, and the men were greatly afraid.

17 And the king said to all his wise men, "Please, Interpret the dream which I dreamed, that I may know it."

18 And Bil'am the son of Beor answered the king and said to him, "This means nothing else but a great evil that will spring up against Mitsrayim in the latter days. 19 For a son will be born to Yisra'el who will destroy all Mitsrayim and its inhabitants, and bring forth the Yisra'elites from Mitsrayim with a mighty hand. 20 Now therefore, O king, take counsel upon this matter, that you may destroy the hope of the children of Yisra'el and their expectation, before this evil arise against Mitsrayim."

21 And the king said to Bil'am, "And what shall we do to Yisra'el? Surely after a certain manner did we at first counsel against them and could not prevail over them. 22 Now therefore give your advice against them by which we may prevail over them."

23 And Bil'am answered the king, saying, "Send now and call your two counsellors, and we will see what their advice is upon this matter and afterward your servant will speak."

24 And the king sent and called his two counsellors Reuel the Midianite and Iyyov the Utsite, and they came and sat before the king.

25 And the king said to them, "Behold you have both heard the dream which I have dreamed, and the interpretation of it; now therefore give counsel and know and see what is to be done to the children of Yisra'el, and how we may prevail over them, before their evil shall spring up against us."

26 And Reuel the Midianite answered the king and said, "May the king live, may the king live forever. 27 If it seem good to the king, let him cease from *afflicting* the Hebrews and leave them, and let him not stretch forth his hand against them. 28 For these are whom 𐤉𐤄𐤅𐤄 chose in days of old, and took as the lot of His inheritance from among all the nations of the earth and the kings of the earth; and who is there that stretched his hand against them freely, of whom their Elohim was not avenged? 29 Surely you know that when Avraham went down to Mitsrayim, Pharaoh, the former king of Mitsrayim, saw Sarah his wife, and took her for a wife, because Avraham said, 'She is my sister,' for he was afraid, lest the men of Mitsrayim would kill him on account of his wife. 30 And when the king of Mitsrayim had taken Sarah then Elohim struck him and his household with heavy plagues, until he restored Sarah his wife to Avraham, then was he healed.

31 "And Avimelekh the Gerarite, king of the Philistines: Elohim punished *him* on account of Sarah wife of Abraham, in stopping up every womb from man to beast. 32 When their Elohim came to Avimelekh in the dream of night and terrified him in order that he might restore Sarah whom he had taken, to Avraham, and afterward all the people of Gerar were punished on account of Sarah, and Avraham prayed to his Elohim for them, and He was entreated by him, and He healed them. 33 And Avimelekh feared all this evil that came upon him and his people, and he returned to Avraham his wife Sarah, and gave him with her many gifts.

34 "He did so also to Yitsḥaq when he had driven him from Gerar, and Elohim had done wonderful things to him, that all the water courses of Gerar were dried up, and their productive trees did not bring forth 35 until Avimelekh of Gerar, and Achuzzath one of his friends, and Pikhol the captain of his host, went to him and they bent and bowed down before him to the ground.
36 And they asked him to petition for them, and he prayed to 𐤉𐤄𐤅𐤄 for them, and 𐤉𐤄𐤅𐤄 was entreated by him and He healed them.

37 "Ya'aqov also, the plain man, was delivered through his integrity from the hand of his brother Esaw, and the hand of Lavan the Aramean his

mother's brother, who had sought his life;
likewise from the hand of all the kings of
Kana'an who had come together against him and
his children to destroy them, and 𐤉𐤄𐤅𐤄 delivered
them out of their hands, that they turned on them
and struck them, for who had ever stretched forth
his hand against them freely?

38 "Surely Pharaoh the former, your father's
father, raised Yoseph the son of Ya'aqov above
all the princes of the land of Mitsrayim, when he
saw his wisdom, for through his wisdom he
rescued all the inhabitants of the land from the
famine. **39** After which he ordered Ya'aqov and
his children to come down to Mitsrayim, in order
that through their virtue, the land of Mitsrayim
and the land of Goshen might be delivered from
the famine. **40** Now therefore if it is good in your
eyes, cease from destroying the children of
Yisra'el; but if it is not your will that they shall
dwell in Mitsrayim, send them forth from here,
that they may go to the land of Kana'an, the land
where their ancestors sojourned."

41 And when Pharaoh heard the words of Yithro
he was very angry with him, so that he rose with
shame from the king's presence, and went to
Midian, his land, and took Yoseph's stick[a] with
him.

42 And the king said to Iyyov the Utsite, "What
do you say Iyyov, and what is your advice
concerning the Hebrews?"

43 So Iyyov said to the king, "Behold all the
inhabitants of the land are in your power: let the
king do as it seems good in his eyes."

44 And the king said to Bil'am, "What do you
say, Bil'am? Speak your word that we may hear
it."

45 And Bil'am said to the king, "Of all that the
king has counselled against the Hebrews they
will be delivered, and the king will not be able to
prevail over them with any counsel. **46** For if you
think to reduce them by the flaming fire, you
cannot prevail over them, for surely their Elohim
delivered Avraham their father from Ur of the
Kaldeans; and if you think to destroy them with
a sword, surely Yitsḥaq their father was
delivered from it, and a ram was placed in his
stead. **47** And if, with hard and rigorous labor,
you think to reduce them, you will not prevail
even in this, for their father Ya'aqov served
Lavan in all manner of hard work, and
prospered. **48** Now therefore, O king, hear my
words, for this is the counsel which is counselled
against them, by which you will prevail over
them, and from which you should not depart.
49 If it pleases the king, let him order all their
children which shall be born from this day
forward, to be thrown into the water, for by
doing this you can wipe away their name, for
none of them, nor of their fathers, were tried in
this manner."

50 And the king heard the words of Bil'am, and
the word pleased the king and the princes, and
the king did according to the word of Bil'am.

51 And the king ordered a proclamation to be
issued and a decree to be made throughout the
land of Mitsrayim, saying, "Every male child
born to the Hebrews from this day forward shall
be thrown into the water."

52 And Pharaoh called to all his servants, saying,
"Go now and seek throughout the land of Goshen
where the children of Yisra'el are, and see that
every son born to the Hebrews is cast into the
river, but every daughter you shall let live."

53 And when the children of Yisra'el heard this
thing which Pharaoh had commanded, to cast
their male children into the river, some of the
people separated from their wives and others
clung to them. **54** And from that day forward,
when the time of delivery arrived to those
women of Yisra'el who had remained with their
husbands, they went to the field to bring forth
there, and they brought forth in the field, and left
their children upon the field and returned home.
55 And 𐤉𐤄𐤅𐤄 who had sworn to their ancestors to
multiply them, sent one of His serving

---

[a] **67:41** Stick – Hebrew word 𐤌𐤈𐤄 (*ma'teh*) meaning literally "branch." Most often translated as "tribe" (such as the "tribe of Asher" or "tribe of Levi") in the sense of a branch of the whole group.

messengers which are in the heavens to wash each child in water, to anoint and swathe him and to put into his hands two smooth stones; from one of which he sucked milk and from the other honey, and He caused his hair to grow to his knees, by which he might cover itself; to comfort him and to cleave to it, through His compassion for him.

56 And when Elohim had compassion over them and had desired to multiply them upon the face of the land, He ordered His earth to receive them to be preserved there until the time of their growing up, after which the earth opened its mouth and vomited them forth and they sprouted forth from the city like the herb of the earth, and the grass of the forest, and they returned each to his family and to his father's house, and they remained with them.

57 And the infants of the children of Yisra'el
were upon the earth like the herb of the field,
through the favor of Elohim to them. 58 And
when all the Mitsrites saw this, they went forth,
each to his field with his yoke of oxen and his
ploughshare, and they ploughed it up as one
ploughs the earth at seed time. 59 And when they
ploughed they were unable to hurt the infants of
the children of Yisra'el, so the people increased
and grew exceedingly. 60 And Pharaoh ordered
his officers daily to go to Goshen to seek for the
infants of the children of Yisra'el.

61 And when they had sought and found one, they took him from his mother's bosom by force, and threw him into the river. But the female children they left with their mother; thus the Mitsrites did to the Yisra'elites all the days.

68 1 And it was at that time the Ruaḥ of Elohim was upon Miryam the daughter of Amram the sister of Aharon, and she went forth and prophesied about the house, saying, "Behold a son will be born to us from my father and mother this time, and he will save Yisra'el from the hands of Mitsrayim."

2 And when Amram heard the words of his daughter, he went and took his wife back to the house, after he had driven her away at the time when Pharaoh ordered every male child of the house of Ya'aqov to be thrown into the waters.
3 So Amram took Yokheved his wife, three years
after he had driven her away, and he came to her
and she conceived. 4 And at the end of seven
new moons from her conception she brought
forth a son, and the whole house was filled with
great light as of the light of the sun and moon at
the time of their shining.[a] 5 And when the
woman saw the child that he was good and
pleasing to the sight, she hid him for three
months in an inner room.

6 In those days the Mitsrites conspired to destroy
all the Hebrews there. 7 And the Mitsrite women
went to Goshen where the children of Yisra'el
were, and they carried their young ones on their
shoulders, their infants who could not speak yet.
8 And in those days, when the women of the
children of Yisra'el brought forth, each woman
had hidden her son from before the Mitsrites,
that the Mitsrites might not know of their
bringing forth, and might not destroy them from
the land. 9 And the Mitsrite women came to
Goshen and their children, who could not speak,
were upon their shoulders. And when a Mitsrite
woman came into the house of a Hebrew woman
her infant began to cry. 10 And when he cried the
child that was in the inner room answered it, so
the Mitsrite women went and told it at the house
of Pharaoh. 11 And Pharaoh sent his officers to
take the children and kill them; thus the Mitsrites
did to the Hebrew women all the days.

12 And it was at that time, about three new
moons from Yokheved's concealment of her son,
that the thing was known in Pharaoh's house.
13 And the woman hurried to take away her son
before the officers came. And she took an ark of
bulrushes for him, and smeared it with tar and
with pitch, and put the child in it, and she laid it
in the reeds by the river's mouth. 14 And his
sister Miryam stood afar off to know what would
be done to him, and what would become of her
words.

15 And Elohim sent forth a terrible heat in the land of Mitsrayim at that time, which burned up the flesh of man like the sun in his circuit, and it

[a] **68:3** Compare Ḥanokh **106:1-2**.

greatly oppressed the Mitsrites. 16 And all the
Mitsrites went down to bathe in the river, on
account of the consuming heat which burned up
their flesh. 17 And Batyah, the daughter of
Pharaoh, went also to bathe in the river, owing to
the consuming heat, and her maidens walked at
the river side, and all the women of Mitsrayim as
well. 18 And Batyah lifted up her eyes to the
river, and she saw the ark upon the water, and
sent her maid to fetch it. 19 And she opened it
and saw the child, and behold the infant cried.
And she had compassion on him, and she said,
"This is one of the Hebrew children."

20 And all the women of Mitsrayim walking on
the riverside desired to nurse him, but he would
not nurse, for this thing was from 𐤉𐤄𐤅𐤄, in order
to restore him to his mother's breast.

21 And Miriam his sister was at that time was
among the Mitsrite women at the riverside, and
she saw this thing and she said to Pharaoh's
daughter, "Shall I go and fetch a nurse of the
Hebrew women, that she may nurse the child for
you?"

22 And Pharaoh's daughter said to her, "Go," and
the girl went and called the child's mother.

23 And Pharaoh's daughter said to Yokheved,
"Take this child away and nurse him for me, and
I will pay you your wages: two pieces of silver
daily." And the woman took the child and nursed
him.

24 And at the end of two years, when the child
grew up, she brought him to the daughter of
Pharaoh, and he was to her as a son, and she
called his name Mosheh[a], for she said, "Because
I drew him out of the water."

25 And Amram his father called his name Ḥavar[b],
for he said it was for him that he joined with his
wife whom he had sent away.

26 And Yokheved his mother called his name
Yequtiel[c], because, she said, "I have hoped for
him to the Almighty, and Elohim restored him to
me."

27 And Miryam his sister called him Yered[d], for
she descended after him to the river to know
what his end would be.

28 And Aharon his brother called his name Avi
Zanuaḥ[e], saying, "My father rejected my mother
and returned to her on his account."

29 And Qohath, the father of Amram, called his
name Avi Gador[f], because on his account Elohim
repaired the walls of the house of Ya'aqov, that
they could no longer throw their male children
into the water.

30 And their nurse called him Avi Sovo[g], saying,
"In his tabernacle he was hidden for three
months, on account of the children of Ḥam."

31 And all Yisra'el called his name Shemayah[h],
son of Nathanel[i], for they said, "In his days

---

[a] **68:24** Mosheh – Hebrew word (𐤌𐤔𐤄) derived from another word of same spelling, different vowels, *mashah*, meaning "to draw." Mosheh means "drawing out."

[b] **68:25** Ḥavar – Hebrew word (𐤇𐤁𐤓) meaning "joined." This is in reference to Amram having become joined to Yokheved after he had previously sent her away.

[c] **68:26** Yequtiel – Hebrew word (𐤉𐤒𐤅𐤕𐤉𐤀𐤋) of disputed meaning. It could possibly be derived from 𐤕𐤒𐤅𐤄 (*tiq'vah*) meaning "hope," thus preserving the wordplay and giving it the meaning of "hope of El." However, it could also be derived from 𐤉𐤒𐤄 (*ya'qeh*) meaning "to hear" or "to obey." Thus the name Yequtiel would mean, "El has heard."

[d] **68:27** Yered – Hebrew word (𐤉𐤓𐤃) meaning "descended."

[e] **68:28** Hebrew word Avi (𐤀𐤁𐤉) means "my father" and Zanuaḥ (𐤆𐤍𐤅𐤇) means "rejected." Thus Avi Zanuaḥ means "my father rejcted."

[f] **68:29** Hebrew word Avi (𐤀𐤁𐤉) means "my father" and Gador (𐤂𐤃𐤅𐤓) means "wall." Thus Avi Gador means "my father has walled."

[g] **68:30** Hebrew word Avi (𐤀𐤁𐤉) means "my father" and Sovo (𐤎𐤅𐤁𐤅) is debated. Most likely it derives from 𐤎𐤁𐤁 (*so'vav*) meaning "surrounded," possibly in reference to the children of Ḥam. However, it is also possible that the word Sovo, spelled Samekh-Vav-Bet-Vav, is actually a misspelling of the word 𐤎𐤅𐤊𐤅 (*so'kho*), spelled Samekh-Vav-Khaf-Vav, which is related to the word 𐤎𐤅𐤊𐤄 (*su'khah*) used here for "tabernacle."

[h] **68:31** Hebrew word Shemayah is formed by the words 𐤔𐤌𐤏 (*sh'ma*) meaning "hear" and 𐤉𐤄 (*Yah*) the shortened form of the Name of Elohim. Thus the name means "Yah hears" or "Yah has heard."

[i] **68:31** Hebrew word Nathanel is formed by the words 𐤍𐤕𐤍 (*na'tan*) meaning "give" and 𐤀𐤋 (*El*). Thus the name means "El has given."

Elohim has heard their cries and rescued them from their oppressors."

32 And Mosheh was in Pharaoh's house, and was a son to Batyah, Pharaoh's daughter, and Mosheh grew up among the king's children.

69 1 And the king of Edom died in those days, in the eighteenth year of his reign, and was buried in his temple which he had built for himself as his royal residence in the land of Edom. 2 And the children of Esaw sent to Pethorah, which is upon the river, and they fetched from there a young man of beautiful eyes and handsome appearance, whose name was Sha'ul, and they made him king over them in the place of Samlah. 3 And Sha'ul reigned over all the children of Esaw in the land of Edom for forty years.

4 And Pharaoh king of Mitsrayim saw that the counsel which Bil'am had advised concerning the children of Yisra'el did not succeed, but that still they were fruitful, multiplied and increased throughout the land of Mitsrayim. 5 Then Pharaoh commanded in those days that a proclamation should be issued throughout Mitsrayim to the children of Yisra'el, saying, "No man shall reduce his daily labor in any way. 6 And the man who shall be found with reduced labor which he performs daily, whether in mortar or in bricks, then his youngest son shall be put in his place."

7 And the labor of Mitsrayim strengthened upon the children of Yisra'el in those days, and behold if one brick was reduced in any man's daily labor, the Mitsrites took his youngest boy by force from his mother, and put him into the building in the place of the brick which his father had left wanting. 8 And the men of Mitsrayim did so to all the children of Yisra'el day by day, all the days for a long period.

9 But the tribe of Levi did not at that time work with the Yisra'elites their brethren, from the beginning, for the children of Levi knew the cunning of the Mitsrites which they exercised at first toward the Yisra'elites.

70 1 And in the third year from the birth of Mosheh, Pharaoh was sitting at a banquet, with Alparanith the queen was sitting at his right and Batyah at his left, and the lad Mosheh was lying upon her bosom. And Bil'am the son of Beor with his two sons, and all the princes of the kingdom were sitting at table in the king's presence.

2 And the lad *Mosheh* stretched forth his hand upon the king's head, and took the crown from the king's head and placed it on his own head. 3 And when the king and princes saw the work which the boy had done, the king and princes were terrified, and one man to his neighbor expressed astonishment.

4 And the king said to the princes who were before him at table, "What do you speak and what do you say, princes, in this matter? And what is to be the judgment against the boy on account of this act?"

5 And Bil'am the son of Beor the magician answered before the king and princes, and he said, "Remember now, O my master and king, the dream which you dreamed many days ago, and that which your servant interpreted for you. 6 Now therefore this is a child from the Hebrew children, in whom is the Ruaḥ of Elohim; do not let my master the king imagine that this youth did this thing without knowledge. 7 For he is a Hebrew boy, and he has wisdom and understanding, even though he is still a child. And with wisdom he has done this and chosen for himself the kingdom of Mitsrayim. 8 For this is the manner of all the Hebrews: to deceive kings and their nobles, to do all these things cunningly, in order to make the kings of the earth and their men tremble.

9 "Surely you know that Avraham their father acted this way; who deceived the army of Nimrod king of Bavel, and Avimelekh king of Gerar, and that he possessed the land of the children of Ḥeth and all the kingdoms of Kana'an. 10 And that he descended into Mitsrayim and said of Sarah his wife, 'she is my sister,' in order to mislead Mitsrayim and her king.

11 "His son Yitsḥaq also did so when he went to Gerar and dwelled there, and his strength prevailed over the army of Avimelekh king of the Philistines. 12 He also thought of making the kingdom of the Philistines stumble, saying Rivqah his wife "is my sister."

13 "Ya'aqov also dealt treacherously with his brother, and took his birthright and his blessing from his hand. 14 He went then to Padan-aram to the house of Lavan his mother's brother, and cunningly obtained from him his daughters, his cattle, and all belonging to him, and fled away and returned to the land of Kana'an to his father.

15 "His sons sold their brother Yoseph, who went down into Mitsrayim and became a slave, and was placed in the prison house for twelve years. 16 Until the former Pharaoh dreamed dreams, and withdrew him from the prison house, and magnified him above all the princes in Mitsrayim on account of his interpreting his dreams to him. 17 And when Elohim caused a famine throughout the land he sent for and brought his father and all his brothers, and the whole of his father's household, and supported them without price or reward, and bought the Mitsrites for slaves.

18 "Now therefore my master and king, behold this child has risen up in their stead in Mitsrayim, to do according to their deeds and to trifle with every king, prince and judge. 19 If it pleases the king, let us now spill his blood upon the ground, lest he grow up and take away the reign from your hand, and the hope of Mitsrayim perish after he shall have reigned."

20 And the king said to Bil'am, "Let us moreover call for all the judges of Mitsrayim and the wise men, and let us know if the judgment of death is due to this boy as you said, and then we will slay him."

21 And Pharaoh sent and called for all the wise men of Mitsrayim and they came before the king, and a messenger of 𐤉𐤄𐤅𐤄 came among them, and he was like one of the wise men of Mitsrayim.

22 And the king said to the wise men, "Surely you have heard what this Hebrew boy, who is in the house, has done. And thus has Bil'am judged in the matter. 23 Now therefore you also judge and see what is due to the boy for the act he has committed."

24 And the messenger, who seemed like one of the wise men of Pharaoh, answered and said, before all the wise men of Mitsrayim and before the king and the princes:

25 "If it pleases the king, let the king send for men who shall bring before him an onyx stone and a coal of fire, and place them before the child. And if the child shall stretch forth his hand and take the onyx stone, then we will know that with wisdom has the youth done all that he has done, and we must kill him. 26 But if he stretches his hand forth upon the coal, then shall we know that it was not with knowledge that he did this thing, and he shall live."

27 And the thing seemed good in the eyes of the king and the princes, so the king did according to the word of the messenger of 𐤉𐤄𐤅𐤄. 28 And the king ordered the onyx stone and coal to be brought and placed before Mosheh.

29 And they placed the boy before them, and the boy went to stretch forth his hand to the onyx stone, but the messenger of 𐤉𐤄𐤅𐤄 took his hand and placed it upon the coal, and the coal became extinguished in his hand. And he lifted it up and put it into his mouth, and burned part of his lips and part of his tongue, and he became heavy in mouth and tongue. 30 And when the king and princes saw this, they knew that Mosheh had not acted with wisdom in taking off the crown from the king's head. 31 So the king and princes refrained from killing the child, so Mosheh remained in Pharaoh's house, growing up, and 𐤉𐤄𐤅𐤄 was with him. 32 And while the boy was in the king's house, he was clothed with purple and he grew among the children of the king. 33 And when Mosheh grew up in the king's house, Batyah the daughter of Pharaoh considered him as a son, and all the household of Pharaoh honored him, and all the men of Mitsrayim were afraid of him. 34 And he daily went forth and came into the land of Goshen, where his brethren the children of Yisra'el were, and Mosheh saw them daily in shortness of breath and hard labor.

35 And Mosheh asked them, saying, "Why is this labor handed out to you day by day?"

36 And they told him all that had happened to them, and all the injunctions which Pharaoh had put upon them before his birth. **37** And they told him all the counsels which Bil'am the son of Beor had counselled against them, and what he had also counselled against him in order to kill him when he had taken the king's crown from off his head. **38** And when Mosheh heard these things his anger was kindled against Bil'am, and he sought to kill him, and he was waiting for him day by day.

39 And Bil'am was afraid of Mosheh, and he and his two sons rose up and went forth from Mitsrayim, and they fled and delivered their beings and went to the land of Kush to Qiqanos, king of Kush. **40** And Mosheh was in the king's house going out and coming in. And 𐤉𐤄𐤅𐤄 gave him favor in the eyes of Pharaoh, and in the eyes of all his servants, and in the eyes of all the people of Mitsrayim, and they loved Mosheh exceedingly. **41** And the day arrived when Mosheh went to Goshen to see his brethren, that he saw the children of Yisra'el in their burdens and hard labor, and Mosheh was grieved on their account. **42** And Mosheh returned to Mitsrayim and came to the house of Pharaoh, and came before the king, and Mosheh bowed down before the king.

43 And Mosheh said to Pharaoh, "Please my master, I have come to seek a small request from you; do not turn away my face empty;" and Pharaoh said to him, "Speak."

44 And Mosheh said to Pharaoh, "Let there be one day of rest from their labor given to your servants, the children of Yisra'el, who are in Goshen."

45 And the king answered Mosheh and said, "Behold I have lifted up your face in this thing to grant your request."

46 And Pharaoh ordered a proclamation to be issued throughout Mitsrayim and Goshen, saying, **47** "To you, all the children of Yisra'el, thus says the king: 'for six days you shall do your work and labor, but on the seventh day you shall rest, and shall not do any work. Thus you shall do all the days, as the king and Mosheh the son of Batyah have commanded.'"

48 And Mosheh rejoiced at this thing which the king had granted to him, and all the children of Yisra'el did as Mosheh ordered them. **49** For this thing was from 𐤉𐤄𐤅𐤄 to the children of Yisra'el, for 𐤉𐤄𐤅𐤄 had begun to remember the children of Yisra'el to save them for the sake of their fathers. **50** And 𐤉𐤄𐤅𐤄 was with Mosheh and his fame went throughout Mitsrayim. **51** And Mosheh became great in the eyes of all the Mitsrites, and in the eyes of all the children of Yisra'el, seeking good for his people Yisra'el and speaking words of peace regarding them to the king.

71

1 And when Mosheh was eighteen years old, he desired to see his father and mother and he went to them to Goshen, and when Mosheh had come near Goshen, he came to the place where the children of Yisra'el were engaged in work, and he observed their burdens, and he saw a Mitsrite striking one of his Hebrew brethren. **2** And when the man who was struck saw Mosheh, he ran to him for help, for the man Mosheh was greatly respected in the house of Pharaoh. And he said to him, "My master attend to me, this Mitsrite came to my house in the night, bound me, and came in to my wife in my presence, and now he seeks to take my life away."

3 And when Mosheh heard this wicked thing, his anger was kindled against the Mitsrite, and he turned this way and the other, and when he saw there was no man there he struck the Mitsrite and hid him in the sand, and delivered the Hebrew from the hand of him that struck him. **4** And the Hebrew went to his house, and Mosheh returned to his home, and went forth and came back to the king's house. **5** And when the man had returned home, he thought of divorcing his wife, for it was not right in the house of Ya'aqov, for any man to come in to his wife after she had been defiled. **6** And the woman went and told her brothers, and the woman's brothers sought to kill him, and he fled to his house and escaped.

7 And on the second day Mosheh went forth to his brethren, and saw, and behold two men were quarreling, and he said to the wicked one, "Why do you strike your neighbor?"

8 And he answered and said to him, "Who has set you as prince and judge over us? Do you think to kill me as you killed the Mitsrite?" and Mosheh was afraid and he said, "Surely the thing is known."

9 And Pharaoh heard of this affair, and he ordered Mosheh to be killed, so Elohim sent His messenger, and he appeared to Pharaoh in the likeness of a captain of the guard. 10 And the messenger of 𐤉𐤄𐤅𐤄 took the sword from the hand of the captain of the guard, and took his head off with it, for the likeness of the captain of the guard was turned into the likeness of Mosheh. 11 And the messenger of 𐤉𐤄𐤅𐤄 took hold of the right hand of Mosheh, and brought him forth from Mitsrayim, and placed him from outside the borders of Mitsrayim, a distance of forty days' journey.

12 And Aharon his brother alone remained in the land of Mitsrayim, and he prophesied to the children of Yisra'el, saying, 13 "Thus says 𐤉𐤄𐤅𐤄 Elohim of your ancestors: 'Throw away, each man, the abominations of his eyes, and do not defile yourselves with the idols of Mitsrayim.'"

14 And the children of Yisra'el rebelled and would not listen to Aharon at that time. 15 And 𐤉𐤄𐤅𐤄 thought to destroy them, were it not that 𐤉𐤄𐤅𐤄 remembered the covenant which He cut with Avraham, Yitsḥaq, and Ya'aqov.

16 In those days the hand of Pharaoh continued to be severe against the children of Yisra'el, and he crushed and oppressed them until the time when Elohim sent forth His word and took notice of them.

72 1 And it was in those days that there was a great war between the children of Kush and the children of the east and Aram, and they rebelled against the king of Kush in whose hands they were. 2 So Qiqanos king of Kush went forth with all the children of Kush, a people numerous as the sand, and he went to fight against Aram and the children of the east, to bring them under subjection. 3 And when Qiqanos went out, he left Bil'am the magician, with his two sons, to guard the city, and the lowest sort of the people of the land.

4 So Qiqanos went forth to Aram and the children of the east, and he fought against them and struck them, and they all fell down wounded before Qiqanos and his people. 5 And he took many of them captives and he brought them under subjection as at first, and he encamped upon their land to take tribute from them as usual.

6 And Bil'am the son of Beor, when the king of Kush had left him to guard the city and the poor of the city, he rose up and advised with the people of the land to rebel against king Qiqanos, not to let him enter the city when he should come home. 7 And the people of the land listened to him, and they swore to him and made him king over them, and his two sons for captains of the army. 8 So they rose up and raised the walls of the city at the two corners, and they built an exceeding strong building. 9 And at the third corner they dug ditches without number, between the city and the river which surrounded the whole land of Kush, and they made the waters of the river burst forth there. 10 At the fourth corner they collected numerous naḥashim by their incantations and enchantments, and they fortified the city and dwelled in it, and no one went out or in before them.

11 And Qiqanos fought against Aram and the children of the east and he subdued them as before, and they gave him their usual tribute, and he went and returned to his land. 12 And when Qiqanos the king of Kush approached his city and all the captains of the forces with him, they lifted up their eyes and saw that the walls of the city were built up and greatly elevated, so the men were astonished at this.

13 And they said one to the other, "It is because they saw that we were delayed in battle, and were greatly afraid of us, therefore they have done this thing and raised the city walls and fortified them so that the kings of Kana'an might not come in battle against them."

14 So the king and the troops approached the city door and they looked up and behold, all the gates of the city were closed, and they called out to the sentinels, saying, "Open to us, that we may enter the city."

15 But the sentinels refused to open to them by
the order of Bil'am the magician, their king; they
did not allow them to enter their city. **16** So they
raised a battle with them opposite the city gate,
and one hundred and thirty men of the army at
Qiqanos fell on that day. **17** And on the next day
they continued to fight and they fought at the
side of the river; they endeavored to pass but
were not able, so some of them sank in the pits
and died. **18** So the king ordered them to cut
down trees to make rafts, upon which they might
pass to them, and they did so.

19 And when they came to the place of the
ditches, the waters revolved by mills, and two
hundred men upon ten rafts were drowned.
20 And on the third day they came to fight at the
side where the naḥashim were, but they could not
approach there, for the naḥashim killed one
hundred and seventy men of them. And they
ceased fighting against Kush, and they besieged
Kush for nine years, *and* no person came out or
in.

21 At that time that the war and the siege were
against Kush, Mosheh fled from Mitsrayim from
Pharaoh who sought to kill him for having killed
the Mitsrite. **22** And Mosheh was eighteen years
old when he fled from Mitsrayim from the
presence of Pharaoh, and he fled and escaped to
the camp of Qiqanos, which at that time was
besieging Kush. **23** And Mosheh was in the camp
of Qiqanos king of Kush nine years. All the time
that they were laying siege to Kush, Mosheh
went out and came in with them. **24** And the king
and princes and all the fighting men loved
Mosheh, for he was great and worthy; his stature
was like a noble lion, his face was like the sun,
and his strength was like that of a lion, and he
was counsellor to the king.

25 And at the end of nine years, Qiqanos was
seized with a mortal disease, and his illness
prevailed over him, and he died on the seventh
day. **26** So his servants embalmed him and
carried him and buried him opposite the city gate
to the north of the land of Mitsrayim. **27** And
they built over him an elegant, strong, and high
building, and they placed great stones below.
28 And the king's scribes engraved upon those
stones all the might of their king Qiqanos, and all
his battles which he had fought, behold they are
written there to this day.

29 Now after the death of Qiqanos king of Kush,
his men and troops grieved greatly on account of
the war.

30 So they said one to the other, "Give us counsel
what we are to do at this time, as we have
resided in the wilderness nine years away from
our homes. **31** If we say we will fight against the
city many of us will fall wounded or killed, and
if we remain here in the siege we will also die.
32 For now all the kings of Aram and of the
children of the east will hear that our king is
dead, and they will attack us suddenly in a
hostile manner, and they will fight against us and
leave no remnant of us. **33** Now therefore let us
go and make a king over us, and let us remain in
the siege until the city is delivered up to us."

34 And they wished to choose on that day a man
for king from the army of Qiqanos, and they
found no object of their choice like Mosheh to
reign over them. **35** And they hurried and
stripped off each man his garments and cast them
upon the ground, and they made a great heap and
placed Mosheh on it.

36 And they rose up and blew with shofars and
called out before him, and said, "May the king
live, may the king live!"

37 And all the people and nobles swore to him to
give him for a wife Adoniyah the queen, the
Kushite, wife of Qiqanos, and they made
Mosheh king over them on that day.

38 And all the people of Kush issued a
proclamation on that day, saying, "Every man
must give something to Mosheh of what is in his
possession."

39 And they spread out a sheet upon the heap,
and every man cast something of what he had
into it: one a gold earring and the other a coin.
40 Also of onyx stones, bdellium, pearls and
marble did the children of Kush cast to Mosheh
upon the heap; also silver and gold in great
abundance. **41** And Mosheh took all the silver
and gold, all the vessels, and the bdellium and
onyx stones, which all the children of Kush had
given to him, and he placed them among his

treasures. 42 And Mosheh reigned over the
children of Kush on that day, in the place of
Qiqanos king of Kush.

73 1 In the fifty-fifth year of the reign of
Pharaoh king of Mitsrayim, that is in the hundred
and fifty-seventh year of the Yisra'elites going
down into Mitsrayim, Mosheh reigned in Kush.
2 Mosheh was twenty-seven years old when he
began to reign over Kush, and he reigned forty
years. 3 And 𐤉𐤄𐤅𐤄 granted Mosheh favor and
kindness in the eyes of all the children of Kush,
and the children of Kush loved him exceedingly,
so Mosheh was favored by 𐤉𐤄𐤅𐤄 and by men.
4 And in the seventh day of his reign, all the
children of Kush assembled and came before
Mosheh and bowed down to him to the ground.

5 And all the children spoke together in the
presence of the king, saying, "Give us counsel
that we may see what is to be done to this city.
6 For it is now nine years that we have laying
siege to the city, and have not seen our children
and our wives."

7 So the king answered them, saying, "If you will
listen to my voice in all that I command you,
then 𐤉𐤄𐤅𐤄 will give the city into our hands and
we shall subdue it. 8 For if we fight with them as
in the former battle which we had with them
before the death of Qiqanos, many of us will fall
wounded as before. 9 Now therefore behold here
is counsel for you in this matter, if you will listen
to my voice; then will the city be delivered into
our hands."

10 So all the forces answered the king, saying,
"All that our master shall command, that will we
do."

11 And Mosheh said to them, "Pass through and
proclaim a voice in the whole camp to all the
people, saying, 12 'Thus says the king, "Go into
the forest and bring with you of the young ones
of the stork, each man a young one in his hand.
13 And any person transgressing the word of the
king, who shall not bring his young one, he shall
die, and the king will take all belonging to him."'
14 And when you bring them you will guard
them; you will raise them until they grow up, and
you shall teach them to dart upon, as is the way
of the young ones of the hawk."

15 So all the children of Kush heard the words of
Mosheh, and they rose up and caused a
proclamation to be issued throughout the camp,
saying, 16 "To you, all the children of Kush, the
king's order is that you go all together to the
forest, and catch there the young storks each man
his young one in his hand, and you shall bring
them home. 17 And any person transgressing the
order of the king shall die, and the king will take
all that belongs to him."

18 And all the people did so, and they went out to
the wood and they climbed the fir trees and
caught, each man a young one in his hand, all the
young of the storks, and they brought them into
the wilderness and raised them by order of the
king, and they taught them to dart upon, similar
to the young hawks. 19 And after the young
storks were raised, the king ordered them to be
starved for three days, and all the people did so.

20 And on the third day, the king said to them,
"Strengthen yourselves and become valiant men,
and put on, each man, his armor and put his
sword upon him, and each man ride his horse
and take his young stork in his hand. 21 And we
will rise up and fight against the city at the place
where the naḥashim are;" and all the people did
as the king had ordered.

22 And they took each man his young one in his
hand, and they went away, and when they came
to the place of the naḥashim the king said to
them,
"Send forth each man his young stork upon the
naḥashim."

23 And they sent forth each man his young stork
at the king's order, and the young storks ran upon
the naḥashim and they devoured them all and
destroyed them out of that place. 24 And when
the king and people had seen that all the
naḥashim were destroyed in that place, all the
people set up a great shout. 25 And they
approached and fought against the city and took
it and subdued it, and they entered the city.
26 And there one thousand and one hundred men
of the people of the city died that day, of all that

inhabited the city; but of the people laying siege,
not one died.

27 So all the children of Kush went each to his
home, to his wife and children and to all
belonging to him.

28 And Bil'am the magician, when he saw that
the city was taken, he opened the gate and he and
his two sons and eight brothers fled and returned
to Mitsrayim to Pharaoh king of Mitsrayim.
29 They are the sorcerers and magicians who are
mentioned in the book of the Torah, opposing
Mosheh when 𐤉𐤄𐤅𐤄 brought the plagues upon
Mitsrayim.[a]

30 So Mosheh took the city by his wisdom, and
the children of Kush placed him on the throne
instead of Qiqanos king of Kush. 31 And they
placed the royal crown upon his head, and they
gave him for a wife Adoniyah the Kushite queen,
wife of Qiqanos. 32 And Mosheh feared 𐤉𐤄𐤅𐤄
Elohim of his fathers, so that he did not come to
her, nor did he turn his eyes to her.

33 For Mosheh remembered how Avraham had
made his servant Eliezer swear, saying to him,
"You shall not take a wife for my son Yitsḥaq
from among the daughters of Kana'an."

34 Also what Yitsḥaq did when Ya'aqov had fled
from his brother, when he commanded him,
saying, "You shall not take a wife from the
daughters of Kana'an, nor make alliance with any
of the children of Ḥam. 35 For 𐤉𐤄𐤅𐤄 our Elohim
gave Ḥam the son of Noaḥ, and his children and
all his seed, as slaves to the children of Shem
and to the children of Yepheth, and to their seed
after them for slaves, forever."

36 Therefore Mosheh did not turn his heart nor
his eyes to the wife of Qiqanos all the days that
he reigned over Kush. 37 And Mosheh feared
𐤉𐤄𐤅𐤄 his Elohim all his life, and Mosheh walked
before 𐤉𐤄𐤅𐤄 in truth, with all his heart and being;
he did not turn from the right way all the days of
his life. He did not decline from the way, either
to the right or to the left, in which Avraham,
Yitsḥaq, and Ya'aqov had walked. 38 And
Mosheh strengthened himself in the kingdom of
the children of Kush, and he guided the children
of Kush with his usual wisdom, and Mosheh
prospered in his kingdom.

39 And at that time Aram and the children of the
east heard that Qiqanos king of Kush had died,
so Aram and the children of the east rebelled
against Kush in those days. 40 And Mosheh
gathered all the children of Kush, a very mighty
people, about thirty thousand men, and he went
forth to fight with Aram and the children of the
east. 41 And they went at first to the children of
the east, and when the children of the east heard
their report, they went to meet them, and
engaged in battle with them. 42 And the war was
severe against the children of the east, so 𐤉𐤄𐤅𐤄
gave all the children of the east into the hand of
Mosheh, and about three hundred men fell down
killed.

43 And all the children of the east turned back
and retreated, so Mosheh and the children of
Kush followed them and subdued them, and put
a tax upon them, as was their custom. 44 So
Mosheh and all the people with him passed from
there to the land of Aram for battle. 45 And the
people of Aram also went to meet them, and they
fought against them, and 𐤉𐤄𐤅𐤄 delivered them
into the hand of Mosheh, and many of the men
of Aram fell down wounded. 46 And Aram also
were subdued by Mosheh and the people of
Kush, and also gave their usual tax.

47 And Mosheh brought Aram and the children
of the east under subjection to the children of
Kush, and Mosheh and all the people who were
with him, turned to the land of Kush. 48 And
Mosheh strengthened himself in the kingdom of
the children of Kush, and 𐤉𐤄𐤅𐤄 was with him,
and all the children of Kush were afraid of him.

74

1 After *some* years Sha'ul king of Edom died,
and Ba'al Ḥanan the son of Akhvor reigned in his
place. 2 In the sixteenth year of the reign of
Mosheh over Kush, Ba'al Ḥanan the son of
Akhvor reigned in the land of Edom over all the
children of Edom for thirty-eight years. 3 In his
days Moav rebelled against the power of Edom,

---

[a] **73**:**29** See also Timotheos B [**2** Timothy] **3**:**8**.
Compare also Yashar **79**:**27**.

having been under Edom since the days of
Hadad the son of Bedad, who struck them and
Midian, and brought Moav under subjection to
Edom. **4** And when Ba'al Ḥanan the son of
Akhvor reigned over Edom, all the children of
Moav withdrew their allegiance from Edom.

5 And Angias king of Afriqah died in those days,
and Azadruval his son reigned in his stead.

6 And in those days died Yaniosh king of the
children of Kittim, and they buried him in his
temple which he had built for himself in the
plain of Kanopia for a residence, and Latiynos
reigned in his stead. **7** In the twenty-second year
of the reign of Mosheh over the children of
Kush, Latiynos reigned over the children of
Kittim forty-five years. **8** And he also built for
himself a great and mighty tower, and he built an
elegant temple in it for his residence, to conduct
his government, as was the custom. **9** In the third
year of his reign he caused a proclamation to be
made to all his skilful men, who made many
ships for him. **10** And Latiynos assembled all his
forces, and they came in ships, and went therein
to fight with Azadruval son of Angias king of
Afriqah, and they came to Afriqah and engaged
in battle with Azadruval and his army. **11** And
Latiynos prevailed over Azadruval, and Latiynos
took the aqueduct from Azadruval which his
father had brought from the children of Kittim,
when he took Yania the daughter of Utsu for a
wife, so Latiynos overthrew the bridge of the
aqueduct, and struck the whole army of
Azadruval a severe blow.

12 And the remaining strong men of Azadruval
strengthened themselves, and their hearts were
filled with envy, and they courted death, and
again engaged in battle with Latiynos king of
Kittim. **13** And the battle was severe upon all the
men of Afriqah, and they all fell wounded before
Latiynos and his people, and Azadruval the king
also fell in that battle. **14** And the king Azadruval
had a very beautiful daughter, whose name was
Ushpezinah, and all the men of Afriqah
embroidered her likeness on their garments, on
account of her great beauty and comely
appearance. **15** And the men of Latiynos saw
Ushpezinah, the daughter of Azadruval, and
praised her to Latiynos their king. **16** And
Latiynos ordered *for* her to be brought to him,
and Latiynos took Ushpezinah for a wife, and he
turned back on his way to Kittim.

17 And it was after the death of Azadruval son of
Angias, when Latiynos had turned back to his
land from the battle, that all the inhabitants of
Afriqah rose up and took Anival the son of
Angias, the younger brother of Azadruval, and
made him king instead at his brother over the
whole land at Afriqah. **18** And when he reigned,
he resolved to go to Kittim to fight with the
children of Kittim, to avenge the cause of
Azadruval his brother, and the cause of the
inhabitants of Afriqah, and he did so. **19** And he
made many ships, and he came in them with his
whole army, and he went to Kittim. **20** So Anival
fought with the children of Kittim, and the
children of Kittim fell wounded before Anival
and his army, and Anival avenged his brother's
cause.

21 And Anival continued the war for eighteen
years with the children of Kittim, and Anival
dwelled in the land of Kittim and encamped
there for a long time. **22** And Anival struck the
children of Kittim very severely, and he killed
their great men and princes, and of the rest of the
people he struck about eighty thousand men.
23 And after days and many years, Anival
returned to his land of Afriqah, and he reigned
securely in the place of Azadruval his brother.

75

1 It happened, in the hundred and eightieth
year of the Yisra'elites going down into
Mitsrayim, there went forth from Mitsrayim
valiant men, thirty thousand on foot, from the
children of Yisra'el, who were all of the tribe of
Yoseph, of the children of Ephrayim the son of
Yoseph. **2** For they said the period was
completed which 𐤉𐤄𐤅𐤄 had appointed to the
children of Yisra'el in the times of old, which He
had spoken to Avraham.

3 And these men girded themselves, and they put
each man his sword at his side, and every man
his armor upon him, and they trusted in their
strength, and they went out together from
Mitsrayim with a mighty hand. **4** But they
brought no provision for the road, only silver and
gold; not even bread for that day did they bring
in their hands, for they thought of getting their

provision for pay from the Philistines, and if not they would take it by force. 5 And these men were very mighty and valiant men; one man could pursue a thousand and two could route ten thousand. So they trusted to their strength and went together as they were. 6 And they directed their course toward the land of Gath, and they went down and found the shepherds of Gath feeding the cattle of the children of Gath.

7 And they said to the shepherds, "Give us some of the sheep for pay, that we may eat, for we are hungry, for we have eaten no bread this day."

8 And the shepherds said, "Are they our sheep or cattle that we should give them to you even for pay?" so the children of Ephrayim approached to take them by force.

9 And the shepherds of Gath shouted over them that their cry was heard at a distance, so all the children of Gath went out to them. 10 And when the children of Gath saw the evil doings of the children of Ephrayim, they returned and assembled the men of Gath, and they put on each man his armor, and came forth to the children of Ephrayim for battle. 11 And they engaged with them in the valley of Gath, and the battle was severe, and they struck from each other a great many on that day.

12 And on the second day the children of Gath sent to all the cities of the Philistines that they should come help them, saying, 13 "Come up to us and help us, that we may strike the children of Ephrayim who have come forth from Mitsrayim to take our cattle, and to fight against us without cause."

14 Now the beings of the children of Ephrayim were exhausted with hunger and thirst, for they had eaten no bread for three days. And forty thousand men went forth from the cities of the Philistines to the assistance of the men of Gath. 15 And these men were engaged in battle with the children of Ephrayim, and 𐤉𐤄𐤅𐤄 delivered the children of Ephrayim into the hands of the Philistines. 16 And they struck all the children of Ephrayim, all who had gone forth from Mitsrayim, none were remaining but ten men who had run away from the engagement.

17 For this evil was from 𐤉𐤄𐤅𐤄 against the children of Ephrayim, for they transgressed the word of 𐤉𐤄𐤅𐤄 in going forth from Mitsrayim, before the period had arrived which 𐤉𐤄𐤅𐤄, in the days of old, had appointed to Yisra'el. 18 And of the Philistines also there fell a great many, about twenty thousand men, and their brethren carried them and buried them in their cities. 19 And the killed of the children of Ephrayim remained forsaken in the valley of Gath for many days and years, and were not brought to burial, and the valley was filled with men's bones.

20 And the men who had escaped from the battle came to Mitsrayim, and told all the children of Yisra'el all that had befallen them. 21 And their father Ephrayim mourned over them for many days, and his brethren came to console him. 22 And he came to his wife and she bore a son, and he called his name Beriah[a], for it was evil in his house.

76 1 And Mosheh the son of Amram was still king in the land of Kush in those days, and he prospered in his kingdom, and he conducted the government of the children of Kush in justice, in righteousness, and integrity. 2 And all the children of Kush loved Mosheh all the days that he reigned over them, and all the inhabitants of the land of Kush were greatly afraid of him. 3 And in the fortieth year of the reign of Mosheh over Kush, Mosheh was sitting on the royal throne while Adoniyah the queen was before him, and all the nobles were sitting around him.

4 And Adoniyah the queen said before the king and the princes, "What is this thing which you, the children of Kush, have done for this long time? 5 Surely you know that for forty years that this man has reigned over Kush he has not approached me, nor has he served the elohim of the children of Kush. 6 Now therefore hear, O children of Kush, and do not let this man reign over you anymore, as he is not of our flesh. 7 Behold Menakhros my son is grown up, let him

---

[a] **75:22** Beriah – Hebrew word (𐤁𐤓𐤉𐤏𐤄) derived from 𐤓𐤏 (*rah*) meaning "evil."

reign over you, for it is better for you to serve the
son of your master, than to serve a foreigner, a
slave of the king of Mitsrayim."

8 And all the people and nobles of the children
of Kush heard the words which Adoniyah the
queen had spoken in their ears. **9** And all the
people were preparing until the evening, and in
the morning they rose up early and made
Menakhros, son of Qiqanos, king over them.
10 And all the children of Kush were afraid to
stretch forth their hand against Mosheh, for 𐤉𐤄𐤅𐤄
was with Mosheh, and the children of Kush
remembered the oath which they swore to
Mosheh, therefore they did no harm to him.
11 But the children of Kush gave many presents
to Mosheh, and sent him from them with great
honor.

12 So Mosheh went forth from the land of Kush,
and went home and ceased to reign over Kush,
and Mosheh was sixty-six years old when he
went out of the land of Kush, for the thing was
from 𐤉𐤄𐤅𐤄, for the period had arrived which he
had appointed in the days of old, to bring forth
Yisra'el from the affliction of the children of
Ḥam.

13 So Mosheh went to Midian, for he was afraid
to return to Mitsrayim on account of Pharaoh,
and he went and sat at a well of water in Midian.
14 And the seven daughters of Reuel the
Midianite went out to feed their father's flock.
15 And they came to the well and drew water to
water their father's flock. **16** So the shepherds of
Midian came and drove them away, and Mosheh
rose up and helped them and watered the flock.
17 And they came home to their father Reuel, and
told him what Mosheh did for them.

18 And they said, "A Mitsrite man has delivered
us from the hands of the shepherds, he drew up
water for us and watered the flock."

19 And Reuel said to his daughters, "And where
is he? Why have you left the man?"

20 And Reuel sent for him and fetched him and
brought him home, and he ate bread with him.
21 And Mosheh related to Reuel that he had fled
from Mitsrayim and that he reigned forty years
over Kush, and that they afterward had taken the
government from him, and had sent him away in
peace with honor and with presents.

22 And when Reuel had heard the words of
Mosheh, Reuel said within himself, "I will put
this man into the prison house, so as to appease
the children of Kush, for he has fled from them."

23 And they took and put him into the prison
house, and Mosheh was in prison ten years. And
while Mosheh was in the prison house,
Tsipporah the daughter of Reuel took pity on
him, and supported him with bread and water all
the days.

24 And all the children of Yisra'el were yet in the
land of Mitsrayim serving the Mitsrites in all
manner of hard work, and the hand of Mitsrayim
continued in severity over the children of
Yisra'el in those days. **25** At that time 𐤉𐤄𐤅𐤄
struck Pharaoh king of Mitsrayim, and He
afflicted *him* with the plague of leprosy from the
sole of his foot to the crown of his head. Because
of the cruel treatment of the children of Yisra'el,
this plague was, at that time, from 𐤉𐤄𐤅𐤄 upon
Pharaoh king of Mitsrayim. **26** For 𐤉𐤄𐤅𐤄 had
listened to the prayer of His people the children
of Yisra'el, and their cry reached Him on account
of their hard labor.

27 Still his anger did not turn from them, and the
hand of Pharaoh was still stretched out against
the children of Yisra'el, and Pharaoh hardened
his neck before 𐤉𐤄𐤅𐤄, and he increased his yoke
over the children of Yisra'el, and embittered their
lives with all manner of hard work. **28** And when
𐤉𐤄𐤅𐤄 had inflicted the plague upon Pharaoh king
of Mitsrayim, he asked his wise men and
sorcerers to cure him.

29 And his wise men and sorcerers said to him
that if the blood of little children were put into
the wounds he would be healed. **30** And Pharaoh
listened to them, and sent his ministers to
Goshen to the children of Yisra'el to take their
little children. **31** And Pharaoh's ministers went
and took the infants of the children of Yisra'el
from the bosoms of their mothers by force, and
they brought them to Pharaoh daily, a child each
day, and the physicians killed them and applied
them to the plague; thus did they all the days.

32 And the number of the children which
Pharaoh killed was three hundred and seventy-
five. 33 But 𐤉𐤄𐤅𐤄 did not listen to the physicians
of the king of Mitsrayim, and the plague went on
increasing mightily. 34 And Pharaoh was
afflicted ten years with that plague, *and yet* still
the heart of Pharaoh was more strengthened
against the children of Yisra'el. 35 And at the end
of ten years 𐤉𐤄𐤅𐤄 continued to afflict Pharaoh
with destructive plagues.

36 And 𐤉𐤄𐤅𐤄 struck him with a bad tumor and
sickness at the stomach, and that plague turned
to a severe boil.

37 At that time the two attendants of Pharaoh
came from the land of Goshen where all the
children of Yisra'el were, and went to the house
of Pharaoh and said to him, "We have seen the
children of Yisra'el slacken in their work and
negligent in their labor."

38 And when Pharaoh heard the words of his
attendants, his anger was kindled against the
children of Yisra'el exceedingly, for he was
greatly grieved at his bodily pain.

39 And he answered and said, "Now that the
children of Yisra'el know that I am ill, they turn
and scoff at us. Therefore harness my chariot for
me, and I myself will go to Goshen and will see
the scoff of the children of Yisra'el with which
they are deriding me;" so his servants harnessed
the chariot for him.

40 And they took and made him ride upon a
horse, for he was not able to ride of himself.
41 And he took with him ten horsemen and ten
footmen, and went to the children of Yisra'el to
Goshen. 42 And when they had come to the
border of Mitsrayim, the king's horse passed into
a narrow place, elevated in the hollow part of the
vineyard, fenced on both sides, the low, plain
country being on the other side. 43 And the
horses ran rapidly in that place and pressed each
other, and the other horses pressed the king's
horse. 44 And the king's horse fell into the low
plain while the king was riding upon it, and
when he fell the chariot turned over the king's
face and the horse lay upon the king, and the
king cried out, for his flesh was very sore.
45 And the flesh of the king was torn from him,
and his bones were broken and he could not ride,
for this thing was from 𐤉𐤄𐤅𐤄 to him, for 𐤉𐤄𐤅𐤄
had heard the cries of His people the children of
Yisra'el and their affliction.

46 And his servants carried him upon their
shoulders lightly, and they brought him back to
Mitsrayim, and the horsemen who were with him
came also back to Mitsrayim. 47 And they placed
him in his bed, and the king knew that his end
was come to die, so Aparanith the queen his wife
came and cried before the king, and the king
wept a great weeping with her. 48 And all his
nobles and servants came on that day and saw
the king in that affliction, and wept a great
weeping with him. 49 And the princes of the king
and all his counselors advised the king to cause
one to reign in his stead in the land, whomsoever
he should choose from his sons.

50 And the king had three sons and two daughters
which Aparanith the queen his wife had borne to
him, besides the king's children of concubines.
51 And these were their names: the firstborn
Othri, the second Adiqam, and the third Moryon,
and their sisters, the name of the elder Batyah
and of the other Akhuzit.

52 And Othri the firstborn of the king was a fool,
impulsive and hurried in his words.

53 But Adiqam was a cunning and wise man and
knowing in all the wisdom of Mitsrayim, but of
unseemly appearance, thick in flesh, and very
short in stature; his height was one cubit. 54 And
when the king saw Adiqam his son intelligent
and wise in all things, the king resolved that he
should be king in his stead after his death. 55 And
he took for him a wife Gedidah daughter of
Avilot, and he was ten years old, and she bore
him four sons.

56 And he afterward went and took three wives
and brought forth eight sons and three daughters.
57 And the disorder greatly prevailed over the
king, and his flesh stank like the flesh of a
carcass cast upon the field in summer time,
during the heat of the sun. 58 And when the king
saw that his sickness had greatly strengthened
itself over him, he ordered his son Adiqam to be
brought to him, and they made him king over the
land in his place.

59 And at the end of three years, the king died, in
shame, disgrace, and disgust, and his servants
carried him and buried him in the tomb of the
kings of Mitsrayim in Tsoan Mitsrayim.

60 But they did not embalm as usual with kings,
for his flesh was putrid, and they could not
approach to embalm him on account of the
stench, so they buried him quickly. 61 For this
evil was from 𐤉𐤄𐤅𐤄 to him, for 𐤉𐤄𐤅𐤄 had repaid
him evil for the evil which in his days he had
done to Yisra'el. 62 And he died with terror and
with shame, and his son Adiqam reigned in his
place.

77 1 Adiqam was twenty years old when he
reigned over Mitsrayim, he reigned four years.
2 In the two hundred and sixth year of Yisra'el's
going down to Mitsrayim Adiqam reigned over
Mitsrayim, but he did not continue long in his
reign over Mitsrayim as his fathers had
continued their reigns. 3 For Melol his father
reigned ninety-four years in Mitsrayim, but he
was ten years sick and died, for he had been very
wicked before 𐤉𐤄𐤅𐤄.

4 And all the Mitsrites called the name of
Adiqam Pharaoh like the name of his fathers, as
was their custom to do in Mitsrayim. 5 And all
the wise men of Pharaoh called the name of
Adiqam, Akhuz, for Akhuz means 'short' in the
Mitsrite tongue.

6 And Adiqam was evil in appearance, and he
was a cubit and a span and he had a great beard
which reached to the soles of his feet. 7 And
Pharaoh sat upon his father's throne to reign over
Mitsrayim, and he conducted the government of
Mitsrayim in his wisdom. 8 And while he
reigned, he exceeded his father and all the
preceding kings in wickedness, and he increased
his yoke over the children of Yisra'el. 9 And he
went with his servants to Goshen to the children
of Yisra'el, and he strengthened the labor over
them and he said to them, "Complete your work,
each day's task, and do not let your hands slack
from our work from this day forward as you did
in the days of my father."

10 And he placed officers over them from among
the children of Yisra'el, and over these officers
he placed taskmasters from among his servants.
11 And he placed over them a measure of bricks
for them to do according to that number, day by
day, and he turned back and went to Mitsrayim.

12 At that time the taskmasters of Pharaoh
ordered the officers of the children of Yisra'el
according to the command of Pharaoh, saying,
13 "Thus says Pharaoh, 'Do your work each day,
and finish your task, and observe the daily
measure of bricks; do not diminish anything.
14 And it shall come to pass that if you are
deficient in your daily bricks, I will put your
young children in your stead.'"

15 And the taskmasters of Mitsrayim did so in
those days as Pharaoh had ordered them. 16 And
whenever any deficiency was found in the
children of Yisra'el's measure of their daily
bricks, the taskmasters of Pharaoh would go to
the wives of the children of Yisra'el and take
infants of the children of Yisra'el to the number
of bricks deficient, they would take them by
force from their mother's laps, and put them in
the building instead of the bricks, 17 while their
fathers and mothers were crying over them and
weeping when they heard the weeping voices of
their infants in the wall of the building.

18 And the taskmasters prevailed over Yisra'el,
that the Yisra'elites should place their children in
the building, so that a man placed his son in the
wall and put mortar over him, while his eyes
wept over him, and his tears ran down upon his
child. 19 And the taskmasters of Mitsrayim did
so to the infants of Yisra'el for many days, and
no one pitied or had compassion over the infants
of the children of Yisra'el. 20 And the number of
all the children killed in the building was two
hundred and seventy, some whom they had built
upon instead of the bricks which had been left
deficient by their fathers, and some whom they
had drawn out dead from the building. 21 And
the labor imposed upon the children of Yisra'el
in the days of Adiqam exceeded in hardship that
which they performed in the days of his father.

22 And the children of Yisra'el sighed every day
on account of their heavy work, for they had said
to themselves, "Behold when Pharaoh dies, his
son will rise up and lighten our work!"

23 But he increased the latter work more than the
former, and the children of Yisra'el sighed at this
and their cry ascended to Elohim on account of
their labor.

24 And Elohim heard the voice of the children of
Yisra'el and their cry in those days, and Elohim
remembered His covenant which He cut with
Avraham, Yitsḥaq, and Ya'aqov. 25 And Elohim
saw the burden of the children of Yisra'el, and
their heavy work in those days, and He
determined to deliver them.

26 And Mosheh the son of Amram was still
confined in the dungeon in those days, in the
house of Reuel the Midianite, and Tsipporah the
daughter of Reuel supported him with food
secretly day by day. 27 And Mosheh was
confined in the dungeon in the house of Reuel
for ten years.

28 And at the end of ten years which was the first
year of the reign of Pharaoh over Mitsrayim, in
the place of his father, 29 Tsipporah said to her
father Reuel, "No man inquires or seeks after the
Hebrew man, whom you bound in prison now
ten years. 30 Now therefore, if it seems good in
your eyes, let us send and see whether he is
living or dead," but her father did not know that
she had supported him.

31 And Reuel her father answered and said to
her, "Has such a thing ever happened, that a man
should be shut up in a prison without food for ten
years, and that he should live?"

32 And Tsipporah answered her father, saying,
"Surely you hast heard that the Elohim of the
Hebrews is great and awful, and does wonders
for them at all times. 33 It was He who delivered
Avraham from Ur of the Kaldeans, and Yitsḥaq
from the sword of his father, and Ya'aqov from
the messenger of 𐤉𐤄𐤅𐤄 who wrestled with him at
the ford of Yabbok. 34 He has also done many
things with this man: He delivered him from the
river in Mitsrayim, and from the sword of
Pharaoh, and from the children of Kush; so also
can He deliver him from famine and make him
live."

35 And the thing seemed good in the eyes of
Reuel, and he did according to the word of his
daughter, and sent to the pit to see what became
of Mosheh. 36 And he saw, and behold the man
Mosheh was living in the pit, standing upon his
feet, praising and praying to the Elohim of his
ancestors. 37 And Reuel commanded Mosheh to
be brought out of the pit. So they shaved him and
he changed his prison garments and ate bread.
38 And afterward Mosheh went into the garden
of Reuel which was behind the house, and he
there prayed to 𐤉𐤄𐤅𐤄 his Elohim, who had done
mighty wonders for him.

39 And it was that while he prayed he looked
opposite to him, and behold a sapphire stick was
placed in the ground, which was planted in the
midst of the garden. 40 And he approached the
stick and he looked, and behold the Name of
𐤉𐤄𐤅𐤄 Elohim Tsevaot was engraved on it,
written and displayed upon the stick. 41 And he
read it and stretched forth his hand and he
plucked it like a forest tree from the thicket, and
the stick was in his hand.

42 And this is the stick with which all the works
of our Elohim were performed, after He had
created the heavens and the earth, and all their
host; seas, rivers, and all their fishes. 43 And
when Elohim had driven Adam from the garden
of Eden, he took the stick in his hand and went
and tilled the ground from which he was taken.
44 And the stick came down to Noaḥ and was
given to Shem and his descendants, until it came
into the hand of Avraham the Hebrew. 45 And
when Avraham had given all he had to his son
Yitsḥaq, he also gave him this stick. 46 And
when Ya'aqov had fled to Padan-aram, he took it
into his hand, and when he returned to his father
he had not left it behind him.

47 Also when he went down to Mitsrayim he
took it into his hand and gave it to Yoseph, one
portion above his brethren, for Ya'aqov had
taken it by force from his brother Esaw. 48 And
after the death of Yoseph, the nobles of
Mitsrayim came into the house of Yoseph, and
the stick came into the hand of Reuel the
Midianite, and when he went out of Mitsrayim,
he took it in his hand and planted it in his garden.
49 And all the mighty men of the Qenites tried to
pluck it when they endeavored to get Tsipporah
his daughter, but they were unsuccessful. 50 So
the stick remained planted in the garden of

Reuel, until he came who had a right to it and
took it.

51 And when Reuel saw the stick in the hand of
Mosheh, he wondered at it, and he gave him his
daughter Tsipporah for a wife.

78 1 At that time Ba'al Ḥannan son of Akhbor,
king of Edom died, and was buried in his house
in the land of Edom. 2 And after his death the
children of Esaw sent to the land of Edom, and
took from there a man who was in Edom, whose
name was Hadad, and they made him king over
them in the place of Ba'al Ḥannan, their king.
3 And Hadad reigned over the children of Edom
forty-eight years.

4 And when he reigned he resolved to fight
against the children of Moav, to bring them
under the power of the children of Esaw as they
were before, but he was not able, because the
children of Moav heard this thing, and they rose
up and hurried to elect a king over them from
among their brethren. 5 And they afterward
gathered together a great people, and sent to the
children of Ammon their brethren for help to
fight against Hadad king of Edom. 6 And Hadad
heard the thing which the children of Moav had
done, and was greatly afraid of them, and
refrained from fighting against them.

7 In those days Mosheh, the son of Amram, in
Midian, took Tsipporah, the daughter of Reuel
the Midianite, for a wife. 8 And Tsipporah
walked in the ways of the daughters of Ya'aqov:
she was not short of the righteousness of Sarah,
Rivqah, Raḥel, and Leah.

9 And Tsipporah conceived and bore a son and
he called his name Gershom, for he said, "I was a
sojourner in a foreign land;" but he did not
circumcise his foreskin, at the command of
Reuel his father-in-law.

10 And she conceived again and bore a son, but
circumcised his foreskin, and called his name
Eliezer, for Mosheh said, "Because the Elohim
of my fathers was my help, and delivered me
from the sword of Pharaoh."

11 And Pharaoh king of Mitsrayim greatly
increased the labor of the children of Yisra'el in
those days, and continued to make his yoke
heavier upon the children of Yisra'el. 12 And he
ordered a proclamation to be made in Mitsrayim,
saying, "Give no more straw to the people with
which to make bricks; let them go and gather
themselves straw as they can find it."

13 Also the requirement of bricks which they
shall make, let them give each day, and diminish
nothing from them, for they are idle in their
work. 14 And the children of Yisra'el heard this,
and they mourned and sighed, and they cried to
𐤉𐤄𐤅𐤄 on account of the bitterness of their beings.

15 And 𐤉𐤄𐤅𐤄 heard the cries of the children of
Yisra'el, and saw the oppression with which the
Mitsrites oppressed them. 16 And 𐤉𐤄𐤅𐤄 was
jealous for His people and His inheritance, and
heard their voice, and He resolved to take them
out of the affliction of Mitsrayim, to give them
the land of Kana'an for a possession.

79 1 And in those days Mosheh was
shepherding the flock of Reuel the Midianite his
father-in-law, beyond the wilderness of Sin, and
the stick which he took from his father-in-law
was in his hand. 2 And it happened one day that a
kid strayed from the flock, and Mosheh pursued
it and it came to the mountain of Elohim to
Ḥorev.

3 And when he came to Ḥorev, 𐤉𐤄𐤅𐤄 appeared to
him there in the bush, and he found the bush
burning with fire, but the fire had no power over
the bush to consume it. 4 And Mosheh was
greatly astonished at this sight, why the bush was
not consumed, and he approached to see this
mighty thing, and 𐤉𐤄𐤅𐤄 called to Mosheh out of
the fire and commanded him to go down to
Mitsrayim, to Pharaoh king of Mitsrayim, to
send the children of Yisra'el from his service.

5 And 𐤉𐤄𐤅𐤄 said to Mosheh, "Go, return to
Mitsrayim, for all those men who sought your
life are dead, and you shall speak to Pharaoh to
send forth the children of Yisra'el from his land."

6 And 𐤉𐤄𐤅𐤄 showed him to do signs and
wonders in Mitsrayim before the eyes of Pharaoh
and the eyes of his subjects, in order that they
might believe that 𐤉𐤄𐤅𐤄 had sent him.

7 And Mosheh listened to all that 𐤉𐤄𐤅𐤄 had
commanded him, and he returned to his father-
in-law and told him the thing, and Reuel said to
him, "Go in peace."

8 And Mosheh rose up to go to Mitsrayim, and
he took his wife and sons with him. And *while*
he was at an inn in the road, a messenger of
Elohim came down, and sought an occasion
against him. 9 And he wished to kill him on
account of his firstborn son, because he had not
circumcised him, and had transgressed the
covenant which 𐤉𐤄𐤅𐤄 cut with Avraham. 10 For
Mosheh had listened to the words of his father-
in-law which he had spoken to him, not to
circumcise his firstborn son, therefore he
circumcised him not.

11 And Tsipporah saw the messenger of 𐤉𐤄𐤅𐤄
seeking an occasion against Mosheh, and she
knew that this thing was owing to his not having
circumcised her son Gershom. 12 And Tsipporah
hurried and took of the sharp rock stones that
were there, and she circumcised her son, and
delivered her husband and her son from the hand
of the messenger of 𐤉𐤄𐤅𐤄.

13 And Aharon the son of Amram, the brother of
Mosheh, was in Mitsrayim walking at the river
side on that day.

14 And 𐤉𐤄𐤅𐤄 appeared to him in that place, and
he said to him, "Go now toward Mosheh in the
wilderness," and he went and met him in the
mountain of Elohim, and he kissed him.

15 And Aharon lifted up his eyes, and saw
Tsipporah the wife of Mosheh and her children,
and he said to Mosheh, "Who are these to you?"

16 And Mosheh said to him, "They are my wife
and sons, which Elohim gave to me in Midian;"
and the thing grieved Aharon on account of the
woman and her children.

17 And Aharon said to Mosheh, "Send away the
woman and her children that they may go to her
father's house," and Mosheh listened to the
words of Aharon, and did so.

18 And Tsipporah returned with her children, and
they went to the house of Reuel, and remained
there until the time arrived when 𐤉𐤄𐤅𐤄 had
visited His people, and brought them forth from
Mitsrayim from the hand at Pharaoh.

19 And Mosheh and Aharon came to Mitsrayim
to the community of the children of Yisra'el, and
they spoke to them all the words of 𐤉𐤄𐤅𐤄, and
the people rejoiced an exceedingly great
rejoicing. 20 And Mosheh and Aharon rose up
early on the next day, and they went to the house
of Pharaoh, and they took in their hands the stick
of Elohim.

21 And when they came to the king's gate, two
young lions were confined there with iron
instruments, and no person went out or came in
from before them, unless those whom the king
ordered to come, when the conjurors came and
withdrew the lions by their incantations, and this
brought them to the king. 22 And Mosheh hurried
and lifted up the stick upon the lions, and he
loosed them, and Mosheh and Aharon came into
the king's house. 23 The lions also came with
them in joy, and they followed them and rejoiced
as a dog rejoices over his master when he comes
from the field.

24 And when Pharaoh saw this thing he was
astonished at it, and he was greatly terrified at
the report, for their appearance was like the
appearance of the sons of Elohim.

25 And Pharaoh said to Mosheh, "What do you
want?" and they answered him, saying, "𐤉𐤄𐤅𐤄
Elohim of the Hebrews has sent us to you, to say,
'Send forth My people that they may serve Me.'"

26 And when Pharaoh heard their words he was
greatly terrified before them, and he said to
them, "Go today and come back to me
tomorrow," and they did according to the word
of the king.

27 And when they had gone Pharaoh sent for
Bil'am the magician and to Yanus and Yambrus
his sons, and to all the magicians and conjurors
and counsellors which belonged to the king, and
they all came and sat before the king.

28 And the king told them all the words which
Mosheh and his brother Aharon had spoken to
him, and the magicians said to the king, "But
how did the men come to you on account of the
lions which were confined at the gate?"

29 And the king said, "Because they lifted up
their rod against the lions and loosed them, and
came to me, and the lions also rejoiced at them
as a dog rejoices to meet his master."

30 And Bil'am the son of Beor the magician
answered the king, saying, "These are none else
than magicians like ourselves. 31 Now therefore
send for them, and let them come and we will
test them," and the king did so.

32 And in the morning Pharaoh sent for Mosheh
and Aharon to come before the king, and they
took the rod of Elohim, and came to the king and
spoke to him, saying, 33 "Thus said 𐤉𐤄𐤅𐤄 Elohim
of the Hebrews, 'Send My people that they may
serve Me.'"

34 And the king said to them, "But who will
believe you that you are the messengers of
Elohim and that you come to me by his order?
35 Now therefore give a wonder or sign in this
matter, and then the words which you speak will
be believed."

36 And Aharon hurried and threw the rod out of
his hand before Pharaoh and before his servants,
and the rod turned into a monster[a]. 37 And the
sorcerers saw this and they cast each man his rod
upon the ground and they became monsters.
38 And the monster of Aharon's rod lifted up its
head and opened its mouth to swallow the rods
of the magicians.

39 And Bil'am the magician answered and said,
"This thing has been from the days of old, that a
monster should swallow its fellow, and that
living things devour each other. 40 Now therefore
restore it to a rod as it was at first, and we will
also restore our rods as they were at first, and if
your rod shall swallow our rods, then shall we
know that the Ruaḥ of Elohim is in you, and if
not, you art only a magician like us."

41 And Aharon hurried and stretched forth his
hand and caught hold of the monster's tail and it
became a rod in his hand, and the sorcerers did
the like with their rods, and they got hold, each
man of the tail of his monster, and they became
rods as at first. 42 And when they were restored
to rods, the rod of Aharon swallowed up their
rods.

43 And when the king saw this thing, he ordered
the book of records that related to the kings of
Mitsrayim, to be brought, and they brought the
book of records, the chronicles of the kings of
Mitsrayim, in which all the idols of Mitsrayim
were inscribed, for they thought of finding in it
the Name of 𐤉𐤄𐤅𐤄, but they did not find it.

44 And Pharaoh said to Mosheh and Aharon,
"Behold I have not found the Name of your
Elohim written in this book, and I do not know
His Name."

45 And the counsellors and wise men answered
the king, "We have heard that the Elohim of the
Hebrews is a son of the wise, the son of ancient
kings."

46 And Pharaoh turned to Mosheh and Aharon
and said to them, "I do not know 𐤉𐤄𐤅𐤄 whom
you have declared, neither will I send His
people."

47 And they answered and said to the king,
"𐤉𐤄𐤅𐤄 Eloah of Elohim is His Name, and He
proclaimed His Name over us from the days of
our ancestors, and sent us, saying, 'Go to
Pharaoh and say to him, "Send My people that
they may serve Me."'"

48 "Now therefore send us, that we may take a
journey for three days in the wilderness, and
slaughtering *offerings* to Him, for from the days
of our going down to Mitsrayim, He has not
taken from our hands either ascension offering,
slaughtering, or *freewill* offering; and if you will
not send us, His anger will be kindled against
you, and He will strike Mitsrayim either with the
plague or with the sword."

49 And Pharaoh said to them, "Tell me now His
power and His might;" and they said to him, "He
created the heavens and the earth, the seas and
all their fishes. He formed the light, created the
darkness, caused rain upon the earth and watered

[a] **79:36** Hebrew word 𐤕𐤍𐤉𐤍 (*ta'niyn*) is usually rendered as "serpent." However, the word is the same as is used in Bereshiyt [Genesis] **1:21** for "Sea monsters." The *tannin* is believed by many to actually be a crocodile.

it, and made the herbage and grass to sprout. He created man and beast and the animals of the forest, the birds of the heavens and the fish of the sea, and by His mouth they live and die. **50** Surely He created you in your mother's womb, and put the breath of life into you, and raised you and placed you upon the royal throne of Mitsrayim. And He will take your breath and being from you, and return you to the ground from which you were taken."

51 And the anger of the king was kindled at their words, and he said to them, "But who among all the elohim of the nations can do this? My river is my own, and I have made it for myself."[a]

52 And he drove them from him, and he ordered the labor upon Yisra'el to be more severe than it was the previous day and before. **53** And Mosheh and Aharon went out from the king's presence, and they saw the children of Yisra'el in an evil condition for the taskmasters had made their labor exceedingly heavy. **54** And Mosheh returned to 𐤉𐤄𐤅𐤄 and said, "Why have You treated Your people this way? For since I came to speak to Pharaoh, which is what You sent me for, he has exceedingly used the children of Yisra'el."

55 And 𐤉𐤄𐤅𐤄 said to Mosheh, "Behold you will see that with an outstretched hand and heavy plagues, Pharaoh will send the children of Yisra'el from his land."

56 And Mosheh and Aharon dwelled among their brethren the children of Yisra'el in Mitsrayim. **57** And as for the children of Yisra'el, the Mitsrites embittered their lives with the heavy work which they imposed upon them.

𐤐𐤓𐤔𐤕 𐤁𐤀 – *Parashat Bo*

80 **1** And at the end of two years, 𐤉𐤄𐤅𐤄 again sent Mosheh to Pharaoh to bring forth the children of Yisra'el, and to send them out of the land of Mitsrayim.

2 And Mosheh went and came to the house of Pharaoh, and he spoke to him the words of 𐤉𐤄𐤅𐤄 who had sent him; but Pharaoh would not listen to the voice of 𐤉𐤄𐤅𐤄. And Elohim roused His might in Mitsrayim upon Pharaoh and his subjects, and Elohim struck Pharaoh and his people with very great and sore plagues. **3** And 𐤉𐤄𐤅𐤄 sent by the hand of Aharon and turned all the waters of Mitsrayim into blood, with all their streams and rivers. **4** And when a Mitsrite came to drink and draw water, he looked into his pitcher, and behold all the water was turned into blood; and when he came to drink from his cup the water in the cup became blood. **5** And when a woman kneaded her dough and cooked her provisions, their appearance was turned to that of blood.

6 And 𐤉𐤄𐤅𐤄 sent again and caused all their waters to bring forth frogs, and all the frogs came into the houses of the Mitsrites. **7** And when the Mitsrites drank, their bellies were filled with frogs and they danced in their bellies as they dance when in the river. **8** And all their drinking water and cooking water turned to frogs, also when they went to lie in their beds their perspiration bred frogs.

9 Despite all this the anger of 𐤉𐤄𐤅𐤄 did not turn from them, and His hand was stretched out against all the Mitsrites to strike them with every heavy plague. **10** And He sent and struck their dust *and there were* gnats.[b] And the gnats became the height of two cubits upon the earth in Mitsrayim. **11** The gnats were also very numerous, in the flesh of man and beast, in all the inhabitants of Mitsrayim, also upon the king and queen 𐤉𐤄𐤅𐤄 sent the gnats, and it grieved Mitsrayim exceedingly on account of the gnats.

12 Despite this, the anger of 𐤉𐤄𐤅𐤄 did not turn away, and His hand was still stretched out over Mitsrayim.

13 And 𐤉𐤄𐤅𐤄 sent all kinds of beasts of the field into Mitsrayim, and they came and destroyed all Mitsrayim, man and beast, and trees, and all things that were in Mitsrayim.

---

[a] **79:51** Compare Yechezqel [Ezekiel] **29:3**.

[b] **80:10** Hebrew word 𐤊𐤍 (kein) translated as "gnat" identifies a species which is debated. Some translations read "lice" though there is no known species of lice that affects man and beast.

14 And 𐤉𐤄𐤅𐤄 sent fiery naḥashim, scorpions,
mice, weasels, turtles, together with others
creeping in dust.

15 Flies, hornets, fleas, bugs and mixed swarms,
each swarm according to its kind.

16 And all creeping things and winged animals
according to their kind came to Mitsrayim and
grieved the Mitsrites exceedingly.

17 And the fleas and flies came into the eyes and
ears of the Mitsrites.

18 And the hornet came upon them and drove
them away, and they removed from it into their
inner rooms, and it pursued them.

19 And when the Mitsrites hid themselves on
account of the swarm of animals, they locked
their doors after them, and Elohim ordered the
Silonit[a] which was in the sea, to come up and go
into Mitsrayim. 20 And she had long arms, ten
cubits in length of the cubit of a man. 21 And she
went upon the roofs and uncovered the raftering
and flooring and cut them, and stretched forth
her arm into the house and removed the lock and
the bolt, and opened the houses of Mitsrayim.
22 Afterward came the swarm of animals into the
houses of Mitsrayim, and the swarm of animals
destroyed the Mitsrites, and it grieved them
exceedingly.

23 Despite this the anger of 𐤉𐤄𐤅𐤄 did not turn
away from the Mitsrites, and His hand was still
stretched forth against them.

24 And Elohim sent the pestilence, and the
pestilence pervaded Mitsrayim, in the horses and
donkeys, and in the camels, in herds of oxen and
sheep and in man. 25 And when the Mitsrites
rose up early in the morning to take their cattle to
pasture they found all their cattle dead. 26 And
there remained of the cattle of the Mitsrites only
one in ten, and of the cattle belonging to Yisra'el
in Goshen not one died.

27 And Elohim sent a burning inflammation in
the flesh of the Mitsrites, which burst their skins,
and it became a severe itch in all the Mitsrites
from the soles of their feet to the crowns of their
heads. 28 And many boils were in their flesh, that
their flesh wasted away until they became rotten
and putrid.

29 Despite this the anger of 𐤉𐤄𐤅𐤄 did not turn
away, and His hand was still stretched out over
all Mitsrayim.

30 And 𐤉𐤄𐤅𐤄 sent a very heavy hail, which struck
their vines and broke their fruit trees and dried
up all they fell upon. 31 Also every green herb
became dry and perished, for a mingling fire
descended with the hail; therefore the hail and
the fire consumed all things. 32 Also men and
beasts that were found abroad died of the flames
of fire and of the hail, and all the young lions
were exhausted.

33 And 𐤉𐤄𐤅𐤄 sent and brought numerous locusts
into Mitsrayim, the locust, devastating locust,
cricket, and grasshopper, locusts each after its
kind, which devoured all that the hail had left
remaining. 34 Then the Mitsrites rejoiced at the
locusts, although they consumed the produce of
the field, and they caught them in abundance and
salted them for food. 35 And 𐤉𐤄𐤅𐤄 turned a
mighty wind of the sea which took away all the
locusts, even those that were salted, and thrust
them into the Sea of Reeds; not one locust
remained within the boundaries of Mitsrayim.

36 And Elohim sent darkness upon Mitsrayim,
that the whole land of Mitsrayim and Pathros
became dark for three days, so that a man could
not see his hand when he lifted it to his mouth.
37 At that time many of the people of Yisra'el
died who had rebelled against 𐤉𐤄𐤅𐤄 and who

---

[a] **80:19** Silonit – Hebrew word of uncertain derivation. In Samuel's translation this was written as "Sulanuth." It is most likely derived from the Hebrew word 𐤎𐤋𐤅𐤍 (*sil'on*) meaning "brier" or "thorn." This word is derived from the root word 𐤎𐤋𐤄 (*sa'lah*) meaning "to reject" or "to have contempt for." Given the description of the creature, if the story is true, it could be a giant squid. This may also be related to the Kraken as described in Greek mythology.

would not listen to Mosheh and Aharon, and did
not believe in them, that Elohim had sent them.

38 And *those* who said, "We will not go forth
from Mitsrayim lest we perish with hunger in a
desolate wilderness," and *those* who would not
listen to the voice of Mosheh. 39 And 𐤉𐤄𐤅𐤄
plagued them in the three days of darkness, and
the Yisra'elites buried them in those days,
without the Mitsrites knowing of them or
rejoicing over them. 40 And the darkness was
very great in Mitsrayim for three days, and any
person who was standing when the darkness
came, remained standing in his place, and he that
was sitting remained sitting, and he that was
lying continued lying in the same state, and he
that was walking remained walking upon the
ground in the same spot; and this thing happened
to all the Mitsrites, until the darkness had passed
away.

41 And the days of darkness passed away, and
𐤉𐤄𐤅𐤄 sent Mosheh and Aharon to the children of
Yisra'el, saying, "Celebrate your Feast and make
your Pesaḥ[a], for behold I come in the midst of
the night among all the Mitsrites, and I will
strike all their firstborn, from the firstborn of a
man to the firstborn of beast. And when I see
your Pesaḥ, I will pass over you."

42 And the children of Yisra'el did according to
all that 𐤉𐤄𐤅𐤄 had commanded Mosheh and
Aharon, thus they did in that night. 43 And it
happened in the middle of the night, that 𐤉𐤄𐤅𐤄
went forth in the midst of Mitsrayim, and struck
all the firstborn of the Mitsrites, from the
firstborn of man to the firstborn of beast. 44 And
Pharaoh rose up in the night, he and all his
servants and all the Mitsrites, and there was a
great cry throughout Mitsrayim in that night, for
there was not a house in which there was not a
corpse. 45 Also the likenesses of the firstborn of
Mitsrayim, which were carved in the walls at
their houses, were destroyed and fell to the
ground. 46 Even the bones of their firstborn who
had died previously, and whom they had buried
in their houses, were raked up by the dogs of
Mitsrayim on that night and dragged before the
Mitsrites and cast before them. 47 And all the
Mitsrites saw this evil which had suddenly come
upon them, and all the Mitsrites cried out with a
loud voice. 48 And all the families of Mitsrayim
wept on that night, each man for his son and each
man for his daughter, being the firstborn, and the
tumult of Mitsrayim was heard at a distance on
that night.

49 And Batyah the daughter of Pharaoh went
forth with the king on that night to seek Mosheh
and Aharon in their houses, and they found them
in their houses, eating and drinking and rejoicing
with all Yisra'el.

50 And Batyah said to Mosheh, "Is this the
reward for the good which I have done to you? *I*,
who raised you and stretched you out, and you
have brought this evil upon me and my father's
house?"

51 And Mosheh said to her, "Surely 𐤉𐤄𐤅𐤄
brought ten plagues upon Mitsrayim; did any
evil accrue to you from any of them? Did one of
them affect you?" and she said, "No."

52 And Mosheh said to her, "Although you are
the firstborn to your mother, you shall not die,
and no evil shall reach you in the midst of
Mitsrayim."

53 And she said, "What advantage is it to me,
when I see the king, my brother, and all his
household and subjects in this evil, whose
firstborn perish with all the firstborn of
Mitsrayim?"

54 And Mosheh said to her, "Surely your brother
and his household, and subjects, the families of
Mitsrayim, would not listen to the words of
𐤉𐤄𐤅𐤄, therefore this evil came upon them."

55 And Pharaoh king of Mitsrayim approached
Mosheh and Aharon, and some of the children of

---

[a] **80:41** Pesaḥ – Hebrew word (𐤐𐤎𐤇) usually rendered as "Passover." Derived from the word *pasaḥ* (same spelling, different vowels) meaning "to pass" or "two spring." The word Pesaḥ refers both to the Day of Passover (Pesaḥ) as well as to the animal victim (sacrifice) of the ceremony.

Yisra'el who were with them in that place, and he
prayed to them, saying, 56 "Rise up and take your
brethren, all the children of Yisra'el who are in
the land, with their sheep and oxen, and all
belonging to them, they shall leave nothing
remaining; only pray for me to 𐤉𐤄𐤅𐤄 your
Elohim."

57 And Mosheh said to Pharaoh, "Behold though
you are my mother's firstborn, yet fear not, for
you will not die, for 𐤉𐤄𐤅𐤄 has commanded that
you shall live, in order to show you His great
might and strong outstretched arm."

58 And Pharaoh ordered the children of Yisra'el
to be sent away, and all the Mitsrites
strengthened themselves to send them, for they
said, "We are all dying."

59 And all the Mitsrites sent the Yisra'elites forth,
with great riches, sheep and oxen and precious
things, according to the oath of 𐤉𐤄𐤅𐤄 between
Him and our father Avraham.

60 And the children of Yisra'el delayed going
forth at night, and when the Mitsrites came to
them to bring them out, they said to them, "Are
we thieves, that we should go forth at night?"

61 And the children of Yisra'el asked of the
Mitsrites, vessels of silver, and vessels of gold,
and garments, and the children of Yisra'el
plundered the Mitsrites. 62 And Mosheh hurried
and rose up and went to the river of Mitsrayim,
and brought up from there the coffin of Yoseph
and took it with him. 63 The children of Yisra'el
also brought up, each man, his father's coffin
with him, and each man the coffins of his tribe.

81

1 And the children of Yisra'el journeyed
from Rameses to Sukkoth, about six hundred
thousand men on foot, besides the little ones and
their wives. 2 Also a mixed multitude went up
with them, and flocks and herds, even much
cattle. 3 And the sojourning of the children of
Yisra'el, who dwelled in the land of Mitsrayim in
hard labor, was two hundred and ten years. 4 And
at the end of two hundred and ten years, 𐤉𐤄𐤅𐤄
brought forth the children of Yisra'el from
Mitsrayim with a strong hand.

5 And the children of Yisra'el traveled from
Mitsrayim and from Goshen and from Rameses,
and encamped in Sukkoth on the fifteenth day of
the first month. 6 And the Mitsrites buried all
their firstborn whom 𐤉𐤄𐤅𐤄 had struck, and all the
Mitsrites buried their dead for three days.

7 And the children of Yisra'el traveled from
Sukkoth and encamped in Ethim, at the end of
the wilderness. 8 And on the third day after the
Mitsrites had buried their firstborn, many men
rose up from Mitsrayim and went after Yisra'el
to make them return to Mitsrayim, for they were
sorry that they had sent the Yisra'elites away
from their servitude.

9 And one man said to his neighbor, "Surely
Mosheh and Aharon spoke to Pharaoh, saying,
'We will go a three days' journey in the
wilderness and slaughter to 𐤉𐤄𐤅𐤄 our Elohim.'
10 Now therefore let us rise up early in the
morning and cause them to return, and it shall be
that if they return with us to Mitsrayim, to their
masters, then we shall know that there is faith in
them; but if they will not return, then will we
fight with them, and make them come back with
great power and a strong hand."

11 And all the princes of Pharaoh rose up in the
morning, and with them about seven hundred
thousand men, and they went forth from
Mitsrayim on that day, and came to the place
where the children of Yisra'el were. 12 And all
the Mitsrites saw and behold Mosheh and
Aharon and all the children of Yisra'el were
sitting before Pi-haḥiroth, eating and drinking
and celebrating the Feast of 𐤉𐤄𐤅𐤄.

13 And all the Mitsrites said to the children of
Yisra'el, "Surely you said, 'We will go a journey
for three days in the wilderness and slaughter to
our Elohim and return.' 14 Now therefore this day
makes five days since you went, why do you not
return to your masters?"

15 And Mosheh and Aharon answered them,
saying, "Because 𐤉𐤄𐤅𐤄 our Elohim has
witnessed in us, saying, 'You shall no more
return to Mitsrayim,' but we will go to a land
flowing with milk and honey, as 𐤉𐤄𐤅𐤄 our
Elohim had sworn to our fathers to give to us."

16 And when the princes of Mitsrayim saw that
the children of Yisra'el did not listen to them, to
return to Mitsrayim, they girded themselves to
fight with Yisra'el. 17 And 𐤉𐤄𐤅𐤄 strengthened the
hearts of the children of Yisra'el over the
Mitsrites, that they gave them a severe beating,
and the battle was heavy upon the Mitsrites, and
all the Mitsrites fled from before the children of
Yisra'el, for many of them died by the hand of
Yisra'el.

18 And the princes of Pharaoh went to Mitsrayim
and told Pharaoh, saying, "The children of
Yisra'el have fled, and will no more return to
Mitsrayim, and in this manner did Mosheh and
Aharon speak to us."

19 And Pharaoh heard this thing, and his heart
and the hearts of all his subjects were turned
against Yisra'el, and they were sorry that they
had sent Yisra'el; and all the Mitsrites advised
Pharaoh to pursue the children of Yisra'el to
make them come back to their burdens.

20 And they said each man to his brother, "What
is this which we have done, that we have sent
Yisra'el from our servitude?"

21 And 𐤉𐤄𐤅𐤄 strengthened the hearts of all the
Mitsrites to pursue the Yisra'elites, for 𐤉𐤄𐤅𐤄
desired to overthrow the Mitsrites in the Sea of
Reeds. 22 And Pharaoh rose up and harnessed his
chariot, and he ordered all the Mitsrites to
assemble, not one man was left excepting the
little ones and the women. 23 And all the
Mitsrites went forth with Pharaoh to pursue the
children of Yisra'el, and the camp of Mitsrayim
was an exceedingly large and heavy camp, about
ten hundred thousand men. 24 And the whole of
this camp went and pursued the children of
Yisra'el to bring them back to Mitsrayim, and
they reached them encamping by the Sea of
Reeds.

25 And the children of Yisra'el lifted up their
eyes, and saw all the Mitsrites pursuing them,
and the children of Yisra'el were greatly terrified
at them, and the children of Yisra'el cried to
𐤉𐤄𐤅𐤄. 26 And on account of the Mitsrites, the
children of Yisra'el divided themselves into four
divisions, and they were divided in their
opinions, for they were afraid of the Mitsrites,
and Mosheh spoke to each of them.[a]

27 The first division was of the children of
Reuven, Shimon, and Yissakhar, and they
resolved to cast themselves into the sea, for they
were exceedingly afraid of the Mitsrites.

28 And Mosheh said to them, "Fear not, stand
still and see the salvation of 𐤉𐤄𐤅𐤄 which He will
do for you today."

29 The second division was of the children of
Zevulun, Benyamin and Naphtali, and they
resolved to go back to Mitsrayim with the
Mitsrites.

30 And Mosheh said to them, "Fear not, for as
you have seen the Mitsrites today, so shall you
see them no more forever."

31 The third division was of the children of
Yehudah and Yoseph, and they resolved to go to
meet the Mitsrites to fight with them.

32 And Mosheh said to them, "Stand in your
places, for 𐤉𐤄𐤅𐤄 will fight for you, and you shall
remain silent."

33 And the fourth division was of the children of
Levi, Gad, and Asher, and they resolved to go
into the midst of the Mitsrites to confound them,
and Mosheh said to them, "Remain in your
stations and do not fear; only call to 𐤉𐤄𐤅𐤄 that
He may save you out of their hands."

34 After this Mosheh rose up from the midst of
the people and prayed to 𐤉𐤄𐤅𐤄 and he said,

35 "O 𐤉𐤄𐤅𐤄 Elohim of the whole earth, save
Your people now, whom You brought forth from
Mitsrayim, and do not let the Mitsrites boast that
power and might are theirs."

36 So 𐤉𐤄𐤅𐤄 said to Mosheh, "Why do you cry to
Me? Speak to the children of Yisra'el that they
shall proceed, and stretch out your rod upon the

---

[a] **81**:**26** Each of the statements to the different divisions here in verses **27-33** are written as one comprehensive statement in Shemoth [Exodus] **14**:**13-14**.

sea and divide it, and the children of Yisra'el
shall pass through it."

37 And Mosheh did so, and he lifted up his rod
upon the sea and divided it. 38 And the waters of
the sea were divided into twelve parts, and the
children of Yisra'el passed through on foot, with
shoes, as a man would pass through a prepared
road. 39 And 𐤉𐤄𐤅𐤄 manifested His wonders to
the children of Yisra'el in Mitsrayim, and in the
sea, by the hand of Mosheh and Aharon.

40 And when the children of Yisra'el had entered
the sea, the Mitsrites came after them, and the
waters of the sea resumed upon them, and they
all sank in the water, and not one man was left
except Pharaoh, who gave thanks to 𐤉𐤄𐤅𐤄 and
believed in Him. Therefore 𐤉𐤄𐤅𐤄 did not cause
him to die at that time with the Mitsrites. 41 And
𐤉𐤄𐤅𐤄 ordered a messenger to take him from
among the Mitsrites, and cast him upon the land
of Nineveh and he reigned over it for a long
time.

42 And on that day 𐤉𐤄𐤅𐤄 saved Yisra'el from the
hand of Mitsrayim, and all the children of
Yisra'el saw that the Mitsrites had died, and they
saw the great hand of 𐤉𐤄𐤅𐤄, in what He had
performed in Mitsrayim and in the sea.

43 Then Mosheh and the children of Yisra'el sang
this song to 𐤉𐤄𐤅𐤄, on the day when 𐤉𐤄𐤅𐤄 caused
the Mitsrites to fall before them.

44 And all Yisra'el sang in unison, saying, "I will
sing to 𐤉𐤄𐤅𐤄 for He is greatly exalted, the horse
and his rider He has cast into the sea; behold it is
written in the book of the Torah of Elohim."

45 After this the children of Yisra'el proceeded
on their journey, and encamped in Marah, and
𐤉𐤄𐤅𐤄 gave to the children of Yisra'el statutes and
judgments in that place in Marah, and 𐤉𐤄𐤅𐤄
commanded the children of Yisra'el to walk in all
His ways and to serve Him. 46 And they
journeyed from Marah and came to Elim, and in
Elim were twelve springs of water and seventy
date trees, and the children encamped there by
the waters. 47 And they journeyed from Elim and
came to the wilderness of Sin, on the fifteenth
day of the second month after their departure
from Mitsrayim.

48 At that time 𐤉𐤄𐤅𐤄 gave the manna to the
children of Yisra'el to eat, and 𐤉𐤄𐤅𐤄 caused food
to rain from the heavens for the children of
Yisra'el day by day. 49 And the children of
Yisra'el ate the manna for forty years, all the
days that they were in the wilderness, until they
came to the land of Kana'an to possess it. 50 And
they proceeded from the wilderness of Sin and
encamped in Alush. 51 And they proceeded from
Alush and encamped in Rephidim.

52 And when the children of Yisra'el were in
Rephidim, Amaleq the son of Eliphaz, the son of
Esaw, the brother of Tsepho, came to fight with
Yisra'el. 53 And he brought with him eight
hundred and one thousand men, magicians and
conjurers, and he prepared for battle with
Yisra'el in Rephidim.

54 And they carried on a great and severe battle
against Yisra'el, and 𐤉𐤄𐤅𐤄 handed Amaleq and
his people into the hands of Mosheh and the
children of Yisra'el, and into the hand of
Yehoshua, the son of Nun, the Ephrathite, the
servant of Mosheh.

55 And the children of Yisra'el struck Amaleq
and his people with the edge of the sword, but
the battle was very heavy upon the children of
Yisra'el.

56 And 𐤉𐤄𐤅𐤄 said to Mosheh, "Write this thing
as a memorial for you in a book, and place it in
the hand of Yehoshua, the son of Nun, your
servant. And you shall command the children of
Yisra'el, saying, 'When you come to the land of
Kana'an, you shall utterly blot out the
remembrance of Amaleq from under the
heavens.'"

57 And Mosheh did so, and he took the book and
wrote upon it these words, saying, 58 "Remember
what Amaleq has done to you in the road when
you went forth from Mitsrayim. 59 Who met you
in the road and struck your rear, even those that
were feeble behind you when you were faint and
weary. 60 Therefore it shall be when 𐤉𐤄𐤅𐤄 your
Elohim gives you rest from all your enemies
round about in the land which 𐤉𐤄𐤅𐤄 your Elohim
gives you for an inheritance, to possess it, that
you shall blot out the remembrance of Amaleq
from under the heavens, you shall not forget *to*

do it. 61 And the king who shall have pity on Amaleq, or upon his memory or upon his seed, behold I will require it of him, and I will cut him off from among his people."

62 And Mosheh wrote all these things in a book, and he charged the children of Yisra'el respecting all these matters.

82 1 And the children of Yisra'el proceeded from Rephidim and they encamped in the wilderness of Sinai, in the third month from their going forth from Mitsrayim.

2 At that time Reuel the Midianite, the father-in-law of Mosheh, came with Tsipporah his daughter and her two sons, for he had heard of the wonders of 𐤉𐤄𐤅𐤄 which He had done to Yisra'el, *and* that He had delivered them from the hand of Mitsrayim. 3 And Yithro came to Mosheh to the wilderness where he was encamped, where the mountain of Elohim was. 4 And Mosheh went forth to meet his father-in-law with great honor, and all Yisra'el was with him. 5 And Yithro and his children remained among the Yisra'elites for many days, and Reuel knew 𐤉𐤄𐤅𐤄 from that day forward.[a]

6 And in the third new moon from the children of Yisra'el's departure from Mitsrayim, on the sixth day *of the new moon,* 𐤉𐤄𐤅𐤄 gave Yisra'el the Ten Words on Mount Sinai. 7 And all Yisra'el heard all these words, and all Yisra'el rejoiced exceedingly in 𐤉𐤄𐤅𐤄 on that day. 8 And the glory of 𐤉𐤄𐤅𐤄 rested upon Mount Sinai, and He called to Mosheh, and Mosheh came in the midst of a cloud and ascended the mountain. 9 And Mosheh was upon the mountain forty days and forty nights; he ate no bread and drank no water, and 𐤉𐤄𐤅𐤄 instructed him in the statutes and judgments in order to teach the children of Yisra'el. 10 And 𐤉𐤄𐤅𐤄 wrote the Ten Words, which He had commanded the children of Yisra'el, upon two tablets of stone, which He gave to Mosheh to command the children of Yisra'el. 11 And at the end of forty days and forty nights, when 𐤉𐤄𐤅𐤄 had finished speaking to Mosheh on Mount Sinai, then 𐤉𐤄𐤅𐤄 gave Mosheh the tablets of stone, written with the finger of Elohim.

12 And when the children of Yisra'el saw that Mosheh tarried to come down from the mountain, they gathered around Aharon, and said, "As for this man Mosheh, we do not know what has become of him. 13 Now therefore rise up, make us an elohim who shall go before us, so that you shall not die."

14 And Aharon was greatly afraid of the people, and he ordered them to bring him gold and he made it into a molten calf for the people.

15 And 𐤉𐤄𐤅𐤄 said to Mosheh, before he had come down from the mountain, "Get down, for your people whom you brought forth from Mitsrayim have corrupted themselves. 16 They have made to themselves a molten calf, and have bowed down to it. Now therefore leave Me, that I may consume them from off the earth, for they are a stiff-necked people."

17 And Mosheh sought the face of 𐤉𐤄𐤅𐤄, and he prayed to 𐤉𐤄𐤅𐤄 for the people on account of the calf which they had made, and he afterward descended from the mountain and in his hands were the two tablets of stone, which Elohim had given him to command the Yisra'elites.

18 And when Mosheh approached the camp and saw the calf which the people had made, the anger of Mosheh was kindled and he broke the tablets under the mountain. 19 And Mosheh came to the camp and he took the calf and burned it with fire, and ground it until it became fine dust, and cast it upon the water and gave it to the Yisra'elites to drink. 20 And about three thousand men died of the people by the swords of each other who had made the calf.

21 And on the next day Mosheh said to the people, "I will go up to 𐤉𐤄𐤅𐤄. Perhaps I may make atonement for your sins which you have sinned against 𐤉𐤄𐤅𐤄."

---

[a] **2-5** Hebrew text here uses both of the names of Reuel: Reuel (𐤓𐤏𐤅𐤀𐤋) and Yithro (𐤉𐤕𐤓𐤅). These both refer to Mosheh's father-in-law. Compare Shemoth [Exodus] **18:1** with Bemidbar [Numbers] **10:29**.

22 And Mosheh again went up to 𐤉𐤄𐤅𐤄, and he
remained with 𐤉𐤄𐤅𐤄 forty days and forty nights.
23 And during the forty days Mosheh entreated
𐤉𐤄𐤅𐤄 on behalf of the children of Yisra'el, and
𐤉𐤄𐤅𐤄 listened to the prayer of Mosheh, and 𐤉𐤄𐤅𐤄
was entreated by him on behalf of Yisra'el.

24 Then 𐤉𐤄𐤅𐤄 spoke to Mosheh, *commanding*
him to cut two stone tablets and to bring them up
to 𐤉𐤄𐤅𐤄, who would write upon them the Ten
Words. 25 Now Mosheh did so, and he came
down and cut the two tablets and went up to
Mount Sinai to 𐤉𐤄𐤅𐤄, and 𐤉𐤄𐤅𐤄 wrote the Ten
Words upon the tablets. 26 And Mosheh
remained with 𐤉𐤄𐤅𐤄 another forty days and forty
nights, and 𐤉𐤄𐤅𐤄 instructed him in statutes and
judgments to impart to Yisra'el. 27 And 𐤉𐤄𐤅𐤄
commanded him concerning the children of
Yisra'el that they should make a dwelling-place
for 𐤉𐤄𐤅𐤄, that His Name might rest in it. And
𐤉𐤄𐤅𐤄 showed him the likeness of the dwelling-
place and the likeness of all its vessels. 28 And at
the end of the forty days, Mosheh came down
from the mount and the two tablets were in his
hand.

29 And Mosheh came to the children of Yisra'el
and spoke to them all the words of 𐤉𐤄𐤅𐤄, and he
taught them Torot, statutes and judgments which
𐤉𐤄𐤅𐤄 had taught him. 30 And Mosheh told the
children of Yisra'el the word of 𐤉𐤄𐤅𐤄, that a
dwelling-place should be made for Him, to dwell
among the children of Yisra'el.

31 And the people rejoiced greatly at all the good
which 𐤉𐤄𐤅𐤄 had spoken to them, through
Mosheh, and they said, "We will do all that 𐤉𐤄𐤅𐤄
has spoken to you."

32 And the people rose up like one man and they
made generous offerings to the dwelling-place of
𐤉𐤄𐤅𐤄, and each man brought the offering of
𐤉𐤄𐤅𐤄 for the work of the dwelling-place, and for
all its service. 33 And all the children of Yisra'el
brought each man of all that was found in his
possession for the work of the dwelling-place of
𐤉𐤄𐤅𐤄: gold, silver, and copper, and everything
that was serviceable for the dwelling-place.
34 And all the wise men who were skilled in
work came and made the dwelling-place of
𐤉𐤄𐤅𐤄, according to all that 𐤉𐤄𐤅𐤄 had
commanded; every man in the work in which he
was skilled; and all the wise men in heart made
the dwelling-place, and its furniture and all the
vessels for the set-apart service, as 𐤉𐤄𐤅𐤄 had
commanded Mosheh.

35 And the work of the dwelling-place of the
Tabernacle was completed at the end of five new
moons, and the children of Yisra'el did all that
𐤉𐤄𐤅𐤄 had commanded Mosheh. 36 And they
brought the dwelling-place and all its furniture to
Mosheh; like the representation which 𐤉𐤄𐤅𐤄 had
shown to Mosheh, so did the children of Yisra'el.
37 And Mosheh saw the work, and behold they
did it as 𐤉𐤄𐤅𐤄 had commanded him, so Mosheh
blessed them.

𐤅𐤉𐤒𐤓𐤀 𐤎𐤐𐤓 – Sefer Vayyiqra

83 1 And in the twelfth new moon, in the
twenty-third day of the new moon, Mosheh took
Aharon and his sons, and he dressed them in
their garments, and anointed them and did to
them as 𐤉𐤄𐤅𐤄 had commanded him. And
Mosheh brought up all the offerings which 𐤉𐤄𐤅𐤄
had commanded him on that day.

2 Mosheh afterward took Aharon and his sons
and said to them, "For seven days shall you
remain at the door of the Tabernacle, as I was
commanded."

3 And Aharon and his sons did all that 𐤉𐤄𐤅𐤄 had
commanded them through Mosheh, and they
remained at the door of the Tabernacle for seven
days. 4 And on the eighth day, being the first day
of the first month, in the second year from the
Yisra'elites' departure from Mitsrayim, Mosheh
erected the dwelling-place. And Mosheh put up
all the furniture of the Tabernacle and all the
furniture of the dwelling-place, and he did all
that 𐤉𐤄𐤅𐤄 had commanded him.

5 And Mosheh called to Aharon and his sons,
and they brought the ascension offering and the
sin offering for themselves and the children of
Yisra'el, as 𐤉𐤄𐤅𐤄 had commanded Mosheh. 6 On
that day the two sons of Aharon, Nadav and
Avihu, took strange fire and brought it before
𐤉𐤄𐤅𐤄 who had not commanded them, and a fire

went forth from before 𐤉𐤄𐤅𐤄, and consumed them, and they died before 𐤉𐤄𐤅𐤄 on that day.[a]

𐤎𐤐𐤓 𐤁𐤌𐤃𐤁𐤓 – Sefer Bemidbar

7 Then on the day when Mosheh finished setting up the dwelling-place, the captains of the children of Yisra'el began to bring their offerings before 𐤉𐤄𐤅𐤄 for the dedication of the altar. 8 And they brought up their offerings, each captain for one day, a captain each day for twelve days. 9 And all the offerings which they brought, each man in his day, one silver dish weighing one hundred and thirty sheqels, one silver bowl of seventy sheqels after the sheqel of the dwelling-place, both of them full of fine flour, mixed with oil for a meat offering. 10 One spoon, weighing ten sheqels of gold, full of incense. 11 One young bull, one ram, one lamb of the first year for a ascension offering. 12 And one kid of the goats for a sin offering. 13 And for a slaughtering of peace offering, two oxen, five rams, five he-goats, five lambs of the first year.

14 Thus the twelve captains of Yisra'el did day by day, each man in his day.

15 And it was after this, in the thirteenth day of the new moon, that Mosheh commanded the children of Yisra'el to observe the Pesaḥ. 16 And the children of Yisra'el kept the Pesaḥ at the appointed time, in the fourteenth day of the month, as 𐤉𐤄𐤅𐤄 had commanded Mosheh, so the children of Yisra'el did.

17 And in the second new moon, on the first day *of the new moon*, 𐤉𐤄𐤅𐤄 spoke to Mosheh, saying, 18 "Number the heads of all the males of the children of Yisra'el from twenty years old and upward; you and your brother Aharon and the twelve captains of Yisra'el."

19 And Mosheh did so, and Aharon came with the twelve captains of Yisra'el, and they numbered the children of Yisra'el in the wilderness of Sinai. 20 And the numbers of the children of Yisra'el by the houses of their fathers, from twenty years old and upward, were six hundred and three thousand, five hundred and fifty. 21 But the children of Levi were not numbered among their brethren the children of Yisra'el.

22 And the number of all the males of the children of Yisra'el from one month old and upward, was twenty-two thousand, two hundred and seventy-three. 23 And the number of the children of Levi from one month old and above, was twenty-two thousand.

24 And Mosheh placed the priests and the Levites, each man, to his service and to his burden to serve the dwelling-place of the Tabernacle, as 𐤉𐤄𐤅𐤄 had commanded Mosheh. 25 And on the twentieth day of the month, the cloud was taken away from the Tabernacle of Witness.

26 At that time the children of Yisra'el continued their journey from the wilderness of Sinai, and they took a journey of three days, and the cloud rested upon the wilderness of Paran; there the anger of 𐤉𐤄𐤅𐤄 was kindled against Yisra'el, for they had provoked 𐤉𐤄𐤅𐤄 in asking him for meat, that they might eat. 27 And 𐤉𐤄𐤅𐤄 listened to their voice, and gave them meat which they ate for one new moon. 28 But after this the anger of 𐤉𐤄𐤅𐤄 was kindled against them, and He struck them with a great slaughter, and they were buried there in that place.

29 And the children of Yisra'el called that place Qivroth Hatta'avah, because there they buried the people that lusted *for* flesh. 30 And they departed from Qivroth Hatta'avah and pitched in Ḥatsoroth, which is in the wilderness of Paran. 31 And while the children of Yisra'el were in Ḥatsoroth, the anger of 𐤉𐤄𐤅𐤄 was kindled against Miryam on account of Mosheh, and she became leprous, white as snow. 32 And she was confined outside the camp for seven days, until she had been received again after her leprosy.

33 The children of Yisra'el afterward departed from Ḥatsoroth, and pitched in the end of the wilderness of Paran.

34 At that time 𐤉𐤄𐤅𐤄 spoke to Mosheh to send twelve men from the children of Yisra'el, one man from each tribe, to go and explore the land

[a] **83:6** See Vayyiqra 10.

of Kana'an. 35 And Mosheh sent the twelve men,
and they came to the land of Kana'an to search
and examine it, and they explored the whole land
from the wilderness of Sin to Reḥov as you come
to Ḥamoth.

36 And at the end of forty days they came to
Mosheh and Aharon, and they brought word as it
was in their hearts, and ten of the men brought
up an evil report to the children of Yisra'el, about
the land which they had explored, saying, "It is
better for us to return to Mitsrayim than to go to
this land, a land that consumes its inhabitants."

37 But Yehoshua the son of Nun, and Kalev the
son of Yephuneh, who were of those that
explored the land, said, "The land is very, very
good. 38 If 𐤉𐤄𐤅𐤄 delights in us, then He will
bring us to this land and give it to us, for it is a
land flowing with milk and honey."

39 But the children of Yisra'el would not listen to
them, and they listened to the words of the ten
men who had brought up an evil report of the
land.

40 And 𐤉𐤄𐤅𐤄 heard the grumblings of the
children of Yisra'el and He was angry and swore,
saying, 41 "Surely not one man of this wicked
generation shall see the land from twenty years
old and upward except Kalev the son of
Yephuneh and Yeoshua the son of Nun. 42 But
surely this wicked generation shall perish in this
wilderness, and their children shall come to the
land and they shall possess it;" so the anger of
𐤉𐤄𐤅𐤄 was kindled against Yisra'el, and He made
them wander in the wilderness for forty years
until the end of that wicked generation, because
they did not follow 𐤉𐤄𐤅𐤄.

43 And the people dwelled in the wilderness of
Paran a long time, and they afterward proceeded
to the wilderness by the way of the Sea of Reeds.

84 1 At that time Qoraḥ the son of Yitshar the
son of Qohath the son of Levi, took many men of
the children of Yisra'el, and they rose up and
quarreled with Mosheh and Aharon and the
whole congregation. 2 And 𐤉𐤄𐤅𐤄 was angry with
them, and the earth opened its mouth, and
swallowed them up, with their houses and all
belonging to them, and all the men belonging to
Qoraḥ. 3 And after this Elohim made the people
go round by the way of Mount Seir for a long
time.

4 At that time 𐤉𐤄𐤅𐤄 said to Mosheh, "Do not
provoke a war against the children of Esaw, for I
will not give to you of anything belonging to
them, as much as the sole of the foot could tread
upon, for I have given Mount Seir for an
inheritance to Esaw."

5 Therefore the children of Esaw fought against
the children of Seir in former times, and 𐤉𐤄𐤅𐤄
had delivered the children of Seir into the hands
of the children of Esaw, and destroyed them
from before them, and the children of Esaw
dwelled in their stead to this day.

6 Therefore 𐤉𐤄𐤅𐤄 said to the children of Yisra'el,
"Do not fight against the children of Esaw your
brethren, for nothing in their land belongs to you,
but you may buy food of them for money and eat
it, and you may buy water of them for money
and drink it."

7 And the children of Yisra'el did according to
the word of 𐤉𐤄𐤅𐤄. 8 And the children of Yisra'el
went about the wilderness, going round by the
way of Mount Sinai for a long time, and did not
touch the children of Esaw, and they continued
in that district for nineteen years.

9 At that time Latiynos king of the children of
Kittim died, in the forty-fifth year of his reign,
which is the fourteenth year of the children of
Yisra'el's departure from Mitsrayim. 10 And they
buried him in his place which he had built for
himself in the land of Kittim, and Avianos
reigned in his place for thirty-eight years.

11 And the children of Yisra'el passed the
boundary of the children of Esaw in those days,
at the end of nineteen years, and they came and
passed the road of the wilderness of Moav.

12 And 𐤉𐤄𐤅𐤄 said to Mosheh, "Do not besiege
Moav, and do not fight against them, for I will
give you nothing of their land."

13 And the children of Yisra'el passed the road of
the wilderness of Moav for nineteen years, and
they did not fight against them. 14 And in the

thirty-sixth year of the children of Yisra'el's
departing from Mitsrayim 𐤉𐤄𐤅𐤄 struck the heart
of Sichon, king of the Amorites, and he waged
war, and went forth to fight against the children
of Moav. 15 And Sichon sent messengers to Beor
the son of Yunus, the son of Bil'am, counsellor
to the king of Mitsrayim, and to Bil'am his son,
to curse Moav, in order that it might be delivered
into the hand of Sichon. 16 And the messengers
went and brought Beor the son of Yunus, and
Bil'am his son, from Pethor in Aram-Naharayim,
so Beor and Bil'am his son came to the city of
Sichon and they cursed Moav and their king in
the presence of Sichon king of the Amorites.

17 So Sichon went out with his whole army, and
he went to Moav and fought against them, and he
subdued them, and 𐤉𐤄𐤅𐤄 delivered them into his
hands, and Sichon killed the king of Moav.
18 And Sichon took all the cities of Moav in the
battle; he also took Ḥeshbon from them, for
Ḥeshbon was one of the cities of Moav, and
Sichon placed his princes and his great ones in
Ḥeshbon, and Ḥeshbon belonged to Sichon in
those days.

19 Therefore the parable speakers Beor and
Bil'am his son uttered these words, saying,
"Come to Ḥeshbon, the city of Sichon will be
built and established. 20 Woe to you, Moav! You
are lost, O people of Kemosh! Behold it is
written in the book of the Torah of Elohim."

21 And when Sichon had conquered Moav, he
placed guards in the cities which he had taken
from Moav, and a considerable number of the
children of Moav fell in battle into the hand of
Sichon, and he made a great capture of them,
sons and daughters, and he killed their king; so
Sichon turned back to his own land. 22 And
Sichon gave numerous presents of silver and
gold to Beor and Bil'am his son, and he
dismissed them, and they went to Aram-
Naharayim to their home and country.

23 At that time all the children of Yisra'el passed
from the road of the wilderness of Moav, and
returned and surrounded the wilderness of Edom.
24 So the whole congregation came to the
wilderness of Sin in the first month of the
fortieth year from their departure from
Mitsrayim, and the children of Yisra'el dwelled
there in Qadesh, of the wilderness of Sin, and
Miryam died there and she was buried there.

25 At that time Mosheh sent messengers to
Hadad king of Edom, saying, "Thus says your
brother Yisra'el: 'Please let me pass through your
land. We will not pass through field or vineyard,
we will not drink the water of the well; we will
walk in the king's road.'"

26 And Edom said to him, "You shall not pass
through my country," and Edom went forth to
meet the children of Yisra'el with a mighty
people. 27 And the children of Esaw refused to
let the children of Yisra'el pass through their
land, so the Yisra'elites removed from them and
did not fight against them.

28 For before this 𐤉𐤄𐤅𐤄 had commanded the
children of Yisra'el, saying, "You shall not fight
against the children of Esaw," therefore the
Yisra'elites removed from them and did not fight
against them.

29 So the children of Yisra'el departed from
Qadesh, and all the people came to Mount Hor.

30 At that time 𐤉𐤄𐤅𐤄 said to Mosheh, "Tell your
brother Aharon that he shall die there, for he
shall not come to the land which I have given to
the children of Yisra'el."

31 And Aharon went up, at the command of
𐤉𐤄𐤅𐤄, to Mount Hor, in the fortieth year, in the
fifth new moon, in the first day of the new moon.
32 And Aharon was one hundred and twenty-
three years old when he died in Mount Hor.

85 1 And king Arad the Kana'anite, who
dwelled in the south, heard that the Yisra'elites
had come by the way of the spies, and he
arranged his forces to fight against the
Yisra'elites. 2 And the children of Yisra'el were
greatly afraid of him, for he had a great and
heavy army, so the children of Yisra'el resolved
to return to Mitsrayim. 3 And the children of
Yisra'el turned back about the distance of three
days' journey to Museroth Beni Ya'aqon, for they
were greatly afraid on account of the king Arad.
4 And the children of Yisra'el would not get back
to their places, so they remained in Beni Ya'aqon
for thirty days.

5 And when the children of Levi saw that the
children of Yisra'el would not turn back, they
were jealous for the sake of 𐤉𐤄𐤅𐤄, and they rose
up and fought against the Yisra'elites their
brethren, and killed a great number of them, and
forced them to turn back to their place, Mount
Hor. 6 And when they returned, king Arad was
still arranging his host for battle against the
Yisra'elites.

7 And Yisra'el vowed a vow, saying, "If You will
deliver this people into my hand, then I will
utterly destroy their cities."

8 And 𐤉𐤄𐤅𐤄 listened to the voice of Yisra'el, and
He delivered the Kana'anites into their hand, and
they utterly destroyed them and their cities, and
they called the name of the place Ḥormah.

9 And the children of Yisra'el journeyed from
Mount Hor and pitched in Ovoth, and they
journeyed from Ovoth and they pitched at Iye-
Ha'avarim, in the border of Moav.

10 And the children of Yisra'el sent to Moav,
saying, "Let us pass now through your land into
our place," but the children of Moav would not
allow the children of Yisra'el to pass through
their land, for the children of Moav were greatly
afraid lest the children of Yisra'el should do to
them as Sichon king of the Amorites had done to
them, who had taken their land and had killed
many of them.

11 Therefore Moav would not allow the
Yisra'elites to pass through his land; and 𐤉𐤄𐤅𐤄
commanded the children of Yisra'el, saying that
they should not fight against Moav, so the
Yisra'elites removed from Moav.

12 And the children of Yisra'el journeyed from
the border of Moav, and they came to the other
side of Arnon, the border of Moav, between
Moav and the Amorites, and they pitched in the
border of Sichon, king of the Amorites, in the
wilderness of Qedemoth.

13 And the children of Yisra'el sent messengers
to Sichon, king of the Amorites, saying, 14 "Let
us pass through your land. We will not turn into
the fields or into the vineyards, we will go along
by the king's highway until we shall have passed
your border," but Sichon would not allow the
Yisra'elites to pass.

15 So Sihon collected all the people of the
Amorites and went forth into the wilderness to
meet the children of Yisra'el, and he fought
against Yisra'el in Yahats. 16 And 𐤉𐤄𐤅𐤄
delivered Sichon king of the Amorites into the
hand of the children of Yisra'el, and Yisra'el
struck all the people of Sichon with the edge of
the sword and avenged the cause of Moav.
17 And the children of Yisra'el took possession of
the land of Sichon from Aram to Yabbok, to *the
land of* the children of Ammon; and they took all
the spoil of the cities. 18 And Yisra'el took all
these cities, and Yisra'el dwelled in all the cities
of the Amorites. 19 And all the children of
Yisra'el resolved to fight against the children of
Ammon, to take their land also.

20 So 𐤉𐤄𐤅𐤄 said to the children of Yisra'el, "Do
not lay siege to the children of Ammon, neither
stir up battle against them, for I will give nothing
to you of their land," and the children of Yisra'el
listened to the word of 𐤉𐤄𐤅𐤄, and did not fight
against the children of Ammon.

21 And the children of Yisra'el turned and went
up by the way of Bashan to the land of Og, king
of Bashan, and Og the king of Bashan went out
to meet the Yisra'elites in battle, and he had with
him many valiant men, and a very strong force
from the people of the Amorites. 22 And Og king
of Bashan was a mighty man of valor, but
Na'arits his son was exceedingly powerful, even
mightier than he was.

23 And Og said in his heart, "Behold now the
whole camp of Yisra'el takes up a space of three
parasot[a], now I will strike them at once without
sword or spear."

24 And Og went up Mount Yahats, and took one
large stone from there, the length of which was
three parasot, and he placed it on his head, and

[a] **85:23** Parasa – Unit of measure. Ten parasot (plural) was said to be the average day's walk. Thus one paras is approximately **2.5** miles.

decided to throw it upon the camp of the children
of Yisra'el, to strike all the Yisra'elites with that
stone.

25 And the messenger of 𐤉𐤄𐤅𐤄 came and pierced
the stone upon the head of Og, and the stone fell
upon the neck of Og that Og fell to the earth on
account of the weight of the stone upon his neck.

26 At that time 𐤉𐤄𐤅𐤄 said to the children of
Yisra'el, "Do not be afraid of him, for I have
given him and all his people and all his land into
your hand, and you shall do to him as you did to
Sichon."

27 And Mosheh went down to him with a small
number of the children of Yisra'el, and Mosheh
struck Og with a stick at the ankles of his feet
and killed him. 28 The children of Yisra'el
afterward pursued the children of Og and all his
people, and they struck and destroyed them until
there was no remnant left of them. 29 Mosheh
afterward sent some of the children of Yisra'el to
spy out Ya'azer, for Ya'azer was a very famous
city. 30 And the spies went to Ya'azer and
explored it, and the spies trusted in 𐤉𐤄𐤅𐤄, and
they fought against the men of Ya'azer. 31 And
these men took Ya'azer and its villages, and
𐤉𐤄𐤅𐤄 gave them into their hand, and they drove
out the Amorites who had been there. 32 And the
children of Yisra'el took the land of the two
kings of the Amorites, sixty cities which were on
the other side of the Yarden, from the brook of
Arnon to Mount Ḥermon. 33 And the children of
Yisra'el journeyed and came into the plain of
Moav which is on this side of the Yarden, by
Yericho.

34 And the children of Moav heard all the evil
which the children of Yisra'el had done to the
two kings of the Amorites, to Sichon and Og, so
all the men of Moav were greatly afraid of the
Yisra'elites.

35 And the elders of Moav said, "Behold the two
kings of the Amorites, Sichon and Og, who were
more powerful than all the kings of the earth,
could not stand against the children of Yisra'el.
How then can we stand before them? 36 Surely
they sent us a message before now, *asking* to
pass through our land on their way, and we
would not allow them; now they will turn upon
us with their heavy swords and destroy us;" and
Moav was distressed on account of the children
of Yisra'el, and they were greatly afraid of them,
and they counselled together what was to be
done to the children of Yisra'el.

37 And the elders of Moav resolved and took one
of their men, Balaq the son of Tsippor the
Moavite, and made him king over them at that
time, and Balaq was a very wise man. 38 And the
elders of Moav rose up and sent to the children
of Midian to make peace with them, for a great
battle and enmity had been in those days
between Moav and Midian, from the days of
Hadad the son of Bedad king of Edom, who
struck Midian in the field of Moav, *even* to these
days. 39 And the children of Moav sent to the
children of Midian, and they made peace with
them, and the elders of Midian came to the land
of Moav to make peace in behalf of the children
of Midian. 40 And the elders of Moav counselled
with the elders of Midian what to do in order to
save their lives from Yisra'el.

41 And all the children of Moav said to the elders
of Midian, "Now therefore the children of
Yisra'el lick up all that are round about us, as the
ox licks up the grass of the field, for thus they
did to the two kings of the Amorites who are
stronger than we are."

42 And the elders of Midian said to Moav, "We
have heard that at the time when Sichon king of
the Amorites fought against you, when he
prevailed over you and took your land, he sent to
Beor the son of Yunus, and to Bil'am his son
from Aram-Naharayim, and they came and
cursed you; therefore the hand of Sichon
prevailed over you, that he took your land.
43 Now therefore send to Bil'am his son, for he
still remains in his land, and give him his hire,
that he may come and curse all the people of
whom you are afraid;" so the elders of Moav
heard this thing, and it pleased them to send to
Bil'am the son of Beor.

44 So Balaq the son of Tsippor king of Moav sent
messengers to Bil'am, saying, 45 "Behold there is
a people come out from Mitsrayim, behold they
cover the face of the earth, and they abide over
against me. 46 Now therefore come and curse this
people for me, for they are too mighty for me;

perhaps I may prevail to fight against them, and drive them out, for I heard that he whom you bless is blessed, and he whom you curse is cursed."

47 So the messengers of Balaq went to Bil'am and brought Bil'am to curse the people to fight against Moav.

48 And Bil'am came to Balaq to curse Yisra'el, and 𐤉𐤄𐤅𐤄 said to Bil'am, "Do not curse this people, for they are blessed."

49 And Balaq urged Bil'am day by day to curse Yisra'el, but Bil'am did not listen to Balaq on account of the word of 𐤉𐤄𐤅𐤄 which He had spoken to Bil'am. 50 And when Balaq saw that Bil'am would not do as he desired, he rose up and went home, and Bil'am also returned to his land and he went from there to Midian.

51 And the children of Yisra'el journeyed from the plain of Moav, and pitched by the Yarden from Beth-Yeshimoth even to Abel-Shittim, at the end of the plains of Moav. 52 And when the children of Yisra'el stayed in the plain of Shittim, they began to whore with the daughters of Moav. 53 And the children of Yisra'el approached Moav, and the children of Moav pitched their tents opposite to the camp of the children of Yisra'el. 54 And the children of Moav were afraid of the children of Yisra'el, and the children of Moav took all their daughters and their wives of beautiful aspect and comely appearance, and dressed them in gold and silver and costly garments. 55 And the children of Moav seated those women at the door of their tents, in order that the children of Yisra'el might see them and turn to them, and not fight against Moav.

56 And all the children of Moav did this thing to the children of Yisra'el, and every man placed his wife and daughter at the door of his tent, and all the children of Yisra'el saw the act of the children of Moav, and the children of Yisra'el turned to the daughters of Moav and desired them, and they went to them. 57 And it happened that when a Hebrew came to the door of the tent of Moav, and saw a daughter of Moav and desired her in his heart, and spoke with her at the door of the tent that which he desired, while they were speaking together the men of the tent would come out and speak to the Hebrew words such as this:

58 "Surely you know that we are brethren, we are all the descendants of Lot and the descendants of Avraham his brother. Why then will you not remain with us, and why will you not eat our bread and our slaughtering?"

59 And when the children of Moav had thus overwhelmed him with their speeches, and enticed him by their flattering words, they seated him in the tent and cooked and slaughtered for him, and he ate of their slaughtering and of their bread. 60 They then gave him wine and he drank and became intoxicated, and they placed before him a beautiful girl, and he did with her as he pleased, for he did not know what he was doing, as he had drunk wine excessively.

61 Thus the children of Moav did to Yisra'el in that place, in the plain of Shittim. And the anger of 𐤉𐤄𐤅𐤄 was kindled against Yisra'el on account of this matter, and He sent a plague among them, and twenty-four thousand men of the Yisra'elites died there.

62 Now there was a man of the children of Shieon whose name was Zimri, the son of Salu, who joined himself to the Midianite *woman* Kosbi, the daughter of Tsur, king of Midian, in the sight of all the children of Yisra'el. 63 And Pinechas the son of Elazar, the son of Aharon the priest, saw this wicked thing which Zimri did. And he took a spear and rose up and went after them, and pierced them both and killed them, and the plague ceased from the children of Yisra'el.

86 1 At that time after the plague, 𐤉𐤄𐤅𐤄 said to Mosheh, and to Elazar the son of Aharon the priest, saying, 2 "Number the heads of the whole congregation of the children of Yisra'el, from twenty years old and upward, all that went forth in the army."

3 And Mosheh and Elazar numbered the children of Yisra'el after their families, and the number of all Yisra'el was seven hundred thousand, seven hundred and thirty. 4 And the number of the children of Levi, from one month old and

upward, was twenty-three thousand, and among
these there was not a man of those numbered by
Mosheh and Aharon in the wilderness of Sinai.
5 For יהוה had told them that they would die in
the wilderness, so they all died, and not one had
been left of them except Kalev the son of
Yephuneh, and Yehoshua the son of Nun.

6 And it was after this that יהוה said to Mosheh,
"Say to the children of Yisra'el to avenge upon
Midian the cause of their brethren the children of
Yisra'el."

7 And Mosheh did so, and the children of
Yisra'el chose from among them twelve thousand
men, being one thousand to a tribe, and they
went to Midian. 8 And the children of Yisra'el
warred against Midian, and they killed every
male, also the five captains of Midian, and
Bil'am the son of Beor they killed with the
sword. 9 And the children of Yisra'el took the
wives of Midian captive, with their little ones
and their cattle, and all belonging to them.
10 And they took all the spoil and all the plunder,
and they brought it to Mosheh and to Elazar to
the plains of Moav. 11 And Mosheh and Elazar
and all the captains of the congregation went
forth to meet them with joy.

12 And they divided all the spoil of Midian, and
the children of Yisra'el had been revenged upon
Midian for the cause of their brethren the
children of Yisra'el.

ספר דברים – *Sefer Devarim*

87 1 At that time יהוה said to Mosheh, "Behold
your days are approaching an end. Now take
Yehoshua the son of Nun, your servant, and
place him in the Tabernacle, and I will command
him," and Mosheh did so.

2 And יהוה appeared in the Tabernacle in a
pillar of cloud, and the pillar of cloud stood at
the entrance of the Tabernacle.

3 And יהוה commanded Yehoshua the son of
Nun and said to him, "Be strong and courageous,
for you will bring the children of Yisra'el to the
land which I swore to give them, and I will be
with you."

4 And Mosheh said to Yehoshua, "Be strong and
courageous, for you will cause the children of
Yisra'el to inherit the land, and יהוה will be
with you; He will not leave you, nor forsake you.
Do not be afraid nor discouraged."

5 And Mosheh called to all the children of
Yisra'el and said to them, "You have seen all the
good which יהוה your Elohim has done for you
in the wilderness. 6 Now therefore guard all the
words of this Torah, and walk in the way of
יהוה your Elohim. Do not turn from the way
which יהוה has commanded you, either to the
right or to the left."

7 And Mosheh taught the children of Yisra'el
statutes and judgments and Torot to do in the
land as יהוה had commanded him. 8 And he
taught them the way of יהוה and His Torot;
behold they are written in the book of the Torah
of Elohim which He gave to the children of
Yisra'el by the hand of Mosheh.

9 And Mosheh finished commanding the children
of Yisra'el, and יהוה spoke to him, saying, "Go
up to the Mount Avarim and die there, and be
gathered to your people as Aharon your brother
was gathered."

10 And Mosheh went up as יהוה had
commanded him, and he died there in the land of
Moav by the order of יהוה, in the fortieth year
from the Yisra'elites going forth from the land of
Mitsrayim. 11 And the children of Yisra'el wept
for Mosheh in the plains of Moav for thirty days,
and the days of weeping and mourning for
Mosheh were completed.

ספר יהושע – *Sefer Yehoshua*

88 1 And it was after the death of Mosheh that
יהוה said to Yehoshua the son of Nun, saying,

2 "Rise up and pass over the Yarden to the land
which I have given to the children of Yisra'el,
and you shall make the children of Yisra'el
inherit the land. 3 Every place where the sole of
your feet walk will belong to you: from the
wilderness of Levanon to the great river, the

Perath River[a] shall be your boundary. 4 No man
shall stand up against you all the days of your
life. As I was with Mosheh, so will I be with
you; only be strong and courageous to guard all
the Torah which Mosheh commanded you. Do
not turn from the way either to the right or to the
left, in order that you may prosper in all that you
do."

5 And Yehoshua commanded the officers of
Yisra'el, saying, "Pass through the camp and
command the people, saying, 'Prepare for
yourselves provisions, for in three days more you
will pass over the Yarden to possess the land.'"

6 And the officers of the children of Yisra'el did
so, and they commanded the people and they did
all that Yehoshua had commanded. 7 And
Yehoshua sent two men to spy out the land of
Yericho, and the men went and spied out
Yericho.

8 And at the end of seven days they came to
Yehoshua in the camp and said to him, "𐤉𐤄𐤅𐤄
has delivered the whole land into our hand, and
the inhabitants of it are melted with fear because
of us."

9 And it happened after that, that Yehoshua rose
up in the morning and all Yisra'el with him, and
they journeyed from Shittim, and Yehoshua and
all Yisra'el with him passed the Yarden; and
Yehoshua was eighty-two years old when he
passed the Yarden with Yisra'el. 10 And the
people went up from Yarden on the tenth day of
the first month, and they encamped in Gilgal at
the eastern corner of Yericho. 11 And the
children of Yisra'el kept the Pesaḥ in Gilgal, in
the plains of Yericho, on the fourteenth day at
the month, as it is written in the Torah of
Mosheh. 12 And the manna ceased at that time on
the day after the Pesaḥ, and there was no more
manna for the children of Yisra'el, and they ate
of the produce of the land of Kana'an. 13 And
Yericho was entirely closed against the children
of Yisra'el, no one came out or went in.

14 And it was in the second month, on the first
day of the month, that 𐤉𐤄𐤅𐤄 said to Yehoshua,
"Rise up; behold I have given Yericho into your
hand with all the people in it; and all your
fighting men shall go around the city, once each
day; thus shall you do for six days. 15 And the
priests shall blow the shofarot, and when you
shall hear the voice of the shofar, all the people
shall give a great shouting, so that the walls of
the city shall fall down; all the people shall go up
every man against his opponent."

16 And Yehoshua did so according to all that
𐤉𐤄𐤅𐤄 had commanded him. 17 And on the
seventh day they went round the city seven
times, and the priests blew upon shofarot.

18 And at the seventh round, Yehoshua said to
the people, "Shout, for 𐤉𐤄𐤅𐤄 has delivered the
whole city into our hands. 19 Only the city and
all that it contains shall be accursed to 𐤉𐤄𐤅𐤄, and
guard yourselves from the accursed thing, lest
you make the camp of Yisra'el accursed and
trouble it. 20 But all the silver and gold and
copper and iron shall be set apart to 𐤉𐤄𐤅𐤄; they
shall come into the treasury of 𐤉𐤄𐤅𐤄."

21 And the people blew upon shofarot and made
a great shouting, and the walls of Yericho fell
down, and all the people went up, every man
straight before him, and they took the city and
utterly destroyed all that was in it, both man and
woman, young and old, ox and sheep and
donkey, with the edge of the sword. 22 And they
burned the whole city with fire; only the vessels
of silver and gold, and copper and iron, they put
into the treasury of 𐤉𐤄𐤅𐤄.

23 And Yehoshua swore at that time, saying,
"Cursed be the man who builds Yericho; he shall
lay the foundation of it with his firstborn, and in
his youngest son shall he set up its gates."

24 And Akhan the son of Karmi, the son of
Zavdi, the son of Zeraḥ, son of Yehudah, acted
treacherously in the accursed thing, and he took
of the accursed thing and hid it in the tent, and
the anger of 𐤉𐤄𐤅𐤄 was kindled against Yisra'el.
25 And it was after this when the children of
Yisra'el had returned from burning Yericho,

[a] **88:3** Perath – The Euphrates River, and probably the etymological origin of the name.

Yehoshua sent men to spy out also Ai, and to
fight against it.

26 And the men went up and spied out Ai, and
they returned and said, "Do not let all the people
go up with you to Ai. Only let about three
thousand men go up and strike the city, for the
men there are but few."

27 And Yehoshua did so, and there went up with
him of the children of Yisra'el about three
thousand men, and they fought against the men
of Ai. 28 And the battle was severe against
Yisra'el, and the men of Ai struck sixty-six men
of Yisra'el, and the children of Yisra'el fled from
before the men of Ai. 29 And when Yehoshua
saw this thing, he tore his garments and fell upon
his face to the ground before 𐤉𐤄𐤅𐤄, he, with the
elders of Yisra'el, and they put dust upon their
heads.

30 And Yehoshua said, "Why, O 𐤉𐤄𐤅𐤄, did You
bring this people over the Yarden? What shall I
say after the Yisra'elites have turned their backs
against their enemies? 31 Now therefore all the
Kana'anites, inhabitants of the land, will hear this
thing, and surround us and cut off our name."

32 And 𐤉𐤄𐤅𐤄 said to Yehoshua, "Why do you fall
upon your face? Arise, get up, for the Yisra'elites
have sinned, and taken of the accursed thing; I
will not be with them anymore unless they
destroy the accursed thing from among them."

33 And Yehoshua rose up and assembled the
people, and brought the Urim by the order of
𐤉𐤄𐤅𐤄, and the tribe of Yehudah was taken, and
Akhan the son of Karmi was taken.

34 And Yehoshua said to Akhan, "Tell me my
son, what have you done?" and Akhan said, "I
saw among the spoil a good-looking garment
from Shinar, and two hundred sheqels of silver,
and a wedge of gold of fifty sheqels weight; I
coveted them and took them, and behold they are
all hidden in the earth in the middle of the tent."

35 And Yehoshua sent men who went and took
them from the tent of Akhan, and they brought
them to Yehoshua. 36 And Yehoshua took Akhan
and these utensils, and his sons and daughters
and all belonging to him, and they brought them
into the valley of Akhor. 37 And Yehoshua
burned them there with fire, and all the
Yisra'elites stoned Akhan with stones, and they
raised over him a heap of stones. Therefore he
called that place the Valley of Akhor; so 𐤉𐤄𐤅𐤄's
anger was appeased, and Yehoshua afterward
came to the city and fought against it.

38 And 𐤉𐤄𐤅𐤄 said to Yehoshua, "Do not fear,
neither be dismayed. Behold I have given Ai into
your hand: her king and her people, and you
shall do to them as you did to Yericho and her
king. Only its spoil and its cattle you shall take
for plunder for yourselves; lay an ambush for the
city behind it."

39 So Yehoshua did according to the word of
𐤉𐤄𐤅𐤄, and he chose from among the sons of war
thirty thousand men of valor, and he sent them,
and they lay in ambush for the city.

40 And he commanded them, saying, "When you
see us, we will flee before them with cunning,
and they will pursue us; then you shall rise out of
the ambush and take the city," and they did so.

41 And Yehoshua fought, and the men of the city
went out toward Yisra'el, not knowing that they
were lying in ambush for them behind the city.
42 And Yehoshua and all the Yisra'elites
pretended to be weary before them, and they fled
by the way of the wilderness with cunning.
43 And the men of Ai gathered all the people
who were in the city to pursue the Yisra'elites,
and they went out and were drawn away from the
city, not one remained, and they left the city
open and pursued the Yisra'elites. 44 And those
who were lying in ambush rose up out of their
places, and hurried to come to the city and took it
and set it on fire, and the men of Ai turned back,
and saw the smoke of the city ascending to the
skies, and they had no means of retreating either
one way or the other. 45 And all the men of Ai
were in the midst of Yisra'el; some on this side
and some on that side, and they struck them so
that not one of them remained.

46 And the children of Yisra'el took Melosh king
of Ai alive, and they brought him to Yehoshua,
and Yehoshua hanged him on a tree and he died.

47 And the children of Yisra'el returned to the
city after having burned it, and they struck all
those that were in it with the edge of the sword.

48 And the number of those that had fallen of the
men of Ai, both man and woman, was twelve
thousand; only the cattle and the spoil of the city
they took to themselves, according to the word
of 𐤉𐤄𐤅𐤄 to Yehoshua.

49 And all the kings on this side of the Yarden,
all the kings of Kana'an, heard of the evil which
the children of Yisra'el had done to Yericho and
to Ai, and they gathered themselves together to
fight against Yisra'el.

50 Only the inhabitants of Givon were greatly
afraid of fighting against the Yisra'elites lest they
should perish, so they acted cunningly, and they
came to Yehoshua and to all Yisra'el, and said to
them, "We have come from a distant land. Now
therefore cut a covenant with us."

51 And the inhabitants of Givon over-reached the
children of Yisra'el, and the children of Yisra'el
cut a covenant with them, and they made peace
with them, and the captains of the congregation
swore to them, but afterward the children of
Yisra'el found that they were neighbors to them
and were dwelling among them. 52 But the
children of Yisra'el did not kill them; for they
had sworn to them by 𐤉𐤄𐤅𐤄. And they became
woodcutters and drawers of water.

53 And Yehoshua said to them, "Why did you
deceive me, to do this thing to us?" and they
answered him, saying, "Because it was told to
your servants all that you had done to all the
kings of the Amorites, and we were greatly
afraid for our beings, and we did this thing."

54 And Yehoshua appointed them on that day to
cut wood and to draw water, and he divided them
for slaves to all the tribes of Yisra'el.

55 And when Adoni-Tsedeq king of
Yerushalayim heard all that the children of
Yisra'el had done to Yericho and to Ai, he sent to
Hoham king of Ḥevron and to Piram king of
Yarmuth, and to Yaphia king of Lakhish and to
Devir king of Eglon, saying, 56 "Come up to me
and help me, that we may strike the children of
Yisra'el and the inhabitants of Givon who have
made peace with the children of Yisra'el."

57 And they gathered themselves together and the
five kings of the Amorites went up with all their
camps, a mighty people numerous as the sand of
the sea shore. 58 And all these kings came and
encamped before Givon, and they began to fight
against the inhabitants of Givon, and all the men
of Givon sent to Yehoshua, saying, "Come up
quickly to us and help us, for all the kings of the
Amorites have gathered together to fight against
us."

59 And Yehoshua and all the fighting people
went up from Gilgal, and Yehoshua came
suddenly to them, and struck these five kings
with a great slaughter. 60 And 𐤉𐤄𐤅𐤄 confused
them before the children at Yisra'el, who struck
them with a terrible slaughter in Givon, and
pursued them along the way that goes up to Beth
Ḥoron to Maqqedah, and they fled from before
the children of Yisra'el. 61 And while they were
fleeing, 𐤉𐤄𐤅𐤄 sent hailstones on them from the
heavens, and more of them died by the
hailstones, than by the slaughter of the children
of Yisra'el. 62 And the children of Yisra'el
pursued them, and they struck them in the road,
and went on and striking them *repeatedly*.

63 And when they were striking *them*, the day
was declining toward evening, and Yehoshua
said in the sight of all the people, "**Sun, stand
still on Givon, and moon in the valley of
Ayalon, until the nation shall have revenged
itself upon its enemies**." [a]

64 And 𐤉𐤄𐤅𐤄 listened to the voice of Yehoshua,
and the sun stood still in the midst of the
heavens, and it stood still thirty-six moments,
and the moon also stood still and did not hurry to
go down a whole day. 65 And there was no day
like that, before it or after it, that 𐤉𐤄𐤅𐤄 listened
to the voice of a man, for 𐤉𐤄𐤅𐤄 fought for
Yisra'el.

89 1 Then Yehoshua spoke this song, on the day
that 𐤉𐤄𐤅𐤄 had given the Amorites into the hand
of Yehoshua and the children of Yisra'el. And he
said in the sight of all Yisra'el, 2 "You have done
mighty things, O 𐤉𐤄𐤅𐤄. You have performed

---

[a] **88:63** See Yehoshua [Joshua] **10:13**.

great deeds; who is like You? My lips shall sing
to Your Name. 3 My goodness and my fortress,
my high tower: I will sing a new song to You. I
will sing to You with thanksgiving. You are the
strength of my salvation. 4 All the kings of the
earth shall praise You, the rulers of the world
shall sing to You, the children of Yisra'el shall
rejoice in Your salvation, they shall sing and
praise Your power.

5 "To You, O 𐤉𐤄𐤅𐤄, did we confide; we said
'You are our Elohim,' for You were our shelter
and strong tower against our enemies. 6 We cried
to You and were not ashamed. We trusted in You
and were delivered. When we cried to You, You
heard our voice. You delivered our beings from
the sword. You showed us Your favor. You gave
us Your salvation. You caused our hearts to
rejoice with Your strength. 7 You went forth for
our salvation. With Your arm You redeemed
Your people. You answered us from the heavens
of Your set-apartness. You saved us from ten
thousands of people.

8 "The sun and moon stood still in the heavens,
and You stood in Your wrath against our
oppressors and commanded Your judgments
over them. 9 All the princes of the earth stood up,
the kings of the nations had gathered themselves
together, they were not moved at Your presence;
they desired Your battles. 10 You rose against
them in Your anger, and brought Your wrath
down upon them. You destroyed them in Your
anger, and cut them off in Your heart.

11 "Nations have been consumed with Your fury.
Kingdoms have declined because of Your wrath.
You wounded kings in the day of Your anger.
12 You poured out Your fury upon them, Your
wrathful anger took hold of them. You turned
their iniquity upon them, and cut them off in
their wickedness. 13 They did spread a trap, they
fell in it. They hid in the net, their foot was
caught.

14 "Your hand was ready for all Your enemies
who said, 'Through their sword they possessed
the land, through their arm they dwelled in the
city.' You filled their faces with shame. You
brought their horns down to the ground. You
terrified them in Your wrath, and destroyed them
in Your anger. 15 The earth trembled and shook
at the sound of Your storm over them. You did
not withhold their beings from death, and
brought down their lives to the grave. 16 You
pursued them in Your storm. You consumed
them in Your whirlwind. You turned their rain
into hail, they fell in deep pits so that they could
not rise.

17 "Their carcasses were like trash cast out in the
middle of the streets. 18 They were consumed
and destroyed in Your anger. You saved Your
people with Your might. 19 Therefore our hearts
rejoice in You, our beings exalt in Your
salvation. 20 Our tongues shall relate Your
might; we will sing and praise Your wondrous
works. 21 For You saved us from our enemies.
You delivered us from those who rose up against
us. You destroyed them from before us and
depress them beneath our feet. 22 Thus shall all
Your enemies die, O 𐤉𐤄𐤅𐤄, and the wicked shall
be like chaff driven by the wind. And Your
beloved shall be like trees planted by the
waters."

23 So Yehoshua and all Yisra'el with him
returned to the camp in Gilgal, after having
struck all the kings, so that not a remnant was
left of them. 24 And the five kings fled alone on
foot from battle, and hid themselves in a cave.
And Yehoshua sought for them in the field of
battle, and did not find them.

25 And afterward it was told to Yehoshua,
saying, "The kings are found and behold they are
hidden in a cave."

26 And Yehoshua said, "Appoint men to be at the
mouth of the cave, to guard them, lest they take
themselves away;" and the children of Yisra'el
did so.

27 And Yehoshua called to all Yisra'el and said
to the officers of battle, "Place your feet upon the
necks of these kings," and Yehoshua said, "So
shall 𐤉𐤄𐤅𐤄 do to all your enemies."

28 And Yehoshua commanded afterward that
they should kill the kings and cast them into the
cave, and to put great stones at the mouth of the
cave. 29 And Yehoshua went afterward with all
the people that were with him on that day to
Maqqedah, and he struck it with the edge of the
sword. 30 And he utterly destroyed the beings

and all belonging to the city, and he did to the
king and people there as he had done to Yericho.
31 And he passed from there to Livnah and he
fought against it, and 𐤉𐤄𐤅𐤄 delivered it into his
hand. And Yehoshua struck it with the edge of
the sword, and all the beings in it, and he did to it
and to its king as he had done to Yericho.

32 And from there he passed on to Lakhish to
fight against it, and Horam king of Gezer went
up to assist the men of Lakhish, and Yehoshua
struck him and his people until there was none
left to him. 33 And Yehoshua took Lakhish and
all its people, and he did to it as he had done to
Livnah.

34 And Yehoshua passed from there to Eglon,
and he took that also, and he struck it and all its
people with the edge of the sword. 35 And from
there he passed to Ḥevron and fought against it
and took it and utterly destroyed it, and he
returned from there with all Yisra'el to Devir and
fought against it and struck it with the edge of
the sword. 36 And he destroyed every being in it;
he left none remaining. And he did to it and its
king as he had done to Yericho.

37 And Yehoshua struck all the kings of the
Amorites from Qadesh-Barnea to Azah, and he
took their country at once, for 𐤉𐤄𐤅𐤄 had fought
for Yisra'el. 38 And Yehoshua with all Yisra'el
came to the camp to Gilgal.

39 When at that time Yavin king of Ḥatsor heard
all that Yehoshua had done to the kings of the
Amorites, Yavin sent to Yovav king of Modan,
and to Lavan king of Shimron, to Yiphil king of
Akhshaph, and to all the kings of the Amorites,
saying, 40 "Come quickly to us and help us, that
we may strike the children of Yisra'el, before
they come upon us and do to us as they have
done to the other kings of the Amorites."

41 And all these kings listened to the words of
Yavin, king of Ḥatsor, and they went forth with
all their camps, seventeen kings; and their people
were as numerous as the sand on the sea shore,
together with horses and chariots innumerable,
and they came and pitched together at the waters
of Merom, and they were met together to fight
against Yisra'el.

42 And 𐤉𐤄𐤅𐤄 said to Yehoshua, "Do not fear
them, for tomorrow about this time I will deliver
them up all dead before you. You shall
hamstring their horses and burn their chariots
with fire."

43 And Yehoshua with all the men of war came
suddenly upon them and struck them, and they
fell into their hands, for 𐤉𐤄𐤅𐤄 had delivered
them into the hands of the children of Yisra'el.
44 So the children of Yisra'el pursued all these
kings with their camps, and struck them until
there were none remaining. And Yehoshua did to
them as 𐤉𐤄𐤅𐤄 had spoken to him.

45 And Yehoshua returned at that time to Ḥatsor
and struck it with the sword and destroyed every
being in it, and burned it with fire. And from
Ḥatsor, Yehoshua passed to Shimron and struck
it and utterly destroyed it. 46 From there he
passed to Akhshaph and he did to it as he had
done to Shimron. 47 From there he passed to
Adulam and he struck all the people in it, and he
did to Adulam as he had done to Akhshaph and
to Shimron.

48 And he passed from them to all the cities of
the kings which he had struck, and he struck all
the people that were left of them and he utterly
destroyed them. 49 Only their plunder and cattle
the Yisra'elites took to themselves as a spoil, but
every human being they struck; they did not
allow a being to live. 50 As 𐤉𐤄𐤅𐤄 had
commanded Mosheh so Yehoshua and all
Yisra'el did. They did not fail in anything.

51 So Yehoshua and all the children of Yisra'el
struck the whole land of Kana'an as 𐤉𐤄𐤅𐤄 had
commanded them, and struck all their kings,
being thirty-one kings, and the children of
Yisra'el took their whole country.

52 Besides the kingdoms of Sichon and Og which
are on the other side of the Yarden, of which
Mosheh had struck many cities. And Mosheh
gave them to the Reuvenites and the Gadites and
to half the tribe of Menasheh. 53 And Yehoshua
struck all the kings that were on this side of the
Yarden to the west, and gave them for an
inheritance to the nine tribes and to the half tribe
of Yisra'el.

54 For five years Yehoshua carried on the war
with these kings, and he gave their cities to the
Yisra'elites, and the land became quieted from
battle throughout the cities of the Amorites and
the Kana'anites.

90 1 At that time in the fifth year after the
children of Yisra'el had passed over the Yarden,
after the children of Yisra'el had rested from
their war with the Kana'anites, at that time great
and severe battles arose between Edom and the
children of Kittim, and the children of Kittim
fought against Edom.

2 And Avianos king of Kittim went forth in that
year; that is, in the thirty-first year of his reign;
and a great force went with him of the mighty
men of the children of Kittim. And he went to
Seir to fight against the children of Esaw.

3 And Hadad the king of Edom heard of his
report, and he went forth to meet him with a
heavy people and strong force, and engaged in
battle with him in the field of Edom. 4 And the
hand of Kittim prevailed over the children of
Esaw, and the children of Kittim killed twenty-
two thousand men of the children of Esaw. And
all the children of Esaw fled from before them.
5 And the children of Kittim pursued them, and
they reached Hadad king of Edom, who was
running before them and they caught him alive,
and brought him to Avianos king of Kittim.
6 And Avianos ordered him to be killed, and
Hadad king of Edom died in the forty-eighth
year of his reign.

7 And the children of Kittim continued their
pursuit of Edom, and they struck them with a
great slaughter and Edom became subject to the
children of Kittim. 8 And the children of Kittim
ruled over Edom, and Edom came under the
hand of the children of Kittim and became one
kingdom from that day. 9 And from that time
they could not lift up their heads any more, and
their kingdom became one with the children of
Kittim.

10 And Avianos placed officers in Edom and all
the children of Edom became subject and
tributary to Avianos, and Avianos turned back to
his own land, Kittim. 11 And when he returned
he renewed his government and built for himself
a large and fortified palace for a royal residence,
and reigned securely over the children of Kittim
and over Edom.

12 In those days, after the children of Yisra'el had
driven away all the Kana'anites and the
Amorites, Yehoshua was old and advanced in
days.

13 And 𐤉𐤄𐤅𐤄 said to Yehoshua, "You are old,
advanced in days, and a great part of the land
remains to be possessed. 14 Now therefore divide
this land for an inheritance to the nine tribes and
to the half tribe of Menasheh," and Yehoshua
rose up and did as 𐤉𐤄𐤅𐤄 had spoken to him.

15 And he divided the whole land to the tribes of
Yisra'el as an inheritance according to their
divisions. 16 But he gave no inheritance to the
tribe at Levi. The offerings of 𐤉𐤄𐤅𐤄 are their
inheritance as 𐤉𐤄𐤅𐤄 had spoken of them by the
hand of Mosheh. 17 And Yehoshua gave Mount
Ḥevron to Kalev the son of Yephuneh, one
portion above his brethren, as 𐤉𐤄𐤅𐤄 had spoken
through Mosheh. 18 Therefore Ḥevron became an
inheritance to Kalev and his children to this day.

19 And Yehoshua divided the whole land by lots
to all Yisra'el for an inheritance, as 𐤉𐤄𐤅𐤄 had
commanded him. 20 And the children of Yisra'el
gave cities to the Levites from their own
inheritance, and suburbs for their cattle, and
property, as 𐤉𐤄𐤅𐤄 had commanded Mosheh so
the children of Yisra'el did. And they divided the
land by lot whether great or small. 21 And they
went to inherit the land according to their
boundaries, and the children of Yisra'el gave to
Yehoshua the son of Nun an inheritance among
them.

22 By the word of 𐤉𐤄𐤅𐤄 they gave him the city
which he required, Timnath-Seraḥ in Mount
Ephrayim, and he built the city and dwelled
therein.

23 These are the inheritances which Elazar the
priest and Yehoshua the son of Nun and the
heads of the fathers of the tribes portioned out to
the children of Yisra'el by lot in Shiloh, before
𐤉𐤄𐤅𐤄, at the door of the Tent of Appointment,
and they left off dividing the land.

24 And 𐤉𐤄𐤅𐤄 gave the land to the Yisra'elites,
and they possessed it as 𐤉𐤄𐤅𐤄 had spoken to
them, and as 𐤉𐤄𐤅𐤄 had sworn to their ancestors.
25 And 𐤉𐤄𐤅𐤄 gave the Yisra'elites rest from all
their enemies around them, and no man stood up
against them, and 𐤉𐤄𐤅𐤄 delivered all their
enemies into their hands, and not one thing failed
of all the good which 𐤉𐤄𐤅𐤄 had spoken to the
children of Yisra'el. Yes, 𐤉𐤄𐤅𐤄 performed
everything.

26 And Yehoshua called to all the children of
Yisra'el and he blessed them, and commanded
them to serve 𐤉𐤄𐤅𐤄, and afterward he sent them
away, and they went each man to his city, and
each man to his inheritance. 27 And the children
of Yisra'el served 𐤉𐤄𐤅𐤄 all the days of
Yehoshua, and 𐤉𐤄𐤅𐤄 gave them rest from all
around them, and they dwelled securely in their
cities.

28 And it happened in those days, that Avianos
king of Kittim died, in the thirty-eighth year of
his reign, that is the seventh year of his reign
over Edom, and they buried him in his place
which he had built for himself, and Latiynos
reigned in his stead fifty years. 29 And during his
reign he brought forth an army, and he went and
fought against the inhabitants of Brintia and
Bimnia, the children of Elisha son of Yavan, and
he prevailed over them and made them tributary.
30 He then heard that Edom had revolted from
under the hand of Kittim, and Latiynos went to
them and struck them and subdued them, and
placed them under the hand of the children of
Kittim, and Edom became one kingdom with the
children of Kittim all the days. 31 And for many
days there was no king in Edom, and their
government was with the children of Kittim and
their king. 32 And it was in the twenty-sixth year
after the children of Yisra'el had crossed the
Yarden, that is the sixty-sixth year after the
children of Yisra'el had departed from
Mitsrayim, that Yehoshua was old, advanced in
days, being one hundred and eight years old in
those days.

33 And Yehoshua called to all Yisra'el, to their
elders, their judges and officers, after 𐤉𐤄𐤅𐤄 had
given to all the Yisra'elites rest from all their
enemies round about, and Yehoshua said to the
elders of Yisra'el, and to their judges, "Behold I
am old, advanced in days. You have seen what
𐤉𐤄𐤅𐤄 has done to all the nations whom He has
driven away from before you, for it is 𐤉𐤄𐤅𐤄 who
has fought for you. 34 Now therefore strengthen
yourselves to guard and to do all the words of the
Torah of Mosheh, not to deviate from it to the
right or to the left, and not to come among those
nations who are left in the land. Neither shall you
make mention of the name of their elohim, but
you shall cling to 𐤉𐤄𐤅𐤄 your Elohim, as you
have done to this day."

35 And Yehoshua greatly exhorted the children
of Yisra'el to serve 𐤉𐤄𐤅𐤄 all their days.

36 And all the Yisra'elites said, "We will serve
𐤉𐤄𐤅𐤄 our Elohim all our days, we and our
children, and our children's children, and our
seed forever."

37 And Yehoshua cut a covenant with the people
on that day, and he sent away the children of
Yisra'el, and they went each man to his
inheritance and to his city. 38 And it was in those
days, when the children of Yisra'el were
dwelling securely in their cities, that they buried
the coffins of the tribes of their ancestors, which
they had brought up from Mitsrayim, each man
in the inheritance of his children. The children of
Yisra'el buried the twelve sons of Ya'aqov, each
man in the possession of his children.

39 And these are the names of the cities where
they buried the twelve sons of Ya'aqov, whom
the children of Yisra'el had brought up from
Mitsrayim.

40 And they buried Reuven and Gad on this side
of the Yarden, in Romia, which Mosheh had
given to their children.

41 And Shimon and Levi they buried in the city
Manda, which he had given to the children of
Simeon, and the suburb of the city was for the
children of Levi.

42 And Yehudah they buried in the city of Benya
opposite Beth-lechem.

43 And the bones of Yissakhar and Zevulun they
buried in Tsidon, in the portion which fell to
their children.

44 And Dan was buried in the city of his children in Eshtael, and Naphtali and Asher they buried in Qadesh-Naphtali, each man in his place which he had given to his children.

45 And the bones of Yoseph they buried in Shekhem, in the part of the field which Ya'aqov had purchased from Ḥamor, and which came to Yoseph for an inheritance.

46 And they buried Benyamin in Yerushalayim opposite the Yevusite, which was given to the children of Benyamin; the children of Yisra'el buried their fathers each man in the city of his children.

47 And at the end of two years, Yehoshua the son of Nun died, one hundred and ten years old, and the time which Yehoshua judged Yisra'el was twenty-eight years. And Yisra'el served 𐤉𐤄𐤅𐤄 all the days of his life. **48** And the other affairs of Yehoshua and his battles and his reproofs with which he reproved Yisra'el, and all which he had commanded them, and the names of the cities which the children of Yisra'el possessed in his days, behold they are written in the book of the words of Yehoshua to the children of Yisra'el, and in the book of the wars of 𐤉𐤄𐤅𐤄,[a] which Mosheh and Yehoshua and the children of Yisra'el had written. **49** And the children of Yisra'el buried Yehoshua in the border of his inheritance, in Timnath-Seraḥ, which was given to him in Mount Ephrayim. **50** And Elazar the son of Aharon died in those days, and they buried him in a hill belonging to Pinechas his son, which was given him in Mount Ephrayim.

𐤎𐤐𐤓 𐤔𐤐𐤈𐤉𐤌 – Sefer Shoftim

91 **1** At that time, after the death of Yehoshua, the children of the Kana'anites were still in the land, and the Yisra'elites resolved to drive them out.

2 And the children of Yisra'el asked of 𐤉𐤄𐤅𐤄, saying, "Who shall first go up for us to the Kana'anites to fight against them?" and 𐤉𐤄𐤅𐤄 said, "Yehudah shall go up."

3 And the children of Yehudah said to Shimon, "Go up with us into our lot, and we will fight against the Kana'anites, and we likewise will go up with you, in your lot," so the children of Shimon went with the children of Yehudah.
4 And the children of Yehudah went up and fought against the Kana'anites, so 𐤉𐤄𐤅𐤄 delivered the Kana'anites into the hands of the children of Yehudah, and they struck them in Bezeq, ten thousand men. **5** And they fought with Adoni-Bezeq in Bezeq, and he fled from before them, and they pursued him and caught him, and they took hold of him and cut off his thumbs and great toes.

6 And Adoni-Bezeq said, "Seventy kings having their thumbs and great toes cut off, gathered their meat under my table; as I have done, so Elohim has repaid me," and they brought him to Yerushalayim and he died there.

7 And the children of Shimon went with the children of Yehudah, and they struck the Kana'anites with the edge of the sword. **8** And 𐤉𐤄𐤅𐤄 was with the children of Yehudah, and they possessed the mountain, and the children of Yoseph went up to Beth-El, the same is Luz, and 𐤉𐤄𐤅𐤄 was with them. **9** And the children of Yoseph spied out Beth-El, and the watchmen saw a man going forth from the city, and they caught him and said to him, "Show us the entrance of the city now and we will be kind to you."

10 And that man showed them the entrance of the city, and the children of Yoseph came and struck the city with the edge of the sword. **11** And they sent away the man with his family, and he went to the Ḥittites and he built a city, and he called its name Luz, so all Yisra'el dwelled in their cities, and the children of Yisra'el served 𐤉𐤄𐤅𐤄 all the days of Yehoshua, and all the days of the elders, who had outlived Yehoshua, and saw the great work of 𐤉𐤄𐤅𐤄, which He had performed for Yisra'el. **12** And the elders judged Yisra'el after the death of Yehoshua for seventeen years.
13 And all the elders also fought the battles of Yisra'el against the Kana'anites and 𐤉𐤄𐤅𐤄 drove the Kana'anites from before the children of

[a] **90:48** See Bemidbar [Numbers] **21:14**.

Yisra'el, in order to place the Yisra'elites in their land.

14 And He accomplished all the words which He
had spoken to Avraham, Yitsḥaq, and Ya'aqov,
and the oath which He had sworn: to give the
land of the Kana'anites to them and to their
children. 15 And 𐤉𐤄𐤅𐤄 gave the children of
Yisra'el the whole land of Kana'an, as He had
sworn to their ancestors, and 𐤉𐤄𐤅𐤄 gave them
rest from those around them, and the children of
Yisra'el dwelled securely in their cities.

16 Blessed be 𐤉𐤄𐤅𐤄 forever, amein, and amein.

17 Strengthen yourselves, and let the hearts of all you that trust in 𐤉𐤄𐤅𐤄 be courageous.

R. H. Charles' Preface: Jubilees

[Editor's note: The following is the preface from R. H. Charles' 1902 edition of *The Book of Jubilees or The Little Genesis*. My preface follows after.]

I had hoped to issue this Commentary on the Book of Jubilees quite six years ago, as a sequel to my edition of the Ethiopic and other fragmentary versions of this work; but after writing a large portion of it, I was obliged to abandon the task, as I felt that somehow I had failed to give a satisfactory interpretation of the text, though at the time I could not understand wherein my disability lay. A year or two later when making a special study of the Testaments of the XII. Patriarchs, I came to discover that the source of my failure lay in my acceptance of the traditional view that Jubilees was written in the first century of the Christian era. So long as I wrote from this standpoint, my notes became more and more a laboured apologetic for the composition of this work in the first century. The earliest approximation to the right date appeared in my article on the "Testaments of the XII. Patriarchs" in the *Encyclopaedia Biblica*, i. 241, 1899, where, after giving grounds for the view that the main bulk of that work was written before 100 B.C., I concluded that we should "regard both works (i.e. the Testaments and Jubilees) as almost contemporary, and as emanating from the same school of thought." This view was advocated in the following year by Bohn and by Bousset on various grounds, and it is from this standpoint that the present Commentary is written. The difficulties that beset almost every page of Jubilees vanish for the most part when once we understand that it was written by a Pharisaic upholder of the Maccabean dynasty, who was also probably a priest.

It is difficult to exaggerate the value of Jubilees. The fact that it is the oldest commentary in the world on Genesis, is in itself a distinction. But it is not on this ground that we value it, but rather for the insight it gives us into the religious beliefs of Judaism in the second century B.C. Its interests are many sided. It appeals to the textual critic, as it attests the form of the Hebrew text, which was current in that century. It appeals to the Old Testament scholar, as exhibiting further developments of ideas and tendencies which are only in their incipient stages in the Old Testament. It appeals to the New Testament scholar, as furnishing the first literary embodiment of beliefs which subsequently obtained an entrance into the New Testament, and as having in all probability formed part of the library of some of the apostolic writers. It appeals to the student, of theological doctrine, as providing certain indispensable links in the process of development. Finally, to the Jewish scholar, a Pharisaic work of the second century B.C. cannot fail to be of transcendent interest, as it gives the earlier forms of certain legislative enactments that appear in the Mishna, and of legends which in later Judaism have undergone much transformation.

Although half a century has elapsed since the discovery of Jubilees in its complete form in the Ethiopic Version, no scholar has hitherto attempted a commentary on the entire work. Some thirty years ago Rönsch edited a very learned and laborious work on the Latin Fragments, which constitute slightly more than one-fourth of the original writing, but since his time scholars have contented themselves with short studies on various views of our author.

I cannot conclude without thanking Mr. Cowley for his help in verifying references in the Talmud.

Editor's Preface: Jubilees

Introduction

With a long and muddled history, the Book of Jubilees is one that has seen a rollercoaster of attention. Also known as "The Little Genesis" or "The Lesser Genesis", the Book of Jubilees has been loved, hated, and almost forgotten. Early in the first centuries BCE and CE, it was very well-known by Jews and Christians alike. Its author was clearly a Jew, probably living around the second century BCE. While there are varying theories as to what sect of Judaism the author subscribed to, it is the opinion of the present editor that he was in some ways a Pharisee, though probably more aligned with the Essenes or their predecessors. More of this is discussed in the *Provenance* section.

The Book of Jubilees comes to us in its most complete form in the Ge'ez (Ethiopic) language, much like the Book of 1 Enoch. Indeed, the most important scholarly work performed prior to the mid-1900s CE was by R. H. Charles. While it is canonized by the Ethiopian Orthodox Church and Beta Israel Ethiopian Jews – to whom it is known as "The Book of Division" – it was subsequently rejected by both traditional Judaism as well as Christianity. It was a very prominent book for Jews and Christians during the first few centuries CE, while tensions between the two religions were on the rise. It was quoted by numerous Christian authors and indeed in a select few cases, some of the best and earliest witnesses to its text that we possess come from these very quotations. But also much like 1 Enoch, the scholarly (and layman) interest in the book has only begun to rise over the last 20 years.

The popularity of the book was spurred on by its discovery among the Dead Sea Scrolls at Qumran. Indeed, there are more fragmented manuscripts of Jubilees found at Qumran than there were of most books of the Hebrew Bible. This caused a shockwave among scholars of the book, who until then had seen no evidence of a pre-Christian existence for the book. These fragments, constituting numerous portions throughout the book, are written in Hebrew. This fully confirmed Charles' theory that the book was originally written in Hebrew, though he himself had never found any Hebrew texts of it.

Dead Sea Scrolls scholar James C. VanderKam outlined the history of the book and its numerous renditions and translations as follows:

- Jubilees was originally written in Hebrew.
- It was translated from Hebrew into Greek and Syriac Aramaic.
- It was translated from Greek into Latin and Ethiopic.[a]

If Charles were alive today, I have no doubts that he would completely agree with this assessment. Charles' translation, which I have chosen as my base English version to revise and emend, was translated almost entirely from Ethiopic. However, he also compared

---

[a] J. C. VanderKam, *Textual and Historical Studies in the Book of Jubilees,* p. vi. See Table of Contents.

numerous Greek, Latin, and Syriac texts. As noted by VanderKam, the Ethiopic version is "...in most respects an accurate and literalistic translation."[a]

The Texts

The manuscripts (MSS.) that come down to us are actually fairly consistent. Extant wholly only in Ethiopic, just as the Book of Enoch, there are considerable portions of the book in Latin as well. There are four primary Ethiopic MSS. that Charles worked from, as these four were most complete. Of these MSS. – titled A through D – Charles relied most heavily on MS. B, which his analysis revealed to be the least corrupted by translation and transmission error. This text was the primary basis for his English translation, which I have chosen to revise in the present edition. There are close to 20 known Ethiopic MSS. of Jubilees now, most of which are fragmentary. Manuscript B, considered most reliable, is itself only a 16th Century copy.

Aside from these Ethiopic MSS. there is about one-third of the entire book preserved in a Latin fragment. While the Ethiopic and Latin were, by all indications, both translations from Greek, the Latin witness is nevertheless a very useful text, in that it is about 1,000 years older than the most reliable Ethiopic text (MS. B). For my revision, I chose a Latin reading a number of times over the Ethiopic that Charles preferred. When these alterations were made, I noted them in footnotes.

In addition to the Latin fragment there are also a handful of quotations that exist in Greek. The book was heavily quoted by some Greek writers, such as Jerome, Justin Martyr and Origen; in some cases it was also written in summary form. Likewise there are a few Syriac fragments, though the Syriac is notorious for its paraphrasing of the text, and is highly truncated.

What is undeniably the most important find regarding manuscript evidence for the book are the fragments found at Qumran and Masada among the Dead Sea Scrolls. At the time of this publication (2015) there are roughly 15 fragmentary MSS. of Jubilees in Hebrew. Some of these cover essentially whole chapters, while others just a handful of verses.

For the edition set forth in this publication I have revised Charles' English translation while also consulting the Hebrew texts that were not known by Charles in his day. In most cases, the differences are negligible. However, there are a few variants which provide a considerable difference. Likewise, as mentioned above, I also showed preference to the Latin in some cases where Charles preferred the Ethiopic. My reasoning for this is that the Latin fragments tend to follow the Hebrew more closely, and the Latin are many hundreds of years older than the Ethiopic, and thus more likely to be free of corruption.

One of the more noticeable differences in this present text from all previous texts, is the alteration of many of the terms. The largest of these is the name of the book itself, which I have chosen to use in Hebrew: יובלים (Yovelim). While it is generally understood what a Jubilee is, the word itself is an Anglicized form of a Latin word. I prefer Hebrew terminology over all, since it is closer to the original. Thus the term "jubilee" which would

---

[a] J. C. VanderKam, "Jubilees, Book of" in L. H. Schiffman and J. C. VanderKam (eds.), *Encyclopedia of the Dead Sea Scrolls*, Oxford University Press (2000), Vol. I, p. 435.

otherwise be prevalent throughout most English translations has actually been written as "yovel" and the plural form, "yovelim."

Divisions in the Text

While Jasher is split into divisions by Torah portion (and by book after that) and Enoch is split into divisions by book, Jubilees contains no natural divisions. That is, the manuscripts themselves do not split the book into divisions, other than the natural flow of chapter breaks. However it is clear that Jubilees is written in a sort of divided form, as the book breaks quite evenly into 50 sections; this is most likely intentional, since the number 50 represents a Jubilee.

Beyond this, section headings have been added by the present editor. These headings were added for the primary purpose of assisting the reader in locating specific stories. These section headings are **not** found in the underlying source texts, but were added by the editor.

Provenance

Jubilees does not identify its author directly, but rather claims to be an account of an angel speaking to Moses, while still on Mount Sinai. It takes the position of an angel referred to as the "messenger of the presence." Many sections of the book are written in first-person, appearing to be a sort of dictation. That is, it appears that the angel is speaking in first-person, telling Moses the stories, and telling him what to write.

The author of the book was undoubtedly a Jew, though to which sect he belonged is still widely debated. It is the opinion of the present author that he was of a sect similar to the Pharisees in many aspects, though holding to the calendar of the Qumran community, be that Essene or otherwise. Many statements are made in Jubilees that lead to the conclusion of a sectarian doctrine. First and foremost is, of course, the calendrical statements. The author most assuredly borrowed from the Book of Enoch when writing about the calendar, and these statements match other Qumran texts that describe their calendar.

Second, a few statements are made regarding specific "laws" that are not found present in the Torah itself. Yovelim 50:8 states that whoever "lies with his wife" on the Sabbath is to be given the death penalty. Likewise, it then lists numerous other infractions that, if committed on the Sabbath, warrant the death of the offender. These specific statements, however, are found nowhere in the Torah – aside from its general prohibition on work – and thus cannot be attributed to the "Torah" as chapter 50 states. These types of prohibitions, however, are common among different Jewish sectarian groups, and some similar statements are found in numerous other Jewish works.

Regardless of his sect, the author clearly wants the reader to understand and interpret the events of Genesis in the manner that he does. In many instances he goes to great lengths to explain passages from the Hebrew Bible that may otherwise be difficult to understand. An example of this is seen in chapter 3, where the author uses the length of time that Adam and Eve were outside of the Garden to explain the puzzling passage found in Leviticus 12.

Conclusion

Jubilees shows a great number of consistencies with other pieces of ancient literature, including the Testaments of the Twelve Patriarchs (T12P). However, it also shows a few places of disagreement, mostly with the Book of Jasher. Yet it should be noted that because of these disagreements, we have an even more valuable account. Since these texts show places of disagreement – however minor they may be – we know that one account is not merely a copy of another. This means that these different books can be viewed as separate witnesses, and in the places where they all agree on a story or fact only increases the likelihood of that story or fact's authenticity.

As with the other books in this publication, whether they should be accepted as canon or not is not a point I desire to make. Rather, at the very least, these books help to put the reader into the mind of a 2nd century Jew, who lived in Bible places, during Bible times, studying the Bible. This alone should give enough reason to study the book.

*This is the history of the division of the days of
the Torah and of the witness, of the events of the
years, of their year-weeks, of their yovelim
throughout all the years of the world, as 𐤉𐤄𐤅𐤄
spoke to Mosheh on Mount Sinai when he went
up to receive the tables of the Torah and of the
command, according to the voice of 𐤉𐤄𐤅𐤄 as He
said to him, "Go up to the top of the Mount."*

Mosheh is Summoned

1 1 And it happened in the first year of the
exodus of the children of Yisra'el out of
Mitsrayim, in the third month, on the sixteenth
day of the month, that 𐤉𐤄𐤅𐤄 spoke to Mosheh,
saying, "Come up to Me on the Mount, and I
will give you two tablets of stone of the Torah
and of the command, which I have written, that
you may teach them."

2 And Mosheh went up into the mount of 𐤉𐤄𐤅𐤄,
and the glory of 𐤉𐤄𐤅𐤄 stayed on Mount Sinai,
and a cloud overshadowed it *for* six days. 3 And
He called to Mosheh on the seventh day out of
the midst of the cloud, and the appearance of the
glory of 𐤉𐤄𐤅𐤄 was like a flaming fire on the top
of the mount. 4 And Mosheh was on the Mount
forty days and forty nights, and 𐤉𐤄𐤅𐤄 taught
him what was and what will be, *and* the division
of all the days of the Torah and of the witness.

5 And He said, "Incline your heart to every
word which I will speak to you on this mount,
and write them in a book in order that their
generations may know that I have not forsaken
them for all the evil which they have worked in
transgressing the covenant which I established
between Me and you for their generations this
day on Mount Sinai. 6 And thus it will come to
pass when all these things come upon them, that
they will recognize that I am more righteous
than they in all their judgments and in all their
actions, and they will recognize that I have been
truly with them.

Rebellion of the People Foretold

7 "And write for yourself all these words which
I declare to you today, for I know their rebellion
and their stiff neck. Before I bring them into the
land of which I swore to their fathers, to
Avraham and to Yitsḥaq and to Ya'aqov,
saying: 'To your seed I will give a land flowing
with milk and honey.' 8 And they will eat and be
satisfied, and they will turn to strange elohim, to
those who cannot deliver them from any of their
affliction. And this witness shall be heard for a
witness against them. 9 For they will forget all
My commands, *even* all that I command them,
and they will walk after the nations, and after
their uncleanness, and after their shame, and
will serve their elohim, and these will become a
stumbling block to them, and an affliction, and a
torment, and a snare.

10 "And many will perish and they will be taken
captive, and will fall into the hands of the
enemy, because they have forsaken My
judgments and My commands, and the Feasts of
My covenant, and My Sabbaths, and My set-
apart place which I have set apart for Myself in
their midst; and My Tabernacle, and My
dwelling-place, which I have set apart for
Myself in the midst of the land, that I should set
My Name upon it, and that it should dwell
there. 11 And they will make high places and
groves and engraved images for themselves.
And they will worship, each his own *engraved
image*, so as to go astray. And they will
slaughter their children to demons, and to all the
works of the error of their hearts.

12 "And I will send witnesses to them, that I
may witness against them, but they will not
hear, and will kill the witnesses also, and they
will pursue those who study the Torah, and they
will alter everything so as to work evil before
My eyes. 13 And I will hide My face from them,
and I will deliver them into the hand of the
nations for captivity, and for a prey, and for
devouring, and I will remove them from the
midst of the land, and I will scatter them among
the nations.

14 "And they will forget all My Torah and all
My commands and all My judgments, and will
go astray as to new moons, and Sabbaths, and
Feasts, and yovelim, and covenant. 15 And after
this they will turn to Me from among the
nations with all their heart and with all their
being and with all their strength, and I will
gather them from among all the nations, and
they will seek Me, so that I shall be found of

them, when they seek Me with all their heart
and with all their being.

16 "And I will reveal to them abounding peace
with righteousness. And with all My heart and
with all My being I will plant them as a
righteous plant. And they will be for a blessing
and not for a curse, and they shall be the head
and not the tail. 17 And I will build My
dwelling-place in their midst, and I will dwell
with them, and I will be their Elohim and they
shall be My people in truth and righteousness.
18 And I will not forsake them nor fail them; for
I am 𐤉𐤄𐤅𐤄 their Elohim."

Mosheh's Prayer of Intercession

19 And Mosheh fell on his face and prayed and
said, 'O 𐤉𐤄𐤅𐤄 my Elohim, do not forsake Your
people and Your inheritance, so that they should
wander in the error of their hearts. And do not
deliver them into the hands of their enemies, the
nations, lest they should rule over them and
cause them to sin against You. 20 Let your
favor, O Master, be lifted up on Your people,
and create in them an upright spirit, and do not
let the spirit of Beliyya'al[a] rule over them to
accuse them before You, and to ensnare them
from all the paths of righteousness, so that they
may perish from before Your face. 21 But they
are Your people and Your inheritance, which
You have delivered with Your great power from
the hands of the Mitsrites. Create in them a
clean heart and a set-apart spirit, and do not let
them be ensnared in their sins from now on until
eternity."

𐤉𐤄𐤅𐤄 Foretells a Restoration of the People

22 And 𐤉𐤄𐤅𐤄 said to Mosheh, "I know their
defiance and their thoughts and their
stubbornness. And they will not be obedient
until they confess their own sin and the sin of
their fathers. 23 And after this they will turn to
Me in all uprightness and with all *their* heart
and with all *their* being, and I will circumcise
the foreskin of their heart and the foreskin of the
heart of their seed, and I will create in them a
set-apart spirit, and I will cleanse them so that
they shall not turn away from Me from that day
to eternity. 24 And their beings will cling to Me
and to all My commands, and they will fulfil
My commands, and I will be their Father and
they shall be My children. 25 And they all shall
be called children of the living El, and every
messenger and every spirit shall know, yes, they
shall know that these are My children, and that I
am their Father in uprightness and
righteousness. And that I love them.

26 "And you: write down for yourself all these
words which I declare to you on this mountain,
the first and the last, which will come to pass in
all the divisions of the days in the Torah and in
the witness and in the weeks and the yovelim to
eternity, until I descend and dwell with them in
all ages of eternity."

27 And He said to the messenger of the
presence, "Write for Mosheh from the
beginning of creation until My dwelling-place
has been built among them for all eternity.
28 And 𐤉𐤄𐤅𐤄 will appear to the eyes of all, and
all will know that I am the Elohim of Yisra'el
and the Father of all the children of Ya'aqov,
and King on Mount Tsion for all eternity. And
Tsion and Yerushalayim shall be set-apart."

Tablets of the Divisions

29 And the messenger of the presence who went
before the camp of Yisra'el took the tablets of
the divisions of the years -from the time of the
creation of the Torah and of the witness of the
weeks of the yovelim, according to the
individual years, according to all the number of
the yovelim according, to the individual years,
from the day of the new creation when the
heavens and the earth shall be renewed and all
their creation according to the powers of the
heavens, and according to all the creation of the
earth, until the dwelling-place of 𐤉𐤄𐤅𐤄 shall be
made in Yerushalayim on Mount Tsion, and all
the lights be renewed for healing and for peace
and for blessing for all the elect of Yisra'el, and

---

[a] **1:20** Beliyya'al – In Hebrew this is 𐤁𐤋𐤉𐤏𐤋 (*be'liy'ya'al*) meaning "worthless." Ethiopic texts records this as በልሖር (*bel'ḥor*).

that thus it may be from that day and to all the days of the earth.

Six Days of Creation

2 1 And the messenger of the presence spoke to Mosheh according to the word of 𐤉𐤄𐤅𐤄, saying: "Write the complete account of the creation, how on the sixth day 𐤉𐤄𐤅𐤄 Elohim finished all His works and all that He created, and guarded Sabbath on the seventh day and set it apart for all ages. 2 And *He* set it as a sign for all His works. For on the first day He created the heavens which are above, and the earth and the waters and all the spirits which serve before him: the messengers of the presence, and the messengers of setting apart, and the messengers of the spirit of fire and the messengers of the spirit of the winds, and the messengers of the spirit of the clouds, and of darkness, and of snow and of hail and of hoarfrost, and the messengers of the voices and of the thunder and of the lightning, and the messengers of the spirits of cold and of heat, and of winter and of spring and of autumn and of summer and of all the spirits of His creatures which are in the heavens and on the earth. He created the abysses and the darkness – evening and night – and the light – morning and day – which He has prepared in the knowledge of His heart. 3 Then we saw His works, and blessed Him, and praised before Him on account of all His works; for He created seven great works on the first day.

4 "And on the second day He created the expanse in the midst of the waters, and the waters were divided on that day. Half of them went up above, and half of them went down below the expanse that was in the midst over the face of the whole earth. And this was the only work He created on the second day.

2 "And on the third day He commanded the waters to pass from off the face of the whole earth into one place, and the dry land to appear. 6 And the waters did so as He commanded them, and they turned aside from off the face of the earth into one place outside of this expanse; and the dry land appeared. 7 And on that day He created for them all the seas according to their separate gatherings, and all the rivers, and the gatherings of the waters in the mountains and on all the earth, and all the lakes, and all the dew of the earth, and the seed which is sown, and all sprouting things, and fruit-bearing trees, and trees of the wood, and the Garden of Eden, in Eden and all. 𐤉𐤄𐤅𐤄 created these four great works on the third day.

8 "And on the fourth day He created the sun and the moon and the stars, and set them in the expanse of the heavens, to give light upon all the earth, and to rule over the day and the night, and divide the light from the darkness. 9 And 𐤉𐤄𐤅𐤄 appointed the sun to be a great sign on the earth for days and, for Sabbaths, and for months, and for Feasts, and for years, and for Sabbaths of years, and for yovelim, and for all seasons of the years. 10 And it separates the light from the darkness, so that all things may prosper which shoot and grow on the earth. He made these three kinds on the fourth day.

11 "And on the fifth day He created great sea monsters in the depths of the waters, for these were the first things of flesh that were created by his hands: the fish and everything that moves in the waters; 12 and everything that flies, the birds and all their kind. And the sun rose above them to cause them to prosper, and above everything that was on the earth, everything that shoots out of the earth, and all 13 fruit-bearing trees, and all flesh. These three kinds He created on the fifth day.

14 "And on the sixth day He created all the animals of the earth, and all cattle, and everything that moves on the earth. And after all this He created mankind, a man and a woman, He created them. And *He* gave him dominion over all that is upon the earth, and in the seas, and over everything that flies, and over beasts and over cattle, and over everything that moves on the earth, and over the whole earth, and over all this He gave him dominion. 15 And these four kinds He created on the sixth day. And there were altogether twenty-two kinds.

The Sabbath

16 "And He finished all his work on the sixth day: all that is in the heavens and on the earth, and in the seas and in the abysses, and in the

light and in the darkness, and in everything.
17 And He gave us a great sign, the Sabbath
day, that we should work six days, but guard
Sabbath on the seventh day from all work.
18 And He told us – all the messengers of the
presence, and all the messengers of setting
apart, these two great classes – He has that we
may guard the Sabbath with Him in heaven and
on earth. 19 And He said to us, "Behold, I will
separate to Myself a people from among all the
peoples, and they shall guard the Sabbath day,
and I will set them apart to Myself as My
people, and will bless them. As I have set the
Sabbath day apart, and do still set it apart to
Myself, even so will I bless them, and they shall
be My people and I will be their Elohim. 20 And
I have chosen the seed of Ya'aqov from among
all that I have seen, and have written him down
as My firstborn son, and have set him apart to
Myself for ever and ever; and I will teach them
the Sabbath day, that they may guard Sabbath
from all work."

21 "And thus He created a sign in accordance
with which they should guard the Sabbath with
us on the seventh day, to eat and to drink, and to
bless Him who has created all things, as He has
blessed and set apart to Himself a peculiar
people above all peoples, and that they should
keep Sabbath together with us. 22 And He
caused His commands to ascend as a sweet
aroma, acceptable before Him all the days.

23 "There were twenty-two heads of mankind
from Adam to Ya'aqov, and twenty-two kinds
of work were made until the seventh day; this is
blessed and set-apart; and the former also is
blessed and set-apart; and this one serves with
that one for setting apart and blessing. 24 And to
Ya'aqov and his seed it was granted that they
should always be the blessed and set-apart ones
of the first witness and Torah, even as He had
set apart and blessed the Sabbath day on the
seventh day. 25 He created heaven and earth and
everything that He created in six days, and
𐤉𐤄𐤅𐤄 made the seventh day set-apart, for all His
works. Therefore He commanded on its behalf
that, whoever does any work on it shall die, and
that he who defiles it shall surely die. 26 Why do
you command the children of Yisra'el to guard
this day, that they may keep it set-apart and not
do any work on it, and not to defile it? It is more
set-apart than all other days. 27 And whoever
profanes it shall surely die, and whoever does
any work on it shall surely die eternally, that the
children of Yisra'el may guard this day
throughout their generations, and not be
removed out of the land, for it is a set-apart and
a blessed day.

28 "And everyone who guards it, and keeps
Sabbath on it from all his work, will be set-apart
and blessed throughout all days like us.
29 Declare and say to the children of Yisra'el:
the Torah of this day both that they should
guard Sabbath on it, and that they should not
forsake it in the error of their hearts. It is not
lawful to do any work on it which is unseemly,
to do their own pleasure, and that they should
not prepare anything to be eaten or drunk on it,
and it is not lawful to draw water, or bring in, or
take out through their gates any burden, which
they had not prepared for themselves on the
sixth day in their dwellings. 30 And they shall
not bring in nor take out from house to house on
that day, for that day is more set-apart and
blessed than any yovel day of the yovelim. On
this we guarded Sabbath in the heavens before it
was made known to any flesh to guard Sabbath
on the earth. 31 And the Creator of all things
blessed it, but He did not set apart all peoples
and nations to guard Sabbath on *the seventh
day*, but Yisra'el alone. Them alone He
permitted to eat and drink and to guard Sabbath
on the earth. 32 And the Creator of all things
blessed this day which He had created for
blessing and set-apartness and glory above all
days. 33 This Torah and witness was given to
the children of Yisra'el as a Torah forever to
their generations.

Naming the Animals

3 1 And on the six days of the second week,
according to the word of 𐤉𐤄𐤅𐤄, we brought all
the beasts, and all the cattle, and all the birds,
and everything that moves on the earth, and
everything that moves in the water, according to
their kinds, and according to their types to
Adam: the beasts on the first day; the cattle on
the second day; the birds on the third day; and
all that which moves on the earth on the fourth

day; and that which moves in the water on the
fifth day. **2** And Adam named them all by their
respective names, and as he called them, so was
their name. **3** And on these five days Adam saw
all these, male and female, according to every
kind that was on the earth, but he was alone and
found no helpmeet for him.

Forming of Woman

4 And 𐤉𐤄𐤅𐤄 said to us, "It is not good that the
man should be alone: let us make a helpmeet for
him." **5** And 𐤉𐤄𐤅𐤄 our Elohim caused a deep
sleep to fall upon him, and he slept, and He took
for the woman one rib from among his ribs, and
this rib was the origin of the woman from
among his ribs, and He built up the flesh in its
stead, and built the woman.

6 And He awakened Adam out of his sleep and
on awaking he rose on the sixth day, and He
brought her to him, and he knew her, and said to
her, "This is now bone of my bones and flesh of
my flesh; she shall be called my wife, because
she was taken from her husband."

7 Therefore shall man and wife be one, and
therefore a man shall leave his father and his
mother, and cling to his wife, and they shall be
one flesh. In the first week was Adam created,
and the rib – his wife. **8** In the second week He
showed her to him, and for this reason the
commandment was given to keep in their
defilement, for a male seven days, and for a
female twice seven days. **9** And after Adam had
completed forty days in the land where he had
been created, we brought him into the Garden of
Eden to serve and guard it, but his wife they
brought in on the eightieth day, and after this
she entered into the Garden of Eden. **10** And for
this reason the commandment is written on the
heavenly tablets in regard to her that gives birth,
"If she bears a male *child*, she shall remain in
her uncleanness seven days according to the
first week of days, and thirty-three days shall
she remain in the blood of her purifying, and
she shall not touch any set-apart thing, nor enter
into the set-apart place, until she accomplishes
these days which for the case of a male child.
11 But in the case of a female child she shall
remain in her uncleanness two weeks of days,
according to the first two weeks, and sixty-six
days in the blood of her purification, and they
will be in all eighty days.[a]"

12 And when she had completed these eighty
days we brought her into the Garden of Eden,
for it is more set-apart than all the rest of the
earth, and every tree that is planted in it is set-
apart. **13** Therefore there was ordained,
regarding her who bears a male or a female
child, the statute of those days that she should
touch no set-apart thing, nor enter into the set-
apart place until these days for the male or
female child are accomplished. **14** This is the
Torah and witness which was written down for
Yisra'el, in order that they should guard it all the
days.

First Week of Years in Eden; The Fall

15 And in the first week of the first yovel, Adam
and his wife were in the Garden of Eden for
seven years serving and guarding it, and we
gave him work and we instructed him to do
everything that is suitable for serving. **16** And he
served the garden, and was naked, and did not
know it, and was not ashamed. And he protected
the garden from the birds and beasts and cattle,
and gathered its fruit, and ate, and put aside the
remainder for himself and for his wife, and put
aside that which was being kept.

17 And after the completion of the seven years,
which he had completed there, seven years
exactly, and in the second month, on the
seventeenth day of the month, the naḥash came
and approached the woman, and the naḥash said
to the woman, "Has 𐤉𐤄𐤅𐤄 commanded you,
saying, 'You shall not eat of every tree of the
garden?'"

18 And she said to it, "Of all the fruit of the trees
of the garden 𐤉𐤄𐤅𐤄 has said to us, 'Eat;' but of
the fruit of the tree which is in the midst of the
garden 𐤉𐤄𐤅𐤄 has said to us, 'You shall not eat of
it, neither shall you touch it, lest you die.'"

19 And the naḥash said to the woman, "You
shall not surely die. For 𐤉𐤄𐤅𐤄 knows that on the
day you eat of it, your eyes will be opened, and

[a] **3:10-11** See Vayyiqra [Leviticus] **12:1-5**.

you will be as Elohim, and you will know good and evil."

20 And the woman saw the tree that it was good and pleasant to the eye, and that its fruit was good for food, and she took of it and ate. 21 And when she had first covered her shame with figleaves, she gave it to Adam and he ate, and his eyes were opened, and he saw that he was naked. 22 And he took figleaves and sewed them together, and made a loincloth for himself, and covered his shame.

23 And 𐤉𐤄𐤅𐤄 cursed the naḥash, and was angry with it forever.[a] 24 And He was angry with the woman, because she listened to the voice of the naḥash, and ate. And He said to her, "I will greatly multiply your sorrow and your pains; in sorrow you will bring forth children, and your turning[b] shall be to your husband, and he will rule over you."

25 And to Adam also He said, "Because you listened to the voice of your wife, and have eaten of the tree which I commanded you not to eat of, cursed be the ground for your sake. It shall bring forth thorns and thistles to you, and you shall eat your bread in the sweat of your face, until you return to the earth from which you were taken. For you are earth, and to earth you shall return."

26 And He made for them coats of skin, and clothed them, and sent them forth from the Garden of Eden. 27 And on that day on which Adam went forth from the Garden, he offered as a sweet aroma an offering: frankincense, galbanum, and stacte, and spices in the morning with the rising of the sun from the day when he covered his shame.[c]

28 And on that day the mouth of all beasts, and of cattle, and of birds, and of whatever walks, and of whatever moves, was closed so that they could no longer speak: for they had all spoken one with another with one lip and with one tongue.

Expulsion from Eden

29 And He sent all flesh out of the Garden of Eden; all that which was in the Garden of Eden, and all flesh was scattered according to its kinds, and according to its types to the places which had been created for them. 30 And to Adam alone did He give *something* to cover his shame, of all the beasts and cattle. 31 On account of this, it is prescribed on the heavenly tablets as touching all those who know the judgment of the Torah that they should cover their shame, and should not uncover themselves as the nations uncover themselves.

32 And on the new moon of the fourth month, Adam and his wife went forth from the Garden of Eden. 33 And they dwelled in the land of Elda in the land of their creation. 34 And Adam called the name of his wife Ḥavvah. And they had no son until the first yovel, and after this he knew her. 35 Now he served the land as he had been instructed in the Garden of Eden.

Qayin and Havel

4 1 And in the third week in the second yovel she gave birth to Qayin; and in the fourth she gave birth to Havel, and in the fifth she gave birth to Awan, his daughter. 2 And at the beginning of the third yovel, Qayin killed Havel because the slaughtering of Havel was accepted, but the offering of Qayin was not accepted.
3 And he killed him in the field: and his blood cried from the ground to heaven, complaining because he had killed him. 4 And 𐤉𐤄𐤅𐤄 rebuked Qayin because of Havel, because he killed him;

---

[a] **3**:**23** In Charles' English translation, he noted that he found numerous ancient witnesses that claim to quote Yovelim, stating that the naḥash (serpent) had four legs prior to his being cursed. This text is never found in Yovelim, though Charles included a lacuna after verse **23** supposing it to have been original.
[b] **3**:**24** While most English Bibles read in the book of Bereshiyt [Genesis], "…and your desire shall be to your husband…" here the Ethiopic text uses the word ምድር (*m'd'r*) meaning "to turn." In the Hebrew Masoretic Text of the Bible, we find the word 𐤕𐤔𐤅𐤒𐤄 (tesh'uw'qah). This word is usually translated as "desire." However, the Greek Septuagint uses ἀποστροφή (*apos'traphe*) meaning "turning away." Thus it appears the author of Yovelim took the term *teshuqah* to mean "turning" rather than "desire" in accordance with the Septuagint. Syriac Peshitta uses ܬܬܦܢܝܢ (*tat'pei'nin*) which also means "turning."
[c] **3**:**26** See Ḥanokh **31**.

and He made him a fugitive on the earth
because of the blood of his brother, and He
cursed him upon the earth.

5 And on this account it is written on the
heavenly tables, "Cursed is he who strikes his
neighbor treacherously, and let all who have
seen and heard say, 'Amein'; and 6 the man who
has seen and not declared, let him be cursed as
the other."

Descendants of Adam

6 And for this reason we announce when we
come before 𐤉𐤄𐤅𐤄 our Elohim all the sin which
is committed in heaven and on earth, and in
light and in darkness, and everywhere. 7 And
Adam and his wife mourned for Havel four
weeks of years, and in the fourth year of the
fifth week they became joyful. And Adam knew
his wife again, and she bore him a son, and he
called his name Sheth, for he said "𐤉𐤄𐤅𐤄 has
raised up a second seed to us on the earth
instead of Havel, for Qayin killed him."

8 And in the sixth week he brought forth his
daughter Azura. 9 And Qayin took Awan his
sister to be his wife and she bore him Ḥanokh at
the end of the fourth yovel. And in the first year
of the first week of the fifth yovel, houses were
built on the earth, and Qayin built a city, and
called its name after the name of his son
Ḥanokh. 10 And Adam knew Ḥavvah his wife
and she bore nine more sons.

11 And in the fifth week of the fifth yovel, Sheth
took Azura his sister to be his wife, and in the
fourth year of the sixth week she bore him
Enosh. 12 He began to call on the Name of
𐤉𐤄𐤅𐤄 on the earth. 13 And in the seventh yovel
in the third week Enosh took Noam his sister to
be his wife, and she bore him a son in the third
year of the fifth week, and he called his name
Qenan. 14 And at the end of the eighth yovel,
Qenan took to himself a wife, Mualeleth his
sister, to be his wife, and she bore him a son in
the ninth yovel, in the first week in the third
year of this week, and he called his name
Mahalalel.

15 And in the second week of the tenth yovel
Mahalalel took to himself a wife: Dinah, the
daughter of Baraki'el the daughter of his father's
brother, as wife. She bore him a son in the third
week in the sixth year, and he called his name
Yared, for in his days the messengers of 𐤉𐤄𐤅𐤄
descended on the earth, those who are named
the Watchers, that they should instruct the
children of men, and that they should perform
judgment and uprightness on the earth.

Birth and Mission of Ḥanokh

16 And in the eleventh yovel Yared took to
himself a wife, and her name was Baraka, the
daughter of Rasui'el, a daughter of his father's
brother, in the fourth week of this yovel, and
she bore him a son in the fifth week, in the
fourth year of the yovel, and he called his name
Ḥanokh. 17 This one was the first among men
that are born on earth who learned writing[a] and
knowledge and wisdom, and who wrote down
the signs of heaven according to the order of
their months in a book, that men might know
the seasons of the years according to the order
of their separate months. 18 And he was the first
to write a witness and he witnessed to the sons
of men among the generations of the earth, and
recounted the weeks of the yovelim, and made
known to them the days of the years, and set in
order the months and recounted the Sabbaths of
the years as we made known to him. 19 And
what was and what will be he saw in a vision of
his sleep; as it will happen to the children of
men throughout their generations until the day
of judgment; he saw and understood everything,
and wrote his witness, and placed the witness on
earth for all the children of men and for their
generations.

20 And in the twelfth yovel, in the seventh
week, he took to himself a wife, and her name
was Edna, the daughter of Dani'el, the daughter
of his father's brother, and in the sixth year in
this week she bore him a son and he called him
Methushelaḥ. 21 And he was with the
messengers of Elohim these six yovelim of
years, and they showed him everything which is

[a] **4:17** See Ḥanokh **12:3**.

on earth and in the heavens: the rule of the sun; and he wrote down everything.

22 And he witnessed to the Watchers, who had sinned with the daughters of men. For these had begun to unite themselves, so as to be defiled, with the daughters of men, and Ḥanokh witnessed against *them* all. 23 And he was taken from among the children of men, and we brought him into the Garden of Eden in majesty and honor, and behold there he writes down the condemnation and judgment of the world, and all the wickedness of the children of men.[a]
24 And because of him none of the waters of the flood were brought upon all the land of Eden; for there he was set as a sign and that he should bear witness against all the children of men, that he should recount all the deeds of the generations until the day of condemnation.

25 And he burned the incense of the set-apart place; sweet spices acceptable before 𐤉𐤄𐤅𐤄 in the evening at the set-apart place on Mount Qater[b]. 26 For 𐤉𐤄𐤅𐤄 has four places on the earth: the Garden of Eden, the Mount of the East, this mountain which you are on today, Mount Sinai, and Mount Tsion *which* will be set apart in the new creation for the setting apart of the earth. Through it the earth will be set apart from all *its* guilt and its uncleanness throughout the generations of the world.

Generations from Ḥanokh to Noaḥ

27 And in the fourteenth yovel Methushelaḥ took to himself a wife, Edna the daughter of Azri'el, the daughter of his father's brother, in the third week, in the first year of this week, and he brought forth a son and called his name Lamekh. 28 And in the fifteenth yovel in the third week Lamekh took to himself a wife, and her name was Batenosh[c] the daughter of Baraki'el, the daughter of his father's brother, and in this week she bore him a son and he called his name Noaḥ, saying, "This one will comfort me for my trouble and all my work, and for the ground which 𐤉𐤄𐤅𐤄 hath cursed."

Death of Adam

29 And at the end of the nineteenth yovel, in the seventh week in the sixth year, Adam died. And all his sons buried him in the land of his creation[d], and he was the first to be buried in the earth. 30 And he lacked seventy years of one thousand years; for one thousand years are as one day[e] in the witness of the heavens and therefore was it written concerning the tree of knowledge, "On the day that you eat of it you will die." For this reason he did not complete the years of this day; for he died during it.

31 At the end of this yovel Qayin was killed after him in the same year; for his house fell upon him and he died in the midst of his house, and he was killed by its stones; for with a stone he had killed Havel, and by a stone was he killed in righteous judgment.[f] 32 For this reason it was ordained on the heavenly tablets, "With the instrument with which a man kills his neighbor with the same shall he be killed; after the manner that he wounded him, in like manner shall they deal with him." [g]

---

[a] **4:23** See Ḥanokh **50:8**; **70:1-3**.

[b] **4:25** Qater – Ethiopic word ቀትር (*kh't'r*) can be translated as "noon." However, it is more likely that this is a corrupted form of the Hebrew root 𐤒𐤈𐤓 (*qa'tar*) which means "incense." Given that the passage already speaks of burning incense, this is most likely the case, as it preserves the wordplay and poetry.

[c] **4:28** Batenosh – Ethiopic text reads ቤቴኖስ (*be'te'nos*) which is most likely a corruption of the Hebrew 𐤁𐤕-𐤀𐤍𐤅𐤔 (*Bat-Enosh*). Batenosh means "daughter of Enosh."

[d] **4:19** Given the phrase form Yovelim **3:9** and Bereshiyt [Genesis] **2:8** that Adam was "formed" and then "placed in the Garden" the author of Yovelim apparently takes this to mean Adam was created outside of Eden, and thus was subsequently buried outside of it as well.

[e] **4:30** See also Tehillim [Psalms] **90:4**; Kepha 𐤁 [2 Peter] **3:8**.

[f] **4:31** This account runs contradictory to Yashar **2:26-29**.

[g] **4:32** Most likely a paraphrased version of Shemoth [Exodus] **21:24-25**; Vayyiqra [Leviticus] **24:19-20**. The Jerusalem Targum contains a similar narrative. In it, it designates different forms of capital punishment dependent on different crimes. These include stoning, strangling, and killing by sword, all dependent on the crime committed.

33 And in the twenty-fifth yovel Noaḥ took to himself a wife, and her name was Emzara[a], the daughter of Rake'el, the daughter of his father's brother, in the first year in the fifth week. And in the third year she bore him Shem, in the fifth year she bore him Ḥam, and in the first year in the sixth week she bore him Yepheth.[b]

Corruption of All Flesh

5 1 And it happened, when the children of men began to multiply on the face of the earth and daughters were born to them, that the messengers of 𐤉𐤄𐤅𐤄 saw them on a certain year of this yovel, that they were beautiful to look upon; and they took themselves wives of all whom they chose, and they bore them sons, and they were giants.[c]

2 And lawlessness increased on the earth and all flesh corrupted its way: men and cattle and beasts and birds and everything that walks on the earth; all of them corrupted their ways and their orders, and they began to devour each other, and lawlessness increased on the earth and every imagination of the thoughts of all men *was* only evil continually. 3 And 𐤉𐤄𐤅𐤄 looked upon the earth, and behold it was corrupt, and all flesh had corrupted its orders, and all that were on the earth had worked all manner of evil before His eyes.

4 And He said that He would destroy man and all flesh upon the face of the earth which He had created. 5 But Noaḥ found favor in the eyes of 𐤉𐤄𐤅𐤄.

Punishment of the Messengers

6 And against the messengers, whom He had sent upon the earth, He was exceedingly angry. And He commanded for them to be rooted out of all their dominion. And He told us to bind them in the depths of the earth,[d] and behold they are bound in the midst of them, and are *kept* separate. 7 And against their sons went forth a command from before His face that they should be struck with the sword, and be removed from under heaven.

8 And He said "My Ruaḥ shall not always abide on man; for they also are flesh. And their days shall be one hundred and twenty years."

9 And He sent His sword into their midst that each should kill his neighbor, and they began to kill each other until they all fell by the sword and were destroyed from the earth.[e] 10 And their fathers were witnesses *of their destruction*. And after this they were bound in the depths of the earth forever, until the day of the great condemnation, when judgment is executed on all those who have corrupted their ways and their works before 𐤉𐤄𐤅𐤄. 11 And He destroyed all from their places, and not one of them was left of whom He did not judge according to all their wickedness.

12 And He made for all His works a new and righteous nature, so that they would not sin in their whole nature forever, but would all be righteous, each in his kind, always. 13 And the judgment of all is ordained and written on the heavenly tablets in righteousness; even *the judgment of* all who depart from the path which is ordained for them to walk in; and if they do not walk in it, judgment is written down for every creature and for every kind. 14 And there is nothing in heaven or on earth, or in light or in darkness, or in Sheol or in the abyss, or in the place of darkness *which is not judged*; and all their judgments are ordained and written and engraved.

15 In regard to all He will judge; the great according to his greatness, and the small according to his smallness, and each according to his way. 16 And He is not one who regards persons, nor is He one who will receive bribes. If He says that He will execute judgment on each, if one gave everything that is on the earth, He would not regard the bribes or the person,

---

[a] **4:33** Emzara – Ethiopic word ዕምዘራ (*'m'za'ra*) has an uncertain meaning. Yashar **5** names the wife of Noaḥ as Na'amah.

[b] **4:33** Yashar **5:17** records Yepheth as firstborn, followed by Shem.

[c] **5:1** See Ḥanokh **7:2**; **15:3-8**.

[d] **5:6** See Ḥanokh **10:12**.

[e] **5:9** See Ḥanokh **10:9-12**.

nor accept anything at his hands, for He is a righteous judge.

17 And of the children of Yisra'el it has been written and ordained, if they turn to Him in righteousness He will forgive all their transgressions and pardon all their sins. It is written and ordained that He will show mercy to all who turn from all their guilt once each year. 19 And as for all those who corrupted their ways and their thoughts before the flood, no man's person was accepted except that of Noaḥ alone; for his person was accepted on behalf of his sons, who were saved from the waters of the flood on his account. For his heart was righteous in all his ways, according as it was commanded regarding him, and he had not departed from anything that was ordained for him.

The Flood

20 And 𐤉𐤄𐤅𐤄 said that He would destroy everything which was upon the earth, both men and cattle, and beasts, and fowls of the heavens, and that which moves on the earth. 21 And He commanded Noaḥ to make an ark, that he might save himself from the waters of the flood. 22 And Noaḥ made the ark in all respects as He commanded him, in the twenty-seventh yovel of years, in the fifth week in the fifth year on the new moon of the first month.

23 And he entered in the sixth year, in the second month, on the new moon of the second month, until the sixteenth. And he entered, and all that we brought to him, into the ark, and 𐤉𐤄𐤅𐤄 closed it from outside on the seventeenth evening. 24 And 𐤉𐤄𐤅𐤄 opened seven flood-gates of heaven, and the mouths of the fountains of the great deep, seven mouths in number. 25 And the flood-gates began to pour down water from the heavens forty days and forty nights. And the fountains of the deep also sent up waters, until the whole world was full of water.

26 And the waters increased upon the earth; fifteen cubits the water rose fifteen cubits above all the high mountains. And the ark was lift up above the earth, and it moved upon the face of the waters. 27 And the water prevailed on the face of the earth five months: one hundred and fifty days. 28 And the ark went and rested on the top of Lubar, one of the mountains of Ararat. 29 And in the fourth month the fountains of the great deep were closed and the flood-gates of heaven were restrained; and on the new moon of the seventh month all the mouths of the abysses of the earth were opened, and the water began to descend into the deep below.

30 And on the new moon of the tenth month the tops of the mountains were seen, and on the new moon of the first month the earth became visible. 31 And the waters disappeared from above the earth in the fifth week in the seventh year, and on the seventeenth day in the second month the earth was dry. 32 And on the twenty-seventh *day* he opened the ark, and sent forth from it beasts, and cattle, and birds, and every moving thing.

Exiting the Ark; Noaḥ's Offerings

6 1 And on the first of the third month he went forth from the ark, and built an altar on that mountain. 2 And he made atonement for the earth, and took a kid *of a goat* and made atonement by its blood for all the sins of the earth; for everything that had been on it had been destroyed, except those that were in the ark with Noaḥ. 3 And he placed its fat on the altar, and he took an ox, and a goat, and a sheep and kids, and salt, and a turtle-dove, and the young of a dove, and placed a ascension offering on the altar, and poured an offering mingled with oil on it, and sprinkled wine and strewed frankincense over everything, and caused a sweet aroma to arise, acceptable before 𐤉𐤄𐤅𐤄.

Covenant with Noaḥ

4 And 𐤉𐤄𐤅𐤄 smelled the sweet aroma, and He cut a covenant with him so that there would not be flood waters to destroy the earth anymore; that all the days of the earth seed-time and harvest should never cease; cold and heat, and summer and winter, and day and night should not change their order, nor cease forever.

5 "As for you, increase and multiply upon the earth, and become many upon it, and be a blessing upon it. I will put the fear of you and

the dread of you in everything that is on earth
and in the sea. **6** And behold I have given all
beasts to you, and all winged things, and
everything that moves on the earth, and the fish
in the waters, and all things for food; as the
green herbs, I have given you all things to eat.
7 But flesh, with the life in it, with the blood,
you shall not eat – for the life of all flesh is in
the blood – lest the blood of your lives be
required. At the hand of every man, at the hand
of every *beast* I will require the blood of man.
8 Whoever sheds man's blood, by man shall his
blood be shed, for in the image of 𐤉𐤄𐤅𐤄 He
made man. **9** And you, increase and multiply on
the earth."

10 And Noaḥ and his sons swore that they would
not eat any blood that was in any flesh, and he
cut a covenant before 𐤉𐤄𐤅𐤄 Elohim forever
throughout all the generations of the earth in
this month. **11** Therefore He spoke to you that
you should cut a covenant with the children of
Yisra'el in this month upon the mountain with
an oath, and that you should sprinkle blood on
them because of all the words of the covenant,
which 𐤉𐤄𐤅𐤄 cut with them forever. **12** And this
witness is written concerning you that you
should observe it continually, so that you should
not eat, on any day, any blood of beasts or birds
or cattle during all the days of the earth. And the
man who eats the blood of beast or of cattle or
of birds during all the days of the earth, he and
his seed shall be uprooted.

13 And command the children of Yisra'el to eat
no blood, so that their names and their seed may
be before 𐤉𐤄𐤅𐤄 our Elohim continually. **14** And
for this Torah there is no limit of days, for it is
forever. They shall guard it throughout their
generations, so that they may continue
petitioning on your behalf with blood before the
altar. Every day, and at the time of morning and
evening, they shall seek forgiveness on your
behalf perpetually before 𐤉𐤄𐤅𐤄 that they may
guard it and not be uprooted.

15 And He gave to Noaḥ and his sons a sign that
there would not be a flood on the earth *again*.
16 He set His bow in the cloud for a sign of the
eternal covenant that there should not again be a
flood on the earth to destroy it all the days of
the earth.

Feast of Shavuot

17 For this reason it is ordained and written on
the heavenly tablets, that they should celebrate
the Feast of Shavuot[a] in this month once a year,
to renew the covenant every year. **18** And this
whole Feast was celebrated in heaven from the
day of creation until the days of Noaḥ: twenty-
six yovelim and five weeks of years. And Noaḥ
and his sons guarded it for seven yovelim and
one week of years, until the day of Noaḥ's
death. And from the day of Noaḥ's death his
sons did away with *it*, until the days of
Avraham, and they ate blood. **19** But Avraham
guarded it, and Yitsḥaq and Ya'aqov, and his
children guarded it up to your days, and in your
days the children of Yisra'el forgot it until you
celebrated it fresh on this mountain.

20 And command the children of Yisra'el to
guard this Feast in all their generations for a
command to them: one day in the year in this
month they shall celebrate the Feast. **21** For it is
the Feast of Shavuot and the Feast of first-fruits.
This Feast is twofold and of a double nature.
According to what is written and engraved
concerning it, celebrate it. **22** For I have written
in the book of the first Torah, in that which I
have written for you, that you should celebrate
it in its season, one day in the year, and I
explained to you its slaughterings that the
children of Yisra'el should remember and
should celebrate it throughout their generations
in this month, one day in every year.

23 And on the first of the first month, and on the
first of the fourth month, and on the first of the
seventh month, and on the first of the tenth
month are the days of remembrance, and the
days of the seasons in the four divisions of the
year. These are written and ordained as a

---

[a] **6:17** Shavuot – Ethiopic word ሴቡዖት (*Se'bu'ot*) literally means "weeks." However, this is actually a corruption of the Hebrew word 𐤔𐤁𐤅𐤏𐤕 (*sha'vu'ot*) which also means "weeks." Likewise Shavuot is also called the Feast of Weeks and it occurs in the **3**rd month. It is sometimes called *Pentecost* after the Greek πεντηκοντη meaning "fifty."

witness forever. 24 And Noaḥ ordained them for
himself as feasts for the generations forever, so
that they have become thereby a memorial to
him. 25 And on the first of the first month he
was told to make for himself an ark, and on that
day the earth became dry and he opened *the ark*
and saw the earth. 26 And on the first of the
fourth month the mouths of the depths of the
abyss beneath were closed. And on the first of
the seventh month all the mouths of the abysses
of the earth were opened, and the waters began
to descend into them. 27 And on the first of the
tenth month the tops of the mountains were
seen, and Noaḥ was glad. 28 Therefore he
ordained them for himself as feasts for a
memorial forever, and thus are they ordained.

29 And they placed them on the heavenly
tablets, each having thirteen weeks; from one to
another *passed* their memorial, from the first to
the second, and from the second to the third,
and from the third to the fourth. 30 And all the
days of the command will be fifty-two weeks of
days, and *these will make* the entire year
complete. Thus it is engraved and ordained on
the heavenly tablets. 31 And there is no
neglecting *this* for a single year or from year to
year.

Calendrical Warnings

32 And command the children of Yisra'el that
they guard the years according to this
reckoning: three hundred and sixty-four days,
and *these* will constitute a complete year, and
they will not disturb its time from its days and
from its feasts; for everything will fall out in
them according to their witness, and they will
not leave out any day nor disturb any feasts.

33 But if they are transgressed, and they do not
guard them according to His command, then
they will corrupt appointed times, and the years
will be moved from this *order*, and they will
disturb the appointed times and the years will be
moved and they will corrupt their ordinances.
34 And all the children of Yisra'el will forget
and will not find the path of the years, and will
forget the new moons, and appointed times, and
Sabbaths and they will go wrong as to all the
order of the years. 35 For I know and now will I
declare it to you, and it is not of my own heart,
for the book is written before me, and is
ordained on the heavenly tablets of the division
of days; lest they forget the feasts of the
covenant and walk in the feasts of the nations;
after their error and after their ignorance.

36 For there will be those who examine the
moon diligently because it will corrupt the
appointed times and it will advance from year to
year, ten days. 37 Therefore, the years will come
to them as they corrupt and make an abominable
day the day of witness, and an unclean day a
feast day, and they will mix all the days, the set-
apart with the unclean, and the unclean day with
the set-apart; for they will go wrong as to the
months and Sabbaths and feasts and yovelim.
38 Therefore I command and witness to you that
you may witness to them; for after your death
your children will be corrupted so that they will
not make the year only three hundred and sixty-
four days. Therefore they will go wrong as to
the new moons and appointed times and
Sabbaths and festivals, and they will eat all
kinds of blood with all kinds of flesh.

Noaḥ's Vineyard

7 1 And in the seventh week in the first year, in
this yovel, Noaḥ planted vines on the mountain
on which the ark had rested, named Lubar, one
of the Mountains of Ararat, and they produced
fruit in the fourth year. And he protected their
fruit, and gathered it in this year in the seventh
month. 2 And he made wine from them and put
it into a vessel, and kept it until the fifth year
until the first day, on the first of the first month.
3 And he celebrated with joy the day of this
feast, and he made a ascension offering to
𐤉𐤄𐤅𐤄, one young ox and one ram, and seven
sheep, each a year old, and a kid of the goats,
that he might make atonement for himself and
his sons. 4 And he prepared the kid first, and
placed some of its blood on the flesh that was
on the altar which he had made, and all the fat
he laid on the altar where he made the ascension
offering, and the ox and the ram and the sheep,
and he laid all their flesh upon the altar. 5 And
he placed all their offerings mingled with oil
upon it, and afterwards he sprinkled wine on the
fire which he had previously made on the altar,
and he placed incense on the altar and caused a

sweet aroma to ascend, acceptable before 𐤉𐤄𐤅𐤄
his Elohim. **6** And he rejoiced and drank of this
wine, he and his children with joy. **7** And it was
evening, and he went into his tent, and being
drunken he lay down and slept, and was
uncovered in his tent as he slept.

Curse of Kana'an; Blessing of Shem

8 And Ḥam saw Noaḥ his father naked, and
went forth and told his two brothers outside.
9 And Shem took his garment and arose, he and
Yepheth, and they placed the garment on their
shoulders and went backward and covered the
shame of their father, and their faces were
backward.

10 And Noaḥ awoke from his sleep and knew all
that his younger son had done to him, and he
cursed his son and said, "Cursed be Kana'an, an
enslaved servant he will be to his brethren."
11 And he blessed Shem, and said, "Blessed be
𐤉𐤄𐤅𐤄 Elohim of Shem, and Kana'an shall be his
servant. **12** May 𐤉𐤄𐤅𐤄 enlarge Yepheth, and
may 𐤉𐤄𐤅𐤄 dwell in the dwelling-place of Shem.
And Kana'an shall be his servant."

13 And Ḥam knew that his father had cursed his
younger son, and he was displeased that he had
cursed his son. And he parted from his father,
he and his sons with him, Kush and Mitrayim
and Put and Kana'an.

The Cities of the Sons of Noaḥ

14 And he built for himself a city and called its
name after the name of his wife Ne'elatama'uk.
15 And Yepheth saw it, and became jealous of
his brother, and he too built for himself a city,
and he called its name after the name of his wife
'Adataneses. **16** And Shem dwelled with his
father Noaḥ, and he built a city close to his
father on the mountain, and he too called its
name after the name of his wife Sedeqetelebab.

17 And behold these three cities are near Mount
Lubar; Sedeqetelebab on the front of the
mountain on its east; and Na'eltama'uk on the
south; 'Adatan'eses towards the west.

18 And these are the sons of Shem: Elam, and
Asshuwr, and Arpakhshad, who was born two
years after the flood, and Lud, and Aram.

19 The sons of Yepheth: Gomer and Magog and
Madai and Yavan, Tuval and Meshekh and
Tiras. These are the sons of Noaḥ.

Noaḥ's Commands to His Children

20 And in the twenty-eighth yovel, Noaḥ began
to command his sons' sons the statutes and
commands, and all the judgments that he knew.
And he exhorted his sons to guard
righteousness, and to cover the shame of their
flesh, and to bless their Creator, and honor
father and mother, and love their neighbor, and
guard their beings from whoring and
uncleanness and all iniquity. **21** For because of
these three things, the flood came upon the
earth. Namely, because of the whoring of the
Watchers against the Torah of their statutes,
who went whoring after the daughters of men,
and took wives to themselves of all which they
chose: and they made the beginning of
uncleanness.[a]

22 And they brought forth sons, the Naphidim[b],
and they were all different. And they devoured
one another; and the giants killed the Naphil[c],
and the Naphil killed the Elyo, and the Elyo
killed mankind, and one man another.[d] **23** And
every one sold himself to work lawlessness, and
to shed much blood, and the earth was filled
with lawlessness.

24 And after this they sinned against the beasts
and birds, and all that moves and walks on the
earth, and much blood was shed on the earth,
and every imagination and desire of men was

---

[a] **7:21** See Ḥanokh **10:2**.

[b] **7:22** Naphidim – Ethiopic word ናፊዲም (*na'fi'dim*) is most likely a corruption of the Hebrew 𐤍𐤐𐤉𐤋𐤉𐤌 (*ne'phi'lim*). This is the name given to the descendants of the "Sons of Elohim" and the "daughters of men" from Bereshiyt [Genesis] **6**. This word derives from the Hebrew root 𐤍𐤐𐤋 (*na'phal*) meaning "to fall."

[c] **7:22** Naphil – Ethiopic word ናፊል (*na'phil*) is most likely a corruption of the Hebrew *Nephilim*, in the singular form. Nephilim is plural by nature.

[d] **7:22** Compare this account of the 'Naphil' (Nephilim) and 'Elyo' (Elioud) with Ḥanokh chapters **6** and **7**, including accompanying footnotes.

worthless and evil continually. **25** And 𐤉𐤄𐤅𐤄
destroyed everything from off the face of the
earth; because of the wickedness of their deeds,
and because of the blood which they had shed in
the midst of the earth He destroyed everything.

26 "And we were left, I and you, my children,
and everything that entered with us into the ark.
And behold I see your works before me that you
do not walk in righteousness; for you have
begun to walk in the path of destruction, and
you are parting one from another, and are
jealous one of another, and *so it comes* that you
are not in harmony, my children, each with his
brother. **27** For I see, and behold, the demons
have begun *their* seductions against you and
against your children. And now I fear on your
behalf, that after my death you will shed the
blood of men upon the earth, and that you, too,
will be destroyed from the face of the earth.
28 For whoever sheds man's blood, and whoever
eats the blood of any flesh, will be destroyed
from the earth.

29 "And there shall not be left any man that eats
blood, or that sheds the blood of man on the
earth, nor shall there be left to him any seed or
descendants living under heaven. For into Sheol
shall they go, and into the place of
condemnation shall they descend, and into the
darkness of the deep shall they all be removed
by a violent death.[a] **30** There shall be no blood
seen upon you of all the blood there shall be all
the days in which you have killed any beasts or
cattle or whatever flies upon the earth; and work
a good work to your beings by covering that
which has been shed on the face of the earth.
31 And you shall not be like him who eats *things*
with blood, but guard yourselves that none may
eat blood before you. Cover the blood, for thus
have I been commanded to witness to you and
your children, together with all flesh.

32 "And do not allow the being to be eaten with
the flesh, that your blood, which is your life,
may not be required at the hand of any flesh that
sheds *it* on the earth. **33** For the earth will not be
clean from the blood which has been shed upon
it; for *only* through the blood of him that shed it
will the earth be purified throughout all its
generations.[b]

First Fruits

34 "And now, my children, listen: work
judgment and righteousness that you may be
planted in righteousness over the face of the
whole earth, and your honor lifted up before my
Elohim, who saved me from the waters of the
flood.[c] **35** And behold, you will go and build for
yourselves cities, and plant in them all the
plants that are upon the earth, and all *kinds of*
fruit-bearing trees. **36** For three years the fruit of
everything that is eaten will not be gathered,[d]
and in the fourth year its fruit will be considered
set-apart. And let them offer the first-fruits,
acceptable before the 𐤉𐤄𐤅𐤄 Most High, who
created heaven and earth and all things. Let
them offer in abundance the first of the wine
and oil *as* first-fruits on the altar of 𐤉𐤄𐤅𐤄, who
receives it, and what is left let the servants of
the house of 𐤉𐤄𐤅𐤄 eat before the altar which
receives *it*.[e]

37 "And in the fifth[f] year make the release so
that you release it in righteousness and
uprightness, and you shall be righteous, and all
that you plant shall prosper. **38** For thus did
Ḥanokh, the father of your father, command
Methushelaḥ, his son, and Methushelaḥ
commanded his son Lamekh, and Lamekh
commanded me all the things which his fathers
commanded him. **39** And I also will give you
command, my sons, as Ḥanokh commanded his
son in the first yovelim, while still living, the
seventh in his generation,[g] he commanded and

---

[a] **7:29** See Ḥanokh **103**:**7-8**.

[b] **7:33** See also Bemidbar [Numbers] **35:33**.

[c] **7:34** See also Yirmeyahu [Jeremiah] **11**:**17**; Amos **9**:**15**.

[d] **7:36** See also Vayyiqra [Leviticus] **19**:**23-25**.

[e] **7:36** See also Devarim [Deuteronomy] **18**:**1-5**.

[f] **7:37** All known Ethiopic manuscripts read ኃምስ (*ḥam's*) meaning "fifth." However, according to Devarim [Deuteronomy] **15** the seventh year is the year of release. It is possible that the author mistook the word "fifth" (ኃምስ) for the word "seventh" (ሰብዕ). Also, it may be drawing a parallel between Noaḥ's practice back in verse **2**, and the statement found in Vayyiqra [Leviticus] **19**:**25**.

[g] **7:39** See Ḥanokh **60**:**8**; **93**:**3**; Yehudah [Jude] **14**.

witnessed to his son and to his son's sons until the day of his death."

Kainan's Discovery of Astrological Writings

8 1 In the twenty-ninth yovel, in the first week, at its beginning Arpakhshad took to himself a wife and her name was Rasuyah, the daughter of Shushan, the daughter of Elam, and she bore him a son in the third year in this week, and he called his name Kainan. 2 And the child grew, and his father taught him writing, and he went to seek for himself a place where he might seize for himself a city. 3 And he found a writing which former *generations* had carved on the rock, and he read what was on it, and he transcribed it and sinned because of it. For it contained the teaching of the Watchers in accordance with which they used to observe the omens of the sun and moon and stars in all the signs of heaven. 4 And he wrote it down and said nothing regarding it; for he was afraid to speak to Noaḥ about it, lest he should be angry with him because of it.

Descendants of Kainan

5 And in the thirtieth yovel, in the second week, in the first year, he took to himself a wife, and her name was Melka, the daughter of Madai, the son of Yepheth, and in the fourth year he brought forth a son, and called his name Shelaḥ, for he said, "Truly I have been sent." [a] 6 And in the fourth year he was born, and Shelaḥ grew up and took to himself a wife, and her name was Mu'ak, the daughter of Kesed, his father's brother, in the one and thirtieth yovel, in the fifth week, in the first year.

7 And she bore him a son in the fifth year, and he called his name Ever: and he took to himself a wife, and her name was 'Azurad, the daughter of Nebrod, in the thirty-second yovel, in the seventh week, in the third year. 8 And in the sixth year, she bore him son, and he called his name Peleg; for in the days when he was born the children of Noaḥ began to divide the earth among themselves. For this reason he called his name Peleg. 9 And they divided it in evil among themselves, and told it to Noaḥ.

Division of the Earth

10 And it happened in the beginning of the thirty-third yovel that they divided the earth into three parts, for Shem, Ḥam, and Yepheth, according to the inheritance of each, in the first year in the first week, when one of us who had been sent was with them. 11 And he called his sons, and they drew near to him, they and their children, and he divided the earth into the lots, which his three sons were to take in possession, and they reached forth their hands, and took the writing out of the bosom of Noaḥ, their father.

Shem's Portion

12 And there came forth on the writing as Shem's lot the middle of the earth which he should take as an inheritance for himself and for his sons for the generations of eternity, from the middle of the mountain range of Rafa, from the mouth of the water from the river Tina[b], and his portion goes towards the west through the midst of this river, and it extends until it reaches the water of the abysses, out of which this river goes forth and pours its waters into the sea Me'at[c], and this river flows into the great sea. And all that is towards the north is Yepheth's, and all that is towards the south belongs to Shem. 13 And it extends until it reaches Karaso: this is in the bosom of the tongue which looks towards the south. 14 And his portion extends along the great sea, and it extends in a straight line until it reaches the west of the tongue which looks towards the south: for this sea is named the tongue of the Mitsrite Sea. 15 And it turns from here towards the south towards the mouth of the great sea on the shore of *its* waters, and it extends to the west to 'Afra[d], and it extends until it reaches the waters of the river Giḥon[e], and to the south of the waters of Giḥon, to the banks of

---

[a] **8:5** Shelaḥ – In Hebrew, the name Shelaḥ is spelled שלח, which is identical to the word *shalah*, meaning "to send." Thus the wordplay in his naming.

[b] **8:12** Tina River – The boundary between the land of Shem and the land of Yepheth. The three "lots" are most likely an early attempt to separate the three major continents in the area: Europe, Africa, and Asia.

[c] **8:12** Me'at – Most likely Lake Maeotis.

[d] **8:15** 'Afra – Most likely Africa.

[e] **8:15** Giḥon – Apparently identified with the Nile.

this river. **16** And it extends towards the east, until it reaches the Garden of Eden, to the south, to the south and from the east of the whole land of Eden and of the whole east, it turns to the east and proceeds until it reaches the east of the mountain named Rafa, and it descends to the bank of the mouth of the river Tina.

17 This portion came forth by lot for Shem and his sons, that they should possess it forever to his generations for evermore. **18** And Noaḥ rejoiced that this portion came forth for Shem and for his sons, and he remembered all that he had spoken with his mouth in prophecy; for he had said, "Blessed be 𐤉𐤄𐤅𐤄 Elohim of Shem. And may 𐤉𐤄𐤅𐤄 dwell in the dwelling-place of Shem."

19 And he knew that the Garden of Eden is the most set-apart place[a], and the dwelling of 𐤉𐤄𐤅𐤄, and Mount Sinai the center of the wilderness, and Mount Tsion, the center of the navel of the earth. These three were created as set-apart places facing each other. **20** And he blessed the Elohim of elohim, who had put the word of 𐤉𐤄𐤅𐤄 into his mouth, and *also the word of* the Eternal El for evermore. **21** And he knew that a blessed portion and a blessing had come to Shem and his sons to the generations forever; the whole land of Eden and the whole land of the Sea of Reeds, and the whole land of the east and Hodu[b], and on the Sea of Reeds and the mountains, and all the land of Bashan, and all the land of Levanon and the islands of Kaphtor, and all the mountains of Sanir and 'Amana, and the mountains of Ashuwr in the north, and all the land of Elam, Ashuwr, and Bavel, and Shushan and Media, and all the mountains of Ararat, and all the region beyond the sea, which is beyond the mountains of Ashuwr towards the north, a blessed and spacious land, and all that is in it is very good.

Ḥam's Portion

22 And for Ḥam came forth the second portion, beyond the Giḥon towards the south to the right of the Garden, and it extends towards the south and it extends to all the mountains of fire, and it extends towards the west to the sea of 'Atel and it extends towards the west until it reaches the sea of Ma'uk; that *sea* into which everything which is not destroyed descends. **23** And it goes forth towards the north to the limits of Gadir, and it goes forth to the coast of the waters of the sea to the waters of the great sea until it draws near to the river Giḥon, and goes along the river Giḥon until it reaches the right of the Garden of Eden. **24** And this is the land which came forth for Ḥam as the portion which he was to occupy forever for himself and his sons to their generations forever.

Yepheth's Portion

25 And for Yepheth came forth the third portion beyond the river Tina to the north of the outflow of its waters, and it extends north-eastern to the whole region of Gog, and to all the country east of it. **26** And it extends northward to the north, and it extends to the mountains of Qelt towards the north, and towards the sea of Ma'uk, and it goes forth to the east of Gadir as far as the region of the waters of the sea. **27** And it extends until it approaches the west of Fereg and it returns towards 'Afreg, and it extends east to the waters of the sea of Me'at. **28** And it extends to the region of the river Tina in a north-eastern direction until it approaches the boundary of its waters towards the mountain Rafa, and it turns around towards the north. **29** This is the land which came forth for Yepheth and his sons as the portion of his inheritance which he should possess for himself and his sons, for their generations forever. Five great islands, and a great land in the north.

30 But it is cold, and the land of Ḥam is hot, and the land of Shem is neither hot nor cold, but it is of blended cold and heat.

Portions of the Descendants of Ḥam, Shem, and Yepheth

9 **1** And Ḥam divided among his sons, and the first portion came forth for Kush towards the east, and to the west of him for Mitsrayim, and to the west of him for Put, and to the west of

[a] **19** Most set-apart place – commonly called "holy of holies."

[b] **8:21** Hodu – That is, India.

him, and to the west of it, on the sea for Kana'an.

2 And Shem also divided among his sons, and the first portion came forth for Elam and his sons, to the east of the Tigris River until it approaches the east, the whole land of Hodu, and on the Sea of Reeds on its coast, and the waters of Dedan, and all the mountains of Mebri and Elam, and all the land of Shushan and all that is on the side of Pharnak to the Sea of Reeds and the river Tina.

3 And for Ashuwr came forth the second portion, all the land of Ashuwr and Nineveh and Shinar and to the border of Hodu, and it ascends and skirts the river.

4 And for Arpakhshad came forth the third portion, all the land of the region of the Kaldeans to the east of the Perath, bordering on the Sea of Reeds, and all the waters of the wilderness close to the tongue of the sea which looks towards Mitsrayim, all the land of Levanon and Sanir and 'Amana to the border of the Perath.

5 And for Aram there came forth the fourth portion, all the land of Aram-Naharayim between the Tigris and the Perath to the north of the Kaldeans to the border of the mountains of Ashuwr and the land of Ararat.

6 And there came forth for Lud the fifth portion, the mountains of Ashuwr and all pertaining to them until it reaches the Great Sea, and until it reaches the east of Ashuwr his brother.

7 And Yepheth also divided the land of his inheritance among his sons.

8 And the first portion came forth for Gomer to the east from the north side to the river Tina; and in the north there came forth for Magog all the inner portions of the north until it reaches to the sea of Me'at.

9 And for Madai came forth as his portion that he should posses from the west of his two brothers to the islands, and to the coasts of the islands.

10 And for Yavan came forth the fourth portion; every island and the islands which are towards the border of Lud.

11 And for Tuval there came forth the fifth portion in the midst of the tongue which approaches towards the border of the portion of Lud to the second tongue, to the region beyond the second tongue to the third tongue.

12 And for Meshekh came forth the sixth portion, all the region beyond the third tongue until it approaches the east of Gadir.

13 And for Tiras there came forth the seventh portion, four great islands in the midst of the sea, which reach to the portion of Ḥam and the islands of Kamaturi came out by lot for the sons of Arpakhshad as his inheritance.

Curse for Violating Boundaries

14 And thus the sons of Noaḥ divided to their sons in the presence of Noaḥ their father, and he bound them all by an oath, speaking a curse on everyone that sought to seize the portion which had not fallen *to him* by his lot.

15 And they all said, "Amein and amein." for themselves and their sons forever throughout their generations until the day of judgment, on which 𐤉𐤄𐤅𐤄 Elohim shall judge them with a sword and with fire for all the unclean wickedness of their errors, wherewith they have filled the earth with transgression and uncleanness and whoring and sin.

Noaḥ's Prayer against the Demons

10 1 And in the third week of this yovel the unclean demons began to lead astray the children of the sons of Noaḥ, and to lead them to folly and destroy them. 2 And the sons of Noaḥ came to Noaḥ their father, and they told him concerning the demons which were leading astray and blinding and killing his sons' sons.

3 And he prayed before 𐤉𐤄𐤅𐤄 his Elohim, and said, "Elohim of the spirits of all flesh, who has shown favor to me and has saved me and my sons from the waters of the flood, and has not caused me to perish as You did the sons of perdition; For Your favor has been great

towards me, and great has been Your favor to
my being. Let Your favor be lifted up upon my
sons, and do not let wicked spirits rule over
them, lest they should destroy them from the
earth.

4 "But bless me and my sons, that we may
increase and multiply and replenish the earth.
5 And You know how Your Watchers, the
fathers of these spirits, acted in my day. And as
for these spirits which are living, imprison them
and hold them fast in the place of
condemnation, and do not let them bring
destruction on the sons of Your servant, my
Elohim; for these are malignant *ones*, and
created in order to destroy. 6 And do not let
them rule over the spirits of the living. For You
alone can exercise dominion over them. 7 And
let them not have power over the sons of
righteousness from now on and for evermore."

8 And יהוה our Elohim told us to bind all. And
the chief of the spirits, Mastema[a], came and
said, "Master, Creator, let some of them remain
before me, and let them listen to my voice, and
do all that I say to them. For if some of them are
not left to me, I shall not be able to execute the
power of my will on the sons of men. For these
are for corruption and leading astray before my
judgment, for great is the wickedness of the
sons of men."

Nine Tenths of Demons Removed

9 And He said, "Let one tenth of them remain
before him, and let nine tenths descend into the
place of condemnation."

10 And He commanded one of us that we should
teach Noaḥ all their medicines. For He knew
that they would not walk in uprightness, nor
strive in righteousness. 11 And we did according
to all His words. All the malignant evil ones we
bound in the place of condemnation and one
tenth of them we left, that they might be subject
to Satan on the earth. 12 And we explained to
Noaḥ all the medicines of their diseases,
together with their seductions, how he might
heal them with herbs of the earth.

13 And Noaḥ wrote down all things in a book as
we instructed him concerning every kind of
medicine. Thus the evil spirits were prohibited
from *harming* the sons of Noaḥ. 14 And he gave
all that he had written to Shem, his eldest son;
for he loved him exceedingly above all his sons.

Death of Noaḥ

15 And Noaḥ slept with his fathers, and was
buried on Mount Lubar in the land of Ararat.
16 Nine hundred and fifty years he completed in
his life: nineteen yovelim and two weeks and
five years. 17 And in his life on earth he
surpassed the children of men – except for
Ḥanokh – because of the righteousness in which
he was perfect. For the work of Ḥanokh was
ordained for a witness to the generations of the
world, so that he should recount all the deeds of
generation to generation, until the day of
judgment.

Tower of Bavel

18 And in the thirty-third yovel, in the first year
in the second week, Peleg took to himself a
wife, whose name was Lomna the daughter of
Sina'ar, and she bore him a son in the fourth
year of this week, and he called his name Reu[b];
for he said, "Behold the children of men have
become evil through the wicked purpose of
building for themselves a city and a tower in the
land of Shinar."

19 For they departed from the land of Ararat
eastward to Shinar; for in his days they built the
city and the tower, saying, "Go to, let us ascend
by this into heaven."

20 And they began to build, and in the fourth
week they made brick with fire, and the bricks

[a] **10:8** Mastema – Ethiopic word መስቴማ (*mas'te'ma*) is a transliteration of the Hebrew word משטמה (*mas'tei'mah*) meaning "hostility." This word is derived from the word שטם (*sa'atm*) meaning "to be against" or "to harass." This name may have originated as a play on the word שטן (*sa'tan*) meaning "adversary." Given the parallel between Mastema and Satan in verse **11**, this is most likely the case.

[b] **10:18** Reu – In Hebrew, this name is רעו (*re'u*). The author of Yovelim apparently connected this name with the Hebrew word רע (*ra*) meaning "evil."

served them for stone, and the clay with which
they cemented them together was asphalt which
comes out of the sea, and out of the fountains of
water in the land of Shinar. **21** And they built it.
It took them forty-three years to build it; its
width was two hundred and three bricks, and the
height *of a brick* was one third its length; its
height amounted to five thousand, four hundred
and thirty-three cubits and two palms. And *the
extent of one* wall was thirteen stades and of the
other thirty stades.

22 And 𐤉𐤄𐤅𐤄 our Elohim said to us, "Behold,
they are one people, and they begin to do *this*.
And now nothing will be withheld from them.
Come, let us go down and confuse their
language, that they may not understand one
another's speech, and they may be dispersed
into cities and nations, and one purpose will no
longer abide with them until the day of
judgment."

23 And 𐤉𐤄𐤅𐤄 descended, and we descended with
Him to see the city and the tower which the
children of men had built. **24** And He confused
their language, and they no longer understood
one another's speech, and they stopped building
the city and the tower. **25** For this reason the
whole land of Shinar is called Bavel, because
𐤉𐤄𐤅𐤄 confused all the language of the children
of men, and from there they were dispersed into
their cities, each according to his language and
his nation.

26 And 𐤉𐤄𐤅𐤄 sent a mighty wind against the
tower and overthrew it upon the earth, and
behold it was between Ashuwr and Bavel in the
land of Shinar, and they called its name 'the
Overthrow'.

Treachery of Kana'an

27 In the fourth week in the first year in its
beginning, in the thirty-fourth yovel, they were
dispersed from the land of Shinar. **28** And Ḥam
and his sons went into the land which he was to
occupy, which he acquired as his portion in the
land of the south. **29** And Kana'an saw the land
of Levanon to the river of Mitsrayim, that it was
very good, and he did not go into the land of his
inheritance to the west, *that is to* the sea, and he
dwelled in the land of Levanon *instead*,
eastward and westward from the border of the
Yarden and from the border of the sea.

30 And Ḥam, his father, and Kush and
Mitsrayim his brothers said to him, "You have
settled in a land which is not yours, and which
did not fall to us by lot. Do not do this. For if
you do, you and your sons will fall in the land
and *be* cursed with troublemaking; for by
troublemaking you have settled, and by
troublemaking your children will fall, and you
will be uprooted forever. **31** Do not dwell not in
the dwelling of Shem; for it came to Shem and
his children by their lot. **32** You are cursed, and
you will be cursed beyond all the sons of Noaḥ,
by the curse by which we bound ourselves by an
oath in the presence of the set-apart judge, and
in the presence of Noaḥ our father."

33 But he did not listen to them, and dwelled in
the land of Levanon from Ḥamath to the
entrance of Mitsrayim, he and his sons until this
day. **34** And for this reason that land is named
Kana'an. **35** And Yepheth and his sons went
towards the sea and dwelled in the land of their
portion, and Madai saw the land of the sea and
it did not please him, and he begged for a
portion from Ḥam and Ashuwr and
Arpakhshad, his wife's brother, and he dwelled
in the land of Media, near his wife's brother
until this day. **36** And he called his dwelling-
place, and the dwelling-place of his sons,
Media, after the name of their father Madai.

Birth of Serug

11 **1** And in the thirty-fifth yovel, in the third
week, in the first year, Reu took to himself a
wife, and her name was 'Ora[a], the daughter of
'Ur, the son of Kesed[b], and she bore him a son,
and he called his name Seroh, in the seventh

---

[a] **11:1** 'Ora – Ethiopic word ኦራ (*'ora*) is a transliteration of the Hebrew word 𐤀𐤅𐤓 (*ore*) meaning "light." This is the feminine version of *Ur*, which also means "light." The author of Yovelim is apparently showing that 'Ora was named after her father, Ur.

[b] 11:1 Kesed – Ethiopic word ኬሴድ (*ke'sed*) is a transliteration of the Hebrew word 𐤊𐤔𐤃 (*ke'sed*). This is the singular form of 𐤊𐤔𐤃𐤉𐤌 (*kas'dim*) which is the name of the Kaldean people. It appears the author of Yovelim is associating this Kesed as being the father of the Kaldeans.

year of this week in this yovel. 2 And the sons of Noaḥ began to war against each other, to take captive and to kill each other, and to shed the blood of men on the earth, and to eat blood, and to build strong cities, and walls, and towers, and men *began* to exalt themselves above the nation, and to found the beginnings of kingdoms, and to go to war, people against people, and nation against nation, and city against city, and all *began* to do evil, and to acquire weapons, and to teach their sons war, and they began to capture cities, and to sell male and female slaves.

3 And 'Ur, the son of Kesed, built the city of Ur Kasdim, and called its name after his own name and the name of his father. 4 And they made for themselves molten images, and they each worshipped the idol, the molten image which they had made for themselves. And they began to make engraved images and unclean likenesses, and malignant spirits assisted and led them to committing sin and uncleanness. 5 And the prince, Mastema, exerted himself to do all this, and he sent forth other spirits, those which were put under his hand, to do all manner of wrong and sin, and all manner of transgression, to corrupt and destroy, and to shed blood upon the earth. 6 For this reason he called the name of Seroh, Serug, for everyone turned to do all manner of sin and transgression.

Birth of Naḥor, Avram's Grandfather

7 And he grew up, and dwelled in Ur Kasdim, near to the father of his wife's mother, and he worshipped idols, and he took to himself a wife in the thirty-sixth yovel, in the fifth week, in the first year. And her name was Milkhah, the daughter of Kaber, the daughter of his father's brother. 8 And she bore him Naḥor, in the first year of this week, and he grew and dwelled in Ur Kasdim, and his father taught him the studies of the Kaldeans to divine and *practice* astrology, according to the signs of heaven.

Birth of Teraḥ, Avram's Father

9 And in the thirty-seventh yovel in the sixth week, in its first year he took to himself a wife, and her name was Yiskah, the daughter of Nestag of the Kaldeans. 10 And she bore him Teraḥ in the seventh year of this week.

11 And the prince, Mastema, sent ravens and birds[a] to devour the seed which was sown in the land, in order to destroy the land, and rob the children of men of their labors. Before they could plough in the seed, the ravens picked *it* from the surface of the ground. 12 And for this reason he called his name Teraḥ, because the ravens and the birds reduced them to destitution and devoured their seed. 13 And the years began to be barren, owing to the birds, and they devoured all the fruit of the trees from the trees: it was only with great effort that they could save a little of all the fruit of the earth in their days.

14 And in this thirty-ninth yovel, in the second week in the first year, Teraḥ took to himself a wife, and her name was 'Edna, the daughter of Avram, the daughter of his father's sister.

Birth of Avram

15 And in the seventh year of this week she bore him a son, and he called his name Avram, by the name of the father of his mother; for he had died before his daughter had conceived a son.

16 And the child began to understand the errors of the earth that all went astray after engraved images and after uncleanness, and his father taught him writing, and he was two weeks of years old, and he separated himself from his father, that he might not worship idols with him. 17 And he began to pray to the Creator of all things that He might save him from the errors of the children of men, and that his portion should not fall into error after uncleanness and scorn.

18 And the seed-time came for the sowing of seed upon the land, and they all went forth together to protect their seed against the ravens, and Avram went forth with those that went, and the child was a lad of fourteen years. 19 And a cloud of ravens came to devour the seed, and Avram ran to meet them before they settled on the ground, and cried to them before they settled

[a] **11:11** Mastema, the ruler of demons (unclean spirits), is also associated with "ravens and birds." Compare Hit'galut [Revelation] **18:1-2**.

on the ground to devour the seed, and said, "Do
not descend. Return to the place from which
you came," and they proceeded to turn back.
20 And he caused the clouds of ravens to turn
back that day seventy times. And of all the
ravens throughout all the land where Avram
was, not even one settled there. 21 And all who
were with him throughout all the land saw him
cry out, and all the ravens turn back, and his
name became great in all the land of the
Kaldeans. 22 And there came to him this year all
those that wished to sow, and he went with
them until the time of sowing ceased. And they
sowed their land, and that year they brought
enough grain home and ate, and were satisfied.[a]

23 And in the first year of the fifth week Avram
taught those who made implements for oxen,
the skilled carpenters, and they made a vessel
above the ground, facing the frame of the
plough, in order to put the seed on it, and the
seed fell down upon the share of the plough, and
was hidden in the earth, and they no longer
feared the ravens. 24 And after this manner they
made *vessels* above the ground on all the frames
of the ploughs, and they sowed and tilled all the
land, as Avram commanded them, and they no
longer feared the birds.

Avram's Plea to Avoid Idolatry

12 1 And it happened in the sixth week, in the
seventh year, that Avram said to Teraḥ his
father, "Father!" And he said, "Behold, here am
I, my son."

2 And he said, "What help and profit do we get
from those idols which you worship and bow
yourself down before? 3 For there is no spirit in
them. For they are dumb likenesses, and a
misleading of the heart. Do not worship them.
4 Worship the Elohim of heaven, who causes
the rain and the dew to descend on the earth,
and does everything upon the earth. He has
created everything by His word, and all life is
from before His face. 5 Why do you worship
things that have no spirit in them? For they are
the work of *human* hands, and you carry them
on your shoulders. And you have no help from
them. But they are a great cause of shame to
those who make them, and a misleading of the
heart to those who worship them. Do not
worship them."

6 And his father said to him, "I know this as
well, my son. But what shall I do with a people
who have made me to serve before them? 7 And
if I tell them the truth, they will kill me; for their
being clings to them, to worship them and honor
them. Keep silent, my son, lest they kill you."

8 And he spoke these words to his two brothers,
and they were angry with him and he kept
silent.

Marriages of the Sons of Teraḥ

9 And in the fortieth yovel, in the second week,
in the seventh year Avram took to himself a
wife, and her name was Sarai, the daughter of
his father, and she became his wife. 10 And
Haran, his brother, took to himself a wife in the
third year of the third week, and she bore him a
son in the seventh year of this week, and he
called his name Lot. 11 And Naḥor, his brother,
took to himself a wife.

Avram Burns the House of Idols

12 And in the sixtieth year of the life of Avram,
that is, in the fourth week, in the fourth year,
Avram arose by night, and burned the house of
the idols, and he burned all that was in the
house and no man knew it.[b] 13 And they arose in
the night and sought to save their elohim from
the midst of the fire. 14 And Haran hurried to
save them, but the fire burned over him, and he
was burned in the fire, and he died in Ur
Kasdim before Teraḥ his father, and they buried
him in Ur Kasdim.

---

[a] **11:22** The incident of Avram with the ravens was also quoted by Jerome and Ephrem the Syrian, both about the 4th century. Charles believed both of these to be derived from the account here in Yovelim.

[b] **12:12** This story does not agree with the account from Yashar in detail. However, it nonetheless retains the overall purpose of the narrative. That is, that Avram had disdain for idols and destroyed those that his father made. Similarly it retains the story of the death of Haran by burning. See Yashar **11:33**; **12:26**.

15 And Teraḥ went forth from Ur Kasdim, he
and his sons, to go into the land of Levanon and
into the land of Kana'an, and he dwelled in the
land of Ḥaran, and Avram dwelled with Teraḥ
his father in Ḥaran two weeks of years.

16 And in the sixth week, in the fifth year
Avram sat up throughout the night on the new
moon of the seventh month to observe the stars
from the evening to the morning, in order to see
what would be the character of the year with
regard to the rains, and he was alone as he sat
and observed. 17 And a word came into his heart
and he said, "All the signs of the stars, and the
signs of the moon and of the sun are all in the
hand of 𐤉𐤄𐤅𐤄. Why do I search *them* out? 18 If
He desires, He causes it to rain, morning and
evening. And if He desires, He withholds it,
And all things are in His hand."

19 And he prayed that night and said, "My
Elohim, El Elyon, You alone are my Elohim.
And I have chosen You and Your dominion.
And You have created all things, and all things
are the work of Your hands. 20 Deliver me from
the hands of evil spirits who have dominion
over the thoughts of men's hearts, and do not let
them lead me astray from You, my Elohim. And
establish me and my seed forever, that we go
not astray from now on and for evermore." [a]

21 And he said, "Shall I return to Ur Kasdim
who seek my face that I may return to them? Or
am I to remain here in this place? Prosper the
right path before You in the hands of Your
servant, that he may fulfil it, and that I may not
walk in the deceitfulness of my heart, O my
Elohim."

Avram Called to the Promised Land

22 And he made an end of speaking and praying,
and behold the word of 𐤉𐤄𐤅𐤄 was sent to him
through me, saying, "Get up from your country,
and from your family, and from the house of
your father; *go* to a land which I will show you,
and I shall make you a great and numerous
nation. 23 And I will bless you. And I will make
your name great. And you will be blessed in the
earth. And in you shall all families of the earth
be blessed. And I will bless them that bless you,
and curse them that curse you. 24 And I will be
Elohim to you and your son, and to your son's
son, and to all your seed. Do not fear, from now
on and to all generations of the earth I am your
Elohim."

Avram is taught Hebrew

25 And 𐤉𐤄𐤅𐤄 Elohim said, "Open his mouth and
his ears, that he may hear and speak with his
mouth, with the language which has been
revealed;" for it had ceased from the mouths of
all the children of men from the day of The
Overthrow. 26 And I opened his mouth, and his
ears, and his lips, and I began to speak with him
in Hebrew, in the tongue of the creation. 27 And
he took the books of his fathers, and these were
written in Hebrew, and he transcribed them, and
he began to study them then, and I made known
to him that which he could not *comprehend*, and
he studied them during the six rainy months.

28 And it happened in the seventh year of the
sixth week that he spoke to his father and
informed him that he would leave Ḥaran to walk
in the land of Kana'an to see it, and return to
him.

Teraḥ's Blessing

29 And Teraḥ his father said to him, "Go in
peace; may the Eternal Elohim make your path
straight. And 𐤉𐤄𐤅𐤄 *be* with you, and protect you
from all evil, [and give you kindness, favor, and
compassion before those who see you.][b] And
may none of the children of men have power
over you to harm you. Go in peace. 30 And if
you see a land *that is* pleasant to your eyes to
dwell in, then arise and bring me to you, and
take Lot with you, the son of Haran your
brother, as your own son. May 𐤉𐤄𐤅𐤄 be with
you. 31 But Naḥor your brother leave with me
until you return in peace, and we go with you all
together."

---

[a] **12:20** Compare the likeness of Avram's prayer in verses **19** & **20** to the model prayer of Mattithyahu [Matthew] **6** & Loukas [Luke] **11**.

[b] **12:29** Bracketed section indicates reading present in Ethiopic texts but absent from Hebrew fragments from Qumran.

Avram's Sojourn at Beth-El

13 1 And Avram journeyed from Ḥaran, and he
took Sarai, his wife, and Lot, his brother Haran's
son, to the land of Kana'an, and he came into
Ashuwr, and proceeded to Shekhem, and
dwelled near a lofty oak. 2 And he saw, and
behold, the land was very pleasant from the
entering of Ḥamath to the lofty oak.

3 And 𐤉𐤄𐤅𐤄 said to him, "To you and to your
seed will I give this land."

4 And he built an altar there, and he offered a
ascension offering on it to 𐤉𐤄𐤅𐤄, who had
appeared to him. 5 And he went from there into
the mountain, with Beth-El on the west and Ai
on the east, and pitched his tent there. 6 And he
saw and behold, the land was wide and very
good, and everything was growing on it: vines
and figs and pomegranates, oaks and ilexes, and
terebinths and oil trees, and cedars and
cypresses and date trees, and all trees of the
field, and there was water on the mountains.[a]
7 And he blessed 𐤉𐤄𐤅𐤄 who had led him out of
Ur Kasdim, and had brought him to this land.

8 And it happened in the first year, in the
seventh week, on the new moon of the first
month, that he built an altar on this mountain,
and called on the Name of 𐤉𐤄𐤅𐤄, *saying*, "You,
the Eternal Elohim, are my Elohim."

9 And he offered a ascension offering on the
altar to 𐤉𐤄𐤅𐤄 that He should be with him and
not forsake him all the days of his life.

Avram Travels to Ḥevron and Mitsrayim

10 And he went from there and went towards the
south, and he came to Ḥevron and Ḥevron was
built at that time, and he dwelled there two
years. And he went *from there* into the land of
the south, to Bealoth, and there was a famine in
the land. 11 And Avram went into Mitsrayim in
the third year of the week, and he dwelled in
Mitsrayim five years before his wife was torn
away from him. 12 Now Tanis of Mitsrayim was
built then; seven years after Ḥevron. 13 And it
happened when Pharaoh seized Sarai, the wife
of Avram that 𐤉𐤄𐤅𐤄 plagued Pharaoh and his
house with great plagues because of Sarai,
Avram's wife. 14 And Avram was very glorious
by reason of possessions in sheep, and cattle,
and donkeys, and horses, and camels, and
manservants, and maidservants, and in silver
and gold exceedingly. And Lot also, his
brother's son, was wealthy.

15 And Pharaoh gave back Sarai, the wife of
Avram, and he sent him out of the land of
Mitsrayim, and he journeyed to the place where
he had pitched his tent at the beginning, to the
place of the altar, with Ai on the east, and Beth-
El on the west, and he blessed 𐤉𐤄𐤅𐤄 his Elohim
who had brought him back in peace.

Avram is Promised the Land

16 And it happened in the forty-first yovel in the
third year of the first week, that he returned to
this place and offered a ascension offering, and
called on the Name of 𐤉𐤄𐤅𐤄, and said, "You, El
Elyon, are my Elohim forever and ever."

17 And in the fourth year of this week, Lot left
him, and Lot dwelled in Sodom, and the men of
Sodom were sinners exceedingly. 18 And it
grieved him in his heart that his brother's son
had left him; for he had no children. 19 In that
year when Lot was taken captive, 𐤉𐤄𐤅𐤄 said to
Avram, after Lot had left him, in the fourth year
of this week, "Lift up your eyes from the place
where you are dwelling, northward and
southward, and westward and eastward. 20 For
all the land which you see I will give to you and
to your seed forever. And I will make your seed
as the sand of the sea. [Though a man may
number the dust of the earth, yet][b] your seed
shall not be numbered. 21 Arise, walk the length
of *the land* and the width of it, and see it all; for
I will give it to your seed."

---

[a] **13:6** The exact identification of some of these trees are unknown. The naming in Ethiopic of vine, fig, pomegranate, and olive are clear. However, the words for cypress, cedar, terebinth, oak, and date appear to be Ethiopic transcriptions for the Greek names of these trees, though their exact classification is still debated.

[b] **13:20** Bracketed section indicates reading present in Ethiopic texts, but absent from Latin fragments.

Avram's Response to Lot's Capture

22 And Avram went to Ḥevron, and dwelled
there. And in this year came Kedorlaomer, king
of Elam, and Amraphel, king of Shinar, and
Arioch king of Ellasar, and Tidal, king of
Goyim, and killed the king of Gomorrah, and
the king of Sodom fled, and many fell through
wounds in the Valley of Siddim, by the Salt
Sea.[a] 23 And they took captive Sodom and
Adam and Tseboyim, and they also took Lot
captive, the son of Avram's brother, and all his
possessions, and they went to Dan. 24 And one
who had escaped came and told Avram that his
brother's son had been taken captive. 25 And he
armed his household servants [...][b] for Avram,
and for his seed, a tenth of the first-fruits to
𐤉𐤄𐤅𐤄, and 𐤉𐤄𐤅𐤄 ordained it as an ordinance
forever that they should give it to the priests
who served before Him, that they should
possess it forever. 26 And to this Torah there is
no limit of days; for He has ordained it for the
generations forever, that they should give to
𐤉𐤄𐤅𐤄 the tenth of everything, of the seed and of
the wine and of the oil and of the cattle and of
the sheep. 27 And He gave *it* to His priests to eat
and to drink with joy before Him.

28 And the king of Sodom came to him and
bowed himself before him, and said, "Our
master, Avram, give us the beings which you
rescued, but let the spoil be yours."

29 And Avram said to him, "I lift up my hands
to El Elyon, that from a thread to a shoelace, I
shall not take anything that is your, lest you say,
'I have made Avram rich;' except only what the
young men have eaten, and the portion of the
men who went with me: Aner, Eskhol, and
Mamre. These shall take their portion."

Avram's Dream

14 1 After these things, in the fourth year of
this week, on the new moon of the third month,
the word of 𐤉𐤄𐤅𐤄 came to Avram in a dream,
saying, "Do not fear, Avram; I am your
defender. And your reward will be exceedingly
great."

2 And he said, "O Master, Master, what will
You give me, seeing I go childless, and the son
of Maseq,[c] the son of my handmaid, is Eliezer
of Dammeseq? He will be my heir, and You
have not given me any seed."

3 And He said to him, "This *one* will not be
your heir, but one that will come out of your
own loins, he will be your heir." 4 And He took
him outside, and said to him, "Look toward the
heavens and number the stars, if you are able to
number them."

5 And he looked toward the heavens, and saw
the stars. And He said to him, "So shall your
seed be." 6 And he believed 𐤉𐤄𐤅𐤄, and it was
counted to him for righteousness.

7 And He said to him, "I am 𐤉𐤄𐤅𐤄 who brought
you out of Ur Kasdim, to give you the land of
the Kana'anites to possess it forever. And I will
be Elohim to you and to your seed after you."

8 And he said, "Master, Master, how will I
know that I will inherit *it*?" 9 And He said to
him, "Bring Me a heifer of three years, and a

---

[a] **13:22** Names of the kings listed here are rendered according to how they are written in the Hebrew Bible. The Ethiopic text of Yovelim, however, appears to follow a Greek pronunciation for 'Ellasar' (written as "Sellasar") and 'Tidal' (written as "Tergal").

[b] **13:25** Bracketed ellipsis indicates an obvious lacuna in the Ethiopic text. The entire story of Avram pursuing the kings, rescuing Lot, and encountering Malkitsedeq is absent. One Syriac fragment includes the phrase, "and he pursued the kings and he returned everything which they had taken captive from Sodom." Given the passage immediately following, it is plausible to assume that the missing section contains the Malkitsedeq encounter.

[c] **14:2** Ethiopic phrase "son of Maseq" is ወወልደ ማሴቅ (*wa'wal'da ma'sek*). This follows the Greek phrase υιος Μασεκ (*u'i'oss ma'sek*) meaning "son of Maseq." However, in Hebrew this phrase is 𐤅𐤁𐤍 𐤌𐤔𐤒 (*u'ben ma'sheq*). This phrase appears only once in the Hebrew Bible, in Bereshiyt [Genesis] **15:2**, where it is rendered as "heir." It is believed to derive from an unused Hebrew root meaning "possession" in the sense of a steward, or heir. However, it may be that since Eliezer, the servant being referenced, was from Dammeseq (Damascus), the "meseq" (𐤌𐤔𐤒) is related to the name of Eliezer's ancestor.

goat of three years, and a sheep of three years, and a turtle-dove, and a pigeon."

10 And he took all these in the middle of the month. And he was dwelling at the oak of Mamre, which is near Ḥevron. 11 And he built there an altar, and slaughtered all these *animals*; and he poured their blood upon the altar, and divided them in the middle, and laid them over against each other; but he did not divide the birds. 12 And birds came down upon the pieces, and Avram drove them away, and did not allow the birds to touch them.

13 And it happened, when the sun had set, that a terror fell upon Avram, and see, a horror of great darkness fell upon him, and it was said to Avram, "Surely know that your seed will be a sojourner in a land *that is* not theirs, and they shall bring them into bondage, and afflict them four hundred years. 14 And the nation also to whom they will be in bondage I will judge, and after that they shall come forth from there with much substance. 15 And you will go to your fathers in peace, and be buried in a good old age. 16 But in the fourth generation they shall return here; for the iniquity of the Amorites is not yet full."

The Covenant with Avram

17 And he awoke from his sleep, and he arose, and the sun had set; and there was a flame, and behold, a furnace was smoking, and a flame of fire passed between the pieces. 18 And on that day 𐤉𐤄𐤅𐤄 cut a covenant with Avram, saying, "To your seed will I give this land, from the river of Mitsrayim to the great river, the Perath River: the Qenites, the Qenizzites, the Kadmonites, the Perizzites, and the Rephaim, the Phaqorites, and the Ḥivites, and the Amorites, and the Kana'anites, and the Girgashites, and the Yevusites."

19 And the day passed, and Avram offered the pieces, and the birds, and their fruit offerings, and their drink offerings, and the fire devoured them. 20 And on that day we cut a covenant with Avram, just as we had covenanted with Noaḥ in this month; and Avram renewed the Feast and ordinance for himself forever.

Hagar and Yishma'el

21 And Avram rejoiced, and told all these things to Sarai his wife. And he believed that he would have seed, but she did not bear. 22 And Sarai advised her husband Avram, and said to him, "Go in to Hagar, my Mitsrite handmaid. It may be that I will build up seed to you by her."

23 And Avram listened to the voice of Sarai his wife, and said to her, "Do *so*." And Sarai took Hagar, her handmaid, the Mitsrite, and gave her to Avram, her husband, as wife. 24 And he went in to her, and she conceived and bore him a son, and he called his name Yishma'el, in the fifth year of this week; and this was the eighty-sixth year in the life of Avram.

First Fruits; Changing Avram's Name

15 1 And in the fifth year of the fourth week of this yovel, in the third month, in the midst of the month, Avram celebrated the Feast of the first-fruits of the grain harvest. 2 And he offered new offerings on the altar, the first-fruits of the produce, to 𐤉𐤄𐤅𐤄, a heifer and a goat and a sheep on the altar as a ascension offering to 𐤉𐤄𐤅𐤄; their fruit offerings and their drink offerings he offered on the altar with frankincense.

3 And 𐤉𐤄𐤅𐤄 appeared to Avram, and said to him, "I am El Shaddai; [be pleasing][a] before Me and be perfect. 4 And I will cut My covenant between Me and you, and I will multiply you exceedingly."

5 And Avram fell on his face, and 𐤉𐤄𐤅𐤄 spoke with him, and said, 6 "Behold My ordinance is with you. And You will be the father of many

---

[a] **15:3** The phrase "be pleasing" is found in the Ethiopic text of Yovelim, and is attested in the Greek Septuagint (LXX), Syriac Peshitta, and the Ethiopic version of Bereshiyt [Genesis] **17:1** as well. In the Hebrew however, this reads, "walk before Me" instead. It is not clear whether the author of Yovelim was using a Hebrew Vorlage which pre-dated the text on which the Hebrew Masoretic was based (which read "be pleasing"), or if a later copyist altered the Ethiopic text to bring it in line with the LXX and Ethiopic Bible.

nations. 7 And your name will not be called
Avram anymore. But your name from now on,
even forever, shall be Avraham. For I have
made you the father of many nations. 8 And I
will make you very great. And I will make you
into *many* nations. And kings shall come forth
from you. 9 And I will establish My covenant
between Me and you, and your seed after you,
throughout their generations, for an eternal
ordinance, so that I may be Elohim to you, and
to your seed after you. 10 And I will give [to
you and to your seed after you][a] the land of your
sojourning; the land of Kana'an, that you may
possess it forever. And I will be their Elohim."

11 And 𐤉𐤄𐤅𐤄 said to Avraham, "And as for you,
guard My covenant, you and your seed after
you. And circumcise every male among you,
and circumcise your foreskins, and it shall be a
sign of an eternal covenant between Me and
you. 12 And you shall circumcise the child on
the eighth day; every male throughout your
generations, him that is born in the house, or
whom you have bought with money from any
stranger, whom you have acquired who is not of
your seed. 13 He that is born in your house shall
surely be circumcised, and those whom you
have bought with money shall be circumcised,
and My covenant shall be in your flesh for an
eternal ordinance. 14 And the uncircumcised
male, *the one* who is not circumcised in the
flesh of his foreskin on the eighth day, that
being shall be cut off from his people, for he has
broken My covenant."

15 And 𐤉𐤄𐤅𐤄 said to Avraham, "As for Sarai
your wife, her name shall no more be called
Sarai, but Sarah shall be her name. 16 And I will
bless her, and give you a son by her, and I will
bless him, and he shall become a nation, and
kings of nations shall proceed from him."

Avram's Plea for Yishma'el

17 And Avraham fell on his face, and rejoiced,
and said in his heart, "Shall a son be born to him
that is a hundred years old? And shall Sarah,
who is ninety years old, bring forth?" 18 And
Avraham said to 𐤉𐤄𐤅𐤄, "O that Yishma'el might
live before You!"

19 And 𐤉𐤄𐤅𐤄 said, "Yes, but Sarah also shall
bear you a son, and you shall call his name
Yitsḥaq, and I will establish My covenant with
him; an everlasting covenant, and for his seed
after him. 20 And as for Yishma'el also I have
heard you, and behold I will bless him, and
make him great, and multiply him exceedingly.
And he shall bring forth twelve princes, and I
will make him a great nation. 21 But My
covenant will be established with Yitsḥaq,
whom Sarah will bear to you, in these days, in
the next year." 22 And He finished speaking
with him, and 𐤉𐤄𐤅𐤄 went up from Avraham.

Circumcision

23 And Avraham did as 𐤉𐤄𐤅𐤄 had said to him,
and he took Yishma'el his son, and all that were
born in his house, and whom he had bought
with his money, every male in his house, and
circumcised the flesh of their foreskin. 24 And
on the same day Avraham was circumcised, and
all the men of his house, [and all of the servants
of his house][b] and all those whom he had
bought with money from the children of the
stranger, were circumcised with him.

25 This Torah is for all the generations forever,
and there is no circumcising[c] of the days, and no
omission of one day out of the eight days; for it
is an eternal ordinance, ordained and written on
the heavenly tablets. 26 And everyone that is
born, the flesh of whose foreskin is not
circumcised on the eighth day, does not belong
to the children of the covenant which 𐤉𐤄𐤅𐤄 cut
with Avraham, but to the children of

[a] **15:10** Bracketed section indicates reading absent from Ethiopic text. This section was added based on the parallel reading from Bereshiyt [Genesis] **17:8**. Without it, the text has obvious lack, and a break in sentence structure.

[b] **15:24** Bracketed section indicates reading present in Latin text, but absent from Ethiopic text.

[c] **15:25** "There is no circumcising of the days" – Poetic wordplay by author, stating that not a single day should be cut off or removed from the total of **8** days.

destruction; nor is there, moreover, any sign on
him that he is 𐤉𐤄𐤅𐤄's, but *is destined* to be
destroyed and killed from the earth, and to be
uprooted from the earth, for he has broken the
covenant of 𐤉𐤄𐤅𐤄 our Elohim. 27 For all the
messengers of the presence and all the
messengers of setting apart have been created
this way from the day of their creation, and
before the messengers of the presence and the
messengers of setting apart He has set Yisra'el
apart, that they should be with Him and with
His set-apart messengers.

28 And command the children of Yisra'el and let
them guard the sign of this covenant for their
generations as an eternal ordinance, and they
will not be uprooted from the land. 29 For the
command is ordained for a covenant, that they
should guard it forever among all the children of
Yisra'el. 30 For 𐤉𐤄𐤅𐤄 did not draw Yishma'el
and his sons and his brothers and Esaw, and He
did not choose them, because they are the
children of Avraham, because He knew them,
but He chose Yisra'el to be His people.

31 And He set it apart, and gathered it from
among all the children of men; for there are
many nations and many peoples, and all are His,
and He has placed spirits in authority to lead
them astray from Him.[a] 32 But over Yisra'el He
did not appoint any messenger or spirit, for He
alone is their ruler, and He will preserve them
and require them at the hand of His messengers
and His spirits, and at the hand of all His
powers in order that He may preserve them and
bless them, and that they may be His and He
may be theirs from now on and forever.

Prophecy of Future Apostasy

33 And now I announce to you that the children
of Yisra'el will deny this ordinance, and they
will not circumcise their sons according to all
this Torah; for in the flesh of their circumcision
they will omit this circumcision of their sons,
and all of them, sons of Beliyya'al, will leave
their sons uncircumcised as they were born.
34 And there will be great wrath from 𐤉𐤄𐤅𐤄
against the children of Yisra'el. Because they
have forsaken His covenant and turned aside
from His word, and provoked and blasphemed;
inasmuch as they do not guard the ordinance of
this Torah. For they have treated their members
like the nations, so that they may be removed
and uprooted from the land. And there will no
more be pardon or forgiveness to them, [so that
there should be forgiveness and pardon][b] for all
the sin of this eternal error.

Sarah Laughs

16 1 And on the new moon of the fourth month
we appeared to Avraham at the oak of Mamre,
and we talked with him, and we announced to
him that a son would be given to him by Sarah
his wife. 2 And Sarah laughed, for she heard
that we had spoken these words with Avraham,
and we admonished her, and she became afraid,
and denied that she had laughed on account of
the words. 3 And we told her the name of her
son, as his name is ordained and written in the
heavenly tablets: Yitsḥaq. 4 And *that* when we
returned to her at a set time, she would have
conceived a son.

Destruction of Sodom; Sin of Lot's Daughters

5 And in this month 𐤉𐤄𐤅𐤄 executed His
judgments on Sodom, and Gomorrah, and
Tseboyim, and all the region of the Yarden, and
He burned them with fire and brimstone, and
destroyed them until this day, just as He
declared to you, "Behold I make known all their
works, that they are wicked and sinners
exceedingly, and that they defile themselves and
commit whoring in their flesh, and work
uncleanness on the earth."

6 And, in like manner, 𐤉𐤄𐤅𐤄 will execute
judgment on the places where they have done
according to the uncleanness of the Sodomites,
like the judgment of Sodom. 7 But Lot we
saved; for 𐤉𐤄𐤅𐤄 remembered Avraham, and sent
him out from the midst of the overthrow. 8 And
he and his daughters committed sin upon the
earth, such as had not been on the earth since

---

[a] **15:31** "Lead them astray" – referring to the evil spirits that resulted from the mating of Watchers with humans. See Yovelim **10**.

[b] **15:34** Bracketed section indicates reading not present in all Ethiopic texts. Charles considered the reading to be spurious.

the days of Adam until his time; for the man lay with his daughters. **9** And behold, it was commanded and engraved concerning all his seed, on the heavenly tablets, to remove them and uproot them, and to execute judgment upon them like the judgment of Sodom, and to leave no seed of the man on earth on the day of condemnation.

10 And in this month Avraham moved from Ḥevron, and departed and dwelled between Qadesh and Shur in the mountains of Gerar. **11** And in the middle of the fifth month he moved from there, and dwelled at the Well of the Oath.[a]

Birth of Yitsḥaq

12 And in the middle of the sixth month 𐤉𐤄𐤅𐤄 visited Sarah and did to her as He had spoken, and she conceived. **13** And she bore a son in the third month, and in the middle of the month, at the time of which 𐤉𐤄𐤅𐤄 had spoken to Avraham; on the Feast of the first-fruits of the harvest, Yitsḥaq was born. **14** And Avraham circumcised his son on the eighth day: he was the first that was circumcised according to the covenant which is ordained forever.

15 And in the sixth year of the fourth week we came to Avraham, to the Well of the Oath, and we appeared to him [as we had told Sarah that we should return to her, and she would have conceived a son. **16** And we returned in the seventh month, and found Sarah with child before us][b] and we blessed him, and we announced to him all the things which had been decreed concerning him, that he should not die until he would bring forth six more sons, and should see *them* before he died. But in Yitsḥaq his name and seed be would called. **17** And *that* all the seed of his sons should be nations, and be reckoned with the nations; but from the sons of Yitsḥaq one should become a set-apart seed, and should not be reckoned among the nations. **18** For he should become the portion of Elyon, and all his seed had fallen into the possession of Elohim, that it should be to 𐤉𐤄𐤅𐤄 a people for to possess above all nations and that he should become a kingdom of priests and a set-apart nation.[c] **19** And we went our way, and we announced to Sarah all that we had told him, and they both rejoiced with exceedingly great joy.

Avraham Celebrates Feast of Tabernacles

20 And he built there an altar to 𐤉𐤄𐤅𐤄 who had delivered him, and who was making him rejoice in the land of his sojourning, and he celebrated a Feast of joy in this month seven days, near the altar which he had built at the Well of the Oath. **21** And he built tabernacles for himself and for his servants on this Feast, and he was the first to celebrate the Feast of Tabernacles on the earth. **22** And during these seven days he brought each day to the altar a ascension offering to 𐤉𐤄𐤅𐤄, two oxen, two rams, seven sheep, one he-goat, for a sin offering, that he might atone for himself and for his seed with it. **23** And, as a freewill offering, seven rams, seven kids, seven sheep, and seven he-goats, and their fruit offerings and their drink offerings; and he burned all their fat on the altar, a chosen offering to 𐤉𐤄𐤅𐤄 for a sweet smelling aroma. **24** And morning and evening he burned fragrant substances, frankincense and galbanum, and stacte, and nard, and myrrh, and spice, and costum; all these seven he offered, crushed, mixed together in equal parts *and* pure.[d] **25** And he celebrated this Feast for seven days, rejoicing with all his heart and with all his being, he and all those who were in his house, and there was no foreigner with him, nor any that was uncircumcised.

26 And he blessed his Creator who had created him in his generation, for He had created him according to His good pleasure. For He knew

---

[a] **16:11** Well of the Oath – This is the literal translation of the Hebrew phrase 𐤔𐤁𐤏 𐤁𐤀𐤓 (*be'er she'va*): Beersheva.

[b] **16:15-16** Bracketed section indicates possible later addition. While the section is attested in both the Ethiopic text and the Latin fragment, it disturbs the flow of the entire section.

[c] **16:18** See also Shemoth [Exodus] **19:5-6**; Devarim [Deuteronomy] **4:20**; Kepha 𐤀 [**1** Peter] **2:9**; Hit'galut [Revelation] **5:10**.

[d] **16:24** While the Ethiopic words for frankincense, myrrh, nard, and spice are well known, the exact definition and classification of the words for costum, galbanum, and stacte are debated.

and perceived that from him would arise a planting of righteousness for eternal generations, and from him a set-apart seed, so that it should become like Him who had made all things.[a] **27** And he blessed and rejoiced, and he called the name of this Feast the Feast of 𐤉𐤄𐤅𐤄, a joy acceptable to El Elyon.

28 And we blessed him forever, and all his seed after him throughout all the generations of the earth, because he celebrated this Feast in its appointed time, according to the witness of the heavenly tablets. **29** For this reason it is ordained on the heavenly tablets concerning Yisra'el, that they shall celebrate the Feast of Tabernacles seven days with joy, in the seventh month, acceptable before 𐤉𐤄𐤅𐤄 *as* a statute forever throughout their generations every year. **30** And to this there is no limit of days; for it is ordained forever regarding Yisra'el that they should celebrate it and dwell in tabernacles, and set wreaths upon their heads, and take leafy boughs, and willows from the brook. **31** And Avraham took branches of palm trees, and the fruit of goodly trees, and every day going round the altar with the branches seven times per day in the morning, he praised and gave thanks to his Elohim for all things in joy.

Weaning of Yitsḥaq

17 **1** And in the first year of the fifth week Yitsḥaq was weaned in this yovel, and Avraham made a great banquet in the third month, on the day his son Yitsḥaq was weaned. **2** And Yishma'el, the son of Hagar, the Mitsrite, was before the face of Avraham, his father, in his place, and Avraham rejoiced and blessed 𐤉𐤄𐤅𐤄 because he had seen his sons and had not died childless. **3** And he remembered the word which He had spoken to him on the day on which Lot had parted from him, and he rejoiced because 𐤉𐤄𐤅𐤄 had given him seed upon the earth to inherit the earth, and he blessed, with all his mouth, the Creator of all things.

Banishment of Hagar and Yishma'el

4 And Sarah saw Yishma'el playing and dancing, and Avraham rejoicing with great joy, and she became jealous of Yishma'el and said to Avraham, "Cast out this girl and her son; for the son of this girl will not be heir with my son, Yitsḥaq."

5 And the thing was grievous in Avraham's sight, because of his maidservant and because of his son, that he should drive them from him.

6 And 𐤉𐤄𐤅𐤄 said to Avraham, "Do not let it be grievous in your eyes, because of the child and the girl. In all that Sarah has said to you, listen to her words and do *them.* For in Yitsḥaq shall your name and seed be called. **7** But as for the son of this girl, I will make him a great nation, because he is of your seed."

8 And Avraham rose up early in the morning, and took bread and a bottle of water, and placed them on the shoulders of Hagar and the child, and sent her away. **9** And she departed and wandered in the wilderness of Beersheva, and the water in the bottle was spent, and the child thirsted, and was not able to go on, and fell down. **10** And his mother took him and cast him under an olive tree, and went and sat her down over against him, at the distance of a bow-shot. She said, "Let me not see the death of my child," and as she sat she wept.

11 And a messenger of 𐤉𐤄𐤅𐤄, one of the set-apart ones, said to her, "Why do you weep, Hagar? Arise, take the child, and hold him in your hand. For 𐤉𐤄𐤅𐤄 has heard your voice, and has seen the child." **12** And she opened her eyes, and she saw a well of water, and she went and filled her bottle with water, and she gave her child to drink, and she arose and went towards the wilderness of Paran.

13 And the child grew and became a hunter, and 𐤉𐤄𐤅𐤄 was with him, and his mother took him a wife from among the daughters of Mitsrayim. **14** And she bore him a son, and he called his name Nevaioth[b]; for she said, "𐤉𐤄𐤅𐤄 was near to me when I called upon him."

---

[a] **16**:**26** See Ḥanokh **10**:**16**.

[b] **17**:**14** Nevaioth – Ethiopic word ናቤዎት (*na'be'wot*) is a transliteration of the Hebrew 𐤍𐤁𐤉𐤅𐤕 (*ne'va'yoth*). This is derived from 𐤍𐤁𐤈 (*ne'vat*) meaning "to look, to pay attention."

Mastema's Plan

15 And it happened in the seventh week, in the
first year, in the first month in this yovel, on the
twelfth of this month, there were voices in
heaven regarding Avraham, that he was faithful
in all that He told him, and that he loved 𐤉𐤄𐤅𐤄,
and that in every affliction he was faithful.

16 And Prince Mastema came and said before
Elohim, "Behold, Avraham loves Yitsḥaq his
son, and he delights in him above all things else.
Tell him to offer him as a burnt-offering on the
altar, and You will see if he will do this
command, and You will know if he is faithful in
everything which You try him." [a]

17 And 𐤉𐤄𐤅𐤄 knew that Avraham was faithful in
all his afflictions; for He had tried him through
his country and with famine, and had tried him
with the wealth of kings, and had tried him
again through his wife, when she was torn *from
him*, and with circumcision; and had tried him
through Yishma'el and Hagar, his maidservant,
when he sent them away. 18 And in everything
in which He had tried him, he was found
faithful, and his being was not impatient, and he
was not slow to act; for he was faithful and a
lover of 𐤉𐤄𐤅𐤄.

The Offering of Yitsḥaq

18 1 And 𐤉𐤄𐤅𐤄 said to him, "Avraham,
Avraham;" and he said, "Behold, *here* am I."

2 And He said, "Take your beloved son, whom
you love, *even* Yitsḥaq, and go to the high
country, and offer him on one of the mountains
which I will point out to you."

3 And he rose early in the morning and saddled
his donkey, and took his two young men with
him, and Yitsḥaq his son, and chopped the
wood of the ascension offering, and he went to
the place on the third day, and he saw the place
far off. 4 And he came to a well of water, and he
said to his young men, "Stay here with the
donkey, and I and the boy shall go *there*, and
when we have worshipped we shall come again
to you." 5 And he took the wood of the burnt-
offering and laid it on Yitsḥaq his son, and he
took in his hand the fire and the knife, and they
went both of them together to that place.

6 And Yitsḥaq said to his father, "Father;" and
he said, "Here am I, my son." And he said to
him, "Behold the fire, and the knife, and the
wood; but where is the lamb for the burnt-
offering, father?"

7 And he said, "𐤉𐤄𐤅𐤄 will provide for Himself a
lamb for a burnt-offering, my son." And they
drew near to the place of the mount of 𐤉𐤄𐤅𐤄.
8 And he built an altar, and he placed the wood
on the altar, and bound Yitsḥaq his son, and
placed him on the wood which was upon the
altar, and stretched forth his hand to take the
knife to kill Yitsḥaq his son.

9 And I stood before him, and before Prince
Mastema, and 𐤉𐤄𐤅𐤄 said, "Tell him not to lay
his hand on the boy, nor to do anything to him,
for I have shown that he fears 𐤉𐤄𐤅𐤄."

10 And I called to him from the heavens, and
said to him, "Avraham, Avraham;" and he was
terrified and said, "Behold, *here* am I."

11 And I said to him, "Do not lay your hand on
the boy, neither do anything to him; for now I
have shown that you fear 𐤉𐤄𐤅𐤄, and have not
withheld your son, your first-born son, from
Me."

12 And Prince Mastema was put to shame; and
Avraham lifted up his eyes and looked, and,
behold a ram caught [in a thicket][b] by his horns.
And Avraham went and took the ram and
offered it for a burnt-offering instead of his son.
13 And Avraham called that place "𐤉𐤄𐤅𐤄 has
seen," so that it is said "[in the mountain][c] 𐤉𐤄𐤅𐤄
has seen." That is Mount Tsion.

---

[a] **17:16** Compare Yashar **22:46-55**.

[b] **18:12** Bracketed section indicates reading not present in Ethiopic texts. However, it is found in one Latin fragment. The Ethiopic has a meaningless phrase that reads, "and he came." The restoration based on the Latin fragment is obvious.

[c] **18:13** Bracketed section indicates reading present in Latin fragment but absent from Ethiopic texts.

14 And 𐤉𐤄𐤅𐤄 called Avraham by his name a second time from the heavens, as He caused us to appear to speak to him in the name of 𐤉𐤄𐤅𐤄.

15 And He said, "By Myself have I sworn, says 𐤉𐤄𐤅𐤄. Because you have done this thing, and have not withheld your son, your beloved[a] son, from Me, that in blessing I will bless you. And in multiplying I will multiply your seed as the stars of the heavens, and as the sand which is on the seashore. And your seed shall inherit the cities of their enemies. 16 And in your seed shall all nations of the earth be blessed. Because you have obeyed My voice, and I have shown to all that you are faithful to Me in all that I have said to you. Go in peace."

17 And Avraham went to his young men, and they arose and went together to Beersheva, and Avraham dwelled by the Well of the Oath. 18 And he celebrated this Feast every year, seven days with joy, and he called it the Feast of 𐤉𐤄𐤅𐤄 according to the seven days during which he went and returned in peace. 19 And accordingly has it been ordained and written on the heavenly tablets regarding Yisra'el and their seed, that they should observe this Feast seven days with the joy of feasting joy.

Death and Burial of Sarah

19 1 And in the first year of the first week in the forty-second yovel, Avraham returned and dwelled opposite Ḥevron, that is Qiryath-Arba, two weeks of years.

2 And in the first year of the third week of this yovel the days of the life of Sarah were accomplished, and she died in Ḥevron. 3 And Avraham went to mourn over her and bury her, and we tried him to see if his spirit was patient, and if he was not indignant in the words of his mouth. And he was found patient in this, and was not disturbed. 4 For in patience of spirit he conversed with the children of Ḥeth, to the intent that they should give him a place in which to bury his dead.

5 And 𐤉𐤄𐤅𐤄 gave him favor before all who saw him, and he requested of the sons of Ḥeth in gentleness, and they gave him the land of the cave of Makhpelah[b] over against Mamre, that is Ḥevron, for [four hundred][c] pieces of silver.

6 And they requested him saying, "We shall give it to you for nothing;" but he would not take it from their hands for nothing, for he gave the price of the place, the money in full, and he bowed down before them twice, and after this he buried his dead in the cave of Makhpelah.

7 And all the days of the life of Sarah were one hundred and twenty-seven years[d]; that is, two yovelim and four weeks and one year: these are the days of the years of the life of Sarah.

8 This is the tenth trial by which Avraham was tried, and he was found faithful *and* patient in spirit. 9 And he did not say a single word regarding the rumor in the land: that 𐤉𐤄𐤅𐤄 had said that He would give it to him and to his seed after him, and he begged a place there to bury his dead; for he was found faithful, and was recorded on the heavenly tablets as the friend of 𐤉𐤄𐤅𐤄.[e]

Marriage of Yitsḥaq and Rivqah

10 And in the fourth year he took a wife for his son Yitsḥaq and her name was Rivqah [the daughter of Bethuel, the son of Naḥor, the brother of Avraham][f] the sister of Lavan and

[a] **18:15** Some Ethiopic texts read, "firstborn" here instead of "beloved." Latin fragment reads, "only-begotten."

[b] **19:5** Charles' translation was based on the Ethiopic text which read, "…land of the cave of double." This was a translated form of the Hebrew word 𐤌𐤊𐤐𐤋𐤄 (*makh'pe'lah*). This word is derived from 𐤊𐤐𐤋 (*ka'phal*) meaning "double." However, two Hebrew fragments found at Qumran contain the word Makhpelah here, thus the restoration is obvious. Also in verse **6**.

[c] **19:5** Bracketed section indicates reading present in Latin fragment. Ethiopic texts read "forty" here. Compare Bereshiyt [Genesis] **23:16**, which also reads, "four hundred."

[d] **19:7** See Yashar **24:1**; Bereshiyt [Genesis] **23:1**.

[e] **19:9** See Ya'aqov [James] **2:23**.

[f] **19:10** Bracketed section indicates difficult reading. While both readings are slightly different, the Ethiopic and Latin versions both appear to have suffered during transmission. This may be due to a

daughter of Bethuel. And Bethuel was the son of Milkhah, who was the wife of Naḥor, the brother of Avraham.

11 And Avraham took to himself a third wife, and her name was Qeturah, from among the daughters of his household servants, for Hagar had died before Sarah. 12 And she bare him six son: Zimran, and Yoqshan, and Medan, and Midian, and Yishbaq, and Shuaḥ, in the two weeks of years.

Birth of Ya'aqov and Esaw

13 And in the sixth week, in the second year, Rivqah bore to Yitsḥaq two sons: Ya'aqov and Esaw. Ya'aqov was a smooth and upright man, and Esaw was fierce, a man of the field, and hairy, and Ya'aqov dwelled in tents. 14 And the youths grew, and Ya'aqov learned writing;[a] but Esaw did not learn, for he was a man of the field and a hunter. And he learned war, and all his deeds were fierce.

Avraham Blesses Ya'aqov

15 And Avraham loved Ya'aqov, but Yitsḥaq loved Esaw. 16 And Avraham saw the deeds of Esaw, and he knew that in Ya'aqov should his name and seed be called; and he called Rivqah and gave commandment regarding Ya'aqov, for he knew that she *also* loved Ya'aqov much more than Esaw.

17 And he said to her, "My daughter, watch over my son Ya'aqov, for he shall be in my stead on the earth. And *he shall be* for a blessing in the midst of the children of men, and for the glory of the whole seed of Shem. 18 For I know that 𐤉𐤄𐤅𐤄 will choose him to be a [set-apart people][b] to Himself, above all [nations][c] that are on the face of the earth. 19 And behold, Yitsḥaq my son loves Esaw more than Ya'aqov, but I see that you truly love Ya'aqov. 20 Add still further to your kindness to him. And let your eyes be upon him in love. For he shall be a blessing to us on the earth from now on to all generations of the earth. 21 Let your hands be strong, and let your heart rejoice in your son Ya'aqov. For I have loved him far beyond all my sons. He shall be blessed forever, and his seed shall fill the whole earth.

22 "If a man can number the sand of the earth, his seed also shall be numbered. 23 And all the blessings with which 𐤉𐤄𐤅𐤄 has blessed me and my seed shall belong to Ya'aqov and his seed always. 24 And in his seed shall my name be blessed, and the name of my fathers, Shem, and Noaḥ, and Ḥanokh, and Mahalalel, and Enosh, and Sheth, and Adam. 25 And these shall serve to lay the foundations of the heavens, and to strengthen the earth, and to renew all the luminaries which are in the expanse."

26 And he called Ya'aqov before the eyes of Rivqah his mother, and kissed him, and blessed him, and said, "Ya'aqov, my beloved son, whom my being loves, may Elohim from above the expanse bless you, and may He give you all the blessings with which He blessed Adam, and Ḥanokh, and Noaḥ, and Shem. 27 And all the things of which He told me, and all the things which He promised to give me, may He cause to cling to you and to your seed forever, according to the days of the heavens above the earth. 28 And the Spirits of Mastema shall not rule over you, or over your seed, to turn you from 𐤉𐤄𐤅𐤄, your Elohim from now on and forever. 29 And may 𐤉𐤄𐤅𐤄 Elohim be a father to you, and you the first-born son, and to the people always. Go in peace, my son."

30 And they both went forth together from Avraham. 31 And Rivqah loved Ya'aqov, with all her heart and with all her being, much more than Esaw; but Yitsḥaq loved Esaw more than Ya'aqov.

---

faulty copy of the Greek text from which they were translated.

[a] **19:14** See Yashar **26**:17.

[b] **19:18** Bracketed section indicates reading present in Latin fragment. Ethiopic text reads, "a people who will rise up."

[c] **19:18** Bracketed section indicates reading present in Latin fragment but absent from Ethiopic texts.

Avraham's Testament to His Children

20 1 And in the forty-second yovel, in the first year of the seventh week, Avraham called Yishma'el, and his twelve sons, and Yitsḥaq and his two sons, and the six sons of Qeturah, and their sons. 2 And he commanded them that they should guard the way of 𐤉𐤄𐤅𐤄, that they should work righteousness, and each love his neighbor, and act in this way among all men; that they should each walk this *way* with regard to them as to do judgment and righteousness on the earth. 3 That they should circumcise their sons, according to the covenant which He had made with them, and not deviate to the right hand or the left of all the paths which 𐤉𐤄𐤅𐤄 had commanded us. And that we should guard ourselves from all whoring and uncleanness, and renounce from among us all whoring and uncleanness.

4 And if any woman or maiden whores amongst you, burn her with fire, and let them not whore with her after their eyes and their heart. Do not let them take to themselves wives from the daughters of Kana'an; for the seed of Kana'an will be uprooted from the land.

5 And he told them of the judgment of the giants, and the judgment of the Sodomites, how they had been judged on account of their wickedness, and had died on account of their whoring, and uncleanness, and corruption among themselves through whoring.

6 "And guard yourselves from all whoring and uncleanness, and from all pollution of sin, lest you make our name a curse, and your whole life a hissing, and all your sons to be destroyed by the sword, and you become accursed like Sodom, and all your remnant as the sons of Gomorrah. 7 I implore you, my sons, love the Elohim of the heavens and cling to all His commands. And do not walk after their idols, and after their uncleannesses. 8 And do not make for yourselves molten or engraved elohim.[a] For they are vain, and there is no spirit in them. For they are work of *men's* hands, and all who trust in them, trust in nothing.[b]

9 "Do not serve them, and do not worship them. But serve El Elyon, and worship Him continually. And hope for His countenance always, and work uprightness and righteousness before Him, that He may have pleasure in you and grant you His favor. And *that He may* send rain upon you morning and evening, and bless all your works which you have wrought upon the earth, and bless your bread and your water. And bless the fruit of your womb and the fruit of your land, and the herds of your cattle, and the flocks of your sheep. 10 And you will be for a blessing on the earth, and all nations of the earth will desire you. Bless your sons in my name, that they may be blessed as I am."

11 And he gave to Yishma'el and to his sons, and to the sons of Qeturah, gifts, and sent them away from Yitsḥaq his son. And he gave everything to Yitsḥaq his son. 12 And Yishma'el and his sons, and the sons of Qeturah and their sons, went together and dwelled from Paran to the entering in of Bavel in all the land which is towards the East facing the wilderness. 13 And these mingled with each other, and their name was called Arabs[c], and Yishma'elites.

Avraham's Testament to Yitsḥaq

21 1 And in the sixth year of the seventh week of this yovel Avraham called Yitsḥaq his son, and commanded him, saying, "I am old, and do not know the day of my death. And I am full of my days. 2 And behold, I am one hundred and seventy-five years old, and throughout all the days of my life I have remembered 𐤉𐤄𐤅𐤄, and sought with all my heart to do His will, and to walk uprightly in all His ways. 3 My being has

---

[a] **20:8** See Shemoth [Exodus] **20:4-5**.

[b] **20:8** See Yirmeyahu [Jeremiah] **10:1-9**.

[c] **20:13** Arabs – Ethiopic word ዓረበ (*a'ra'ba*). In the Latin fragment it is written as Arabiis. These are both transliterations of the Greek Αραβας (*arabas*). All of these are most likely stand-ins for the Hebrew 𐤏𐤓𐤁 (*a'rav*). The cognates of *arav* all refer to a mixture. *Erev* (same spelling different vowels) is the word meaning "evening" which is a mixture of the end of light and beginning of darkness. Similarly this word is used in Shemoth [Exodus] **12:38** to describe a "mixed" multitude. Thus its usage here is most likely intended to mean that the Yishmaelites and sons of Qeturah would all be "mixed" with the people of the East.

hated idols, [and I have rejected those who
serve them. And I have][a] given my heart and
spirit that I might guard to do the will of Him
who created me. 4 For He is the living El, and
He is set-apart and faithful, and He is righteous
beyond all, and there is no partiality with Him,[b]
and no accepting of bribes, for Elohim is
righteous, and executes judgment on all those
who transgress His commands and despise His
covenant.[c]

5 "And you, my son, guard His commands and
His statutes and His judgments, and do not walk
after the abominations and after the engraved
images and after the molten images. 6 And do
not eat blood at all of animals or cattle, or of
any bird which flies in the heavens. 7 And if you
kill a slaughtering as an acceptable peace
offering, kill it, and pour out its blood upon the
altar, and all the fat of the offering offer on the
altar with fine flour and the meat offering
mingled with oil, with its drink offering. Offer
them all together on the altar of ascension
offering; it is a sweet aroma before 𐤉𐤄𐤅𐤄. 8 And
you will offer the fat of the slaughtering of
freewill offering on the fire which is upon the
altar, and the fat which is on the belly, and all
the fat on the inwards and the two kidneys, and
all the fat that is on them, and upon the loins
and liver you shall remove, together with the
kidneys. 9 And offer all these for a sweet aroma
acceptable before 𐤉𐤄𐤅𐤄, with its meat-offering
and with its drink-offering, for a sweet aroma.
And the bread of the offering to 𐤉𐤄𐤅𐤄.

10 "And eat its meat on that day and on the
second day, and do not let the sun go down on
the second day until it is eaten, and let nothing
be left over for the third day; for it is not
approved, and it will not be accepted; and let it
no longer be eaten, and all who eat of it will
bring sin upon themselves. For thus I have
found it written in the books of my forefathers,
and in the words of Ḥanokh, and in the words of
Noaḥ.

11 "And on all your offerings you shall cast salt,
and do not let the salt of the covenant be lacking
in all your offerings before 𐤉𐤄𐤅𐤄. 13 And
regarding the wood of the slaughterings, beware
lest you bring *other* wood for the altar in
addition to these: cypress, bay, almond, fir,
pine, cedar, savin, fig, olive, myrrh, laurel,
aspalathus.[d] And of these kinds of wood lay
upon the altar under the slaughtering, such as
have been tested as to their appearance. And do
not lay any split or dark wood *on it, but only*
hard and clean *wood*, without fault; a sound and
new growth; and do not lay old wood *on it*, for
its fragrance is gone for there is no longer
fragrance in it as before. 14 Besides these kinds
of wood there is none other that you shall place
on the altar, for the fragrance is dispersed, and
the smell of its fragrance will not go up to the
heavens.

15 "Guard this command and do it, my son, that
you may be upright in all your deeds. 16 And at
all times be clean in your body, and wash
yourself with water before you approach to
offer on the altar, and wash your hands and your
feet before you draw near to the altar; and when
you are done slaughtering, wash your hands and
feet again. 17 And let no blood appear upon you
nor upon your clothes; be on your guard, my
son, against blood, be on your guard
exceedingly; cover it with dust. 18 And do not
eat any blood for it is the being; eat no blood
whatever. 19 And take no bribes for the blood of
man, lest it be shed at will, without judgment.
For it is the blood that is shed that causes the
earth to sin, and the earth cannot be cleansed
from the blood of man except by the blood of
him who shed it. 20 And take no present or bribe
for the blood of man: blood for blood, that you
may be accepted before 𐤉𐤄𐤅𐤄, El Elyon. For He
is the defense of the good. And that you may be
preserved from all evil, and that He may save
you from every kind of death.

21 "I see, my son, that all the works of the
children of men are sin and wickedness. And all

---

[a] **20:3** Bracketed section indicates reading present in Latin fragment but absent from Ethiopic texts.
[b] **20:4** See Devarim [Deuteronomy] **10:17**; Romaious [Romans] **2:11**; Iyyov [Job] **34:19**; Ma'asei [Acts] **10:34**.
[c] **20:4** Compare Melakhim 𐤁 [2 Kings] **18:11-12**.
[d] **20:13** While the exact translation and classification of 'olive' is known, the other eleven trees have debated translations and classifications.

their deeds are uncleanness and abominable and
a pollution. And there is no righteousness with
them. 22 Beware, lest you walk in their ways
and tread in their paths, and sin a sin to death
before El Elyon. *Or* else He will hide His face
from you and give you back into the hands of
your transgression and uproot you from the
land, and your seed likewise from under the
heavens. And your name and your seed shall
perish from the whole earth. 23 Turn away from
all their deeds and all their uncleanness. Guard
the statute of El Elyon, and do His will and be
upright in all things. 24 And He will bless you in
all your deeds, and will raise up a planting of
righteousness from you through all the earth,
throughout all generations of the earth. And my
name and your name shall not be forgotten
under the heavens forever.

25 "Go in peace, my son. May El Elyon, my
Elohim and your Elohim, strengthen you to do
His will. And may He bless all your seed and
the remnant of your seed for the generations
forever, with all righteous blessings, that you
may be a blessing on all the earth."

26 And he went out from him rejoicing.

Avraham's Celebration of First Fruits

22 1 And it happened in the first week in the
forty-fourth yovel, in the second year, that is,
the year in which Avraham died, that Yitsḥaq
and Yishma'el came from the Well of the Oath –
to celebrate Shavuot, that is, the Feast of the
first-fruits of the harvest – to Avraham, their
father, and Avraham rejoiced because his two
sons had come. 2 For Yitsḥaq had many
possessions in Beersheva, and Yitsḥaq desired
to go and see his possessions and to return to his
father. 3 And in those days Yishma'el came to
see his father, and they both came together, and
Yitsḥaq offered a slaughtering for a ascension
offering, and presented it on the altar of his
father which he had made in Ḥevron. 4 And he
offered a freewill offering and made a Feast of
joy before Yishma'el, his brother. And Rivqah
made new cakes from the new grain, and gave
them to Ya'aqov, her son, to take them to
Avraham, his father, from the first-fruits of the
land, that he might eat and bless the Creator of
all things before he died.
5 And Yitsḥaq, too, sent by the hand of Ya'aqov
to Avraham a best freewill offering, that he
might eat and drink. 6 And he ate and drank,
and blessed El Elyon, who created the heavens
and earth. Who made all the fat things of the
earth, and gave them to the children of men that
they might eat and drink and bless their Creator.

7 "And now I give thanks to You, my Elohim,
because You have caused me to see this day.
Behold, I am one hundred and seventy-five
years old; an old man and full of days, and all
my days have been peace to me. 8 The sword of
the adversary has not overcome me in all that
You have given me and my children all the days
of my life until this day. 9 My Elohim, may
Your kindness and Your peace be upon Your
servant, and upon the seed of his sons, that they
may be to You a chosen nation and an
inheritance from among all the nations of the
earth from now on, to all the days of the
generations of the earth, to all the ages."

Avraham's Blessing for Ya'aqov

10 And he called Ya'aqov and said, "My son
Ya'aqov, may the Elohim of all bless you and
strengthen you to do righteousness, and His will
before Him, and may He choose you and your
seed that you may become a people for His
inheritance according to His will always. And
now, my son, Ya'aqov, draw near and kiss me."

11 And he drew near and kissed him, and he
said, "Blessed be my son Ya'aqov, and all the
sons of El Elyon, to all the ages. May 𐤉𐤄𐤅𐤄 give
you a seed of righteousness. And may He set
apart some of your sons in the midst of the
whole earth. May nations serve you, and all the
nations bow themselves before your seed. 12 Be
strong in the presence of men, and rule over all
the seed of Sheth. Then your ways and the ways
of your sons will be declared right, so that they
shall become a set-apart nation.

13 "May El Elyon give you all the blessings
with which He has blessed me and with which
He blessed Noaḥ and Adam. May they rest on
the set-apart head of your seed from generation
to generation forever. 14 And may He cleanse
you from all unrighteousness and uncleanness,
that you may be forgiven all the transgressions

which you committed ignorantly. And may He
strengthen you, and bless you. And may you
inherit the whole earth. 15 And may He renew
His covenant with you. That you may be to Him
a nation for His inheritance for all the ages. And
that He may be to you and to your seed an
Elohim in truth and righteousness throughout all
the days of the earth. 16 And now, my son
Ya'aqov, remember my words, and guard the
commands of Avraham you father. Separate
yourself from the nations, and do not eat with
them. And do not do according to their works,
and do not become their associate. For their
works are unclean, and all their ways are a
pollution and an abomination and uncleanness.

17 "They offer their slaughterings to the dead
and they worship evil spirits,[a] and they eat over
the graves, and all their works are vain and
empty. 18 They have no heart to understand and
their eyes do not see what their works are, and
how they err in saying to a piece of wood, 'You
are my elohim,' and to a stone, 'You are my
master and you are my deliverer.' And they have
no heart. 19 And as for you, my son Ya'aqov,
may El Elyon help you. And the Elohim of the
heavens bless you and remove you from their
uncleanness and from all their error. 20 Be on
guard, my son Ya'aqov, of taking a wife from
any seed of the daughters of Kana'an. For all his
seed is to be uprooted from the earth.

21 "For because of the transgression of Ḥam,
Kana'an erred, and all his seed shall be
destroyed from off the earth and all the remnant
of it. And none springing from him shall be
saved on the day of judgment. 22 And as for all
the worshippers of idols and the profane, there
is no hope for them in the land of the living. For
they will go to down into Sheol. And into the
place of judgment they will walk, and there
shall be no remembrance of them on the earth.
As the children of Sodom were taken away from
the earth, so will all those who worship idols be
taken away.

23 "Do not fear, my son Ya'aqov, and be not
dismayed, O son of Avraham. May El Elyon
preserve you from destruction, and may He
deliver you from all the paths of error. 24 This
house have I built for myself that I might put
my name on it in the earth. It is given to you
and to your seed forever, and it will be named
the house of Avraham. It is given to you and to
your seed forever. For you will build my house
and establish my name before Elohim forever.
Your seed and your name will stand throughout
all generations of the earth."

25 And he ceased commanding him and blessing
him. 26 And the two lay together on one bed.
And Ya'aqov slept in the bosom of Avraham,[b]
his father's father, and he kissed him seven
times, and his affection and his heart rejoiced
over him. 27 And he blessed him with all his
heart and said, "El Elyon, the Elohim of all, and
Creator of all, who brought me forth from Ur
Kasdim that He might give me this land to
inherit it forever, and that I might establish a
set-apart seed, blessed be the Most High
forever."

28 And he blessed Ya'aqov and said, "My son,
over whom with all my heart and my affection I
rejoice, may Your favor and Your kindness be
lifted up upon him and upon his seed always.
29 And do not forsake him, nor bring him to
nothing, from now on to the days of eternity,
and may Your eyes be opened on him and on
his seed, that You may preserve him, and bless
him, and set him apart as a nation for Your
inheritance. 30 And bless him with all Your
blessings from now on to all the days of
eternity, and renew Your covenant and Your
favor with him and with his seed according to
all Your good pleasure to all the generations of
the earth."

Death and Burial of Avraham

23 1 And he placed two of Ya'aqov's fingers on
his eyes, and he blessed the Elohim of elohim,
and he covered his face and stretched out his
feet and slept the sleep of eternity, and was
gathered to his fathers. 2 And despite all this
Ya'aqov was lying in his bosom, and did not

---

[a] **22:17** See Vayyiqra [Leviticus] **17:7**; Korinthious A [**1** Corinthians] **10:20**.

[b] **22:26** Compare Loukas [Luke] **16**.

know that Avraham, his father's father, was
dead.

3 And Ya'aqov awoke from his sleep, and
behold Avraham was cold as ice, and he said
'Father, father'; but there was no answer, and he
knew that he was dead. 4 And he arose from his
bosom and ran and told Rivqah, his mother; and
Rivqah went to Yitsḥaq in the night, and told
him; and they went together, and Ya'aqov with
them, and a lamp was in his hand, and when
they had gone in they found Avraham lying
dead. 5 And Yitsḥaq fell on the face of his father
and wept and kissed him. 6 And the voices were
heard in the house of Avraham, and Yishma'el
his son arose, and went to Avraham his father,
and wept over Avraham his father, he and all
the house of Avraham, and they wept with a
great weeping.

7 And his sons Yitsḥaq and Yishma'el buried
him in the cave of Makhpelah, near Sarah his
wife, and they wept for him forty days; all the
men of his house, and Yitsḥaq and Yishma'el,
and all their sons, and all the sons of Qeturah in
their places; and the days of weeping for
Avraham were ended. 8 And he lived three
yovelim and four weeks of years, one hundred
and seventy-five years, and completed the days
of his life, being old and full of days.

Discussion on the Decline of Lifespan

9 For the days of the forefathers, of their life,
were nineteen yovelim; and after the Flood they
began to grow less than nineteen yovelim, and
to decrease in yovelim, and to grow old quickly,
and to be full of their days due to much
affliction, and the wickedness of their ways,
with the exception of Avraham. 10 For Avraham
was perfect in all his deeds with 𐤉𐤄𐤅𐤄, and
well-pleasing in righteousness all the days of his
life; and behold, he did not complete four
yovelim in his life; when he had grown old due
to the wickedness *of men*, and was full of his
days.

11 And all the generations which shall arise
from this time until the day of the great
judgment shall grow old quickly, before they
complete two yovelim, and their knowledge
shall forsake them due to their old age [and all
their knowledge shall vanish away][a]. 12 And in
those days, if a man live a yovel and a half of
years, they shall say regarding him, "He has
lived long, and the greater part of his days are
pain and sorrow and affliction, and there is no
peace. 13 For calamity follows on calamity, and
wound on wound, and affliction on affliction,
and evil news on evil news, and illness on
illness, and all evil judgments such as these, one
with another, illness and overthrow, and snow
and frost and ice, and fever, and chills, and
stupor, and famine, and death, and sword, and
captivity, and all plagues and pains."

14 And all these shall come on an evil
generation, which transgresses on the earth.
Their works are uncleanness and whoring, and
pollution, and abominations. 15 Then they shall
say, "The days of the forefathers were many,
even to a thousand years, and were good; but
behold, the days of our life, if a man has lived
many, are seventy years; and, if he is strong,
eighty years.[b] And *for* those evil, there is no
peace in the days of this evil generation."

Prophecy of Future Evil Generation

16 And in that generation the sons will convict
their fathers and their elders of sin and
unrighteousness, and of the words of their
mouth and the great wickednesses which they
perpetrate, and concerning their forsaking the
covenant which 𐤉𐤄𐤅𐤄 cut between them and
Him, that they should guard and do all His
commands and His judgments and all His Torot,
without departing either to the right hand or the
left. 17 For all have done evil, and every mouth
speaks iniquity and all their works are an
uncleanness and an abomination, and all their
ways are pollution, uncleanness and
destruction.[c]

18 Behold the earth shall be destroyed on
account of all their works, and there shall be no
seed of the vine, and no oil; for their works are

---

[a] **23:11** Bracketed section indicates reading present in Ethiopic texts, but absent from Latin fragment.

[b] **23:15** See Tehillim [Psalms] **90:10**.

[c] **23:17** See Romaious [Romans] **3:23**; Melakhim 𐤀 [1 Kings] **8:46**; Qoheleth [Ecclesiastes] **7:20**.

altogether faithless, and they shall all perish
together, beasts and cattle and birds, and all the
fish of the sea, on account of the children of
men. **19** And some shall strive with one another,
the young with the old, and the old with the
young, the poor with the rich, the lowly with the
great, and the beggar with the prince, on
account of the Torah and the covenant; for they
have forgotten the command, and covenant, and
Feasts, and months, and Sabbaths, and yovelim,
and all judgments. **20** And they shall stand [with
bow and][a] with swords, and *make* war to turn
them back into the way; but they shall not return
until much blood has been shed on the earth, by
one another.

21 And those who have escaped shall not return
from their wickedness to the way of
righteousness, but they shall all exalt
themselves to deceit and wealth, that they may
each take all that is his neighbor's, and they
shall name the great Name, but not in truth and
not in righteousness, and they shall defile the
Most Set-apart Place[b] with their uncleanness
and the corruption of their pollution.

Punishment, Repentance of Future Generation

22 And a great plague shall fall on the deeds of
this generation from 𐤉𐤄𐤅𐤄, and He will give
them over to the sword and to judgment and to
captivity, and to be plundered and devoured.
23 And He will wake up against them the
sinners of the nations, who have neither
kindness nor compassion, and who do not
respect the person of anyone, neither old nor
young, nor anyone, for they are more wicked
and strong to do evil than all the children of
men. And they shall use violence against
Yisra'el and transgression against Ya'aqov. And
much blood shall be shed upon the earth. And
there shall be none to gather and none to bury.

24 In those days they shall cry aloud, and call
and pray that they may be saved from the hand
of the sinners, the nations, but none shall be
saved. **25** And the heads of the children shall be
white with grey hair, and a child of three weeks
shall appear old like a man of one hundred
years, and their stature shall be destroyed by
affliction and oppression. **26** And in those days
the children shall begin to study the Torah, and
to seek the commands, and to return to the path
of righteousness. **27** And the days shall begin to
grow many and increase among those children
of men until their days draw near to one
thousand years. And to a greater number of
years than *before* was the number of the days.
28 And there shall be no old man, nor one who
is full of days; for all shall be *as* children and
youths. **29** And all their days they shall complete
and live in peace and in joy. And there shall be
no Satan nor any evil destroyer. For all their
days shall be days of blessing and healing.

30 And at that time 𐤉𐤄𐤅𐤄 will heal His servants.
And they shall rise up and see great peace, and
drive out their adversaries. And the righteous
shall see and be thankful, and rejoice with joy
forever and ever, and shall see all their
judgments and all their curses on their enemies.
31 And their bones shall rest in the earth, and
their spirits shall have much joy. And they shall
know that it is 𐤉𐤄𐤅𐤄 who executes judgment,
and shows kindness to hundreds and thousands
and to all that love Him. **32** And you, Mosheh,
write down these words; for thus are they
written, and they record *them* on the heavenly
tablets for a witness for the generations forever.

Ya'aqov Buys the Birthright

24 **1** And it happened after the death of
Avraham, that 𐤉𐤄𐤅𐤄 blessed Yitsḥaq his son,
and he arose from Ḥevron and went and dwelled
at the Well of the Vision[c] in the first year of the
third week of this yovel *for* seven years. **2** And
in the first year of the fourth week a famine
began in the land, besides the first famine,
which had been in the days of Avraham.

3 And Ya'aqov stewed lentil soup, and Esaw
came from the field hungry. And he said to

---

[a] **23:20** Bracketed section indicates reading present in Latin fragment, but absent from Ethiopic texts.
[b] **23:21** Most Set-apart Place – Traditionally translated as "Holy of Holies."
[c] **24:1** Well of the Vision – Beer Lahai-roi. See Bereshiyt [Genesis] **16**.

Ya'aqov his brother, "Give me of this red[a]
soup." And Ya'aqov said to him, "Sell me your
birthright and I will give you bread, and also
some of this lentil soup."

4 And Esaw said in his heart, "I shall die; what
profit to me is this birthright?" And he said to
Ya'aqov, "I give it to you."

5 And Ya'aqov said, "Swear to me today," and
he swore to him. 6 And Ya'aqov gave his
brother Esaw bread and soup, and he ate until he
was satisfied, and Esaw despised his birthright;
for this reason Esaw's name was called Edom,
on account of the red soup which Ya'aqov gave
him for his birthright. 7 And Ya'aqov became
the elder, and Esaw was brought down from his
dignity.

Yitsḥaq and Avimelekh

8 And the famine was over the land, and
Yitsḥaq departed to go down into Mitsrayim in
the second year of this week, and went to the
king of the Philistines to Gerar, to Avimelekh.
9 And 𐤉𐤄𐤅𐤄 appeared to him and said to him,
"Do not go down into Mitsrayim; dwell in the
land that I tell you, and sojourn in this land, and
I will be with you and bless you. 10 For to you
and to your seed will I give all this land, and I
will establish My oath which I swore to
Avraham your father, and I will multiply your
seed as the stars of the heavens, and will give to
your seed all this land. 11 And in your seed shall
all the nations of the earth be blessed, because
your father obeyed My voice, and guarded My
charge and My commands, and My Torot, and
My judgments, and My covenant. And now,
obey My voice and dwell in this land."

12 And he dwelled in Gerar three weeks of
years. 13 And Avimelekh charged concerning
him, and concerning all that was his, saying,
"Any man that touches him or anything that is
his shall surely die." 14 And Yitsḥaq grew
strong among the Philistines, and he gained
many possessions: oxen and sheep and camels
and donkeys and a great household. 15 And he
sowed in the land of the Philistines and brought
in a hundred-fold, and Yitsḥaq became
exceedingly great, and the Philistines envied
him.

Yitsḥaq's Wells

16 Now all the wells which the servants of
Avraham had dug during the life of Avraham,
the Philistines had stopped them after the death
of Avraham, and filled them with earth. 17 And
Avimelekh said to Yitsḥaq, "Go from us, for
you are much mightier than we," and Yitsḥaq
departed there in the first year of the seventh
week, and sojourned in the valleys of Gerar.
18 And they dug the wells of water again, which
the servants of Avraham, his father, had dug,
and which the Philistines had closed after the
death of Avraham his father. And he called their
names as Avraham his father had named them.
19 And the servants of Yitsḥaq dug a well in the
valley, and found living water, and the
shepherds of Gerar strove with the shepherds of
Yitsḥaq, saying, "The water is ours;" and
Yitsḥaq called the name of the well Harshness',
because "they have been harsh with us."

20 And they dug a second well, and they strove
for that also, and he called its name 'Hostility'.
And he arose from there and they dug another
well, and they did not fight for that one, and he
called the name of it 'Breadth', and Yitsḥaq said,
"Now 𐤉𐤄𐤅𐤄 has made a wide *place* for us, and
we have increased in the land."

21 And he went up from there to the Well of the
Oath in the first year of the first week in the
forty-fourth yovel. 22 And 𐤉𐤄𐤅𐤄 appeared to
him that night, on the new moon of the first
month, and said to him, "I am the Elohim of
Avraham your father; do not fear, for I am with
you, and will bless you and shall surely multiply
your seed as the sand of the earth, for the sake
of Avraham My servant."

---

[a] **24:3** The Ethiopic text actually reads "wheat" here instead of "red." However, Charles noted that this is most likely a scribal error carried over from the Greek, as there is a Greek word πυρος (*puros*) which means "wheat" and there is a Greek word πυρρος (*purros*) which means "fire-colored; red." Given the narrative of Bereshiyt [Genesis] **25**, and the wordplay (Edom means "red" in Hebrew), this is only preserved if the stew were "red" not "wheat."

23 And he built an altar there, which Avraham
his father had first built, and he called upon the
name of 𐤉𐤄𐤅𐤄, and he offered slaughtering to
the Elohim of Avraham his father. 24 And they
dug a well and they found living water. 25 And
the servants of Yitsḥaq dug another well and did
not find water, and they went and told Yitsḥaq
that they had not found water, and Yitsḥaq said,
"I have sworn today to the Philistines and this
thing has been announced to us."

26 And he called the name of that place the Well
of the Oath; for there he had sworn to
Avimelekh, and Achuzzath his friend, and
Phikhol the commander of his host. 27 And
Yitsḥaq knew that day that under constraint he
had sworn to them to make peace with them.

Yitsḥaq Curses the Philistines

28 And on that day Yitsḥaq cursed the
Philistines and said, "Cursed be the Philistines
to the day of wrath and indignation from the
midst of all nations; may 𐤉𐤄𐤅𐤄 make them a
scorn and a curse and an object of wrath and
indignation in the hands of the sinners, the
nations, and in the hands of the Kittim. 29 And
whoever escapes the sword of the enemy and
the Kittim, may the righteous nation uproot in
judgment from under the heavens; for they shall
be the enemies and foes of my children
throughout their generations upon the earth.
30 And no remnant shall be left to them, nor one
that shall be saved on the day of the wrath of
judgment. For destruction and uprooting and
expulsion from the earth is for the whole seed of
the Philistines. And there shall no longer be left
for these Kaphtorim a name or a seed on the
earth.

31 "For though he ascend to the heavens, from
there he will be brought down. And though he
make himself strong on earth, from there he will
be dragged forth. And though he hide himself
among the nations, even from there he will be
uprooted. And though he descend into Sheol,
there also shall his condemnation be great. And
there also he shall have no peace. 32 And if he
go into captivity, by the hands of those that seek
his life shall they kill him on the way, and
neither name nor seed shall be left to him on all
the earth. For he will walk into an eternal
curse."

33 And thus is it written and engraved
concerning him on the heavenly tablets, to do to
him on the day of judgment, so that he may be
uprooted from the earth.

Rivqah Instructs Ya'aqov

25 1 And in the second year of this week in this
yovel, Rivqah called Ya'aqov her son, and
spoke to him, saying, "My son, do not take a
wife of the daughters of Kana'an, as did Esaw
your brother, who took two wives of the
daughters of Kana'an, and they have embittered
my being with all their unclean deeds. For all
their deeds are whoring and lust, and there is no
righteousness with them, for *their works* are
evil. 2 And I love you, my son, exceedingly; and
my heart and my affection bless you every hour
of the day, and *every* watch of the night. 3 And
now, my son, listen to my voice, and do the will
of your mother. Do not take a wife of the
daughters of this land, but only of the house of
my father, and of my father's relatives. You
shall take a wife of the house of my father, and
El Elyon will bless you. And your children shall
be a righteous generation and a set-apart seed."

4 And then Ya'aqov spoke to Rivqah, his
mother, and said to her, "Behold, mother, I am
nine weeks of years old, and I have not known
or touched any woman, nor have I betrothed
myself to any, nor even think of taking a wife
from the daughters of Kana'an. 5 For I
remember, mother, the words of Avraham, our
father, for he commanded me not to take a wife
of the daughters of Kana'an, but to take a wife
from the seed of my father's house and from my
relatives. 6 I have heard before that daughters
have been born to Lavan, your brother, and I
have set my heart on them to take a wife from
among them. 7 And for this reason I have
guarded myself in my spirit against sinning or
being corrupted in all my ways throughout all
the days of my life; for Avraham my father gave
me many commands with regard to lust and
whoring. 8 And, despite all that he has
commanded me, these twenty-two years my
brother has fought with me, and spoken
frequently to me and said, "My brother, take for

a wife a sister of my two wives;" but I refuse to
do as he has done. 9 I swear before you, mother,
that all the days of my life I will not take a wife
from the daughters of the seed of Kana'an, and I
will not act wickedly as my brother has done.
10 do not fear, mother; be assured that I shall do
your will and walk in uprightness, and not
corrupt my ways forever."

Rivqah Blesses Ya'aqov

11 And then she lifted up her face to the heavens
and extended the fingers of her hands, and
opened her mouth and blessed El Elyon, who
had created the heavens and the earth, and she
gave Him thanks and praise.

12 And she said, "Blessed be 𐤉𐤄𐤅𐤄 Elohim, and
may His set-apart Name be blessed forever and
ever, who has given me Ya'aqov as a pure son
and a set-apart seed. For he is Yours, and his
seed shall be Yours continually, and throughout
all the generations forever. 13 Bless him, O
𐤉𐤄𐤅𐤄, and place in my mouth the blessing of
righteousness, that I may bless him."

14 And at that hour, when the spirit of
righteousness descended into her mouth, she
placed both her hands on the head of Ya'aqov,
and said, 15 "Blessed are You, Master of
righteousness, Elohim of the ages. And may He
bless you beyond all the generations of men.
May He give you, my son, the path of
righteousness, and reveal righteousness to your
seed. 16 And may He make your sons many
during your life. And may they arise according
to the number of the months of the year. And
may their sons become many and great beyond
the stars of the heavens, and their numbers be
more than the sand of the sea. 17 And may He
give them this goodly land – as He said He
would give it to Avraham and to his seed after
him always – and may they hold it as a
possession forever. 18 And may I see blessed
children *born* to you during my life, and may all
your seed be a blessed and set-apart seed.

19 "And as you have refreshed your mother's
spirit during her life, the womb of her that bore
you blesses you thus. My affection and my
breasts bless you, and my mouth and my tongue
praise you greatly. 20 Increase and spread over
the earth, and may your seed be perfect in the
joy of the heavens and earth forever. And may
your seed rejoice, and on the great day of peace
may they have peace.

21 "And may your name and your seed endure
to all the ages. And may El Elyon be their
Elohim, and may the Elohim of righteousness
dwell with them, and by them may His set-apart
place be built to all the ages. 22 Blessed be he
that blesses you, and all flesh that curses you
falsely, may it be cursed."

23 And she kissed him, and said to him, "May
the Master of the world love you as the heart of
your mother and her affection rejoice in you and
bless you." And she ceased from blessing.

Ya'aqov gets the Blessing

26 1 And in the seventh year of this week
Yitsḥaq called Esaw, his elder son, and said to
him, "I am old, my son, and behold my eyes are
dim in seeing, and I do not know the day of my
death. 2 And now take your hunting weapons,
your quiver and your bow, and go out to the
field, and hunt and catch me *game*, my son, and
make me savory meat, such as my being loves,
and bring it to me that I may eat, and that my
being may bless you before I die."

3 But Rivqah heard Yitsḥaq speaking to Esaw.
4 And Esaw went forth early to the field to hunt
and catch *game* and bring it home to his father.

5 And Rivqah called Ya'aqov, her son, and said
to him, "Behold, I heard Yitsḥaq, your father
speak to Esaw, your brother, saying, 'Hunt for
me, and make me savory meat, and bring *it* to
me that I may eat *it* and bless you before 𐤉𐤄𐤅𐤄
before I die.' 6 And now, my son, obey my voice
in that which I command you. Go to your flock
and fetch me two good kids of the goats, and I
will make them *into* savory meat for your
father, such as he loves, and you shall bring *it* to
your father that he may eat and bless you before
𐤉𐤄𐤅𐤄 before he die, and that you may be
blessed."

8 And Ya'aqov said to Rivqah his mother,
"Mother, I shall not withhold anything which
my father would eat, and which would please
him. Only I fear, my mother, that he will

recognize my voice and wish to touch me.
8 And you know that I am smooth, and Esaw,
my brother, is hairy, and I will look like a
deceiver in his eyes, and shall do a deed which
he had not commanded me, and he will be angry
with me, and I shall bring upon myself a curse,
and not a blessing."

9 And Rivqah, his mother, said to him, "Your
curse be upon me, my son; only obey my
voice."

10 And Ya'aqov obeyed the voice of Rivqah, his
mother, and went and fetched two good and fat
kids of the goats, and brought them to his
mother, and his mother made them into savory
meat, such as he loved. **11** And Rivqah took the
goodly garments of Esaw, her elder son, which
was with her in the house, and she clothed
Ya'aqov, her younger son, *with them*, and she
put the skins of the kids on his hands and on the
exposed parts of his neck. **12** And she gave the
meat and the bread which she had prepared into
the hand of her son Ya'aqov.

13 And Ya'aqov went to his father and said, "I
am your son. I have done as you told me. Arise
and sit and eat of that which I have caught,
father, that your being may bless me."

14 And Yitsḥaq said to his son, "How have you
found *game* so quickly, my son?"

15 And Ya'aqov said, "Because your Elohim
directed me."

16 And Yitsḥaq said to him, "Come near, that I
may feel you, my son, *to see* if you are my son
Esaw or not."

17 And Ya'aqov went near to Yitsḥaq, his father,
and he felt him and said, **18** "The voice is
Ya'aqov's voice, but the hands are the hands of
Esaw," and he did not know him, because the
change was from the heavens in order to remove
his power of perception; and Yitsḥaq did not
know, for his hands were hairy like the hands of
Esaw [his bother][a], so that he blessed him.

19 And he said, "Are you my son Esaw?" and he
said, "I am your son;" and he said, "Bring *the
game* near to me that I may eat of that which
you caught, my son, that my being may bless
you."

20 And he brought near to him, and he did eat,
and he brought him wine and he drank.

21 And Yitsḥaq, his father, said to him, "Come
near and kiss me, my son." And he came near
and kissed him.

22 And he smelled the smell of his garment, and
he blessed him and said, "Behold, the smell of
my son is as the smell of a [full][b] field which
𐤉𐤄𐤅𐤄 has blessed. **23** And may 𐤉𐤄𐤅𐤄 give you
the dew of the heavens and the dew of the earth,
and plenty of corn and oil. Let nations serve
you, and peoples bow down to you. **24** Be
master over your brethren, and let your mother's
sons bow down to you. And may all the
blessings with which 𐤉𐤄𐤅𐤄 has blessed me and
blessed Avraham, my father, be imparted to you
and to your seed forever. Cursed be he that
curses you, and blessed be he that blesses you."

25 And it happened as soon as Yitsḥaq had made
an end of blessing his son Ya'aqov, and Ya'aqov
had gone forth from Yitsḥaq his father, that he
hid himself and Esaw, his brother, came in from
his hunting. **26** And he also made savory meat,
and brought *it* to his father, and said to his
father, "Let my father arise, and eat of my
game, that your being may bless me."

27 And Yitsḥaq, his father, said to him, "Who
are you?" And he said to him, "I am your
firstborn, your son Esaw. I have done as you
commanded me."

28 And Yitsḥaq was very greatly astonished, and
said, "Who is he that hunted and caught *game*
and brought *it* to me? I have eaten all before you
came, and have blessed him, *and* he shall be
blessed, and all his seed forever."

29 And it happened when Esaw heard the words
of his father Yitsḥaq that he cried with an
exceedingly great and bitter cry, and said to his
father, "Bless me, me also, father."

---

[a] **26:18** Bracketed section indicates reading present in Latin fragment but absent from Ethiopic texts.

[b] **26:22** Bracketed section indicates reading present in Latin fragment but absent from Ethiopic texts.

30 And he said to him, "Your brother came
craftily, and has taken away your blessing." And
he said, "Now I know why his name is named
Ya'aqov; behold, he has supplanted me these
two times: he took away my birthright, and now
he has taken away my blessing."

31 And he said, "Have you not reserved a
blessing for me, father?" and Yitsḥaq answered
and said to Esaw, "Behold, I have made him
your master. And I given all his brethren to him
for servants. And I have strengthened him with
plenty of corn and wine and oil. And what now
shall I do for you, my son?"

32 And Esaw said to Yitsḥaq, his father, "Do
you only have one blessing, O father? Bless me,
me also, father."

33 And Esaw lifted up his voice and wept. And
Yitsḥaq answered and said to him, "Behold,
your dwelling shall be far from the dew of the
earth. And far from the dew of the heavens
above. 34 And by your sword you will live, and
you will serve your brother. And it will happen,
when you become great, and shake his yoke
from off your neck, you will sin a complete sin
to death, and your seed will be uprooted from
under the heavens."

35 And Esaw kept threatening Ya'aqov because
of the blessing with which his father blessed
him, and he said in his heart, "May the days of
mourning for my father come quick, so that I
may kill my brother Ya'aqov."

Rivqah and Yitsḥaq Counsel Ya'aqov

27 1 And the words of Esaw, her elder son,
were told to Rivqah in a dream, and Rivqah sent
and called Ya'aqov her younger son, and said to
him, 2 "Behold, Esaw your brother will take
vengeance on you so as to kill you. 3 Now,
therefore, my son, obey my voice, and arise and
flee to Lavan, my brother, to Ḥaran, and stay
with him a few days until your brother's anger
turns away, and he remove his anger from you,
and forgets all that you did. Then I will send
and fetch you from there."

4 And Ya'aqov said, "I am not afraid. If he
wishes to kill me, I will kill him."

5 But she said to him, "Do not cause me to lose
both of my sons in one day."

6 And Ya'aqov said to Rivqah his mother,
"Behold, you know that my father has become
old, and does not see because his eyes are dull.
If I leave him it will be evil in his eyes, because
I leave him and go away from you, and my
father will be angry, and will curse me. I will
not go; when he sends me, only then will I go."

7 And Rivqah said to Ya'aqov, "I will go in and
speak to him, and he will send you away."

8 And Rivqah went in and said to Yitsḥaq, "I
detest my life because of the two daughters of
Ḥeth, whom Esaw has taken as wives. If
Ya'aqov takes a wife from among the daughters
of the land such as these, then what is my life to
me, for the daughters of Kana'an are evil."

9 And Yitsḥaq called Ya'aqov and blessed him,
and admonished him and said to him, 10 "Do not
take a wife of any of the daughters of Kana'an;
arise and go to Aram-Naharayim, to the house
of Bethuel, your mother's father, and take a wife
from there of the daughters of Lavan, your
mother's brother. 11 And may El Shaddai bless
you and increase and multiply you that you may
become a company of nations; and *may He* give
you the blessings of my father Avraham, to you
and to your seed after you, that you may inherit
the land of your sojourning and all the land
which 𐤉𐤄𐤅𐤄 gave to Avraham. Go in peace, my
son."

Ya'aqov goes to Ḥaran

12 And Yitsḥaq sent Ya'aqov away, and he went
to Aram-Naharayim, to Lavan the son of
Bethuel the Aramean, the brother of Rivqah,
Ya'aqov's mother. 13 And it happened after
Ya'aqov had arisen to go to Aram-Naharayim
that the spirit of Rivqah was grieved after her
son, and she wept.

14 And Yitsḥaq said to Rivqah, "My sister, do
not weep on account of Ya'aqov, my son; for he
goes in peace, and in peace he will return. El
Elyon will preserve him from all evil, and will
be with him; for He will not forsake him all his
days. 16 For I know that his ways will be
prospered in all things wherever he goes, until

he returns in peace to us, and we see him in peace. **17** Do not fear on his account, my sister, for he is on the upright path and he is a perfect man; and he is faithful and will not perish. Do not weep." **18** And Yitsḥaq comforted Rivqah on account of her son Ya'aqov, and blessed him.

Ya'aqov's Dream

19 And Ya'aqov went from the Well of the Oath to go to Ḥaran on the first year of the second week in the forty-fourth yovel, and he came to Luz on the mountains, that is, Beth-El, on the new moon of the first month of this week, and he came to the place at even and turned from the way to the west of the road that night: and he slept there; for the sun had set. **20** And he took one of the stones of that place [and placed it at his head][a] and laid under the tree, and he was journeying alone, and he slept. **21** And he dreamed that night, and behold a ladder set up on the earth, and the top of it reached to the heavens, and behold, the messengers of 𐤉𐤄𐤅𐤄 ascended and descended on it: and behold, 𐤉𐤄𐤅𐤄 stood upon it.

22 And he spoke to Ya'aqov and said, "I am 𐤉𐤄𐤅𐤄 Elohim of Avraham, your father, and the Elohim of Yitsḥaq; I will give to you and to your seed after you the land on which you are lying. **23** And your seed will be as the dust of the earth, and you shall increase to the west and to the east, to the north and the south, and in you and in your seed shall all the families of the nations be blessed. **24** And behold, I will be with you, and will keep you wherever you go, and I will bring you again into this land in peace; for I will not leave you until I do everything that I told you."

25 And Ya'aqov awoke from his sleep, and said, "Truly this place is the house of 𐤉𐤄𐤅𐤄, and I did not know." And he was afraid and said, "Dreadful is this place which is none other than the house of 𐤉𐤄𐤅𐤄, and this is the gate of the heavens."

26 And Ya'aqov arose early in the morning, and took the stone which he had put under his head and set it up as a pillar for a sign, and he poured oil upon the top of it. And he called the name of that place Beth-El; but the name of the place was Luz at the first.

27 And Ya'aqov vowed a vow to 𐤉𐤄𐤅𐤄, saying, "If 𐤉𐤄𐤅𐤄 will be with me, and will keep me in this way that I go, and give me bread to eat and garments to put on, so that I come again to my father's house in peace, then shall 𐤉𐤄𐤅𐤄 be my Elohim, and this stone which I have set up as a pillar for a sign in this place shall be the house of 𐤉𐤄𐤅𐤄, and of all that You give me, I shall give the tenth to You, my Elohim."

Lavan's Treachery

28 **1** And he picked up his feet and journeyed, and came to the land of the east, to Lavan, the brother of Rivqah, and he was with him, and served him for Raḥel his daughter one week.

2 And in the first year of the third week he said to him, "Give me my wife, for whom I have served you seven years;" and Lavan said to Ya'aqov, "I will give you your wife."

3 And Lavan made a banquet, and took Leah his elder daughter, and gave *her* to Ya'aqov as a wife, and gave her Zilpah his handmaid for a handmaid. And Ya'aqov did not know, for he thought that she was Raḥel. **4** And he went in to her, and behold, she was Leah; and Ya'aqov was angry with Lavan, and said to him, "Why have you done this to me? Did not I serve you for Raḥel, and not for Leah? Why have you wronged me? Take your daughter, and I will go; for you have done evil to me."

5 For Ya'aqov loved Raḥel more than Leah; for Leah's eyes were weak, but her appearance was very beautiful; but Raḥel had beautiful eyes and a good and very beautiful appearance.

6 And Lavan said to Ya'aqov, "It is not so done in our country, to give the younger before the elder." And it is not right to do this; for thus it is ordained and written in the heavenly tablets, that no one should give his younger daughter before the elder; but the elder one he gives first,

---

[a] **27:20** Bracketed section indicates reading present in Latin fragment but absent from Ethiopic texts.

and after her the younger. And the man who does so, they set down guilt against him in the heavens, and none is righteous that does this thing, for this deed is evil before 𐤉𐤄𐤅𐤄.

7 And command the children of Yisra'el that they do not this thing; let them neither take nor give the younger before they have given the elder, for it is very wicked.

8 And Lavan said to Ya'aqov, "Let the seven days of the banquet of this one pass, and I will give you Raḥel, that you may serve me another seven years, that you may pasture my sheep as you did in the former week."

Marriage to Raḥel

9 And on the day when the seven days of the banquet of Leah had passed, Lavan gave Raḥel to Ya'aqov, that he might serve him another seven years, and he gave Bilhah, the sister of Zilpah, to Raḥel as a handmaid. **10** And he served yet other seven years for Raḥel, for Leah had been given to him for nothing.

11 And 𐤉𐤄𐤅𐤄 opened the womb of Leah, and she conceived and bore Ya'aqov a son, and he called his name Reuven, on the fourteenth day of the ninth month, in the first year of the third week. **12** But the womb of Raḥel was closed, for 𐤉𐤄𐤅𐤄 saw that Leah was hated and Raḥel *was* loved. **13** And again Ya'aqov went in to Leah, and she conceived, and bore Ya'aqov a second son, and he called his name Shimon, on the twenty-first of the tenth month, and in the third year of this week.

14 And again Ya'aqov went in to Leah, and she conceived, and bare him a third son, and he called his name Levi, on the first day of the first month in the sixth year of this week. **15** And again Ya'aqov went in to her, and she conceived, and bore him a fourth son, and he called his name Yehudah, on the fifteenth of the third month, in the first year of the fourth week.

16 And on account of all this Raḥel envied Leah, for she did not bear, and she said to Ya'aqov, "Give me children;" and Ya'aqov said, "Have I withheld the fruits of your womb from you? Have I forsaken you?" **17** And when Raḥel saw that Leah had borne four sons to Ya'aqov – Reuven and Shimon and Levi and Yehudah – she said to him, "Go in to Bilhah my handmaid, and she will conceive, and bear a son to me."

18 [And she gave *him* Bilhah her handmaid to wife][a]. And he went in to her, and she conceived, and bore him a son, and he called his name Dan, on the ninth *day* of the sixth month, in the sixth year of the third week. **19** And Ya'aqov went in again to Bilhah a second time, and she conceived, and bore Ya'aqov another son, and Raḥel called his name Naphtali, on the fifth of the seventh month, in the second year of the fourth week.

20 And when Leah saw that she had stopped and did not bear, she envied Raḥel, and she also gave her handmaid, Zilpah, to Ya'aqov as wife; and she conceived, and bore a son, and Leah called his name Gad, on the twelfth *day* of the eighth month, in the third year of the fourth week. **21** And he went in again to her, and she conceived, and bore him a second son, and Leah called his name Asher, on the second *day* of the eleventh month, in the fifth year of the fourth week.

22 And Ya'aqov went in to Leah, and she conceived, and bore a son, and she called his name Yissakhar, on the fourth *day* of the fifth month, in the fourth year of the fourth week, and she gave him to a nurse. **23** And Ya'aqov went in to her again, and she conceived, and bore two *children*, a son and a daughter. And she called the name of the son Zevulun, and the name of the daughter Dinah, in the seventh *day* of the seventh month, in the sixth year of the fourth week.

24 And 𐤉𐤄𐤅𐤄 was favorable to Raḥel, and opened her womb, and she conceived, and bore a son, and she called his name Yoseph, on the first day of the fourth month, in the sixth year in this fourth week. **25** And in the days when Yoseph was born, Ya'aqov said to Lavan, "Give me my wives and sons, and let me go to my

---

[a] **28:18** Bracketed section indicates reading present in Latin fragment but absent from Ethiopic texts.

father Yitsḥaq, and let me make me a house; for I have completed the years in which I have served you for your two daughters, and I will go to the house of my father."

26 And Lavan said to Ya'aqov, "Stay with me for your wages, and pasture my flock for me again, and take your wages."

27 And they agreed with one another that he should give him as his wages those of the lambs and kids which were born black and spotted and white: *these* were to be his wages. 28 And all the sheep brought forth spotted and speckled and black, variously marked, and they brought forth again lambs like themselves, and all that were spotted were Ya'aqov's and those which were not were Lavan's. 29 And Ya'aqov's possessions multiplied exceedingly, and he possessed oxen and sheep and donkeys and camels, and manservants and maidservants. 30 And Lavan and his sons envied Ya'aqov, and Lavan took back his sheep from him, and he observed him with evil intent.

Ya'aqov Flees to Gilad

29 1 And it happened when Raḥel had borne Yoseph, that Lavan went to shear his sheep; for they were distant from him, a three days' journey. 2 And Ya'aqov saw that Lavan was going to shear his sheep, and Ya'aqov called Leah and Raḥel, and spoke to them *from* the heart, that they should come with him to the land of Kana'an. 3 For he told them how he had seen everything in a dream, even all that He had spoken to him, that he should return to his father's house. And they said, "To every place where you go, we will go with you."

4 And Ya'aqov blessed the Elohim of Yitsḥaq his father, and the Elohim of Avraham his father's father, and he arose and loaded up his wives and his children, and took all his possessions and crossed the river, and came to the land of Gilad, and Ya'aqov hid his intention from Lavan and did not tell him.

Oath between Ya'aqov and Lavan

5 And in the seventh year of the fourth week Ya'aqov turned toward Gilad in the first month, on the twenty-first *day*. And Lavan pursued after him and overtook Ya'aqov in the mountain of Gilad in the third month, on the thirteenth *day*.

6 And 𐤉𐤄𐤅𐤄 did not allow him to harm Ya'aqov; for He appeared to him in a dream by night. And Lavan spoke to Ya'aqov. 7 And on the fifteenth of those days Ya'aqov made a banquet for Lavan, and for all who came with him, and Ya'aqov swore to Lavan that day, and Lavan also to Ya'aqov, that neither should cross the mountain of Gilad to the other with evil purpose. 8 And he made there a heap for a witness, so the name of that place is called 'The Heap of Witness,' after this heap. 9 But before they used to call the land of Gilad 'The Land of the Rephaim;' for it was the land of the Rephaim. And the Rephaim were born giants, whose height was ten, nine, eight down to seven cubits *tall*. 10 And their habitation was from the land of the children of Ammon to Mount Ḥermon, and the seats of their kingdom were Qarnayim and Ashtaroth, and Edrei, and Misur, and Beon. 11 And 𐤉𐤄𐤅𐤄 destroyed them because of the evil of their deeds; for they were very cruel, and the Amorites dwelled in their stead; wicked and sinful, and there is no people today which has worked equal to all their sins. And therefore they do not have length of life on the earth.

12 And Ya'aqov sent Lavan away, and he departed into Aram-Naharayim, the land of the East, and Ya'aqov returned to the land of Gilad. 13 And he passed over the Yabboq in the ninth month, on the eleventh *day*. And on that day Esaw, his brother, came to him, and he was reconciled to him, and departed from him to the land of Seir, but Ya'aqov dwelled in tents.

Contrast between Ya'aqov and Esaw

14 And in the first year of the fifth week in this yovel he crossed the Yarden, and dwelled beyond the Yarden, and he pastured his sheep from the sea of the heap to Bethshan, and to Dothan and to the forest of Aqrabbim. 15 And he sent to his father Yitsḥaq of all his possessions, clothing, and food, and meat, and drink, and milk, and butter, and cheese, and some dates of the valley. 16 And to his mother Rivqah, also four times a year, between the

appointed times of the months, between
ploughing and reaping, and between autumn
and the rain *season* and between winter and
spring, to the tower of Avraham. 17 For Yitsḥaq
had returned from the Well of the Oath and
gone up to the tower of his father Avraham, and
he dwelled there apart from his son Esaw.
18 For in the days when Ya'aqov went to Aram-
Naharayim, Esaw took to himself a wife,
Mahalath, the daughter of Yishma'el, and he
gathered together all the flocks of his father and
his wives, and went up and dwelled on Mount
Seir, and left Yitsḥaq his father at the Well of
the Oath alone. 19 And Yitsḥaq went up from
the Well of the Oath and dwelled in the tower of
Avraham his father on the mountains of Ḥevron.
20 And there Ya'aqov sent all that he was
sending to his father and his mother from time
to time, all they needed, and they blessed
Ya'aqov with all their heart and with all their
being.

Levi and Shimon Avenge Dinah

30 1 And in the first year of the sixth week he
went up to Salem, to the east of Shekhem, in
peace, in the fourth month.

2 And there Dinah, the daughter of Ya'aqov,
was carried away to the house of Shekhem, the
son of Ḥamor, the Ḥivite, the prince of the land,
and he lay with her and defiled her, and she was
little, a child of twelve years. 3 And he asked his
father and her brothers that she might be given
to him as wife. And Ya'aqov and his sons were
angry because of the men of Shekhem; for they
had defiled Dinah, their sister, and they spoke to
them with evil intent and dealt deceitfully with
them and deceived them.

4 And Shimon and Levi came unexpectedly to
Shekhem and executed judgment on all the men
of Shekhem, and killed all the men whom they
found in it, and left not a single one remaining
in it; they killed all in torments because they
had dishonored their sister Dinah. 5 And thus let
it not again be done from now on that a
daughter of Yisra'el be defiled; for judgment is
ordained in the heavens against them that they
should destroy with the sword all the men of the
Shekhemites because they had worked shame in
Yisra'el. 6 And 𐤉𐤄𐤅𐤄 delivered them into the
hands of the sons of Ya'aqov that they might
destroy them with the sword and execute
judgment upon them, and that it might not be
done again in Yisra'el that a virgin of Yisra'el
should be defiled.

Prohibition of Marriage to Foreigners

7 And if there is any man who wishes in Yisra'el
to give his daughter or his sister to any man
who is of the seed of the nations he shall surely
die, and they shall stone him with stones; for he
has worked shame in Yisra'el; and they shall
burn the woman with fire, because she has
dishonored the name of the house of her father,
and she shall be uprooted from Yisra'el. 8 And
do not let an adulteress or uncleanness be found
in Yisra'el throughout all the days of the
generations of the earth, for Yisra'el is set-apart
to 𐤉𐤄𐤅𐤄, and every man who causes defilement
shall surely die: they shall stone him with
stones.

9 For thus has it been ordained and written in
the heavenly tablets regarding all the seed of
Yisra'el: he who causes defilement shall surely
die, and he shall be stoned with stones. 10 And
to this Torah there is no limit of days, and no
remission, nor any atonement: but the man who
has caused the defilement of his daughter shall
be uprooted in the midst of all Yisra'el, because
he has given of his seed to Moloch, and worked
profanely so as to cause defilement.

11 And you, Mosheh, command the children of
Yisra'el and exhort them not to give their
daughters to the nations, and not to take for their
sons any of the daughters of the nations, for this
is abominable before 𐤉𐤄𐤅. 12 For this reason I
have written for you in the words of the Torah
all the deeds of the Shekhemites, which they
worked against Dinah, and how the sons of
Ya'aqov spoke, saying, "We will not give our
daughter to a man who is uncircumcised; for
that is a reproach to us." 13 And it is a reproach
to Yisra'el, to those who live, and to those that
take the daughters of the nations; for this is
unclean and abominable to Yisra'el. 14 And
Yisra'el will not be free from this uncleanness if
it has a wife of the daughters of the nations, or
has given any of its daughters to a man who is
of any of the nations. 15 For there will be plague

upon plague, and curse upon curse, and every judgment and plague and curse will come if he does this thing, or hides his eyes from those who commit uncleanness, or those who defile the set-apart place of 𐤉𐤄𐤅𐤄, or those who profane His set-apart Name, *then* will the whole nation together be judged for all the uncleanness and profanation of this man. **16** And there will be no accepting of persons [and no regarding of appearance][a] and no receiving at his hands of fruits and offerings and burnt-offerings and fat, nor the smell of sweet aroma, so as to accept it. And so is every man or woman in Yisra'el who defiles the set-apart place. **17** For this reason I have commanded you, saying, "Witness this witness to Yisra'el: see what happened to the Shekhemites and their sons, how they were delivered into the hands of two sons of Ya'aqov, who killed them under tortures, and it was *reckoned* to them for righteousness, and it is written down to them for righteousness.

Levi Chosen for Priesthood

18 And the seed of Levi was chosen for the priesthood, and to be Levites, that they might minister before 𐤉𐤄𐤅𐤄, as we do, continually, and that Levi and his sons may be blessed forever; for he was zealous to execute righteousness and judgment and vengeance on all those who arose against Yisra'el. **19** And so they inscribe as a witness in his favor on the heavenly tablets blessing and righteousness before the Elohim of all. **20** And we remember the righteousness which the man fulfilled during his life, at all periods of the year; until a thousand generations they will record it, and it will come to him and to his descendants after him, and he has been recorded on the heavenly tablets as a friend and a righteous man. **21** All this account I have written for you, and have commanded you to say to the children of Yisra'el, that they should not commit sin nor transgress the judgments nor break the covenant which has been ordained for them, *but* that they should fulfil it and be recorded as friends.
22 But if they transgress and work uncleanness in every way, they will be recorded on the heavenly tablets as adversaries, and they will be blotted out of the book of life,[b] and they will be recorded in the book of those who will be destroyed, and with those who will be uprooted from the earth. **23** And on the day when the sons of Ya'aqov killed Shekhem, a writing was recorded in their favor in the heavens, that they had executed righteousness and uprightness and vengeance on the sinners, and it was written for a blessing. **24** And they brought Dinah, their sister, out of the house of Shekhem, and they took captive everything that was in Shekhem: their sheep and their oxen and their donkeys, and all their wealth, and all their flocks, and brought them all to Ya'aqov their father. **25** And he reproached them because they had put the city to the sword, for he feared those who dwelled in the land: the Kana'anites and the Perizzites. **26** And the dread of 𐤉𐤄𐤅𐤄 was upon all the cities which are around about Shekhem, and they did not rise to pursue after the sons of Ya'aqov; for terror had fallen upon them.

Preparation for Journey to Beth-El

31 **1** And on the first of the month Ya'aqov spoke to all the people of his house, saying, "Purify yourselves and change your garments, and let us arise and go up to Beth-El, where I vowed a vow to Him on the day when I fled from the face of Esaw my brother, because He has been with me and brought me into this land in peace; put away the strange elohim that are among you." **2** And they gave up the strange elohim and that which was in their ears and which was on their necks and the idols which Raḥel stole from Lavan her father she gave wholly to Ya'aqov. And he burned and broke them to pieces and destroyed them, and hid them under an oak which is in the land of Shekhem.

3 And he went up on the first of the seventh month to Beth-El. And he built an altar at the place where he had slept, and he set up a pillar there, and he sent word to his father Yitsḥaq to come to him to his slaughtering, and to his mother Rivqah.

---

[a] **30:16** Bracketed section indicates reading present in Ethiopic texts but absent from Latin fragment.

[b] **30:22** See Tehillim [Psalms] **69:28**; Hit'galut [Revelation] **3:5**; **13:8**; **17:8**; **20:15**.

4 And Yitsḥaq said, "Let my son Ya'aqov come,
and let me see him before I die."

Ya'aqov Visits Yitsḥaq

5 And Ya'aqov went to his father Yitsḥaq and to
his mother Rivqah, to the house of his father
Avraham, and he took two of his sons with him,
Levi and Yehudah, and he came to his father
Yitsḥaq and to his mother Rivqah. 6 And
Rivqah came forth from the tower to the front of
it to kiss Ya'aqov and embrace him; for her
spirit had revived when she heard:, "Behold
Ya'aqov your son has come;" and she kissed
him.

7 And she saw his two sons, and she recognized
them, and said to him, "Are these your sons, my
son?" and she embraced them and kissed them,
and blessed them, saying, "In you shall the seed
of Avraham become illustrious, and you will be
a blessing on the earth."

8 And Ya'aqov went in to Yitsḥaq his father, to
the chamber where he lay, and his two sons
were with him, and he took the hand of his
father, and stooping down he kissed him, and
Yitsḥaq clung to the neck of Ya'aqov his son,
and wept upon his neck. 9 And the darkness left
the eyes of Yitsḥaq, and he saw the two sons of
Ya'aqov, Levi, and Yehudah, and he said, "Are
these your sons, my son? For they are like you."

10 And he said to him that they were truly his
sons, "And you have truly seen that they are
truly my sons."

Blessing of Levi

11 And they came near to him, and he turned
and kissed them and embraced them both
together. 12 And the spirit of prophecy came
down into his mouth, and he took Levi by his
right hand and Yehudah by his left.

13 And he turned to Levi first, and began to
bless him first, and said to him, "May the
Elohim of all, 𐤉𐤄𐤅𐤄 of all ages, bless you and
your children throughout all the ages. 14 And
may 𐤉𐤄𐤅𐤄 give to you and to your seed
greatness and great glory, and cause you and
your seed, from among all flesh, to approach
Him to serve in His set-apart place as the
messengers of the presence and as the set-apart
ones. *Even* as they are, so shall the seed of your
sons be for glory and greatness and holiness,
and may He make them great to all the ages.
15 And they will be judges and princes, and
chiefs of all the seed of the sons of Ya'aqov.
They will speak the word of 𐤉𐤄𐤅𐤄 in
righteousness. And they will judge all His
judgments in righteousness. And they will
declare My ways to Ya'aqov And My paths to
Yisra'el. The blessing of 𐤉𐤄𐤅𐤄 shall be given in
their mouths to bless all the seed of the beloved.
16 Your mother has called your name Levi, and
rightly so; you will be joined to 𐤉𐤄𐤅𐤄, and be
the companion of all the sons of Ya'aqov.[a] Let
His table be yours, and you and your sons eat of
it. And may your table be full to all generations,
and your food fail not to all the ages. 17 And let
all who hate you fall down before you.[b] And let
all your adversaries be uprooted and die. And
blessed be he that blesses you, and cursed be
every nation that curses you."

Blessing of Yehudah

18 And to Yehudah he said, "May 𐤉𐤄𐤅𐤄 give
you strength and power to tread down all that
hate you. You will be a prince, you and one of
your sons, over the sons of Ya'aqov. May your
name and the name of your son go forth and
travel every land and region. Then shall the
nations fear before your face, and all the nations
shall quake. [And all the nations shall quake][c].
19 In you shall be the help of Ya'aqov, and in
you the salvation of Yisra'el will be found.
20 And when you sit on the throne of the honor
of your righteousness, there shall be great peace
for all the seed of the sons of the beloved.
Blessed be he that blesses you, and all that hate
you and afflict you and curse you shall be
uprooted and destroyed from the earth and be
accursed."

21 And turning he kissed him again and
embraced him, and rejoiced greatly; for he had

---

[a] **31:16** Hebrew name 𐤋𐤅𐤉 (*le'vi*) means "to cling; be joined."

[b] **31:17** See Bemidbar [Numbers] **10:35**.

[c] **31:18** Bracketed section indicates what is most likely a textual corruption. This was most likely repeated through dittography by mistake.

seen the sons of Ya'aqov his son in truth. 22 And
he went forth from between his feet and fell
down and bowed down to him, and he blessed
them and rested there with Yitsḥaq his father
that night, and they ate and drank with joy.
23 And he made the two sons of Ya'aqov sleep,
the one on his right hand and the other on his
left, and it was counted to him for
righteousness.

24 And Ya'aqov told his father everything
during the night, how 𐤉𐤄𐤅𐤄 had shown him
great favor, and how He had prospered all his
ways, and protected him from all evil. 25 And
Yitsḥaq blessed the Elohim of his father
Avraham, who had not withdrawn His favor and
His righteousness from the sons of His servant
Yitsḥaq. 26 And in the morning Ya'aqov told his
father Yitsḥaq the vow which he had vowed to
𐤉𐤄𐤅𐤄, and the vision which he had seen, and
that he had built an altar, and that everything
was ready for the slaughtering to be made
before 𐤉𐤄𐤅𐤄 as he had vowed, and that he had
come to set him on a donkey.

Yitsḥaq's Farewell to Ya'aqov

27 And Yitsḥaq said to Ya'aqov his son, "I am
not able to go with you for I am old and not able
to bear the way. Go in peace, my son. For I am
one hundred and sixty-five years this day; I am
no longer able to journey; set your mother *on a
donkey* and let her go with you. 28 And I know,
my son, that you have come because of me, and
may this day be blessed on which you have seen
me alive, and I also have seen you, my son.
29 May you prosper and fulfil the vow which
you vowed; and do not put off your vow; for
you will be called to account for the vow. Now
therefore hurry to perform it, and may He be
pleased who has made all things, to whom you
vowed the vow."

30 And he said to Rivqah, "Go with Ya'aqov
your son;" and Rivqah went with Ya'aqov her
son, and Deborah with her, and they came to
Beth-El. 31 And Ya'aqov remembered the
prayer with which his father had blessed him
and his two sons, Levi and Yehudah, and he
rejoiced and blessed the Elohim of his fathers,
Avraham and Yitsḥaq.

32 And he said, "Now I know that I have an
eternal hope, and my sons also, before the
Elohim of all;" and thus is it ordained
concerning the two; and they record it as an
eternal witness to them on the heavenly tablets
how Yitsḥaq blessed them.

Ya'aqov's Tithe and Offering

32 1 And he stayed that night at Beth-El, and
Levi dreamed that they had ordained and made
him the priest of El Elyon, him and his sons
forever; and he awoke from his sleep and
blessed 𐤉𐤄𐤅𐤄. 2 And Ya'aqov rose early in the
morning, on the fourteenth of this month, and
he gave a tithe of all that came with him, both of
men and cattle, both of gold and every vessel
and garment, yes, he gave tithes of all.

3 And in those days Raḥel became pregnant
with her son Benyamin. And Ya'aqov counted
his sons from him upwards and Levi fell to the
portion of 𐤉𐤄𐤅𐤄, and his father clothed him in
the garments of the priesthood and filled his
hands.

4 And on the fifteenth *day* of this month, he
brought to the altar fourteen oxen from among
the cattle, and twenty-eight rams, and forty-nine
sheep, and seven lambs, and twenty-one kids of
the goats as a burnt-offering on the altar of
slaughtering, well pleasing for a sweet aroma
before Elohim.[a] 5 This was his offering from the
vow which he had vowed that he would give a
tenth, with their fruit-offerings and their drink-
offerings. 6 And when the fire had consumed it,
he burned incense on the fire over the fire, and
for a freewill-offering two oxen and four rams
and four sheep, four he-goats, and two sheep of
a year old, and two kids of the goats; and thus
he did daily for seven days. 7 And he and all his
sons and his men were eating with joy there
seven days and blessing and thanking 𐤉𐤄𐤅𐤄,

---

[a] **32**:**4** Latin text reads "seven" and "twenty-one" here, while the Ethiopic texts read "sixty" and "twenty-nine" respectively. The cause of this corruption is unknown. Given the multiples of seven, it is doubtful the reading of "sixty" and "twenty-nine" is original.

who had delivered him out of all his affliction and had given him his vow.

8 And he tithed all the clean animals, and made a ascension offering, but he did *not*[a] give the unclean animals to Levi his son. And he gave him all the beings of the men. 9 And Levi served as priest at Beth-El before Ya'aqov his father *apart from* his ten brothers, and he was a priest there, and Ya'aqov gave his vow. Thus he tithed again the tithe to 𐤉𐤄𐤅𐤄 and set it apart, and it became set-apart to Him.

10 And for this reason it is ordained on the heavenly tablets as a Torah to tithe again the tithe to eat before 𐤉𐤄𐤅𐤄 from year to year, in the place where it is chosen that His Name should dwell, and to this Torah there is no limit of days forever. 11 This judgment is written that it may be fulfilled from year to year in eating the second tithe before 𐤉𐤄𐤅𐤄 in the place where it has been chosen, and nothing shall remain over from it from this year to the year following. 12 For the seed shall be eaten in its year, until the days of the gathering of the seed of the year, and the wine until the days of the wine, and the oil until the days of its season. 13 And all that is left of it and becomes old, let it be regarded as unclean: let it be burned with fire, for it is unclean. 14 And thus let them eat it together in the set-apart place, and let them not allow it to become old. 15 And all the tithes of the oxen and sheep shall be set-apart to 𐤉𐤄𐤅𐤄, and shall belong to His priests, which they will eat before Him from year to year; for thus is it ordained and engraved regarding the tithe on the heavenly tablets.

Ya'aqov's Vision

16 And on the second night, on the twenty-second day of this month, Ya'aqov resolved to build that place, and to surround the court with a wall, and to set it apart and make it set-apart forever, for himself and his children after him.

17 And 𐤉𐤄𐤅𐤄 appeared to him by night and blessed him and said to him, "Your name shall not be called Ya'aqov, but they will now call you Yisra'el." 18 And He said to him again, "I am 𐤉𐤄𐤅𐤄 who created the heavens and the earth, and I will increase you and multiply you exceedingly, and kings shall come forth from you, and they shall judge everywhere wherever the foot of the sons of men has walked. 19 And I will give to your seed all the earth which is under the heavens, and they will judge all the nations according to their desires, and after that they will gain possession of the whole earth and inherit it forever."

20 And He finished speaking with him, and He went up from him. And Ya'aqov looked until He had ascended into the heavens. 21 And he saw in a vision of the night, and behold a messenger descended from the heavens with seven tablets in his hands, and he gave them to Ya'aqov, and he read them and knew all that was written in them which would happen to him and his sons throughout all the ages. 22 And he showed him all that was written on the tablets, and said to him, "Do not build this place, and do not make it an eternal set-apart place, and do not dwell here; for this is not the place. Go to the house of Avraham your father and dwell with Yitsḥaq your father until the day of the death of your father. 23 For in Mitsrayim you shall die in peace, and in this land you shall be buried with honor in the tomb of your fathers, with Avraham and Yitsḥaq. 24 Do not fear, for as you have seen and read it, thus shall it all be; and write down everything as you have seen and read."

25 And Ya'aqov said, "𐤉𐤄𐤅𐤄, how can I remember all that I have read and seen?" And He said to him, "I will bring all things to your remembrance.[b]"

26 And he went up from him, and he awoke from his sleep, and he remembered everything which he had read and seen, and he wrote down all the words which he had read and seen.

---

[a] **32:8** The manuscripts lack the negative here, but the sense of the sentence given the counter statement "but" requires it; as does the context.

[b] **32:25** Compare Yoḥanan [John] **14:26**.

Feast of the 8th Day Instituted

27 And he celebrated there yet another day, and he slaughtered on *that day* according to all that he slaughtered on the former days, and called its name 'Addition,' for this day was added and the previous days he called 'The Feast.'

28 And thus it was manifested that it should be, and it is written on the heavenly tablets: why it was revealed to him that he should celebrate it, and add it to the seven days of the Feast. 29 And its name was called 'Addition,' because it was recorded [among the days][a] of the Feast Days, according to the number of the days of the year.

Death of Devorah; Departure of Rivqah

30 And in the night, on the twenty-third of this month, Devorah, Rivqah's nurse died, and they buried her beneath the city under the oak of the river, and he called the name of this place, 'The River of Devorah,' and the oak, 'The Oak of the Mourning of Devorah.' 31 And Rivqah went and returned to her house to his father Yitsḥaq, and Ya'aqov sent by her hand rams and sheep and he-goats that she should prepare a meal for his father such as he desired. 32 And he went after his mother until he came to the land of Kabratan, and he dwelled there.

Birth of Benyamin; Death of Raḥel

33 And Raḥel bore a son in the night, and called his name 'Son of My Sorrow;' for she suffered in giving birth. But his father called his name Benyamin, on the eleventh *day* of the eighth month in the first of the sixth week of this yovel. 34 And Raḥel died there and she was buried in the land of Ephrath, the same is Beth-lechem, and Ya'aqov built a pillar on the grave of Raḥel, on the road above her grave.

Reuven's Sin with Bilhah

33 1 And Ya'aqov went and dwelled to the south of Migdal-Eder at Ephrath[b]. And he went to his father Yitsḥaq, he and Leah his wife, on the first of the tenth month.

2 And Reuven saw Bilhah, Raḥel's handmaid, the concubine of his father, bathing in water in a secret place, and he desired her. 3 And he hid himself at night, and he entered the house of Bilhah, and he found her sleeping alone on a bed in her house. 4 So he lay with her, and she awoke and saw, and behold Reuven was lying with her in the bed, and she uncovered the border of her covering and seized him, and cried out, and discovered that it was Reuven. 5 And she was ashamed because of him, and she let go of him, and he fled. 6 And she lamented because of this thing exceedingly, and did not tell it to anyone. 7 And when Ya'aqov returned and sought her, she said to him, "I am not clean for you, for I have been defiled to you; for Reuven has defiled me, and has lain with me in the night, and I was asleep, and did not discover until he uncovered my skirt and slept with me."

8 And Ya'aqov was exceedingly angry with Reuven because he had lain with Bilhah, because he had uncovered his father's skirt. And Ya'aqov did not approach her again because Reuven had defiled her. 9 And as for any man who uncovers his father's skirt his deed is exceedingly wicked, for he is abominable before 𐤉𐤄𐤅𐤄.

Discussion on Incest

10 For this reason it is written and ordained on the heavenly tablets that a man should not lie with his father's wife, and should not uncover his father's skirt, for this is uncleanness: they shall surely die together, the man who lies with his father's wife and the woman also, for they have worked uncleanness on the earth. 11 And

[a] **32:29** Bracketed section indicates reading present in Latin fragment. This reads as additio est in dies. Ethiopic texts read ያዐርጉ: ይእቲ: በስምዕ: (*ya'a'rgu y'a'ti bas'm'ti*) meaning "in the attestation." This was an emendation made by Charles in his Ethiopic text as well as his English translation; I have chosen to stick with it.

[b] **33:1** Ethiopic text reads መግደላድራኤፍ (*mag'dalad'ra'ef*) here. Latin fragment reads Magdale der Efratam. Both of these are corruptions of the Hebrew 𐤌𐤂𐤃𐤋 𐤏𐤃𐤓 𐤀𐤐𐤓𐤕 (*mig'dal eder eph'rath*): Migdal-Eder of Ephrath. Migdal-Eder (the "Tower of Eder" or "Tower of the Flock") is mentioned in Bereshiyt [Genesis] **35:21**.

there shall be nothing unclean before our
Elohim in the nation which He has chosen for
Himself as a possession. **12** And again, it is
written a second time, "Cursed be he who lies
with the wife of his father, for he has uncovered
his father's shame;" and all the set-apart ones of
𐤉𐤄𐤅𐤄 said "Amein; amein." **13** And you,
Mosheh, command the children of Yisra'el that
they guard this word; for it *includes* a
punishment of death; and it is unclean, and there
is no atonement forever to atone for the man
who has committed this, but he is to be put to
death and killed, and stoned with stones, and
uprooted from the midst of the people of our
Elohim. **14** For it is not permitted to any man in
Yisra'el to remain alive a single day on the earth
who does so, for he is abominable and unclean.
15 And let them not say, "to Reuven was granted
life and forgiveness after he had lain with his
father's concubine, and to her also though she
had a husband, and her husband Ya'aqov, his
father, was still alive." **16** For until that time
there had not been revealed the statute and
judgment and Torah in its entirety for all
mankind, but in your days *it has been revealed*
as a Torah of appointed times and of days, and
an everlasting Torah for the everlasting
generations. **17** And for this Torah there is no
end of days, and no atonement for it, but they
must both be uprooted in the midst of the
nation: on the day which they committed it they
shall kill them.[a]

Mosheh to Instruct the People on Defilement

18 And you, Mosheh, write *it* down for Yisra'el
that they may guard it, and do according to
these words, and not commit a sin to death; for
𐤉𐤄𐤅𐤄 our Elohim is Judge, who does not respect
persons and does not accept bribes. **19** And tell
them these words of the covenant, that they may
hear and guard, and be on their guard with
respect to them, and not be destroyed and
uprooted from the land. For an uncleanness, and
an abomination, and a contamination, and a
pollution are all those who commit it on the
earth before our Elohim. **20** And there is no
greater sin than the whoring which they commit
on earth; for Yisra'el is a set-apart nation to
𐤉𐤄𐤅𐤄 their Elohim, and a nation of inheritance,
and a royal priestly nation; and for *His own*
possession. There shall be no such uncleanness
in the midst of the set-apart nation.

Children of Ya'aqov before Yitsḥaq

21 And in the third year of this sixth week
Ya'aqov and all his sons went and dwelled in
the house of Avraham, near Yitsḥaq his father
and Rivqah his mother. **22** And these were the
names of the sons of Ya'aqov: the first-born
Reuven, Shimon, Levi, Yehudah, Yissakhar,
Zevulun, the sons of Leah. And the sons of
Raḥel, Yoseph and Benyamin. And the sons of
Bilhah, Dan and Naphtali. And the sons of
Zilpah, Gad and Asher. And Dinah, the
daughter of Leah, the only daughter of Ya'aqov.
23 And they came and bowed themselves to
Yitsḥaq and Rivqah, and when they saw them
they blessed Ya'aqov and all his sons, and
Yitsḥaq rejoiced exceedingly, for he saw the
sons of Ya'aqov, his younger son and he blessed
them.

War between Ya'aqov and the Amorites

34 **1** And in the sixth year of this week of this
forty-fourth yovel, Ya'aqov sent his sons to
pasture their sheep, and his servants with them
to the pastures of Shekhem. **2** And the seven
kings of the Amorites assembled themselves
together against them, to kill them, hiding
themselves under the trees, and to take their
cattle as a prey. **3** And Ya'aqov and Levi and
Yehudah and Yoseph were in the house with
Yitsḥaq their father; for his spirit was sad, and
they could not leave him; and Benyamin was
the youngest, and for this reason remained with
his father.

4 And there came the king of Taphu[b] and the
king of 'Aresa[c], and the king of Seragan[d], and
the king of Selo[e], and the king of Ga'as[f], and the

---

[a] **33:17** See also Testament of Reuven **3:10-15**.

[b] **34:4** Taphu – Most likely a corruption of Tapuaḥ. Compare Yovelim **34** with Yashar **37**.

[c] **34:4** 'Aresa – Most likely a corruption of Ḥatsor.

[d] **34:4** Seragon – Most likely a corruption of Sarton.

[e] **34:4** Selo – Most likely a corruption of Shiloh.

[f] **34:4** Ga'as – Most likely a corruption of Ga'ash.

king of Bethoron[a], and the king of Ma'anisakir[b],
and all those who dwell in these mountains *and*
who dwell in the woods in the land of Kana'an.

5 And they announced this to Ya'aqov saying,
"Behold, the kings of the Amorites have
surrounded your sons, and plundered their
herds."

6 And he arose from his house, he and three of
his sons and all the servants of his father, and
his own servants, and he went against them with
six thousand men, who carried swords. 7 And he
killed them in the pastures of Shekhem, and
pursued those who fled, and he killed them with
the edge of the sword, and he killed 'Aresa and
Taphu and Saregan and Selo and 'Amanisakir
and Ga'as, and he recovered his herds. 8 And he
prevailed over them, and imposed a tax on them
that they should pay him tribute: five fruit
products of their land. And he built Robel and
Tamnatares. 9 And he returned in peace, and
made peace with them, and they became his
servants, until the day that he and his sons went
down into Mitsrayim.

10 And in the seventh year of this week he sent
Yoseph to learn about the welfare of his
brothers from his house to the land of Shekhem,
and he found them in the land of Dothan.

Yoseph's Brothers Sell Him

11 And they dealt treacherously with him, and
formed a plot against him to kill him; but
changing their minds, they sold him to
Yishma'elite merchants, who brought him down
into Mitsrayim, and they sold him to Potiphar,
the eunuch of Pharaoh, the chief of the cooks[c],
priest of the city of 'Elew[d].

12 And the sons of Ya'aqov slaughtered a kid,
and dipped the coat of Yoseph in the blood, and
sent *it* to Ya'aqov their father on the tenth *day* of
the seventh month. 13 And he mourned all that
night, for they had brought it to him in the
evening, and he became feverish with mourning
for his death, and he said, "An evil beast has
devoured Yoseph;" and all the members of his
house were grieving and mourning with him all
that day. 14 And his sons and his daughter rose
up to comfort him, but he refused to be
comforted for his son.

Death of Bilhah and Dinah

15 And on that day Bilhah heard that Yoseph
had perished, and she died mourning him, and
she was living in Qafratef, and Dinah also, his
daughter, died after Yoseph had perished.
16 And these three mournings came upon
Yisra'el in one month. And they buried Bilhah
over against the tomb of Raḥel, and Dinah, his
daughter, they also buried there. 17 And he
mourned for Yoseph one year, and did not
cease, for he said, "Let me go down to the grave
mourning for my son."

Day of Atonement as a Memorial for Yoseph

18 For this reason it is ordained for the children
of Yisra'el that they should afflict themselves on
the tenth *day* of the seventh month. On the day
that the news which made him weep for Yoseph
came to Ya'aqov his father, that they should
make atonement for themselves with with a
young goat on the tenth *day* of the seventh
month, once a year, for their sins; for they had
grieved the affection of their father regarding
Yoseph his son. 19 And this day has been
ordained that they should grieve for their sins,
and for all their transgressions and for all their
errors, so that they might cleanse themselves on
that day once a year.

---

[a] **34:4** Bethoron – Most likely a corruption of Bethḥoron.

[b] **34:4** Ma'anisakir – Most likely a corruption of Machanehem.

[c] **34:11** Chief of the cooks – Ethiopic phrase ሊቀ: ዐቀብት (*li'kha akh'b't*). This was most likely caused by misunderstanding the Hebrew word 𐤈𐤁𐤇 (*tab'bach*). Tabbach literally means "one who butchers." However, it is used throughout the Tanakh to mean "guard" (see Bereshiyt [Genesis] **37**:**36**; **39**:**1**; **40**:**3-4**). Thus the term for "butcher" or "cook" was used in Ethiopic, despite the idiomatic expression having the intended meaning of "bodyguard."

[d] **34:11** 'Elew – Ethiopic word ኤሌው (*ele'w*) is most likely a corruption of the Greek ἡλιου (*he'liou*) meaning "sun." This in turn is a corruption of Heliopolis, meaning "City of the Sun."

Wives of the Twelve Patriarchs

20 And after Yoseph perished, the sons of Ya'aqov took to themselves wives. The name of Reuven's wife is 'Ada[a]. And the name of Shimon's wife is 'Adiba'a[b], a Kana'anite. And the name of Levi's wife is Melkha[c], of the daughters of Aram, of the seed of the sons of Teraḥ. And the name of Yehudah's wife, Betasu'el[d], a Kana'anite. And the name of Yissakhar's wife, Hezaqa[e]. And the name of Zevulun's wife, Ni'iman[f]. And the name of Dan's wife, 'Egla[g]. And the name of Naphtali's wife, Rasu'u[h], of Aram-Naharayim. And the name of Gad's wife, Maka[i]. And the name of Asher's wife, 'Iyona[j]. And the name of Yoseph's wife, Asenath, the Mitsrite. And the name of Benyamin's wife, Yiskah[k]. **21** And Shimon repented, and took a second[l] wife from Aram-Naharayim as his brothers.

Rivqah's Prophecy of her Death

35 **1** And in the first year of the first week of the forty-fifth yovel Rivqah called Ya'aqov, her son, and commanded him regarding his father and regarding his brother, that he should honor them all the days of his life.

2 And Ya'aqov said, "I will do everything you have commanded me; for this thing will be honor and greatness to me, and righteousness before 𐤉𐤄𐤅𐤄, that I should honor them. **3** And you too, mother, know from the time I was born until this day, all my deeds and all that is in my heart, that I always think good concerning all. **4** And how should I not do this thing which you commanded me, that I should honor my father and my brother? **5** Tell me, mother, what perversity have you seen in me, and I shall turn away from it, and kindness will be upon me."

6 And she said to him, "My son, I have not seen in you, in all my days, any perverse *thing* but *only* upright deeds. And yet I will tell you the truth, my son: I will die this year, and I will not pass through this year alive; for I have seen in a dream the day of my death, that I should not live beyond a hundred and fifty-five years. And behold I have completed all the days of my life which I am to live."

7 And Ya'aqov laughed at the words of his mother, because his mother said that she would die; and she was sitting opposite to him in possession of her strength, and she was not weak; for she went in and out and saw, and her teeth were strong, and no sickness had touched her all the days of her life.

8 And Ya'aqov said to her, "Blessed am I, mother, if my days approach the days of your life, and my strength remain with me as your strength. You will not die, for you are joking with me regarding your death."

---

[a] **34:20** 'Ada – Wife of Reuven. Yashar **45** records her name as Eliuram. It also states she was a Kana'anite, disagreeing here with verse **21**.

[b] **34:20** 'Adiba'a – Wife of Shimon. While Yovelim states Dinah died the same day as Yoseph, Yashar states that the first wife of Shimon was Dinah, his sister, not 'Adiba'a the Kana'anite.

[c] **34:20** Melkha – Wife of Levi. Yashar **45** records her name as Adinah. Yovelim states that she was a descendant of Aram, while Yashar says she was a descendant of Yoktan, making her descended from Arpakhshad, the brother of Aram. See Bereshiyt [Genesis] **10**.

[d] **34:20** Betasu'el – Wife of Yehudah. Yashar **45** records her name as Aliyath. Testament of Yehudah records this as Bathshua (see Test. Of Yeh. **8:2** and accompanying footnote). Betasu'el is probably a corruption of Bathshua.

[e] **34:20** Hezaqa – Wife of Yissakhar. Yashar **45** records her name as Aridah, the sister of Adinah.

[f] **34:20** Ni'iman – Wife of Zevulun. Yashar **45** records her name as Merishah.

[g] **34:20** 'Egla – Wife of Dan. Yashar **45** records her name as Aphlaleth.

[h] **34:20** Rasu'u – Wife of Naphtali. Yashar **45** records her name as Merimah.

[i] **34:20** Maka – Wife of Gad. Yashar **45** records her name as Utsit.

[j] **34:20** 'Iyona – Wife of Asher. Yashar **45** states that the first wife of Asher died. It is not clear if 'Iyona is identified with Adon, his first wife, or Hadurah, his second.

[k] **34:20** Yiskah – Wife of Benyamin. Yashar **45** records her name as Meḥalya.

[l] **34:21** Yashar **45** agrees that Shimon took a second wife, though it states she was a Kana'anite named Bunah.

Rivqah's Petition on behalf of Ya'aqov

9 And she went in to Yitsḥaq and said to him,
"One petition I make to you: cause Esaw to
swear that he will not harm Ya'aqov, nor pursue
him with enmity; for you know Esaw's
inclinations, and how they are evil from his
youth, and there is no good in him; for he
desires after to kill him after your death. 10 And
you know all that he has done since the day
Ya'aqov his brother went to Ḥaran until this
day: how he has forsaken us with his whole
heart, and has done evil to us; he has taken your
flocks to himself, and carried off all your
possessions from before your face. 11 And when
we asked and entreated him for what belonged
to us, he did as a man who was taking pity on
us. 12 And he is bitter against you because you
blessed Ya'aqov, your perfect and upright son;
for there is no evil but only good in him. And
since he came from Ḥaran to this day he has not
robbed us of anything; for he brings us
everything in its season always, and rejoices
with all his heart when we take at his hands and
he blesses us, and has not parted from us since
he came from Ḥaran until this day, and he
remains with us continually at home honoring
us."

13 And Yitsḥaq said to her, "I, too, know and
see the deeds of Ya'aqov who is with us, how he
honors us with his whole heart. But I loved
Esaw formerly more than Ya'aqov, because he
was the firstborn; but now I love Ya'aqov more
than Esaw, for he has done exceedingly evil
deeds, and there is no righteousness in him, for
all his ways are unrighteousness and violence,
[and there is no righteousness around him.]
14 And now my heart is troubled because of all
his deeds, and neither he nor his seed is to be
saved, for they are those who will be destroyed
from the earth and who will be uprooted from
under the heavens, for he has forsaken the
Elohim of Avraham and gone after his wives,
and after their uncleanness, and after their error,
he and his children. 15 And you tell me to cause
him to swear that he will not kill Ya'aqov his
brother; even if he swears he will not keep his
oath, and he will not do good but evil only.
16 But if he desires to kill Ya'aqov his brother,
he will be given into Ya'aqov's hands, and he
will not escape from his hands, for he will
descend into his hands. 17 And do not fear on
account of Ya'aqov; for the guardian of Ya'aqov
is great and powerful and honored, and praised
more than the guardian of Esaw."

Rivqah Petitions Esaw to Love Ya'aqov

18 And Rivqah sent and called Esaw and he
came to her, and she said to him, "I have a
petition, my son, to make to you, and promise to
do it, my son." 19 And he said, "I will do
everything that you say to me, and I will not
refuse your petition."

20 And she said to him, "I ask you that the day I
die, you will take me in, and bury me near
Sarah, your father's mother, and that you and
Ya'aqov will love each other and that neither
will desire evil against the other, but mutual
love only, and *so* you will prosper, my sons, and
be honored in the midst of the land, and no
enemy will rejoice over you, and you will be a
blessing and kindness in the eyes of all those
that love you."

21 And he said, "I will do all that you told me,
and I will bury you on the day you die near
Sarah, my father's mother, as you desired, that
her bones may be near your bones. 22 And
Ya'aqov, my brother, also, I shall love above all
flesh; for I do not have a brother in all the earth
besides him. And this is no great merit for me if
I love him, for he is my brother, and we were
sown together in your body, and together we
came forth from your womb. 23 And if I do not
love my brother, whom shall I love? And I,
myself, beg you to exhort Ya'aqov concerning
me, and concerning my sons, for I know that he
will surely be king over me and my sons, for on
the day my father blessed him, he made him the
higher and me the lower. 24 And I swear to you
that I shall love him, and not desire evil against
him all the days of my life but good only." And
he swore to her regarding all this matter.

25 And she called Ya'aqov before the eyes of
Esaw, and gave him command according to the
words which she had spoken to Esaw. 26 And he
said, "I will do what pleases you; believe me
that no evil will proceed from me or from my

sons against Esaw, and I shall be first in nothing
except in love only."

Death and Burial of Rivqah

27 And they ate and drank, she and her sons that
night, and she died, three yovelim and one week
and one year old, on that night, and her two
sons, Esaw and Ya'aqov, buried her in the cave
of Makhpelah near Sarah, their father's mother.

Yitsḥaq's Testament to Ya'aqov and Esaw

36 1 And in the sixth year of this week Yitsḥaq
called his two sons, Esaw and Ya'aqov, and they
came to him, and he said to them, "My sons, I
am going the way of my fathers, to the eternal
house where my fathers are. 2 So bury me near
Avraham my father, in the cave of Makhpelah
in the field of Ephron the Ḥittite, where
Avraham purchased a tomb to bury in; in the
tomb which I dug for myself: bury me there.
3 And this I command you, my sons, that you
practice righteousness and uprightness on the
earth, so that 𐤉𐤄𐤅𐤄 may bring upon you all that
𐤉𐤄𐤅𐤄 said He would do to Avraham and to his
seed. 4 And love one another, my sons, your
brother, as a man loves his own being, and let
each seek ways that he may benefit his brother,
and act together on the earth. And let them love
each other as their own beings. 5 And
concerning the question of idols, I command
and admonish you to reject them and hate them,
and do not love them, for they are full of
deception for those that worship them and for
those that bow down to them.

6 "Remember, my sons, 𐤉𐤄𐤅𐤄 Elohim of
Avraham your father, and how I too worshipped
Him and served Him in righteousness and in
joy, that He might multiply you and increase
your seed as the stars of the heavens in
multitude, and establish you on the earth as the
plant of righteousness which will not be
uprooted to all the generations forever. 7 And
now I shall make you swear a great oath – for
there is no oath which is greater than it by the
Name glorious and honored and great and
splendid and wonderful and mighty, which
created the heavens and the earth and all things
together – that you will fear Him and worship
Him. 8 And that each will love his brother with
affection and righteousness, and that neither
will desire evil against his brother from now on
forever all the days of your life so that you may
prosper in all your deeds and not be destroyed.

9 "And if either of you devises evil against his
brother, know that from now on everyone that
devises evil against his brother shall fall into his
hand, and shall be uprooted from the land of the
living, and his seed shall be destroyed from
under the heavens. 10 But on the day of turmoil
and insult and indignation and anger, with
flaming consuming fire as He burned Sodom, so
likewise will He burn his land and his city and
all that is his, and he shall be blotted out of the
book of the discipline of the children of men,
and not be recorded in the book of life, but in
that which is appointed to destruction, and he
shall depart into eternal insult; so that their
condemnation may be always renewed in hate
and in insult and in wrath and in torment and in
indignation and in plagues and in disease
forever. 11 I say and witness to you, my sons,
according to the judgment which shall come
upon the man who wishes to harm his brother."

12 And he divided all his possessions between
the two on that day and he gave the larger
portion to him that was the firstborn, and the
tower and all that was about it, and all that
Avraham possessed at the Well of the Oath.

13 And he said, "This larger portion I will give
to the firstborn." 14 And Esaw said, "I have sold
and given my birthright to Ya'aqov; let it be
given to him. I do not have a single word to say
regarding it, for it is his."

15 And Yitsḥaq said, "May a blessing rest upon
you, my sons, and upon your seed this day, for
you have given me rest, and my heart is not
pained concerning the birthright, lest you work
wickedness on account of it. 16 May the El
Elyon bless the man that works righteousness,
he and his seed forever."

Death and Burial of Yitsḥaq

17 And he ended commanding them and
blessing them, and they ate and drank together
before him, and he rejoiced because there was
one mind between them, and they went forth
from him and rested that day and slept. 18 And

Yitsḥaq slept on his bed that day rejoicing; and he slept the eternal sleep, and died one hundred and eighty years old. He completed twenty-five weeks and five years; and his two sons, Esaw and Ya'aqov, buried him. 19 And Esaw went to the land of Edom, to the mountains of Seir, and dwelled there. 20 And Ya'aqov dwelled in the mountains of Ḥevron, in the tower of the land of the sojourning of his father Avraham, and he worshipped 𐤉𐤄𐤅𐤄 with all his heart and according to the visible commands as He had divided the days of his generations.

Death and Burial of Leah

21 And Leah his wife died in the fourth year of the second week of the forty-fifth yovel, and he buried her in the cave of Makhpelah near Rivqah his mother, to the left of the grave of Sarah, his grandmother and all her sons and his sons came to mourn over Leah his wife with him and to comfort him regarding her, because he was lamenting her. 22 For he loved her exceedingly after Raḥel her sister died; for she was perfect and upright in all her ways and honored Ya'aqov, and all the days that she lived with him he did not hear a harsh word from her mouth, for she was gentle and peaceable and upright and honorable. 24 And he remembered all her deeds which she had done during her life and he lamented her exceedingly; for he loved her with all his heart and with all his being.

Esaw's Sons Rebuke Him

37 1 And on the day that Yitsḥaq the father of Ya'aqov and Esaw died, the sons of Esaw heard that Yitsḥaq had given the portion of the elder to his younger son, Ya'aqov, and they were very angry.

2 And they fought with their father, saying, "Why has your father given Ya'aqov the portion of the elder, and passed over you, although you are the elder and Ya'aqov the younger?"

3 And Esaw said to them, "Because I sold my birthright to Ya'aqov for a small portion of lentils, and on the day my father sent me to hunt and catch *game* [and bring him something][a] that he should eat and bless me, he came with deception and brought my father food and drink, and my father blessed him and put me under his hand. 4 And now our father has caused us to swear, me and him, that we shall not mutually devise evil, either against his brother, and that we shall continue in love and in peace each with his brother and not make our ways corrupt."

5 And they said to him, "We shall not listen to you to make peace with him; for our strength is greater than his strength, and we are more powerful than him. We will go against him and kill him, and destroy him and his sons. And if you will not go with us, we will harm you also. 6 And now listen to us. Let us send to Aram and Philistia and Moav and Ammon, and let us choose for ourselves chosen men who are valiant in battle, and let us go against him and do battle with him, and let us exterminate him from the earth before he grows strong."

7 And their father said to them, "Do not go, and do not make war with him, lest you fall before him."

8 And they said to him, "This too, is exactly your method of doing from your youth until this day, and you are putting your neck under his yoke. We will not listen to these words."

War Between Ya'aqov and Esaw

9 And they sent to Aram, and to 'Aduram, to the friend of their father, and they hired – along with them – one thousand fighting men, chosen men of war. 10 And from Moav and from the children of Ammon, there came those who were hired, one thousand chosen men, and from Philistia, one thousand chosen men of war, and from Edom and from the Ḥorites one thousand chosen fighting men, and from Kittim mighty men of war.

11 And they said to their father, "Go forth with them and lead them, or else we will kill you." And he was filled with wrath and indignation on seeing that his sons were forcing him to go

---

[a] **37:3** Bracketed section indicates reading present in Ethiopic texts but absent from Latin and Syriac fragments.

before *them* to lead them against Ya'aqov his brother.

12 But afterward he remembered all the evil which lay hidden in his heart against Ya'aqov his brother; and he did not remember the oath which he had sworn to his father and to his mother: that he would devise no evil all his days against Ya'aqov his brother. 13 And despite all this, Ya'aqov did not know that they were coming against him to battle, and he was mourning for Leah, his wife, until they approached very near to the tower with four thousand warriors and chosen men of war.

14 And the men of Ḥevron sent to him saying, "Behold your brother has come against you, to fight you, with four thousand *men* with swords, and they carry shields and weapons;" for they loved Ya'aqov more than Esaw. 15 So they told him; for Ya'aqov was a more generous and kind man than Esaw. 16 But Ya'aqov would not believe until they came very near to the tower.

17 And he closed the gates of the tower; and he stood on the battlements and spoke to his brother Esaw and said, "Is the comfort with which you have come to comfort me for my wife who has died good?[a] Is this the oath that you swore to your father, and again to your mother, before they died? You have broken the oath. [On the day that you swore to your father you were condemned.][b]"

18 And then Esaw answered and said to him, "Neither the children of men nor the beasts of the earth have any oath of righteousness which in swearing they have sworn *an oath valid* forever; but every day they devise evil one against another, and how each may kill his adversary and enemy. 19 And you hate me and my children forever. And there is no observing the bond of brotherhood with you." [And Ya'aqov said, "Do not do this, my brother. As for me, there is no evil in my heart against you. Do not devise evil against me. Know there Elohim, He sees what is hidden, and repays all *men* according to his deeds. Quiet your anger and do not act so harshly, that your evil comes down on you." Then Esaw turned and said,][c]

20 "Hear these words which I declare to you: If the boar can change its skin and make its bristles as soft as wool, or if it can cause horns to sprout forth on its head like the horns of a stag [or of a sheep][d], then I would observe the bond of brotherhood with you. [And if the breasts separated themselves from their mother, for you have not been a brother to me.][e] 21 And if the wolves make peace with the lambs so as not to devour or harm them, and if their hearts are towards them for good, then there shall be peace in my heart towards you. 22 And if the lion becomes the friend of the ox and makes peace with him, and if he is bound under one yoke with him and ploughs with him, then I will make peace with you. 23 And when the raven becomes white as the stork[f], then know that I have loved you and will make peace with you. You will be uprooted and your sons will be uprooted, and there will be no peace for you."

24 And when Ya'aqov saw that he was evilly disposed towards him with his heart, and with all his being *desired* to kill him, and that he had come springing like the wild boar which comes upon the spear that pierces and kills it, and does not recoil from it; then he spoke to his own *sons* and to his servants that they should attack him and all his companions.

---

[a] **37:17** Most Ethiopic texts do not phrase this sentence as a question. However, without it, the structure is lacking. One major manuscript does, however, make it a question and the Syriac fragment includes the interrogative hm (*mah*) meaning "what?" or "how?" at the beginning of the sentence.

[b] **37:17** Bracketed section indicates reading present in Ethiopic texts but absent from Syriac fragment.

[c] **37:19** Bracketed section indicates reading present in Syriac fragment but absent from Ethiopic texts.

[d] **37:20** Bracketed section indicates reading present in Ethiopic text but absent from Syriac fragment.

[e] **37:20** Bracketed section indicates reading present in Ethiopic but absent from Syriac fragment. However, verses **20-23** have been abbreviated drastically in the Syriac fragment, and thus it does not provide the best witness.

[f] **37:23** Syriac fragment records this as "pelican." Either is viable.

Defeat and Death of Esaw

38 1 And after that Yehudah spake to Ya'aqov,
his father, and said to him, "Bend your bow,
father, and send forth your arrows, and cast
down the adversary and kill the enemy. And
may you have the power, for we will not kill
your brother, for he is near to you, and he is like
you: let us give him *this* honor."

2 Then Ya'aqov bent his bow and sent forth the
arrow and struck Esaw, his brother [on his right
breast][a] and killed him.[b] 3 And again he sent
forth an arrow and struck 'Adoran the
Aramaean, on the left breast, and drove him
backward and killed him. 4 And then the sons of
Ya'aqov, went forth, with their servants,
dividing themselves into companies on the four
sides of the tower.

5 And Yehudah went forth in front, and
Naphtali and Gad with him, and fifty servants
with him on the south side of the tower, and
they killed all they found before them, and not
one individual of them escaped. 6 And Levi and
Dan and Asher went forth on the east side of the
tower, and fifty *men* with them, and they killed
the fighting men of Moav and Ammon. 7 And
Reuven and Yissakhar and Zevulun went forth
on the north side of the tower, and fifty men
with them, and they killed the fighting men of
the Philistines. 8 And Shimon and Benyamin
and Ḥanokh, Reuven's son, went forth on the
west side of the tower, and fifty *men* with them,
and they killed of four hundred men of Edom
and of the Ḥorites, stout warriors; and six
hundred fled, and four of the sons of Esaw fled
with them, and left their father lying dead, as he
had fallen on the hill which is in 'Aduram.

9 And the sons of Ya'aqov pursued after them to
the mountains of Seir. And Ya'aqov buried his
brother on the hill which is in 'Aduram, and he
returned to his house. 10 And the sons of
Ya'aqov encircled the sons of Esaw in the
mountains of Seir, and bowed their necks so
that they became servants of the sons of
Ya'aqov. 11 And they sent to their father *to see*
whether they should make peace with them or
kill them. 12 And Ya'aqov sent word to his sons
that they should make peace, and they made
peace with them, and placed the yoke of
servitude upon them, so that they paid tax to
Ya'aqov and to his sons always. 13 And they
continued to pay tax to Ya'aqov until the day
that he went down into Mitsrayim.

14 And the sons of Edom have not removed the
yoke of servitude which the twelve sons of
Ya'aqov had imposed on them *even* until this
day. 15 And these are the kings that reigned in
Edom before there reigned any king over the
children of Yisra'el until this day in the land of
Edom.

Kings of Edom

16 And Balaq, the son of Beor, reigned in Edom,
and the name of his city was Danaba. 17 And
Balaq died, and Yovav, the son of Zara of
Boser, reigned in his stead. 18 And Yovav died,
and 'Asam, of the land of Teman, reigned in his
stead. 19 And 'Asam died, and 'Adath, the son of
Barad[c], who killed Midian in the field of Moav,
reigned in his stead, and the name of his city
was Avith. 20 And 'Adath died, and Salman,
from 'Amaseqa, reigned in his stead. 21 And
Salman died, and Sha'ul of Ra'aboth *by the*
river, reigned in his stead. 22 And Sha'ul died,
and Ba'elunan, the son of Akhbor, reigned in his
stead. 23 And Ba'elunan, the son of Akhbor
died, and 'Adath reigned in his stead, and the
name of his wife was Maitabith, the daughter of

---

[a] **38:2** Bracketed section indicates reading present in Latin fragment but absent from Ethiopic texts. Charles also noted that Midrash Wayyisau – a classical Rabbinic writing in Hebrew that recorded battles of Ya'aqov's sons – also notes that Esav was killed by an arrow to the right breast.

[b] **38:2** This disagrees with Yashar **56**, which states that Ya'aqov died prior to Esav. Another disagreement shows that Ḥushim, son of Dan, killed Esav after the death of Ya'aqov, while Yovelim states here that Ya'aqov killed Esav himself. See also Testament of Yehudah **9**.

[c] **38:19** Barad – Ethiopic word በረድ (*ba'rad*) is most likely a corruption of the Hebrew 𐤁𐤃𐤃 (*Be'dad*). According to Yashar **85:38** and Bereshiyt [Genesis] **36:35**; D'vrei Ha'Yamim 𐤀 [**1** Chronicles] **1:46**, it was Bedad son of Hadad who killed Midian in the field of Moav. A copyist most likely mistook the first Hebrew letter Dalet [𐤃] for a Resh [𐤓] which was a common copyist error.

Matarat, the daughter of Metabedza'ab. **24** These are the kings who reigned in the land of Edom.

Yoseph in Potiphar's House

39 1 And Ya'aqov dwelled in the land of his father's sojourning in the land of Kana'an.

2 These are the generations of Ya'aqov. And Yoseph was seventeen years old when they took him down into the land of Mitsrayim, and Potiphar, a eunuch of Pharaoh, the chief cook purchased him. **3** And he set Yoseph over all his house and the blessing of 𐤉𐤄𐤅𐤄 came upon the house of the Mitsrite on account of Yoseph, and 𐤉𐤄𐤅𐤄 prospered him in all that he did. **4** And the Mitsrite entrusted everything into the hands of Yoseph; for he saw that 𐤉𐤄𐤅𐤄 was with him, and that 𐤉𐤄𐤅𐤄 prospered him in all that he did.

5 And Yoseph's appearance was good and very handsome, and his master's wife lifted up her eyes and saw Yoseph, and she desired him and entreated him to lie with her. **6** But he did not surrender his being, and he remembered 𐤉𐤄𐤅𐤄 and the words which Ya'aqov, his father, used to read from among the words of Avraham, that no man should whore with a woman who has a husband; that for him the punishment of death has been ordained in the heavens before El Elyon, and the sin will be recorded against him in the eternal books continually before 𐤉𐤄𐤅𐤄. 7 And Yoseph remembered these words and refused to lie with her. **8** And she entreated him for a year,[a] and he refused and would not listen. **9** But she embraced him and held him tight in the house in order to force him to lie with her; and *she* closed the doors of the house and held him tight; but he left his garment in her hands and broke through the door and fled outside from her presence.

10 And the woman saw that he would not lie with her, and accused him in the presence of his master, saying, "Your Hebrew servant, whom you love, tried to force me so that he might lie with me; and it happened when I lifted up my voice that he fled and left his garment in my hands when I held him, and he broke through the door."

Yoseph in Prison

11 And the Mitsrite saw the garment of Yoseph and the broken door, and heard the words of his wife, and cast Yoseph into prison into the place where the prisoners were kept whom the king imprisoned. **12** And he was there in the prison; and 𐤉𐤄𐤅𐤄 gave Yoseph favor in the eyes of the chief of the prison guards and compassion before him, for he saw that 𐤉𐤄𐤅𐤄 was with him, and that 𐤉𐤄𐤅𐤄 made all that he did to prosper. **13** And he entrusted all things into his hands, and the chief of the prison guards knew of nothing that was with him, for Yoseph did everything, and 𐤉𐤄𐤅𐤄 perfected it. And he remained there two years.

14 And in those days Pharaoh, king of Mitsrayim was angry against his two eunuchs, against the chief butler, and against the chief baker, and he put them in prison in the house of the chief cook, in the prison where Yoseph was kept. **15** And the chief of the prison guards appointed Yoseph to serve them; and he served before them. **16** And they both dreamed a dream, the chief cupbearer and the chief baker, and they told it to Yoseph. **17** And as he interpreted to them, so it happened to them, *as Yoseph said;* and Pharaoh restored the chief cupbearer to his office and he killed the [chief][b] baker, as Yoseph had interpreted to them. **18** But the chief cupbearer forgot Yoseph in the prison, although he had informed him what would happen to him, and did not remember to inform Pharaoh how Yoseph had told him, for he forgot.

Yoseph Interprets Pharaoh's Dreams

40 1 And in those days Pharaoh dreamed two dreams in one night concerning a famine which was to be in all the land, and he awoke from his sleep and called all the interpreters of dreams that were in Mitsrayim, and *the* magicians, and told them his two dreams, and they were not able to declare *the meaning*. **2** And then the

[a] **39:8** Yashar **44:73** seems to agree that Yoseph was in the house of Potiphar for one year.

[b] **39:17** Bracketed section indicates reading present in Latin fragment but absent from Ethiopic texts.

chief cupbearer remembered Yoseph and spoke of him to the king, and he brought him forth from the prison, and he told his two dreams before him.

3 And he said before Pharaoh that his two dreams were one, and he said to him, "Seven years will come. Abundance will be over all the land of Mitsrayim, and after that seven years of famine, such a famine as has not been in all the land. **4** And now let Pharaoh appoint [overseers][a] in all the land of Mitsrayim, and let them store up food in every city throughout the days of the years of plenty, and there will be food for the seven years of famine, and the land will not perish through the famine, for it will be very heavy."

5 And 𐤉𐤄𐤅𐤄 gave Yoseph favor and kindness in the eyes of Pharaoh, and Pharaoh said to his servants, "We shall not find such a wise and knowing man as this man, for the Ruaḥ of 𐤉𐤄𐤅𐤄 is with him."

Yoseph Becomes Ruler of Mitsrayim

6 And he appointed him the second in all his kingdom and gave him authority over all Mitsrayim, and caused him to ride in the second chariot of Pharaoh. **7** And he clothed him with byssus garments, and he put a gold chain around his neck, and they proclaimed before him "El El wa 'Abirer," and placed a ring on his hand and made him ruler over all his house, and magnified him, and said to him, "Only on the throne shall I be greater than you."

8 And Yoseph ruled over all the land of Mitsrayim, and all the princes of Pharaoh, and all his servants, and all who did the king's business loved him, for he walked in uprightness, for he was without pride and arrogance, and he had no respect of persons, and did not accept bribes, but he judged all the people of the land in uprightness. **9** And the land of Mitsrayim was at peace before Pharaoh because of Yoseph, for 𐤉𐤄𐤅𐤄 was with him, and gave him favor and kindness for all his generations before all those who knew him and those who heard concerning him, and Pharaoh's kingdom was well ordered, and there was no Satan and no evil *one*.

10 And the king called Yoseph's name 'Sephantiphans,' and gave Yoseph to wife the daughter of Potiphar, the daughter of the priest of Heliopolis, the chief cook. **11** And on the day that Yoseph stood before Pharaoh he was thirty years old [when he stood before Pharaoh][b]. **12** And in that year Yitsḥaq died. And it happened as Yoseph had said in the interpretation of his two dreams, according as he had said it, there were seven years of plenty over all the land of Mitsrayim, and the land of Mitsrayim abundantly produced, one measure *producing* eighteen hundred measures. **13** And Yoseph gathered food into every city until they were full of grain, until they could no longer count and measure it for its multitude.

Yehudah and Tamar

41 **1** And in the forty-fifth yovel, in the second week, in the second year, Yehudah took for his firstborn Er, a wife from the daughters of Aram, named Tamar.[c] **2** But *Er* hated her, and did not lie with her, because his mother was of the daughters of Kana'an, and he wished to take a wife of the relatives of his mother, but Yehudah, his father, would not permit him. **3** And Er, the firstborn of Yehudah, was wicked, and 𐤉𐤄𐤅𐤄 killed him.

4 And Yehudah said to Onan, *Er's* brother, "Go in to your brother's wife and perform the duty of a husband's brother to her, and raise up seed to your brother."

5 And Onan knew that the seed would not be his, *but* his brother's only, and he went into the house of his brother's wife, and spilled the seed

---

[a] **40:4** Bracketed section indicates reading from Latin fragment. Ethiopic texts contain a meaningless phrase.

[b] **40:11** Bracketed section indicates what is most likely a textual corruption. This was most likely repeated through dittography by mistake.

[c] **41:1** This disagrees with Yashar **45**, which states that Tamar was the daughter of Elam. Elam and Aram were brothers according to Bereshiyt [Genesis] **10:22**.

on the ground. And he was wicked in the eyes
of 𐤉𐤄𐤅𐤄, and He killed him *also*.

6 And Yehudah said to Tamar, his daughter-in-
law, "Remain in your father's house as a widow
until Shelah my son is grown up, and I shall
give you to him as wife." 7 And he grew up; but
Bedsu'el[a], the wife of Yehudah, did not permit
her son Shelah to marry. And Bedsu'el, the wife
of Yehudah, died in the fifth year of this week.

8 And in the sixth year Yehudah went up to
shear his sheep at Timnah. And they told
Tamar, "Behold your father-in-law goes up to
Timnah to shear his sheep."

9 And she put off her widow's clothes, and put
on a veil, and beautified herself, and sat in the
gate adjoining the way to Timnah. 10 And as
Yehudah was going along he found her, and
thought her to be a whore, and he said to her,
"Let me come in to you;" and she said to him
"Come in," and he went in. 11 And she said to
him, "Give me my hire;" and he said to her, "I
have nothing in my hand except my ring that is
on my finger, and my cords, and my staff which
is in my hand."

12 And she said to him, "Give them to me until
you send me my hire;" and he said to her, "I will
send to you a kid of the goats;" and he gave
them to her, [and he was with her][b] she
conceived by him. 13 And Yehudah went to his
sheep, and she went to her father's house.
14 And Yehudah sent a kid of the goats by the
hand of his shepherd, an Adullamite, and he did
not fine her. And he asked the people of the
place, saying, "Where is the whore who was
here?" And they said to him, "There is no whore
here with us."

15 And he returned and informed *Yehudah*, and
said to him, "I did not find her, and I asked the
people of the place, and they said to me, 'There
is no whore here.'" And he said, "Let her keep
the items, lest we become a cause of scorn."

16 And when she had completed three months, it
was known that she was with child, and they
told Yehudah, saying, "Behold Tamar, your
daughter-in-law, is with child by whoring."

17 And Yehudah went to the house of her father,
and said to her father and her brothers, "Bring
her forth, and let them burn her, for she has
worked uncleanness in Yisra'el."

18 And it happened when they brought her forth
to burn her that she sent to her father-in-law the
ring and the cords and the staff, saying,
19 "Discern whose are these, for by him am I
with child." And Yehudah acknowledged, and
said, "Tamar is more righteous than I am. And
therefore do not burn her." 20 And for that
reason she was not given to Shelah, and he did
not approach her again. 21 And after that she
bore two sons, Perets and Zeraḥ, in the seventh
year of this second week.

22 And after this the seven years of fruitfulness
were completed, of which Yoseph spoke to
Pharaoh. 23 And Yehudah acknowledged that
the deed which he had done was evil, for he had
lain with his daughter-in-law, and he considered
it hateful in His eyes, and he acknowledged that
he had transgressed and gone astray, for he had
uncovered the skirt of his son. And he began to
lament and to petition before 𐤉𐤄𐤅𐤄 because of
his transgression. 24 And we told him in a
dream that it was forgiven him because he
petitioned earnestly, and lamented, and did not
do it again.

Discussion on Yehudah's Forgiveness in Contrast to Punishment

25 And he received forgiveness because he
turned from his sin and from his ignorance, for
he transgressed greatly before our Elohim. And
anyone that acts thus, anyone who lies with his
mother-in-law, let them burn him with fire that
he may burn in it, for there is uncleanness and
pollution upon them, let them burn them with
fire. 26 And command the children of Yisra'el
that there be no uncleanness among them, for
anyone who lies with his daughter-in-law or
with his mother-in-law has worked uncleanness;
let them burn the man who has lain with her
with fire, and also the woman, and He will turn

[a] **41**:7 Bedsu'el – Recorded in Yovelim **34** as Betasu'el.

[b] **41**:**12** Bracketed section indicates reading present in Syriac fragment but absent from Ethiopic texts.

away wrath and punishment from Yisra'el.
27 And we said to Yehudah that his two sons had not lain with her, and for this reason his seed was stablished for a second generation, and would not be uprooted. 28 For in the integrity of *his* eye he had sought for punishment according to the judgment of Avraham, which he had commanded his sons, so Yehudah sought to burn her with fire.

Years of Famine

42 1 And in the first year of the third week of the forty-fifth yovel the famine began to come into the land, and the rain refused to be given to the earth, for nothing came down. 2 And the earth grew barren. But in the land of Mitsrayim there was food, for Yoseph had gathered the seed of the land in the seven years of plenty and had preserved it. 3 And Mitsrayim came to Yoseph that he might give them food, and he opened the store-houses where was the grain of the first year, and he sold it to the people of the land for gold. 4 [And the famine was very heavy in the land of Kana'an.][a] And Ya'aqov heard that there was food in Mitsrayim, and he sent his ten sons that they should purchase food for him in Mitsrayim; but he did not send Benyamin. [And the ten sons of Ya'aqov][a] arrived [in Mitsrayim][a] among those that went *there*.

5 And Yoseph recognized them, but they did not recognize him, and he spoke to them and questioned them, and he said to them, "Are you not spies, and have you not come to examine the paths of the land?" And he put them in prison.
6 And after that he set them free again, and only imprisoned Shimon and sent off his nine brothers. 7 And he filled their sacks with grain, and he put their gold in their sacks, and they did not know. 8 And he commanded them to bring their younger brother, for they had told him their father was living and their younger brother.

Ya'aqov's Sons Describe their Encounter with the Ruler of Mitsrayim

9 And they went up from the land of Mitsrayim and they came to the land of Kana'an. And they told their father all that happened to them, and how the overseer of the land had spoken roughly to them, and had seized Shimon until they would bring Benyamin.

10 And Ya'aqov said, "You have bereaved me of my children! Yoseph is no more, and Shimon also is no more, and you would take Benyamin away! Your wickedness has come on me."
11 And he said, "My son will not go down with you lest perhaps he fall sick; for their mother gave birth to two sons, and one has perished, and you would also take this one from me. If perhaps he took a fever on the road, you would bring down my old age with sorrow to death."

12 For he saw that their money had been returned to every man in his sack, and for this reason he feared to send him.

Ya'aqov's Sons Forced to Return to Mitsrayim

13 And the famine increased and became heavy in the land of Kana'an, and in all lands except in the land of Mitsrayim, for many of the children of the Mitsrites had stored up their seed for food from the time when they saw Yoseph gathering seed together and putting it in storehouses and preserving it for the years of famine. 14 And the people of Mitsrayim fed themselves on it during the first year of their famine. 15 But when Yisra'el saw that the famine was very heavy in the land, and that there was no deliverance, he said to his sons, "Go again, and purchase food for us so that we will not die."

16 And they said, "We will not go unless our youngest brother goes with us; we will not go."

17 And Yisra'el saw that if he did not send him with them, they would all perish by reason of the famine. 18 And Reuven said, "Give him into my hand, and if I do not bring him back to you, kill my two sons instead of his being." And he said to him, "He shall not go with you."

---

[a] **42:4** Bracketed sections indicate readings present in Latin fragment but absent from Ethiopic texts.

19 And Yehudah came near and said, "Send him
with me, and if I do not bring him back to you,
let me bear the blame before you all the days of
my life."

20 And he sent him with them in the second year
of this week on the first day of the month, and
they came to the land of Mitsrayim with all
those who went, and *they had* presents in their
hands: stacte and almonds and terebinth nuts
and pure honey.

21 And they went and stood before Yoseph, and
he saw Benyamin his brother, and he knew him,
and said to them, "Is this your youngest
brother?" And they said to him, "It is he." And
he said "𐤉𐤄𐤅𐤄 be favorable to you, my son!"

22 And he sent him into his house and he
brought forth Shimon to them and he made a
banquet for them, and they presented to him the
gift which they had brought in their hands.
23 And they ate before him and he gave them all
a portion, but the portion of Benyamin was
seven times larger than that of any of theirs.
24 And they ate and drank and arose and
remained with their donkeys. 25 And Yoseph
devised a plan by which he might learn their
thoughts as to whether thoughts of peace
prevailed among them. 26 And he said to the
steward who was over his house, "Fill all their
sacks with food, and return their money to them
into their vessels, and my cup, the silver cup out
of which I drink, put it in the sack of the
youngest, and send them away."

Yoseph Tests His Brothers

43 1 And he did as Yoseph had told him, and
filled all their sacks for them with food and put
their money in their sacks, and put the cup in
Benyamin's sack. 2 And early in the morning
they departed, and it happened that, when they
had gone from there, Yoseph said to the steward
of his house, "Pursue them and run and seize
them, saying, 'For good you have repaid me
with evil; you have stolen from me the silver
cup out of which my master drinks.' And bring
their youngest brother back to me, and fetch *him*
quickly before I go forth to my seat of
judgment."

3 And he ran after them and said to them
according to these words. 4 And they said to
him, "Elohim forbid that your servants should
do this thing, and steal from the house of your
master any utensil, and the money also which
we found in our sacks the first time, we your
servants brought back from the land of Kana'an.
How then should we steal any utensil? 5 Behold
here are we; search our sacks, and wherever you
find the cup in the sack of any man among us,
let him be killed, and we and our donkeys will
serve your master."

6 And he said to them, "Not so, the man with
whom I find, him only shall I take as a servant,
and you shall return in peace to your house."
7 And as he was searching in their vessels,
beginning with the eldest and ending with the
youngest, it was found in Benyamin's sack.
8 And they tore their garments, and saddled
their donkeys, and returned to the city and came
to the house of Yoseph, and they all bowed
themselves on their faces to the ground before
him.

9 And Yoseph said to them, "You have done
evil." And they said, "What shall we say, and
how shall we defend ourselves? Our master has
discovered the transgression of his servants;
behold we are the servants of our master, and
our donkeys also."

10 And Yoseph said to them, "I too fear 𐤉𐤄𐤅𐤄;
as for you, go to your homes and let your
brother be my servant, for you have done evil.
Do you not know that a man delights in his cup,
as I with this cup? And yet you have stolen it
from me."

11 And Yehudah said, "O my master, let your
servant, please speak a word in my master's ear.
Your servant's mother bore two sons to our
father: one went away and was lost, and has not
been found, and *this one* alone is left of his
mother, and your servant our father loves him,
and his life also is bound up with the life of this
boy. 12 And it will happen, when we go to your
servant our father, and the boy is not with us,
that he will die, and we shall bring down our
father with sorrow to death. 13 Now rather let
me, your servant, stay instead of the boy as a
bondsman to my master, and let the boy go with

his brothers, for I became collateral for him at
the hand of your servant our father, and if I do
not bring him back, your servant will bear the
blame to our father forever."

Yoseph Reveals Himself to His Brothers

14 And Yoseph saw that their hearts were all in
accord in goodness one with another, and he
could not refrain himself, and he told them that
he was Yoseph. 15 And he conversed with them
in the Hebrew tongue and fell on their neck and
wept. But they knew him not and they began to
weep.

16 And he said to them, "Do not weep over me,
but hurry and bring my father to me; and you,
see that it is my mouth that speaks and the eyes
of my brother Benyamin see. 17 For behold this
is the second year of the famine, and there are
still five years without harvest or fruit of trees
or ploughing. 18 Come down quickly, you and
your households, so that you do not perish
through the famine, and do not be grieved for
your possessions, for 𐤉𐤄𐤅𐤄 sent me before you
to set things in order that many people might
live. 19 And tell my father that I am still alive,
and you, behold, you see that 𐤉𐤄𐤅𐤄 has made
me as a father to Pharaoh, and ruler over his
house and over all the land of Mitsrayim.
20 And tell my father of all my glory, and all the
riches and glory that 𐤉𐤄𐤅𐤄 has given me."

Return to Kana'an to Fetch Ya'aqov

21 And by the command of the mouth of
Pharaoh he gave them chariots and provisions
for the way, and he gave them all vari-colored
garments and silver. 22 And to their father he
sent garments and silver and ten donkeys which
carried grain, and he sent them away. 23 And
they went up and told their father that Yoseph
was alive, and was measuring out grain to all
the nations of the earth, and that he was ruler
over all the land of Mitsrayim. 24 And their
father did not believe it, for he was beside
himself in his mind; but when he saw the
wagons which Yoseph had sent, the life of his
spirit revived, and he said, "It is enough for me
if Yoseph lives; I will go down and see him
before I die."

Ya'aqov Observes First Fruits at Beersheva

44 1 And Yisra'el took his journey from Ḥaran[a]
from his house on the first of the third month,
and he went on the way of the Well of the Oath,
and he offered a slaughtering to the Elohim of
his father Yitsḥaq on the seventh of this month.
2 And Ya'aqov remembered the dream that he
had seen at Beth-El, and he feared to go down
into Mitsrayim. 3 And while he was thinking of
sending word to Yoseph to come to him, and
that he would not go down, he remained there
seven days, so that perhaps he may see a vision
as to whether he should remain or go down.

3 And he celebrated the Feast of the harvest of
the first-fruits with old wheat, for in all the land
of Kana'an there was not a handful of seed in
the land, for the famine was over all the beasts
and cattle and birds, and also over man.

𐤉𐤄𐤅𐤄 Appears to Ya'aqov

5 And on the sixteenth *day* 𐤉𐤄𐤅𐤄 appeared to
him, and said to him, "Ya'aqov, Ya'aqov;" and
he said, "Here am I." And He said to him, "I am
the Elohim of your fathers, the Elohim of
Avraham and Yitsḥaq; do not be afraid to go
down into Mitsrayim, for there I will make of a
great nation of you. 6 I will go down with you,
and I will bring you up *again*. In this land you
will be buried, and Yoseph will put his hands
upon your eyes. Do not fear; go down into
Mitsrayim."

7 And his sons rose up, and his sons' sons, and
they placed their father and their possessions
upon chariots. 8 And Yisra'el rose up from the
Well of the Oath on the sixteenth *day* of this
third month, and he went to the land of
Mitsrayim. 9 And Yisra'el sent Yehudah before
him to his son Yoseph to examine the Land of
Goshen, for Yoseph had told his brothers that
they should come and dwell there that they
might be near him. 10 And this was the best *land*

[a] **44:1** Bereshiyt [Genesis] **37:14** states that it was Ḥevron, not Ḥaran that Ya'aqov journeyed from. This could be a simple copyist error.

in all the land of Mitsrayim, and near to him, for all *of them* and also for the cattle.

Descendants of Ya'aqov

11 And these are the names of the sons of Ya'aqov who went into Mitsrayim with Ya'aqov their father: **12** Reuven, the Firstborn of Yisra'el. And these are the names of his sons Ḥanokh, and Pallu, and Ḥezron and Kharmi: five.
13 Shimon and his sons. And these are the names of his sons: Yemuel, and Yamin, and Ohad, and Yakhin, and Tsoḥar, and Sha'ul, the son of the Tsephathite[a] woman: seven. **14** Levi and his sons. And these are the names of his sons: Gershon, and Qehath, and Merari: four.
15 Yehudah and his sons. And these are the names of his sons: Shelah, and Perets, and Zeraḥ-four. **16** Yissakhar and his sons. And these are the names of his sons: Tola, and Puah, and Yashuv, and Shimron: five. **17** Zevulun and his sons. And these are the names of his sons: Sered, and Elon, and Yaḥleel: four. **18** And these are the sons of Ya'aqov and their sons whom Leah bore to Ya'aqov in Aram-Naharayim: six, and their one sister, Dinah and all the beings of the sons of Leah, and their sons, who went with Ya'aqov their father into Mitsrayim, were twenty-nine, and Ya'aqov their father being with them, they were thirty.

19 And the sons of Zilpah, Leah's handmaid, the wife of Ya'aqov, who bore to Ya'aqov Gad and Asher. **20** And these are the names of their sons who went with him into Mitsrayim. The sons of Gad: Tsiphion, and Ḥaggi, and Shuni, and Etsbon, [and Eri,][b] and Areli, and Arodi: eight.
21 And the sons of Asher: Yimnah, and Yishvah, [and Yishvi], and Beriah, and Seraḥ their one sister: six. **22** All these beings were fourteen, and all those of Leah were forty-four.

23 And the sons of Raḥel, the wife of Ya'aqov: Yoseph and Benyamin. **24** And there were born to Yoseph in Mitsrayim before his father came into Mitsrayim, those whom Asenath, daughter of Potiphar priest of Heliopolis bore to him: Menasheh, and Ephrayim: three. **25** And the sons of Benyamin: Bela and Bekher and Ashbel, Gera, and Na'aman, and Eḥi, and Rosh, and Muppim, and Ḥuppim, and Ard: eleven.
26 And all the beings of Raḥel were fourteen.

27 And the sons of Bilhah, the handmaid of Raḥel, the wife of Ya'aqov, whom she bore to Ya'aqov, were Dan and Naphtali. And these are the names of their sons who went with them into Mitsrayim. **28** And the sons of Dan were Ḥushim, and Samon, and Asudi and 'Iyaka, and Sh'lomoh: six. **29** And they died the year in which they entered into Mitsrayim, and there was left to Dan only Ḥushim alone. **30** And these are the names of the sons of Naphtali Yaḥtseel, and Guni and Yetser, and Shallum, and 'Iv. **31** And 'Iv, who was born after the years of famine, died in Mitsrayim. **32** And all the beings of Raḥel were twenty-six. **33** And all the beings of Ya'aqov which went into Mitsrayim were seventy beings. **34** These are his children and his children's children, in all seventy, but five died in Mitsrayim before Yoseph, and had no children. **35** And in the land of Kana'an two sons of Yehudah died, Er and Onan, and they had no children, and the children of Yisra'el buried those who perished, and they were reckoned among the seventy nations.[c]

Yisra'el Settles in Goshen

45 1 And Yisra'el went into the country of Mitsrayim, into the land of Goshen, on the first of the fourth month, in the second year of the third week of the forty-fifth yovel. **2** And

[a] **44:13** Tsephathite – a person from the Kana'anite city of Tsephath. See Shoftim [Judges] **1:17**.
[b] **44:20** Bracketed section indicates reading not present in Ethiopic texts. These names were restored based on Bereshiyt [Genesis] **46**. Given the number of descendants listed here being eight (**8**) there must be one missing. The problem is solved by restoring Eri according to Bereshiyt [Genesis] **46**. The same applies to Yishvi in verse **21**.
[c] **44** Given that there is a discrepancy between the Masoretic Hebrew Text, and the Greek Septuagint and the Dead Sea Scrolls, this may be the author's attempt to explain a variant that existed even in his own day. The Masoretic Hebrew text reads (at Shemoth [Exodus] **1:5**) "All the persons who came from the loins of Ya'aqov were seventy beings." The Greek Septuagint and Hebrew Dead Sea Scrolls read, "All the persons who came from the loins of Ya'aqov were seventy-five beings." It is possible that this explains the variation: seventy-five were born, only seventy entered Mitsrayim.

Yoseph went to meet his father Ya'aqov, to the
land of Goshen, and he fell on his father's neck
and wept.

3 And Yisra'el said to Yoseph, "Now let me die
since I have seen you, and now may 𐤉𐤄𐤅𐤄
Elohim of Yisra'el be blessed, the Elohim of
Avraham and the Elohim of Yitsḥaq who has
not withheld His favor and His kindness from
His servant Ya'aqov. 4 It is enough for me that I
have seen your face while I am still alive; yes,
the vision which I saw at Beth-El is true.
Blessed be 𐤉𐤄𐤅𐤄 my Elohim forever and ever,
and blessed be His Name."

5 And Yoseph and his brothers ate bread before
their father and drank wine, and Ya'aqov
rejoiced with exceedingly great joy because he
saw Yoseph eating with his brothers and
drinking before him, and he blessed the Creator
of all things who had preserved him, and had
preserved for him his twelve sons. 6 And
Yoseph had given to his father and to his
brothers as a gift the right of dwelling in the
land of Goshen and in Rameses and all the
region round about, which he ruled over before
Pharaoh. And Yisra'el and his sons dwelled in
the land of Goshen, the best part of the land of
Mitsrayim, and Yisra'el was one hundred and
thirty years old when he came into Mitsrayim.
7 And Yoseph nourished his father and his
brothers and also their possessions with bread as
much as sufficed them for the seven years of the
famine. 8 And the land of Mitsrayim suffered
because of the famine, and Yoseph acquired all
the land of Mitsrayim for Pharaoh in return for
food, and he gained possession of the people
and their cattle and everything for Pharaoh.
9 And the years of the famine were finished, and
Yoseph gave to the people in the land seed and
food that they might sow *the land* in the eighth
year, for the river had overflowed all the land of
Mitsrayim.[a] 10 For in the seven years of the
famine it had *not* overflowed and had watered
only a few places on the banks of the river; but
now it overflowed and the Mitsrites sowed the
land, and it bore much grain that year.

Death and Burial of Ya'aqov

11 And this was the first year of the fourth week
of the forty-fifth yovel. 12 And Yoseph took the
fifth part of [the grain of the harvest][b] for the
king, and left four parts for *the people* for food
and for seed, and Yoseph made it a statute for
the land of Mitsrayim until this day. 13 And
Yisra'el lived in the land of Mitsrayim
seventeen years, and all the days which he lived
were three yovelim, one hundred and forty-
seven years, and he died in the fourth year of
the fifth week of the forty-fifth yovel.

14 And Yisra'el blessed his sons before he died
and told them everything that would happen to
them in the land of Mitsrayim; and he made
known to them what would come upon them in
the last days, and blessed them and gave to
Yoseph two portions in the land. 15 And he slept
with his fathers, and he was buried in the cave
of Makhpelah in the land of Kana'an, near
Avraham his father, in the grave which he dug
for himself in the cave of Makhpelah in the land
of Ḥevron. 16 And he gave all his books and the
books of his fathers to Levi his son that he
might preserve them and renew them for his
children until this day.

Death of Yoseph's Generation

46 1 And it happened that after Ya'aqov died
the children of Yisra'el multiplied in the land of
Mitsrayim, and they became a great nation, and
they were of one accord in heart, so that brother
loved brother and every man helped his brother,
and they increased abundantly and multiplied
exceedingly, ten weeks of years, all the days of
the life of Yoseph. 2 And there was no Satan[c]

[a] **45:9** In Ancient Mitsrayim the Nile River overflowed each year. This constituted one of the three seasons. These seasons were Inundation, Growth, and Harvest. The overflow of the Nile was the Inundation season. This was the primary irrigation source for watering crops in the land. With the construction of the High Dam at Aswan in **1970**, the annual Inundation season came to an end.

[b] **45:12** Latin fragment reads, "everything that bore fruit" here instead of "the grain of the harvest."

[c] **46:2** Satan – Ethiopic word ሲይጣን (*siy'tan*) is no doubt a transliteration of the Hebrew 𐤍𐤈𐤔 (*sa'than*). *Satan* in Hebrew means "adversary" and does not refer exclusively to 'The Devil.' Thus here it could simply read, "And there was no adversary nor any evil all the days of the life of Yoseph…"

nor any evil all the days of the life of Yoseph which he lived after his father Ya'aqov, for all the Mitsrites honored the children of Yisra'el all the days of the life of Yoseph. 3 And Yoseph, died being a hundred and ten years old; he lived in the land of Kana'an seventeen years, and he was a servant ten years, and in prison three years, and eighty years he was under the king, ruling all the land of Mitsrayim. 4 And he died; and all his brothers *also,* and all that generation. 5 And he commanded the children of Yisra'el before he died that they should carry his bones with them when they went forth from the land of Mitsrayim. 6 And he made them swear regarding his bones, for he knew that the Mitsrites would not bring him forth again and bury him in the land of Kana'an, for Makamaron, king of Kana'an, while dwelling in the land of Ashuwr, fought in the valley with the king of Mitsrayim and killed him there, and pursued after the Mitsrites to the gates of 'Ermon. 7 But he was not able to enter, for a different, new king had become king of Mitsrayim, and he was stronger than he, and he returned to the land of Kana'an, and the gates of Mitsrayim were closed, and none went out and none came in to Mitsrayim. 8 And Yoseph died in the forty-sixth yovel, in the sixth week, in the second year, and they buried him in the land of Mitsrayim, and all his brothers died after him.

War Between Kana'an and Mitsrayim

9 And the king of Mitsrayim went forth to war with the king of Kana'an in the forty-seventh yovel, in the second week in the second year, and the children of Yisra'el brought forth all the bones of the children of Ya'aqov except the bones of Yoseph, and they buried them in the field in the cave of Makhpelah in the mountain. 10 And the most *of them* returned to Mitsrayim, but a few of them remained in the mountains of Ḥevron, and Amram your father remained with them.

Affliction and Slavery of Yisra'el

11 And the king of Kana'an was victorious over the king of Mitsrayim, and he closed the gates of Mitsrayim. 12 And he devised an evil plan against the children of Yisra'el of afflicting them and he said to the people of Mitsrayim, "Behold the people of the children of Yisra'el have increased and multiplied more than we. 13 Come and let us deal wisely with them before they become too many, and let us afflict them with slavery before war comes upon us, and before they fight against us; else they will join themselves to our enemies and get them up out of our land, for their hearts and faces are towards the land of Kana'an."

14 And he set taskmasters over them to afflict them with slavery; and they built strong cities for Pharaoh: Pithom, and Ramses, [and On][a]; and they built all the walls and all the fortifications which had fallen in the cities of Mitsrayim. 15 And they made them serve rigorously, and the more they dealt evilly with them, the more they increased and multiplied. 16 And the people of Mitsrayim regarded the children of Yisra'el as abominable.

Birth of Mosheh

47 1 And in the seventh week, in the seventh year, in the forty-seventh yovel, your father went forth from the land of Kana'an, and you were born in the fourth week, in the sixth year, in the forty-eighth yovel; this was the time of affliction on the children of Yisra'el. 2 And Pharaoh, king of Mitsrayim, issued a command regarding them, that they should cast all their male children which were born into the river. 3 And they cast them in for seven months until the day that you were born. 4 And your mother hid you for three months, and they told about her. And she made an ark for you, and covered it with pitch and tar, and placed it in the reeds on the bank of the river, and she placed you in it seven days, and your mother came by night and nursed you, and by day Miryam, your sister, guarded you from the birds.

5 And in those days Tharmuth, the daughter of Pharaoh, came to bathe in the river, and she heard your voice crying, and she told her maidens to bring you forth, and they brought

---

[a] **46:14** Bracketed section indicates reading present in Latin fragment but absent from Ethiopic texts.

you to her. 6 And she took you out of the ark, and she had compassion on you. 7 And your sister said to her, "Shall I go and call one of the Hebrew women to nurse and nurture this child for you?" And she said *to her,* "Go." 8 And she went and called your mother, Yokheved, and she gave her wages, and she nursed you. 9 And afterwards, when you grew up, they brought you to the daughter[a] of Pharaoh, and you became her son, and Amram your father taught you writing, and after you completed three weeks they brought you into the royal court.

Mosheh Kills a Mitsrite

10 And you were three weeks of years at court until the time when you went forth from the royal court and saw a Mitsrite striking your friend who was of the children of Yisra'el, and you killed him and hid him in the sand. 11 And on the second day you saw two of the children of Yisra'el fighting with one another, and you said to him who was doing the wrong, "Why do you strike your brother?"

12 And he was angry and indignant, and said, "Who made you a prince and a judge over us? Do you think to kill me as you killed the Mitsrite yesterday?" And you feared and fled on account of these words.

Mosheh's Flight to Midian; Encounter with Mastema

48 1 And in the sixth year of the third week of the forty-ninth yovel you departed and dwelled [in the land of Midian][b], five weeks and one year. And you returned to Mitsrayim in the second week in the second year in the fiftieth yovel. 2 And you yourself know what He spoke to you on Mount Sinai, and what prince Mastema desired to do with you when you were returning into Mitsrayim. 3 Did he not, with all his power, seek to kill you and deliver the Mitsrites out of your hand when he saw that you were sent to execute judgment and vengeance on the Mitsrites? 4 And I delivered you out of his hand, and you performed the signs and wonders which you were sent to perform in Mitsrayim against Pharaoh, and against all his house, and against his servants and his people.

Plagues on Mitsrayim

5 And 𐤉𐤄𐤅𐤄 executed a great vengeance on them for the sake of Yisra'el's, and struck them through *the plagues of* blood and frogs, lice and flies, and evil boils that broke forth in blisters; and their cattle by death; and by hailstones, by which He destroyed everything that grew for them; and by locusts which devoured the remnant which had been left by the hail, and by darkness; and *by the death* of the firstborn of men and animals, and 𐤉𐤄𐤅𐤄 took vengeance on all their elohim and burned them[c] with fire.

6 And everything was sent through you hand, that you should declare *these things* before they were done, and you spoke with the king of Mitsrayim before all his servants and before his people. 7 And everything took place according to your words; ten great and terrible judgments came on the land of Mitsrayim that you might execute vengeance on it for Yisra'el. 8 And 𐤉𐤄𐤅𐤄 did everything for Yisra'el's sake, and according to His covenant, which he had established with Avraham, that He would take vengeance on them as they had brought them by force into bondage.

Exodus from Mitsrayim; Mastema's Deeds

9 And the prince Mastema stood up against you, and sought to cast you into the hands of Pharaoh, and he helped the Mitsrite sorcerers, and they stood up and worked evils before you. 10 And indeed we permitted them to work, but the remedies we did not allow to be worked by their hands. 11 And 𐤉𐤄𐤅𐤄 struck them with evil ulcers, and they were not able to stand, for we destroyed them so that they could not perform a single sign. 12 And despite all *these* signs and

---

[a] **47:9** Both the Ethiopic texts and the Latin fragment actually read, "house" instead of "daughter." This was most likely caused by misreading the Hebrew 𐤁𐤕 (*baht*) meaning "daughter" for the Hebrew 𐤁𐤉𐤕 (*beit*) meaning "house."

[b] **48:1** Bracketed section indicates reading present in Latin fragment. Ethiopic texts read, "there."

[c] **48:5** Them – most likely referring to the idols of the elohim of the Mitsrites.

wonders the prince Mastema was [not][a] put to shame because he took courage and cried to the Mitsrites to pursue after you with all the powers of the Mitsrites, with their chariots, and with their horses, and with all the hosts of the peoples of Mitsrayim. **13** And I stood between the Mitsrites and Yisra'el, and we delivered Yisra'el out of his hand, and out of the hand of his people, and 𐤉𐤄𐤅𐤄 brought them through the midst of the sea as if it were dry land. **14** And all the peoples whom he brought to pursue after Yisra'el, 𐤉𐤄𐤅𐤄 our Elohim cast them into the midst of the sea, into the depths of the abyss beneath the children of Yisra'el, even as the people of Mitsrayim had cast their children into the river. He took vengeance on one million *of them.* And one thousand strong and valiant men were destroyed on account of one nursling of the children of your people which they had thrown into the river.

15 And on the fourteenth day and on the fifteenth and on the sixteenth and on the seventeenth and on the eighteenth the prince Mastema was bound and imprisoned behind the children of Yisra'el that he might not accuse them. **16** And on the nineteenth we let them loose that they might help the Mitsrites and pursue the children of Yisra'el. **17** And he hardened their hearts and made them stubborn, and the plot was planned by 𐤉𐤄𐤅𐤄 our Elohim that He might strike the Mitsrites and cast them into the sea.

18 And on the fourteenth[b] we bound him that he might not accuse the children of Yisra'el on the day when they asked the Mitsrites for vessels and garments, vessels of silver, and vessels of gold, and vessels of copper, in order to spoil the Mitsrites in return for the bondage in which they had forced them to serve. **19** And we did not lead the children of Yisra'el forth from Mitsrayim empty handed.

The Pesaḥ

49 **1** Remember the command which 𐤉𐤄𐤅𐤄 commanded you concerning the Pesaḥ, that you should celebrate it at its appointed time, on the fourteenth *day* of the first month; that you should slaughter it before it is evening, so that they may eat it by night on the evening of the fifteenth from the time of the setting of the sun. **2** For on this night – the beginning of the Feast and the beginning of the joy – you were eating the Pesaḥ in Mitsrayim, when all the powers of Mastema had been let loose to kill all the firstborn in the land of Mitsrayim, from the firstborn of Pharaoh to the firstborn of the captive maid-servant in the mill, and to the cattle. **3** And this is the sign which 𐤉𐤄𐤅𐤄 gave them: Every house of which they saw the blood of a lamb of the first year on the lintels, they should not enter that house to kill, but should pass over *it*, that all those should be saved that were in the house because the sign of the blood was on its lintels.

4 And the powers of 𐤉𐤄𐤅𐤄 did everything as 𐤉𐤄𐤅𐤄 commanded them, and they passed by all the children of Yisra'el, and the plague did not come upon them to destroy from among them any being either of cattle, or man, or dog. **5** And the plague was very heavy in Mitsrayim, and there was no house in Mitsrayim where there was not one dead, and weeping and lamentation. **6** And all Yisra'el was eating the flesh of the Pesaḥ lamb, and drinking the wine, and was praising, and blessing, and giving thanks to 𐤉𐤄𐤅𐤄 the Elohim of their fathers, and was ready to go forth from under the yoke of Mitsrayim, and from the evil bondage.

7 And remember this day all the days of your life, and guard it from year to year all the days of your life, once a year, on its day, according to all its Torah, and do not suspend *it* from day to day, or from month to month. **8** For it is an eternal statute, and engraved on the heavenly tablets regarding all the children of Yisra'el that

---

[a] **48:12** Bracketed "not" here indicates an emendation proposed by Charles. The word is present in all known Ethiopic texts, though Charles stated that it "conflicts with the sense" of the verse.

[b] **48:18** Fourteenth – Different Ethiopic texts disagree here. Of the four major texts, B (which Charles preferred) reads, "fourteenth." Manuscripts A and D read, "seventeenth" while manuscript C reads, "fifteenth."

they should guard it every year on its day once a
year, throughout all their generations; and there
is no limit of days, for this is established
forever. **9** And the man who is free from
uncleanness, and does not come to guard it on
its day, so as to bring an acceptable offering
before 𐤉𐤄𐤅𐤄, and to eat and to drink before
𐤉𐤄𐤅𐤄 on the day of its Feast, that man who is
clean and close nearby shall be uprooted;
because he did not bring the gift of 𐤉𐤄𐤅𐤄 in its
appointed time, he shall take his guilt upon
himself.

10 Let the children of Yisra'el come and guard
the Pesaḥ on the day of its appointed time: on
the fourteenth day of the first month, between
the evenings, from the third part of the day to
the third part of the night, for two portions of
the day are given to the light, and a third part to
the evening. **11** This is that which 𐤉𐤄𐤅𐤄
commanded you that you should guard it
between the evenings.

12 And it is not fitting to slaughter it during any
period of the light, but during the period
bordering on the evening, and let them eat it at
the time of the evening, until the third part of
the night, and whatever is left over of all its
flesh from the third part of the night and
onwards, let them burn it with fire. **13** And it is
not fitting that they boil it with water, nor shall
they eat it raw, but roasted on the fire. And they
shall eat it, its head with its inward parts and its
feet they shall roast with fire, and not break any
of its bones, for no bone of the children of
Yisra'el shall be crushed.

14 For this reason 𐤉𐤄𐤅𐤄 commanded the
children of Yisra'el to guard the Pesaḥ on the
day of its appointed time, and they shall not
break a bone of it; for it is a Feast day, and a
day commanded, and there may be no passing
over from *one* day to *another* day, and one
month to *another* month, but on the day of its
Feast let it be kept. **15** And command the
children of Yisra'el to guard the Pesaḥ
throughout their days, every year, once a year
on the day of its appointed time, and it shall
come for a memorial well pleasing before 𐤉𐤄𐤅𐤄,
and no plague shall come upon them to kill or to
strike in that year in which they celebrate the
Pesaḥ at its appointed time in every respect
according to His command. **16** And they shall
not eat it outside the set-apart place of 𐤉𐤄𐤅𐤄,
but before the set-apart place of 𐤉𐤄𐤅𐤄, and all
the people of the congregation of Yisra'el shall
celebrate it at its appointed time.

17 And every man who has come upon its day
shall eat it in the set-apart place of your Elohim
before 𐤉𐤄𐤅𐤄 from twenty years old and upward;
for thus is it written and ordained that they
should eat it in the set-apart place of 𐤉𐤄𐤅𐤄.
18 And when the children of Yisra'el come into
the land which they are to possess, into the land
of Kana'an, and set up the Tabernacle of 𐤉𐤄𐤅𐤄
in the midst of the land in one of their tribes
until the Temple of 𐤉𐤄𐤅𐤄 has been built in the
land, let them come and keep the Pesaḥ in the
midst of the Tabernacle of 𐤉𐤄𐤅𐤄, [and let them
slaughter it before 𐤉𐤄𐤅𐤄 from year to year.][a]

19 And in the days when the House has been
built in the Name of 𐤉𐤄𐤅𐤄 in the land of their
inheritance, they shall go there and slaughter the
Pesaḥ in the evening, at sunset, at the third part
of the day.

20 And they shall offer its blood on the
threshold of the altar, and shall place its fat on
the fire which is upon the altar, and they shall
eat its flesh roasted with fire in the court of the
house which has been set apart in the Name of
𐤉𐤄𐤅𐤄.[b]

21 And they may not keep the Pesaḥ in their
cities, nor in any place except before the
Tabernacle of 𐤉𐤄𐤅𐤄, or before His House where

---

[a] **49:18** Bracketed section indicates reading present in Ethiopic texts but absent from Latin fragment.

[b] **49:20** This seems to be a reiteration Devarim [Deuteronomy] **16**. However, Devarim [Deuteronomy] **16** does not state that the lamb is to be roasted. Rather, after they went into the land of Kana'an, the lamb was to then be "boiled" or "seethed" in contrast to the roasted lamb in Mitsrayim. This is seen in **16:7** which uses the Hebrew word 𐤁𐤔𐤋 (*ba'shal*) which means "to boil" or "to seethe." This was also how it was cooked in Divrei Ha'Yamim 𐤁 [**2** Chronicles] **35:13** during the time of Yoshiyahu [Josiah].

His Name dwells; and they shall not go astray
from 𐤉𐤄𐤅𐤄. 22 And you, Mosheh, command the
children of Yisra'el to guard the judgments of
the Pesaḥ, as it was commanded to you. Declare
to them every year and the day of its days, and
the Feast of unleavened bread, that they should
eat unleavened bread seven days, *and* that they
should guard its Feast, and that they bring a gift
every day during those seven days of joy before
𐤉𐤄𐤅𐤄 on the altar of your Elohim. 23 For you
kept this Feast with haste when you went forth
from Mitsrayim until you entered into the
wilderness of Shur; for on the shore of the sea
you completed it.

Various Sabbath Laws

50 1 And after this Torah, I made known to you
the days of the Sabbaths in the wilderness of
Sin, which is between Elim and Sinai. 2 And I
told you of the Sabbaths of the land on Mount
Sinai, and I told you of the yovel years in the
Sabbaths of years: but its year have I not told
you until you enter the land which you are to
possess.

3 And the land also shall keep its Sabbaths
while they dwell on it, and they shall know the
yovel year. 4 Therefore I have ordained for you
the year-weeks and the years and the yovelim:
there are forty-nine yovelim from the days of
Adam until this day, and one week and two
years: and there are yet forty years distant for
learning the commands of 𐤉𐤄𐤅𐤄, until they pass
over into the land of Kana'an, crossing the
Yarden to the west. 5 And the yovelim shall
pass by, until Yisra'el is cleansed from all guilt
of whoring, and uncleanness, and pollution, and
sin, and error, and dwells with confidence in all
the land, and there shall be no more a Satan or
any evil one, and the land shall be clean from
that time onward.

6 And behold the command regarding the
Sabbaths – I have written *them* down for you –
and all the judgments of its Torot. 7 Six days
you shall labor, but on the seventh day is the
Sabbath of 𐤉𐤄𐤅𐤄 your Elohim. In it you shall
not do any manner of work, you and your sons,
and your manservants and your maidservants,
and all your cattle and the sojourner also who is
with you. 8 And the man that does any work on
it shall die; whoever profanes that day, whoever
lies with *his* wife, or whoever says he will do
something on it, that he will set out on a journey
on it in regard to any buying or selling, and
whoever draws water on it which he had not
prepared for himself on the sixth day, and
whoever takes up any burden to carry it out of
his tent or out of his house shall die.

9 You shall do no work whatsoever on the
Sabbath day except what you have prepared for
yourselves on the sixth day, so as to eat, and
drink, and rest, and keep Sabbath from all work
on that day, and to bless 𐤉𐤄𐤅𐤄 your Elohim,
who has given you a day of Feast and a set-apart
day, and a day of the set-apart kingdom for all
Yisra'el is this day among their days forever.
10 For great is the honor which 𐤉𐤄𐤅𐤄 gave to
Yisra'el that they should eat and drink and be
satisfied on this Feast day, and rest on it from
all labor which belongs to the labor of the
children of men, except burning frankincense
and bringing gifts and slaughterings before
𐤉𐤄𐤅𐤄 for days and for Sabbaths. 11 This work
alone shall be done on the Sabbath-days in the
set-apart place of 𐤉𐤄𐤅𐤄 your Elohim; that they
may atone for Yisra'el with slaughtering
continually from day to day for a memorial[a]
well-pleasing before 𐤉𐤄𐤅𐤄, and that He may
receive them always from day to day, as you
have been commanded.

12 And every man who does any work on it, or
goes a journey, or tills *his* farm, whether in his
house or any other place, and whoever kindles a
fire, or rides on any beast, or travels by ship on
the sea, and whoever strikes or kills anything, or
slaughters a beast or a bird, or whoever catches
an animal or a bird or a fish, or whoever fasts or
makes war on the Sabbaths;[b] 13 that man who
does any of these things on the Sabbath shall
die, so that the children of Yisra'el shall guard
the Sabbaths according to the commands
regarding the Sabbaths of the land, as it is

---

[a] **50**:**11** Compare Ivrim [Hebrews] **10**:**3**.

[b] **50**:**12** Compare Maqabiym 𐤀 [1 Maccabees] **2**:**31-38**.

written in the tablets, which He gave into my hands that I should write out for you the Torah of the appointed times, and the appointed times according to the division of their days.

The account of the division of the days is completed here.

R. H. Charles' Preface: Testaments of the Twelve Patriarchs

[Editor's note: The following is the preface from R. H. Charles' 1908 edition of *The Testaments of the Twelve Patriarchs*. My preface follows after.]

The many laborious years of study of the Testaments of the Twelve Patriarchs see at last their close in the present volume. The labour involved has been very great, at times indeed oppressive, but it has not been without its own compensations ; for the toil has been frequently lightened by the joys of discovery, and the task of research has been often one of sheer delight. The pleasures of fox-hunting are not to be compared with those of the student in full quest of some truth, some new fact showing itself for the first time within his intellectual horizon. But to return. Many of the problems arising from our text had hitherto been wholly unattempted, or else had been wrongly solved in the past — in large part owing in earlier years to the lack of documentary authorities, and in later years to the large demand on the scholar's time that the mastery of these would have entailed. Short but valuable contributions and suggestions have recently been made by Schnapp, Conybeare, Kohler, Gaster, and Bousset, and not a few of the conclusions arrived at by these scholars have been confirmed by my own investigations.

The main questions as regards the date, original language, and object of the author, are, I am convinced, now practically settled beyond the range of dispute. Other questions arise in the text that call for further study and research. For the prosecution of these the student is fully provided with all the documentary materials, so far as the Testaments themselves are concerned, in the present volume and in my Text, which is published by the Oxford University Press. For these two volumes all accessible authorities in Greek, Armenian, Hebrew, Aramaic, and Slavonic have been used, and of these a full account is given in the Introductions to these two books.

The Testaments of the Twelve Patriarchs has, since its rediscovery by Bishop Grosseteste in the thirteenth century till the last decade, been a sealed book, misunderstood and misdated on every hand. The research of the last few years has, however, as I have just indicated, succeeded in discovering its true date, purpose, and character. It now comes forward as a book second in importance to none composed between 200 B.C. and the Christian era. It was written in Hebrew in the last quarter of the second century B.C. by a Chasid on behalf of the high-priesthood of the great Maccabean family, and especially on behalf of the Messianic claims of John Hyrcanus, who, according to Josephus, was the only Israelite who enjoyed the triple offices of prophet, priest, and king. But its claims to historical importance, however great, are overshadowed by its still greater claims as being the sole representative of the loftiest ethical standard ever attained by pre-Christian Judaism, and as such, attesting the existence of a type of religious thought in pre-Christian Judaism that was the natural preparation for the ethics of the New Testament, and especially of the Sermon on the Mount. Not only so, but this book influenced directly the Sermon on the Mount in a few of its most striking thoughts and phrases, and the Pauline Epistles in a great variety of passages.

Some of the Sections in this Introduction will of necessity appear in the Introduction to my Text, which will be published immediately by the University Press.

As the present volume constitutes the first commentary on the Testaments, the editor has had often to pursue untravelled ways, and as he has pushed his discoveries now in this direction, now in that, he is conscious that he cannot when so doing have escaped falling into errors of perception, judgment, or scholarship. For such he can with confidence throw himself on the indulgence of his fellow researchers, who know the difficulties of the pioneer and the ease with which he falls a victim even to obvious errors. I have, however, done my best to avoid such errors. In this I should no doubt have been more successful, if my sheets had been revised by other eyes. But I naturally shrank from imposing the overwhelming labour of revising my Text on any of my friends, and even of reading my Translations and Notes. For all corrections I shall be very grateful.

I cannot conclude without thanking the Publishers for their magnanimity in undertaking yet another of these expensive works. I hope that their virtue in this respect may have something outside of and beyond its own reward.

Editor's Preface: Testaments of the Twelve Patriarchs

Introduction

While the other books in this volume are fairly well-known, the Testaments of the Twelve Patriarchs (T12P) has been given far less attention. And this fact is rather sad, considering the long history this book has had. While there are no established Churches or Jewish factions that accept T12P as canon, it has nonetheless been treasured by Jews and Christians alike. Indeed, some fragments of a few of the Testaments were found among the Dead Sea Scrolls at Qumran. While the vast majority of manuscript evidence is in Greek, there are numerous texts extant in multiple other languages. This includes a rather large manuscript tradition in both Slavonic and Armenian. Indeed, next to the Greek, the Armenian texts appear to offer a very consistent version, having been carefully modeled after the Greek.

The book claims to be the last words of each of the 12 sons of Jacob. Just as the Bible records Jacob's last words to his sons in Genesis 49, so this books claims to have the last words of each of his sons. Each testament is a treatise, of sorts, on moral values and ethics. In addition to general morality, they are specifically tailored towards warning one's descendants against a vice he, himself, struggled with. For instance, it is recorded in the Bible as well as in the Book of Jubilees that Reuben, Jacob's eldest son, slept with Bilhah, Jacob's concubine. In the Testament of Reuben, he warns his children against being seduced by women, and against whoring. Judah, who decided to sell Joseph for money in the Biblical narrative, warns his descendants against greed. The Testament of Levi is filled with apocalyptic literature, and should almost be categorized by itself.

There are a large number of quotes in the Testaments that offers some insight into the penning of the New Testament, as it appears the Apostles made frequent use of the T12P.

The Texts

The primary source for T12P is by far Greek, though there are very useful witnesses found in the Slavonic and Armenian versions as well. I have utilized the collation that Dr. R. H. Charles compiled, and have chosen to emend his English translation, as with Enoch and Jubilees.

In addition to these texts utilized by Charles, however, I have also consulted the Aramaic fragment of the Testament of Levi, as well as the Hebrew fragment of the Testament of Naphtali. Both of these provide few major variations, though where available I have taken their readings over that of the Greek. It is the opinion of the present editor that T12P were originally written in a Semitic language. That is not the general scholarly consensus, though there remains to be any definitive proof one way or another. I believe, as Charles did, that the frequent use of idiomatic expressions and Semitism within the text proves a Semitic original. Other disagree, stating that the very content and nature of the Testaments are Hellenistic. Indeed, in some portions they read similarly to some Stoic philosophy, though that in and of itself is debated.

Regardless, given that the oldest fragments available to us are Semitic, and these are dated to the pre-Christian era, I believe they were originally Semitic. Sadly, there are not large enough sections on these fragments to ascertain the degree of accuracy that the Greek copies retained.

For this edition, as mentioned, Charles' English translation was edited. This means the English was modernized away from the Elizabethan style which he wrote in. In addition, as with all other books in this volume, the names of those involved have been restored to their Hebraic form. As for our Creator's Name, it appears written as 𐤉𐤄𐤅𐤄, as with the other books. Though it can be difficult because, as discussed in the *Volume Preface*, the Greek *Kurios* can be applied to anyone, human or divine, I found comfort in knowing that there is a Semitic original. In Aramaic, given the style it was written, this would most assuredly be the placeholder 𐤌𐤓𐤉𐤀 (*Mar-Ya*), whereas in Hebrew I have no doubt that it, like Jubilees, would have continued to use the tetragrammaton, 𐤉𐤄𐤅𐤄. Sadly, we will not know for certain unless more of a Semitic original is uncovered.

Aside from merely emending the English of Charles' version I checked it against the Greek, Slavonic, Armenian, Aramaic, and Hebrew texts available. I mostly tend to agree with Charles in taking the Greek reading over the Slavonic and Armenian, though in a few places the Armenian provides the only witness. In addition, when the Aramaic and Hebrew texts are available, I gave preferences to their readings. The Aramaic fragments were actually discovered in the Cairo Genizah. While ancient documents were initially reported to be housed in the Cairo Genizah in the 1750s, cataloging did not formally begin for close to 150 years. The Hebrew fragments were discovered at Qumran along with the Dead Sea Scrolls.

One issue with the Aramaic Levi, however, is that some portions of it do not correspond with any known text of the Greek, Slavonic, or Armenian versions. For these sections, I have chosen to stick with the Greek, unless an Aramaic variant was of great import, in which case it is noted in the footnotes.

Provenance

The author of T12P is unknown, and it is still debated whether there was initially one author for all twelve or if different authors penned the testaments. Regardless, however, it is known that many sections were added at the behest of Christian scribes. Charles noted that many of the additions were probably due to interpolations. These interpolations were, in all likelihood, originally written into the margins of the texts they had available to them. They most likely wrote these notes to insert Messiah into the text, attempting to find parallels between the texts and their theology.

After more years of this, the interpolations became heavy in some portions. So much so, that we have reason to believe in some cases even entire chapters were added. As the New Testament neared canonization, it is most likely that more and more interpolations were worked into T12P from the extant New Testament text.

Given the Hellenistic style and phrasing, as well as some possible mention of the Hasmonean dynasty, it is quite likely some or all of T12P were written during the Seleucid

Empire, sometime after Alexander the Great. The author(s) make frequent reference to the "writings of Enoch" yet their quotations do not match any known Enochian literature.

Conclusion

Whether original to the pre-Christian era, or a largely edited book of Christian origin, T12P nonetheless displays great historical significance. While many scoff at its numerous Christian additions and interpolations, these additions are just as telling as the original text. Indeed, even the additions that were added later show that early Christianity was much more similar to a sect within Judaism, than it was to a free-standing religion. T12P has a great number of parallels to other extra-Biblical works such as Jubilees, and has many parallels within the New Testament.

This books has been overlooked for too many years as it stands now, and with this publication, I hope to give it a boost in notoriety.

The Testaments of the Twelve Patriarchs: the Sons of Ya'aqov the Patriarch.

The Testament of Reuven, the First Son of Ya'aqov and Leah

1 1 The copy of the Testament of Reuven, even the commands which he gave his sons before he died in the hundred and twenty-fifth year of his life.[a] 2 Two years after the death of Yoseph his brother, when Reuven fell ill, his sons and his sons' sons were gathered together to visit him.

3 And he said to them, "My children, behold I am dying, and go the way of my fathers." 4 And when he saw there Yehudah, and Gad, and Asher, his brothers, he said to them, "Raise me up, that I may tell my brothers and my children what things I have hidden in my heart, for behold now at length I am passing away."

5 And he arose and kissed them, and said to them, "My brothers, hear; and do, my children: give ear to Reuven your father in the commands which I give you. 6 And behold I call to witness against you this day the Elohim of the heavens, that you should not walk in the sins of youth and whoring, in which I indulged, and defiled the bed of my father Ya'aqov. 7 And I tell you that He struck me with a heavy wound in my loins for seven months; and had my father Ya'aqov not prayed to 𐤉𐤄𐤅𐤄 for me, 𐤉𐤄𐤅𐤄 would have destroyed me. 8 For I was thirty years old when I worked evil before 𐤉𐤄𐤅𐤄, and I was sick to death for seven months. 9 And after this I repented with determination of my being for seven years before 𐤉𐤄𐤅𐤄. 10 And I did not drink wine or strong drink, and flesh entered not into my mouth, and I ate no pleasant food; but I mourned over my sin, for it was great, such as had not been in Yisra'el."

2 1 "And now hear me, my children, what things I saw during my time of repentance concerning the seven spirits of deceit. 2 Seven spirits are appointed against man, and they are the leaders in the works of youth. 3 And seven other spirits are given to man at creation, so that through them every work of man should be done. 4 The first is the spirit of life, with which the substance *of man* is created. The second is the sense of sight, from which desire arises. 5 The third is the sense of hearing, with which comes teaching. The fourth is the sense of smell, with which tastes are given to draw air and breath. 6 The fifth is the power of speech, with which comes knowledge. 7 The sixth is the sense of taste, with which comes the eating of meats and drinks; and by it strength is produced, for food is the foundation of strength. 8 The seventh is the power of sowing *seed* and intercourse, which brings sin through affection of pleasure. For this reason it is the last in order of creation, and the first in that of youth, because it is filled with ignorance, and leads the youth as a blind man to a pit, and as a beast to a cliff."

3 1 "Besides all these there is an eighth spirit of sleep, which brings with it the astonishment of nature and the image of death. 2 These spirits are mingled with the spirits of error. First, the spirit of whoring resides in nature and in the senses. 3 A second, the spirit of insatiability, in the belly; the third, the spirit of fighting, in the liver and gall. 4 The fourth is the spirit of flattery and trickery, that through excessive effort one may appear fair. 5 The fifth is the spirit of pride, that one may be boastful and arrogant. The sixth is the spirit of lying, which with destruction and jealousy to practice deceits, works concealment from family and friends. 6 The seventh is the spirit of injustice, with which are thefts and acts of greed, that a man may fulfill the desire of his heart; for injustice works together with the other spirits by taking bribes.

7 "And with all these the spirit of sleep is joined which is *that* of error and pompousness. 8 And so every young man dies, darkening his mind from the truth, and not understanding the

---

[a] **1:1** Reuven's age at his death, **125**, is consistent with the account given in Yashar **62:1**.

Torah of Elohim, nor obeying the corrections
of his fathers as happened to me also in my
youth.

9 "And now, my children, love the truth, and it
will preserve you. Hear the words of Reuven
your father. 10 Pay no attention to the face of a
woman, nor associate with another man's wife,
nor meddle with affairs of womankind.

11 "For if I had not seen Bilhah bathing in the
covered place, I would not have fallen into this
great lawlessness. 12 For my mind, taking in
the thought of the woman's nakedness, did not
allow me to sleep until I worked the
abominable thing. 13 For while Ya'aqov our
father had gone to Yitsḥaq his father, when we
were in Eder, near to Ephrath in Beth-lechem,
Bilhah became drunk and was asleep
uncovered in her bedchamber. 14 Having gone
in and seeing her nakedness, I worked the
profane *thing* without her knowing it. Leaving
her sleeping I departed.[a] 15 And immediately a
messenger of Elohim revealed to my father
concerning my profanity, and he came and
mourned over me, and he did not touch her
again."

4 1 "Pay no attention, my children, to the
beauty of women, nor set your mind on their
affairs; but walk in singleness of heart in the
fear of 𐤉𐤄𐤅𐤄, and expend labor on good works,
and on study and on your flocks, until 𐤉𐤄𐤅𐤄
gives you a wife, whom He will, that you do
not suffer as I did. 2 For until my father's death
I was not bold *enough* to look in his face, or to
speak to any of my brothers, because of the
reproach. 3 Even until now my conscience
causes me pain on account of my profanity.
4 And yet my father comforted me much and
prayed to 𐤉𐤄𐤅𐤄 for me, that the anger of 𐤉𐤄𐤅𐤄
might pass from me, even as 𐤉𐤄𐤅𐤄 showed.
And from then on until now I have been on my
guard and have not sinned.

5 "Therefore, my children, I say to you, guard
all things that I command you, and you will not
sin. 6 For the sin of whoring is a pit to the
being, separating it from Elohim, and bringing
it near to idols, because it deceives the mind
and understanding, and leading young men into
Sheol before their time. 7 For whoring has
destroyed many; because, though a man be old
or noble, or rich or poor, he brings reproach
upon himself with the sons of men and derision
with Beliyya'al. 8 For you heard regarding
Yoseph, how he guarded himself from a
woman, and purged his thoughts from all
whoring, and found favor in the eyes of Elohim
and men. 9 For the Mitsrite woman did many
things to him, and summoned magicians, and
offered him love potions, but the purpose of his
being admitted no evil desire. 10 Therefore the
Elohim of your fathers delivered him from
every evil *and* hidden death. 11 For if whoring
does not overcome your mind, neither can
Beliyya'al overcome you."

5 1 "For women are evil, my children. Since
they have no power or authority over man, they
plot by their appearance ways that they may
draw him to themselves. 2 And whomever they
cannot enchant by appearance, him they
overcome by deception. 3 For indeed,
concerning them the messenger of 𐤉𐤄𐤅𐤄 told
me, and taught me, that women are overcome
by the spirit of whoring more than men, and in
their heart they plot against men; and by means
of their adornment they deceive first the men's
minds, and by the glance of the eye instill the
poison, and then through the accomplished act
they take them captive. 4 For a woman cannot
force a man openly, but by a whore's attitude
she deceives him.

5 "Therefore my children, flee whoring,[b] and
command your wives and your daughters that
they adorn not their heads and faces to deceive
the mind *of men*, because every woman who
plots such has been reserved for eternal
punishment. 6 For in this way they enticed the
Watchers who were before the flood. 7 For as
these continually looked upon them, they

[a] **3:14** Yovelim **33:4-5** agrees with most of the details. However, its account states that Bilhah awoke and cried out, seizing Reuven's arm.

[b] **5:5** Compare Korinthious A [**1** Corinthians] **6:18**.

lusted after them, and they conceived the act in their mind; for they changed themselves into the shape of men, and appeared to them when they were with their husbands. **8** And the women, lusting in their minds after their forms, gave birth to giants, for the Watchers appeared to them as reaching even to the heavens.[a]"

6 **1** "Therefore beware of whoring. And if you wish to be pure in mind, guard your senses from every woman. **2** And command the women likewise not to associate with men, that they also may be pure in mind. **3** For constant meetings, even if the profane act is not committed, are an incurable disease, and to us a destruction of Beliyya'al and an eternal reproach. **4** For in whoring there is neither understanding nor reverence, and all jealousy dwells in the lust of it.

5 "Therefore I say to you, you will be jealous against the sons of Levi, and will seek to be exalted over them; but you will not be able. **6** For Elohim will avenge them, and you will die an evil death. **7** For Elohim gave the sovereignty to Levi, and to Yehudah with him [and to me also, and to Dan and Yoseph, that we should be for rulers][b]. **8** Therefore I command you to listen to Levi, because he will know the Torah of 𐤉𐤄𐤅𐤄, and will give statutes for judgment and will slaughter for all Yisra'el until the end of the times, as the anointed High Priest, of whom 𐤉𐤄𐤅𐤄 spoke.

9 "I call to witness the Elohim of the heavens, that you do truth, each one, to his neighbor; and to entertain love, each for his brother. **10** And draw near to Levi in humility of heart, that you may receive a blessing from his mouth. **11** For he will bless Yisra'el and Yehudah, because 𐤉𐤄𐤅𐤄 has chosen him to be king over all the nation. **12** And bow down before his seed, for on our behalf it will die in wars visible and invisible, and will be among you an eternal king."

7 **1** And Reuven died, having given these commands to his sons. **2** And they placed him in a coffin until they carried him up from Mitsrayim, and they buried him in Ḥevron in the cave where his father was.[c]

---

[a] **5:6-8** See Ḥanokh chapters **6** & **7**.

[b] **6:7** Bracketed section indicates likely later addition. This was most likely caused by interpolation by a Jewish copyist.

[c] **7:2** This agrees with Yovelim **46:9**, which states that all twelve sons of Ya'aqov, except for Yoseph, were buried in Makhpelah.

The Testament of Shimon, the Second Son of Ya'aqov and Leah

1 1 The copy of the words[a] of Shimon, the
things which he spoke to his sons before he
died, in the hundred and twentieth year of his
life,[b] at which time Yoseph, his brother, died.
2 For when Shimon was sick, his sons came to
visit him, and he strengthened himself and sat
up and kissed them, and said:

2 1 "Listen, my children, to Shimon your
father, and I will declare to you the things I
have in my heart. 2 I was born of Ya'aqov as
my father's second son, and my mother Leah
called me Shimon, because 𐤉𐤄𐤅𐤄 heard her
prayer. 3 Moreover, I became exceedingly
strong; I did not hold back from any
achievement, nor was I afraid of anything.
4 For my heart was hard, and my liver was
immovable, and my bowels without
compassion.

5 "For valor is also given from the Most High
to men in being and body. 6 For from the time
of my youth I was jealous in many things of
Yoseph, because my father loved him beyond
all. 7 And I set my mind against him to destroy
him, and the prince of deceit sent forth the
spirit of jealousy and blinded my mind, so that
I did not regard him as a brother, nor did I even
spare Ya'aqov my father. 8 But his Elohim and
the Elohim of his fathers sent forth His
messenger, and delivered him out of my hands.

9 "For when I went to Shekhem to bring salve
for the flocks, and Reuven to Dothan, where
our supplies and all our stores were, Yehudah
my brother sold him to the Yishma'elites.
10 And when Reuven heard these things he was
grieved, for he wished to restore him to his
father. 11 But on hearing this I was exceedingly
angry against Yehudah, for he let him go away
alive. For five months I continued being angry
toward him. 12 But 𐤉𐤄𐤅𐤄 restrained me, and
withheld from me the power of my hands; for
my right hand was half withered for seven
days. 13 And I knew, my children, that because
of Yoseph, this had happened to me, and I
repented and wept; and I sought 𐤉𐤄𐤅𐤄 Elohim
that my hand might be restored, and that I
might hold back from all corruption and envy
and from all foolishness. 14 For I knew that I
had devised an evil thing before 𐤉𐤄𐤅𐤄 and
Ya'aqov my father, on account of Yoseph my
brother, in that I envied him."

3 1 "And now, my children, listen to me and
beware of the spirit of deceit and envy. 2 For
envy rules over the whole mind of a man, and
does not allow him to eat or drink, nor to do
any good thing. 3 But it always suggest *to him*
to destroy him that he envies; and so long as he
that is envied flourishes, he that envies fades
away.

4 "Therefore I was afflicted in my being for
two years with fasting in the fear of 𐤉𐤄𐤅𐤄, and
I learned that deliverance from envy comes by
the fear of Elohim. 5 For if a man flees to
𐤉𐤄𐤅𐤄, the evil spirit runs away from him, and
his mind is lightened. 6 And from then on he
sympathizes with him whom he envied and
forgives those who are hostile to him, and so
ceases from his envy."

4 1 "And my father asked concerning me,
because he saw that I was sad. 2 And I said to
him, 'I am pained in my liver.' For I mourned
more than they all, because I was guilty of the
selling of Yoseph. 3 And when we went down
into Mitsrayim, and he bound me as a spy, I
knew that I was suffering justly, and I did not
grieve.

4 "Now Yoseph was a good man, and had the
Ruaḥ of Elohim within him; being
compassionate and pitiful, he bore no malice
against me; but loved me even as the rest of his
brothers. 5 Beware, therefore, my children, of
all jealousy and envy, and walk in singleness of
being and with good heart, keeping in mind
Yoseph your father's brother, that Elohim may
give you also favor and glory, and blessing

---

[a] **1:1** Some Greek and Slavonic texts read "testament" instead of "words" here.

[b] **1:1** Shimon's age at his death, **120**, is consistent with the account given in Yashar **61**:**4**.

upon your heads, even as you saw in Yoseph's case. 6 All his days he did not despise us concerning this thing, but loved us as his own being, and glorified us beyond his own sons, and gave us riches, and cattle and fruits.

7 "You also, my children, love each one his brother with a good heart and the spirit of envy will withdraw from you. 8 For *envy* makes the being savage and destroys the body; it causes anger and war in the mind, and stirs up to deeds of blood, and leads the mind into frenzy, and does not allow discretion to act in men. Moreover, it takes away sleep, and causes tumult to the being and trembling to the body. 9 For even in sleep some malicious jealousy, deceiving him, gnaws and, with wicked spirits, disturbs his being, and causes the body to be troubled, and awakens the mind from sleep in confusion; and as a wicked and poisonous spirit, so it appears to men."

5 1 "Therefore was Yoseph handsome and goodly to look upon, because no wickedness dwelled in him. For the face manifests some of the trouble of the spirit.

2 "And now, my children, make your hearts good before 𐤉𐤄𐤅𐤄, and your ways straight before men. And you will find favor before 𐤉𐤄𐤅𐤄 and men. 3 Beware, therefore, of whoring, for whoring is mother of all evils, separating from Elohim, and bringing near to Beliyya'al. 4 For I have seen it inscribed in the writing of Ḥanokh that your sons will be corrupted in whoring, and will harm the sons of Levi with the sword.[a] 5 But they will not be able to withstand Levi; for he will wage the war of 𐤉𐤄𐤅𐤄, and will conquer all your hosts. 6 And they will be few in number, divided in Levi and Yehudah, and there will be none of you for leadership, even as also our father prophesied in his blessings."

6 1 "Behold I have told you all things, that I may be acquitted of your sin. 2 Now, if you remove from you your envy and all stiff-neckedness, my bones will be as a rose that flourish in Yisra'el, and as a lily my flesh in Ya'aqov, and my odor will be as the odor of Libanus. And as cedars will set-apart ones be multiplied from me forever, and their branches will stretch afar off. 3 Then the seed of Kana'an will die, and a remnant will not remain for Amaleq. And all the Kappadokians will die, and all the Ḥittites will be utterly destroyed. 4 Then the land of Ḥam will fail, and all the people will perish. Then all the earth will rest from trouble, and all the world under the heavens from war. 5 Then the Mighty One of Yisra'el will glorify Shem, for 𐤉𐤄𐤅𐤄 Elohim will manifest on earth [as a man][b], and He Himself will save men. 6 Then will all the spirits of deceit be given to be trodden under foot, and men will rule over wicked spirits. 7 Then will I arise in joy, and will bless the Most High because of His marvelous works. [Because Elohim has taken a body and eaten with men and saved men][c].

7 1 "And now, my children, obey Levi and Yehudah, and do not be lifted up against these two tribes, for from them will arise to you the salvation of Elohim. 2 For 𐤉𐤄𐤅𐤄 will raise up from Levi a High Priest, and from Yehudah a King [Elohim and man][d], and He will save all [the nations and][d] the race of Yisra'el. 3 Therefore I give you these commands that you also may command your children that they may guard them throughout their generations."

8 1 And when Shimon had made an end of commanding his sons, he slept with his fathers, being a hundred and twenty years old. 2 And they laid him in a wooden coffin, to take up his bones to Ḥevron. And they took them up

---

[a] 5:4 The referenced writing of Ḥanokh is uncertain.
[b] 6:5 Bracketed section indicates what is most likely a later Christian interpolation.
[c] 6:7 Bracketed section indicates what is most likely a later Christian interpolation.
[d] 7:2 Bracketed sections indicate what are most likely later Christian interpolations.

secretly during a war of the Mitsrites.[a] **3** For the Mitsrites guarded the bones of Yoseph in the tombs of the kings, because the sorcerers told them that on the departure of the bones of Yoseph there would be, throughout all the land, darkness and gloom, and an exceedingly great plague to the Mitsrites, so that even with a lamp a man should not recognize his brother.

9 **1** And the sons of Shimon mourned their father. **2** And they were in Mitsrayim until the day of their departure by the hand of Mosheh.

[a] **8:2** This war may be the same as the war between Mitsrayim and Kana'an mentioned in Yovelim **46**.

The Testament of Levi, the Third Son of Ya'aqov and Leah

1 1 The copy of the words[a] of Levi, the things
which he declared to his sons, according to all
that they should do, and what things would
happen to them until the day of judgment. 2 He
was sound in health when he called them to
him; for it had been revealed to him that he
would die. And when they were gathered
together he said to them:

2 1 "I, Levi, was born in Ḥaran, and I came
with my father to Shekhem. 2 And I was
young, about twenty years of age, when
Shimon and I worked vengeance on Ḥamor for
our sister Dinah. 3 And when I was feeding the
flocks in Havel-Maul, the spirit of the
understanding of 𐤉𐤄𐤅𐤄 came upon me, and I
saw all men corrupting their way, and that
unrighteousness had built walls for itself, and
lawlessness sat upon towers.

4 "And I was grieving for the race of the sons
of men, and I prayed to 𐤉𐤄𐤅𐤄 that I might be
saved. 5 Then a sleep there fell upon me, and I
saw a high mountain, and I was upon it. 6 And
behold, the heavens were opened and a
messenger of Elohim said to me, 'Levi enter.'
7 And I entered from the first heaven, and I
saw a great sea hanging there. 8 And further I
saw a second heaven, far brighter and more
brilliant, for there was a boundless light in it
also.

9 "And I said to the messenger, 'Why is it like
this?' And the messenger said to me, 'Do not
marvel at this, for you will see another heaven
more brilliant and incomparable. 10 And when
you have ascended there, you will stand near
𐤉𐤄𐤅𐤄, and will be His minister. And you will
declare His mysteries to men, and will
proclaim concerning Him that will redeem
Yisra'el. 11 And by you and Yehudah will
𐤉𐤄𐤅𐤄 appear among men, saving every race of
men. 12 And from the portion of 𐤉𐤄𐤅𐤄 will be
your sustenance, and He will be your field and
vineyard, and fruits, gold, and silver.'"

3 1 "'Hear, therefore, regarding the heavens
which have been shown to you. The lowest is
dark for this reason: it sees all the unrighteous
deeds of men. 2 And it has fire, snow, and ice
made ready for the day of judgment, in the
righteous judgment of Elohim; for in it are all
the spirits of the punishment of man. 3 And in
the second *heaven* are the hosts of the armies
which are ordained for the day of judgment, to
work vengeance on the spirits of deceit and of
Beliyya'al. And above them are the set-apart
ones. 4 And in the highest of all, the Great
Glory dwells, far above all set-apartness.

5 "'In it are the Ruling Messengers[b], who
minister and make offerings to 𐤉𐤄𐤅𐤄 for all the
sins of ignorance of the righteous; 6 Offering to
𐤉𐤄𐤅𐤄 a sweet-smelling aroma, a reasonable
and a bloodless offering. 7 And in the heaven
below this are the messengers who bear
answers to the messengers of the presence of
𐤉𐤄𐤅𐤄. 8 And in the heaven next to this are
thrones and dominions, in which always they
offer praise to Elohim.[c] 9 Therefore when 𐤉𐤄𐤅𐤄
looks at us, all of us are shaken; yes, the
heavens, and the earth, and the abysses tremble
at the presence of His majesty. 10 But the sons
of men, not perceiving these things, sin and
provoke the anger of Most High.'"

4 1 "'Now, therefore, know that 𐤉𐤄𐤅𐤄 will
execute judgment upon the sons of men. For
when the rocks are being split, and the sun
quenched, and the waters dried up, and the fire
cowering, and all creation troubled, and the
invisible spirits melting away; and Sheol takes
spoils [through the visitations of the Most

---

[a] **1:1** Some Greek texts read "testament" instead of "words" here.

[b] **3:5** Ruling Messengers – Greek word αρχαγγελος (*arch'agg'elos*) which is usually rendered as "Archangel." However, some Greek and Slavonic texts read "With Him are the messengers of the presence of 𐤉𐤄𐤅𐤄." Compare wording of verse **7**.

[c] **3:8** Compare Kolossaeis [Colossians] **1:16**; Hit'galut [Revelation] **4:4-10**.

High][a], men will be unbelieving and persist in
their unrighteousness. Because of this they will
be judged with punishment. 2 Therefore the
Most High has heard your prayer, to separate
you from unrighteousness[b], and that you should
become to Him a son, and a servant, and a
minister of His presence. 3 You will light up
the light of knowledge in Ya'aqov, and you
will be as the sun to all the seed of Yisra'el.
4 And a blessing will be given to you, and to all
your seed, until 𐤉𐤄𐤅𐤄 visits all the nations in
His affection forever, [although your sons will
lay hands on Him in order to impale Him][c].
5 And therefore counsel and understanding
have been given to you, that you might instruct
your sons concerning this. 6 For they that bless
Him will be blessed, and they that curse Him
will die.'"

5 1 "And then the messenger opened the gates
of heaven to me, and I saw the set-apart
Temple, and the Most High *sitting* upon a
throne of glory. 2 And He said to me, 'Levi, I
have given you the blessings of the priesthood
until I come and sojourn in the midst of
Yisra'el.'

3 "Then the messenger brought me down to the
earth, and gave me a shield and a sword, and
said to me, 'Execute vengeance on Shekhem
because of Dinah, your sister, and I will be
with you because 𐤉𐤄𐤅𐤄 has sent me.' 4 And I
destroyed the sons of Ḥamor at that time, as it
is written in the heavenly tablets. 5 And I said
to him, 'Please, O master, tell me your name,
so I may call on you in a day of affliction.'
6 And he said, 'I am the messenger who
intercedes for the nation of Yisra'el, that they
may not be utterly destroyed, for every evil
spirit attacks it.' 7 And after these things I
awoke, and blessed the Most High, and the
messenger who intercedes for the nation of
Yisra'el and for all the righteous."

6 1 "And when I was going to my father, I
found a copper shield; the name of the
mountain is Aspis, which is near Gebal, to the
south of Abila. 2 And I kept these words in my
heart. 3 And after this I counselled my father,
and Reuven my brother, to tell the sons of
Ḥamor not to be circumcised; for I was zealous
because of the abomination which they had
worked on my sister. 4 And I killed Shekhem
first, and Shimon slew Ḥamor. 5 And after this
my brothers came and struck that city with the
edge of the sword.

6 "And my father heard these things and was
angry, and he was grieved because they had
received the circumcision, and afterwards had
been put to death, and in his blessings he
passed us by. 7 For we sinned because we had
done this thing against his will, and he was sick
on that day. 8 But I saw that the sentence of
Elohim was for evil upon Shekhem; for they
sought to do to Sarah and Rivqah as they had
done to Dinah our sister, but 𐤉𐤄𐤅𐤄 prevented
them. 9 And they persecuted Avraham our
father when he was a sojourner, and they
frustrated his flocks when they were pregnant.
And they shamefully mistreated Eblaen[d], who
was born in his house. 10 And thus they did to
all sojourners, taking away their wives by
force, and banishing them. 11 But the anger of
𐤉𐤄𐤅𐤄 came upon them to the uttermost."

7 1 "And I said to my father Ya'aqov, '𐤉𐤄𐤅𐤄
will destroy the Kana'anites by you, and will
give their land to you and to your seed after
you. 2 For from this day forward Shekhem will
be called "City of Senselessness;" for as a man
mocks a fool, so we mocked them. 3 Because

---

[a] **4:1** Bracketed section indicates what is most likely a later Christian interpolation.

[b] **4:2** Some Greek texts read "lawlessness" instead of "unrighteousness" here.

[c] **4:4** Bracketed section indicates what is most likely a later Christian interpolation. This reading is found in most major Greek, Slavonic, and Armenian texts, though it interrupts the flow in each. Note the word for "impale" is not σταυροω (*sta'ro'o*) as is normally used such as in the Gospels for "crucify" but rather is ανασκολοπισαι (*anas'kolo'pisai*) meaning "impale."

[d] **6:9** Eblaen – Name of an unknown member of the house of Avraham. The different manuscripts offer a wide number of textual variants, such as Iekblai, Iekblae, Deblaen, Ieblaen, Ebal, and more.

they also worked foolishness in Yisra'el by
defiling my sister.' And we departed and came
to Beth-El."

8 1 "And there again I saw a vision like the
previous one, after we had spent seventy days
there. 2 And I saw seven men in white
garments saying to me, 'Arise, put on the robe
of the priesthood, and the crown of
righteousness, and the breastplate of
understanding, and the garment of truth, and
the plate of faith, and the turban of the head,
and the ephod of prophecy.' [a] 3 And they each
carried *these items* and put *them* on me, and
said to me, 'From now on become a priest of
𐤉𐤄𐤅𐤄, you and your seed forever.'

4 "And the first anointed me with set-apart oil,
and gave me the staff of judgment. 5 The
second washed me with pure water, and fed me
with bread and wine *even* the most set-apart
things, and dressed me with a set-apart and
glorious robe. 6 The third clothed me with a
linen vestment like an ephod. 7 The fourth put
a purple belt around me. 8 The fifth gave me a
branch of rich olive. 9 The sixth placed a crown
on my head. 10 The seventh placed a diadem of
priesthood on my head, and filled my hands
with incense, that I might serve as priest to
𐤉𐤄𐤅𐤄 Elohim.

11 "And they said to me, 'Levi, your seed will
be divided into three branches, for a sign of the
glory of 𐤉𐤄𐤅𐤄 who is to come. 12 And the first
portion will be great; yes, none will be greater
than it. 13 The second will be in the priesthood.
14 And the third will be called by a renewed
name, because a king will arise in Yehudah,
and will establish a new priesthood, after the
fashion of the nations to all the nations. 15 And
His presence is beloved, as a prophet of the
Most High, of the seed of Avraham our father.
16 Therefore, every desirable thing in Yisra'el
will be for you and for your seed, and you will
eat everything that looks good, and the table of
𐤉𐤄𐤅𐤄 will be the portion of your seed.

17 "'And some of them will be high priests, and
judges, and scribes; for by their mouth will the
set-apart place be guarded.'

18 "And when I awoke, I understood that this
dream was like the first dream. 19 And I hid
this also in my heart, and did not tell it to any
man upon the earth."

9 1 "And after two days I and Yehudah went
up with our father Ya'aqov to Yitsḥaq our
father's father. 2 And my father's father blessed
me according to all the words of the visions
which I had seen. And he would not come with
us to Beth-El.

3 "And when we came to Beth-El, my father
saw a vision concerning me, that I would be
their priest to Elohim. 4 And he rose up early in
the morning, and paid tithes of all to 𐤉𐤄𐤅𐤄
through me. 5 And so we came to Ḥevron to
dwell there. 6 And Yitsḥaq called me
continually to put me in remembrance of the
Torah of 𐤉𐤄𐤅𐤄, even as the messenger of 𐤉𐤄𐤅𐤄
showed me. 7 And he taught me the Torah of
the priesthood, of slaughterings, ascension
offerings, first-fruits, freewill offerings, and
peace offerings.

8 "And each day that he was instructing me, he
worked on my behalf before 𐤉𐤄𐤅𐤄, and said to
me, 9 'Beware of the spirit of whoring; for this
will continue and by your seed will pollute the
set-apart place. 10 Therefore, take to yourself a
wife without blemish or pollution, while you
are still young; and not of the race of strange
nations. 11 And bathe before entering into the
set-apart place. And when you offer the
slaughterings, wash, and then again when you
finish. 12 And when you finish the
slaughtering, present twelve leafy trees, and
offer them to 𐤉𐤄𐤅𐤄, as Avraham also taught
me.[b] 13 And of every clean beast and bird offer

---

[a] **8:2** See Ephesious [Ephesians] **6:10-17**.
[b] **9:12** Compare Yovelim **21:12**; Yechezqel [Ezekiel] **47:12**; Hit'galut [Revelation] **22:2**. One particular Qumran document related to the Testament of Levi, 4Q**214**b, includes a very similar statement as recorded here. It reads, "Twelve kinds of wood [Avraham] showed me, which are fitting to be on the altar, and the smell which goes up pleasing. These are their names:

a slaughtering to 𐤉𐤄𐤅𐤄. **14** And of all your first-
fruits and of wine offer the first, as an offering
to 𐤉𐤄𐤅𐤄 Elohim; and every slaughtering you
will season with salt."

10 **1** "Therefore children, guard whatever I
command you; for whatever things I have
heard from my fathers I have declared to you.
2 And behold I am innocent of your profanity
and transgression, which you will commit in
the end of the ages, [acting profane against the
Savior of the world, Messiah][a], deceiving
Yisra'el, and stirring up against it great evils
from 𐤉𐤄𐤅𐤄."

3 "And you will deal lawlessly together with
Yisra'el, so He will not bear with Yerushalayim
because of your wickedness; but the veil of the
Temple will be split, so as not to cover your
shame. **4** And you will be scattered as captives
among the nations, and will be for a reproach
and for a curse there. **5** For the house which
𐤉𐤄𐤅𐤄 chooses will be called Yerushalayim, as
is contained in the book of Ḥanokh the
righteous.[b]"

11 **1** "Therefore when I took a wife I was
twenty-eight years old, and her name was
Melkha[c]. **2** And she conceived and bore a son,
and I called his name Gershom, for we were
sojourners in our land.[d] **3** And I saw concerning
him, that he would not be in the first rank.
4 And Qohath was born in the thirty-fifth year
of my life, towards sunrise. **5** And I saw [that
the assembly of all the nation, and the high
priesthood of Yisra'el, would belong to him.][e]
6 Therefore I called his name Qohath [which is,
'beginning of majesty and instruction'][f]. **7** And
she bore me a third son, in the fortieth year of
my life; and since his mother bore him with
difficulty, I called him Merari[g], that is, 'my
bitterness,' because he also nearly died. **8** And
in my sixty-fourth year [I was with *my wife*
again, and she conceived and bore a daughter.
And I called her Yokheved[h], saying, 'As she
has given birth to my honor, so has she given
birth to the glory of Yisra'el. This was the first
day of the seventh month.][i]"

12 **1** "And Gershom took a wife, and she bore
to him Livni and Shimei.[j] **2** And the sons of

---

cedar, juniper, almond, tamarind, pine, ash, cypress, fig, olive, laurel, myrtle, and balsam."

[a] **10:2** Bracketed section indicates what is most likely a later Christian interpolation. Most Greek texts, all Slavonic and Armenian texts, do not contain the word for "Messiah" here.

[b] **10:5** Possible reference to Ḥanokh **89:50**. Here, however, it is not named.

[c] **11:1** Melkha – Wife of Levi. See Yovelim **34:20** and footnote e.

[d] **11:2** Gershom – The naming convention and explanation here shows deep Semitic influence, as the root of Gershom in Hebrew is 𐤂𐤓 (*ger*) meaning "to sojourn."

[e] **11:5** Bracketed section indicates reading present in Aramaic Levi document. Greek, Slavonic, and Armenian texts read, "in a vision that he was standing on high in the midst of all the congregation." Given the content, it is quite possible that an early Greek translator shortened the Aramaic sentence.

[f] **11:6** Bracketed section indicates what is most likely a later addition, though not necessarily a Christian one. Charles noted that this section may actually be a gloss attempting to preserve an explanation from an older text that was no longer extant when the Greek text was copied. The name may be related to the word 𐤒𐤄𐤋 (*qa'hal*) which in Hebrew and Aramaic means "assembly" or "congregation."

[g] **11:7** Merari – From the first-person possessive of the Hebrew 𐤌𐤓𐤓 (*marar*) meaning "bitter": "my bitterness."

[h] **11:8** Yokheved – From a particle of the Divine Name, 𐤉𐤄𐤅𐤄, and 𐤊𐤁𐤃 (ka'vad) meaning "honor" or "glory." Together, it means "𐤉𐤄𐤅𐤄 is glory [honor]."

[i] **11:8** Bracketed section indicates reading present in the Aramaic Levi document. Greek, Slavonic, and Armenian texts read, "Yokheved was born in Mitsrayim, for I was honored then in the midst of my brothers."

[j] **12:1** Greek, Slavonic, and Armenian texts vary widely on these names. Most read Lomen or Lomnen, and Semei or Semi. I have restored them throughout based on Shemoth [Exodus] **6:17** and the Aramaic Levi document.

Qohath: Amram, Yitshar, Ḥevron, and Uzziel.[a]
3 And the sons of Merari: Machli and Mushi.[b]

4 "And in the ninety-fourth year Amram took
Yokheved my daughter to him as wife, for they
were born on the same day, he and my
daughter. 5 I was eight years old when I went
into the land of Kana'an, and eighteen years
when I killed Shekhem. At nineteen years *old* I
became priest, and at twenty-eight years *old* I
took a wife, and at forty-eight I went into
Mitsrayim. 6 And behold, my children, you are
a third generation. [I lived in Mitsrayim ninety-
eight years.][c] 7 In my hundred and eighteenth
year Yoseph died."

13 1 "And now, my children, I command you:
Fear 𐤉𐤄𐤅𐤄 your Elohim with all your heart, and
walk according to all His Torah. 2 And also
teach your children letters, that they may have
understanding all their life, reading the Torah
of Elohim without ceasing. 3 For everyone that
knows the Torah of 𐤉𐤄𐤅𐤄 will be honored, and
will not be a stranger wherever he goes. 4 Yes,
he will gain many more friends than his
parents, and many men will desire to serve
him, and to hear the Torah from his mouth.

5 "Work righteousness on the earth, my
children, that you may have a treasure in
heaven.[d] 6 And sow good things in your beings,
that you may find them in your life. But if you
sow evil things, you will reap every trouble and
affliction.[e]

7 "Get wisdom in the fear of Elohim with
diligence. For though there will be a leading
into captivity, and cities and lands will be
destroyed, and gold and silver and every
possession will perish; nothing can take away
the wisdom of the wise, except the blindness of
profanity, and the hardness *that comes* from
sin. 8 For if he keeps himself from these evil
things, then wisdom will be glory to him, even
among his enemies; in a strange country a
fatherland, and in the midst of foes will prove a
friend. 9 Whoever teaches noble things and
does them, will be enthroned with kings, as
was also Yoseph my brother."

14 1 "Therefore, my children, I have learned
[from the writings of Ḥanokh][f] that at the end
of the ages you will act profanely against
𐤉𐤄𐤅𐤄, stretching out hands to wickedness; and
you will become a scorn to all the nations.
2 For our father Yisra'el is innocent from the
transgressions of the chief priests [who will lay
their hands upon the Savior of the world][g].

3 "For as the heaven is purer in the sight of
𐤉𐤄𐤅𐤄 than the earth, so also you should be, *as*
the lights of Yisra'el, *purer* than all the nations.
4 But if you are darkened through
transgressions, what, therefore, will all the
nations do, who live in blindness? Yes, you
will bring a curse upon our race, because the
light of the Torah – which was given to lighten
every man – you desire to destroy by teaching
commands contrary to the judgments of
Elohim.[h] 5 You will rob the offerings of 𐤉𐤄𐤅𐤄,
and you will steal choice portions from His
portion,[i] eating *them* contemptuously with
whores. 6 And you will teach the commands of
𐤉𐤄𐤅𐤄 out of covetousness; you will pollute
married women, and you will defile the virgins

[a] **12:2** Greek, Slavonic, and Armenian texts vary widely on these names. Most read Ambram, Yissakhar, Ḥevron, and Ozeel. I have restored them throughout based on Shemoth [Exodus] **6:18** and the Aramaic Levi document.

[b] **12:3** Greek, Slavonic, and Armenian texts vary widely on these names. Most read Mooli and Mouses. I have restored them throughout based on Shemoth [Exodus] **6:19** and the Aramaic Levi document.

[c] **12:6** Bracketed section indicates reading present in Aramaic Levi document, but absent from Greek, Slavonic, and Armenian texts. Given the content and form, it is quite likely this section is original.

[d] **13:5** Compare Mattithyahu [Matthew] **6:19-20**; **19:21**; Loukas [Luke] **12:33**; **18:22**.

[e] **13:6** Compare Hoshea [Hosea] **10:12-13**; Galatas [Galatians] **6:6-10**.

[f] **14:1** Bracketed section indicates reading present in some Greek, Slavonic, and Armenian texts, but absent from others. See also Ḥanokh **91:6-7**.

[g] **14:2** Bracketed section indicates what is most likely a later Christian interpolation.

[h] **14:4** Compare Mattithyahu [Matthew] **15:1-9**; Markos [Mark] **7:5-13**.

[i] **14:5** See Malakhi [Malachi] **3:8-15**.

of Yerushalayim; with whores and adulteresses
you will be joined, and you will take the
daughters of the nations as wife, purifying
them with an unlawful purification; and your
union will be like Sodom and Gomorrah. 7 And
you will be puffed up because of your
priesthood, lifting yourselves up against men,
and not only so, but also against the commands
of Elohim. 8 For you will treat the set-apart
things with jests and laughter."

15 1 "Therefore the Temple, which 𐤉𐤄𐤅𐤄
chooses, will be laid waste through your
uncleanness, and you will be captives
throughout all nations. 2 And you will be an
abomination to them, and you will receive
reproach and everlasting shame from the
righteous judgment of Elohim. 3 And all who
hate you will rejoice at your destruction. 4 And
if you were not to receive kindness through
Avraham, Yitsḥaq, and Ya'aqov, our fathers,
not one of our seed would be left on the earth."

16 1 "And now I have learned [in the book of
Ḥanokh][a] that for seventy weeks you will go
astray, and profane the priesthood, and pollute
the slaughterings. 2 And you will make void
the Torah, and set the words of the prophets at
nothing by evil perverseness. 3 [And you will
persecute righteous men, and hate the reverent,
and you will despise the words of the faithful.
And a man who renews the Torah in the power
of the Most High, you will call him a deceiver;
and at last you will rush *upon him* to kill him,
not knowing his dignity, taking innocent blood
through wickedness upon your heads.][b] 4 And
your set-apart places will be laid waste even to
the ground because of him. 5 And you will
have no place that is clean; but you will be a
curse among the nations, and a dispersion until
He will again visit you and in pity, and will
receive you [through faith and water][c]."

17 1 "And whereas you have heard concerning
the seventy weeks, hear also concerning the
priesthood.

2 "For in each yovel there will be a priesthood.
And in the first yovel, the first who is anointed
to the priesthood will be great, and will speak
to Elohim as to a father. And his priesthood
will be perfect with 𐤉𐤄𐤅𐤄, and in the day of his
gladness he will arise for the salvation of the
world. 3 In the second yovel, he that is
anointed will be conceived in the sorrow of
beloved ones; and his priesthood will be
honored and will be glorified by all. 4 And the
third priest will be taken hold of by sorrow.
5 And the fourth will be in pain, because
unrighteousness will gather itself against him
exceedingly, and all Yisra'el will hate each one
his neighbor. 6 The fifth will be taken hold of
by darkness. 7 Likewise also the sixth and the
seventh. 8 And in the seventh will be such
pollution as I cannot express before men, for
they will know it who do these things.

9 "Therefore they will be taken captive and
become plunder, and their land and their
substance will be destroyed. 10 And in the fifth
week they will return to their desolate country,
and will renew the house of 𐤉𐤄𐤅𐤄. 11 And in
the seventh week idolaters, adulterers, lovers of
money, proud, lawless, lewd, abusers of
children and beasts: these will become priests."

18 1 "And after their punishment has come
from 𐤉𐤄𐤅𐤄, the priesthood will fail. 2 Then
𐤉𐤄𐤅𐤄 will raise up a renewed priest. And all
the words of 𐤉𐤄𐤅𐤄 will be revealed to him.
And he will execute a righteous judgment upon
the earth for a multitude of days. 3 And his star
will arise in heaven, as of a king, lighting up
the light of knowledge as the sun the day. And

[a] **16:1** Bracketed section indicates reading present in some Greek, Slavonic, and Armenian texts, but absent from others. See also Ḥanokh **89:59**.

[b] **16:4** Bracketed section indicates what is most likely a later Christian addition. Charles noted that while it is likely to be a later addition, it is unlikely that it is due to simple interpolation. Rather, he believed the entire section was reworked by a Christian author.

[c] **16:5** Bracketed section indicates reading present in some Greek, Slavonic, and Armenian texts, but absent in others.

he will be magnified in the world. 4 He will
shine forth as the sun on the earth, and will
remove all darkness from under heaven, and
there will be peace in all the earth.

5 "The heavens will rejoice in his days, and the
earth will be glad, and the clouds will rejoice.
And the knowledge of 𐤉𐤄𐤅𐤄 will be poured out
on the earth, as the water of the seas. And the
messengers of the glory of the presence of
𐤉𐤄𐤅𐤄 will be glad in him. 6 The heavens will
be opened, and he will be set apart for the
Temple of glory, with the Father's voice as
from Avraham to Yitsḥaq. 7 And the glory of
the Most High will be uttered over him, and the
spirit of understanding and setting apart will
rest upon him in the water. 8 For he will give
the majesty of 𐤉𐤄𐤅𐤄 to His sons in truth
forevermore. There will be none to succeed
him for all generations forever.

9 "And in his priesthood the nations will be
multiplied in knowledge upon the earth, and
enlightened through the favor of 𐤉𐤄𐤅𐤄. [But
Yisra'el will be diminished by her ignorance,
and darkened by her grief.][a] In his priesthood
sin will come to an end, and the lawless *ones*
will cease to do evil. And the just will rest in
him.

10 "And he will open the gates of paradise, and
will remove the threatening sword against
Adam. 11 And he will give to the set-apart ones
to eat from the tree of life, and the spirit of set-
apartness will be on them. 12 And Beliyya'al
will be bound by him, and he will give power
to His children to tread upon the evil spirits.
13 And 𐤉𐤄𐤅𐤄 will rejoice in His children, and
be well-pleased in His beloved ones forever.
14 Then will Avraham and Yitsḥaq and
Ya'aqov rejoice, and I will be glad, and all the
set-apart ones will clothe themselves with joy."
[b]

["All the days of my life have been one hundred and thirty-seven years, and I have seen my sons' sons' sons before my death. Yoseph died in my hundred and eighteenth year, in which I summoned my sons and their sons and began to instruct them all that was in my heart. I said to my sons, 'Listen to the word of Levi your father, and pay attention to the precepts of Elohim. I order you, my children, and I show you the truth, my beloved ones. The principle of all your works should be truth, and let justice and truth stay with you forever. {...} the sower that sows good, harvests good; whoever sows evil, his seed will turn against him. {...} But now my children, teach reading, and instruction, and wisdom to your children, and let wisdom be with you for everlasting honor. He who teaches wisdom will be honored by it, but he who despises wisdom is given over to insult. {...} See then, my sons, how my brother Yoseph taught reading, and instruction, and wisdom...'"][c]

19 1 "And now, my children, you have heard
all; choose, therefore, for yourselves either the
light or the darkness, either the Torah of 𐤉𐤄𐤅𐤄
or the works of Beliyya'al."

2 And his sons answered him, saying, "We will
walk before 𐤉𐤄𐤅𐤄, according to His Torah."

3 And their father said to them, "𐤉𐤄𐤅𐤄 is
witness, and His messengers are witnesses, and
you are witnesses, and I am witness,
concerning the word of your mouth."

4 And his sons said to him, "We are witnesses."
And thus Levi ceased commanding his sons;

[a] **18:9** Bracketed section indicates what is most likely a later Christian addition. Charles noted that while it is found in nearly all the texts he worked with, he highly doubted its authenticity.

[b] **18** One of the primary Armenian texts that Charles used, which he designated A$^{\alpha}$ does not contain chapters **17** and **18** at all.

[c] **18** Bracketed section here is a block of text from the Aramaic Levi document. The Testament of Levi never details his age, as is common with the testaments. Similarly the material presented here fits with the context. It should be noted here that this section is translated from one fragmentary manuscript (hence the ellipses {...} indicating lacunas), and is not attested in any copy of the Greek, Slavonic, or Armenian Testaments. Whether originally part of the Testament of Levi, or a completely different document altogether, I felt it made a worthwhile addition.

and he stretched out his feet on the bed, and was gathered to his fathers, after he had lived a hundred and thirty-seven years. 5 And they laid him in a coffin, and afterwards they buried him in Ḥevron, with Avraham, Yitsḥaq, and Ya'aqov.

The Testament of Yehudah, the Fourth Son of Ya'aqov and Leah

1 1 The copy of the words of Yehudah, the things he spoke to his sons before he died. 2 They gathered themselves together, therefore, and came to him, and he said to them,

3 "Listen, my children, to Yehudah your father. I was the fourth son born to my father Ya'aqov; and Leah my mother named me Yehudah, saying, 'I give thanks to 𐤉𐤄𐤅𐤄, because He has given me a fourth son also.' 4 I was swift in my youth, and obedient to my father in everything. 5 And I honored my mother and my mother's sister. 6 And it happened, when I became a man, that my father blessed me, saying, 'You will be a king, prospering in all things.'"

2 1 "And 𐤉𐤄𐤅𐤄 showed me favor in all my works both in the field and in the house. 2 I know that I raced a hind, and caught it, and prepared the meat for my father, and he ate. 3 And the deer I used to master in the chase, and overtake all that was in the plains. A wild horse I overtook, and caught it and tamed it. 4 I killed a lion and plucked a kid *goat* out of its mouth. 5 I took a bear by its paw and threw it down the cliff, and it was crushed. I outran the wild boar, and seizing it as I ran, I tore it in two. 6 A leopard in Ḥevron leaped upon my dog, and I caught it by the tail, and threw it on the rocks, and it was broken in two. 7 I found a wild ox feeding in the fields, and seizing it by the horns, and whirling it around, stunning it, I threw it from me and killed it."

3 1 "And when the two kings of the Kana'anites came covered in armor against our flocks, and many people with them, I rushed upon the king of Ḥatsor alone, and struck him on the shin-guard and dragged him down, and so I killed him. 2 And the other, the king of Tapuaḥ, as he sat upon his horse, I killed, and so I scattered all his people. 3 Akhor the king, a man of giant stature I found, hurling javelins in front and behind as he sat on horseback; and I took up a stone of sixty pounds weight, and hurled it and struck his horse, and killed it. 4 And I fought with *this* other for two hours; and I split his shield in half, and I chopped off his feet, and killed him. 5 And as I was stripping off his breastplate, behold nine men, his companions, began to fight with me. 6 And I wound my garment on my hand; and I threw stones at them, and killed four of them, and the rest fled. 7 And Ya'aqov my father killed Beelesath, king of all the kings, a giant in strength, twelve cubits tall. 8 And fear fell upon them, and they ceased warring against us. 9 Therefore my father was free from anxiety in the wars when I was with my brothers. 10 For he saw in a vision concerning me that a messenger of might followed me everywhere, that I should not be overcome." [a]

4 1 "And in the south a greater war came upon us than that in Shekhem; and I joined in battle array with my brothers, and pursued a thousand men, and killed two hundred of them, and four kings. 2 And I went up upon the wall, and I killed four mighty men. 3 And so we captured Ḥatsor, and took all the spoil."

5 1 "On the next day we departed to Sarton[b], a city strong and walled and inaccessible, threatening us with death. 2 But Gad and I approached on the east side of the city, and Reuven and Levi on the west.[c] 3 And they that were upon the wall. Thinking that we were alone, they were drawn down against us. 4 And so my brothers secretly climbed up the wall on both sides by stakes, and entered the city, while the men did not know. 5 And we took *the city*

---

[a] **3** See Yashar **34** & **37**; Yovelim **34**.

[b] **5**:**1** Greek texts vary widely on this spelling. Slavonic texts read етеран (*Eteran*). Armenian texts read արիտա (*Arita*). All of these seem to be corruptions of the Greek Αρετον (*Areton*), which is itself a corruption of the Hebrew 𐤎𐤓𐤈𐤍 (*Sarton*). So it has been restored here. See Yashar **37**:7.

[c] **5**:**2** Yashar **38**:**30-31** agrees that Yehudah went to the east of the city. However, there it states that Gad and Asher went to the west, Shimon and Levi to the north, and Dan and Reuven to the south.

with the edge of the sword. And as for those
who had taken refuge in the tower, we set fire
to the tower and took both it and them. 6 And
as we were departing, the men of Tapuaḥ went
after our spoil, and delivering it up to our sons
we fought with them as far as Tapuaḥ. 7 And
we killed them and burned their city, and took
as spoil all that was in it."

6 1 "And when I was at the waters of Kozeva[a],
the men of Yovel[b] came against us to battle.
2 And we fought with them and routed them;
and we killed their allies from Shiloh, and we
did not leave them power to come in against
us. 3 And the men of Makir came upon us the
fifth day, to seize our spoil; and we attacked
them and overcame them in fierce battle, for
there was a host of mighty men among them,
and we killed them before they had gone up the
ascent. 4 And when we came to their city their
women rolled upon us stones from the brow of
the hill on which the city stood. 5 And Shimon
and I hid ourselves behind the town, and seized
upon the heights, and destroyed this city also."

7 1 "And the next day we were told that the
king of the city of Ga'ash was coming against
us with a mighty host. 2 Therefore Dan and I
pretended to be Amorites, and went as allies
into their city. 3 And in the depth of night our
brothers came and we opened the gates to
them. And we destroyed all the men and their
substance, and we took for spoil all that was
theirs, and we cast down their three walls.
4 And we drew near to Thamna, where all the
substance of the hostile kings was. 5 Then
being insulted by them, I was therefore angry,
and rushed against them to the summit; and
they kept slinging stones and spear against me.
6 And had not Dan my brother assisted me,
they would have killed me. 7 We came upon
them, therefore, with anger, and they all fled;
and passing by another way, they sought my
father, and he made peace with them. 8 And we
did no harm to them, and they paid taxes to us,
and we returned the spoil to them. 9 And I built
Thamna, and my father built Rabael.[c] 10 I was
twenty years old when this war happened. And
the Kana'anites feared me and my brothers."

8 1 "And I had much cattle, and I had for chief
herdsman Iram the Adullamite. 2 And when I
went to him I saw Barsaba, king of Adullam;
and he spoke to us, and he made us drinks; and
[when I begged][d], he gave me his daughter
Bathshua[e] as wife. 3 She bore me Er, and Onan
and Shelah; and 𐤉𐤄𐤅𐤄 struck two of them: for
Shelah lived, [and you are his children][f]."

9 1 "And my father lived in peace with his
brother Esaw for eighteen years, and his sons
with us, after we came from Aram-Naharayim,

---

[a] **6:1** Greek, Slavonic, and Armenian texts vary widely on the spelling of this city. However, most still retain a general pronunciation of Kozeba. This refers to 𐤊𐤆𐤁𐤀 (*Kozeva*), the city mentioned in Divrei Ha'Yamim 𐤀 [1 Chronicles] **4:22**.

[b] **6:1** Yovel – City of disputed origin and name. Not to be confused with yovel, the Hebrew term usually translated as Jubilee.

[c] **7:9** One of the primary Greek texts that Charles used reads "And his city was not built" here, rather than "And I built Thamna, and my father built Rabael." However, the primary Slavonic and Armenian sources contain the longer reading, as above.

[d] **8:2** Charles believed this word in Greek, παρακαλεσας (*para'kale'sas*), was a corrupted form of the Hebrew 𐤌𐤍𐤇𐤌 (*me'na'ḥeim*) itself being a corruption of 𐤁𐤇𐤌𐤉 (*be'ḥu'miy*) meaning "in my heat." He believed this referred to the wine causing Yehudah to become intoxicated, and thus did not beg for Bathshua to be his wife, but rather married her while drunk. While that does not seem to be the case here, Charles' theory is supported in **13:6**, where Yehudah states that his eyes were turned aside by the wine.

[e] **8:2** Bathshua – In Greek, this is written in various ways all carrying a similar pronunciation to Βησουε (*Besoue*). In Armenian it appears as Բերսուե (*Bersoue*). Charles noted that all of the variants are apparently corruptions of the Hebrew 𐤁𐤕-𐤔𐤅𐤏 (*Bath-Shua*) which means "daughter of Shua." Compare Yashar **45:4**.

[f] **8:3** Bracketed section indicates reading present in some Greek, Slavonic, and Armenian texts, though absent in others. Given that the descendants of Yehudah are always traced through Perets and Zeraḥ, it is unlikely that this section is original.

from Lavan. 2 And when eighteen years were complete, in the fortieth year of my life, Esaw, the brother of my father, came upon us with a mighty and strong people. 3 And Ya'aqov struck Esaw with an arrow,[a] and he was taken up wounded on Mount Seir, and as he went he died at Anoniram. 4 And we pursued after the sons of Esaw. They had a city with walls of iron and gates of copper, and we could not enter into it, so we encamped around, and laid siege to it. 5 And when they did not open to us in twenty days, I set up a ladder in the sight of all and with my shield upon my head I went up, bearing the attack of stones, weighing close to three talents; and I killed four of their mighty men. 6 And Reuven and Gad killed six others.

7 "Then they asked us to make peace with them; and having taken counsel with our father, we received them as tributaries. 8 And they gave us five hundred cors of wheat, five hundred baths of oil, five hundred measures of wine, until the famine, when we went down into Mitsrayim." [b]

10 1 "And after these things my son Er took Tamar, of Aram-Naharayim, a daughter of Aram, as wife. 2 Now Er was wicked, and he was in need concerning Tamar, because she was not of the land of Kana'an. 3 And on the third[c] night a messenger of 𐤉𐤄𐤅𐤄 struck him. And he had not known her according to the evil deeds of his mother, for he did not wish to have children by her. 4 In the days of the wedding-feast, I gave Onan to her in marriage; and he also, in wickedness, did not know her, though he spent a year with her. 5 And when I threatened him, he went in to her, but he spilled the seed on the ground, according to the command of his mother, and he also died through wickedness. 6 And I wished to give Shelah also to her, but his mother did not permit it; for she worked evil against Tamar, because she was not of the daughters of Kana'an, as she herself was."

11 1 "And I knew that the race of the Kana'anites was wicked, but the impulse of youth blinded my mind. 2 And when I saw her pouring out wine, I was deceived because of intoxication from wine, and took her, although my father had not counselled *it.* 3 And while I was away she went and took for Shelah a wife from Kana'an. 4 And when I knew what she had done, I cursed her in the anguish of my being. 5 And she also died through her wickedness together with her sons."

12 1 "And after these things, while Tamar was a widow, she heard after two years that I was going up to shear my sheep, and adorned herself in bridal attire,[d] and sat in the city Enaim by the gate. 2 For it was a law of the Amorites, that she who was about to marry should sit in whoring seven days by the gate. 3 Therefore being drunk with wine, I did not recognize her; and her beauty deceived me, through the way she was dressed.

4 "And I turned aside to her, and said, 'Let me go in to you.' And she said, 'What will you give me?' And I gave her my staff, and my belt, and the diadem of my kingdom in pledge. 5 And I went in to her, and she conceived. And not knowing what I had done, I wished to kill her; but she secretly sent my pledges, and put me to shame. 6 And when I called her, I heard also the secret words which I spoke when lying with her in my drunkenness; and I could not kill her, because it was from 𐤉𐤄𐤅𐤄.

7 "For I said, 'Lest perhaps she did it in subtlety, having received the pledge from another woman.' 8 But I did not come near her

---

[a] **9:3** See also Yovelim **38:2** and accompanying footnote.

[b] **9** See Yovelim **38:9-13**.

[c] **10:3** Some Greek texts read δευτερα (*deu'tera*) meaning "second." Armenian texts read երկրորդում (*Erk'ror'dowm*) also meaning "second."

[d] **12:1** Bridal attire – While the narrative here offers no further details, the account given in Bereshiyt [Genesis] **38:14-19** shows that Tamar put off her "widow's garments" and covered herself with a veil.

again while I lived, because I had done this abomination in Yisra'el. 9 Moreover, they who were in the city said there was no whore in the gate, because she came from another place, and sat for a while in the gate. 10 And I thought that no one knew that I had gone in to her. 11 And after this we came into Mitsrayim to Yoseph, because of the famine. 12 And I was forty-six years old, and I lived in Mitsrayim for seventy-three years."

13 1 "And now I command you, my children, listen to Yehudah your father, and keep my sayings to perform all the ordinances of 𐤉𐤄𐤅𐤄, and to obey the commands of Elohim. 2 And do not walk after your lusts, nor in the imaginations of your thoughts in pride of heart; and do not glory in the deeds and strength of your youth, for this also is evil in the eyes of 𐤉𐤄𐤅𐤄. 3 Since I also gloried that in wars no beautiful woman's face ever tempted me, and *I* reproved Reuven my brother concerning Bilhah, the wife of my father, the spirits of jealousy and whoring arrayed themselves against me, until I lay with Bathshua the Kana'anite, and Tamar, who was given to my sons.

4 "For I said to my father-in-law, 'I will take counsel with my father, and so will I take your daughter.' But he was unwilling, and he showed me a boundless store of gold on his daughter's behalf; for he was a king. 5 And he dressed her with gold and jewels, and caused her to pour out wine for us at the banquet with the beauty of women. 6 And the wine turned my eyes aside, and pleasure blinded my heart. 7 And I became captivated *with her*, and I lay with her, and transgressed the command of 𐤉𐤄𐤅𐤄 and the command of my fathers, and I took her as wife. 8 And 𐤉𐤄𐤅𐤄 repaid me according to the imagination of my heart, and I had no joy in her children."

14 1 "And now, my children, I say to you: do not be drunk with wine, for wine turns the mind away from the truth, and inspires the passion of lust, and leads the eyes into error. 2 For the spirit of whoring has wine as an attendant to give pleasure to the mind; for these two also take away the mind of man. 3 For if a man drinks wine to drunkenness, it disturbs the mind with unclean thoughts which lead to whoring, and heats the body to fleshly union. 4 And if the cause of the lust is present, he works the sin, and is not ashamed. Such is the drunk man, my children; for he who is drunk does not respect anyone.

5 "For behold, it caused me also to err, so that I was not ashamed of the multitude in the city, in that before the eyes of all I turned aside to Tamar, and I worked a great sin, and I uncovered the covering of my sons' shame. 6 After I had drunk wine I did not respect the command of Elohim, and I took a woman of Kana'an as wife. 7 For the man who drinks wine needs much discretion, my children; and here is discretion in drinking wine: a man may drink so long as he preserves modesty. 8 But if he goes beyond this limit, the spirit of deceit attacks his mind, and it makes the drunkard to speak uncleanness, and to transgress, and not to be ashamed, but even to glory in his shame, and to think himself honorable."

15 1 "He that commits whoring is not aware when he suffers loss, and is not ashamed when put to dishonor. 2 For even though a man be a king and commit whoring, he is stripped of his kingship by becoming the slave of whoring, as I myself also suffered. 3 For I gave my staff, that is, the backbone of my tribe; and my belt, that is, my power; and my diadem, that is, the glory of my kingdom. 4 And indeed I repented of these things; I did not eat wine and meat until my old age, nor did I see any joy. 5 And the messenger of Elohim showed me that women bear rule over king and beggar alike, forever. 6 And they take away glory from the king, and might from the valiant man, and even that little which is the backbone of his poverty from the beggar."

16 1 "Observe, therefore, my children, the right limit in wine; for there are four evil spirits in it: lust, heated passion, wickedness, and greed. 2 If you drink wine in gladness, be

modest in the fear of Elohim. For if in *your*
gladness the fear of Elohim departs, then
drunkenness arises and shamelessness sneaks
in. **3** But if you want to live cautiously, do not
drink wine at all, lest you sin in words of
outrage, and in fightings and slanders, and
transgressions of the commands of Elohim, and
you die before your time. **4** Moreover, wine
reveals the mysteries of Elohim and men, even
as I also revealed the commands of Elohim and
the mysteries of Ya'aqov my father to the
Kana'anite woman Bathshua, which Elohim
told me not to reveal. [**5** And wine is a cause of
both war and confusion.][a]"

17 **1** "And now, I command you, my children,
not to love money, nor to gaze upon the beauty
of women; because of money and beauty I was
led astray to Bathshua the Kana'anite. **2** [For I
know that because of these two things my race
fall into wickedness. **3** For even wise men
among my sons will be ruined by it, and will
cause the kingdom of Yehudah to be
diminished, which 𐤉𐤄𐤅𐤄 gave me because of
my obedience to my father. **4** For I never
caused grief to Ya'aqov, my father: for all
things he commanded, I did. **5** And Yitsḥaq,
the father of my father, blessed me to be king
in Yisra'el, and Ya'aqov further blessed me in
the same manner. **6** And I know that the
kingdom will be established from me."

18 **1** "And I know what evils you will do in
the last days.][b] **2** Beware, therefore, my
children, of whoring, and the love of money,
and listen to Yehudah your father. **3** For these
things withdraw you from the Torah of Elohim,
and blind the inclination of the being. *They*
teach arrogance, and do not allow a man to
have compassion on his neighbor. **4** They rob
his being of all goodness, and oppress him with
toils and troubles, and drive away sleep from
him, and devour his flesh. **5** And he hinders the
slaughterings of Elohim, and he does not
remember the blessing of Elohim. He does not
listen to a prophet when he speaks, and resents
the words of reverence. **6** For he is a slave to
two opposing passions,[c] and cannot obey
Elohim,[d] because they have blinded his being,
and he walks in the day as if it were night."

19 **1** "My children, the love of money leads to
idolatry;[e] because, when led astray through
money, men name as elohim those who are not
elohim, and it causes him who has it to fall into
madness. **2** For the sake of money I lost my
children, and had not my repentance and my
humiliation and the prayers of my father been
accepted, I would have died childless. **3** But the
Elohim of my fathers had kindness on me,
because I did it in ignorance. **4** And the prince
of deceit blinded me, and I sinned as a man and
as flesh, being corrupted through sins; and I
learned my own weakness while thinking
myself to be invincible."

20 **1** "Therefore my children, know that two
spirits wait upon man: the spirit of truth and
the spirit of error.[f] **2** And in between is the
spirit of understanding of the mind, which
inclines wherever it wills. **3** And the works of
truth and the works of error are written on the
hearts of men, and 𐤉𐤄𐤅𐤄 knows each one of
them. **4** And there is no time at which the
works of men can be hidden, for they have
been written down on the heart itself before
𐤉𐤄𐤅𐤄. **5** And the spirit of truth witnesses all
things, and accuses all; and the sinner is burned

---

[a] **16:5** Bracketed section indicates reading present in most Greek, Slavonic, and Armenian texts. Some Greek texts do not contain this section.

[b] **17:2-18:1** Bracketed section indicates what is most likely a later Christian addition. While it is contained in nearly all relevant manuscripts, it disturbs the style and flow of the writing. Charles bracketed this section in his Greek text to denote a Christian interpolation.

[c] **18:6** See also Mattithyahu [Matthew] **6:24**.

[d] **18:6** See also Romaious [Romans] **8:6-8**; Ya'aqov [James] **4:4**.

[e] **19:1** See also Timotheon A [**1** Timothy] **6:10**; Ivrim [Hebrews] **13:5**.

[f] **20:1** See also Yoḥanan 𐤀 [**1** John] **4:5-6**.

up by his own heart, and cannot raise his face
to the judge."

21 1 "And now, my children, I command you,
love Levi, that you may stay, and do not exalt
yourselves against him, lest you be utterly
destroyed. 2 For 𐤉𐤄𐤅𐤄 gave the kingdom to me,
and the priesthood to him, and He set the
kingdom beneath the priesthood. 3 He gave the
things upon the earth to me; and the things in
the heavens to him. 4 As the heaven is higher
than the earth,[a] so is the priesthood of Elohim
higher than the earthly kingdom, unless it falls
away from 𐤉𐤄𐤅𐤄 through sin and is dominated
by the earthly kingdom.

5 "For the messenger of 𐤉𐤄𐤅𐤄 said to me,
'𐤉𐤄𐤅𐤄 chose him rather than you, to draw near
to Him, and to eat of His table and to offer Him
the first-fruits of the choice things of the sons
of Yisra'el; but you will be king of Ya'aqov.
6 And you will be among them as the sea. For
on the sea, just and unjust are tossed about:
some taken into captivity, while some are
enriched; so also will every race of men be in
you. Some will be impoverished, being taken
captive, and others grow rich by plundering the
possessions of others. 7 For the kings will be as
sea-monsters. They will swallow men like fish.
They will enslave the sons and daughters of
free men; they will plunder houses, lands,
flocks, and money. 8 They will wrongfully feed
the ravens and the cranes with the flesh of
many. And they will advance in evil, in
covetousness uplifted, and there will be false
prophets like tempests. 9 And they will
persecute all righteous men."

22 1 "And 𐤉𐤄𐤅𐤄 will bring upon them
divisions one against another. And there will
be continual wars in Yisra'el. 2 And among
men of another race my kingdom will be
brought to an end, until the salvation of
Yisra'el will come – until the appearing of the
Elohim of righteousness – that Ya'aqov [and all
the nations][b] may rest in peace. 3 And He will
guard the might of my kingdom forever. For
𐤉𐤄𐤅𐤄 swore to me with an oath that He would
not destroy the kingdom from my seed
forever."

23 1 "Now I have much grief, my children,
because of your vileness and witchcrafts, and
idolatries which you will practice against the
kingdom, following them that have familiar
spirits, diviners, and demons of error. 2 You
will make your daughters musicians and public
worshipers[c], and you will mingle in the
abominations of the nations. 3 Because of these
things 𐤉𐤄𐤅𐤄 will bring on you famine and
pestilence, death and the sword, harassing by
enemies, and revilings of friends, the slaughter
of children, the rape of wives, the plundering
of possessions, the burning of the dwelling-
place of Elohim, the laying waste of the land,
and the enslavement of yourselves among the
nations. 4 And they will make some of you
eunuchs for their wives.[d] 5 Until 𐤉𐤄𐤅𐤄 visits
you, when you repent with a perfect heart and
walk in all His commands; and He will bring
you up from captivity among the nations."

24 1 "And after these things will a star arise to
you from Ya'aqov in peace, and a man will
arise [from my seed][e], like the sun of
righteousness,[f] walking with the sons of men in
humility and righteousness. And no sin will be
found in him. 2 The heavens will be open to
him, to pour out the spirit, *even* the blessing of
the Set-apart Father. 3 And He will pour out the
spirit of favor upon you. And you will be sons
to Him in truth, and you will walk in His
commands first and last. 4 [This Branch of El

---

[a] **21:4** See also Yeshayahu [Isaiah] **55:9**.

[b] **22:2** Bracketed indicates what is most likely a later Christian interpolation. Armenian texts omit it entirely.

[c] **23:2** Public worshipers – Possible reference to pagan temple prostitutes.

[d] **23:4** Eunuchs commonly worked as bedchamber servants for wealthy women.

[e] **24:1** Bracketed section indicates what is most likely a later Christian interpolation. Armenian texts omit it entirely.

[f] **24:1** Compare Malakhi [Malachi] **4:2**.

Elyon, and this Fountain giving life to all.][a]
5 Then the scepter of my kingdom will shine
forth; and from your root will arise a stem.
6 And from it will grow a rod of righteousness
to the nations, to judge and to save all that call
upon 𐤉𐤄𐤅𐤄."

25 1 "And after these things Avraham and
Yitsḥaq and Ya'aqov will arise to life, and I
and my brothers will be rulers of the tribes of
Yisra'el: Levi first, I second, Yoseph third,
Benyamin fourth, Shimon fifth; Yissakhar
sixth, and so all in order. 2 And 𐤉𐤄𐤅𐤄 blessed
Levi; and the Messenger of the Presence
blessed me; the powers of glory *blessed*
Shimon; the heavens *blessed* Reuven; the earth
blessed Yissakhar; the sea *blessed* Zevulun; the
mountains *blessed* Yoseph; the Tabernacle
blessed Benyamin; the luminaries *blessed* Dan;
Eden *blessed* Naphtali; the sun *blessed* Gad;
the moon *blessed* Asher.

3 "And you will be the people of 𐤉𐤄𐤅𐤄, and
have one tongue. And there will be no spirit of
error of Beliyya'al, for he will be cast into the
fire forever. 4 And they who have died in grief
will arise in joy, and they who were poor for
the sake of 𐤉𐤄𐤅𐤄 will be made rich, and they
who are put to death for the sake of 𐤉𐤄𐤅𐤄 will
awake to life. 5 And the deer of Ya'aqov will
run in joyfulness, and the eagles of Yisra'el
will fly in gladness. And all the people will
glorify 𐤉𐤄𐤅𐤄 forever."

26 1 "Therefore my children, guard all the
Torah of 𐤉𐤄𐤅𐤄, for there is hope for all them
who hold fast to His ways."

2 And he said to them, "Behold, I die before
your eyes this day, a hundred and nineteen
years old.[b] 3 Do not let anyone bury me in
costly apparel, nor tear open my bowels, for
those who are kings will do this; carry me up to
Ḥevron with you."

4 And Yehudah, when he had said these things,
fell asleep; and his sons did according to all he
commanded them, and they buried him in
Ḥevron, with his fathers.

---

[a] **24:4** Bracketed section indicates what is most likely a later Christian interpolation. Some Greek and Armenian texts omit it entirely.

[b] **26:2** Yashar **62:23** records Yehudah's age as **129** at his death.

The Testament of Yissakhar, the Fifth Son of Ya'aqov and Leah.

1 1 The copy of the words of Yissakhar. For he called his sons and said to them, "Listen, my children, to Yissakhar your father; Give ear to the words of him who is beloved of 𐤉𐤄𐤅𐤄. 2 I was born the fifth son to Ya'aqov, by way of hire for the mandrakes[a]. 3 For Reuven my brother brought in mandrakes from the field, and Raḥel met him and took them. 4 And Reuven wept, and at his voice Leah my mother came forth. 5 Now these *mandrakes* were sweet-smelling apples which were produced in the land of Ḥaran below a ravine of water.

6 "And Raḥel said, 'I will not give them to you, but they will be to me instead of children. For 𐤉𐤄𐤅𐤄 despises me, and I have not borne children to Ya'aqov.'

7 "Now there were two apples; and Leah said to Raḥel, 'Is it not enough that you have taken my husband? Will you also take these?' 8 And Raḥel said to her, 'You will have Ya'aqov this night for your son's mandrakes.' 9 And Leah said to her, 'Ya'aqov is mine, for I am the wife of his youth.' 10 But Raḥel said, 'Do not boast, and do not puff yourself up; for he was betrothed to me before you, and he served our father fourteen years for me. 11 And if deception had not increased on the earth and the wickedness of men prospered, you would not see the face of Ya'aqov now. 12 You are not his wife, but you were taken to him through deception in my place. 13 My father deceived me and replaced me that night, not allowing Ya'aqov to see me. For if I had been there, this would not have happened.'

14 "Then Raḥel said, 'I will give wages to a woman for Ya'aqov for one night, in exchange for the mandrakes.' And Ya'aqov laid with Leah, and she conceived and bore me. 15 And I was called Yissakhar because of the wages."

2 1 "Then a messenger of 𐤉𐤄𐤅𐤄 appeared to Ya'aqov, saying, 'Raḥel will *only* bear two children, because she has refused intercourse with her husband, and has chosen abstinence.' 2 And had Leah my mother not paid the two apples in exchange for intercourse, she would have borne eight sons; for this reason she bore six, and Raḥel bore two; for 𐤉𐤄𐤅𐤄 visited her on account of the mandrakes. 3 For He knew that she wanted intercourse with Ya'aqov for the sake of children, and not for the lust of pleasure. 4 For she gave up Ya'aqov again the next day. Therefore, because of the mandrakes 𐤉𐤄𐤅𐤄 listened to Raḥel. 5 For though she desired them, she did not eat them, but offered them in the house of 𐤉𐤄𐤅𐤄, presenting them to the priest of the Most High who was at that time."

3 1 "Therefore, when I grew up, my children, I walked in uprightness of heart, and I became a shepherd for my father and my brothers, and I brought in fruits from the field according to their season. 2 And my father blessed me, for he saw that I walked in righteousness before him. 3 And I was not a nuisance in my doings, nor envious and malicious against my neighbor. 4 I never slandered anyone, nor did I criticize the life of any man, walking as I did in singleness of eye. 5 Therefore, when I was thirty-five years old, I took to myself a wife, for my labor wore away my strength, and I never thought about pleasure with women; but owing to my toil, sleep overcame me.

6 "And my father always rejoiced in my righteousness, because I offered – through the priest – all first-fruits to 𐤉𐤄𐤅𐤄; then to my father also. 7 And 𐤉𐤄𐤅𐤄 increased ten thousand-fold His benefits in my hands; and also Ya'aqov, my father, knew that Elohim aided my singleness. 8 For I gave good things

---

[a] 1:2 Mandrakes – In Greek this is μανδραγορους (*man'drag'or'ous*). This correlates to the Hebrew 𐤃𐤅𐤃𐤀𐤉𐤌 (*du'da'iym*). This is derived from the root 𐤃𐤅𐤃 (*dohd*) meaning "beloved." Mandrakes are sometimes translated as "love-apples." It was believed that they were actually an herb with a forked root, which was thought to aid in conception. This, then, becomes praise for Rachel, who did not eat the mandrakes (in hopes of conceiving) but rather offered them to 𐤉𐤄𐤅𐤄.

of the earth to all the poor and oppressed in the
singleness of my heart."

4 1 "And now, listen to me, my children: walk
in singleness of your heart, for I have seen in
all that is well-pleasing to 𐤉𐤄𐤅𐤄. 2 The single-
minded man does not covet gold; He does not
overreach his neighbor; He does not long after
various dainties; He does not delight in varied
apparel. 3 He does not desire to live a long life,
but only waits for the will of Elohim. 4 And the
spirits of error have no power against him, for
he does not look on the beauty of women, lest
he should pollute his mind with corruption.
5 There is no envy in his thoughts; [No malice
makes his being wither][a], nor worry with
insatiable desire in his mind. 6 For he walks in
singleness of being, and sees all things in
uprightness of heart, shunning evil eyes, *made
so* through the error of the world, lest he see
the perversion of any of the commands of
𐤉𐤄𐤅𐤄."

5 1 "Therefore my children, guard the Torah of
Elohim, and get singleness *of heart*. And walk
without deceit, not being a nuisance with the
business of your neighbor. 2 But love 𐤉𐤄𐤅𐤄 and
your neighbor, and have compassion on the
poor and weak. 3 Bow down your back to
farming, and toil in labors in all manner of
farming, offering gifts to 𐤉𐤄𐤅𐤄 with
thanksgiving. 4 For 𐤉𐤄𐤅𐤄 will bless you with
the first-fruits of the earth, even as He blessed
all the set-apart ones from Havel even until
now. 5 For no portion is given to you other
than the fatness of the earth, whose fruits are
raised by toil. 6 For our father Ya'aqov blessed
me with blessings of the earth and of first-
fruits. 7 And Levi and Yehudah were glorified
by 𐤉𐤄𐤅𐤄 even among the sons of Ya'aqov; for
𐤉𐤄𐤅𐤄 gave them an inheritance, and He gave
the priesthood to Levi, and the kingdom to
Yehudah. 8 Therefore obey them, and walk in
the singleness of your father; [for it has been
given to Gad to destroy the troops that are
coming upon Yisra'el][b]."

6 1 "Therefore my children, know that in the
last times your sons will forsake singleness *of
heart*, and will cling to insatiable desire. And
leaving innocence will draw near to malice.
And forsaking the commands of 𐤉𐤄𐤅𐤄, they
will cling to Beliyya'al. 2 And leaving farming,
they will follow after their own wicked
devices. And they will be dispersed among the
nations, and will serve their enemies. 3 And
therefore give these commands to your
children so that, if they sin, they may more
quickly return to 𐤉𐤄𐤅𐤄. 4 For He is kind, and
will deliver them, even to bring them back into
their land."

7 1 "Behold, therefore, as you see, I am a
hundred and twenty-six years old[c] and am not
conscious of committing any sin. 2 I have not
known any woman except my wife. I never
committed whoring by the uplifting of my
eyes. 3 I did not drink wine to be led astray by
it. I did not covet any desirable thing that was
my neighbor's. 4 Deceit did not arise in my
heart. No lie passed through my lips. 5 If any
man were in distress I joined my sighs with his,
and I shared my bread with the poor. I worked
reverence, and all my days I kept truth; I loved
𐤉𐤄𐤅𐤄; Likewise also every man with all my
heart.[d]

7 "So you also should do these things, my
children. And every spirit of Beliyya'al will
flee from you, and no deed of wicked men will
rule over you. And you will subdue every wild
beast, since you have the Elohim of heaven and
earth with you. Walk with men in singleness of
heart."

8 And having said these things, he commanded
his sons that they should carry him up to

[a] **4:5** Bracketed section indicates reading present in Greek and Slavonic texts but absent from Armenian.

[b] **5:8** Bracketed section indicates what is most likely a later addition or scribal error. The context seems foreign to the section, and some texts omit it.

[c] **7:1** Yashar **62:3** records Yissakhar's age as **122** at his death.

[d] **7:6** See also Vayyiqra [Leviticus] **19:18**; Devarim [Deuteronomy] **6:5**.

Ḥevron, and bury him there in the cave with
his fathers. **9** And he stretched out his feet and
died, at a good old age; with every limb sound,
and without loss of strength; he slept the
eternal sleep.

The Testament of Zevulun, the Sixth Son of Ya'aqov and Leah.

1 1 The copy of the words of Zevulun, which
he enjoined on his sons before he died in the
hundred and fourteenth year of his life,[a] two
years after the death of Yoseph.

2 And he said to them, "Listen to me, you sons
of Zevulun; attend to the words of your father.
3 I, Zevulun, was born a good gift to my
parents. For when I was born my father was
increased exceedingly, both in flocks and
herds; *this was* when he had his portion with
the striped rods. 4 I am not conscious that I
have sinned all my days, except in thought.
5 Nor yet do I remember that I have done any
lawlessness, except the sin of ignorance which
I committed against Yoseph; for I covenanted
with my brothers not to tell my father what had
been done. 6 But I wept in secret many days on
account of Yoseph, for I feared my brother,
because they had all agreed that if anyone
declared the secret, he would be killed. 7 But
when they wished to kill him, I greatly insisted
with tears not to be guilty of this sin."

2 1 "For Shimon and Gad came against
Yoseph to kill him,[b] and he said to them with
tears, 2 'Pity me, my brothers; be kind to the
bowels of Ya'aqov our father; do not lay your
hands on me to shed innocent blood, for I have
not sinned against you. 3 And if indeed I have
sinned, correct me with discipline, my brothers.
But do not lay your hand on me, for the sake of
Ya'aqov our father.' 4 And as he spoke these
words, wailing as he was speaking, I was
unable to bear his lamentations, and began to
weep, and my liver was poured out, and all the
substance of my bowels was loosened. 5 And I
wept with Yoseph, and my heart sounded, and
the joints of my body trembled, and I was not
able to stand. 6 And when Yoseph saw me
weeping with him, and them coming against
him to kill him, he fled behind me, begging
them. 7 But meanwhile Reuven arose and said,
'Come, my brothers, let us not kill him, but let
us cast him into one of these dry pits, which
our fathers dug and found no water.' 8 For
because of this 𐤉𐤄𐤅𐤄 did not allow water to
rise up in them, in order that Yoseph should be
preserved. 9 And they did so, until they sold
him to the Yishma'elites."

3 1 "For I had no share in his price, my
children. 2 But Shimon and Gad and six other
brothers took the price of Yoseph, and bought
sandals for themselves, and their wives, and
their children,[c] 3 saying, 'We will not eat of it,
for it is the price of our brother's blood, but we
will assuredly tread it under foot, because he
said that he would be king over us, and so let
us see what will become of his dreams.'
4 "Therefore it is written in the writing of the
Torah of Mosheh, that whoever will not raise
up seed to his brother, his sandal should be
removed, and they should spit in his face.[d]
5 And the brothers of Yoseph did not desire
that their brother should live, and 𐤉𐤄𐤅𐤄
removed the sandal from them, which they
wore against Yoseph their brother. 6 For when
they came into Mitsrayim they were removed
by the servants of Yoseph outside the gate, and
so they bowed to Yoseph after the fashion of
King Pharaoh. 7 And not only did they bow to
him, but were spit upon also, falling down
before him immediately; and so they were put
to shame before the Mitsrites. 8 For after this
the Mitsrites heard all the evils that they had
done to Yoseph."

4 1 "And after he was sold, my brothers sat
down to eat and drink. 2 But I, through pity for

---

[a] **1:1** This agrees with Yashar **61:3**, that Zevulun was **114** at his death.

[b] **2:1** Yashar **41:25** states that it was indeed Shimon who desired to kill Yoseph, though Gad is not mentioned.

[c] **3:2** The Jerusalem Targum (also called Pseudo-Jonathan) on Bereshiyt [Genesis] **37:28** states, "and they drew and brought up Yoseph out of the pit, and sold Yoseph to the Arabians for twenty pieces of silver; and they bought sandals of them. And they brought Yoseph to Mitsrayim."

[d] **3:4** Devarim [Deuteronomy] **25:5-10**.

Yoseph, did not eat, but watched the pit, since
Yehudah feared lest Shimon, Dan, and Gad
should rush off and kill him. **3** But when they
saw that I did not eat, they set me to watch
him, until he was sold to the Yishma'elites.
4 And when Reuven came and heard that while
he was away *Yoseph* had been sold, he tore his
garments in mourning, *and* said, 'How will I
look on the face of my father Ya'aqov?'
5 "And he took the money and ran after the
merchants, but as he failed to find them he
returned grieving. **6** But the merchants had left
the broad road and marched through the region
of the Troglodytes[a] by a shortcut. **7** But Reuven
was grieved, and did not eat food that day.
8 "Therefore Dan[b] came to him and said, 'Do
not weep, nor grieve; for we have found what
we can say to our father Ya'aqov. **9** Let us kill a
kid of the goats, and dip the coat of Yoseph in
it, and then send it to Ya'aqov, saying, "Know,
is this the coat of your son?"' And they did so.
10 For they stripped Yoseph's coat off of him
when they were selling him, and put the
garment of a slave on him. **11** Now Shimon
took the coat, and would not give it up, for he
wished to tear it with his sword, as he was
angry that Yoseph lived and that he had not
killed him. **12** Then we all rose up and said to
him, 'If you do not give up the coat, we will
say to our father that you alone did this evil
thing in Yisra'el.' **13** And so he gave it to them,
and they did even as Dan had said."

5 **1** "And now, my children, I bid you to guard
the commands of 𐤉𐤄𐤅𐤄, and to show kindness
to your neighbors, and to have compassion
towards all, not towards men only, but also
towards beasts. **2** For 𐤉𐤄𐤅𐤄 because of all these
things, and when all my brothers were sick, I
escaped without sickness, for 𐤉𐤄𐤅𐤄 knows the
purposes of each *person*. **3** Therefore, have
compassion in your hearts, my children,
because as a man does to his neighbor, even so
also will 𐤉𐤄𐤅𐤄 do to him. **4** For the sons of my
brothers were sick and dying on account of
Yoseph, because they did not show kindness in
their hearts; but my sons were preserved
without sickness, as you know. **5** And when I
was in the land of Kana'an, by the sea-coast, I
caught fish for Ya'aqov my father; and when
many were choked in the sea, I continued
unharmed."

6 **1** "I was the first to make a boat to sail upon
the sea, for 𐤉𐤄𐤅𐤄 gave me understanding and
wisdom. **2** And I let down a rudder behind it,
and I stretched a sail along another upright
piece of wood in the midst. **3** And I sailed in it
along the shores, catching fish for the house of
my father until we came to Mitsrayim. **4** [And
through compassion I shared my catch with
every stranger. **5** And if a man were a stranger,
or sick, or aged, I boiled the fish, and dressed
them well, and offered them to all men, as
every man had need, grieving with and having
compassion upon them. **6** And so 𐤉𐤄𐤅𐤄
satisfied me with abundance of fish when
catching fish; for he that shares with his
neighbor receives much more from 𐤉𐤄𐤅𐤄.][c]
7 For five years I caught fish [and gave of them
to every man whom I saw, and provided for all
the house of my father][d]. **8** And in the summer
I caught fish, and in the winter I kept sheep
with my brothers."

7 **1** ["Now I will declare to you what I did. I
saw a man in distress, being naked in winter
time, and had compassion on him, and secretly
took a garment from my father's house, and
gave it to him who was in distress. **2** Therefore
you, my children, should also do, from that

---

[a] **4:6** Troglodytes – Greek word Τρωγλοδυτων (*Trohg'lo'du'tohn*). This word is used in the Greek Septuagint (LXX) in D'vrei Ha'Yamim 𐤁 [2 Chronicles] **12:3** in place of the Hebrew 𐤎𐤊𐤉𐤉𐤌 (*Sukiim*) which is believed to mean "hut-dwellers" or "cave-dwellers."

[b] **4:8** According to Yashar **43:10** it was Yissakhar's idea, not Dan's.

[c] **6:4-6** Bracketed section indicate readings present in only a few Greek texts. Absent from other Greek, Slavonic, and Armenian texts.

[d] **6:7** Bracketed section indicates reading present in only a few Greek texts. Absent from other Greek, Slavonic, and Armenian texts.

which Elohim gives to you, show compassion
and kindness without hesitation to all men, and
give to every man with a good heart. 3 And if
you do not have the means to give to him that
is in need, have compassion for him in bowels
of kindness. 4 I know that my hand did not find
the means to give to him that needed, and I
walked with him weeping for seven furlongs,[a]
and my bowels yearned towards him in
compassion."

8 1 "Therefore, my children, you yourselves
should have compassion towards every man
with kindness, that 𐤉𐤄𐤅𐤄 also may have
compassion and kindness upon you. 2 Because
in the last days Elohim will send His
compassion on the earth, and wherever He
finds bowels of kindness He dwells in him.
3 For in the degree in which a man has
compassion upon his neighbors, in the same
degree has 𐤉𐤄𐤅𐤄 also in him.][b] 4 And when we
went down into Mitsrayim, Yoseph bore no
malice against us. 5 To the ones on guard, you
also, my children, approve yourselves without
malice, and love one another; do not set down
in account, each one of you, evil against his
brother. 6 For this breaks unity and divides all
families, and troubles the being, and wears
away the face."

9 1 "Therefore, guard the waters, and know
when they flow together, they sweep along
stones, trees, earth, and other things. 2 But if
they are divided into many streams, the earth
swallows them up, and they vanish away. 3 So
will you also be if you are divided. 4 Do not be
so, therefore, divided into two heads, for
everything which 𐤉𐤄𐤅𐤄 made has but one head,
and two shoulders, two hands, two feet, and all
the remaining members. 5 For I have learned in
the writing of my fathers, that you will be
divided in Yisra'el, and you will follow two
kings, and will work every abomination. 6 And
your enemies will lead you captive, and you
will be treated with evil among the nations,
with many infirmities and afflictions. 7 And
after these things you will remember 𐤉𐤄𐤅𐤄, and
repent, and He will cause you to return; for He
is kind and compassionate. 8 And He does not
set down evil in account to the sons of men,
because they are flesh. And the spirits of error
deceive them in all their deeds. 9 And after
these things 𐤉𐤄𐤅𐤄 Himself will arise to you,
the light of righteousness, [and healing and
compassion will be in His wings.[c] He will
redeem all the captivity of the sons of men
from Beliyya'al. And every spirit of error will
be trodden down]. 10 And He will bring back
all the nations into zeal for Him. And you will
return to your land, and you will see Him in
Yerushalayim, for His Name's sake. 11 And
again through the wickedness of your works
you will provoke Him to anger, and you will be
cast away by Him until the time of
consummation."

10 1 "And now, my children, do not grieve
that I am dying, nor be cast down because I am
coming to my end. 2 For I will rise again in the
midst of you, as a ruler in the midst of his sons;
and I will rejoice in the midst of my tribe, as
many as will guard the Torah of 𐤉𐤄𐤅𐤄, and the
commands of Zevulun their father. 3 But on the
profane, 𐤉𐤄𐤅𐤄 will bring eternal fire, and
destroy them throughout all generations. 4 But
I am now hastening away to my rest, as did
also my fathers. 5 But fear 𐤉𐤄𐤅𐤄 our Elohim
with all your strength all the days of your life."

6 And when he said these things he fell asleep,
at a good old age. And his sons laid him in a
wooden coffin. 7 And afterwards they carried
him up and buried him in Ḥevron, with his
fathers.

---

[a] **7:4** Seven furlongs ≈ **7/8** of a mile.

[b] **7:1-8:3** Bracketed section indicates readings present in only a few Greek texts. Absent from other Greek, Slavonic, and Armenian texts.

[c] **9:9** See Malakhi [Malachi] **4:2**.

The Testament of Dan, the Seventh Son of Ya'aqov and Bilhah.

1 1 The copy of the words of Dan, which he spoke to his sons in his last days, in the hundred and twenty-fifth year of his life.[a]

2 For he called together his family, and said, "Listen to my words, you sons of Dan; and pay attention to the words of your father. 3 I have proved in my heart, and in my whole life, that truth with just dealing is good and well pleasing to Elohim, and that lying and anger are evil, because they teach man all wickedness. 4 I confess, therefore, today to you, my children, that in my heart I resolved on the death of Yoseph my brother, the true and good man. 5 And I rejoiced that he was sold, because his father loved him more than us. 6 For the spirit of jealousy and arrogance said to me, 'You yourself are also his son.' 7 And one of the spirits of Beliyya'al stirred me up, saying, 'Take this sword, and kill Yoseph with it; then your father will love you, when *Yoseph* is dead.' 8 Now this is the spirit of anger that persuaded me to crush Yoseph as a leopard crushes a kid *goat*. 9 But the Elohim of my fathers did not allow him to fall into my hands, so that I should find him alone and kill him, and cause a second tribe to be destroyed in Yisra'el."

2 1 "And now, my children, behold I am dying, and I tell you of a truth, that unless you keep yourselves from the spirit of lying and of anger, and love truth and patience, you will die. 2 For anger is blindness, and does not allow one to see the face of any man with truth. 3 For though it be a father or a mother, he behaves towards them as enemies; though it be a brother, he does not know him; though it be a prophet of 𐤉𐤄𐤅𐤄, he disobeys him; though a righteous man, he does not regard him; though a friend, he does not acknowledge him. 4 For the spirit of anger encompasses him with the net of error, and blinds his eyes, and darkens his mind through lying, and gives him its own peculiar vision. 5 And how does it encompass his eyes? With hatred of heart, so as to be envious of his brother."

3 1 "For anger is an evil thing, my children, for it troubles even the being itself. 2 And it makes the body of the angry man its own, and it gains control over his being, and it gives the body power that it may work all lawlessness. 3 And when the body does all these things, the being declares what is done right, since it does not see correctly. 4 Therefore he that is angry, if he is a mighty man, has a threefold power in his anger: one by the help of his servants; a second by his wealth, with which he persuades and overcomes wrongfully; and a third, having his own natural power by which he works the evil. 5 And though the angry man be weak, yet has he a power twice that which is by nature; for anger always aids in such lawlessness. 6 This spirit goes always with lying at the right hand of Satan, that with cruelty and lying his works may be worked."

4 1 "Therefore, understand the power of anger, that it is worthless. 2 For it first of all gives provocation by word; then it strengthens him who is angry by works, and disturbs his mind with sharp losses, and so stirs up his being with great anger. 3 Therefore, when anyone speaks against you, do not be moved to anger; and if anyone praises you as set-apart men, be not uplifted; do not be moved either to delight or to disgust. 4 For first it pleases the hearing, and so makes the mind keen to perceive the grounds for provocation; and then being enraged, he thinks that he is rightly angry. 5 If you fall into any loss or ruin, my children, do not be afflicted; for this very spirit makes *one* desire that which is perishable, so that he may be enraged through the affliction. 6 And if you suffer loss voluntarily, or involuntarily, do not be frustrated; for anger with lying arises from frustration. 7 Moreover, anger with lying is twice the mischief; and they assist one another in order to disturb the heart; and when the

---

[a] **1:1** Yashar **62:2** records that Dan was **120** at his death, not **125**.

being is continually disturbed, 𐤉𐤄𐤅𐤄 departs from it, and Beliyya'al rules over it."

5 1 "Therefore, my children, guard the commands of 𐤉𐤄𐤅𐤄, and guard His Torah. Depart from anger, and hateful lying, that 𐤉𐤄𐤅𐤄 may dwell among you, and Beliyya'al may flee from you. 2 Speak truth, each one with his neighbor, so you will not fall into anger and confusion. But you will be in peace, having the Elohim of peace, so will no war prevail over you. 3 Love 𐤉𐤄𐤅𐤄 through all your life, and one another with a true heart.[a] 4 I know that in the last days you will depart from 𐤉𐤄𐤅𐤄, and you will provoke Levi to anger, and fight against Yehudah. But you will not prevail against them, for a messenger of 𐤉𐤄𐤅𐤄 will guide them both; for Yisra'el will stand by them.

5 "And whenever you depart from 𐤉𐤄𐤅𐤄, you will walk in all evil and work the abominations of the nations, going whoring after women of the lawless ones, while all the spirits of wickedness work wickedness in you. 6 [For I have read in the book of Ḥanokh, the righteous, that your prince is Satan, and that all the spirits of wickedness and pride will conspire to attend constantly on the sons of Levi, to cause them to sin before 𐤉𐤄𐤅𐤄.[b] 7 And my sons will draw near to Levi, and sin with them in all things. And the sons of Yehudah will be covetous, stealing other men's goods like lions.][c]
8 Therefore you will be led away [with them][d] into captivity, and there you will receive all the plagues of Mitsrayim, and all the evils of the nations.

9 "And so when you return to 𐤉𐤄𐤅𐤄 you will obtain kindness, and He will bring you into His set-apart place, and He will give you peace.
10 And the salvation of 𐤉𐤄𐤅𐤄 will arise to you, from the tribe of [Yehudah and of][e] Levi; and He will make war against Beliyya'al, and execute an everlasting vengeance on our enemies. 11 And He will take the captivity of [the beings of the set-apart ones][f] from Beliyya'al, and turn disobedient hearts to 𐤉𐤄𐤅𐤄, and give eternal peace to them that call upon Him. 12 And the set-apart ones will rest in Eden, and the righteous will rejoice in the New Yerushalayim, and it will be to the glory of Elohim forever. 13 And no longer will Yerushalayim endure desolation, nor Yisra'el be led captive. For 𐤉𐤄𐤅𐤄 will be in the midst of it, living among men,[g] and the Set-Apart One of Yisra'el will reign over it [in humility and in poverty; and he who believes in Him will reign among men in truth][h]."

6 1 "And now, fear 𐤉𐤄𐤅𐤄, my children, and beware of Satan and his spirits. 2 Draw near to Elohim and to the messenger that mediates for you, for He is a mediator between Elohim and man, and for the peace of Yisra'el He will stand up against the kingdom of the enemy.[i]
3 Therefore the enemy is eager to destroy all that call upon 𐤉𐤄𐤅𐤄. 4 For he knows that on the day on which Yisra'el repents, the kingdom of the enemy will be brought to an end. 5 For the very messenger of peace will strengthen Yisra'el, that it will not fall into the destiny of evil. 6 And it will be in the time of the lawlessness of Yisra'el, that 𐤉𐤄𐤅𐤄 will not depart from them, but will transform them into a nation that does His will, for none of the

---

[a] **5:3** See also Vayyiqra [Leviticus] **19:18**; Devarim [Deuteronomy] **6:5**.

[b] **5:6** No known reference is found in Ḥanokhian writings. However, here Satan is referred to as Dan's prince, possibly in connection with Yirmeyahu [Jeremiah] **8:16-17**. Dan is also omitted from the list of "sealed tribes" found in Hit'galut [Revelation] **7:4-8**.

[c] **5:6-7** Bracketed section indicates readings present in some Greek, Slavonic, and Armenian texts, but absent from others. Charles believed this to be an interpolation.

[d] **5:8** This section is present in the same texts mentioned in footnote b. Charles considered this, too, to be an interpolation.

[e] **5:10** See footnote d.

[f] **5:11** Bracketed section indicates what is most likely a later Christian interpolation.

[g] **5:13** Compare Testament of Yehudah **24:1**.

[h] **5:13** Bracketed section indicates what is most likely a later Christian interpolation.

[i] **6:1** See also Ya'aqov [James] **4:8**; Timotheon A [1 Timothy] **2:5**.

messengers will be equal to him. 7 And His
Name will be in every place in Yisra'el, and
among the nations. 8 Therefore, guard
yourselves, my children, from every evil work,
and cast away anger and all lying, and love
truth and patience.

9 "And the things which you have heard from
your father, also impart to your children [that
the Savior of the nations may receive you; for
He is true and patient, humble and lowly, and
teaches the Torah of Elohim by His works][a].
10 Depart, therefore, from all unrighteousness,
and cling to the righteousness of Elohim, and
your race will be saved forever. And bury me
near my fathers."

7 1 And when he had said these things he
kissed them, and fell asleep at a good old age.
2 And his sons buried him. And after that they
carried up his bones, and placed them near
Avraham, and Yitsḥaq, and Ya'aqov.
3 [Nevertheless, Dan prophesied to them that
they would forget their Elohim, and would be
alienated from the land of their inheritance and
from the race of Yisra'el, and from the family
of their seed.][b]

[a] **6:9** Bracketed section indicates what is most likely a later Christian interpolation.

[b] **7:3** See footnote at **5:6**.

The Testament of Naphtali, the Eighth Son of Ya'aqov and Bilhah.

1 1 The copy of the testament of Naphtali,
which he ordained at the time of his death in
the hundred and thirtieth year of his life.[a]
2 When his sons were gathered together in the
seventh month, on the first day of the month,
while still in good health, he made them a
Feast of food and wine.

3 And after he was awake in the morning, he
said to them, "I am dying;" and they did not
believe him. 4 And as he glorified 𐤉𐤄𐤅𐤄, he
grew strong and said that after the Feast of the
previous day he would die.

5 And he began then to say, "Hear, my
children, you sons of Naphtali; hear the words
of your father. 6 I was born from Bilhah, and
because Raḥel dealt craftily, and gave Bilhah
in place of herself to Ya'aqov, and she
conceived and bore me upon Raḥel's knees;
therefore she called my name Naphtali. 7 For
Raḥel loved me very much because I was born
upon her lap; and when I was still young she
desired to kiss me, and said, 'May I have a
brother of yours from my own womb, like you.'

8 "And Yoseph was like me in all things,
according to the prayers of Raḥel. 9 Now my
mother was Bilhah, daughter of Rotheus, the
brother of Devorah, the nurse of Rivqah, who
was born on the same day as Raḥel. 10 And
Rotheus was of the family of Avraham, a
Kaldean, who feared Elohim; *he was* born free,
and noble. 11 And he was taken captive and
was freed by Lavan; and he gave him Ḥanah[b]
his handmaid as wife, and she bore a daughter,
and called her name Zilpah, after the name of
the village in which he had been taken captive.
12 And next she bore Bilhah[c], saying, 'My
daughter quickly goes after renewed things, for
as soon as she was born, she seized the breast
and hurried to nurse on it.' 13 [...When
Ya'aqov, my father, came fleeing to Lavan
away from Esaw his brother, and when...the
father of Bilhah, my mother. And Lavan led
Ḥanah, my mother's mother, and her two
daughters with him; and he gave one to Leah,
and the other to Raḥel. And since Raḥel did not
bear any sons, she was given to Ya'aqov my
father. And as he was given Bilhah, my
mother, she bore my brother Dan, and
myself.][d]"

2 1 "And I was swift on my feet like the deer,
and my father Ya'aqov appointed me for all
messages, and as a deer did he give me his
blessing.[e] 2 For as the potter knows the vessel,
how much it needs to contain, and brings clay
in the right amount, so also does 𐤉𐤄𐤅𐤄 make
the body after the likeness of the spirit, and He
implants the spirit according to the capacity of
the body. 3 And the one does not fall short of
the other by *the length of* one-third of a hair;
for by *such* weight, and measure, and rule was
all the creation made. 4 And as the potter
knows the use of each vessel, what it is made
for, so also 𐤉𐤄𐤅𐤄 knows the body, how far it
will persist in goodness, and when it begins in
evil. 5 For there is no inclination or thought
which 𐤉𐤄𐤅𐤄 does not know, for He created
every man after His own image. 6 As a man's
strength, so also is his work; and as his mind,
so also is his skill; and as his purpose, so also
is his achievement; and as his heart, so also is
his mouth; as his eye, so also is his sleep; as his
being, so also is his word, either in the Torah
of 𐤉𐤄𐤅𐤄 or in the works of Beliyya'al.

7 "And as there is a division between light and
darkness, between seeing and hearing, so also

[a] **1:1** Yashar **62:24** records Naphtali's age as **132**, not **130**.

[b] **1:11** Ḥanah – Name of Rotheus' wife. Greek spellings widely vary, usually presenting the name Euna, or Enan. I have restored this name to Ḥanah based on a Hebrew fragment of the Testament of Naphtali found among the Dead Sea Scrolls. Here it is spelled 𐤇𐤍𐤄.

[c] **1:12** The name Bilhah (𐤁𐤋𐤄𐤄) derives from the root word 𐤁𐤄𐤋 (*ba'hal*) meaning "to hasten, to hurry" often in the sense of amazement.

[d] **1:12** Bracketed section indicates text found in the Hebrew fragment, but absent from Greek, Slavonic, and Armenian texts. The ellipses (...) represent portions of the text that is either damaged or otherwise not readable.

[e] **2:1** See Bereshiyt [Genesis] **49:21**.

is there a division between man and man, and between woman and woman; and it is not to be said that the one is like the other either in face or in mind. **8** For Elohim made all things good in their order: the five senses in the head, the joining of the neck to the head; adding to it the hair also for beauty and glory,[a] then the heart for understanding, the gut for excrement, and the stomach for *grinding*, the windpipe for taking in *breath*, the liver for anger, the gall for bitterness, the spleen for laughter, the thighs for prudence, the muscles of the loins for power, the lungs for drawing in *breath*, the loins for strength, and so forth. **9** So then, my children, let all your works be done in order with good intent in the fear of Elohim, and do nothing disorderly in scorn or out of its due season. **10** For if you tell the eye to hear, it cannot; so neither while you are in darkness can you do the works of light." [b]

3 **1** "Therefore do not be eager to corrupt your doings through covetousness or with worthless words to deceive your beings; for if you keep silence in purity of heart, you will understand how to hold fast to the will of Elohim, and to cast away the will of Beliyya'al. **2** Sun and moon and stars do not change their order;[c] so you also do not change the Torah of Elohim in the disorder of your doings. **3** The nations went astray, and forsook 𐤉𐤄𐤅𐤄, and changed their order, and obeyed wood and stone, spirits of error. **4** But you will not be so, my children, recognizing in the expanse *of the heavens*, in the earth, and in the sea, and in all created things, 𐤉𐤄𐤅𐤄 who made all things, that you will not become like Sodom, which changed the order of nature. **5** In the same way the Watchers also changed the order of their nature,[d] so 𐤉𐤄𐤅𐤄 cursed them at the flood; on account of them He made the earth without inhabitants and fruitless."

4 **1** "I say these things to you, my children, for I have read in the writing of Ḥanokh that you yourselves will also depart from 𐤉𐤄𐤅𐤄, walking according to all the lawlessness of the nations, and you will do according to all the wickedness of Sodom. **2** And 𐤉𐤄𐤅𐤄 will bring captivity upon you, and you will serve your enemies there, and you will be bowed down with every affliction and trial, until 𐤉𐤄𐤅𐤄 consumes you all. **3** And after you have become reduced and made few, you will return and acknowledge 𐤉𐤄𐤅𐤄 your Elohim; and He will bring you back into your land, according to His abundant kindness. **4** And it will be, that after that they come into the land of their fathers, they will forget 𐤉𐤄𐤅𐤄 again, and become profane. **5** And 𐤉𐤄𐤅𐤄 will scatter them upon the face of all the earth, until the compassion of 𐤉𐤄𐤅𐤄 comes: a man working righteousness and kindness to all them that are afar off,[e] and to them that are near."

5 **1** "For in the fortieth year of my life, I saw a vision on the Mount of Olives, on the east of Yerushalayim; the sun and the moon were standing still. **2** And behold Yitsḥaq, the father of my father, said to us, 'Run and lay hold of them, each one according to his strength; and the sun and moon will belong to the one who seizes them.'

3 "And all of us ran together, and Levi laid hold of the sun, and Yehudah caught the moon, and they were both exalted with them. **4** And when Levi became as a sun, behold, a certain young man gave him twelve branches of palm *trees*; and Yehudah was bright as the moon, and under their feet were twelve rays. **5** [And the two, Levi and Yehudah, ran, and laid hold of the others.][f]

6 "And *behold,* a bull upon the earth, with two great horns, and an eagle's wings upon its back;

---

[a] **2:8** Compare Mishle [Proverbs] **16:31**; **20:29**; Korinthious A [**1** Corinthians] **11:15**.
[b] **2:10** See Yoḥanan [John] **12:35**; Romaious [Romans] **13:12-13**.
[c] **3:2** Compare Yirmeyahu [Jeremiah] **31:35**.
[d] **3:5** See Yovelim **7:21-25**; Ḥanokh **6** & **7**.
[e] **4:5** See also Yirmeyahu [Jeremiah] **31:10-11**.
[f] **5:5** Bracketed section is most likely an accidental repeat of verse **3** through dittography.

and we tried to seize him, but could not. 7 But
Yoseph came, and seized him, and ascended up
with him on high. 8 And I saw, for I was there,
and behold a set-apart writing appeared to us,
saying, 'Ashuwrites[a], Medes, Parsites[b],
Kaldeans, Arameans: *these* will possess the
twelve tribes of Yisra'el in captivity.'" [c]

6 1 "And again, after seven days[d], I saw our
father Ya'aqov standing by the sea of Yavneel,
and we were with him. 2 And behold, there
came a ship sailing by, without sailors or pilot;
and written on the ship was, 'The Ship of
Ya'aqov.'

3 "And our father said to us, 'Come, let us
embark on our ship.' 4 And when he had gone
on board, there arose a violent storm, and a
mighty tempest of wind; and our father, who
was holding the helm, departed from us. 5 And
we, being tossed with the tempest, were carried
along over the sea; and the ship was filled with
water, *being* pounded by mighty waves, until it
was broken up. 6 And Yoseph fled away upon
a little boat, and we were all divided upon nine
planks, and Levi and Yehudah were together.
7 And we were all scattered to the ends of the
earth. 8 Then Levi, dressed in sackcloth, prayed
to 𐤉𐤄𐤅𐤄 for us all. 9 And when the storm
ceased, the ship reached the land as it were in
peace. 10 And our father came, and we all
rejoiced with one accord."

7 1 "I told these two dreams to my father, and
he said to me, 'These things must be fulfilled in
their season, after Yisra'el endures many
things.'

2 "Then my father said to me, 'I believe Elohim
that Yoseph lives, for I see that 𐤉𐤄𐤅𐤄 always
numbers him with you.' 3 And he said,
weeping, 'O, my son Yoseph, you live, though
I do not see you, and you do not see Ya'aqov
that brought you forth.'

4 He caused me also, therefore, to weep by
these words, and I burned in my heart to
declare that Yoseph had been sold, but I feared
my brothers."

8 1 "And see, my children, I have shown you
the last times, how everything will come to
pass in Yisra'el. 2 Therefore, charge your
children that they be united to Levi and to
Yehudah. For through them will salvation arise
to Yisra'el, and in them will Ya'aqov be
blessed. 3 For through their tribes will Elohim
appear dwelling among men on earth, to save
the race of Yisra'el, and to gather together the
righteous from among the nations. 4 If you
work that which is good, my children, both
men and messengers will bless you, and
Elohim will be glorified among the nations
through you, and the devil will flee from you,
and the wild beasts will fear you, and 𐤉𐤄𐤅𐤄
will love you, [and the messengers will cling to
you][e].

5 "As a man who has trained a child well is
kept in kindly remembrance, so also for a good
work there is a good remembrance before
Elohim. 6 But him that does not do that which
is good, both messengers and men will curse,
and Elohim will be dishonored among the
nations through him, and the devil will make
him as his own peculiar instrument, and every
wild beast will rule him, and 𐤉𐤄𐤅𐤄 will hate

---

[a] **5:8** Ashuwrites – Generally translated as "Assyrians."

[b] **5:8** Parsites – Generally translates as "Persians."

[c] **5** The entirety of chapter **5** is reminiscent of Daniel **10-11**. Similarly, the nations mentioned here are written out of chronological order. The Ashuwrites came in first to take away the Northern Kingdom, then Ten Tribes of Yisra'el. After this the Kaldeans (Babylonians) came in took away the Southern Kingdom of Yehudah. After this the Medo-Parsite empire came in, followed by the Greeks. The Greek empire later split into two kingdoms, the Ptolemies of Mitsrayim and Seleukids of Aram (Syria). The Hasmonean (Maccabean) dynasty arose during the time of these two kingdoms. The two horns of the bull may be indicative of this split.

[d] **6:1** Some Greek and Slavonic texts read "months" instead of "days" here.

[e] **8:4** Bracketed section indicates what is most likely a later Christian interpolation. Charles noted that while all but one of his texts did include this reading, the preceding line finished a proper stanza. Adding this line disrupted the flow.

him. 7 For the commands of the Torah are
twofold, and through carefulness they must be
fulfilled. 8 For there is a season for a man to
embrace his wife, and a season to abstain from
it for his prayer.[a] 9 So, then, there are two
commands; and, unless they be done in due
order, they bring very great sin upon men. So
also is it with the other commands.
10 Therefore be wise in Elohim, my children,
and prudent, understanding the order of His
commands, and every word of the Torah, that
𐤉𐤄𐤅𐤄 may love you."

9 1 And when he had charged them with many
such words, he exhorted them that they should
remove his bones to Ḥevron, and that they
should bury him with his fathers. 2 And when
he had eaten and drunken with a merry heart,
he covered his face and died. 3 And his sons
did according to all that Naphtali their father
had commanded them.

---

[a] **8:8** see Korinthious A [1 Corinthians] **7:4-5**.

The Testament of Gad the Ninth Son of Ya'aqov and Zilpah.

1 1 The copy of the testament of Gad, the things he spoke to his sons, in the hundred and twenty fifth year of his life,[a] saying to them: "2 Listen, my children, I was the ninth son born to Ya'aqov, and I was valiant in keeping the flocks. 3 Accordingly I guarded the flock at night; and whenever the lion came, or the wolf, or any wild beast against the fold, I pursued it, and overtaking *it*, I seized its foot with my hand and hurled it about a stone's throw, and so killed it.

4 "Now Yoseph my brother was feeding the flock with us for nearly thirty days, and being young, he fell sick by reason of the heat. 5 And he returned to Ḥevron to our father, who made him lie down near him, because he loved him greatly. 6 And Yoseph told our father that the sons of Zilpah and Bilhah were killing the best of the flock and eating them against the judgment of Reuven and Yehudah. 7 For he saw that I had delivered a lamb out of the mouth of a bear, and put the bear to death; but had killed the lamb, being grieved concerning it that it could not live, and that we had eaten it. 8 And I was angry with Yoseph because of this until the day that he was sold. And the spirit of hatred was in me, and I did not want to hear Yoseph with *my* ears, or see him with *my* eyes, because he rebuked us to our faces saying that we were eating of the flock without Yehudah. 9 For whatever things he told our father, he believed him."

2 1 "I confess now my sin, my children, that oftentimes I desired to kill him, because I hated him from my heart. 2 Moreover, I hated him yet more for his dreams; and I desired to lick him up from the land of the living, even as an ox licks up the grass of the field. 3 Therefore Shimon and I sold him to the Yishma'elites [for thirty pieces of gold, and ten of them we hid, and showed the twenty to our brothers][b]. 4 And thus through covetousness we were bent on killing him. 5 And the Elohim of my fathers delivered him from my hands, that I would not work lawlessness in Yisra'el."

3 1 "And now, my children, listen to the words of truth to work righteousness, and all the Torah of the Most High, and go not astray through the spirit of hatred, for it is evil in all the doings of men. 2 Whatever a man does, the one who hates sees him as abominable; and though a man works the Torah of 𐤄𐤅𐤄𐤉, he does not praise him; though a man fears 𐤄𐤅𐤄𐤉, and takes pleasure in that which is righteous, he does not love Him. 3 He dispraises the truth, he envies him that prospers, he welcomes evil-speaking, he loves arrogance, for hatred blinds his being; as I also then looked on Yoseph."

4 1 "Therefore my children, beware of hatred; for it works lawlessness even against 𐤄𐤅𐤄𐤉 Himself. 2 For it will not hear the words of His commands concerning the loving of one's neighbor, and it sins against Elohim. 3 For if a brother stumbles, it delights immediately to proclaim it to all men, and is urgent that he should be judged for it, and be punished and be put to death. 4 And if it be a servant it stirs him up against his master, and with every affliction he devises against him, if perhaps he can be put to death, for hatred works with envy also against those that prosper; so long as it hears of or sees their success, it always languishes.

6 "For as love would quicken even the dead, and would call back them that are condemned to die, so hatred would kill the living, and those that had sinned not leading to death, it would not allow to live.[c] 7 For the spirit of hatred works together with Satan, through hastiness of spirit, in all things to men's death;

---

[a] **1:1** Yashar **62:5** agrees with the Gad being **125** at his death.

[b] **2:3** Bracketed section indicates reading present in most Greek, Slavonic, and Armenian texts, but absent from other Greek texts.

[c] **4:6** See Yoḥanan 𐤀 [1 John] **5:15-18**.

but the spirit of love works together with the
Torah of Elohim in patience to the salvation of
men.[a]"

5 1 "Therefore, hatred is evil, for it constantly
mates with lying, speaking against the truth;
and it makes small things to be great, and
causes the light to be darkness, and calls the
sweet bitter,[b] and teaches slander, and kindles
wrath, and stirs up war, and violence and all
covetousness; it fills the heart with evils and
devilish poison. 2 Therefore, I say these things
to you from experience, my children, that you
may drive hatred away, which is of the devil,
and cling to the love of Elohim.
3 Righteousness casts out hatred, humility
destroys envy. For he that is just and humble is
ashamed to do what is unjust, being reproved
not by another, but by his own heart, because
𐤉𐤄𐤅𐤄 looks on his inclination. 4 He does not
speak against a set-apart man, because the fear
of Elohim overcomes hatred. 5 For fearing lest
he should offend 𐤉𐤄𐤅𐤄, he will not do wrong to
any man, even in thought.

6 "These things I learned at last, after I had
repented concerning Yoseph. 7 For true
repentance after a reverent sort destroys
ignorance, and drives away the darkness, and
enlightens the eyes, and gives knowledge to the
being, and leads the mind to salvation. 8 And
those things which it has not learned from man,
it knows through repentance. 9 For Elohim
brought a disease of the liver upon me; and had
not the prayers of Ya'aqov my father preserved
me, it had hardly failed but my spirit had
departed. 10 For in the way a man transgresses,
by the same also is he punished. 11 Therefore,
since my liver was set mercilessly against
Yoseph, I suffered mercilessly in my liver, and
was judged for eleven months, for so long a
time as I had been angry against Yoseph."

6 1 "And now, my children, I exhort you, love
each one his brother, and put away hatred from
your hearts; love one another in deed, and in
word, and in the inclination of the being. 2 For
in the presence of my father I spoke peaceably
to Yoseph, and when I had gone out, the spirit
of hatred darkened my mind, and stirred up my
being to kill him. 3 Therefore, love one another
from the heart; and if a man sins against you,
cast forth the poison of hate and speak
peaceably to him, and in your being do not
hold cunning; and if he confess and repent,
forgive him. 4 But if he denies it, do not get
into a passion with him, lest catching the
poison from you, he takes to swearing and so
you sin doubly. 5 [Do not let another man hear
your secrets when engaged in legal strife, lest
he come to hate you and become your enemy,
and commit a great sin against you; for many
times he addresses you cunningly or keeps
himself busy about you with wicked intent.][c]
And though he denies it, and yet have a sense
of shame when reproved, give over reproving
him. 6 For he who denies may repent so as not
to wrong you again; yes, he may also honor
you, and fear, and be at peace with you. 7 And
if he be shameless and persist in his wrong-
doing, even so forgive him from the heart, and
leave the avenging to Elohim."

7 1 "If a man prospers more than you, do not
be frustrated, but pray for him, that he may
have perfect prosperity. 2 For so it is useful for
you. And if he is further exalted, do not be
envious of him, remembering that all flesh will
die; and offer praise to Elohim, who gives
things good and profitable to all men. 3 Seek
out the judgments of 𐤉𐤄𐤅𐤄, and your mind will
rest and be at peace. 4 And though a man
become rich by evil means, even as Esaw, the
brother of my father *was*, do not be jealous; but
wait for the end from 𐤉𐤄𐤅𐤄. 5 For if He takes
away *from a man* wealth gained by evil means,
He forgives him if he repents, but the
unrepentant is reserved for eternal punishment.

[a] **4:7** See Romaious [Romans] **13:10**; Kepha 𐤁 [2 Peter] **3:15**.

[b] **5:1** See Yeshayahu [Isaiah] **5:20**.

[c] **6:5** Bracketed section indicates what is most likely a later Christian interpolation. Charles noted that this section completely breaks up the flow of the text, going from denial to legal strife back to denial.

6 For the poor man, if free from envy, pleases
𐤉𐤄𐤅𐤄 in all things, and is blessed beyond all
men, because he does not have the travail of
vain men. 7 Therefore, put away jealousy from
your beings, and love one another with
uprightness of heart."

8 1 "Therefore, also tell these things to your
children, that they honor Yehudah and Levi,
for from them will 𐤉𐤄𐤅𐤄 raise up salvation to
Yisra'el. 2 [For I know that at the last your
children will depart from Him, and will walk in
all wickedness, and affliction and corruption
before 𐤉𐤄𐤅𐤄.][a]"

3 And when he had rested for a little while, he
said again, "My children, obey your father, and
bury me near to my fathers." 4 And he drew up
his feet, and fell asleep in peace. 5 And after
five years they carried him up to Ḥevron, and
laid him with his fathers.

---

[a] **8:2** Bracketed section indicates what is most likely a later Christian interpolation.

The Testament of Asher, the Tenth Son of Ya'aqov and Zilpah.

1 1 The copy of the Testament of Asher, the
things he spoke to his sons in the hundred and
twenty-fifth year of his life.[a]

2 For while he was still in health, he said to
them, "Listen, you children of Asher, to your
father, and I will declare to you all that is
upright in the sight of 𐤉𐤄𐤅𐤄.

3 "Elohim has given the sons of men two ways,
and two inclinations, and two kinds of action,
and two methods, and two issues.[b] 4 Therefore
all things are by twos, one against the other.
5 For there are two ways of good and evil, and
with these are the two inclinations in our
breasts deciding between them. 6 Therefore if
the being takes pleasure in good, all its actions
are in righteousness; and if it sins, it quickly
repents. 7 For having its thoughts set upon
righteousness, and casting away wickedness, it
quickly overthrows the evil, and uproots the
sin. 8 But if it inclines to the evil inclination, all
its actions are in wickedness, and it drives
away the good, and clings to the evil, and is
ruled by Beliyya'al; even though it works what
is good, he perverts it to evil. 9 For whenever it
begins to do good, he forces the issue of the
action into evil for him, seeing that the treasure
of the inclination is filled with an evil spirit."

2 1 "A man, then, may help the good with
words for the sake of the evil, yet the issue of
the action leads to mischief. 2 There is a man
who shows no compassion on him who serves
his turn in evil; and this thing has two sides,
but the whole is evil. 3 And there is a man that
loves the worker of evil, because he would
prefer even to die in evil for his sake; and
concerning this it is clear that it has two sides,
but the whole is an evil work. 4 Though indeed
he has love, yet he who conceals what is evil
for the sake of the good name is wicked; but
the end of the action tends to evil. 5 Another
steals, does unjustly, plunders, defrauds, and
still pities the poor: this too has two sides, but
the whole is evil. 6 He who defrauds his
neighbor provokes Elohim, and swears falsely
against the Most High, and yet pities the poor.
He considers 𐤉𐤄𐤅𐤄, who commanded the
Torah, as nothing, and provokes, and yet he
refreshes the poor. 7 He defiles the being, and
makes the body happy; he kills many, and
pities few: this, too, has two sides, but the
whole is evil. 8 Another commits adultery and
whoring, and abstains from meats, and when he
fasts he does evil, and by the power of his
wealth overcomes many; and despite his
excessive wickedness he does the commands:
this, too, has two sides, but the whole is evil.
9 Such men are as hares; equally clean in part,
but in very deed are unclean. 10 For Elohim has
declared this in the tables of the commands."

3 1 "But you, my children, do not wear two
faces like them, of goodness and of
wickedness; but cling to goodness only, for
Elohim has His dwelling there, and men desire
it. 2 But flee away from wickedness, destroying
the *evil* inclination by your good works; for
they that are double-faced do not serve Elohim,
but their own lusts, so that they may please
Beliyya'al and men like themselves."

4 1 "For good men, even they that are of one
face, though they be thought by them that are
double-faced to sin, are just before Elohim.
2 For many, in killing the wicked, do two
works, of good and evil; but the whole is good,
because he has uprooted and destroyed that
which is evil. 3 One man hates the kind and
unjust man, and the man who commits adultery
and *the one who* fasts: this, too, has two sides,
but the whole work is good, because he follows
the example of 𐤉𐤄𐤅𐤄, in that he does not accept
what appears good as what is genuinely good.
4 Another desires not to see a good day with

---

[a] **1:1** Yashar **62:4** states that Asher was **123** at his death.

[b] **1:3** See Devarim [Deuteronomy] **30**. Similarly, the late first-century CE book called Didache (also called "The Teaching of the Twelve Apostles") states in Didache **1:1**, "There are two Ways, one of Life and one of Death, and there is a great difference between the two Ways."

them that riot, lest he defile his body and pollute his being: this, too, is double-faced, but the whole is good. **5** For such men are like stags and deer, because similar to wild animals they appear to be unclean, but they are altogether clean; because they walk in zeal for 𐤉𐤄𐤅𐤄 and abstain from what Elohim also hates and forbids by His commands, warding off the evil from the good."

5 **1** "You see, my children, how there are two *sides* in all things: one against the other; and the one is hidden by the other: in wealth *is hidden* covetousness, in hospitality *is hidden* drunkenness, in laughter *is hidden* grief, in marriage *is hidden* licentiousness. **2** Death succeeds to life, dishonor to glory, night to day, and darkness to light; [and all things are under the day, just things under life, unjust things under death;][a] so also eternal life wards off death. **3** It may not be said that truth is a lie, nor that right is wrong; for all truth is under the light, even as all things are under Elohim. **4** All these things, therefore, I proved in my life, and I did not wander from the truth of 𐤉𐤄𐤅𐤄. And I searched out the commands of the Most High, walking according to all my strength, single-mindedly in that which is good."

6 **1** "Therefore, my children, guard the commands of 𐤉𐤄𐤅𐤄, following the truth single-mindedly. **2** For they that are double-minded are guilty of double sin; for they both do the evil thing, and they have pleasure in them that do it, following the example of the spirits of error, and striving against mankind.

3 "Therefore you, my children, guard the Torah of 𐤉𐤄𐤅𐤄, and do not pay attention to evil as to good; but look to the thing that is really good, and guard it in all *the* commands of 𐤉𐤄𐤅𐤄, speaking of them, and resting in them. **4** For the latter ends of men show their righteousness, when they meet the messengers of 𐤉𐤄𐤅𐤄 and of Satan. **5** For when the being departs troubled, it is tormented by the evil spirit which also it served in lusts and evil works. **6** But if he is peaceful he meets the messenger of peace with joy, and he leads him into eternal life."

7 **1** "My children, do not become as Sodom, which sinned against the messengers of 𐤉𐤄𐤅𐤄, and perished forever. **2** For I know that you will sin, and be delivered into the hands of your enemies; and your land will be made desolate, and your set-apart places destroyed, and you will be scattered to the four corners of the earth. **3** And you will be set at nothing in the dispersion, vanishing away as water, until the Most High visits the earth, coming Himself [as man, with men eating and drinking,][b] and breaking the head of the dragon in the water. He will save Yisra'el and all the nations [Elohim speaking in the person of man][c]. Therefore you also, my children, tell these things to your children, that they do not disobey Him. **5** For I have known that you will surely be disobedient, and surely act profanely, not guard the Torah of Elohim, but *instead* the commands of men,[d] being corrupted through wickedness. **6** And therefore you will be scattered, as Gad and Dan my brothers, and you will not know your lands, tribe, and tongue. **7** But 𐤉𐤄𐤅𐤄 will gather you together in faith through His kindness, and for the sake of Avraham, Yitsḥaq, and Ya'aqov."

8 **1** And when he had said these things to them he commanded them, saying, "Bury me in Ḥevron." **2** And he fell asleep and died at a good old age. And his sons did as he had commanded them, and they carried him up to Ḥevron, and buried him with his fathers.

---

[a] **5:2** Bracketed section indicates reading present in some Greek and Slavonic, but absent from others, and Armenian.

[b] **7:3** Bracketed section indicates what is most likely a later Christian interpolation.

[c] **7:3** Bracketed section indicates what is most likely a later Christian interpolation.

[d] **7:5** Compare Mattithyahu [Matthew] **15**; Markos [Mark] **7**.

The Testament of Yoseph, the Eleventh Son of Ya'aqov and Raḥel.

1 1 The copy of the Testament of Yoseph.
When he was about to die he called his sons
and his brothers together, and said to them,
2 "My brothers and my children, listen to
Yoseph the beloved of Yisra'el; give ear, my
sons, to your father. 3 I have seen in my life
envy and death, yet I did not go astray, but
pressed on in the truth of 𐤉𐤄𐤅𐤄.

4 "My brothers here hated me, but 𐤉𐤄𐤅𐤄 loved
me. They desired to kill me, but the Elohim of
my fathers guarded me. They let me down into
a pit, and the Most High brought me up again.
5 I was sold into slavery, and the Master of all
made me free. I was taken into captivity, and
His strong hand supported me. I was
overwhelmed with hunger, and 𐤉𐤄𐤅𐤄 Himself
nourished me. 6 I was alone, and Elohim
comforted me. I was sick, and 𐤉𐤄𐤅𐤄 visited
me. I was in prison, and my Elohim showed
favor to me. *I was* in bonds, and He released
me. *I was* slandered, and He pleaded my cause.
I was bitterly spoken against by the Mitsrites,
and He delivered me. *I was* envied by my
fellow-slaves, and He exalted me."

2 1 "And this chief captain of Pharaoh
entrusted his house to me. 2 And I struggled
against a shameless woman, urging me to
transgress with her; but the Elohim of Yisra'el
my father delivered me from the burning
flame. 3 I was cast into prison, I was beaten, I
was mocked; but 𐤉𐤄𐤅𐤄 allowed me to find
kindness in the eyes of the keeper of the prison.
4 For 𐤉𐤄𐤅𐤄 does not forsake them that fear
Him; not in darkness, nor in bonds, nor in
afflictions, nor in necessities. 5 For Elohim is
not put to shame as a man, nor is He afraid as a
son of man, nor is He weak or scared as one
that is earth-born. 6 But in all those things He
gives protection, and He comforts in many
ways. *Though* for a little while He departed, so
as to try the inclination of the being. 7 In ten
trials He showed me approved, and I endured
them all. For endurance is a great medicine,
and patience gives many good things."

3 1 "How often did the Mitsrite woman
threaten me with death! How often did she give
me over to punishment, and then call me back
and threaten me. 2 And when I was unwilling
to lie with her, she said to me, 'You will be my
master, and all that is in my house, if you will
give yourself to me, and you will be our ruler.'
3 But I remembered the words of my father,
and going into my chamber, I wept and prayed
to 𐤉𐤄𐤅𐤄. 4 And I fasted in those seven years,
and I looked to the Mitsrites like one living
delicately, for they that fast for the sake of
Elohim receive beauty of face.

5 "And if my master were away from home, I
drank no wine; nor for three days did I take my
food, but I gave it to the poor and sick. 6 And I
sought 𐤉𐤄𐤅𐤄 early, and I wept for the Mitsrite
woman of Noph, for she troubled me
unceasingly; and also at night she came to me
under pretense of visiting me. 7 And because
she had no male child she pretended to regard
me as a son, and so I prayed to 𐤉𐤄𐤅𐤄, and she
bore a male child. 8 And for a time she
embraced me as a son, and I did not know it;
but later, she sought to draw me into whoring.
9 And when I perceived it I wept unto death;
and when she had gone out, I came to myself,
and lamented for her many days, because I
recognized her cunning and her deceit. 10 And
I declared the words of the Most High to her, if
only she would turn from her evil lust."

4 1 "Therefore she often flattered me with
words as a set-apart man, and praised my self-
control cunningly in her talk before her
husband, while desiring to ensnare me when
we were alone. 2 For she praised me openly for
self-control, and in secret she said to me, 'Do
not fear my husband, for he is persuaded
concerning your self-control. For even should
one tell him concerning us, he would not
believe.'

3 "Because all these things I lay upon the
ground, and sought Elohim, that 𐤉𐤄𐤅𐤄 would
deliver me from her deceit. 4 And when
nothing she tried worked, she came again to me

under the plea of instruction, that she might learn the word of Elohim.

5 "And she said to me, 'If you desire that I should leave my idols, lie with me, and I will persuade my husband to depart from his idols, and we will walk in the Torah of 𐤉𐤄𐤅𐤄.' 6 And I said to her, '𐤉𐤄𐤅𐤄 does not desire that those who reverence Him should be unclean, nor does He take pleasure in them that commit adultery, but in those that approach Him with a pure heart and undefiled lips.'

7 "But she held her peace, longing to accomplish her evil desire. 8 And I fasted and prayed even more, that 𐤉𐤄𐤅𐤄 would deliver me from her."

5 1 "And again, at another time she said to me, 'If you will not commit adultery then I will kill my husband by poison, and take you to be my husband.' 2 Therefore, when I heard this, I tore my garments, and said to her, 'Woman, fear Elohim, and do not do this evil deed, lest you be destroyed. Know indeed, therefore, that I will declare your plan to all men.' 3 Therefore she was afraid, and sought that I would not declare this plan. 4 And she departed, soothing me with gifts, and sending to me every delight of the sons of men."

6 1 "And afterwards she sent me food mixed with enchantments. 2 And when the eunuch who brought it came, I looked up and saw a terrible man giving me a sword with the dish, and I perceived that *her* scheme was to entice me. 3 And when he had gone out I wept, and did not taste that or any other of her food. 4 So then after one day she came to me and observed the food, and said to me, 'Why have you not eaten the food?'

5 "And I said to her, 'Because you filled it with deadly enchantments. I told you before: I do not come near to idols, but only to 𐤉𐤄𐤅𐤄. 6 Now therefore know that the Elohim of my father has revealed your wickedness to me by His messenger, and I have kept it to convict you, if perhaps you might see and repent. 7 But perhaps you may learn that the wickedness of the profane has no power over them that worship Elohim with self-control; behold I will take it and eat before you.'

8 "And having said this, I prayed, *saying*, 'The Elohim of my fathers and the messenger of Avraham, be with me;' and I ate. 8 And when she saw this she fell upon her face at my feet, weeping; and I raised her up and reproved her, and she promised not to commit this lawlessness any more."

7 1 "But her heart was still set upon evil, and she looked around how to ensnare me, and sighing deeply she became downcast, though she was not sick. 2 And when her husband saw her, he said to her, 'Why is your face fallen?' And she said to him, 'I have a pain in my heart, and the groanings of my spirit oppress me;' and so he comforted her who was not sick.

3 "Then, seizing the opportunity, she rushed to me while her husband was still outside, and said to me, 'I will hang myself, or cast myself over a cliff, if you will not lie with me.' 4 And when I saw the spirit of Beliyya'al was troubling her, I prayed to 𐤉𐤄𐤅𐤄, and said to *the woman*, 5 'Why, wretched woman, are you troubled and disturbed, blinded through sins? Remember that if you kill yourself, Asteho, your husband's concubine and your rival, will beat your children, and you will destroy your memory from off the earth.'

6 "And she said to me, 'See then, you do love me. Let this be enough for me: only strive for my life and my children, and I expect that I will enjoy my desire also.'

7 "But she did not know that I spoke this way because of my master, and not because of her. 8 For if a man falls before the passion of a wicked desire and becomes enslaved by it, even as she *was*, whatever good thing he may hear with regard to that passion, he views through the lens of his wicked desire."

8 1 "Therefore my children, I declare to you, that it was about the sixth hour when she departed from me; and I knelt before 𐤉𐤄𐤅𐤄 all day, and all the night; and about dawn I rose up, weeping the whole time and praying for a release from her. 2 At last, then, she laid hold of my garments, forcibly dragging me to have intercourse with her.

3 "Therefore, when I saw that in her madness she was holding tightly to my garment, I left it behind, and fled away naked. 4 And holding fast to the garment she falsely accused me, and when her husband came he cast me into prison in his house; and on the next day he scourged me and sent me into Pharaoh's prison. 5 And when I was in bonds, the Mitsrite woman was oppressed with grief, and she came and heard how I gave thanks to 𐤉𐤄𐤅𐤄 and sang praises in the dwelling of darkness, and rejoiced with a glad voice, glorifying my Elohim that I was delivered from the lustful desire of the Mitsrite woman."

9 1 "And she sent to me often, saying, 'Agree to fulfill my desire and I will release you from your bonds, and I will free you from the darkness.' And I did not incline to her even in thought. 2 For Elohim loves him who, in a den of wickedness, combines fasting with self-control, rather than the man who combines luxury with license in kings' chambers. 3 And if a man lives in self-control, and also desires glory, and the Most High knows that it is beneficial for him, He gives this also to *men, and* to me. 4 How often, though she were sick, did she come down to me at times she was not sought, and listened to my voice as I prayed! 5 And when I heard her groanings I held my peace. For when I was in her house she revealed her arms, breasts, and legs, that I might lie with her; for she was very beautiful, splendidly adorned in order to entice me. 6 And 𐤉𐤄𐤅𐤄 guarded me from her devices."

10 1 "Therefore, my children, you see how patience works great things, and prayer *too* with fasting. 2 So you also – if you follow after self-control and purity, with patience and prayer, with fasting in humility of heart – 𐤉𐤄𐤅𐤄 will dwell among you, because He loves self-control. 3 And wherever the Most High dwells, even though envy, or slavery, or slander happens, 𐤉𐤄𐤅𐤄 who dwells in him, for the sake of his self-control not only delivers him from evil, but also exalts him even as me. 4 For in every way the man is lifted up, whether in deed, or in word, or in thought. 5 My brothers knew how my father loved me, and yet I did not exalt myself in my mind; although I was a child, I had the fear of Elohim in my heart. 6 For I knew that all things would pass away, and I did not raise myself *against them* with evil intent, but I honored my brothers; and out of respect for them, even when I was being sold, I refrained from telling the Yishma'elites that I was a son of Ya'aqov, a great man and a mighty."

11 1 "Therefore my children, you also have the fear of Elohim in all your works before your eyes, and honor your brothers. For everyone who does the Torah of 𐤉𐤄𐤅𐤄 will be loved by Him. 2 And when I came to the slave-market with the Yishma'elites, they asked me, saying, 'Are you a slave?' And I said that I was a home-born slave, so that I would not put my brothers to shame. 3 And the eldest of them said to me, 'You are not a slave, for even your appearance proves that.' But I said that I was their slave.

4 "Now when we came into Mitsrayim they strove concerning me, which of them should buy me and take me. 5 Therefore it seemed good to all that I would remain in Mitsrayim with the merchant of their trade, until they returned with their merchandise. 6 And 𐤉𐤄𐤅𐤄 gave me favor in the eyes of the merchant, and he entrusted to me his house. 7 And Elohim blessed him on account of me, and increased him in gold and silver and in household servants. 8 And I was with him three months and five days."

12 1 "And about that time the Nophite woman, the wife of Potiphar, came down in a chariot, with great splendor, because she had heard from her eunuchs concerning me. 2 And she told her husband that the merchant had become rich by means of a young Hebrew, and they say that he had surely been stolen out of the land of Kana'an.

3 "'Now, therefore, render justice to him, and take away the youth to your house; so will the Elohim of the Hebrews bless you, for favor from heaven is upon him.'"

13 1 "And Potiphar was persuaded by her words, and commanded the merchant to be brought, and said to him, 'What is this that I hear concerning you, that you steal people out of the land of Kana'an, and sell them for slaves?' 2 But the merchant fell at his feet, and begged him, saying, 3 'Please, my master, I do not know what you are saying.' 4 And Potiphar said to him, 'Where, then, is the Hebrew slave from?' And he said, 'The Yishma'elites entrusted him to me until they return.'

4 "But he did not believe him; rather, *he* commanded him to be stripped and beaten. And when he persisted in this statement, Potiphar said, 'Let the youth be brought.' 5 And when I was brought in, I bowed down to Potiphar, for he was third in rank of the officers of Pharaoh. 6 And he took me apart from him, and said to me, 'Are you a slave, or *are you* free?' 7 And I said, 'A slave.' And he said, 'Whose?' And I said, 'The Yishma'elites.' 8 And he said, 'How did you become their slave?' And I said, 'They bought me out of the land of Kana'an.' 9 And he said to me, 'Truly you lie;' and immediately he commanded me to be stripped and beaten."

14 1 "Now the Nophite woman was looking through a window at me while I was being beaten, for her house was near, and she sent to him saying, 'Your judgment is unjust; for you punish a free man who has been stolen, as though he were a transgressor.' 2 And when I made no change in my statement, though I was beaten, he ordered me to be imprisoned, 'Until,' he said, 'the owners of the boy return.'

3 "And the woman said to her husband, 'Why do you detain the captive and well-born boy in bonds, who should instead be set free, and be waited upon?' 4 For she wanted to see me out of a desire of sin, but I was ignorant concerning all these things. 5 And he said to her, 'It is not the custom of the Mitsrites to take that which belongs to others before proof is given.' 6 He said this concerning the merchant. 'But as for the boy, he must be imprisoned.'"

15 1 "Now after twenty-four days the Yishma'elites returned; for they had heard that Ya'aqov my father was mourning much concerning me. 2 And they came and said to me, 'Why did you tell us that you were a slave? Behold, we have learned that you are the son of a mighty man in the land of Kana'an, and your father still mourns for you in sackcloth and ashes.' 3 When I heard this my bowels were dissolved and my heart melted, and I desired greatly to weep, but I restrained myself, that I would not put my brothers to shame. 4 And I said to them, 'I do not know, I am a slave.'

5 Therefore they took counsel to sell me, that I should not be found in their hands. For they feared my father, lest he should come and execute a grievous vengeance upon them. For they had heard that he was mighty with Elohim and with men. 6 Then the merchant said to them, 'Release me from the judgment of Potiphar.' 7 And they came and requested me, saying, 'Say that you were bought by us with money, and he will set us free.'"

16 1 "Now the Nophite woman said to her husband, 'Buy the youth, for I hear,' she said, 'that they are selling him.' 2 And immediately she sent a eunuch to the Yishma'elites, and asked them to sell me. 3 But since the eunuch would not agree to buy me *at their price* he returned, having tried them; and he told his mistress that they asked a large price for their slave. 4 And she sent another eunuch, saying, 'Even if they demand two minas, give it to them. Do not spare the gold, only buy the boy, and bring him to me.' 5 The eunuch therefore went and gave them eighty pieces of gold, and he received me. But he told the Mitsrite woman, 'I paid a hundred *pieces of gold*.' 6 And

though I knew *this* I held my peace, lest the
eunuch should be put to shame."

17 1 "Therefore my children, you see what
great things I endured that I would not put my
brothers to shame. 2 Therefore you also should
love one another, and hide one another's faults
with patience. 3 For Elohim delights in the
unity of brothers,[a] and in the purpose of a heart
that takes pleasure in love. 4 And when my
brothers came into Mitsrayim they learned that
I had returned their money to them, and did not
rebuke them, and comforted them. 5 And after
the death of Ya'aqov my father I loved them
more abundantly, and all things he commanded
I did very abundantly for them. 6 And I did not
allow them to be afflicted in *even* the smallest
matter; and all that was in my hand I gave to
them. 7 And their children were my children,
and my children as their servants; and their life
was my life, and all their suffering was my
suffering, and all their sickness was my
infirmity. 8 My land was their land, and their
counsel my counsel. And I did not exalt myself
among them in arrogance because of my
worldly glory, but I was as one of the least
among them."

18 1 "Therefore, walk in the commands of
𐤉𐤄𐤅𐤄, my children, and He will exalt you
there, and will bless you with good things
forever and ever. 2 And if anyone seeks to do
evil to you, do good to him, and pray for him,
and you will be redeemed by 𐤉𐤄𐤅𐤄 from all
evil. 3 For, behold, you see that out of my
humility and patience I took as wife the
daughter of the priest of On. And a hundred
talents of gold were given me with her, and
𐤉𐤄𐤅𐤄 made them[b] serve me. 4 And He also
gave me beauty as a flower beyond the
beautiful ones of Yisra'el; and He preserved me
to old age in strength and in beauty, because I
was like in all things to Ya'aqov."

19 1 "Therefore, hear my vision which I saw.
2 I saw twelve deer feeding, and nine of them
were dispersed. Now three were preserved, but
on the following day they also were dispersed.
[3 And I saw that the three deer became three
lambs, and they cried to 𐤉𐤄𐤅𐤄, and He brought
them forth into a flourishing and well-watered
place; yes He brought them out of darkness
into light. 4 And there they cried to 𐤉𐤄𐤅𐤄 until
the nine deer gathered together to them, and
they became as twelve sheep, and after a little
time they increased and became many flocks.

5 "And after these things I saw and behold,
twelve bulls were nursing from one cow, which
produced a sea of milk, and the twelve flocks
and innumerable herds drank from it. 6 And the
horns of the fourth bull went up to heaven and
became as a wall for the flocks, and in the
midst of the two horns there grew another horn.
7 And I saw a heifer which surrounded them
twelve times, and it became a perfect help to
the bulls.][c]

8 "And I saw that a virgin was born from
Yehudah, wearing a linen shawl, and a spotless
lamb was born from her. There was something
like a lion on his left, and all the wild animals
rushed against him, but the lamb overcame and
destroyed them, trampling them underfoot.
9 The messengers, and men, and all the earth
rejoiced because of him. 10 These things will
take place in the last days. 11 Therefore my
children, guard the commands of 𐤉𐤄𐤅𐤄. Honor
Levi and Yehudah, because [the Lamb of
Elohim – who will take away the sin of the
world –][d] will arise from their seed, and will
save all the nations, and Yisra'el. 12 For his
kingdom is an eternal kingdom that will not
pass away. My kingdom will come to an end

[a] **17:3** See Tehillim [Psalms] **133:1**.

[b] **18:3** That is, the Mitsrites.

[c] **19:3-7** This large bracketed section is found only in the Armenian version. Similarly, when the Greek and Slavonic picks back up at verse **8**, it differs widely from the Armenian in **8-12**. I have chosen to give preference to the Greek and Slavonic reading, when it is available. However, the Armenian version is included as Appendix E, to give the reader both variants.

[d] **19:11** Bracketed section indicates what is most likely a later Christian interpolation.

among you, as a guard in an orchard, who
vanishes at the end of the summer."

20 1 "For I know that after my death the
Mitsrites will afflict you, but Elohim will
avenge you, and will bring you into that which
He promised to your fathers. 2 But you will
carry up my bones with you; for when my
bones are being taken up there, 𐤉𐤄𐤅𐤄 will be
with you in light, and Beliyya'al will be in
darkness with the Mitsrites. 3 And carry up
Asenath your mother to the Hippodrome[a], and
bury her near Raḥel your mother."

4 And when he had said these things he
stretched out his feet, and died at a good old
age. 5 And all Yisra'el mourned for him, along
with all Mitsrayim, with a great mourning.
6 And when the children of Yisra'el went out of
Mitsrayim, they took the bones of Yoseph with
them, and they buried him in Ḥevron with his
fathers, and the years of his life were one
hundred and ten years.

---

[a] **20:3** Hippodrome – A sort of outdoor theater where chariot races took place.

The Testament of Benyamin, the Twelfth Son of Ya'aqov and Raḥel

1 1 The copy of the words of Benyamin, which he commanded his sons to observe, after he had lived a hundred and twenty-five years.

2 And he kissed them, and said, "As Yitsḥaq was born to Avraham in his old age, so also was I *born* to Ya'aqov. 3 And since Raḥel my mother died in giving birth to me, I had no milk; therefore I was nursed by Bilhah her handmaid. 4 For Raḥel remained barren for twelve years after she had borne Yoseph; and she prayed to 𐤉𐤄𐤅𐤄 with fasting for twelve days, and she conceived and bore me. 5 For my father loved Raḥel dearly, and prayed that he might see two sons born from her. 6 Therefore I was called Benyamin, that is, a son of days[a]."

2 1 "And when I went into Mitsrayim, to Yoseph, and my brother recognized me, he said to me, 'What did they tell my father when they sold me?' 2 And I said to him, 'They smeared your coat with blood and sent it, and said, "Know whether this is your son's coat."'

3 "And Yoseph said to me, 'Even so, brother, the Kana'anite merchants stole me by force. 4 And it happened that as they went on their way they concealed my garment, as though a wild beast had met me and killed me. 5 And so their associates sold me to the Yishma'elites. 6 And they did not lie in saying this.' For he wished to hide my brothers' deeds from me. And he called his brothers to him and said, 7 'Do not tell my father what you have done to me, but tell him as I have told Benyamin. And let the thoughts among you be such, and do not let these things come to the heart of my father.'"

3 1 "Therefore my children, love 𐤉𐤄𐤅𐤄 Elohim of heaven and earth, and guard His commands, following the example of the good and set-apart man Yoseph. 2 And let your mind be for good, even as you know me; for he that has his mind right sees all things rightly. 3 Fear 𐤉𐤄𐤅𐤄, and love your neighbor; and even though the spirits of Beliyya'al claim you to afflict you with every evil, they will not have dominion over you, even as they did not have it over Yoseph my brother. 4 How many men desired to kill him, and Elohim shielded him! For he that fears Elohim and loves his neighbor cannot be struck by the spirit of Beliyya'al, being shielded by the fear of Elohim. 5 Nor can he be ruled over by the device of men or beasts, for he is helped by 𐤉𐤄𐤅𐤄 through the love which he has towards his neighbor.

6 "For Yoseph also begged our father that he would pray for his brothers, that 𐤉𐤄𐤅𐤄 would not impute sin to them, for whatever evil they had done to him. 7 And thus Ya'aqov cried out, 'My good child, you have prevailed over the bowels of your father Ya'aqov.' 8 And he embraced him, and kissed him for two hours, saying, 'In you the prophecy of heaven [concerning the Lamb of Elohim, and Savior of the world][b] will be fulfilled, that a blameless one will be delivered up for lawless men, and a sinless one will die for unrighteous men [in the blood of the covenant. 9 For the salvation of the nations and of Yisra'el, and will destroy Beliyya'al and his servants][c].

4 1 "Therefore, my children, do you see the end of the good man? Be followers of his compassion, therefore, with a good mind, that you also may wear crowns of glory. 2 For the good man does not have a dark eye; for he shows kindness to all men, even though they are sinners. 3 And though they evil concerning him, he overcomes evil by doing good, being

---

[a] **1:6** Benyamin does not mean "son of days." Rather, it means "son of [my] right hand." However, this may be a reference to Bereshiyt [Genesis] **44:20**, where Benyamin is called the son of Ya'aqov's old age.

[b] **3:8** Bracketed section indicates what is most likely a later Christian interpolation. Armenian texts omit this section.

[c] **3:8-9** Bracketed section indicates what is most likely a later Christian interpolation. Armenian texts omit this section.

shielded by Elohim, and he loves the righteous as his own being. **4** If anyone is glorified, he does not envy him; if anyone is rich, he is not jealous; if anyone is valiant, he praises him; he exalts the virtuous man; he shows kindness to the poor man; he has compassion on the weak; he sings praises to Elohim.

5 "As for the one who has the fear of Elohim, he protects him as with a shield; he helps the one that loves Elohim; he rebukes and turns back the one that rejects the Most High; and he loves as his own being the one that has the kindness of a good spirit."

5 **1** "Therefore, if you also have a good mind, then both wicked men will be at peace with you, and the wasteful will reverence you and turn to good; and the covetous will not only cease from their excessive desire, but even give the objects they covet to those that are afflicted. **2** If you do well, even the unclean spirits will flee from you; and the beasts will dread you. **3** For where there is reverence for good works and light in the mind, even darkness flees away from him. **4** For if anyone does violence to a set-apart man, he repents; for the set-apart man is kind to his reviler, and holds his peace. **5** And if anyone betrays a righteous man, the righteous man prays, though for a little *while* he is humbled, yet not long after *that* he appears far more glorious, as Yoseph my brother was."

6 **1** "The inclination of the good man is not in the power of the error of the spirit of Beliyya'al, for the messenger of peace guides his being. **2** And he does not gaze passionately upon corruptible things, nor does he gather together riches through a desire of pleasure. **3** He does not delight in pleasure; [he does not grieve for his neighbor][a]; he does not satisfy himself with luxuries; he does not err in the uplifting of the eyes; 𐤉𐤄𐤅𐤄 is his portion. **4** The good inclination receives neither glory nor dishonor from men, and it does not know any treachery, or lie, or fighting or reviling; for 𐤉𐤄𐤅𐤄 dwells in him and lights up his being, and he rejoices towards all men always.

5 "The good mind does not have two tongues, *one* of blessing and *one* of cursing; *one* of contempt and *one* of honor; *one* of sorrow and *one* of joy; *one* of quietness and *one* of confusion; *one* of hypocrisy and *one* of truth; *one* of poverty and *one* of wealth; but it has one disposition, uncorrupt and pure, concerning all men. **6** It has no double sight, nor double hearing; for in everything which he does, or speaks, or sees, he knows that 𐤉𐤄𐤅𐤄 looks on his being. **7** And he cleanses his mind that he may not be condemned by men as well as by Elohim. **8** And in the same way, the works of Beliyya'al are twofold, and there is no singleness in them."

7 **1** "Therefore, my children, I tell you: flee from the malice of Beliyya'al. For he gives a sword to them that obey him. **2** And the sword is the mother of seven evils. First, the mind conceives through Beliyya'al, and first there is bloodshed; second *is* ruin; third *is* affliction; fourth *is* exile; fifth *is* famine; sixth *is* panic; seventh *is* destruction. **3** Therefore Qayin was also delivered over to seven vengeances by Elohim, for in every hundred years 𐤉𐤄𐤅𐤄 brought one plague upon him. **4** And when he was two hundred years old he began to suffer, and in the nine-hundredth year he was destroyed. For on account of Havel his brother, he was judged with all the evils; but Lamekh with seventy times seven. **5** Because those who are like Qayin, *who are* envious and hate their brothers forever, *they* will be punished with the same judgment."

8 **1** "And you, my children, flee evil-doing, envy, and hatred of brothers, and cling to goodness and love. **2** He that has a pure mind in love, does not look at a woman with eyes to whoring; for he has no defilement in his heart, because the Ruaḥ of Elohim rests on him. **3** For

---

[a] **6:3** Bracketed section indicates what is most likely a later Christian interpolation.

as the sun is not defiled by shining on dung and
mire – but rather dries up both and drives away
the evil smell – so also the pure mind – though
surrounded by the defilements of the earth –
instead cleanses *them*, and is not defiled itself."

9 1 "And I believe that there will be also evil-
doings among you, from the words of Ḥanokh
the righteous:[a] that you will commit whoring
with the whoring of Sodom, and will perish, all
but a few, and will renew cruel deeds with
women. And the kingdom of 𐤉𐤄𐤅𐤄 will not be
among you, for immediately He will take it
away. 2 Nevertheless the Temple of Elohim
will be in your portion, and the last *Temple* will
be more glorious than the first. And the twelve
tribes will be gathered together there, and all
the nations, until the Most High sends forth His
salvation in the visitation of an only-begotten
prophet. 3 [And He will enter into the first
Temple, and there will the Master be treated
with outrage, and He will be lifted up on a tree.
4 And the veil of the Temple will be torn, and
the Ruaḥ of Elohim will pass on to the nations
as fire pours forth. 5 And He will ascend from
Sheol and will pass from earth into heaven.
And I know how lowly He will be upon earth,
and how glorious in heaven.][b]"

10 1 "Now when Yoseph was in Mitsrayim, I
longed to see his figure and the form of his
face; and through the prayers of Ya'aqov my
father I saw him, while awake in the daytime,
even his entire figure exactly as he was."
2 And after he had said these things, he said to
them, "Therefore my children, know that I am
dying. 3 So do truth and righteousness each one
to his neighbor, and judgment to confirmation,
and guard the Torah of 𐤉𐤄𐤅𐤄 and His
commands. 4 For I leave you these things
instead of inheritance. Therefore, also give
them to your children for an everlasting
possession; for Avraham, and Yitsḥaq, and
Ya'aqov did likewise. 5 For all these things
they gave us for an inheritance, saying, 'Guard
the commands of Elohim, until 𐤉𐤄𐤅𐤄 reveals
His salvation to all nations.'

6 "And then will you see Ḥanokh, and Noaḥ,
and Shem, and Avraham, and Yitsḥaq, and
Ya'aqov, rising on the right hand in gladness.
7 Then will we also rise, each one over our
tribe, worshipping the King of heaven, [who
appeared upon earth in the form of a man in
humility. And as many as believe on Him on
the earth will rejoice with Him][c]. 8 Then also
all men will rise, some to glory and some to
shame.[d] And 𐤉𐤄𐤅𐤄 will judge Yisra'el first, for
their unrighteousness; [for when He appeared
as Elohim in the flesh to deliver them they did
not believe Him][e]. 9 And then will He judge all
the nations, [as many as did not believe Him
when He appeared on earth][f]. 10 And He will
convict Yisra'el through the chosen ones of the
nations, even as He reproved Esaw through the
Midianites, who deceived[g] their brothers, [so
that they fell into whoring, and idolatry; and
they were alienated from Elohim][h], becoming
children in the portion of those who fear 𐤉𐤄𐤅𐤄.
11 Therefore my children, if you walk set-apart
according to the commands of 𐤉𐤄𐤅𐤄, you will
dwell securely again with me, and all Yisra'el

---

[a] **9:1** Exact reference to words of Ḥanokh is unknown.

[b] **9:3-5** Bracketed section indicates a rather obvious Christian interpolation. The Armenian version varies widely in these verses, thus they have been included in Appendix E.

[c] **10:7** Bracketed section indicates what is most likely a later Christian interpolation.

[d] **10:8** See Daniel **12:2**.

[e] **10:8** Bracketed section indicates what is most likely a later Christian interpolation. Armenian texts omit this section.

[f] **10:9** Bracketed section indicates what is most likely a later Christian interpolation. Armenian texts omit this section.

[g] **10:10** Armenian (and a single Greek) texts read "loved" here instead of deceived. Charles noted that it is actually more likely to be an original reading, and the bracketed section following (footnote h) was most likely added to explain this deception. In Greek, the word απατησασιν (*apa'tes'asin*) meaning "to deceive" is a corruption of αγαπησασιν (*aga'pes'asin*) meaning "to love."

[h] **10:10** Bracketed section indicates what is most likely a later Christian interpolation. Armenian texts omit this section.

will be gathered to 𐤉𐤄𐤅𐤄."

11 1 "And I will no longer be called a
ravening wolf on account of your ravages,[a] but
a worker of 𐤉𐤄𐤅𐤄, distributing food to them
that work what is good. 2 And there will rise up
from my seed in the latter times one beloved of
𐤉𐤄𐤅𐤄, hearing His voice on the earth, and a
doer of the good pleasure of His will,
enlightening all the nations with new
knowledge, even the light of knowledge,
bursting in upon Yisra'el for salvation and
tearing it away from them like a wolf, and
giving it to the synagogue of the nations.
3 Until the end of the age, he will be in the
synagogues of the nations, and among their
rulers, as a strain of music in the mouth of all.
4 And he will be inscribed in the set-apart
books, both his work and his word, and he will
be a chosen one of Elohim forever. And
through them he will go to and fro as Ya'aqov
my father, saying, 'He will fill up that which
lacks of your tribe'." [b]

12 1 And when he finished his words, he said,
"I command you, my children, to carry up my
bones out of Mitsrayim, and bury me at
Ḥevron, near my fathers."

2 So Benyamin died a hundred and twenty-five
years old, at a good old age, and they placed
him in a coffin. 3 And in the ninety-first year
from the entrance of the children of Yisra'el
into Mitsrayim, they and their brothers brought
up the bones of their fathers secretly during the
Kana'anite war; and they buried them in
Ḥevron, by the feet of their fathers. 4 And they
returned from the land of Kana'an and dwelled
in Mitsrayim until the day of their departure
from the land of Mitsrayim.

---

[a] **11:1** See Bereshiyt [Genesis] **49:27**.

[b] **11** Chapter **11** varies widely in among Greek, Slavonic, and Armenian texts. The majority of Greek and Slavonic texts read as I have rendered above. In these texts, the individual most likely refers to Sha'ul the Shaliaḥ (Apostle Paul). Some Greek texts state that the prophesied man to come is form the lines of Levi and Yehudah, not from Benyamin himself, thus more likely pointing to Messiah. The Armenian version diverges heavily, and is greatly truncated. The Armenian version's reading in included in Appendix E.

Appendix A
Explanatory Notes

Aram-Naharayim. Aram-Naharayim is the transliteration of the Hebrew 𐤀𐤓𐤌 (*aram*) meaning "Aram" and 𐤍𐤄𐤓𐤉𐤌 (*na'ha'ra'yim*) meaning "rivers." This literally means "Aram *between* rivers." It is usually rendered as "Mesopotamia" because of its Greek name, Μεσοποταμια (*Meso'po'tamia*) from the Greek words μεσος (*mesos*) meaning "middle" or "between" and ποταμος (*po'ta'mos*) meaning "river." This refers to a geographic area usually called "the fertile crescent" including the land between the Tigris and Euphrates rivers.

Being. The Hebrew (and Aramaic) word 𐤍𐤐𐤔 (*nephesh*) is almost universally rendered as "soul" for most translations. It has also been rendered as "being" in this publication. This is true of *nephesh* and its Greek counterpart, ψυχη (*psuche*), which carries the same meaning. It should be noted, however, that these words are separate from the words for "spirit" in both Hebrew and Greek (see entry **Ruaḥ**). Simply put, humans are souls (beings), and have a spirit. In Ethiopic it is a bit more difficult, as the word used for being [soul] is the same word used for spirit: ነፍስ (*na'fas*). This is a cognate to the Hebrew *nephesh*.

Beliyya'al. The Hebrew word 𐤁𐤋𐤉𐤏𐤋 (*beliy'ya'al*) is a combination of the Hebrew words 𐤁𐤋𐤉 (*beli*) which means "without" and 𐤉𐤏𐤋 (*ya'al*) meaning "profit, worth." It often appears in the phrase "son of Beliyya'al" which is normally translated as "worthless man." However, translated literally it should read as, "son of worthlessness." For this publication, however, I have simply rendered it as "Beliyya'al." In the Greek texts, such as Testaments, it often appears written as Βελιαρ (*Beliar*) which is, itself, a corruption of the Hebrew.

Messenger. The word "angel" has been replaced with the more accurate and appropriate "messenger." The Hebrew (and Aramaic) word in question is 𐤌𐤋𐤀𐤊 (*malakh*), the Greek is αγγελος (*angelos*), and the Ethiopic is መልአክ (*ma'la'k*), all meaning "messenger." These words can be applied both to men (eg. Yehoshua [Joshua] 6:17 and Loukas [Luke] 7:24) and heavenly messengers (eg. Shemoth [Exodus] 3:2 and Mattithyahu [Matthew] 1:20). As such, in order to keep a consistent translation, all instances have been rendered as "messenger."

Naḥash. The Hebrew word 𐤍𐤇𐤔 (*na'chash*) is most often rendered "serpent." The word is derived from the word *nawchash* (same word, different vowels) which means "divination." The association is most likely due to the "hiss" of whispering a spell, in connection with the noise a serpent makes. However, it is also etymologically connected to the word 𐤍𐤇𐤔𐤕 (*ne'cho'sheth*) meaning "copper." The connection with copper is believed to be on account of it being a metal used in divination, or possibly the "ringing" sound of copper resembling the "hiss" or "whisper" mentioned in the use of divination.

Regardless, the exact classification of animal (serpent, snake, etc.) is unknown, and thus has been transliterated in Genesis Retold.

Nations. The Hebrew word rendered "nation" is 𐤂𐤅𐤉 (*goy*) and literally means "nation." It is usually used in the plural form *goyim*, which is "nations." Strictly defined, it refers to anyone that is not a Yisra'elite.

The Greek word rendered "nation" is εθνος (*ethnos*) and means the same as its Hebrew counterpart. This word is generally translated as "Gentile" but I have chosen a more literal translation.

New. In Hebrew, there is a word meaning "new" and a word meaning "to renew" which are both spelled 𐤇𐤃𐤔 (*chadash*). However, in Greek, there are two different words: Νεος (*neos*) and Καινος (*Kainos*). *Neos* means "new" in the sense of being young, never-seen-before. *Kainos* means "fresh, renewed." While most translators use the two words interchangeably, I have chosen to differentiate between them. So when something has been translated from Greek (most in Testaments) and the word "renewed" is encountered, it is because in Greek the word used is *Kainos*. If it reads "new" then the word is *Neos*.

New Moon. The Hebrew word 𐤇𐤃𐤔 (*chodesh*) is usually rendered as "month." However, the word itself is derived from the word *chadash* (see entry **New**) meaning "new." As such, the word is more accurately translated as "renewal." There is also the Hebrew word ירח (*yeraḥ*) which does mean "moon." In order to keep the translation consistent, *chodesh* has been translated as "new moon" throughout, since it specifically carries the connotation of a renewal cycle; *yeraḥ* has been translated as "month." Note that this applies when the source text is Hebrew, primarily in Yashar.

Ruaḥ. The word "spirit" has been left alone in many cases. However, whenever it applies directly to יהוה, it is rendered as "Ruaḥ." רוח (*Ruaḥ*) means "spirit," "breath," or "wind." Thus, to differentiate between just a "spirit" and the Set-apart Spirit of יהוה, it is rendered as the transliterated form "Ruaḥ." It should also be noted that in the Greek writings, the word πνευμα (*pneuma*) is used, but is rendered as spirit or Ruaḥ depending on what (or whom) it is applied to.

Set-apart. The common English rendering of "Holy" has been changed to "Set-apart." The Hebrew (and Aramaic) word commonly rendered as "Holy" is קדוש (*qadosh*) and means literally "set-apart." While "Holy" is usually defined as "something dedicated to God" the meaning of *qadosh* is slightly different. The Greek word in question is ἅγιος (*hagios*) and means the same as *qadosh*. In Ethiopic, this word is ቅዱስ (*k'dusa*) which is a cognate to the Hebrew *qadosh*. Likewise, rather than use a separate word for "consecrate" it is simply written as an action, without the hyphen. So the adjective – and noun – ("Holy") becomes set-apart, while the verb ("consecrate") becomes set apart.

Sheol. The Hebrew (and Aramaic) word שאול (*Sheol*) is usually rendered as "grave" or is left un-translated. Sheol is literally the grave; it is a physical place where the dead are buried. Its Greek counterpart is Αδης (Hades). The Ethiopic word used is ሲኦል (*si'ol*) which is a cognate to the Hebrew *Sheol*. All have been rendered as "Sheol."

Shofar. The Hebrew word שופר (*shofar*) comes from the word שפר (*shafar*) meaning "beautiful" or "goodly." *Shofar* refers to the instrument of the ram's horn itself. For Genesis Retold this word has been transliterated. The plural of *shofar* is *shofarot*.

Teraphim. The Hebrew word תרפים (*Ter'aph'iym*) is a type of household idol. According to some of the Targumim (Aramaic paraphrases of the Tanakh), the Teraphim were human heads that were salted for preservation. A golden tablet with spells written on it was then placed under the tongue, and it was believed that these heads could speak. This is the type of idol that Raḥel stole from Lavan.

Torah. The Hebrew word תורה (*Torah*) is best rendered as "instructions" and not the commonly translated word "law." To the Hebrew mind, Torah is always seen in a positive light. As such, Torah has simply been transliterated and not translated. The Aramaic word is, typically, אוריתא (*ora'iyta*). In Syriac Aramaic, however, the word used is actually a loan-word from Greek, which is ܢܡܘܣܐ (*n'musa*). The Greek word is νομος (*nomos*), and the Ethiopic word is ኦሪት (*'oriyt*) which is a cognate of the Aramaic *ora'iyta*. In Genesis Retold these words are usually rendered as law, except: (1) when the Hebrew text reads "Torah" and (2) when the context of the section clearly indicates that the Torah is the law being referenced.

Tsevaot. The Hebrew word צבאות (*Tsevaot*) is usually rendered as "armies" or "hosts." It is one of the Titles of יהוה, and is seen over 200 times in the Scriptures as "יהוה Tsevaot" though this is normally translated as "Lord of Hosts." As with most terms for Genesis Retold, I prefer the transl*iteration* over the transl*ation*. Thus, in the text, it is rendered simply as "Tsevaot."

Yovel. The Hebrew word יובל (*yovel*) is usually rendered "jubilee." It comes from the word יבל (*yaval*) which means "to bring," "to carry," or "to flow." Literally, this refers to the trumpeting sound of the instrument itself, in the sense of the sound "carrying" or "flowing" out. The English word "jubilee" comes from the Latin *jubilaeus*.

Names of the Messengers

Note: Almost all of the names listed below contain the Hebrew word 𐤀𐤋 (El). This word has been left transliterated in Genesis Retold. However, it is normally translated as "God." The plural form of this is 𐤀𐤋𐤄𐤉𐤌 (Elohim).

Anan'el: From the Hebrew 𐤏𐤍𐤍 (*an'an*) meaning "cloud" and 𐤀𐤋 (*El*). Thus together it means "Cloud of El."

Ar'taqoph: From the Aramaic word 𐤀𐤓𐤏 (*ara*) meaning "earth" and 𐤕𐤒𐤐 (*ta'qoph*) meaning "strong." Thus together it means "Strength of the earth."

Asa'el: From the Hebrew 𐤍𐤔𐤀 (*na'sa*) meaning "to make" and 𐤀𐤋 (*El*). Thus together it means "El has made." In the Greek and Ethiopic versions, this name is often mistakenly replaced by the name of a separate messenger, Azaz'el.

Azaz'el: There are two possible origins for the name Azaz'el. The first appears in Vayyiqra [Leviticus] 16, where the name is spelled 𐤏𐤆𐤀𐤆𐤋 (*az'azel*) and is normally translated as "scapegoat." This word is formed by combining two different Hebrew words: 𐤏𐤆 (*ez*) meaning "goat" and 𐤀𐤆𐤋 (*az'al*) meaning "gone" or "removed." Thus it is understood to mean "Goat of removal." This seems to suit the context of Vayyiqra [Leviticus] 16 very well. The other spelling is attested in some other Qumran documents, and is spelled 𐤏𐤆𐤆𐤀𐤋 (*az'az'el*) and is formed by the words 𐤏𐤆𐤆 (*az'az*) meaning "to prevail, to be strong" and 𐤀𐤋 (*El*). Thus together it means "El prevails." Over time, as the book of Enoch was carried into Greek, then into Ethiopic and Latin, the name Azaz'el came to replace the actual messenger mentioned, who was Asa'el. This was most likely a corruption carried over on account of existing Azaz'el myths and legends, and thus Asa'el was mistaken for Azaz'el in the process of transmission and translation. However, in 69:2 both Asa'el and Azaz'el are mentioned. In this case, it is likely that Azaz'el was added completely.

Baraq'el: From the Hebrew 𐤁𐤓𐤒 (*ba'raq*) meaning "lightning" and 𐤀𐤋 (*El*). Thus together it means "Lightning of El."

Dani'el: From the possessive form of the Hebrew 𐤃𐤍 (*dahn*) meaning "judge" and 𐤀𐤋 (*El*). Thus together it means "El is my judge."

Gavri'el: From the Hebrew word 𐤂𐤁𐤓 (*ga'var*) meaning "mighty" and 𐤀𐤋 (*El*). Thus together it means "El is mighty."

Ḥermoni: From the adjective form of 𐤇𐤓𐤌𐤅𐤍 (*Ḥermon*) referring to the mountain. Thus it means "Ḥermonite."

Kokhav'el: From the Hebrew 𐤊𐤅𐤊𐤁 (*ko'khav*) meaning "star" and 𐤀𐤋 (*El*). Thus together it means "Star of El."

Matar'el: From the Hebrew 𐤌𐤈𐤓 (*ma'tar*) meaning "rain" and 𐤀𐤋 (*El*). Thus together it means "Rain from El."

Mikha'el: From the Hebrew word 𐤌𐤉 (*miy*) meaning "who?" and 𐤀𐤋 (*El*), with the khaf-prefix (𐤊), meaning "like El." Thus together it means "Who is like El?"

Phanu'el: From the Hebrew 𐤐𐤍𐤉 (*p'nei*) meaning "face" and 𐤀𐤋 (*El*). Thus together it means "Face of El." It could also mean "Before El" in the sense of a messenger of the presence. Phanu'el is believed by some scholars to be another name for Uri'el.

Ram'el: From the Hebrew 𐤓𐤏𐤌 (*ra'am*) meaning "thunder" and 𐤀𐤋 (*El*). Thus together it means "Thunder of El."

Rami'el: From the Hebrew 𐤓𐤅𐤌 (*room*) meaning "exalted" and 𐤀𐤋 (*El*). Thus together it means "El is exalted."

Ramt'el: From the Hebrew word 𐤓𐤌𐤄 (*ra'mah*) meaning "high place" and 𐤀𐤋 (*El*). Thus together it means "High place of El."

Raphael: From the Hebrew word 𐤓𐤐𐤄 (*ra'fah*) meaning "to heal" and 𐤀𐤋 (*El*). Thus together it means "El is healer."

Rau'el: From the Hebrew 𐤓𐤏𐤉 (*ro'iy*) meaning "shepherd" and 𐤀𐤋 (*El*). Thus together it means "El is shepherd."

Sahari'el: From the Hebrew 𐤔𐤄𐤓 (*sa'har*) meaning "[crescent] moon" and 𐤀𐤋 (*El*). Thus together it means "[Crescent] Moon of El."

Sari'el: From the Hebrew 𐤔𐤓 (*sar*) meaning "prince" and 𐤀𐤋 (*El*). Thus together it means "Prince of El."

Sataw'el: From the Hebrew 𐤎𐤕𐤅 (*sa'tav*) meaning "winter" and 𐤀𐤋 (*El*). Thus together it means "Winter of El."

Shamshi'el: From the Hebrew 𐤔𐤌𐤔 (*she'mesh*) meaning "sun" and 𐤀𐤋 (*El*). Thus together it means "Sun of El."

Shemiḥazah: From the Hebrew word 𐤔𐤌 (*shem*) meaning "name" and 𐤇𐤆𐤄 (*chazah*) meaning "to reveal" or "to make seen." Thus together it means "My name has revealed" or "My name has [been] revealed."

Tami'el: From either the Hebrew 𐤕𐤌𐤌 (*ta'mam*) meaning "complete" or 𐤈𐤌𐤍 (*ta'man*) meaning "concealed" and 𐤀𐤋 (*El*). Thus together it could be "El has completed" or "El has concealed."

Tummi'el: From the Hebrew 𐤕𐤌𐤌 (*ta'mam*) meaning "perfect" and 𐤀𐤋 (*El*). Thus together it means "Perfection of El."

Turi'el: From the Aramaic 𐤈𐤅𐤓 (*tuwr*) meaning "mountain" and 𐤀𐤋 (*El*). Thus together it means "Mountain of El."

Uri'el: From the Hebrew 𐤀𐤅𐤓 (*uwr*) meaning "light" and 𐤀𐤋 (*El*). Thus together it means "Light of El."

Yehaddi'el: From the Hebrew 𐤄𐤃𐤄 (*ha'dah*) meaning "to guide" and 𐤀𐤋 (*El*). Thus together it means "El will guide."

Yomi'el: From the Hebrew 𐤉𐤅𐤌 (*yowm*) meaning "day" and 𐤀𐤋 (*El*). Thus together it means "Day of El."

Ziqi'el: From the Aramaic 𐤆𐤉𐤒 (*zyq*) meaning "lightning flash" and 𐤀𐤋 (*El*). Thus together it means "Lightning-flash of El."

Though there are other messengers' names in Sefer Ḥanokh, not all of them have corresponding sections available in Aramaic and/or Hebrew. Those listed here are the best attempt at reconstruction currently available. Most of these are taken from the Aramaic fragments, back to a Hebrew original. However, since Aramaic and Hebrew share many cognates, it is just as possible that many more of these are Aramaic than I have presented here.

Appendix C: Alphabets

Hebrew / Aramaic	English Equivalent (Hebrew & Aramaic)	Greek	English Equivalent (Greek)
𐤀 (Alef)	Depends on vowel	Α α (Alpha)	A
𐤁 (Bet)	B	Β β (Beta)	B
𐤂 (Gimel)	G	Γ γ (Gamma)	G
𐤃 (Dalet)	D	Δ δ (Delta)	D
𐤄 (Hey)	H	Ε ε (Epsilon)	E
𐤅 (Vav/Waw)	V/W/U	Ζ ζ (Zeta)	Z
𐤆 (Zayin)	Z	Η η (Eta)	Ee
𐤇 (Ḥet)	Ch [Ḥ]	Θ θ (Theta)	Th
𐤈 (Tet)	T	Ι ι (Iota)	I
𐤉 (Yod)	Y	Κ κ (Kappa)	K
𐤊 (Khaf)	K/Kh [Ḥ]	Λ λ (Lambda)	L
𐤋 (Lamed)	L	Μ μ (Mu)	M
𐤌 (Mem)	M	Ν ν (Nu)	N
𐤍 (Nun)	N	Ξ ξ (Xi)	X
𐤎 (Samekh)	S	Ο ο (Omicron)	O
𐤏 (Ayin)	Depends on Vowel	Π π (Pi)	P
𐤐 (Pe)	P/F	Ρ ρ (Rho)	R
𐤑 (Tsadi)	Ts	Σ σ (Sigma) ς (Final Sigma)	S
𐤒 (Qof)	Q	Τ τ (Tau)	T
𐤓 (Resh)	R	Υ υ (Upsilon)	U
𐤔 (Shin)	S/Sh	Φ φ (Phi)	F
𐤕 (Tav/Taw)	T	Χ χ (Chi)	Ch [Ḥ]
		Ψ ψ (Psi)	Ps
		Ω ω (Omega)	Oh

* Sofit letters are final forms. That is, they appear in this form only at the end of a word.

Ge'ez	English Equivalent	ä	u	i	a	e	ə	o	wa	yä
Hoy	H	ሀ	ሁ	ሂ	ሃ	ሄ	ህ	ሆ	-	-
Lawe	L	ለ	ሉ	ሊ	ላ	ሌ	ል	ሎ	ሏ	-
Ḥawt	Ch [Ḥ]	ሐ	ሑ	ሒ	ሓ	ሔ	ሕ	ሖ	ሗ	-
May	M	መ	ሙ	ሚ	ማ	ሜ	ም	ሞ	ሟ	ፙ
Śawt	Ś	ሠ	ሡ	ሢ	ሣ	ሤ	ሥ	ሦ	ሧ	-
Rə's	R	ረ	ሩ	ሪ	ራ	ሬ	ር	ሮ	ሯ	ፘ
Sat	S	ሰ	ሱ	ሲ	ሳ	ሴ	ስ	ሶ	ሷ	-
Khaf	Kh [Ḥ]	ቀ	ቁ	ቂ	ቃ	ቄ	ቅ	ቆ	ቋ	-
Bet	B	በ	ቡ	ቢ	ባ	ቤ	ብ	ቦ	ቧ	-
Tawe	T	ተ	ቱ	ቲ	ታ	ቴ	ት	ቶ	ቷ	-
Ḫarm	Ḫ	ኀ	ኁ	ኂ	ኃ	ኄ	ኅ	ኆ	ኋ	-
Nahas	N	ነ	ኑ	ኒ	ና	ኔ	ን	ኖ	ኗ	-
'Alf	Depends on Vowel	አ	ኡ	ኢ	ኣ	ኤ	እ	ኦ	ኧ	-
Kaf	K	ከ	ኩ	ኪ	ካ	ኬ	ክ	ኮ	ኳ	-
Wawe	W	ወ	ዉ	ዊ	ዋ	ዌ	ው	ዎ	-	-
'Ayn	Depends on Vowel	ዐ	ዑ	ዒ	ዓ	ዔ	ዕ	ዖ	-	-
Zay	Z	ዘ	ዙ	ዚ	ዛ	ዜ	ዝ	ዞ	ዟ	-
Yaman	Y	የ	ዩ	ዪ	ያ	ዬ	ይ	ዮ	-	-
Dant	D	ደ	ዱ	ዲ	ዳ	ዴ	ድ	ዶ	ዷ	-
Gaml	G	ገ	ጉ	ጊ	ጋ	ጌ	ግ	ጎ	ጓ	-
Tayt	Ṭ	ጠ	ጡ	ጢ	ጣ	ጤ	ጥ	ጦ	ጧ	-
Payt	P̣	ጰ	ጱ	ጲ	ጳ	ጴ	ጵ	ጶ	ጷ	-
Tsadday	Ts	ጸ	ጹ	ጺ	ጻ	ጼ	ጽ	ጾ	ጿ	-
Ṣappa	Ṣ	ፀ	ፁ	ፂ	ፃ	ፄ	ፅ	ፆ	-	-
Af	F	ፈ	ፉ	ፊ	ፋ	ፌ	ፍ	ፎ	ፏ	ፚ
Psa	P	ፐ	ፑ	ፒ	ፓ	ፔ	ፕ	ፖ	ፗ	-

Note: In Ge'ez Ethiopic, the alphabet uses different characters to indicate vowels that follow a letter. For example, the letter Af (ፍ) makes the sound of the English "F." However, when written as (ፌ) it makes the sound "FE." When written as (ፋ) it makes the sound "FA." When written as (ፏ) it makes the sound "FWA." Thus each of the letters are assigned a vowel sound based on the way the letter is written. This means the Ge'ez alphabet, though it only has 13 letters, actually has 115 different characters. Whenever a letter in the (ə) column is used, it represents the consonant itself without a following vowel.

Appendix D: Glossary of Terms

Pronunciation Key							
AH	a in "father"	**AI**	eye	**EI**	ay in "pray"	**TS**	ts in "cats"
EE	ee in "tree"	**EH**	e in "pet"	**E**	e in "pet"	**OH**	o in "bone"
OO	oo in "soon"	**Ḥ/ch/kh**	Guttural "h" in Bach or Loch				

SQV	Pronunciation	Anglicized
𐤉𐤄𐤅𐤄	~	LORD
Adoni-Tsedeq	Ad-oh-nee Tseh-dek	Adonizedek
Aharon	Ah-ha-ROHN	Aaron
Aiyalon	Ai-ya-LOHN	Ajalon
Amaleq	Am-ah-lek	Amalek
Amein	Ah-mein	Amen
Aram	Ar-ahm	Syria
Aram-Naharayim	Ar-ahm Nah-hah-rah-yeem	Mesopotamia
Ashuwr	Ah-SHOO-wr	Assyria
Avarim	Av-ar-EEM	Abarim
Avihu	Av-EE-hoo	Abihu
Avimelekh	Av-ee-MEL-ek	Abimelech
Avraham	Av-RAH-hahm	Abraham
Avram	Av-RAHM	Abram
Azazel	Ahz-ah-ZEL	Scapegoat
Balaq	Bah-LAHK	Balak
Bavel	Bah-vehl	Babel / Babylon
Beersheva	Beh-ehr-SHEI-vah	Beersheba
Being	BEE-EENG	Soul
Beliyya'al	Beh-LEE-yah-ahl	Belial
B'midbar	Beh-MEED-bahr	Numbers
Benyamin	Bein-yah-MEEN	Benjamin
Bereshiyt	Behr-eh-SHEET	Genesis
Beth-El	Beith-el	Bethel
Beth-lechem	Beith-leh-chehm	Bethlehem
Bil'am	Beel-ahm	Balaam
Botsrah	Bohts-rah	Bozrah
Dammeseq	Dahm-ess-ehk	Damascus
D'varim	Deh-vahr-EEM	Deuteronomy
Devorah	Deh-vor-ah	Deborah
Diqlah	DEEK-lah	Diklah
Divrei Ha'Yamim	Dee-vrei-hah-yah-MEEM	Chronicles
Edom	Eh-DOHM	Edom / Idumea
El	Ehl	God
el	ehl	god
El Shaddai	Ehl Shah-DAI	God Almighty
Elazar	Ehl-ah-zahr	Eleazar (also Lazarus)
Elohim	Ehl-oh-HEEM	God
elohim	ehl-oh-heem	gods
Elyaqim	Ehl-yah-KEEM	Eliakim
Elyon	Ehl-YOHN	Most High
Ephesious	Eh-pheh-SEE-os	Ephesians
Ephrayim	Eph-rah-YEEM	Ephraim
Eqron	Ek-ROHN	Ekron
Esaw	Eh-sahv	Esau
Ever	Eh-vehr	Eber
Eyval	Ei-vahl	Ebal
Hit'galut	Gah-lah	Revelation
Galatas	Gah-lah-teis	Galatians
Gavri'el	Gahv-REE-ehl	Gabriel
Giḥon	Gee-CHOHN	Giḥon
Gilad	Gee-LAHD	Gilead
Givon	Gee-VOHN	Gibeon
Havel	Hah-vehl	Abel
Ḥam	Ḥahm	Ham
Ḥanokh	Ḥahn-OHCH	Enoch (also Hanoch)
Ḥaran	Ḥah-rahn	Haran
Ḥatsor	Ḥahts-OHR	Hazor
Ḥavilah	Ḥahv-EE-lah	Havilah
Ḥavvah	Ḥah-vah	Eve
Ḥeshbon	Ḥesh-BOHN	Heshbon
Ḥetsron	Ḥets-ROHN	Hezron

Ḥittite	Ḥeet-AIT	Hittite
Ḥivite	Ḥiv-AIT	Hivite
Ḥorev	Ḥohr-ehv	Horeb
Hoshea	Hoh-shei-ah	Hosea
Ivrim	Eev-REEM	Hebrews
Iyyov	Ee-yohv	Job
Kaldea	Kal-DEE-ah	Chaldea
Kana'an	Kah-nah-ahn	Canaan
Kerub	Keh-roob	Cherub
Kittim	Kit-TEEM	Chittim
Kolossaeis	Kol-oss-ei-iss	Colossians
Korinthious	Kor-in-thee-oos	Corinthians
Kush	KOO-sh	Cush (also Ethiopia)
Lamekh	Lah-mehk	Lamech
Lavan	Lah-vahn	Laban
Levanon	Lev-ah-nahn	Lebanon
Livnah	Leev-nah	Libnah
Livyathan	Leev-yah-thahn	Leviathan
Loukas	Loo-kahs	Luke
M'lakhim	Meh-lah-KHEEM	Kings
Ma'asei	Mah-ah-sei	Acts
Malakhi	Mah-lah-kee	Malachi
Menasheh	Meh-nah-sheh	Manasseh
Markos	Mahr-koss	Mark
Mattithyah /-yahu	Maht-tith-yah	Matthew
Messiah	Me-sai-uh	Christ
Mikha'el	Mee-kah-ehl	Michael
Miryam	Meer-yahm	Mary (also Miriam)
Mishlei	Meesh-lei	Proverbs
Mitsrayim	Meets-rah-YEEM	Egypt (also Mizraim)
Moav	MOH-ahv	Moab
Mosheh	Moh-sheih	Moses
Noaḥ	Noh-ach	Noah
Noph	Noh-ph	Memphis
Paras	Pahr-ahs	Persia
Perets	Peh-rehts	Perets
Pesaḥ	Pei-sahch	Passover
Perath	Peh-rahth	Euphrates
Philippesious	Phil-ih-pee-see-oos	Philippians

Pinechas	Peen-chas	Phineas
Put	Poot	Libya (also Phut)
Qadesh	Kah-dehsh	Kadesh
Qayin	Kai-een	Cain
Qedar	Keh-dahr	Kedar
Qemuel	Keh-moo-ehl	Kemuel
Qenan	Keh-nahn	Cainan
Qenaz	Keh-nahz	Kenaz
Qeturah	Keh-too-rah	Keturah
Qiryath	Keer-yahth	Kirjath
Qohath	Koh-hath	Kohath
Qoheleth	Qoh-heh-leth	Ecclesiastes
Qoraḥ	Kor-ach	Korah
Reuven	Reh-oo-vein	Reuben
Rivqah	REEV-kah	Rebecca
Ruaḥ	ROO-ach	Spirit
Sha'ul	Shah-OOL	Saul (also Paul)
Shekhem	Sheh-chem	Shechem
Shemoth	Sh'-MOHT	Exodus
Shemu'el	Shem-OO-ehl	Samuel
Sheth	Sheh-th	Seth
Shimon	Shee-mohn	Simon (also Simeon)
Shir Ha'Shirim	Sheer-HAH-sheer-EEM	Song of Songs
Shofar	SHOH-fahr	Trumpet
Shoftim	Shohf-TEEM	Judges
Tehillim	Teh-heel-EEM	Psalms
Timotheos	Teem-oh-thei-oss	Timothy
Torah	Toh-rah	Law
Torot	Toh-roht	Laws
Tsevaot	Tseh-vah-oht	Hosts
Tsidon	Tsee-DOHN	Sidon
Tsion	Tsee-OHN	Zion
Tsipporah	Tsee-por-ah	Zipporah
Tsivon	Tsee-VOHN	Zibeon
Tsor	Tsor	Tyre
Uts	Oots	Uz
Vayyiqra	Vah-yee-krah	Leviticus
Ya'aqov	Yah-akohv	Jacob (also James)
Yarden	Yahr-dein	Jordan

Yashuv	Yah-SHOOV	Jashub
Yavan	Yah-vahn	Greece (also Javan)
Yevusite	Yehv-OO-sait	Jebusite
Yechezqel	Yeh-chez-kehl	Ezekiel
Yehoshua	Yeh-hoh-shoo-ah	Joshua
Yehudah	Yeh-hoo-dah	Judah (also Judas; Judea; Jude)
Yehudim	Yeh-hoo-DEEM	Jews
Yehudite	Yeh-hoo-dait	Jew
Yeptheth	Yeh-pheth	Japheth
Yericho	Yeh-ree-choh	Jericho
Yerushalayim	Yeh-roo-shah-lah-YEEM	Jerusalem
Yeshayah /-yahu	Yeh-shah-yah	Isaiah
Yirmeyah /-yahu	Yeer-meh-yah	Jeremiah
Yishma'el	Yeesh-mah-ehl	Ishmael
Yiskah	Yees-kah	Ishcah
Yisra'el	Yees-rah-ehl	Israel
Yissakhar	Yees-sah-ḫar	Issachar
Yithro	Yeeth-roh	Jethro
Yitsḫaq	Yeets-chahk	Isaac
Yitshar	Yeets-hahr	Izhar
Yoḫanan	Yoh-chah-nahn	John (also Johanan)
Yoel	Yoh-ehl	Joel
Yokheved	Yoh-keh-vehd	Jokebed
Yoseph	Yoh-sehph	Joseph
Yoshiyah /-yahu	Yoh-shee-yahu	Josiah
Yovav	Yoh-vahv	Jobab
Yovel	Yoh-vehl	Jubilee
Zevulun	Zeh-voo-loon	Zebulun

Appendix E: Major Textual Variants

1) 1 Enoch 105. The text present in this publication is based on a translation of the Aramaic fragments of this section. The Ethiopic version, however, differs greatly in these verses. As such, the Ethiopic version's translation is listed here for comparison.

> 1 In those days, He says, "The Master will be patient and cause the children of the earth to hear. 2 Reveal it to them with your wisdom, for you are their guides; and you are a reward upon the whole earth. 3 Until I and My Son are united with them forever in the upright paths in their lifetime; and there shall be peace to you, rejoice, you children of truth. Amein."

2) Testament of Yoseph 19:8-12. The text present in this publication is based on a translation of the Greek version of this section. The Armenian version, however, differs greatly in these verses. As such, the Armenian version's translation is listed here for comparison.

> 8 And I saw in the midst of the horns a certain virgin, wearing a vari-colored shawl, and a lamb came forth from her. All kinds of wild animals and creeping things were rushing from the north, and the lamb conquered them all. 9 The bull rejoiced because of him, and the cow and deer were also glad. 10 These things must take place in their appointed time. 11 And you, my children, must honor Levi and Yehudah, because the salvation of Yisra'el will rise from them. 12 For my kingdom will have an end among you, like an orchard guard who disappears after the summer.

3) Testament of Benyamin 9:3-5. The text present in this publication is based on the Greek version of this section. The Armenian version, however, differs greatly in these verses. As such, the Armenian version's translation is listed here for comparison.

> 3 And 𐤉𐤄𐤅𐤄 will be treated with outrage, and be despised. 4 And He will depart from the heavens, and will know indeed what is theirs from the earth to the heavens, 5 and what is their measure, and what is their place, and what is their way.

4) Testament of Benyamin 11. The text present in this publication is based on the Greek version of this section. The Armenian version, however, differs greatly in these verses. As such, the Armenian version's translation is listed here for comparison.

> 1 And I will no longer be called a ravening wolf on account of your ravages; 2 but rather *I will be called* the beloved of 𐤉𐤄𐤅𐤄, a doer of the good pleasure of His will.

Appendix F: New Testament Parallel Verses

The following is a list of verses that appear in the New Testament of the Bible on the left, with their corresponding passage in Enoch, Jasher, Jubilees, and T12P on the right. Note that not all of these can be considered direct quotes. While this list is by no means exhaustive, it does provide a general understanding of how frequently these texts match up with the New Testament.

New Testament	Genesis Retold
Matthew	~
Matthew 5:28	Test. of Benjamin 8:2
Matthew 6:16	Test. of Zebulun 8:6; Joseph 3:4
Matthew 6:22	Test. of Issachar 3:4
Matthew 12:35	Test. of Asher 1:9
Matthew 12:45	Test. of Reuben 2:2-4
Matthew 18:15	Test. of Gad 6:3
Matthew 19:23	1 Enoch 62:5
Matthew 19:28	1 Enoch 108:12
Matthew 19:29	1 Enoch 40:9
Matthew 22:37-39	Test. of Dan 5:3
Matthew 25:35-36	Test. of Joseph 1:5-7
Matthew 25:41	1 Enoch 54:4-5
Matthew 26:24	1 Enoch 38:2
Matthew 28:18	1 Enoch 62:6
Mark	~
Mark 3:22	Jubilees 10:8; 48:9-12
Luke	~
Luke 1:52	1 Enoch 46:4
Luke 2:19	Test. of Levi 6:2
Luke 2:37	Test. of Joseph 4:7-8
Luke 9:35	1 Enoch 40:5
Luke 11:49	Jubilees 1:12
Luke 12:45	Test. of Joseph 3:5-6
Luke 16:8	1 Enoch 108:11
Luke 16:9	1 Enoch 63:10
Luke 18:7	1 Enoch 47:1-2
Luke 21:2	1 Enoch 51:2
Luke 23:35	1 Enoch 40:5
John	~
John 1:9	Test. of Levi 14:4
John 3:19	Test. of Naphtali 2:10
John 5:22-27	1 Enoch 69:27
John 12:36	1 Enoch 108:11
John 14:2	1 Enoch 39:4
John 14:26	Jubilees 32:25
Acts	~
Acts 3:14	1 Enoch 53:6
Acts 4:12	1 Enoch 48:7
Acts 7:15-16	Jubilees 46:9
Acts 7:23	Jubilees 47:10-12
Acts 7:30	Jubilees 48:1

Acts 7:53	Jubilees 1:14,27
Acts 10:4	1 Enoch 99:3
Acts 12:11	Test. of Simeon 2:8
Acts 17:31	1 Enoch 41:9
Romans	~
Romans 1:21	Test. of Reuben 3:8
Romans 1:31	Test. of Asher 6:2
Romans 2:15	Test. of Judah 20:5
Romans 8:34	1 Enoch 61:10
Romans 9:5	1 Enoch 77:1
Romans 12:1	Test. of Levi 3:6
Romans 12:8	Test. of Issachar 3:8
Romans 12:21	Test. of Benjamin 4:3
1 Corinthians	~
1 Corinthians 4:4	Test. of Issachar 7:1
1 Corinthians 6:11	1 Enoch 48:7
1 Corinthians 6:18	Test. of Reuben 5:5
1 Corinthians 7:5	Test. of Naphtali 8:8
1 Corinthians 11:32	Test. of Benjamin 6:7
1 Corinthians 13:6	Test. of Simeon 4:8
2 Corinthians	~
2 Corinthians 4:6	1 Enoch 38:4
2 Corinthians 5:17	Jubilees 5:12
2 Corinthians 6:14-15	Test. of Levi 19:1
2 Corinthians 6:18	Jubilees 1:24
2 Corinthians 7:10	Test. of Gad 5:7
2 Corinthians 11:31	1 Enoch 77:1
Galatians	~
Galatians 1:4	1 Enoch 48:7
Galatians 2:15	Jubilees 23:23
Ephesians	~
Ephesians 1:21	1 Enoch 61:10
Ephesians 1:9	1 Enoch 49:4
Ephesians 5:6	Test. of Naphtali 3:1
Ephesians 5:8	1 Enoch 108:11
Ephesians 5:18	Test. of Judah 16:1-5
Philippians	~
Philippians 2:10	1 Enoch 48:5
Colossians	~
Colossians 1:16	1 Enoch 61:10
Colossians 2:2-3	1 Enoch 46:3
1 Thessalonians	~
1 Thessalonians 2:16	Test. of Levi 6:11
1 Thessalonians 5:3	1 Enoch 62:4
1 Thessalonians 5:5	1 Enoch 108:11
2 Thessalonians	~
2 Thessalonians 1:7	1 Enoch 61:10
2 Thessalonians 2:3	Jubilees 10:3
1 Timothy	~
1 Timothy 1:9	1 Enoch 93:4
1 Timothy 1:15	1 Enoch 94:1
1 Timothy 5:21	1 Enoch 39:1
1 Timothy 6:15	1 Enoch 9:4

1 Timothy 6:16	1 Enoch 14:21
2 Timothy	~
2 Timothy 3:8	Jasher 79:27
2 Timothy 4:8	Test. of Levi 8:2
Hebrews	~
Hebrews 4:13	1 Enoch 9:5
Hebrews 11:10	1 Enoch 90:29
Hebrews 12:9	1 Enoch 37:2
Hebrews 12:22	1 Enoch 90:29
James	~
James 1:2	Test. of Dan 4:5
James 1:8	1 Enoch 91:4
James 1:27	Test. of Joseph 4:6
James 4:7	Test. of Naphtali 8:4
James 5:1-6	1 Enoch 94:8-11; 46:7; 63:10; 96:4-8
1 Peter	~
1 Peter 3:3-5	Test. of Reuben 5:5
1 Peter 3:19-20	1 Enoch 10:1-13; 19:1; 20:1
2 Peter	~
2 Peter 2:3	Jubilees 7:20-39
2 Peter 2:4	1 Enoch 10:1-13; 12:5; 13:2
2 Peter 3:8	Jubilees 4:30
2 Peter 3:13	1 Enoch 45:4-5; Jubilees 1:29
1 John	~
1 John 1:7	1 Enoch 92:4
1 John 2:1	1 Enoch 53:6
1 John 2:8	1 Enoch 58:5
1 John 2:15	1 Enoch 108:8
1 John 3:2	1 Enoch 90:37-38
Jude	~
Jude 4	1 Enoch 48:10
Jude 6	1 Enoch 12:4; 10:1-13
Jude 7	Test. of Naphtali 3:4
Jude 13	1 Enoch 18:15; 21:2-6
Jude 14	1 Enoch 60:8
Jude 14-15	1 Enoch 1:9; 5:4; 27:2
Revelation	~
Revelation 1:4	1 Enoch 90:21
Revelation 1:6	Jubilees 16:18
Revelation 2:7; 22:2-14	1 Enoch 25:4-6
Revelation 3:5	1 Enoch 90:31
Revelation 3:10	1 Enoch 37:5
Revelation 3:12	1 Enoch 90:29; Test. of Dan 5:12
Revelation 3:17	1 Enoch 97:8
Revelation 3:20	1 Enoch 62:14
Revelation 3:21	1 Enoch 108:12
Revelation 4:6	1 Enoch 40:2
Revelation 4:8	1 Enoch 39:13
Revelation 6:10	1 Enoch 47:2
Revelation 6:15-16	1 Enoch 62:3-5
Revelation 7:1	1 Enoch 69:22
Revelation 7:15	1 Enoch 45:4
Revelation 9:1	1 Enoch 86:1

Revelation 9:20	1 Enoch 99:7
Revelation 11:19	Test. of Levi 5:1
Revelation 12:10	1 Enoch 40:7
Revelation 13:14	1 Enoch 54:6
Revelation 14:9-10	1 Enoch 48:9
Revelation 14:20	1 Enoch 100:3
Revelation 17:14	1 Enoch 9:4
Revelation 20:12	1 Enoch 90:20; 47:3
Revelation 20:13	1 Enoch 51:1
Revelation 20:15	1 Enoch 90:26
Revelation 22:3	1 Enoch 25:6